Integral Research and Societal Regeneration in Africa

Anselm Adodo /
Ronnie Lessem /
Alexander Schieffer

Integral Research and Societal Regeneration in Africa

From University to Communiversity

PETER LANG

Berlin - Bruxelles - Chennai - Lausanne - New York - Oxford

Library of Congress Cataloging-in-Publication Data
A CIP catalog record for this book has been applied for at the Library of Congress.

Bibliographic Information published by the Deutsche Nationalbibliothek
The Deutsche Nationalbibliothek lists this publication in the Deutsche Nationalbibliografie; detailed bibliographic data is available online at http://dnb.d-nb.de.

ISBN 978-3-631-91966-8 (Print)
E-ISBN 978-3-631-91967-5 (E-PDF)
E-ISBN 978-3-631-91968-2 (E-PUB)
10.3726/b22153

© 2024 Peter Lang Group AG, Lausanne
Published by Peter Lang GmbH, Berlin, Germany

info@peterlang.com - www.peterlang.com

All rights reserved.

All parts of this publication are protected by copyright. Any utilisation outside the strict limits of the copyright law, without the permission of the publisher, is forbidden and liable to prosecution. This applies in particular to reproductions, translations, microfilming, and storage and processing in electronic retrieval systems.

Contents

Preface 9

Foreword 13

Part 1 Orientation

Chapter 1 New African Research, University and Economic Paradigm. Technological/Social Innovation; University/Communiversity; Capitalism and Socialism/Communitalism 17

Chapter 2 *Centring* Cosmology: Healing Wisdom Out of Africa Amplified Worldwide. South/Africa, East/Asia, North/Europe, Integral West/ America and Centre/MENA 47

Chapter 3 Integral Research and Innovation in Southern, East, North and West Africa. Paths and Trajectories: Communiversity to Communitalism 77

Chapter 4 Originating Integral Research in African South. Feel Local, Intuit Local-Global, Think Newly Global, Act Global-Local 101

Part 2 The Relational Path Out of *Southern* Africa: Towards Nhakanomics

Chapter 5 From Descriptive Methods (S1) to *Southern* Phenomenology (S2). Engage with Your Local-Global Southern Life World 129

Chapter 6 From Phenomenology to Southern Feminism. Re-Inventing Africa 153

Chapter 7 From Feminism to Participatory Action Research in Africa and the Global South. Ujaama in Tanzania to Six S's in the Sahel 183

Integral Case Story 1: Integral Kumusha/Nhakanomics in Zimbabwe: Taranhike's 207

Part 3 The Renewal Path Out of South-*East* Africa: Towards Yurugu-nomics

Chapter 8 Narrative Methods to African Hermeneutic Methodological Foundation Fusing South-Eastern Horizons 235

Chapter 9 From Hermeneutics to African Critical Theory Towards Yurugu-Nomics. Develop a Dialectical Argument 263

Chapter 10 From Critical Theory to Co-Operative Inquiry in Africa AMP, MSET, CIDA: Integral PHD, Green Zimbabwe and Beyond 287

Integral Case Story 2: Good African Story and *Yurugu-nomics* **in Uganda/ Rugisara** 317

Part 4 Path of Reason Out of South-*North* Africa: Towards the Economics of Love

Chapter 11   Grounded Theory to Critical Rationalist African Foundation: Towards the Economy of Love. Build up a Theoretical Perspective 345

Chapter 12   Southern-*Northern* African Post-Modernism: Theory of the South. Feel Local – Tswana Go Dira; Intuit Local/Global – Multiple Discourses; Newly Global Theory of the South; Global-Local Pre-Post Modern Africa 373

Chapter 13   From Postmodernism to African Integral Design. Towards an Integral Enterprise 397

Integral Case Story 3: Sekem and the *Economics of Love* in Egypt/Abouleish 425

Part 5 Realization Path Out of South-*West* Africa/ Diaspora: Communitalism

Chapter 14   Case Study Method to African Empirical Foundation. Positivism to Naturalism 451

Chapter 15 From Empiricism to Critical African
            Realism. Discover Underlying African
            Reality 477

Chapter 16 From Critical Realism to Afrocentric
            Action Research. Become an African
            Scientist in Action 503

Integral Case Story 4: Pax Herbals and *Communitalism*
in Nigeria/Adodo 533

Part 6 University to Communiversity/Capitalism/Socialism
to Communitalism

Chapter 17 Cooperative Inquiry/Trans-Doctoral
            Program: Towards Societal Re-Gene-
            Ration in and Through Africa 577

Chapter 18 Towards a Societal PHD Community,
            Corporation, Communiversity,
            Communitalism 609

Index 639

Preface

In the heart of this tale, *"Integral Research and Social Regeneration in Africa,"* lies a tapestry woven from the threads of Africa's intricate history, unspoken aspirations, and uncharted potential. Beyond the mere pages of academic discourse, this opus is an elegy sung in celebration, a pioneering odyssey. It beckons forth a fervent plea for change, resonating with the pulse of our diverse cultures and the harmonies of our collective yearning for a brighter world. Amidst the whirlwind of globalisation, we do not yield; instead, we orchestrate a dance – a symphony intertwining local and global rhythms. Each chapter reverberates with the lyrical echoes of our ancestral lands, transforming rigid institutions into vibrant "communiversities," where innovation and progress converge. Step into the heart of Integral Cosmology, a transformation journey where economics transmutes and "Communitalism" emerges as a beacon for a fresh economic paradigm. We delve into the rich tapestry of our quadrilateral lineage, finding solace in the core of our African heritage.

This book transcends a mere roadmap; it is a mosaic interwoven by integral research and regeneration, traversing the realms of analytical insight and visionary foresight. The GENE rhythms, Grounding and Emergence, Navigation and Effect, serve as our steadfast pillars, supporting the construction of an ever-evolving society. Here, at the crossroads of cultural authenticity and scholarly pursuit, we embrace empirical phenomenology and conceptual learning – pillars of genesis reflecting the diverse hues of our cultural orientations.

Within the expanse of southern Africa, we honour indigenous and exogenous wisdom while championing the profound influence of Ubuntu. Feminism emerges not solely as a movement but as a methodology – a mirror reflecting the vibrant matriarchal tapestry of our African communities. The call of integral case stories resounds, each narrative embroidered with the resilience and innovation that define nations. These tales echo the dynamic cadence of community growth and economic ingenuity across Egypt, Nigeria, Zimbabwe, and Uganda.

Beyond the confines of postmodern speculations, we tread the path of sociotechnical design rooted in ancient cosmology – a journey from grounded theory to critical rationalism. We transcend empirical observations to explore the realm of experiential elements. More than ink on parchment, these essays compose a symphony, harmonising the diversity of the African continent. They summon scholars, educators, and visionaries to carve a path towards an integral paradigm shift beyond the pursuit of propositional knowledge towards also experiential, imaginal and practical modes of cooperative inquiry. Join us on this expedition as we traverse the nexus of community and consciousness, academia and industry, witnessing theories transmute into tangible societal applications. Let us not merely peruse Africa's revival but engage actively, crafting a narrative that echoes our shared experiences.

The chapters unveil vistas of transformation, illuminating how African universities can evolve into communities nurturing both social innovation and technological prowess. They beckon the transformation of standardised institutions into dynamic hubs resonating with local and global contexts. Addressing the pressing challenges of environmental degradation and societal fractures, our exploration plunges into the bedrock of social innovation and societal regeneration. We advocate not just for change but for a transformative ideology – communitalism – a beacon that transcends the rigid confines of socialism and capitalism. It is an anthem resounding across Africa, carrying the regional echoes of "Nhakanomics," "Yurugu-nomics," and the enchanting "Economics of Love." These variants are not just economic models; they are melodies harmonising tradition with progress, Chapter 1 opening with local wisdom with global aspirations, and solidarity with regenerative innovation.

Chapter 2 emerges as a crucible of transformation – Integral Research and Innovation – a symphony that orchestrates analytical prowess and transformative visions across transcultural pathways. Here, within the rhythmic cadence of GENE – grounding, emerging, navigating, and effecting – we unearth the essence of methodological evolution. It is not just a roadmap; it is a metamorphosis – a journey that heralds a new epoch in research, transcending geographical boundaries to sculpt a holistic approach to knowledge creation.

The subsequent chapters paint an altogether integral, and regenerative, tableau, showcasing the historical tapestry of Southern Africa's research methodologies. Each methodology – Southern rich description, Eastern unfolding narrative, Northern complicated theorising, and Western survey and experimentation – stands as a testament to cultural diversity and orientation. It is not merely a chronicle of methods but a mosaic of narratives, inviting us to comprehend the intricacies of thought that shaped and continue to shape African scholarship.

Following the experiential, imaginal, conceptual and practical tapestry, as Chapters 3-4 unfold, Chapter 5 emerges as a fulcrum, where phenomenology blooms into a philosophy rooted not in mere descriptions but also in immersive experiential learning – a tribute to the essence of Southern African research. Here, the shift from the clinical to the experiential encapsulates the soul of African scholarship – a voyage through words and lived realities.

Chapter 6 unfurls feminism as more than a movement – it is a catalyst for liberation, tracing its evolutionary waves amidst the cultural tapestry of Africa. It fosters the genesis of authentic research and innovation by emphasising not just theory but cultural context, experiential wisdom, and descriptive methodologies. It is a symphony that does not just advocate for gender equality; it celebrates diverse voices, nurturing an inclusive paradigm of knowledge creation. These Chapters 1-6, transcend the boundaries of academic discourse; they are conduits of transformation, guiding us towards a panoramic understanding of Africa's intellectual heritage. Each page is not just a repository of knowledge; it is an invitation to weave together the myriad threads of culture, experience, and wisdom, crafting a narrative that reverberates with the richness of African thought and innovation.

Preface   11

In Chapter 7, South African Participatory Action Research unfurls its vibrant tapestry, illuminating grassroots movements and heralding the champions of societal metamorphosis. It's a celebration of voices from the ground, an anthem for the marginalised, emphasising the convergence and the harmonious dance between theory and practice. This methodology, rooted in the pulse of communities, weaves together the threads of academia and lived experiences, echoing the symphony of change orchestrated by those on the frontlines of societal evolution. Within the intricate web of chapters encompassing hermeneutics, critical theory, cooperative inquiry, and critical rationalism lies the heart of African intellectual exploration. Each chapter is a luminary guiding us through the labyrinth of knowledge, urging us to embrace the holistic tapestry of comprehension. These methodologies are not just academic musings; they are lanterns illuminating the path towards societal metamorphosis, if not regeneration, prompting us to seek a comprehensive understanding that transcends mere discourse.

Coursing through the chapter that follow, we ultimately turn to "western" Empiricism, followed by Critical Realism, also turning to east-west Meta-Reality, unfurling their vibrant banners in Chapters 14 and 15, beckoning us to depart from the confines of Western paradigms. They invite us to perceive beyond the surface, encouraging us to unearth the multilayered tapestry of realities. These chapters do not just challenge existing power dynamics; they ignite a revolution of thought, inviting us to transcend conventional lenses and perceive the world through a kaleidoscope of perspectives.

As the voyage reaches its crescendo within Chapters 16–18, it touches upon the essence of action research, signalling the transition from Afrocentrism to Afrikology and embracing Communitalism's pivotal role in reshaping Africa's educational, research and ultimately societally regenerative landscapes. These chapters are not mere conclusions; they are prologues to a new epoch, a testament to Africa's intellectual renaissance, and an invocation to reimagine paradigms that honour diverse narratives and foster collective growth.

Far from a mere compass, this book resonates as a symphony – a vibrant call to reimagine, reinvent, and reshape Africa's narrative. It is a siren's song that echoes across academia, inviting scholars, visionaries, and changemakers to compose a new dawn – a canvas painted with the hues of our shared heritage and collective destiny. It is a testament to the transformative power of knowledge, beckoning us to co-author a story that stitches our wisdom into the tapestry of global REGENERATION.

Foreword

I am honoured to write the foreword for this groundbreaking book "Integral Research and Social Regeneration in Africa". This book represents years of dedicated research, practical experience, and leadership in the field. It is a valuable and timely contribution to the literature and discourse on integral research and social regeneration in Africa.

This narrative is a jubilant journey, an innovative quest for transformation echoing through diverse cultures and the shared desire for a brighter future. The authors guide us through a metamorphic dance, blending local and global rhythms and transforming institutions into dynamic "communiversities." Beyond a mere guide, this book unfolds as a carefully crafted mosaic, intertwining integral research and regeneration – a harmonious symphony of analytical insight and visionary foresight.

The rhythms of foundation and emergence, navigation, and impact act as steadfast pillars, nurturing an ever-evolving society. The exploration delves into experiential elements, reshaping economics into the paradigm of "communitalism." Acknowledging the wisdom of Southern Africa, the authors uphold Ubuntu, portraying feminism not merely as a movement but as a methodology reflecting the matriarchal fabric of African communities. Across Egypt, Nigeria, Zimbabwe, and Uganda, integral case stories resonate, adorned with resilience and innovation.

As the chapters unfold, they reveal the metamorphosis of African universities into centres fostering social innovation and technological excellence. Tackling challenges, the exploration champions "Communalism" – a transformative ideology blending tradition with progress. They paint an inclusive picture, showcasing Southern Africa's historical research methodologies. These chapters surpass academic rhetoric, prompting scholars and visionaries to pave the way for an integral paradigm shift. Spotlighting South African Participatory Action Research, the chapters honour voices from the ground, highlighting the convergence of theory and practice. Building on the discourse provided thereafter, the three concluding chapters signify the shift from Afrocentrism to Afrikology and embracing the role of Communitalism in reshaping Africa's educational, research, and societal frameworks.

The book echoes as a symphony – a vibrant call to reimagine, redefine, and reshape Africa's narrative. This book is a testament to the transformative power of knowledge, urging scholars and visionaries to compose a new dawn – a canvas painted with the hues of shared heritage and collective destiny.

The authors make us realise that we are in charge of our lives. It is both empowering and inspiring, challenging us to do more and be more than we are. Join Lessem, Adodo and Schieffer as they share their acquired wisdom and insights as scholars over the past few decades. The reported lived experiences and insights from their research and reflections will ultimately help you to think differently, reflect, and start reaping the rewards of successfully embracing integral research and social regeneration in Africa. Without a doubt, this is a must-read book.

I found the integrated approach advocated by the authors enlightening and of great practical value. The reflections provided, the contextual interpretation, rich insights into important conversations, and the words of wisdom are real inspirations.

This book also celebrates the joint efforts progressing well in establishing a research centre focusing on integral research in an African context, to be housed at the Da Vinci Institute for Technology Management in collaboration with RE-GENE-AFRIKA. The research centre aims to foster interdisciplinary and transdisciplinary research addressing Africa's complex and interrelated challenges. The centre also seeks to promote the co-creation of knowledge and solutions with local communities, stakeholders, and policymakers in line with the principles of Ubuntu and communalism.

I highly recommend this book to anyone who is serious about our beautiful continent's regeneration.

Prof. HB Klopper,
CEO, The Da Vinci Institute for Technology Management

Part 1 Orientation

Chapter 1 New African Research, University and Economic Paradigm. Technological/Social Innovation; University/Communiversity; Capitalism and Socialism/Communitalism

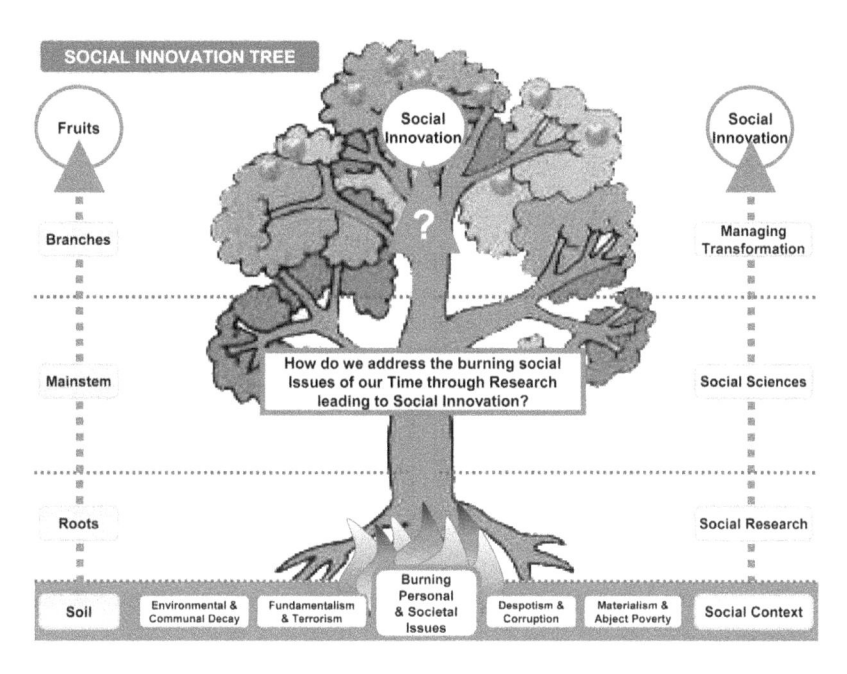

Figure 1.1: *Can Research lead to Social Innovation?*

Summary: Towards a New Research-and-Innovation Paradigm

- The core question underlying integral research, our volume 1, in Africa if not also in worlds at large, is: "How can social research as thereby a regenerative process be turned into social as opposed to technological, innovation?" We ask this question, because of the distinct lack of such a process of social innovation on the one hand, and, of the desperate need for such in society in general, and in the global South in particular.

- We address, therefore, students and practitioners, consultants and policy makers, individually and communally, organisationally and societally, most especially in Africa and its diaspora who want to become innovators in the social and economic arena, by applying the process if Integral Research and Innovation to their research and development work, applied, socio-economically and substantively to amplifying the healing wisdom of Africa (our volumes 2 and 3), communitalism-wise, set inter-institutionally within a new communiversity form (our volume 4),

- In the process of such, university social sciences and humanities departments in Africa and the African diaspora, as integral research academies, alongside learning communities, associated with individual transformation journeys, was well as socio-economic laboratories, gain their rightful place as sources of knowledge creation, social innovation, and ultimately societal regeneration, dealing with burning issues that are particular to their society, drawing on the particular gifts they uniquely bring to the world, in association with others.

- In research and innovation terms, as in "real life", socially if not also technologically, it is the western and the northern approach that dominate (with some exceptions), while the southern and eastern ones have been left out. That is the reason, this being one of our core arguments, why the world generally is "on fire", and Africa/Africans specifically have not realised their full potential.

- We also reconnect with the social philosophies, both from Africa and worlds-wide, which are vital for all research and innovation, as a bridge between process and substance. All too often we fail to recognize the philosophical foundations of research methodologies, epistemologies and ontologies, which in most social science research is disconnected from the research content/substance and issues at hand.

- While closely connected over two decades, one of us authors, Father Dr Anselm Adodo, was born and bred as a Yoruba in rural Nigerian heartlands, and is thereby an African indigenously inside out, south-north, the other of us Professor Ronnie Lessem, born in Zimbabwe of central European, Lithuanian-Austrian parentage, is thereby Euro-African, exogenously outside-in, north-south

- The route we take, thereby combining worlds, toward Integral Research and Innovation is an integral one, encompassing, for us, southern and eastern, as well as northern and western paths, each of which has a fourfold, re-GENE-rative trajectory: local Grounding and origination, local-global Emergent foundation, newly global emancipatory Navigation and global-local transformative Effect: our integral GENE rhythm
- For such a regenerative process, in this volume, we encompass south and east, north and west Africa, spanning most specifically South Africa and Zimbabwe; Tanzania and Uganda; Egypt and Tunisia; Nigeria and Benin, alongside the worlds at large
- Such an Integral Research process is institutionalised through a Societally Regenerative Research Centre (SRRC), set alongside, and building on, Learning Communities and transformation journeys, aligned with Socio-Economic Laboratories, as an African Communiversity within, and overall with the Healing Wisdom of Africa

1.1. Introduction: The Quest for Social Innovation

For Africans, the community is a place of creativity, healing, and relationships. Even though the community embraces both the visible and invisible, the natural and supernatural worlds, like the world of spirits, it should be noted that the point of interaction is always the visible community. The earth is where we live, relate, procreate, and discover our creativity. As a person, I am born into a certain place, on a certain date, at a certain time, into a certain family. These facts play a key role in determining my destiny, my orientation, and my sense of self. I am not just a vague entity. I belong to a place. No one becomes a global citizen at birth. Each individual is a local entity.

Anselm Adodo   Nature Power

Economies at large, as well as business enterprises around the globe then, if they and their societies are to prosper together over the long term, need to draw more purposefully and creatively on their indigenous, alongside their exogenous, cultural and philosophical soils. While the business and economic ethos in America is superficially ("topsoil"-wise) different from that in China – and these two countries combined have recently dominated the business world – further variants, including those within Europe, Africa and much of Asia today, and in Japan hitherto, remain now substantially hidden. It is as if a business and economic geologist has been unable to differentiate, at least in any fundamental way, granite economic and enterprise formations in the Pyrenees from limestone business cliffs in Wales! The implication is, as it were, that volcanic rock in Japan (ever less so today), limestone formations (only superficially visible) in China, and coal shale in America are the only identifiable formations in the "econosphere". Now, moreover, it seems that even the volcanic rock is being eroded, leaving us, if we're not careful, with only "world class" coal shale, or limestone formations, with which to do business!

Ronnie Lessem   Managing in Four Worlds

1.1.1. Backdrop to Social Innovation in Africa: Inside/Out and Outside/In

Integral Research and Innovation, Communiversity, Communitalism in Africa

We are setting out on an ambitious journey, out of Africa, to overturn globalization, economically if not also politically, by GENE-rically co-evolving local identity toward global integrity. Grounding ourselves locally, naturally and communally in Africa is Father Anselm Adodo, relationally from his rural Ewu community in central Nigeria. Father Anselm, moreover, globally-locally, economically and enterprise-wise, through Paxherbals as a socio-economic enterprise he founded over two decades ago, is realizing a formidable transformative Effect. Ronnie Samanyanga Lessem meanwhile, a graduate of Harvard and the LSE, based in the UK but of Southern African heritage, now author of some 50 books on socio-economic re-GENE-ration in Africa, Asia, Europe and the Americas, provides worlds-wide, thereby integral, social scientific, newly global Navigation. Finally, the three authors, in close association with others in Southern, East, North and West Africa, have been engaging over the past decade in a transformation journey, providing the local-global Emergent, cultural foundation for what is now integrally to follow.

What follows then is our re-GENE-rative process of research and social innovation in south, east, north and west Africa, set alongside our communitalist substance Africa and worldwide and a communiversity form in theory and practice. Altogether and processally then, we feel local (Grounding), intuit locally-globally (Emergence), think newly globally (Navigation), and act globally-locally (Effect) on each of four research and innovation relational (southern), renewal (eastern) paths, as well as paths of reason (northern) and realization (western). Following such, substantively, will be the transformation of capitalism and communitalism, Africa-wide and worlds-wide, building on the healing wisdom of Africa, middle-up-down-across. All of the above, moreover, will be continually placed in context, both Africa and worlds wide.

The outcome will be the transformation of the African university into a communiversity, through *learning communities* (instead of individual community service), *transformation journeys* (instead of individual education and training), a *research academy* (instead of individual research), and *socio-economic laboratories* (instead of individual secondments). Furthermore, and communitalism-wise, transcending capitalism, *Nhakanomics* in Zimbabwe (southern Africa), *Yurugu-nomics* in Uganda (east Africa), the *Economics of Love* in Egypt (north Africa), and overall

Communitalism in Nigeria (West Africa) will altogether ensue, altogether building on Africa's healing wisdom, naturally, culturally, scientifically and technologically, politically and economically.

1.1.2. Beyond the Innovation Buzzword: Process, Substance, Form and Context

Innovation is the "buzzword of our day". Each business is concerned with it and claims that it will soon be "out of the market" if it loses its power to innovate. Entire societies, governments and political parties nail their colours to the innovation mast, altogether promoting "economic growth", and thereby claiming to be doing everything to promote such. They thereby commit themselves to developing a legal, financial, educational and communicational infrastructure to promote such (implied technological) innovation, with businesses inevitably expected to take the "innovative" lead. Governments, however, and indeed people in general, have little understanding of what "social", as distinct from conventional technological innovation, might actually mean, more especially when lodged in a particular community or society, be it, for example, in Buhera or Benin.

As such, and more especially, such research and innovation is now specifically contextualised within, and thereby born out of, a particular natural and cultural context, specifically for us here, one in Africa and its diaspora. This then is the primary issue, through firstly our *process* of integral research-and-innovation, secondly by way of *substance*, within the integral realms of nature, culture, social science and technology, polity and economy, thirdly the inter-institutional *form* in which such needs to be lodged, that of a so-called Communiversity, and finally, by way of *context*, explicitly within Africa and its Diaspora. Process, substance, form and context then need to be integrally co-evolved for social innovation to occur.

As we have said then, the term innovation is invariably used to represent "technical and technological innovation". It reflects advancement in core industries (from automotive to communications, from information technology to chemistry and biotechnology, from solar energy to medical products, from the financial industry to logistics, from airline to space technology, and now, most notably, from desktop computing to the new social media). Billions of dollars are pumped into research and development to enable technological innovation to take place in those sectors. Of course, all this is very important. But, while parts of the world have become highly innovative in technological terms, what we term "social innovation" lags way, way behind, which is why, for us, Ukraine and Russia, Palestine and Israel, Yemen and Sudan – the list is endless – are all on fire!

For us, such "innovation" in a particular society accompanied by a communiversity and communitalism, and ultimately the healing wisdom of Africa, as we shall see, in Africa or its Diaspora, if not world-wide, is comprised of:

- a local communal grounding and origination/learning community and Nhaka-economy supported by Community Building (nor marketing);
- a local-global trans-cultural, emergent foundation/transformation journey and Yurugu-economy, supported by Conscious Evolution (not HR); thereafter
- a "newly global", emancipatory, scientific navigation/research academy and economics of love supported by Knowledge Creation (not operations), and
- global-local transformative economic effect/Communitalism supported by Sustainable Development (not finance).

Such altogether then constitutes "social" innovation. Moreover, in specifically Re-GENE-rative integral research terms, we ground such innovation in original research "method", emerge foundationally through a research "methodology", navigate in emancipatory guise via research critique, and effect innovation transformatively through "action" research, altogether and in turn, on one or other research path.

So, alongside these technological advances, socially bereft of the above, the world generally and Africa specifically suffers increasingly from the downsides of such technological, and now also financial, innovation, without social innovation to counteract it. Moreover, in Africa, being generally "relational" in our "southern" research orientation, *social* innovation should occupy pride of place. Altogether though we are faced with environmental destruction and economic crises, all too often serving to increase the gaps between the rich and the poor, while at the same time, crazy as it seems, there is more and more work that needs to be done while unemployment – people thereby being "out of work" – proliferates.

As materialism advances, there is an increasing sense of unrest, insecurity and lack of rootedness, psychologically and spiritually. Then, we turn again to economics and technology to find the solutions to such problems. We want our industries to become more environmentally friendly; we want our pharmaceutical companies and globally initiated health initiatives to solve our health problems, we want technology to be developed to resolve the digital divide, we want trade and growth to create wealth for all-comers, and so on, and so on.

Therefore, we of the "west" and the "north", whether within industrialised societies or without, believe that once the poor countries have developed economies, with technology thereby playing a major part, many of the current problems will be solved automatically, and Africa will be "rising", just was we did in the "west" and indeed parts now of the "east". But of course this is not taking place, in African societies as a whole (all too often only the elites are rising), because there is no social innovation, albeit that in Africa and its Diaspora, for example, thousands and thousands of students are conducting "research". Where are we going wrong?

1.1.3. Beyond Technology

Our claim, therefore, is not that we should abandon technological innovation but that we are seeing such innovation in far too one-dimensional terms, with AI today being at the top of the technical list. There is more to life and work than technological and economic innovation. There is social, including ecological and cultural, innovation, and in our integral enterprises, as we shall see in the African case stories that follow, we demonstrate why social innovation is equally important and how it can be achieved structurally through institutionalising such and functionally by evolving social research, re-GENE-relatively, accordingly. Such a newly regenerative approach towards research, moreover, needs to be purposefully lodged in specific natural and cultural soils, thereby intimately connected with the social sciences generally, as well as the humanities in particular, in the process of addressing burning issues and drawing on particular gifts/capacities. Structurally speaking, as we shall see, a Centre for Integral Research and Societal Re-GENEration is being co-evolved, therefore, at the heart of, or networked alongside, learning communities, transformation journeys, and socio-economic laboratories to build purposefully on Africa's healing wisdom.

Indeed, one of us, Anselm Adodo as we shall see, promoted such learning communities amongst his local farmers, and has developed transformation journeys by way of a Masters in Transformation Studies for individuals and communities in Nigeria, and has founded Pax Herbals (Adodo2017) as a socio-economic laboratory, in fact a leading such example of deploying healing wisdom, naturally and economically, in the whole of Africa.

The other one of us, Ronnie Lessem, together with his former partner at Trans4m, Alexander Schieffer, developed the overall approach to *Integral Research and Innovation* (Lessem and Schieffer 2010), alongside *Integral Economics* (Lessem and Schieffer 2010) and *Transformation Management* (Lessem and Schieffer (2009), upon which our work was initially based. Together moreover, Ronnie, Anselm, and Tony Bradley (2019, have developed *The Idea of the Communiversity* and also *Afrikology (Adodo and Lessem, 2021),* each in turn, altogether paving the way, also now with Sandile Ndlungwane in South Africa, for a Centre for *Integral Research and Innovation in Africa* So why, overall, and more specifically, are we embarking on this ambitious journey?

1.2. Why Social Innovation Falls Behind Technological Innovation

1.2.1. Enterprise and University Bereft of Humanity

When we ask many of our business or academic colleagues how they are advancing thelot of mankind generally, or indeed Africa and its diaspora, specifically, through their commercial activities, on the one business hand, or their "research" papers or indeed degree courses, on the academic other, we usually we get incredulous looks. There are, of course, exceptions to this rule, but such are few and far between. After all, individual students are wrapped up in their formal studies, individual researchers with their academic papers, and individual practitioners with their business priorities, rather than building learning or, indeed, knowledge-creating communities rather than engaging in deeply rooted and broadly based transformation journeys.

Moreover, when we ask colleagues in the corporate world how their research is contributing to resolving our pensions crisis, social injustice, human poverty around the globe, or, more recently, the global financial crisis, we get similarly blank looks though as an exception, some may now be concerned with the problem of world climate change, albeit as part of their corporate remit. On the one hand, then, "that's all very well", the academics say, "our students just want to get a degree", or "I have a PhD to complete". On the other hand, for business or management practitioners, "I have targets to meet", "it's up to the government or you people at the universities to solve the world's problems, not us". Indeed, the business of marketing, operations, finance, or indeed of HR has little to do with community building or even knowledge creation, never mind with healing society!

The prospect that business or academe, of course alongside the public and civic sectors, may be advancing the lot of mankind, purposefully through social – alongside technological – innovations, is therefore seldom considered. When it is, moreover, such social "innovation" is conceived of in terms of the development of some new product or service, whereby such "development" has nothing to do with formalised research in sociology or psychology, philosophy or geography, ecology or anthropology. Imagine a technological innovator who does not delve into physics or chemistry, biology or ecology, bioengineering or biotechnology. In fact, and in the course of the 2008 financial crisis, it is amazing that nobody seemed to look towards the universities or research institutes as either a source of the problem or as the source of its solution.

Thought and action, most especially that of a radical, transformative nature, at least in the social and economic arena, especially lodged within a particular society's natural and cultural context, seldom institutionally meet. More so, for us, and especially in parts of the world or *a* world, which are supposedly "lagging behind", the university, as it currently stands, together with others, is failing to play its part in regenerating a society. Indeed, while in the natural sciences, industry and academia, most especially with "high tech" oriented "science parks", combine forces prolifically, in the social sciences, no such equivalent exists. It is for that very reason what we are crying out for a "high touch", as opposed to high tech, communiversity!

In Figure 1.2. below we sketch this out, to feed, perhaps, our imagination, if not also to enhance our powers of research and analysis, as well as ultimately, and specifically, social innovation. We now turn, specifically, to academically, and indeed practically, based social research, and will build up our social innovation process, Communion form, communitatism-like healing substance, and African context integrally from there.

SOCIAL INNOVATION TREE

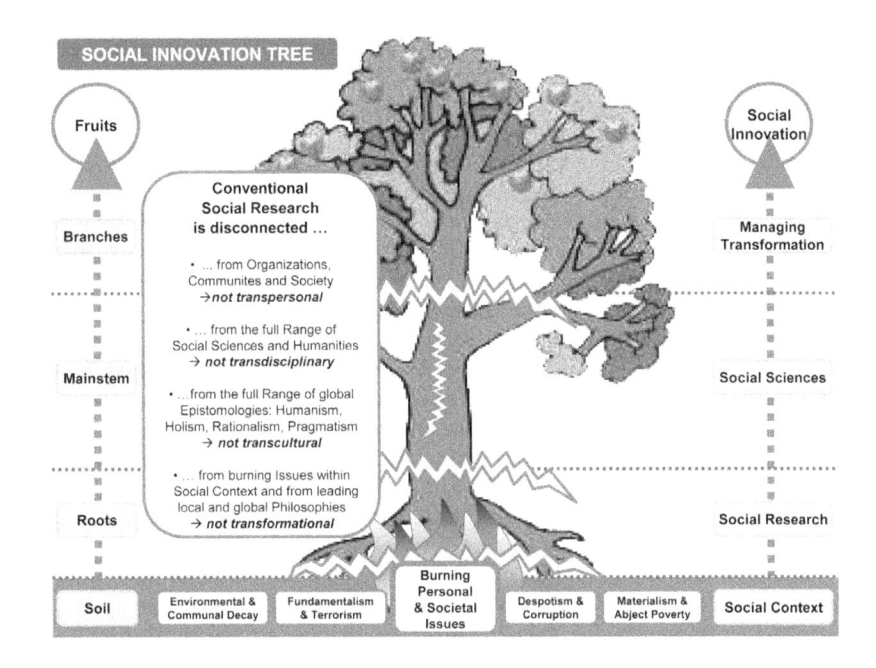

Figure 1.2: *Dysfunctional Research*

1.3. Waking Up to Our Research and Innovation Potential

1.3.1. First Wake-Up Call: Social Research Devoid of Innovation

Method and Methodology Are Part of an Integral Process as a Whole

How, we might ask process-wise, to begin with, is social and economic research positioned in universities, if not also within social research institutes, as well as corporations? Research "method", as conventionally conceived of in the social sciences, ranging from quantitative to qualitative, is a form of "data processing" drawn, for example, from census data, interviews, questionnaires, focus groups or case studies, rather than as a very *Grounding* of such research and innovation.

Few researchers, as such, are aware of the fact that *research method and methodology are each part of a more integral whole*, thereby incorporated into what we term one or other relational ("southern"), renewal ("eastern"), reason ("northern") or realisation ("western") research path, each with our "integral research trajectory", or re-GENE-native rhythm, from origination to transformation. Indeed it is in that same guise that economics generally and management, or indeed now leadership, specifically, is caught in "flatlands", also bereft of such a rhythm or trajectory, never mind bestowed with alternately southern, eastern, northern and western paths. Instead, TINA (There is no alternative) rules!

In fact, most researchers, within universities and without, engage with method or research as a technique rather than with "methodology" or research methodology, without realizing the difference between one and the other, and without encompassing a research trajectory – see above – as such. Moreover, at least in the social sciences and the humanities, such research, confined to the university, disconnected from community and laboratory, and devoid of a transformation journey, is duly limited to analysis as opposed to re-GENE-ration, whereby with the method the researcher makes a Grounding start. Indeed, the same technical pre-emphasis applies to econometrically based economics and "scientifically" based functional management, increasingly today.

In fact, and on the one hand, one of us (Ronnie Lessem) had been put off such research methods, in fact, for four decades, by an initially tedious (par for the course), stand-alone undergraduate economics module on "statistical research methods", at the University of Rhodesia and Nyasaland. The other of us (Anselm Adodo), while fully engaged hitherto in research and innovation, in relation to the natural sciences, through Pax Herbals, had been unaware, , of the potentially transformative impact of integral research methodology, not to mention also integral economics and enterprise, in the social sciences.

So it took us many long years of travelling through such a social and economic research desert, from Africa to Europe, onto American and Asia, indeed ultimately across four continents, also including MENA – Middle East and North Africa – in the centre, before, as we shall see, several wake-up calls came along to transform our perspective. *The key that opened such a transformative door was our discovery that* differentiated inevitably "westernised" research paths could be reconceived as leading, *integrally* as we shall soon see, research-wise from method (data processing technique) onto research methodology (research paradigm) and beyond, and, innovation wise, from origination to transformation. The same indeed applied to management and to economics, where each economic or managerial function or sub-discipline, could be considered originally – nature wise, according to local feel; could be intuited locally-globally, transculturally; could be thought about in emancipatory, scientific guise, newly globally; and ultimately acted upon globally-locally in terms of variegated southern, eastern, northern or western effect. Indeed finally, a communiversity itself had such an re-GENE-rative rhythm to it from learning community (original Grounding) to integral laboratory (transformative Effect).

Yet Research Method and Methodology Fail to Meet

There was, then, a vast gulf between *methodology (incorporating philosophy) and method (incorporating technique)* of which only the enlightened few had become aware. We had discovered that, amongst colleagues and students alike, *reference to method and methodology tended to be intertwined rather than clearly differentiated.* This mix of terms was replicated in much of the literature. We had found it virtually impossible to discover any research texts that dealt, sequentially and complementarily, with methodology-philosophy and method-technique.

Moreover, when our practitioner colleagues referred to "market research" or to "morale surveys" it was invariably to such research methods, whether "interview" or "questionnaire" based, to which they referred, and they were oblivious to any idea of methodology, or indeed to research as philosophy. The same applies for one of us (Ronnie Lessem) observing his daughter's psychology undergraduate studies at the Open University. Though pedagogically such learning methodologies are second to none, research-wise the overwhelming pre-emphasis is on method/technique with almost zero orientation to research philosophy/paradigm. Furthermore, such seemingly "incomprehensible" academic notions as ontology (theory of reality) and epistemology (theory of knowledge) were entirely foreign to most, be they research students or management/economic practitioners alike.

The trouble is, then, that *methodology, or philosophy,* remains disconnected from method or practicality, not to mention the fact that action research is all too often left out of the picture altogether, and hence innovation, process-wise is curbed. As such the corrosive gap between the research ivory tower as perceived (methodology and philosophy) and research muck and brass (method and technique) is reinforced. Research methodologies were often profound in scope, but they were all too often, as we shall see, very difficult to follow or indeed apply. Moreover, while methods may have been easier to comprehend, it was difficult to decide what method applied to which methodology. Finally, it was only in the context of a doctoral programme that any attention to methodology was given at all, and yet, if we were to claim to be social innovators, method or technique alone would get us pretty well nowhere.

In summary, there were virtually no attempts to bridge the gap between methodology, as research philosophy, and method, as research activity. Each stood in splendid isolation from the other, so that ultimately the process of social innovation – never mind substance and form which is a separate consideration for us – which needed methodology (philosophy) and method (technique), as well as research critique and action was massively short changed. We now come to our second wake-up call.

1.3.2. Second Wake Up Call: Lacking in Integrity

Colonization of the Minds

As our journey of discovery progressed, we came to the next revealing realisation that, whereas *methodology was predominantly European* in origin and *method was more likely to be American,* the *rest of the world virtually did not get a look in at all.*

Indeed, the same applies to the study of economics and management as a substantive whole, not to mention the university's form, whereby in all such processal, substantive and form-laden cases, either Europe or America dominates.

In other words, whether researchers, as students, came from South Africa or the Middle East, China or India, as well as Europe and the U.S., their research orientation would invariably be European or American. The same, of course, would apply to practitioners who engaged with us in "research" projects from China or India, South Africa or the Arab world. Somehow, that "north-western" predominance did not make sense to us. No wonder the world was on fire. Furthermore, the very fact that the philosophical "northern" Europeans predominated methodologically, and the practical "western" Americans prevailed where the method was concerned, meant that there was bound to be a gap in the mid-Atlantic!

Academe Has Given up Its Knowledge Birthright

Furthermore, we found ourselves confused in between two knowledge domains with very different "rules of the game". For on the one hand, there was the field of business administration where knowledge management, or indeed knowledge creation, had recently become the order of the day. Therein, as was the case for the "knowledge-creating company", popularised by the two Japanese organizational sociologists, Nonaka and Takeuchi (1995), it was the norm to integrate diverse knowledge perspectives, thereby, for the formidable Japanese duo, originating or socialising (our southern), dialoguing or externalising (our eastern), systematising or combining (our northern) and practising or internalising (our western).

However, on the other hand, when it came to academic research in the social sciences, the norm was to specialize in one "Western" research method or "Northern" *methodology*. So it seemed, at least in Nonaka's knowledge-creating terms, that one knowledge world predominated over the others, so that, in our terms, in research, there was a lack of worldly integrity. Moreover, whereas Nonaka's *knowledge-creating company* was a seminal work in the field of management, by way of an "eastern" Japanese exception to the "western" American norm, universities carried on in their same old way, with their individual research and education, bereft of organisational knowledge creation, especially in the social sciences and humanities.

Moreover, while Nonaka's approach to knowledge creation was exclusively organizational, no such approach, which we term social innovation, existed at the societal level. In fact, where there is, increasingly, reference to social as well as business entrepreneurship and "innovation", there is no connection, in the latter case, with academically based research in the social sciences. Unlike the case, as we indicated, in the natural sciences, social research and social – as opposed to technological – innovation, are completely split apart.

But we had two more fundamental discoveries to make before finally putting together our thoughts on Integral Research, and, in parallel, on *Integral Economics* (Lessem and Schieffer 2010) and *Integral Enterprise* (Lessem and Schieffer 2010), followed by our *Idea of the Communiversity* (Lessem et al 2019). In fact, with the third wake-up call we would come back full circle to where one of us (Ronnie Lessem) had started as an undergraduate in Africa.

1.3.3. Third Wake Up Call: Need for the Integral, for Integrity and Integration

Origination Precedes Foundation

Our third, wake up call, had several connected parts to it, paving the way for social research-and-innovation that is ultimately integral (re-GENE-rative trajectory), integrity (worldly-wise) laden, and integrating (I to U in Synergy).

Firstly then, now that we had discovered the fact that research methodology was indeed philosophy, we were duly uplifted, but too much so. Our feet had left the ground so that we, and also our research students, were up in the clouds. So-called "phenomenology" and "critical rationalism", "postmodernism" and "critical realism", for example, were truly revolutionary in nature and scope, particularly when we were able to touch base with their founding fathers, like:

- *Moravia's Edmund Husserl:* the founder of phenomenology, who heralded, in the 1930s, a crisis in the European sciences
- *Austria's Karl Popper:* the founder of critical rationalism, a refugee from Nazism, who, in the 1940s, made his call for an open society, against its fascist enemies
- *France's Michel Foucault:* founder of postmodernism, who was a leading light in the 1960s in the radical, anti-capitalist student movement of the time
- *Anglo-Indian Roy Bhaskar:* founder of critical realism, an ex Marxist, who saw his critical realism as an antidote to an empirically based free market society

However, there was a twist in the revolutionary tale. For these research philosophies were difficult for your everyday student, practitioner, or indeed researcher, to grasp, from the ground up. No wonder social innovation is all too often short-changed. Moreover, because such research methodologies, or philosophies, were "studied" by individual researchers, in academe, they were not easily accessed by society at large. They were certainly far too difficult, if not esoteric, to be grasped by "real world" practitioners, so that their revolutionary influence was severely circumscribed.

In fact, and in the final analysis, the fact that the farther reaches of such research methodology had become an individual, more often than not "doctoral" pursuit, meant that community, organisation and society were left out in the cold. In our terms then, there was no integration between self and community, organisation and society, research-wise, which meant that social innovation was bound to go begging. Indeed, we were intrigued to find that community activists were all too often as far removed from such transformative methodologies as management practitioners.

The worlds of communal learning, transformative education, institutionalised research and economic enterprise, each in societal context, which we were seeking to bridge through our communiversity were invariably split apart. Moreover, and especially frustrating for us, was that for all the proliferation of universities, worlds-wide, research academies that explicitly drew on the unique contexts in which they were set, while simultaneously serving societal needs – as opposed to outstanding, individual public intellectuals who of course existed – were almost impossible to find. No wonder TINA still prevailed!

Imagine, by way of contrast, assuming that technological innovation was a matter for individuals, not for organizations or societies. What an absurd thought. Yet, when it comes to social research and innovation, that's an individual matter! So then it came to us: the more accessible research method needed to be reconceived as a form of origination, or a point of access, prior to what then became a methodological research foundation. Census data, producer or consumer attitude surveys, for example, were organisationally and societally, as well as individually oriented. So that was a good place for us to start, but definitely not to end. In other words, and with a view to social innovation, such research method, as a point of origination, needed to be followed by the application of research methodology, to provide a deeper, and broader, foundation. Indeed the same logic applied, process-wise for example, organisationally, to the distinction between human relations and organisational development, or to operations management versus organisational knowledge creation.

Emancipation Succeeds Foundation

What we simultaneously discovered, moreover, with a little help from Australian research philosopher Norman Blaikie (2016), was that what he termed "classical" and "contemporary" research methodologies were qualitatively different from each other. Whereas the longstanding *classical* ones – empiricism and the like – were foundational, so to speak, the more contemporary *critical* ones – like "critical theory" so called, were for us indeed *emancipatory*.

So we decided not only to differentiate method (origination) from methodology (foundation), but also critique (emancipation) from both of the other two. So the overall rhythm, or what we now termed our re-GENE-rative *research trajectory,* as indicated above, went from origination (Grounding) to foundation (Emergence) to emancipation (Navigation) as a combined prelude to transformation (Effect). Moreover, as we evolved from Grounding origination (method) toward Emergent foundation (methodology) and Emancipatory navigation (critique), so we assumed an ever deeper, and broader, societal reach, ultimately ending up with action research, by way of Effective transformation, altogether constituting our GENE.

As we can see, such a re-GENE-rative trajectory extends, at least process-wise (substance and form still to come in future volumes) from research towards innovation, ending up with transformation. Although the emancipatory approaches were more radical and transformative in intent than what came before, they still were primarily means of reflection rather than action. At the same time, the processes of origination (method), establishing a research foundation (methodology) and thereafter emancipation (critique) paved the way for transformation (action), whereby social research turns into innovation, at least process-wise, along one path or another.

We now turn to action research.

Emancipation onto Transformative Action

Kurt Lewin (2015), who founded action research in the 1950s, and was himself a refugee to the UK from Nazi Germany, claimed that research in the social sciences lacked authenticity, if it did not involve action, to test out the otherwise inauthentic theory. Moreover, as we were soon to discover, there were four fundamentally different, albeit related, approaches to such action research: generic action research (AR), socio-technical design (STD), co-operative inquiry (CI), and participatory action research (PAR). Lo and behold, we then concluded, each embodied, in particular, one or other of our Four Worlds: western (AR), northern (STD), eastern (CI) and southern (PAR). What they did not reveal, though, and as will be recognized through the course of this text, is that each of these needs to be further contextualised so as to constitute Integral Research and Innovation in Africa, that is apart from the need for substantiation (content) and form.

At this transformative point moreover, building upon this ultimately action research orientation, we have left the individual researcher way behind, and have entered the realms of communal, organisational and societal transformation, whereby the integrating of the individual, the institutional and the societal becomes for real. The fourth and culminating wake-up call, the one with which we are currently still preoccupied, is that neither the subject matter of economics and management, with which such a university is primarily engaged, in substance as well as in African context, nor the university in and of itself, in its form, especially in the social sciences and humanities with which we are engaged, is up to the social innovation and regeneration task.

1.3.4. Institutionalising Social Innovation: The Fourth Wake-Up Call

1.3.4.1. What Gets in the Way of Inter-Institution Building

Individual Research Predominates

Characteristically and ironically, "social" science research, conventionally led by universities, is individually oriented, while natural science research and development, typically conducted and thereby institutionalised, within corporate or governmental research laboratories, is team-oriented. Indeed, and to complicate matters further, on the one hand, whatever attempts have been made to collectivise research and learning, at least conceptually, have not come from the relational cultures of "southern" guise, certainly not from Africa, notwithstanding the superb, scholarly work, of late, from the likes of Ndlovu Gatsheni (2018) and more, on "de-colonising" episteme. On the other hand, when it comes to consideration of the institution, or indeed society at large, it is not specifically attuned to Africa, neither in social scientific substance nor in natural and cultural context.

In fact, and firstly then, one of the major stumbling blocks to assimilating the wide range of research methods and methodologies to which we have alluded, is that there are too many for the individual mind to absorb. Indeed, not only does authentic social innovation, re-GENE-ratively speaking, require an initial method (original Grounding), an established methodology (Emergent foundation), a radical critique (emancipatory Navigation)and ultimately transformative action (Trans4mative Effect) – hence leading from research to innovation – but it also needs to be trans-disciplinary.

To address environmental and communal decay then, to take one example, needs ideally a team of ecologists, physical geographers, anthropologists, social historians, sociologists and economists, if not also business minded researchers, as well as some of those, additionally, schooled in the humanities. Yet there are virtually no institutional forms, no "social laboratories" so to speak, to promote such. The closest we got to this, for example historically in the 20th century, was with the composite "Area Studies", involving say China or the Middle East, instigated by the U.S. government after the last war. There may then have been interdisciplinary research into such, but certainly no social innovation to regeneratively follow. Moreover today, the theory and practice of economics and management, is predominantly, as we have seen, "north-western" rather than "south-eastern". In the same way as we need variegated research paths and trajectories – southern, eastern, northern and western – the same applies to the substance of the social sciences and humanities.

Bereft of Integral Research and Societal Regeneration

In other words, in social research, culminating in thoroughgoing social innovation, not only are a multiplicity of disciplines involved, but there needs to be, as we shall see, a wide range of research paths, as well as economic and managerial contexts, each with a societally regenerative trajectory. In contrast, as is the "research" norm, social scientists, invariably working as individuals rather than as research teams, go for the lowest common denominator. While, on the one hand, they stick to a single discipline, be it economics or psychology, on the other hand each researcher adopts a single research method – for example an empirically oriented, questionnaire based, approach to "data processing" – bereft of a research – or economic or managerial – trajectory.

This is even more the case in developing countries, where human and physical resources are especially scarce. In developed countries, in the social sciences, the alternative may be to plump for one particular methodology favoured by a university department, say phenomenology, preferably a combination of method (technique) and methodology (philosophy), such as so called "interpretive phenomenological analysis" (IPA) in psychology.

The overall result, all too often, is arid and pedestrian individual, monodisciplinary based, research, bereft of any integral research and societal re-GENE-ration, conducted within a single program, rather than contained within an institutional structure. At best, there may be a research centre, so called, but it will invariably be dependent on the talent and charisma of an individual "guru", such as the corporate strategist Michael Porter (2004) at Harvard Business School, or the development economist Jeffrey Sachs at Columbia University, whereby and respectively competitive strategy/Porter's *Techniques for Analysing Industries and Competitors* and SDG's (Sustainable Development Goals)/Sachs' – *Sustainable Development Report* (Sachs et al 2022) invariably predominate in "north-western" guise over all comers.

Absence of a Composite Research-and-Innovation Team

As we have also indicated then, while in the typical, university department, in the social sciences or the humanities, the focus is on the researcher as an individual, this is absolutely not the case in the corporate R and D laboratory, in the natural sciences, where the focus is on the research and development team. As such, and in this latter case, whereas one of the team members, as a fundamental researcher, would be both multidisciplinary in orientation, and also inclined to span a fully regenerative research trajectory, others, in the innovation team, would be more specialised in design, engineering, production or sales.

In other words, and more conventionally speaking, the individual inventor, in such a technology-based innovation team, needs to be surrounded by product engineers, designers, operations and sales people, who, in effect, turn such an invention from an original concept into a commercial success. In the case, say, of pharmaceuticals, this may take ten years, from research (fundamental) and development (applied) to market (commercialisation), and cost a billion dollars in all.

Social research, in contrast, is reckoned not to have those kinds of resources attached to it. In fact, we would argue that such a "lack of resources" is a symptom rather than a cause. The cause, for us, is the overriding belief that it is up to politicians, locally, nationally and internationally, if not also, in a very loose sense, civil society, to deal with intractable social and economic problems, such as recurring warfare, unemployment and environmental decay. The result is what we see in Russia or in Iran for example today, with billions spent on military hardware, accompanied by the tragic loss of human lives, with seemingly no social innovation in place to prevent such horrendous outcomes from occurring, even recurring, in the first place.

Indeed, and in the overall scheme of things, the humanities through art and culture, though more easily contextualised in a particular society than the natural and social sciences, does not even feature, but are rather restricted to exhibitions, museums, festivals and events, to be enjoyed, on the side. In fact, if it is not politicians, it is natural scientists, and technologists, who are called upon to address social problems, aside from the odd, footloose "think tank", now in support of NATO for example, so that is where the bulk of the financial resources go. We fail then to recognize that the social sciences and humanities generally, and that social researchers, specifically, can both address our burning societal needs, and serve to harness our unique natural and cultural capacities, indeed to forestall warfare, poverty and strife.

Yet, ironically, over centuries, we have pointed to individual social philosophers and scientists, ranging from Aristotle to St Thomas Aquinas, from John Locke to Adam Smith, and more recently from John Maynard Keynes to Milton Friedman, to address these issues. Indeed, and during the neo-liberal heyday of the past thirty years, the best, and perhaps only, example we have of a team of social innovators, ultimately ruinous ones we would reckon at that, were the "Chicago Boys", where Friedman and his social scientific cronies were based, that's is in the University of Chicago economics department. In the final analysis, they were never short of resources!

Research-Innovation; University-Communiversity; Capitalism-Communitalism

Ultimately then, the conclusion we came to, both in theory (Adodo 2017) and in practice (Zilberg 2012), hitherto through our *Idea of the Communiversity* (Lessem) and the institutionalisation of such around Pax Herbals, as a *Integral Community Enterprise in Africa* (Adodo), was that social innovation, generally, and the move from integral research to societal regeneration of a particular society, in African part or whole, needs to be grounded in *learning communities*, not in individual education. Further to such, individually westernised education needs to be turned into trans-culturally contextualised transformation, a transformation journey from call to contribution.

Thirdly, individuals and communities need to co-evolve with one or more particular and evolved enterprises, which we term *socio-economic laboratories*. Finally, as is our primary concern here, a Centre for Integral Research and Societal Re-GENEration in Africa is required. Represented from the outset naturally and culturally, scientifically and economically – indigenously (inside/out) and exogenously (outside/in) – actively and reflectively by ourselves, Adodo (Afro-Yoruba) and Lessem (Euro-African) in turn, thereafter amplified by relevant others. Moreover, in the African case, such an academy needs to be concerned with the development of a form of economy and enterprise that befits its being, becoming, knowing and doing, centred in the healing wisdom of Africa. That is a tall order, but one that needs to be addressed if, and in response to current events, streams of boat people are stop crossing over to European shores, crime rates amongst the perennially unemployed are to be reduced, and climate change thwarted, over the long term.

1.4.2. Towards Research and Development in the Social Sciences and Humanities

The Integral Trajectory and Technological Innovation

The natural sciences then, on the one hand as we have now seen, at least in the industrialised world, provides many good examples of such a trans-disciplinary as well as trans-sectoral research orientations, as for example with biochemistry, genetic engineering, socio-biology, lodged within corporate, governmental, or even non-governmental research departments, leading to fundamental, indeed generative, technological breakthroughs. On the other hand, when it comes to the social sciences, while there are such trans-disciplinary fields as social psychology, or cultural anthropology, as well as, historically at least, political economics, each of these tends to be dominated by the major discipline (psychology, anthropology, and economics in turn). Moreover, and from our longstanding experience, sponsored research is invariably compartmentalised, bureaucratised, and instrumentalised, thereby seldom leading to the kind of social and contextualised innovation that can lead to a functional polity in Russia or Iran, to ongoing peace between Israelis and Palestinians, or to a functional economy in South Africa or Nigeria, that benefits all its peoples.

Specific disciplines might give rise to research centres, say in Social Economics (Economics) or in Chaos and Complexity Theory (Political Science), but the research undertaken seldom, if ever, gives rise to any social innovation, thereby making a transformative impact, in a particular context, on the ground, as illustrated above. Moreover, the humanities, for example, music and dance, art and sculpture, literature and drama, are closely aligned with a particular, say, Senegalese African context, whereby such research and application will be far removed from the areas of technology, economy and polity that ultimately "make things happen". In our own integral terms, nature and culture are separated from technology, economy and polity, which is what we are therefore seeking to overcome.

Technological innovation, moreover, aside from its trans-disciplinary and trans-sectoral orientation, also involves a "research and development – or research and innovation – trajectory" which goes roughly like this:

- fundamental research, say in physics, chemistry, biology
- applied research, for example in electronics, biotechnology, nanotechnology
- development, including product and process design and engineering
- commercialization: including finance, operations, project management, sales.

Altogether then, in a corporate context, we can talk of the trajectory of research *and* development, together with commercialisation, leading ultimately to technological innovation. We are aware, with one notable contemporary African exception highlighted below, in Zimbabwe, of no real articulated equivalent in the social sciences and humanities (even the superb Japanese organisational sociologists Nonaka and Takeuchi as above relate their knowledge creating company to technological innovation). Indeed, it is not even commonplace to talk of fundamental (basic or blue-sky) versus applied social research, never mind development and commercialization, in economics or sociology (social science), in history or fine arts (humanities). So what hope is there of all-round social innovation and regeneration?

The Integral Research Trajectory and Societal Re-GENE-ration

So we have had to invent what we call our research-and-innovation *trajectory*, as well as, ultimately, one such for an African economy and enterprise at large, that is from local grounding, naturally, and local-grounding emergence, trans-culturally, to newly global navigation, scientifically and global-local effect, politically and economically, in southern, east, northern and west Africa. Unsurprisingly such ultimate societal re-GENE-ration follows the logic of our GENE – original local natural and communal **Grounding**, **Emergent** local-global trans-cultural foundation, emancipatory "newly global" scientific and humanistic **Navigation** and ultimately global-local transformative economic **Effect** – because social research inevitably applies to a particular society, if not also to an individual, organisation and community. It is in that guise that we shall come up with variegated examples of African Communitalism such as Nhakanomics (south), Yurugu-nomics (east), the Economics of Love (north) and Communitalism (west), each drawing differently on African healing wisdom.

So we have to start the social, including natural and cultural, process by recognizing the particular Grounds in which we stand, while also, and subsequently, acknowledging that these local grounds never stand in global isolation (with the ever decreasing exception of still isolated, indigenous peoples). This blending of the local and the global, as indeed is represented by ourselves as Yoruba-African and Euro-African, is what we term emergent development. However, and in addition, for social innovation to fully occur, such natural grounding (nature power in Adodo's case as we shall see) and trans-cultural emergence (local Yoruba and global Benedictine in his case) needs to be consolidated, in terms of newly constituted concepts and frameworks, which we term scientific Navigation (Communiversity to Communitalism). Finally, such conceptual frameworks, institutional designs, or political constitutions need to be put into enterprise Effect, Pax Herbals for Adodo.

Arguably then, grounding can be likened to fundamental research, albeit that latter is rooted in a discipline (physics or chemistry) rather than a community (Beninois or Bengali). Emergence, then, can be aligned with applied research, in the natural sciences, in that is more attuned to a particular context, albeit informed by science in general. Navigation is closely linked with development (design, engineering), and Effecting can be connected with commercialisation. All of such then needs to be applied to the research-and-development of economy and enterprise in Africa, newly globally in our emancipatory terms, in each societal case, following the local feel and intuited local-global connection that comes before, be it in Zimbabwe or Uganda, Egypt or Nigeria, in our exemplary cases in south, east, north, west respective point.

Though these links between our integral trajectory and the research-to-innovation process, in science and technology, are rough and ready, and thereby only indicative of what is missing from social research, it does serve to explain why there is so little social innovation. In other words, and analogously, in social research, so to speak, research origination, foundation, emancipation and transformation can be respectively aligned with fundamental and applied research, development and commercialisation, respectively. Moreover, all of such, as in biochemistry or quantum physics, needs to be applied to `Communitalism, centred, as we shall see, in African healing wisdom. Because then there is usually no such equivalent in the social sciences, explicitly at last, we have had to invent one, as we shall see over the course of this book, and indeed research academy. In fact, it is a dual trajectory: analytical and transformative, as we shall now see.

A Rare Case of African Integral Research to Societal Re-GENE-ration

Before turning to such, though, we cite the one glaring exception, generally unrecognized as such, of. kind of integral research, linking the proverbial "two cultures" – the arts and the sciences – that is the advent of "shona sculpture" in Zimbabwe (originally Rhodesia) from the 1950s, as superbly represented in his PhD thesis by art historian/researcher Jonathan Zilberg (Lessem et al 2019), on *Pandora's Conundrum: The Ties That Bind Modern African Art from Zimbabwe to European Art History*:

> .. the Shona sculpture tradition, rather than being a modern tribal art is a complex amalgamation of multiple histories. There are as of yet dimly understood or established connections to the arts and cultures of such diverse Southern African peoples as the Cewa, Sena, Yao, Mbunda and others and there are also stunningly serendipitous connections to distant and diverse art forms. These include, connections not only with the traditional African art of the masquerade but with the West African Yoruba Christian art of Oyo-Ekiti and even further afield to modern Balinese painting and Melanesian tourist art. By re-routing this instance of invented ethnic simplicity into complexity, this historical investigation into origins reaffirms the central axiom of art historical analysis. It is always possible to trace the origin of an idea, a technique or a style if one can delve closely enough into the initial historical context from which the form emerged. Instead of uniformity we find hybridity and heterogeneity.

For in its heyday (commercialisation for transformative effect), in the 1980s, the exports of "shona" sculpture, second to tobacco, generated the country's highest export value. Artistic and social innovation, as such, were intimately linked. The catalyst in chief, Frank McEwen, wrote in the *Rhodesian Herald* in 1957:

> Design, architecture, and art in its widest sense from all epochs and countries can be studied in the Gallery's library and reading room – from Lascaux cave paintings to the present day, from Vasari to Herbert Read. In the heart of Africa in this centre, a student can keep abreast of his time with reviews from London, Paris, Rome, Rio and New York.

As just one case, for Zilberg, indicating the link between tradition and modernity:

> Munyaradzi's fame and fortune came about not only because of his extreme technical dexterity and appreciation for form, finish and harmony but in some great part as early

in his career he perfected a trademark signature which is often received as archetypically modern in it's sensibility and simplicity. His stylization is emblematic of the influence of traditional Central African art on the works created by the non-Shona Tengenenge (Tengenenge being the farm Ton Blomfiled donated to also personally steward groups of sculptors) sculptors – mainly Yao and Cewa. This primitivist treatment of the face, which is so reminiscent of Klee, Picasso, Giacometti, Brancusi, Miro or Moore, is derived from a connection with the Chewa nyau cult, a funeral society to which many of the non-Shona sculptors belonged.

Sad to say, the above is a very rare example of such social innovation, to scale, from fundamental research to commercialisation, in Africa. We now turn to our two re-GENE-rative trajectories, in theory if not also in practice.

Analytical Trajectory: Research and Development Research GENE: Method, Methodology, Critique, Action

The analytical trajectory is the one that can be directly likened, analytically so to speak, with fundamental and applied research in the natural sciences, development and commercialisation. This involves in our corresponding, social/aesthetic terms, as we have seen in the case of "shona" sculpture above:

- research *method* or mode: **Grounding** – fundamental research (Zilberg)
- research *methodology*: **Emergence** – applied research (McEwan)
- emancipatory *critique*: **Navigation** – development (Munyaradzi et al), and
- *action* research: **Effecting** – commercialisation/operations, sales (multiple).

At the same time, such an analytically based trajectory (the GENE) is also lodged within one or more conventional social science, if not also humanities-based, disciplines. Finally, we need to bear in mind that in the social sciences, unlike the natural sciences, there are, overall, four major research paths (instead of the invariably confusing multiplicity of methodologies conventionally articulated), corresponding to our four worlds, that is relational (southern) and renewal (eastern) research paths, as well as paths of reason (northern) and realisation (western). This markedly distinguishes social from technological innovation. We now turn from the analytical to the transformative trajectory.

Transformative Trajectory: Invention to Innovation: Releasing GENE-ius: Origination, Foundation, Emancipation, Transformation

The transformative trajectory, in the natural sciences, proceeds from invention to innovation. Though it involves those same analytical elements as before – fundamental and applied research, development and commercialisation – these are now cast in more dynamic light.

The inventor, who gets the whole thing rolling, with a view innovation, often needs what we may term a *catalyst* alongside him or her, who can build bridges between product/concept and market/society, between emerging provision and need. Both inventor and catalysts, moreover, need a *steward*, within an organisation or in the community at large, who can chart a path for the emerging innovation, can protect it from the slings and arrows of its critics, while at the same time upholding, if not indeed enhancing, the wider vision that it embodies. Finally, and to some extent simultaneously – as this is not a strictly linear sequence – there needs to be people and processes that ultimately facilitate, or *develop*, the innovation. Indeed such an overall "innovation ecosystem", as in the Zimbabwean sculptural for us, replaces the more static and hierarchal, educational model of teacher and student, or principal and assistant researcher.

So if we now liked the transformation trajectory in the natural and the social sciences, as well as the humanities, for example in our Zimbabwean sculptural case, in our newly conceived integral research (origination to transformation) and societally re-GENE-rative terms, we may see:

- *origination*: Grounding – stewardship (Blomfield)
- *foundation*: Emergence – catalysation (McEwan)
- *emancipation*: Navigation – research and innovation (Munyaradzi et al)
- *transformation*: Effect – facilitation or development (multiple galleries)

The focus, through this now integral trajectory, from research to innovation, is on the overall transformation process, from local grounding (origination), to local-global emergence (foundation), onto global navigation (emancipation), and then global-local effect (transformation). Its grounding in particular soils as well as within specific fundamental disciplines, in response to a burning need, fuelled by burning desire, and building upon unique gifts as in the Zimbabwean-Southern African sculptural case, kicks the process off. It then needs to be lodged in deeper and broader methodological foundations, so as to extent its reach, provide it with philosophical as well as social substance, as well as broaden its base. Thereafter, and inevitably, given the inertia of established institutions and customary norms, it needs to rise above the conventional fray, and build up a systemic, if also newly evolved, institutional presence. Finally, and ultimately, transformation needs to be managed.

As such, and moreover, in the same way as research and innovation, in and of themselves, involve a trajectory, so the same applies to our communiversity on the one hand, and to communitalism on the other, centred in African healing wisdom:

- Communal learning, community building, nhakanomics
- Transformation journey, conscious evolution, yurugu-nomics
- Research academy, knowledge creation, economics of love
- Socio/economic laboratory, sustainable development, communitalism

However, and as we have said from the outset, the very nature of the social sciences, and the humanities, necessitates more than one path to research-and-innovation, because of the diversity of cultures and natures on our planet. We have devised four of these to somehow balance unity-and-diversity.

1.4.3. Towards Research Integrity

Relational, Renewal, Reason, Realisation

As we have already intimated, the major differences between research in the natural, and that in the social, sciences, and in the humanities, is that in the former case there is considered to be *a* scientific method, albeit duly incorporated into an R & D trajectory. In the latter cases, however, there are many such social/humanistic "scientific" paths, the *relational* path and trajectory, of re-GENE-ration for us, comes most naturally to researchers/innovators in the "south". The adjacent trajectory, for us, involved descriptive method (original Grounding); phenomenological methodology (Emergent foundation); feminist critique (emancipatory Navigation) and ultimately participatory action research (transformative Effect).

In fact, because there are so many paths, and thereby mixed-up methods/methodologies, the social researcher usually ends up not being able to see the wood for the trees. For that reason, we have grouped such integral research approaches, and their regenerative trajectories, into four overall paths: relational, renewal, reason and realisation, in the same way as we have done for the integral enterprise: community building, conscious evolution, knowledge creation and sustainable development in turn. Each research-and-innovation path, moreover, can be aligned with a field of research, for example nature and community in the "southern" case. Moreover, each plays its part, if you like, in integral economic, and societal, development as a whole. In the African economic case, substantively in alignment as we shall see, while Nhakanomics is relational, and Yurugu-nomics promotes renewal, the Economics of Love follows the path of reason and Communitalism the path of realisation. Finally, formatively and correspondingly in communiversity terms, a learning community, transformation journey, research academy and integral laboratory follows.

Specifically then, we identify, alternatively and altogether, duly aligning integral research with our integral enterprise, economy and communiversity, the four paths:

- *Relational*: south: nhakanomics: community building: learning community
- *Renewal*: east: yurugu-nomics: conscious evolution: trans4mation journey
- *Reason*: northern: economics of love: knowledge creation: research academy
- *Realisation*: western: communitalism: sustainable development: integral lab

In fact, our research students, particularly in the most marginalised parts of the world, that is generally in the "south", feel a sense of pride and relief when they find that there is a legitimate research path, specifically the "relational" one, that is socially and culturally attuned to their own world, together with enterprise, economic and university functioning to go with. But that relief of having found an authentic path for doing research is only a starting point. Equally important, though of course challenging, is the sense of empowerment that any Integral Researcher or such a Research Community feels, when they discover that each path is designed to bring about social innovation, through the pursuit of a corresponding path of re-GENE-ration. Such a path and trajectory, moreover, needs to address one or more burning issues, drawing on the innate gifts of the relevant individuals and communities, organisation and societies, as well as the burning desires and unique gifts of the researchers-and-innovators concerned, and be aligned with a communiversity and communitalism at large in some shape or form.

Relational Path: To Give the World a Human Face

We now turn to each of the research paths, and to the regenerative trajectory of each in turn, to reveal how, together, they may, overall, be operationalised, bearing in mind that the relational path is the most likely – with inevitable individual variations – to be attuned to Africa. You may recall the late and great Steve Biko (1987) in South Africa claimed that the unique gift that Africa had top give to the world was "to give the world a human face". At this stage, in fact, we shall be merely providing an overview, an illustration of each. As our work unfolds, we shall go into much more detail. Before we do such, though, we have one more "integrating" step to go, the one related to institutional, or better inter-institutional, form.

1.4.4. Communiversity Integrating Self, Community, Organization and Society

Emerging through Self and Others – Transformation Journey: 4 C's

Most educational programmes, and the research undertaken in that context, simultaneously gain and lose from the focus is on the development of the individual. The gain, of course, is that, over an extended period of time, if there are the right enabling conditions, an individual can concentrate on his or her own development, as a learner and/or researcher. We term such, overall, a *transformation journey*, from Call to Contribution in a particular trans-cultural Context, in the process Co-creating with others. The disadvantage is that he or she is conventionally disconnected from any organisation, and a particular community and indeed society, naturally and culturally, if not also cosmologically-ontologically.

Grounded in a Learning Community in the African/Diasporan South: CARE

To that extent we seek to align our approach to a particular community, relevant to an individual concerned, while seeking to compare and contrast one with another. The focus, as such, is anthropological, ecological and psychological, if not also philosophical and spiritual. Overall, such CARE – communal learning – involves Community activation, Awakening integral consciousness, Research/innovation, and ultimately Embodying development.

Moreover, and in that context, we not only focus on the researcher, as an individual, but also their community, and the course of their combined individuation over time. To that extent we are able to align the GENE, that is in this case the release of individual genius, through grounding (Communal activation), emergence (Awakening integral consciousness), navigation (institutionalised Research and innovation) and effect (Embodying development).

Research Academy: Connecting Self and Community with Organisation

A fundamental disconnect, we find, in most societies, albeit in some perhaps more than others, is between activism (community based), enterprise (corporately based) and intellect (university based), our Centre for Integral Research and Societal Re-GENE-ration seeking to bridge these divided worlds. In fact, we find that while the focus on "self" as individually, psychologically and spiritually, predominated in the "west" (psychological) and the "east" (spiritual), there is a strong communal focus in the "south", albeit in close connection with the self.

The orientation toward organisation, we find though, is especially strong in the "north", including, for example in the American case, what we might term the "north-west". So the interconnection between self-community-organisation, in an integrated way, arises is only very rare cases. Moreover, and institutionally, it falls in between all stools as it were, whereby the individual, educational focus of a conventional university is supplemented, organisationally, more usually by bureaucratic "university administration" than by a research led, institutional vision and form.

That having been said, there are distinctive fields or disciplines, that is most particularly sociology and complexity theory in general, as well as management and leadership in particular, that focuses on the structure and dynamics of organisations. Whereas, as such, there is a distinct lack of organisational theory connected with different parts of the world, thereby providing such with integrity, integrally speaking, there are concepts of organisational development, renewal, learning and individuation that can be aligned with our overall approach.

So much then for connecting self and community with organisation, in theory. In practice, at one and the same time, if we are to realise an integration between self, community and organisation, in a particular societal context, as in Africa, the researchers concerned need to be embedded in particular institutions, while, and through which they engage in social innovation, we need a Communiversity. Through the course of this Volume 1 then, and ever more so in Volume 4 in this series, we shall be illustrating how communiversity form and research paths interact, also substantively aligned with varieties of African communitalism (expanded in Volumes 2 and 3 Africa and worlds-wide), altogether building on African healing wisdom.

This is invariably a difficult two-way (self and organisation), or indeed three-way (self, community and organisation), stretch. Indeed, we find it a feasible, though very difficult stretch, for an individual researcher, thereby, and through our active encouragement, engaging purposefully with community and organisation, in pursuit of social innovation. On the other hand, we find it virtually impossible to start from the organisation, to invoke the kind of individual and communal attentiveness, to pursue social innovation on those three, interconnected fronts. There is never the time for reflection, accompanying action, allowed for such. That is why the communiversity is so important to us. Our ongoing and cumulative efforts are particularly illustrated by our test case in Nigeria, where one of our members, Anselm Adodo, exemplifies this approach through his work with Paxherbals/Pax Africana.

Connecting Self and Community, Organisation and Society

We now turn to the most difficult task of all, and yet most important one if we are to realise our overall, integrated goals. Societies are contained within a global, if not also cosmological order, whereby international studies, comparative and development economics, and cosmology itself, not to mention the newly emerging systems theories, all have their place. The question then is, how to we encompass, societally, all of such, alongside our focus on individual, organisation and community, to realize social innovation? More especially, how does such innovation specifically address such burning issues as the alleviation of poverty, to development of an open society, the promotion of a cultural and spiritual renaissance, as well as overcoming environmental and communal decay, most especially in Africa, and its diaspora?

To all of such we now turn, with a view to actualising integral research, research integrity, and the integration of individual and collective research

1.5. Concluding Integral Research, Communiversity, Communitalism

1.5.1. The Social Innovation Tree

We started this chapter with the question, whether and how research in the social sciences can be turned into social innovation.

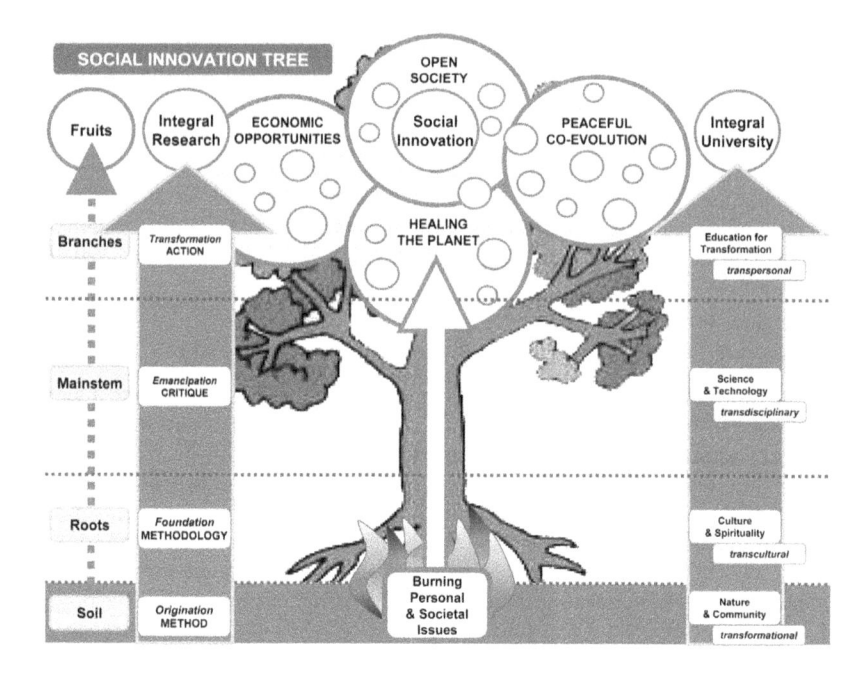

Figure 1.5: *Integral Research and Integral University (Communiversity)*

We have been working with this question for many years now, trying to address the burning issues we, our organizations and societies are facing, also encompassing the unique gifts that individual researchers and their communities as well as enterprises, most especially in Africa (south), and to a lesser extent the gifts that Asia (east), Europe (west) and the Americas (west), bring uniquely to bear, if not also the MENA centre.

Working with Masters students and Doctoral researchers from all over the world, as well as prospective post-docs, we have developed a fundamentally new approach towards the *process* research in the social sciences, designed to bring about social innovation, when aligned with a re-GENE-rative substance and form.

By applying Integral Research, you, individually or preferably as a research group, engage with particular burning issues in your specific contexts, also pursuing a double-layered trajectory, along a specific research path, towards social innovation, set in the context of a Communiversity, as if you like an Integral University, and ultimately Communitalism.

1.5.2. Social Science for the 21st Century

We close this chapter by citing the redoubtable Yale University based sociologist Immanuel Wallerstein (1999), one of the most prolific contemporary advocates of a new approach to knowledge creation, also with a passion for Africa, in his *Social Science for the 21st Century*, an approach that allows for reuniting the social sciences with the humanities:

> Can we tear down the old structure of social science while simultaneously constructing new pillars for some kind of roof? And will the roof be limited to just social science or rather encompass a reunited single world of knowledge that knows no division between humans and nature, no divorce between philosophy and science, no separation of the search for the true and the search for the good. Can we unthink social science while reconstructing the structure of knowledge?

By introducing the *process* of Integral Research and Innovation, in alignment with Communitalism (*substance)*, and a Communiversity (*form*) in an overall African *context,* we echo Wallerstein's claim. In the next chapter we introduce the cosmological centring of such integral and re-GENE-rative orientation towards research and knowledge creation, promoting a fundamentally new approach towards the social sciences. We start with a tour de world, re-searching different approaches to knowledge creation and social innovation from the four corners of the globe.

1.6. References

Adodo A (2017) *Integral Community Enterprise In Africa. Communitalism As An Alternative to Capitalism..* Abingdon. Routledge

Adodo A and **Lessem** R (2021) *Afrikology: Deconstructing and Reconstructing Knowledge and Value in Africa.* Manchester. Beacon Academic

Biko S (1987) *I Write What I Like.* London. Heinemann African Writes Series

Blaikie N et al (2016) *Social Science: Paradigms in Action.* Cambridge. Polity

Lessem R and **Schieffer** A (2010) *Integral Economics: Releasing the Economic Genius of Your Society.* Abingdon. Routledge

Lessem R and **Schieffer** A (2010) *Integral Research and Innovation: Transforming Enterprise and Society.* Abingdon. Routledge

Lessem R and **Schieffer** A (2010) *Transformation Management: Toward the Integral Enterprise.* Abingdon. Routledge

Lessem R, **Adodo** A and **Bradley** T (2019) *The Idea of the Communiversity. Releasing the Natural, Cultural, Technological and Economic GENE-ius of Societies.* Manchester. Beacon Academic

Lewin N (2015) *Principles of Topological Psychology.* Connecticut. Martino Fine Books

Ndlovu-Gatsheni S (2018) *Epistemic Freedom in Africa: Deprovincialisation and Decolonisation.* Abingdon. Routledge

Nonaka I and **Takeuchi** H (1995) *The Knowledge Creating Company.* Oxford. Oxford University Press

Porter M (2004) *Competitive Strategy: Techniques for Analysing Industries and Competitors.* New York. Free Press

Sachs J et al (2022) *Sustainable Development Report.* Cambridge. Cambridge University Press

Wallerstein I (1999) *Social Science for the 21st Century: The End of the World as We Know It.* Minnesota. University of Minnesota Press

Zilberg J (2012) *Pandora's Conundrum: The Ties That Bind Modern African Art from Zimbabwe to European Art History.* Centre for African Studies. University of Illinois. Urbana- Champaign.

Chapter 2 *Centring* Cosmology: Healing Wisdom Out of Africa Amplified Worldwide. South/Africa, East/Asia, North/Europe, Integral West/America and Centre/MENA

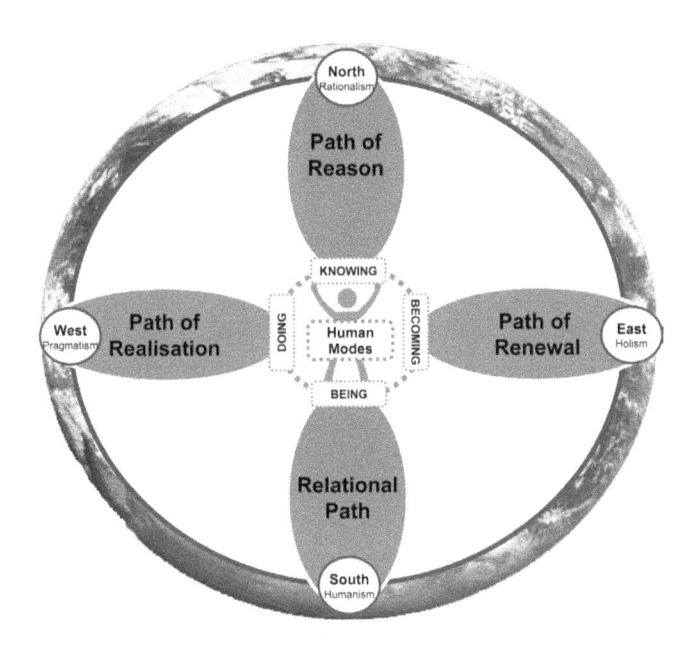

Figure 2.1: *Paths of Integral Research*

> **Summary: Centring Cosmology: Healing Wisdom Out of Africa**
>
> - In order to actualise a process of social innovation, learning communities, engaged in transformation journeys, aligned with a research academy, and integral laboratory, building on relevant substance, need to (a) connect with the creativity (historic creative achievements) of the culture it is applied to, hence being centred cosmologically and (b) serve to re-GENE-rate such.
>
> - Societies in Africa in particular, and generally worlds-wide, have, in particular times, have developed an integral, four-world perspective, which formed their particular cosmology, duly centred, showing how these elements could be held in a dynamic balance. Such modes of being and becoming, knowing and doing found their way into the socio-cultural design of those societies, and thereby provided an orientation for a particular civilisation.
>
> - While each society embodies the above-mentioned modes, there are regions in the world that have over time developed a particular strength in one field as opposed to the others. In research-and-innovation terms we found that there is a "southern" humanistic "relational path" (being), an "eastern" holistic "path of renewal" (becoming), a "northern" rational "path of reason" (knowing) and a "western" pragmatic "path of realisation" (doing).
>
> - We recognized that when a society was at its peak, it managed to keep a kind of dynamic balance between its various parts and modes, thereby locally, and also locally-globally, with a view to co-evolving "newly globally". It practised "unity in variety", both internally, through interconnecting its different societal functions, and externally by interacting, on equal terms, with different cultures.
>
> - You and your integral research academy, start by immersing yourself in the very soils of the creative source of your society, as well as those of others, before entering a particular research path authentic to you, though characteristically building in the "southern" *relational* path, and trajectory, in African guise, building up learning communities, leading ultimately to social innovation.
>
> - Such a creative source, or centreing, in an overall African context, we have identified in terms of the Healing Wisdom of Africa, which is also constituted of its elemental fourfold, building up from, and towards, its overall cosmological centreing.
>
> - Overall cosmologically, such centring in healing and regeneration, out of Africa in the "south", emerges in Asia as healing divides in the "east", navigates in Europe by way of making connections, effected in the "integral west", in America, on the art of association, and in MENA connecting paths, potentially if not actually, between one people and another.

In Dagara cosmology, the image and structure of the circle, or wheel, organise perceptions of the world. The indigenous tendency is therefore to perceive all of life within the context of this cycle or integrating cosmology. The medicine wheel of the Dagara, as for the native Americans, is a symbolic representation of the relationships between the five elements of the cosmos. Earth is the centre and touches all the other elements. Water in the east is adjacent to fire in the south. Minerals lie in the north, and nature lies in the west.

Malidoma Patrice Some (1987)   *The Healing Wisdom of Africa*

2.1. Origins of Social Innovation

2.1.1. Centred Cosmologically: Beyond the Known University and Economy

In Chapter 1 we highlighted the need for social, as opposed to merely technological, innovation, integral research-wise, and the kind of Communiversity, comprised of learning communities (relational path), transformation journeys (renewal path), socio-economic laboratories (path of realisation) and an overarching, integral research academy (path of reason), that would be required to promote such. We also intimated, enterprise wise, that a new kind of Community Building, Conscious Evolution, Knowledge Creation and Sustainable Development – as opposed to marketing, HR, operations and finance, respectively, was required.

Finally, though at this point we merely hinted at such, as a more healthy, integral alternative to capitalism and socialism, that is Communitalism in various guises for all African comers, Nhakanomics in the South, Yurugu-nomics in the East, the Economics of Love in the North, and ultimately Communitalism from the West, of Africa, was called for, altogether centred in the healing wisdom of Africa.

2.1.2. Giving the World a Human Face/The Healing Wisdom of Africa

In this chapter we tap into the cosmological centring of such social innovation, in Africa and worlds-wide. For unlike technological innovation, which, like the European Enlightenment, emerged supposedly out of an emerging "age of reason", social innovation, in our integral guise, has, at least to some degree, a fourfold heritage, though in an African context, as we have said, the relational has pride of place. As South African icon Steve Biko (1987) notably claimed, in *ubuntu* guise (I am because you are), the role of Africa worlds-wide is "to give the world a human face". For his African sage-like compatriot moreover, Burkino Faso born, California based, Malidoma Some (1997), in his seminal work on *The Healing Wisdom of Africa*, as also elaborated in the opening quote above:

> At the opposite end of healing is the illness of not being able to accept or even tolerate those who are different from us. Worse, this inability encourages suspicion, fear, and resentment. Thus, it is an illness of the collective psyche when different cultures don't

understand one another. The history of humankind is plagued by this psychic disease that has caused much pain and disappointment in the world, as we still see today. Methods of healing, then, must take into account the energetic or spiritual condition that is in turmoil, thereby affecting the physical condition.

2.1.3. Centreing, Grounding, Emerging, Navigating, Effecting

In other words, such *social* innovation is as much to do with being (our local, communal original Grounding), and becoming (our local-global trans-culturally Emergent foundation), as with knowing (our newly global emancipatory social scientific Navigation) and doing (our global-local transformative economic Effect), altogether underpinned by regional, even continental (e.g. African), centring (IUS).

It addresses and builds on all these four or five modes, with a view to releasing GENE-ius, building thereby on the moral core, or centre, of a particular individual and community, organisation and, especially, society, that is on a society in each of the four corners of our world. As such, whereas the original industrial revolution emerged out of uniquely English soils, its subsequent impact, around the world, has been all too often to displace, globally-locally, rather than build on, locally-globally/indigenously-exogenously, indigenous knowledge.

The process of uncovering and releasing a particular society's cosmological centre (integration), such as Africa's healing wisdom (see above); nature (origination), grounding or being; culture (foundation), emergence, or becoming; it can thereafter activate, and articulate, its own innate process of knowing or emancipatory navigation, scientifically and technologically; ultimately (transformation) effecting such integral politically and economically. That said, for example and by way of comparison, "soulfully" speaking, the U.S., as California based philosopher Jacob Needleman (2003) has brilliantly articulated, in *The American Soul: Rediscovering the Wisdom of the Founders*, has its "south" (African American), its "east" (Native Indian), its "north" (continental European) and "west" (Anglo-Saxon), whereby the United States is centred, cosmologically, surprisingly, not in the individualistic, "westernised", American Dream but in *the art of association*, in the integral West!

2.1.4. Releasing Your GENE-ius

The role then of our Centre for Integral Research and Societal Re-GENE-ration is to:

- connect to the creative centre (historic creative achievements) of the region with which you are concerned, in Africa at large its healing wisdom
- transformationally combine this locally indigenous with the globally exogenous, duly centred, to support the further evolution and sustainability of your community, your self, your society, and your organisation, specifically from local to local-global to then "newly global" and ultimately global-local

- purposefully engage in (fundamental as well as applied) research and development, within and across the social sciences and humanities, naturally, culturally, technologically and economically, to promote fully-fledged social innovation.

It is the creative interaction of diverse elements that is needed for innovation. But such a process of social innovation can only take place, if a dynamic balance between the interacting elements is retained, including the balance between being and becoming, knowing and doing, underpinned by cosmological centreing. Similarly, *process* (integral research), *substance* (communitalism) and *form* (communiversity), the latter two contributing to societal regeneration, need to be aligned.

All societies have developed over time their own kind of knowledge about the design of their social and material creations and how to maintain a healthily dynamic balance with creation, or indeed co-creation (cultural synthesis) itself. Again and again, societies tested, or over-reached, the limits of this balance, while failing to reach their potential, which – in its worst cases – led to wars, to destruction and extinction. In the pan-African case moreover (see Figure 2.1.2. below) healing wisdom is at the centre.

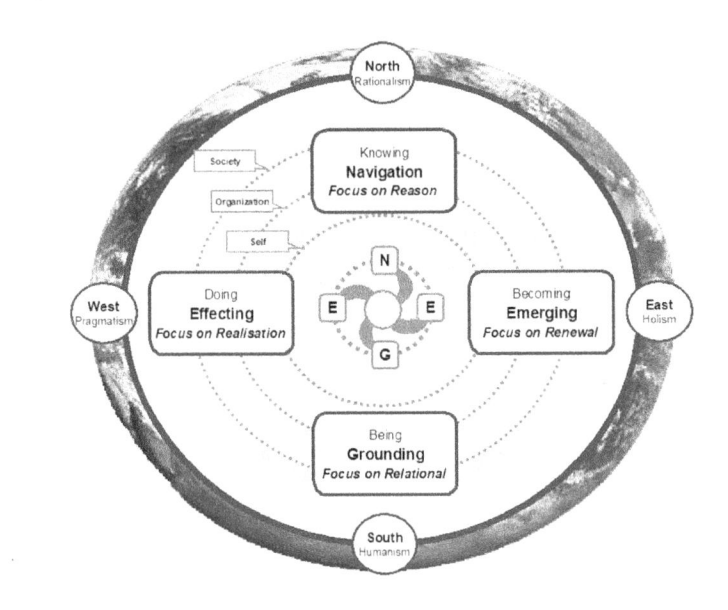

Figure 2.1.2: *Releasing Your Individual/Collective GENE-ius*

Invariably though, a particular community or society becomes out of touch with its knowledge of how to continually recreate its genius, and there is no institutional, or better institutional agency, like a communiversity, to rectify such, nor does our predominantly capitalist form of economy, or entrepreneurial enterprise, promote such integration. That leads us to the role we need to play here, processally, substantively and formatively, centred within an African context.

2.1.5. Focus on Developing Capabilities

Nobel Laureate Amartya Sen (2006) argues that poverty should be seen as a deprivation of capabilities. By focusing on developing capabilities, rather than merely on income, various social aspects of life can be enhanced, contributing to overall development. Sen emphasizes that understanding and using social design processes can improve livelihoods. Therefore, for us, social innovation that aims to bring about a unique social improvement should explicitly draw on the social sciences. This innovation needs to bring a dynamic balance to the four factors that form the underlying and integral social design we have developed, based on our Integral Worlds Model (Lessem et al., 2015).

- Relational: Nature and Community/Community Building/Nhakanomics
- Renewal: Culture and Spirituality/Conscious Evolution/Yurugu-nomics
- Reason: Science and Technology/Knowledge Creation/Economics of Love
- Realisation: Economics and Enterprise/Sustainable Development/ Communitalism

altogether aligned through an integrally functional polity. We now turn to such cultural design behind social innovation in more detail.

2.2. Designs Behind Social Innovation

Underlying Circle and Spiral: From Dogon
"South" to Native American "West"

You have noticed that the model we have presented of social design and social innovation has been conveyed in circular fashion, also following Some (see opening quote) containing an outer four-foldness and an inner centre, the latter, in and African context, constituted of healing wisdom. These serve to express a specifically and dynamically balanced interaction of particularly diverse factors, also true to our shared African heritage where, if you like, the underlying circle encompasses first (being/grounding), followed by the spiral (becoming/emergence) and then only the overarching network (knowing/navigation) and the culminating point (doing/effect).

In our transcultural research around the world, we have discovered that the core visual design, or indeed guiding metaphor, of many cultures is expressed either in a cycle (or, as variation, in a spiral) or a fourfold or a combination of both. All of them embodied a philosophical and/or spiritual understanding of a dynamically balanced order of communities, societies, and individuals in relation to nature and their particular version of God. Of course what has not yet materialised, worlds-wide, is the expression of such cosmological centreing, or manifestations, of such inner, aesthetic designs, in outer, functional scientific and technological, political and economic forms, thereby duly "north-westernised" AI for example, on the one hand, or free markets and liberal democracies dominate. Moreover, and as a reaction to such, in the "global South" all too often autocracies and oligarchies rule the roots, for us because of such a failure to centre, ground, emerge, navigate and effect integration.

The circle/cycle, as we shall later see, is perhaps the single most distinct visual design, that can be found, in one form or the other, at the core of the self-perspective of many cultures. So, for examples, in various cultures the cycle was a symbol for the absolute as well as for unity. It has been used as a symbol of a cosmic egg by the Dogon in West Africa, of absolute beauty (Platonic ancient Greek interpretation) and for emptiness (Hinduism). The cycle embodies harmony of all spiritual forces (Zen), and it is a symbol of time and eternity, in the Japanese "east", while the circular medicine wheel stands for healing wisdom in the Native American "west".

According to mythological interpretation, the four is one of the core order-giving principles (four directions, four elements, four seasons, four temperaments, and currently our four research paths). The most elemental visual expressions of the fourfold is the geometric form of the square. On a symbolic level, the square was a symbol for the earth and for the cooperation of the four elements. It stood for absolute beauty (Platonic interpretation); in Islam it represented the heart (as per four sources of inspiration). And in China, as for the Dogon, and the Yoruba like one of us as we shall see, it stood for the Cosmos as a whole.

The Cyclical Process Element as Illustrated in Dagara African Cosmology

The circular designs that various cultures created over time often include discrete, integral elements, as we saw in the African Dagara case: centring in the integrating *earth;* emerging in *water*-like becoming guise in the "east"; grounded in *fire*-like energy in its "southern" being; navigating in mineral-like form, for example likened to silicon chips, in the knowledge creating "north"; displaying a willful *nature* of doing in the "west". – in addition to the circle or the square (or a combination of both of them). Such an elemental cycle is both dynamic and stabilising.

Such designs were always an expression of a "balanced order" or unity between diverse elements, duly centred. On a societal level, for us here, the core defining elements, subject to such centreing, can be understood as firstly nature and community, secondly culture and spirituality, thirdly science and technology and fourthly polity and economy. On a personal level, such defining elements can be viewed as being, becoming, knowing and doing. These dimensions can be found in each personality and civilization. Moreover, at a communiversity level, these are represented by learning community (being), transformation journey (becoming), research academy (knowing) and socio-economic laboratory (doing) in turn. And each of these three, in order to survive on a long-term basis, needed then, and needs now, a kind of healthy and dynamically evolving balance between these core elements, which is only possible if a cosmological centre holds them together.

Four Worlds as Part and Whole

In our studies, we have made another discovery. While each society embodies the Four Worlds of nature/community, culture/spirituality, science/technology and politics/economics, there are parts of the world that have over time developed a particular strength in one particular field, as opposed to the others. Figure 2.2.1. illustrates this finding.

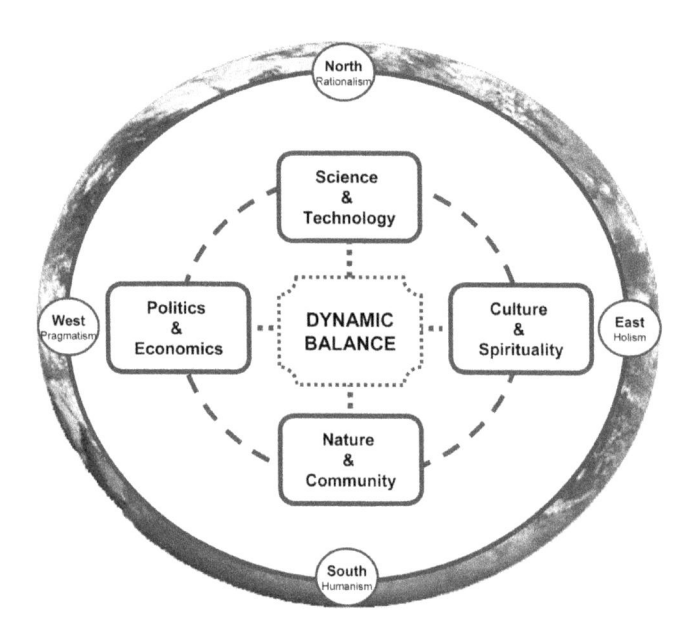

Figure 2.2.1: *Integral Societal Design – Orientations of the Four Worlds Model*

This pattern suggests that in order to have a dynamic balance on a global level, each part needs to bring its unique contribution – that is when it is functioning at its "functional" best – into the whole in order to ensure "unity in diversity". Figure 2.3. shows which particular element each world does contribute. Moreover, as we shall see later, the four research paths each represent a part of an integral whole. In other words, and paradoxically, for example, for the "south" to altogether re-GENE-rate its natural and communal self (Grounding), it needs to draw on "eastern" culture and spirituality (Emergence), "northern" science and technology

(Navigation), as well as "western" polity and economy (Effect), both from within and without, altogether centred within its own healing cosmology.

Of course, you find these "archetypal features" in every society, in every organization, in every individual, implicitly, and culturally, but not explicitly and politically-economically-technologically. We are not saying that, for example, Humanism/Naturalism or Being is only rooted in the south (hence in Africa), or that Holism or Becoming is only rooted in the east (hence in countries like Japan and China). We argue that each world region has evolved over time one inner dimension (interior design) that seems to be more strongly developed than the others. However, while each region of the world, potentially, has all Four Worlds embodied within it, actually one or other world predominates, so that each part of the world needs to consciously seek after what we term "global integrity", by recognizing and evolving, rather than by-passing or enclosing, itself within its local identity. Moreover, and in the final analysis, our African Communiversity, Economy and Enterprise as a whole needs to embody all four elements, duly centred.

The east has arguably the longest and deepest tradition in the area of holism, spirituality and non-material aspects, as we shall see for our path of renewal while, for example, the west has developed an enormous capacity for the pragmatic and material self-expression, our path of realisation. And it is the centre (countries in the Middle East) that has historically been, more so than any other world region, not only a crossroads for the most diverse cultures, but it has also experienced various epochs, most notably in the 9th to 14th centuries AD, when a "creative synthesis" between different cultures and religions did prolifically happen.

Even Islam itself could be seen as "creative synthesis" and further evolution of Judaism and Christianity – and has in itself been a major social innovation for the region, and ultimately for the world. At its best, the Middle East and Islam have demonstrated an enormous ability to generate a dynamic balance between most diverse parts. That's why we see the integrative ability of "creative synthesis" as the particular contribution of the centre, including our own ability to "centre" ourselves, when at our integrative best as opposed to dissipative worst.

56   *Centring* Cosmology

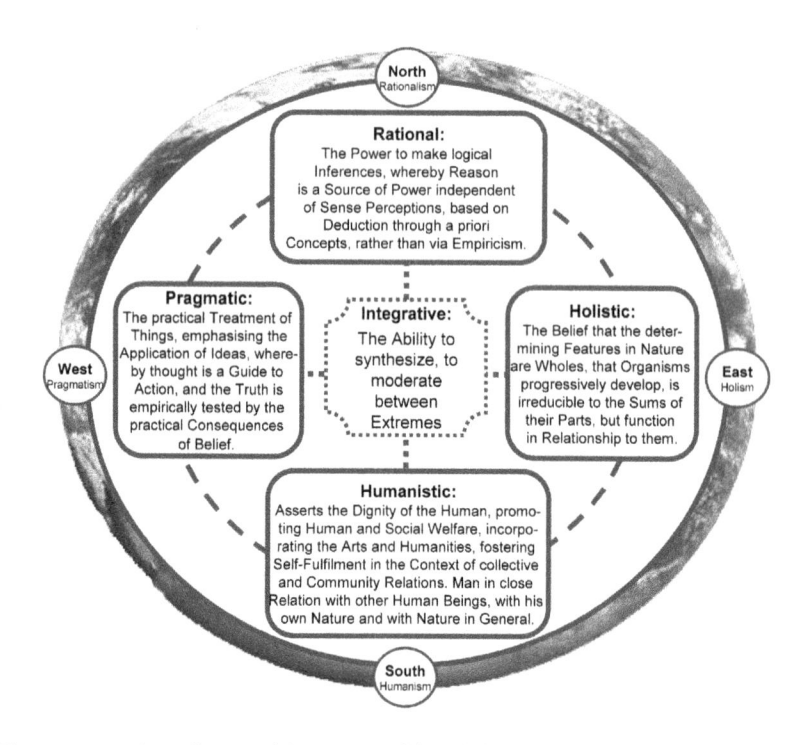

Figure 2.2.2: *Contribution of the Four Worlds and the Centre*

You could say that what we can observe on a global level also mirrors the inner designs, images, worldviews or archetypes of each individual and society, though, as we have been saying, expressed inwardly and aesthetically but generally not outwardly and materially. Each of us has our potential south, its east, its north, its west and centre. At the same time each of us has developed a particular strength in one or two areas, and only a few individuals, organizations, communities and societies "manage" to keep a harmonic, yet dynamic balance between the four elements. Yet all four elements, the relational circle and spiral of renewal, a line or network of reason, and points of realisation that builds on all that has come before – as we shall see, at least to some degree, in our four African cases presented, are required.

This archetypal social and psychological design is a distillation of our research and observations in different cultures and personalities. It is also a design that resonates with core cultural and artistic artefacts (visual designs) that occur in most societies. We shall demonstrate that an outer design in its more explicit manifestation needs to be linked with the inner design of a culture or psyche as a whole, as we shall see for example in the case of Sekem (our northern African case in Egypt) whereby such a psychic design can be regarded as the underlying spirit of its material expression. It is hence important to understand this deeper layer, and we shall now explore such and their inner and outer expressions in various cultures.

2.3. Images Behind the Innovation Paths
2.3.1. Centring Paths of Creative Synthesis

We shall start by exploring what kind of "inherently sustainable and dynamically balanced social designs" have been developed as diverse regional cosmologies and how these have been expressed inwardly (design) as well as outwardly (symbol). In the case of each of our worlds, mediated by our worldly "centre", we shall find an all-encompassing design, in each case with a particular orientation, towards, respectively, a research path of realisation (western), renewal (eastern), reason (northern) and a relational path (southern), as well as an ultimately integral one. Such prospectively applies as much to communitalism, economy and, enterprise-wise, substantively, as to communiversity, academy-wise, formatively, as it does to social innovation, processally, though our major focus in this volume is on the last of these.

The outer symbol representing the cosmology of a particular society has an explicit, static outer structure, which is represented, in turn and at a deeper level, an implicit, dynamic inner or process dimension. These archetypal and relational *images* moreover, as we have discussed in *Transformation Management* (Lessem and Schieffer, 2009), in terms of a *transformational topography,* need to be manifested as societal *ideologies*, organizational *institutions* and individual *inclinations* that are resonant with one another.

When each of our world civilisations were at their peak, centring was at its most integrally manifest, becoming a field of force if you like, leading to a fruitful exchange amongst its diverse elements: centring (integral) being (relational), becoming (renewal), knowing (reason), as well as doing (realisation). The same of course applies to an individual or an organization. At such a time, each such entity was able to keep its unity and to orchestrate its diversity in a way that it was fertile for all its parts.

Indeed, the great African Muslim philosopher Ali Mazrui (1986) defines a civilisation as a "creative synthesis" of diverse parts, related not only to the combination of the rich "interior design" of a society, but also bearing upon the civilisation's interaction with other civilisations, thereby embodying unity-in-diversity. When "creative synthesis" was at its best, so was the inner process of innovation.

When societies lose their power to socially innovate, through following these research paths as it were, thereby interlinking the explicit structural form (outer design) with the implicit dynamic process (inner design) neither the deeper meaning of the symbol, nor its power to connect, is any longer present. So, the symbol of the cross, for example, as a bridge between reason (lines of reasoning) and faith (*religere* as renewal), loses its fusion power. To take another example, in the Arab world, their buildings, both inside and out, are still richly laden with Arabesque forms, but few people know what these structurally symbolize, or indeed the force field, which they dynamically represent. Moreover, such a cosmological design, born out of an appreciation of nature and culture, needs to consciously be built into an approach to science and technology that arises out of such, and then applied economically and politically. Indeed, as we shall see in the Sekem case in Egypt, below, such a "fourfold" is intrinsic to the functioning of the enterprise as a whole.

Many of us, therefore, enjoy visits to museums, where the static artefacts of civilisations are aesthetically displayed for us to get to know. We admire the artefacts that ancient generations of our own and other cultures have created, from a distance, even how innovative they had been. But we make no conscious connection between material or practical innovations of the past, and the spiritual or mental process that allowed these to come into being, thereby taking into conscious account the current ability of a society to be creative, by turning its nature and culture into technologies and enterprises, centred in an overarching cosmological design.

We now start with an exploration of social innovation in the *relational* south, in fact from the neglected grounds of indigenous African civilisation with which this volume is primarily concerned, albeit thereafter connecting with other such integral designs, worlds-wide. So thereafter we reach out to the other polarities, that is the east, north and west, before we turn towards the centre.

2.3.2. South – Yoruba African Cosmology: Initiating Healing and Regeneration

Obatala, Esu, Ogun, Sango: Creation to Integration

In the "south", to begin with, the relational thrives, but renewal, reason and realisation has been thwarted by influences from both within and without. The spiritual worldview of Nigeria's Yoruba people, representing one of us (Anselm Adodo) for example, influenced a large number of African religious traditions, which nowadays are practiced, aside from Nigeria itself, in a number of Latin American countries, as well as North American states, spread throughout the African diaspora. The core cosmology is rooted in an inseparable cosmos, in which the conscious and the unconscious are held together in a kind of relational balance through the life energy, or indeed Yoruba healing wisdom, Ashé. There is no polarisation of good and bad.

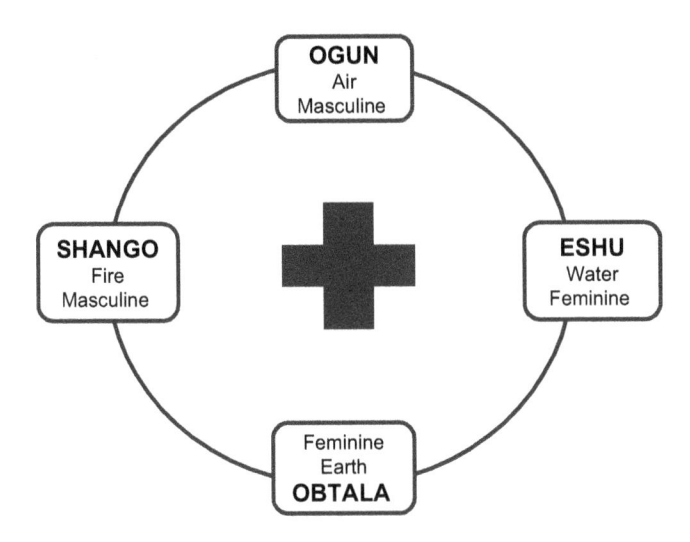

Figure 2.3.2: *Fourfold "Inner World" of the Yoruba (according to Frobenius)*

Within this cosmos, Yoruba religion speaks about a fourfold activation within the human being, which we shall later see embodied in Pax Herbals specifically, and in the Pax Africana Communiversity in Nigeria. This fourfold is represented by Orisas: these divinities are contained not outside the individual but deep within; and the individual possesses the gods and goddesses as a way of repossessing those divine aspects of the self. "Obatala", as such, is creative, compassionate, and patient, one prepared to accept his lot; benefactor of humanity; dedicated to friendship and the maintenance of the social fabric. "Esu" is the inner guide – that part of ourselves leading us to life-changing and life-sustaining insights and revelations. "Sango" was famous as a king passionately devoted to war and a master magician. He presents us with the tenacious aspect of the human personality – will, determination, commitment. *"Ogun",* finally, is the dynamic centre of the psyche capable of containing, integrating, synthesizing, healing, regenerating and even transcending the many opposing forces that operate within us (Adodo, 2017). At the heart of this fourfold system is a Yoruba cross – indeed a sign of African healing wisdom – uniting a horizontal axis known as the "chief way" with a vertical axis, the "Secondary Way".

Healing and Regeneration: Using Sound for Bringing New Things into Creation

For the similarly West African Bambara people, the centre of the cross is symbolically the "kuru" or God Point; here, the Bambara say, life emerges from divinity through birth and merges back into divinity through death, and through this notably cyclical transformation immortality is achieved (Ford 2000).

Indeed if you take a look at the human cosmos as illustrated (as we shall see later in this chapter) the Cree and Objiway Native American people from Northern America – arguably our west-south – one notices, that they link sound (music and rhythm) to the "people of black colour" and describe them as people "using sound for bringing new things into creation", as is further revealed in his Nigerian-Paxherbals case story by one of us (Anselm Adodo). Indeed, music, dance and rhythm are still today cultural expressions of underlying African cosmology and there is hardly any other form of art that has such an immediate relational power as music and dance.

For Africans it is indeed a "way of knowing"; knowing the rhythm of the eternal dance called life. Indeed, for leading English research philosopher John Heron (1994) on whose *Feeling and Personhood* we draw upon extensively below, as well as, and especially, on his (1997) action research orientation towards *Cooperative Inquiry*, such musically laden feeling and emotion constitutes the very grounding of research and learning, as the transformative effect of our "eastern" path of renewal. We now turn from "southern" cosmology, focusing in particular on the Yoruba, to the "east".

2.3.3. East – India to China in Asia: Healing Divides

Continual Becoming

The quest for knowledge in the East was oriented, more than in other parts of the world, towards a path of ongoing renewal rooted in dynamic forces within nature and culture, such as, for the ancient Chinese, the forces of yin (feminine-responsive) and yang (masculine-assertive). You could reason things out or realise the truth, but only if you renewed your connection with the grounds of your being. Moreover, the truth was not what could be seen and touched, but somewhere "in between".

In fact, notably today in China, especially from an economic point of view, renewal is lodged somewhere in between the east and the west, as had been the case in Japan in the second half of the last century. Dialogue, as such, means "between the words"; it is about knowledge that is "flowing through" past, present and future, in a process of continual becoming. Hence, it needs to be continuously re-acquired, as the entire cosmos itself underlies continuous change and transformation. The path of renewal is a spiralling one, continually reaching back, to ever present origins, and then forward again. Two core visualisations of this are the Wheel of Life and the Mandala.

Images Behind the Innovation Paths 61

Figure 2.3.3.1: *Wheel of Life (Centre, Outer Cycle plus a Double Fourfold) (left) and a Tibetan Mandala (Fourfold in a Cycle) (right)*

The Way of the East

In Buddhism, which emerged from ancient India, the wheel of life is a symbol for the Eightfolded Way, aiming for freedom from reincarnation or rebirth. It is also found in Indian Hinduism, Jainism, Sikhism and other related religions.

Mandala (Sanskrit for "circle", "completion") is a term used to refer to various objects. It is of Hindu origin, but is also used in other Dharmic religions, such as Buddhism. In the Tibetan branch of Vajrayana Buddhism, they have been developed into sandpainting, expressing the belief that knowledge cannot be fixed but needs to be regenerated again and again. In practice, mandala has become a generic term for any plan, chart or geometric pattern that represents the cosmos metaphysically or symbolically, a microcosm of the universe from the human perspective.

A mandala, especially its centre, can be used during meditation as an object for focusing attention. The symmetrical geometric shapes tend to draw attention towards their centre. The Swiss Psychologist Carl Gustav Jung saw the mandala as "a representation of the unconscious self", and believed his paintings of mandalas enabled him to identify emotional disorders and work towards wholeness and integration in personality (Jaffe 2001).

Holistic Design: Existence and Non-Existence

Taoism, for the ancient Chinese, represents the force behind all natural order. Tao can be roughly stated to be the flow of the universe (Cane 2002). It is believed to be the influence that keeps the universe balanced and ordered. Tao is associated with nature, due to a belief that nature demonstrates the Tao (Martinson 1987). The flow of qi, as the essential energy of action and existence, is compared to the universal order of Tao. It is often considered to be the source of both existence and non-existence. And hence, it does not search for knowledge and enhanced awareness through distinction and differentiation (either / or) but embodies the ability of embracing paradox (and holding opposites as equal forces, not valuing them as good or bad).

Taoists believe that man is a microcosm for the universe (Robinet 1997). The body ties directly into the Chinese five elements. The five organs correlate with the five elements, the five directions (including our Four Worlds and a centre) and the seasons (Kohn 2000). Akin to the "neoplatonic maxim" of "as above, so below", Taoism posits that by understanding himself, and in particular his path of becoming, man may gain knowledge of the universe. The "Taijitu" (yin and yang) symbol is a keynote of Taoist symbolism. While almost all Taoist philosophies make use of the yin and yang symbol, one could also call it Confucian, Neo-Confucian or pan-Chinese (Little et al 2000).

Healing Divides: Yin-Yang

The five directions as conceived by the ancient Chinese (east, south, west, north, centre) can be linked to the yin and yang symbols; each have their own attributes, as follows in the chart below. (Little et al 2000). As we can see, flow and interconnectivity is a feature of the east, and renewal goes, linking past, present and future, together with such. That all said, and in all the above cited cases, the centring design, needs to be not only grounded explicitly in nature, and represented in the societal culture, but also, herein lies to key, embodied in technology, and applied within the economy, such altogether being all to seldom the case. Not surprisingly moreover, it is *east* Africa, which has been most influenced by the wider world's "east", that is most especially the Indian sub-continent and the Arab world.

Table 2.3.2. *The Cyclical Yin-Yang in Relation to the Fourfold (5 Elements / 4 Seasons) and the Centre*

Element	Season	Force
Wood	Spring	Yang
Fire	Summer	Yang
Metal	Autumn	Yin
Water	Winter	Yin
Earth	None	Neutral

We now turn from *healing and regeneration* in the African-Yoruba "south", and *healing the Yin-Yang feminine-masculine divides* in the Chinese "east", to the symbol of *the cross as the means of connection* in the "north" that is within Europe. Moreover, it is important to realise that, from an integral, cosmological perspective, one centring path needs ultimately to build on another. In this case, the "eastern" development spiral is much more powerful if it builds on the prior "southern" circle of communion. When "northern" means of connection is added, to complement rather than supplant what has come before, such "healing" potency increases ever more.

2.3.4. North – Ancient Greek/Judeo-Christian Means of Connection

The Cross: Holding Opposites Together

Europe's civilisation in our "north" has been influenced mostly by two major sources: the Judaic-Christian influence and its Greek heritage. The single strongest symbol in Christianity is the cross and its variations, including the Monogram of Christ. On a superficially explicit Level, it is a static, structural Symbol of a torture instrument, which led to the death of Jesus, not to mention since all the Christian wars that have been waged. However, in its deeper implicit, indeed dynamic and thereby integral meaning, the cross could be understood as a symbol that holds opposites together, that incorporates the ability of embracing paradoxes. As such, it is a means of connection not only between earth (matter/mother) and heaven (spirit/father), but also between the past and the future (embracing eternity).

Specifically, moreover, the cross (see Figures 2.3.4.1. below) stands for horizontal and vertical connections, and, in contemporary management consultancy terms, for graphs, for matrices, self assessment inventories, and other such analytical devices for gauging your business or management performance and prospects. On the other hand, if taken out of its dynamic context, a cross is simply a static form. Every time an athlete or other performer "crosses him or herself" such a static form is reinforced.

64 Centring Cosmology

Figure 2.3.4.1: *Monogram of Christ / Cross / Canterbury Cross (used by Anglian Church)*

For a certain period Christianity was indeed the cultural driving force in Western Europe not only in religious and spiritual matters, but also in the arts and the sciences. Especially as several Monasteries became true centres of civilisation; they emerged as showcases of social and economic transformation, where communities based on brotherhood, enhanced not only the Christian spiritual tradition, but also fostered the arts and sciences, cultivated the land, and even became economically successful. However, at a certain stage the church used its enormous influence on politics and economics, on culture and nature, for domination rather than for liberation, for persecution rather than for healing.

Renaissance Man: Focusing on the Power of Reason

The Enlightenment period, however, from the 14th century onwards, connecting the ancient European past with its modern present and future, was of particular importance for the birth of a modern society in Europe and it freed the continent from the oppressive medieval form of Christianity. Now man, not God, was in the centre of the universe. Now, so it was believed, it was man who kept the world going (see da Vinci's Vitruvian Man), not God. Man could do it with the power of his mind and his own imagination. While in the symbol of the "fourfold" cross the centre is where the two lines meet (many paintings place here the "eye of god"), da Vinci's expression of the Renaissance Man, moves the "centre of power to the mind of the human being".

In fact, da Vinci himself became the embodiment of imagination, science, and innovation. Some claim, da Vinci was one of the last men in European history embodying universal knowledge, linking science and arts in a most innovative manner.

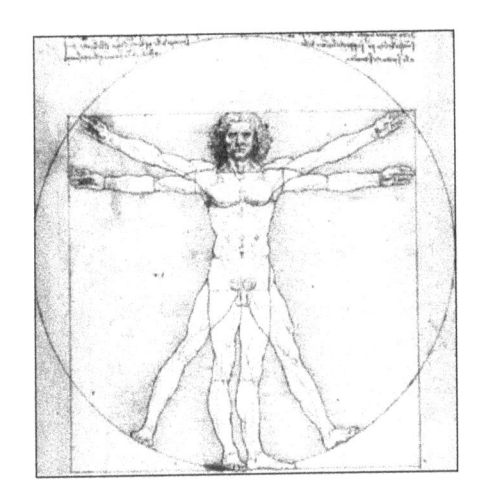

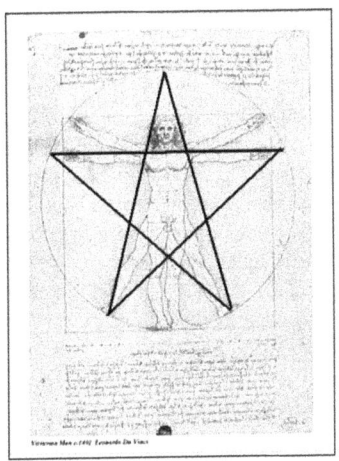

Figure 2.3.4.2: *Leonardo da Vinci's Vitruvian Man (The Mind on Top of the Hierarchy)*

The period of the Enlightenment, which in arts and design was called "Renaissance" (rebirth), re-animated the second pillar of European civilisation: the Greek tradition. It was the Greek philosophers and their focus on reasoning and democratic interaction of minds who enabled one of the most innovative periods within Europe to take place: when the Greek civilisation was at its peak, so was their innovative power with regard to politics, arts and science. Interestingly enough it was the middle *eastern* Arabs who played a major part in recovering the classical Greek tradition. The Odyssey and the Iliad, as the two core myths of that time, tell stories about the intelligence of man, which helped him, especially in the case of Odysseus, to triumph even over the gods.

Lacking Paths towards an Integrated Future

However, the sole focus on the power of human reasoning has led to a new kind of distortion. For decades now, Europe has been suffering from a spiritual vacuum. The "more than human" world (Abram 1997) is evidently missing. Many analysts claim that Christianity has failed to renew itself and to refill this spiritual gap. In contrast, a growing number of Western European (and the US-American) population have taken their spiritual journey in their own hands and are looking for "alternative offerings"; often trying to "re-root" themselves in other belief systems, such as Buddhism and Islam, rather than renew their own "northern" path, as indeed, as we shall see, the "postmodernists" have attempted to do.

Furthermore, the sole focus on rationality and mind has increasingly created work and communication processes that are not in synch with nature in general and with human nature specifically. Technology and economics as a single "northwestern" world or dimension has taken precedence over all other worlds, and is often out of touch with nature, culture, politics and social sciences. The awareness of this misfit is, however, gradually increasing throughout the globe. Yet we lack social designs for a more integrated future. In effect the "north" (reason) and the "west" (action) dominate over the rest, and, at least for the time being, the "middle" ground has lost its way.

There are however amazing examples of social innovators, from Austrian polymath Rudolf Steiner (1977) to Swiss German psychotherapist C.G. Jung (both influenced by the "east" if not also the "south"), who started to pave the way towards more integrated perspectives of the various dimensions of human psyche and society. In our work, we concertedly build on them, acknowledging that they are very much the "northern" and integral exception, rather than the rule. Interestingly enough, and as we shall see later in the Sekem case in Egypt, not only has Egypt generally rubbed shoulders prolifically with Europe, both for good and for ill, but so has Sekem specifically, most especially with Austria's Rudolph Steiner, and anthroposophy, as above.

We now turn from healing and regeneration in the "south", healing divided in the "east", and making connections in the "north", to the "west", starting with the original Native Americans, and ending with the *art of association* between native Americans, Afro Americans, Euro and Anglo-Americans in the American "east", "south", "north" and "west", respectively, not geographically, but by cosmological origination.

2.3.5. Integral West – Towards the Art of Association

Native Medicine Wheel: Harmonising Black, Red, Yellow and White Peoples

The "integral west" today, as opposed to the conventional, proverbial "west", is most vividly embodied in the United States of America as a whole. In fact, we identified some astonishing examples of balanced fourfold designs in a number of indigenous (what we term "southern") societies from North America. They are, if you like, deep expressions of the original "southern" and also "eastern" dimension of what we now call the "west" or North America. As such, we begin with the "original" west, as opposed to the "derivative" western frontier spirit, as exhibited historically, and still to this day, by the American "cowboy" and footloose "get up and go".

Native Americans, to begin with, the "east-west", as it were, are renowned for their indigenous, so-called "medicine wheel" (see Figured 2.3.5. below). The cosmos of the Cree and Objiway people (a native American tribe), for example, includes all of the knowledge required to live in harmony with creation; that is, the knowledge of body and mind and the ability to disseminate knowledge through communication. According to this perspective, all those attributes are necessary to form a holistic (nature) and humanistic (culture) worldview. These Native Americans recognized particular strengths in specific ethnic groups, who together, once again, constitute a "creative synthesis". It is interesting now to see how they were able to recognize the unique contribution of the "white (wo)man", who, after all, until this day, did not embrace the Native American heritage in his or her own cosmos.

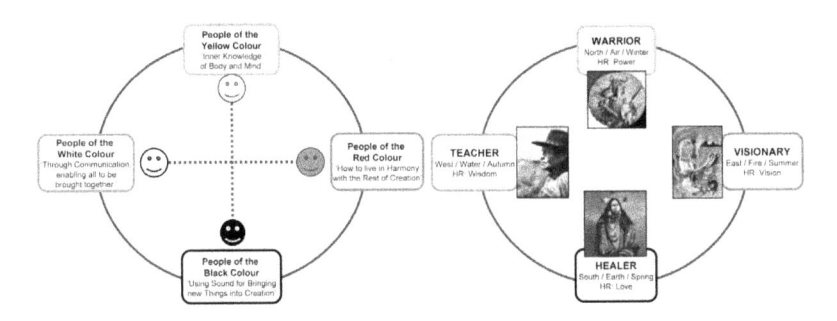

Figure 2.3.5: *Fourfold Design of the Human Cosmos of Cree and Objiway People (left) Fourfold of an Ancient Medicine Wheel (Native American Origin) (right)*

In ancient medicine wheels, attributed to Native American civilisations, it is often different personality types that form a fourfold. In one example (Arrien 1993), each of the four types in the human spectrum, the healer, the visionary, the warrior and the teacher is connected to a specific direction, element, season and human resource (HR): love, vision, power and wisdom. Individuals represent a certain type or a combination of two or more types, and their individual developmental path is influenced by that type. Each type, according to the medicine wheel, is also represented by a particular instrument, emphasizing the strong connection, the "human south" has to music and rhythm. Indeed, music may even be seen as a "way of knowing" and a way to know oneself and the other in a deeper way.

Oriented Towards What Is Materially Realisable

North America today is a "melting pot" of all kinds of cultures and personalities, ironically exclusive – rather than inclusive – of the native Indian, who is shut off with a native "reserve". In a most fascinating way, the "United States" has managed to develop out of this enormously diverse cultural amalgam, a society whose economic and technological forces come to the fore. It is active, future oriented and pragmatic like no other country; and it has quite obviously enabled lots of technologically and economically laden "creative synthesis" within the country, focusing on what is materially *realisable*. However, it is also increasingly evident, that the US has lost its ability to engage in such "creative synthesis", both within its own psychic being, and also together with other countries and civilisations. It still interacts most easily with those countries and personalities, which are most comparable to the US – western style economies and democracies, and similar behavioural orientations towards work and life. But it seems to be unable to embrace diversity on a global level, especially when it comes to other religious and cultural, individual and institutional forms and outlooks that do not want to follow the "American Way".

It may be worthwhile to explore to what extent this "out of balance" perspective is also a manifestation of North America's inability to embrace the cultural and spiritual heritage and knowledge that the indigenous Native American cultures had to offer. Such an exploration is such an obvious one, when we recognize that among the greatest of problems that the US faces is its difficulty in engaging with other cultures, including its indigenous own, as well as with nature and environment. America, overall then, is much more at home in exercising reason and in the process realising its material objectives, than at socially relating and spiritually renewing itself.

There are, however, very promising "western" exceptions. There is an increasing number of social scientists trying to reconcile the primary focus on economics, politics and natural science, with culture, community and nature. Paul Hawken's, Amory and Hunter Lovins' *Natural Capitalism* (1999) and David Peak's *Blackfoot Physics* (2005) are just two recent expressions of such. However, and for example in the former case, Lovin's locally *natural* perspective has not been evolved into an integral American trans-cultural local-global one, which then in turn can be developed into a "newly global" scientific orientation that transcends the all pervasive "north-western" outlook that currently prevails.

American Soul and the Art of Association

In fact, the United States of America, as such, for leading U.S. social philosopher Jacob Needleman (2003) based until his death at San Francisco State University, is the fact, the symbol, and the promise of a new beginning, a new dawn, for the world as a whole. Such an opening "western" premise is very different from the proverbial notion of America as individualistic, enterprising, and indeed militaristic.

Our world today, led by the USA, as we see and hear on all sides, is drowning in materialism, commercialism, and consumerism. But the problem, for Needleman, is not really there. What we ordinarily speak of as materialism is a symptom, not a cause. For him, the *root of materialism is a poverty of ideas about the inner and outer world.* Less and less does our contemporary culture have, or even seek, commerce with great ideas, as indeed we are seeking to articulate here, and it is that lack that is weakening the human spirit. This is the essence of materialism. Materialism, then, is the proverbial, everyday version of such, lodged in commodity fetishism. It is a disease of the mind starved of ideas, not the more common interpretation of such.

Obviously, no search for the meaning of American can turn away from the fact that the U.S. was built on the destruction of its native "eastern" American Indian peoples and the exploitation of its "southern" African slaves. When the real feeling, the deep sense of pondering of each side of this contradiction, does appear in the American soul, something entirely new may be glimpsed in its heart and in its actions. People need to apprehend what is good in America, without self-inflation, and what is evil, without self-flagellation.

The great art form of America, quintessentially for Needleman, is the art of association in general and government in particular. Other nations and cultures have produced cathedrals, epics, poems, music, and systems of philosophy that far surpass what America has brought forth. In this art form, it seems to Needleman that *America is pointing toward the most essential art of the future – the art of human association, the art of working together as individuals and groups and communities. This is the essential art form of the coming humanity.* Without it, nothing else can help us. It is through the group, the community, that moral power and a higher level of intelligence can be sought, if only we can discover the way of constructing associations with others in communities, groups, and combinations of men and women. Interestingly enough, this associative form, unbeknown to most, drew on the Iroquois Native American nation that came before.

Yet another strong voice is that of the Israeli peace activist Jesaiah Ben-Aharon (2002) who, in outlining "America's Global Responsibility", argues that an evolving western culture must rather serve to integrate than to isolate or dominate the south, east, north and centre. He argues that the major destabilising power in the modern era is the modern economy. For Ben-Aharon, globalisation has the capacity to tear away from the state its economic, political and cultural (and natural) assets. Only therefore a clear relational understanding and thereby practical and social implementation of the human interactions and relationships among the various sectors of society will yield the power to replace the pure focus on the economy with more adequate modern social design. We now turn, finally, to the centre of the Four Worlds, represented by the most "synthetic" or integral form of monotheist religion, that is Islam, albeit that voices from within and without have served to distort such an integral orientation.

2.3.6. Centred Imagination: Connecting Paths

Infinity, Balance, and Architectural Beauty in the Islamic World

The interaction between "self and the other" generally, or between Muslim, Roman, Persian and Byzantine architecture specifically, as an evolutionary catalyst for creation and innovation, is evident in the most important architectural expression of the Islamic world, that is the mosque. The mosque is the "sacred architecture" of Islam par excellence. It is, in its religious and aesthetic origination, ironically enough, but a recreation of the harmony, order and peace inherent in nature.

Distinguishing motifs of Islamic architecture have always been ordered repetition, radiating structures, and rhythmic, metric patterns. In this respect, fractal geometry had been a key feature, especially for mosques and palaces. Many argue that Islamic architecture also borrows heavily from the Persian and in many ways can be called an extension and further evolution of such.

A Meeting of Islamic and Judeo-Christian Cultures

The Moorish architecture (to be found mainly in North Africa and on the Iberian Peninsula) is another example of when a civilisation reaches its peak by predominantly peaceful and constructive interactions with others. The Moorish period in Spain is indeed famous for the atmosphere of peaceful coexistence and creative interaction between Muslims, Christians and Jews. Core examples are the Great Mosque of Cordoba (the Mezquita) and the Alhambra, the magnificent palace-fortress of Granada. Interestingly enough, as of February 2023, it has been reported that in Abu Dabi, following the so called Abrahamic Accord (The National News), a mosque-church-synagogue complex is being constructed to bring together the peoples of the book.

The Arabesque: Displaying Unity in Diversity

The Arabesque is an elaborate application of repeating geometric forms. Geometric artwork was not widely used in the Islamic world until the golden age of Islam came into full bloom. During this time, ancient texts were translated from their original Greek and Latin into Arabic at the House of Wisdom, an academic research institution in Baghdad. Like the Renaissance in Europe that followed much later, mathematics, science, literature and history were infused into the Islamic world with mostly positive repercussions. The works of Plato and especially of Euclid became popular among the literate. In fact, it was Euclid's geometry along with the foundations of trigonometry codified by Pythagoras that were expounded on by Al-Jawhari (ca. 800 to 860) whose *Commentary on Euclid's Elements* (De Young 1997) became the impetus of the art for that was to become the Arabesque. Plato's idea about the existence of a separate reality that was perfect in form and function and crystalline in character also would contribute to the development of the Arabesque.

Hence the Arabesque is a symbol of the particular worldview that Islam developed.

There are two modes to arabesque art: the first reflects the principles that govern the order of the world. These principles included the bare basics of what makes objects structurally sound, and, by extension, beautiful. In this first mode, each repeating geometric form has a built-in symbolism ascribed to it. For example, the square, with its four equilateral sides, is symbolic of the equally important elements of nature: earth, air, fire and water. Without any one of the four, the physical world, represented by a circle that inscribes the square, would collapse and cease

Images Behind the Innovation Paths 71

to exist. The second mode is based upon the flowing nature of plant forms. This mode recalls the feminine nature of life giving. In addition, upon inspection of many examples of Arabesque art, some would argue that there is in fact a third mode, the mode of Arabic calligraphy.

Figure 2.3.6: *Arabesques (Fourfold, Circular and Process Elements, Centre)*

As figurative art was considered to be idolatrous and was forbidden (haram) in Mosques, calligraphy and abstract figures became the main methods of artistic expression in Islamic cultures. Arabic, Persian and Ottoman Turkish calligraphy is associated with geometric Islamic art on the walls and ceilings of mosques as wells as in books. Contemporary artists in the Islamic world draw on the heritage of calligraphy. The guiding principles of infinity, balance and beauty can also easily be found in Islamic calligrams. At the peak of Muslim civilisation "creative synthesis" worked at its best: knowledge was able to flow.

In the so-called Islamic Golden Age (Kraemer 2008), in Baghdad and in Egypt, between the 9th and 13th centuries, as well as in Cordoba in Spain, there was also rich interaction between all three peoples of the book, until that began to wain thereafter. Interestingly enough, in this day and age, Ibrahim Abouleish, the founder of Sekem in Egypt, as we shall see, drew on both his Islamic and his European heritage explicitly, as well as his African-Egyptian heritage, at least implicitly, to evoke his integral Sekem design in relation to what we (Lessem and Schieffer 2009) term *society building*. We are now ready for overall cosmology, world-wide, originally emerging out of Africa.

2.4. Conclusion: Healing and Regeneration- Connecting Paths

2.4.1. Out of the Healing Wisdom of Africa

In our "tour de world", we started out in West Africa, in the African "south-west", specifically with the Yoruba people of Nigeria, illustrating how their *orisa* laden, centring cosmology, focused on *healing and regeneration,* echoing that of Malidoma Some's Dagara communities, also in West Africa. Thereafter we turned from south to "east", most specifically to China in Asia, where the Taoist notion of "Yin-Yang" oriented us, cosmologically, to *healing divides* between most specifically the masculine and the feminine.

In then turning "north-west" to Europe, now most specifically to Christianity on that continent, the holy cross symbolised the *making of connections* between spirit and matter, heaven and earth, also thereafter the making of conceptual connections between one kind of theory and another. Penultimately, in North America, within what we have termed an "integral West", we highlighted the *art of association,* according to philosopher Joseph Needleman America's greatest gift to the world. Finally then, in the Middle East, the geographical centre of the world, we identified Islam, in spirit if not in everyday matter as we can see, *connecting paths* between one peoples and another. All of such then emerges, cosmologically – healing divides, making connections, the art of association, and now connecting paths, out of such original African healing wisdom.

2.4.2. Symbolised by a Circle, Spiral, Matrix, Point

We have attributed to each cosmological region a particular symbol, which most evidently represents its particular quality:

- *The African South:* symbolized by a *circle*, representing togetherness in nature (full moon, sun etc.) and community (family and community cycles), to be embodied in our case story of the Integral Kumusha in Southern Africa, generally, and in a learning community and communal steward specifically
- *The Asian East:* symbolized by a *spiral*, representing continuous, interconnected cycles of renewal, as well as continuous storylines, interconnecting past, present and future (civilisational spiral), to be embodied in the *Good African Coffee Story* in East Africa, generally, and in a transformation journey and catalyst specifically
- *The European North:* symbolized by a line or *matrix*, representing lines of reasoning, order within manmade social systems (institutions, enterprises etc.) or constitutions (e.g. laws) to be embodied in Sekem in North Africa, generally, and in a research academy together with educators and researchers specifically
- *The American Integral West:* symbolized by a *point*, representing the focus on personal, organizational and community goals, realising the material point of our endeavours, embodied by one of us (Anselm Adodo) in Paxherbals in

Conclusion: Healing and Regeneration- Connecting Paths 73

West Africa, generally, and in our Integral Laboratory and in such development specifically.

From an innovation perspective, circle, spiral, line and point need to mutually reinforce one another, not only visually but also viscerally, so to speak. Furthermore, it is no accident that we talk in terms of a "line of reasoning", and the "point of an argument". Each symbolizes a particular, cultural or individual mentality. Interestingly enough, in English at least, we have no such positive colloquialisms for the other two archetypal forms: cycle and spiral. In fact, we allude negatively to someone "going around in circles", and "getting nowhere" as a result. Spirals, proverbially as such, are not even on our radar screens. Finally, what we have left out of overall account in the *Middle* East, or indeed MENA, which potentially, if not yet actually, serves to bring all of the above together, albeit that arguably, in our own African context, Sekem, plays a dual role as both northern and mediating as such.

In Figure 2.4.3. below we distill the four if not five cosmologies and symbols

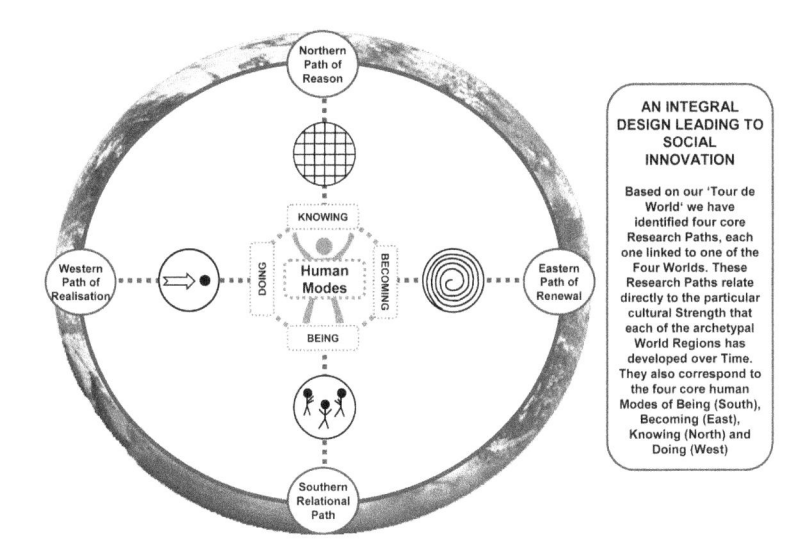

Figure 2.4.3: *Integral Cosmologies*

Finally, we turn from a horizontal "tour de world", so to speak, to a vertical one, from local roots, in a manner of speaking to global-local fruits.

2.4.5. Local Roots, Local-Global Mainstem, Newly Global Branches, Global-Local Fruits: Integral Tree of Life

The core defining factors of our Integral Tree of Life, are summarised as follows:

- *Building on Local Roots:* reconnecting the researcher, enterprise and community with the innovative power of his or her own civilisation as a starting point for his/ her, their path; ensuring the researcher/innovator is true to his own culture
- *Local-Global Mainstem:* integrating and equally valuing different worlds, and hence different approaches to research methodology and knowledge creation
- *Newly Global Branches:* enabling creative synthesis of diverse dimensions within a social organism (self, organization, society) and between social organisms (between organization, between societies) connecting different knowledge paths
- *Global-Local Fruits:* through the integration of knowledge paths and the enabling of creative synthesis, *Integral Research, Enterprise and Economy* foster a gradual evolution from local roots (local identity) to global reach (contributing to an integrated, balanced perspective on a global level). The local and global connection also helps to enable forms of social innovation that, while reaching globally, stay true and authentic to the local context where they are ultimately applied.

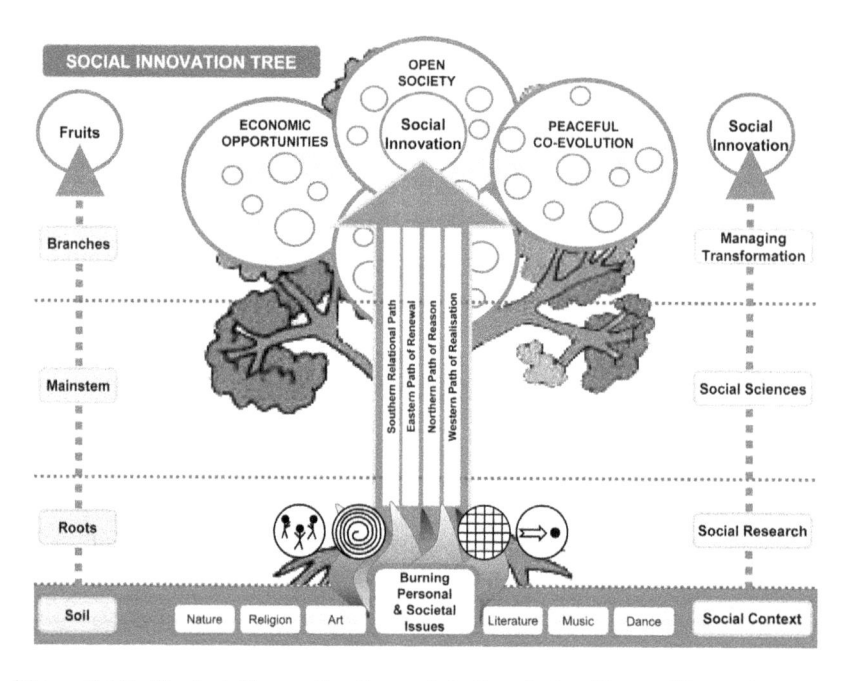

Figure 2.4.5: *The Social Innovation Tree and the Four Paths of Integral Research*

The above illustration of our social innovation tree, Figure 2.4.5., translates once more our core architecture into an organic picture, linking the process of integral research and innovation. with the substance of the social sciences.

Altogether, we have seen how particular societies and civilisations have developed implicit knowledge about maintaining a healthy and dynamic balance, naturally and aesthetically, but have seldom managed to make such explicit, technologically, economically and altogether politically, not least because there is no composite societal agency to accomplish such. This is, we maintain, as we shall see, where out inter-institutional communiversity comes in. Such innovation power, moreover, is born out of the interaction between cultures, what we term transcultural transformational, transdisciplinary and transpersonal, as was the case for the Muslim world at its height (in the 9th–14th centuries), and for America in the 19th and first half of the 20th centuries.

We now turn more specifically to the paths, and trajectories, of integral research and innovation, albeit set alongside integral enterprise and economics in an overall African context.

2.5. References

Abram D (1997) *The Spell of the Sensuous.* New York. Random House

Adodo A (2017) *Integral Community Enterprise in Africa: Communitalism as an Alternative to Capitalism.* Abingdon. Routledge

Arrien A (1993) *The Four-Fold Way – Walking the Paths oft he Warrior, Teacher, Healer and Visionary.* San Francisco. Harper

Ben Aharon J (2002) *America's Global Responsibility.* Herdon. Lindisfarne

Biko S (1987) *I Write What I Like.* London. Heinemann African Series

Cane EP (2002) *Harmony: Radical Taoism Gently Applied.* Victoria. Trafford Publishing

De Young G (1997) Al-Jawhari's Additions to Book V of Euclid's Elements. *Zeitschrift fur Geschichte der Arabisch-Islamischen Wissenschaften* 11 (10): 153–178

Ford C (2000) *The Hero with an African Face – The Mystic Wisdom of Africa.* New York. Bantam

Hawken P, Lovins A and Lovins H (1999) *Natural Capitalism: The Next Industrial Revolution.* Boston. Little Brown

Heron J (1994) *Feeling and Personhood.* Abingdon. Routledge

Heron J (1997) *Cooperative Inquiry.* London. Sage

Jaffe A (2001) *Erinnerungen, Träume and Gedanken von C.G. Jung.* Zurich. Walter

Kohn L (ed) (2000) *Daoism Handbook.* Leiden. Brill

Kraemer J (2008) *Maimonides: The Life and World of One of the Civilisation's Greatest Minds.* New York. Doubleday

Lessem R and **Schieffer** A (2009) *Transformation Management: Toward the Integral Enterprise*. Abingdon. Routledge

Lessem R et al (2013) *Integral Dynamics: Cultural Dynamics, Political Economy and the Future oft he University*. Abingdon. Routledge

Lessem R, **Abouleish** A, **Pogacnik** M and **Herman** L (2015) *Integral Polity: Aligning Nature, Culture, Society and Economy*. Abingdon. Routledge

Little S et al (2000) *Taoism and the Arts of China*. Chicago. Chicago Art Institute

Martinson PV (1987) *A Theology of World Religions: Interpreting God, Self and World in Semitic, Indian and Chinese Thought*. Augsburg. Augsburg Publishing

Mazrui A (1986) *The Africans – A Triple Heritage*. London. Guild Publishing

Needleman J (2003) *The American Soul: Rediscovering the Wisdom of the Founders*. New York. Jeremy Tarcher

Needleman J (2003) *The American Soul: Rediscovering the Wisdom of the Founders*. New York. Jeremy Tarcher

Peat D (2005) *Blackfoot Physics: A Journey into the Native American Universe*. New York. Weiser

Robinet I (1997) *Taoism: Growth of a Religion*. Stanfrod, CA. Stanford University Press

Sen A (2006) *The Argumentative Indian: Writings on Indian History, Culture, and Identity*. London. Penguin

Some M (1997) *The Healing Wisdom of Africa*. New York. Jeremy Tarcher

Steiner R (1977) *Towards Social Renewal*. Forest Row. Rudolf Steiner Press

The National News. https://www.thenationalnews.com/opinion/comment/2022/01/22/the-abrahamic-family-house-is-not-about-merging-faiths/

Chapter 3 Integral Research and Innovation in Southern, East, North and West Africa. Paths and Trajectories: Communiversity to Communitalism

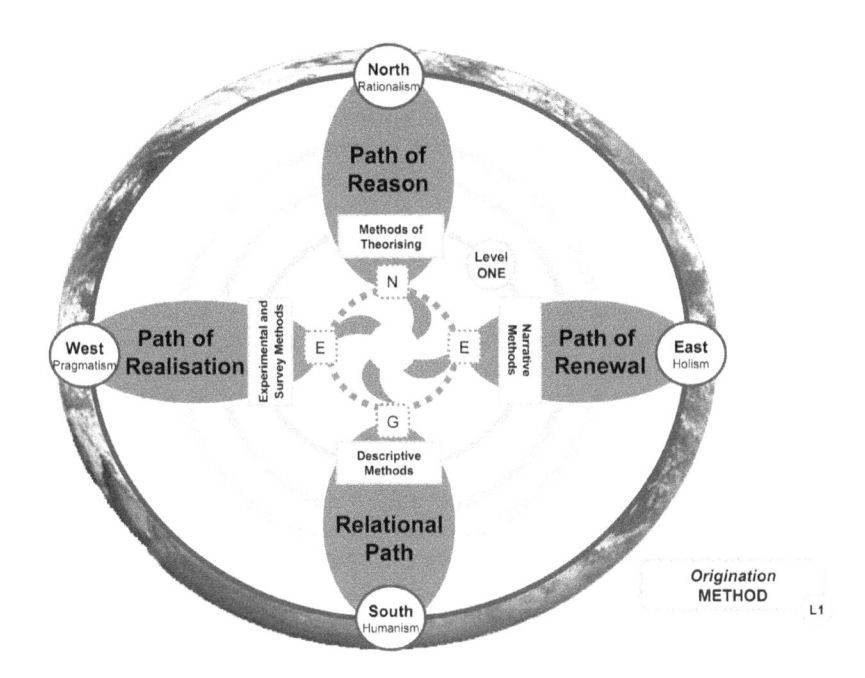

Figure 3.1: *Overview Chapter 4 – Method*

Summary: Integral Research and Innovation

- **Integral Trajectory:** We distinguish from the outset between research method as grounding and origination; research methodology, as emergent local-global foundation; research critique, as emancipatory navigation; and action research as transformative effect, for each of four worlds

- **Research Paths:** We identify, overall, four research paths, each with their trajectory from origination to transformation, that is the relational (southern) and renewal (eastern) paths, as well as the paths of reason (northern) and realisation (western)

- **Individual Research Paths and Inter-institutional Communiversity:** Each individual research paths needs to be aligned with an equivalent institutional constituency: the relational path with a learning community; the path of renewal with a transformation journey; the path of reason with a research academy; the path of realisation with a socio-economic laboratory.

- **Research and Innovation:** Each such research paths, and communiversity constituent, is also aligned with its corresponding enterprise and economic functioning: the learning community with community building and self sufficiency; the transformation journey with conscious evolution and a developmental economy; the research academy with knowledge creation and a social economy; the socio-economic laboratory with sustainable development and a living economy

- **Communiversity to Communitalism:** Each such facet of the Communiversity is additionally aligned with one or other facet of Communitalism embodied in Southern Africa in an integral *Kumusha* (homestead) in Zimbabwe; in East Africa in a Ugandan *Good African Story*; in North Africa in Egypt in Sekem's *Economics of Love*; and in West Africa in Nigeria in pax Herbals' *Nature Power*, altogether as a "southern" alternative to "western" capitalism.

- **Crisis of Representation:** Our overall approach to integral research and innovation reflects, in the research methodological arena, as stated by guru's in the field, Denzyn and Lincoln, a *crisis of representation*, whereby particular cultures, specifically "north-western" rule the research roost, and issue we seek integrally to redress

I have walked that long road to freedom. I have tried not to falter; I have made mishaps along the way. But I have discovered the secret that after climbing a great hill, one only finds that there are many more hills to climb. I have taken a moment here to rest, to steal a view of the glorious vistas that surround me, to look back on the distance I have come. But I can rest only for a moment, for with freedom comes responsibilities, and I dare not linger, for my long walk is not yet ended.

Nelson Mandela (1994)   *The Long Walk to Freedom*

3.1. Introduction: A Double-Layered Trajectory

3.1.1. Analytical Research/Transformative Innovation

Within this chapter, we shall lay out in detail the paths and trajectories of Integral Research, both analytical and transformative, in the foreground while retaining integral enterprise and economics in the background. We build, on the one hand, on the four trans-culturally based research paths (integral realities) that we introduced in Chapter 1, and, on the other, on the transformational trajectory (integral rhythm). These four paths within the Integral Worlds framework each follow a double-layered Integral Research trajectory that combines an analytical orientation towards research with a transformative orientation towards innovation.

These paths are also altogether aligned with the fourfold functioning of our integral communiversity, as well as, ultimately, also with communitalism. In the university context, community outreach is accompanied by *communal learning;* individual education by a *transformation journey;* individual research by a *research academy;* and student secondments by a *socio-economic laboratory.* Likewise, in enterprise terms, marketing if accompanied by *community building;* HR by *conscious evolution;* operations by *knowledge creation;* and finance by *sustainable development.*

3.1.2. Method, Methodology, Critique, Action: *Communal Learning, Transformation Journey, Research Academy, Socio-economic Laboratory*

Once you have chosen your particular research path, you work yourself through the four levels of our GENE rhythm, specific to that path. Altogether, the interaction between the two kinds of trajectory serve to "dynamize" your research and innovation, individually on the one hand, and the communiversity-wise, institutionally on the other. Overall then you progressively and cumulatively advance through the following four ultimately transformative levels, formatively, reformatively, newly normatively and indeed transformatively, each also linked with one or other facet, accumulatively, of our communiversity, if not ultimately, also, communitalism:

- *Level 1:* Research *method* linked with *origination* of an innovation, aligned with one or other naturally/communally oriented learning community, alongside, as we shall see through course of this work, community building and nhakanomics.
- *Level 2:* Research *methodology* aligned with a philosophical and paradigmatic *foundation* for such innovation, aligned with your culturally and spiritually contextualised transformation journey, conscious evolution and Yurugu-nomics

- *Level 3:* Research *critique* linked with philosophical sources of *emancipation* behind innovation, aligned with our scientific (social sciences) and artistic (humanities) based <u>research academy</u>, knowledge creation/economics of love
- *Level 4: Action research,* building on all previous levels, realising the necessary *transformation,* to bring about a full-fledged integral innovation, aligned ultimately with a <u>socio-economic laboratory</u>, sustainable development and communitalism.

To make this overall integral research rhythm clearer we now guide you through the two, aligned trajectories. Have in mind, that at each level you simultaneously engage with both trajectories. Our integral approach to research-and-innovation is then an interactive journey between a more analytical (research) and a more transformative (innovation) trajectory, leading towards an integral social innovation. We now turn to the four levels, both analytical and transformative in each of the four cases, in turn, respectively and accumulatively grounding (origination – communal *learning*), emergence (foundation – *transformation* journey), navigation (emancipation – *re-search* academy) and ultimate effect (transformation – socio/economic *laboratory*).

3.1.1. Grounding: Level 1: Method and Local Communal Origination

Method: Communal Research Method

You engage firstly with a particular research method or technique, which is, as we shall see in Chapter 4, closely related to underlying human modes of being and becoming, knowing and doing. Hence, you start, communally, through your chosen path, with either descriptive methods (relational path), narrative methods (path of renewal), methods of theorizing (path of reason) or experimental and survey – including case study/story – methods (path of realisation).

Local Origination: Origination of Your Innovation via Communal Learning

Closely aligned with analytical method is the transformatively oriented origination, in this case of your innovation. You identify and address a burning issue, galvanized by your burning desire, lodged in your particular world (reality), focused on a specific community, polity, economy or enterprise (realm) with a view to a specifically contributing, locally, to communal *learning*. You thereby not only uncover the origins of your own inner calling, but also that of your community, activating its particular local wisdom and learning potential, thereby, enterprise-wise, community building, and economy-wise, locally activating nhakanomics ("nhaka" meaning *legacy*).

3.1.2. Emergence: Level 2: Methodology and Local-Global Cultural Foundation

Methodology: Research Journey from Ontology to Epistemology to Methodology

You engage methodologically and philosophically with existing theories, which have been built up over time to establish a solid analytical basis, or paradigm, for your thereby research and learning journey through ontology, epistemology and methodology. Here you choose, according to your path, and altogether as above, between phenomenology (relational path), hermeneutics (path of renewal), critical rationalism (path of reason) or empiricism (path of realisation).

Local-Global Foundation: Innovation Foundation/Transformation Journey

You develop a philosophical and methodological foundation for your envisioned innovation, lodged in one or other of the social sciences, thereby transforming – deepening and widening – your perspective on such, locally as well as globally. As such you gain profoundly greater contextual insight, culturally and spiritually, into the phenomena you are investigating. Such a transformation journey, communiversity wise, is then accompanied by conscious evolution, enterprise-wise, and by Yurugu-nomics overall, economy wise out of Africa.

3.1.3. Navigation: Level 3: Scientific Critique and Newly Global Emancipation

Critique: Integral Research Academy

You now start to engage with a core contemporary critique within research methodology, further evolving, analytically, your philosophical and methodological position. Here you choose, according to your path, between feminism (relational path), critical theory (path of renewal), postmodernism (path of reason) or critical realism (path of realisation). These critiques are notably more transdisciplinary than the original methodology/philosophy/social science considered on level 2. Your analytical perspective broadens, and you engage more intensely with co-researchers.

Emancipation: Emancipation for Innovation via Newly Global Critical Re-Search

You evolve the foundation to innovation further, now specifically with a view to promoting a "newly global", emancipatory scientific model, if not also institution, in your particular African, if not also another, society. Instead of becoming merely part of a de-colonised "Global South", you position your particular society, uniquely, and "newly globally", as such. Indeed, you thereby follow the critical philosophies with which you have been engaging (feminism, postmodernism etc.). All, at least to some extent, also represent a social movement. As such, your research academy becomes part of such a "de-colonial" African movement, albeit including enterprise and economy as part of such, spanning knowledge creation and the economics of love.

3.1.4. Effect: Level 4: Global-Local Economic Action and Transformation

Action: Action Research

Finally, having worked yourself through levels 1, 2 and 3 you are ready for action. You have built up sufficient experience, theory and critical understanding of your burning issue, and the gifts your community and society bring to bear on the issue at hand, to develop your own knowledge and value base. You are now ready to apply this knowledge and engage with the institution, community or society at hand, in action research. On this ultimate level 4 you choose, according to your path, between participatory action research (relational path), co-operative inquiry (path of renewal), socio-technical design (path of reason) or generic action research (path of realisation).

Moreover, for us in Africa, such action research, most especially participatory action research, becomes aligned with sustainable development, at a micro enterprise level, and with communitalism, at a macro economic level. Your action research, as such, is directed to bringing about an integral innovation addressing your original, communal and societal burning issue (outer calling) and individual desire (inner calling). Based on your emancipated philosophical perspective, you engage in actively realising a transformation within your social context, making a significant, both theoretical and practical, contribution to the community, polity, economy or enterprise (realms) with which you are engaging. The specific vehicle for such becomes a socio-economic laboratory, prospectively now operating globally-locally, having built on what has come locally (communal learning), locally-globally (transformation journey) and newly globally (via a research academy), before.

Introduction: A Double-Layered Trajectory 83

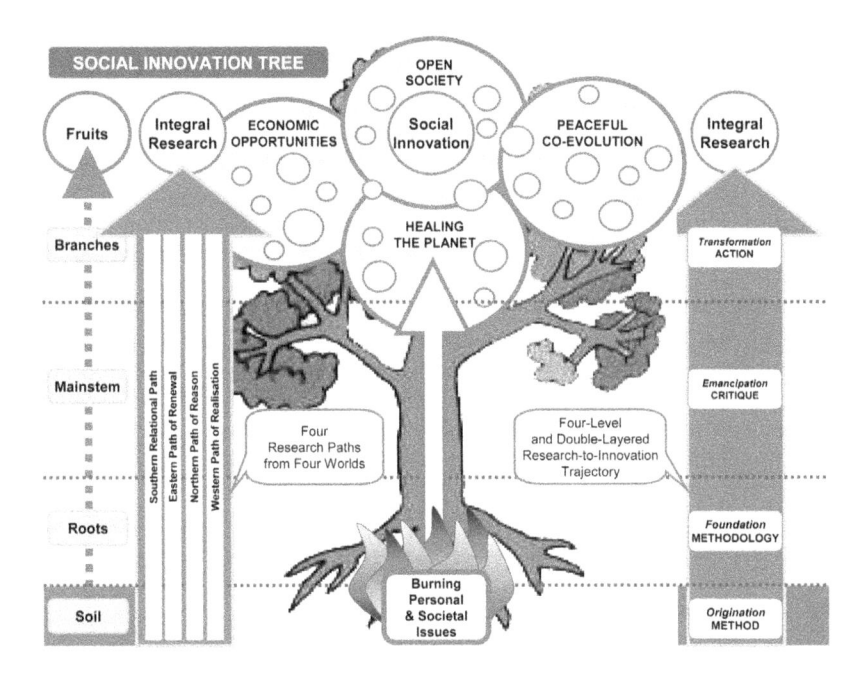

Figure 3.1.4: *The Social Innovation Tree – Four Paths, Four Levels*

Transformation: Action Research to Experimental Socio-Economic Laboratory

The social innovation tree (see Figure 3.1.4. above) summarizes the fourfold Integral Research Trajectory leading to an ultimately integral social innovation. According to your inner and outer calling and the path accordingly taken your research-and-innovation would contribute to (or have generated fruit in) one of the following issues

- *Healing the Planet:* overcoming environmental and communal decay
- *Promoting Peaceful Co-Evolution:* overcoming fundamentalism and terrorism
- *Building Open Societies:* overcoming corruption and despotism
- *Creating Economic Opportunities:* overcoming materialism and abject poverty

We will now start to build systematically from this basis. While the detailed Integral Research framework is presented in linear terms, *Integral Research is quintessentially a back and forth cyclical, spiralling and ultimately original and organic, living process, where the end of "doing well" is created out of the beginning, "doing good".* But let us move forward step by step. So get ready fo(u)r Integral Research and Innovation, get ready to release your GENE-ius as an analytical researcher and transformative innovator. Get ready to co-evolve a communiversity.

Transformation Through and of the Social Sciences Through a Communiversity

Note, that in this book, we use both terms, "social" and "integral" innovation, simultaneously and interactively. We do so to highlight, that our particular approach towards social innovation is an integral one, spanning origination, in particular soils; foundation in social research methodology; emancipation through a transdisciplinary orientation to the social sciences; and ultimate social and economic transformation.

We believe that this is key, not only to come up with truly original and authentic social innovations, but also to gradually build a new knowledge base, which leads to a transformation through and of the social sciences as well as to new educational curricula, enabling future social, and thereby also integral, innovators, through a communiversity. We thereby distinguish ourselves clearly from the generally very loose use of the term social innovation. Integral Research and integral innovation are the two analytical and transformative sides of the same coin.

3.2. The Fourfold GENEtic Code to Social Innovation

3.2.1. Process, Form, Context and Substance

Integral Research is both analytical and transformative, stabilising and *dynamic*, as is our communiversity, through its *learning* community, *transformation* journey, *re-search* academy, and socioeconomic *laboratory*. The paths illustrated here may generate the illusion of a purely linear movement. But they are also expressions of archetypal patterns of creation. You will remember from Chapter 2 that the visual social design (like the illustration of the four research paths) is only the outer expression of an inner dynamic process. It is this transformative inner *process* alongside an analytical, stabilising structure that combine to constitute Integral Research and Innovation, with the Communiversity as its *form*. Invariably this arises, for us, in a particular African *context*, its *substance* encompassing community building and nhakanomics; conscious evolution and Yurugu-nomics; knowledge creation and the economics of love; sustainable development and communitalism.

3.2.2. The GENEtic Process

Such a process is a kind of "vital" force or "attractor" that attracts individuals, organizations, communities and societies towards knowledge and value creation. We have called this process the GENE, an acronym that stands for grounding, emerging, navigating and effecting, and have described it in detail in our previous (2009) work on *Transformation Management (Lessem* and Schieffer, 1994). The Table below introduces the transformative rhythm of the GENE, serving to release GENE-ius/conceive of a communiversity.

The "effecting" step is the final one, and for once it is the south that leads the process, followed by the east and the north. The archetypal west, so our argument, becomes only truly effective if it builds on the other worlds. In other words, you need to uncover the south, east, north and west, metaphorically, not geographically, of your society, while also, and in the process, drawing from these worlds.

The Four World GENE distinguishes between the relational path of research, as well as the research paths of renewal, of reason, and of realisation. As mentioned hitherto in this chapter, as an Integral Researcher you opt for one of the four specific research paths, one that is authentic to yourself and your society. In fact each of our case stories (see Table 3.2.2.) illustrates in particular each phase of our GENE.

Table 3.2.2. *The GENE Release GENE-ius/Conceive of a Communiversity*

Local Grounding and Communal Origination/Learning Community
Southern Africa: Community Building/Kumusha-Nhakanomics
In the Grounding phase, you as an Integral Researcher/Innovator individually and collectively recognize/promote local natural/communal learning in your Life World.
Local-Global Emergent Trans-cultural Foundation/Trans4mation Journey
East Africa: Conscious Evolution/Good African Story -Yurugu/nomics
Trans-cultural Emergence, now locally-globally, thereby indigenously-exogenously, enables you to let go of the old to let in the new, combining tradition and modernity
Newly Global Emancipatory Scientific Navigation/Research Academy
North Africa: Knowledge Creation/Sekem – Economics of Love
The Navigation Phase now building "newly globally" on what has come before, through a centre for social innovation, combines nature and culture, society and economy in a fourfold, associative-anthroposophical union, aligning east and west, north and south
Transformative Global-Local Enterprise Effect: Socio-Economic Laboratory
West Africa: Sustainable Development/PaxHerbals – Communitalism
The Phase of Effecting allows you to develop a Social Innovation, addressing a burning issue lodged in the grounds of your Life World, with ultimately global-local implications

3.3. The Four Level Research-to-Innovation Journey

3.3.1. Overview: Integral Research Leading to Integral Innovation

Integral Research

By now you have received a first introduction to Integral Research and Innovation, as well as to our Communiversity, which is the inter-institutional vehicle, or form, which serves to deliver such an ultimately transformative process, and substance, in context. Integral Research distinguishes between four discrete research paths – relational to renewal, reason to realisation – and within each one, between four levels in a research trajectory – research method and research methodology, research critique and action research. These differentiations constitute an analytical device whereby we help you make sense of what is otherwise a very confusing body of literature, spanning research method and methodology. In fact, the conventional division, or assumed balance, between qualitative and quantitative method, for us, is singularly unhelpful, given that, as we shall see, in spanning research methods, methodologies, critiques, and action research, the vast majority of these are "qualitative".

Instead, we have come up with four mutually exclusive and collectively exhaustive research paths, each with a similar fourfold trajectory, from research method to action research. Moreover, while each of the four paths can be aligned with one or other of our four worlds, each trajectory, as we have demonstrated, follows the course of our GENE, from grounding (method) and emergence (methodology) to navigation (critique) and effect (action). Integral Research therefore provides a coherent set of categories for you to work with and select from in undertaking your research, alongside the literature you search through and the fieldwork you undertake. As such, it is also an *integral* approach to research method and methodology. How then does social innovation compare and contrast with the integral approach to research?

Integral Innovation

While research is analytical, and most conventional doctoral work for example in the social sciences and humanities, be it in the African South or the American West, is analytical, social research-*and*-Innovation is transformative. While research is exclusive and self-contained, innovation is inclusive of, and interconnected with, the burning issue you address, the culture with which you engage, the social sciences, which you deploy, and the enterprise to which you give rise. Indeed, for one of us (Adodo), in addressing the burning issue of poverty in Ewo State, in rural Nigeria, taking due account of his Yoruba culture, deploying his brand of communitalism drawing on nature power, the enterprise he and his community effected was indeed Pax Herbals: duly involving community, journey, academy and laboratory. In fact, and overall as such, the division between social research and innovation, on the one hand, and economy and enterprise on the other, herein in African guise, is overcome.

The link between the burning issue that you and your community – for example Adodo and Ewo above – are addressing and the innovation that you are destined to bring about – for example Pax Herbals underpinned by Communitalism – serves to enfold one level of the trajectory into the other. In that unfolding and progressively transformative respect, research method becomes origination; methodology, becomes a new foundation or research paradigm; research critique heralds social emancipation; finally, and for each of the four paths, action becomes transformation. What then actually turns research into innovation, analysis into transformation?

On the one hand, as we have already intimated, we now focus on the developmental connection as opposed to analytical separation between each level. On the other hand, and even more significantly, the following connections are inclusively made:

- *Transformational Origination Grounded in Communal Learning e.g. Ewu farmers:* The origination of the innovation takes place within the underlying social context (nature and community within a particular society), identifying the burning issue, setting the transformational course for the research-to-innovation journey.
- *Transcultural Foundation Emerging out of Transformation Journey e.g. Adodo:* The innovative foundation is formed out of the relevant philosophical foundation (e.g. critical rationalism) and/or a particular core discipline (e.g. management or sociology). You seek to include solid philosophical foundations related to the issue at hand, including such from your own culture that critically engages with the local context. It is here, where you fully engage with one of the four transculturally oriented paths – relational, renewal, reason or realisation – to innovation, while also, progressively, reaching out to other cultures.
- *Transdisciplinary Emancipation: Research Academy Navigated Scientifically e.g. Communitalism:* The existing theoretical basis is to be further evolved through critical reflection and through transdisciplinary interaction with a variety of social sciences and humanities. It is at this highly dynamic third level that the combination of a socially and economically critical stance, with a strong urge to improve the lot of humankind, leads to an inner and outer mobilization of the researcher, potentially linked with a socio-economic movement, such as feminism, of his or her time.
- *Transpersonal Transformation: Techno-Economic Laboratory Effected Economically e.g. Pax Herbals.* At this culminating level you actively engage with a particular enterprise, community or society. Thereby the personal realm of the individual researcher is transcended. It is here where the full-fledged integral innovation is to be achieved.

Drawing on the same logic that John Heron (1997) uses in his approach to action research, that is co-operative inquiry (see Chapter 10) we argue that origination, foundation, emancipation and transformation form the full transformational trajectory. It is for that reason that we take into account all four, in the same way as communal learning, a transformation journey, research academy and socio-economic laboratory accumulatively serve to make up our communiversity, and indeed, as we shall see, community building/self sufficiency, conscious evolution/developmental economy, knowledge creation/social economy and sustainable development/living economy altogether constitute, for Adodo, communitalism (Adodo 2017) and, for Lessem and Schieffer, integral enterprise and economics at micro (Lessem and Schieffer 2009) and macro (Lessem and Schieffer 2010) levels.

We are responding thereby to a call of our time, where social innovation, as we mentioned in Chapter 1, has failed to match technological innovation. We have particularly emphasized, that this thwarted development has much to do with a domination of western and northern ways of pragmatic-rational knowledge generation, by way of *context*, of the university *form*, the analytical research *process*, and predominating economic, capitalist *substance*. We therefore need to ultimately come to an integral perspective of the different ways, illustrating the specific contributions which each world or research-to-innovation path represents, each of which is needed in order to enable creative synthesis, resulting out of the constructive transcultural interaction within and between the various worlds.

As all truly innovative social scientists have done, we intend to make a contribution to the particular context we are currently living in – a world, where social innovations are too rare to significantly improve the world in which we live. So let us start to uncover now the various layers of Integral Research, with which, when understood and acted upon, will enable you to pursue the full transformational trajectory. Moreover, as we shall see, such a trajectory also underlies our communiversity and communitalism in turn, transcending the university and capitalism respectively.

3.3.2. Method to Action – Origination to Transformation: Being to Doing

Origination: Research Method/Local Grounding of African Enterprise/Economy; African Learning Community

We start out research method (Grounding) from an analytical research perspective, and of local *origination*, altogether constituting the grounding of your endeavours, *Being* individually, and that of the integral enterprise (community building to sustainable development) and economy (nhakanomics to communitalism) in south, east, north and west Africa in turn. As such descriptive and narrative method, grounded theory and case study method, respectively, provides the concrete or experiential starting point, research-wise, for our prospective social innovation, enterprise and economy wise, as will be specifically illustrated in our four cases. In fact the lack of such case stories in Africa means that we have been failing to concretely and experientially ground our would-be innovative endeavours.

Table 3.3.2.1. *Local Origination: Research/Enterprise/Economy: Concrete Method/Learning Community*

<u>Descriptive</u> <u>Methods</u> (South)	Describe Phenomena (relational Path) in intimate Detail: *Root yourself in a particular Life World: Community Building* (S1) *Nhakanomic* Origination in the African *South*: Kumusha
<u>Narrative</u> <u>Methods</u> (East)	Narrate unfolding storylines (Path of Renewal): *Co-evolve a Culture's Local Origins: Conscious Evolution* (E1) Originating *Yurugu-nomics* in *East* Africa: Good African Story
<u>Methods of</u> <u>Theorising</u> (North)	Conjecture (Path of Reason) and form Research Hypotheses: *Reveal Knowledge-Value Base of a Society: Create Knowledge* (N1) Originating *Economics of Love* in the African *North*: Sekem
<u>Case, Survey</u> <u>Methods/</u> <u>Experiment</u> (West)	Case Study, Survey and Experimentation (Path of Realisation): *Experiment with Nature/Enterprise/Sustain Development* (W1) Originating *Communitalism* in the African *West*: Sekem

Foundation: Research Methodology/Locally-Globally Emergent African Enterprise/Economy: African Transformation Journey

Our next local-global emergent foundation, thereby journeying from being to *becoming*, is comprised of more deeply insightful but still conventional methodology.

Table 3.3.2.2. *Local-Global Research Foundation: Enterprise/Economy: Insightful Methodology/Transformation Journey*

<u>Phenomenology</u> (South)	A radical Inquiry into the inner Quality of a World: *Immersed in a Local-Global World: Community Building* (S2) *Nhakanomic* Foundation in the African South: Kumusha
<u>Hermeneutics</u> (East)	Interpret the Past Locally-Globally in Terms of the Present: *Review/Renew Local-Global Origins: Conscious Evolution* (E2) *Yurugu-nomics* Foundation in East Africa: Good African Story
<u>Critical</u> <u>Rationalism</u> (North)	Deduce relevant Theories on your Subject of Concern: *Apply Theory to Deepen Explanations: Knowledge Creation* (N2) Foundation of *Economics of Love* in African North: Sekem
<u>Empiricism</u> (West)	Apply empirically based inductive Analysis: *Address the "Real" World: Sustainable Development* (W2) Foundation of *Communitalism* in African West: Pax Herbals

Our analytical research trajectory serves to locate yourself in one or other of four respectively, now locally-globally, phenomenological or hermeneutic (interpretive), rational and empirical (positivist) classical methodologies, albeit with a view, for us, to now more insightfully delving into, with a view to renewing, your economic and enterprise foundations in Africa, as illustrated by each of our cases in turn. As such the concrete, experiential, local case story becomes a more insightful, indeed more imaginative local-global re-view, thereby illuminated by one or other classical methodologies, albeit now in African as well as generic such guise.

In parallel, the transformative innovation trajectory is serving to form the emerging paradigm or research *foundation* for your ultimate innovation. In your *transformation journey*, as such, evolving from communal grounding, aligned with research method, communally as well as organisationally, a *conscious evolution* is needed, towards more philosophically oriented methodology, societally aligned with a culturally and spiritually based *developmental economy*. In "southern" guise, methodologically then, phenomenology is our first port of call.

Emancipation: Research Critique/Newly Global Navigation of African Enterprise and Economy: Research Academy

Now "newly global" level 3, encompasses the more contemporary, unconventional wisdom, spanning so-called "critical methodologies", which serve to provide an overtly emancipatory and socio-political African outlook promoted now by a Research Academy. In addition, from an innovation perspective, such "knowing", building on prior being and becoming, serves as a basis for social and economic emancipation, building upon a major social movement, underpinned by/navigated via critical methodologies, of your time and place, newly globally aligned with Nhakanomics, Yurugu-nomics, Economics of Love and Communitalism in turn.

Table 3.3.2.3. *Emancipation: Newly Global African Enterprise/Economy Conceptual Critique: Research Academy*

Feminism (South)	Newly Global Feminism promoting personal/social Liberation: *Knowledge Creating Communities: Community Building (S3)* Nhakanomic Emancipation in African South: Kumusha
Critical Theory (East)	Critical Theory as emancipatory Dialectic: *Breakdown Capitalism to evolve Anew: Conscious Evolution (E3)* Yurugu-nomic Emancipation in Africa East: Good Africa Story
Postmodernism (North)	Postmodernism as alternative Discourses: *Post-Industrial Society: Knowledge Creation (N3)* Emancipatory Economics of Love in African North: Sekem
Critical Realism (West)	Critical Realism as stratified Knowledge: *Uncover the generative Forces: Sustainable Development (W3)* Emancipatory Communitalism in West Africa: Pax Herbals

Pride of place here, in "southern" methodological guise, is occupied by *Feminism*, in our case building, "newly globally" in an African context, upon prior *Nature Power*, ecologically, and *Healing Radiance*, culturally and spiritually.

Transformation: Action Research/Socio-Economic Lab/Sustainable Development

Fully transformative Level 4, building on all that has come before, for the first time, by way now of *doing*, ultimately globally-locally, involves *action* research; it serves to finally bring about social *innovation* through a combined process of practical action and theoretical reflection, also involving concrete experience and imaginative insight, indeed Heron's (1997) four modes of knowing, alongside our four worlds and our GENE. More generally, and in communiversity terms, we fully enter *laboratory* realms here, pursuing *sustainable development*, enterprise-wise, alongside *communitalism*

3.3.2.4. *Transformation: Global-Local Enterprise/Economy Action Research/Laboratory*

<u>Participatory</u> <u>Action Research</u> <u>(South)</u>	Communal Problem Solving to promote Self Reliance: *Alleviate communal/environmental Decay; Build Community (S4)* Transformative Nhakanomics in African South: Kumusha
<u>Co-operative</u> <u>Inquiry</u> <u>(East)</u>	Democratising Research and Education *Drawing on Diverse Modes of Knowing: Co-evolution (E4)* Yurugu-nomic Transformation in Africa East: Good Africa Story
<u>Socio-</u> <u>Technical Design</u> <u>(North)</u>	Co-generating democratic Workplaces: *Build Networked Communities: Knowledge Creation (N4)* Transformative Economics of Love in African North: Sekem
<u>Action</u> <u>Research</u> <u>(West)</u>	Continual Cycling between Action and Reflection: *Promote Social Change* (W4) Transformative Communitalism in West Africa: Pax Herbals

At this final point, the individual and the communal, journey and laboratory, need to be mutually aligned to promote social innovation. Overall then, as we can see, as we move through four levels of the research trajectory, from original grounding (method 1) to emergent foundation (methodology 2) onto emancipatory (critique 3) and transformative (action 4), so each world – southern Africa, east Africa, north Africa and west Africa – evolves accordingly, in research, enterprise and economic terms.

We now turn from this analytical structure of Integral Research to its more fully dynamic orientation, as Integral Innovation, ultimately embodied in our four Pan/African paths – southern, eastern, northern and western – micro Community Building to Sustainable Development, macro Nhakanomics towards Communitalism.

3.3.3. Integral *Communitalism*: Towards an Integral Pan-Africanism

Nhakanomics in Southern Africa, Yurugu-nomics in East Africa, Economics of Love in North Africa, Communitalism in West Africa

To provide you with a better sense of how the journey along your paths towards a particular innovation may look and feel, we have translated each fourfold path into a research-and-innovation storyline. Such an outer-directed story, following the transformative trajectory, from research to learning, from organisation to society generally, onto communitalism specifically, is to be read alongside, and in continuous interaction with, the more inner-directed research trajectory. We start with our primary port of call, in the South, and with the *Relational* path, albeit, as we shall see, that each path has a fourfold GENE-tic trajectory, that spans, for example, S (South) 1,2,3 and 4 in turn. Moreover, while the research path is thereby inner-directed, the path of innovation, for us in economic and enterprise guise, is outer directed, and our communiversity lies in between. Finally, there are four such *southern*, *south-eastern*, *south-northern* and *south-western* paths. We codify the inner-directed research paths as (S, E, N, W) in normal capitals and the outer directed innovation path in italics.

Southern African Learning Community: African Research – Inner Relational; African Innovation – Outer Macro Nhakanomic and Micro Community Building

<u>Inwardly Re-Searching via "Southern" Relational Path: Descriptive Method, Phenomenological Methodology, Feminist Critique, PAR: Chapters 4–7: S1–4</u>

Engaging your total self-and-community, as well as your unique gifts and capacities in passionate involvement with a burning issue and collective need, you undertake originally careful, comprehensive *Descriptions* (S1), vivid and accurate renderings of your and others experiences, attributes and needs, rather than conducting measurements. Immersing yourself *Phenomenologically* (S2), in a life world of immediately lived experiences, you concentrate, foundationally, on illuminating the unfolding nature of your "inner self", and that of your society, locating every unique case of your individual, communal and natural history as an episode in a larger societal story.

Aiming, in emancipatory guise, to create social change, through a *Feminist* critique (S3), you see knowledge that leads to such as a means of liberation not domination, of physical and human nature. You also strive thereby to represent diversity. Finally, transformatvely (S4), engaging in Participatory Action Research (PAR) in and through your community, aiming at the exploited, the poor, the oppressed, the marginal, you serve to create awareness of their own resources, mobilizing for self-reliant development, with yourselves as committed participants.

Outwardly Innovating via "Southern" Community Building, Nhakanomics – Integral Kumusha: Integral Case Story 1
Such "southern" *relational* research descriptive method, phenomenological methodology, feminist critique and PAR laden action research, altogether brought to life through *communal learning*, education-wise, is institutionalized via *community building* on a micro scale, and prospectively actualized, altogether on a macro scale, through naturally and communally based *nhakanomics*.

Thereby, and altogether, we outwardly ground *community building* (*S1*), descriptively, in local *Kumusha* (homestead) and *Nhaka* (legacy). The Taranhike's *Integral Kumusha*, as a unique communal phenomenon, or life world, then emerges locally-globally (*S2*) from Buhera in rural Zimbabwe to southern African as a whole, duly connecting nature, culture, technology and enterprise. *Nhakanomics* then becomes the newly global (*S3*) form of emancipatory navigation of a Southern African economic form, also inspired by feminism. Finally, globally-locally, also now informed by PAR, a newly forged *Vakamusha* (*S4*) replaces the western-style business corporation, as an enterprise-in-community.

East African Transformation Journey: African Research – Inner Renewal; African Innovation – Outer Macro Yurugu-nomics and Micro Conscious Evolution

Inwardly Re-Searching via "Eastern" Path of Renewal: Narrative Method, Interpretive Methodology, Critical Theory, CI: Chapters 4, 9–11: E1–4
We now turn from southern to east, Africa, on the inner directed research path of renewal. *Narratively* (E1) we firstly tie together potentials and possibilities of individual, communal, organizational or societal beginnings. Such narrative method is like a plot shaped by many of the larger stories in which it is set, befitting the Good African Coffee Story as it locally-globally unfolds. Secondly, and *Interpretively*, (E2) reconnecting with a historical, cultural and spiritual source, you understand how the world with which you are dealing, like as we shall see Andrew Rugisara's in this case, is constructed, thereby giving relevant others a voice in such.

Thirdly, via *Critical Theory* (E3), your social construction arises out of the everyday problems you faced. Through such you uncover power relations, analysing specifically the suffering of people, thereby explicitly focused on promoting liberation of self and community. Finally, through *Cooperative Inquiry* (E4), you engage in a politically oriented process, doing so in a participative form of inquiry, whereby you are also involved in a four world knowledge-oriented process. While you engage in an alternating current of informative and transformative inquiry, in action-reflection cycles, the validity you seek for your cooperative inquiry is goodness, trustworthiness and authenticity.

Outwardly Innovating via "Eastern" Communitalism: Trans4mation Journey, Conscious Evolution, Yurugu-nomics: Good Africa Story: Integral Case Story 2

The *Good African Coffee Story* is a local narrative (*E1*) in its own right, an unfolding story, a gripping drama, an enterprise plot within a largely economic one, with communal potential in the beginning for a societal East African end. The end is picked up in emergent, local-global guise, in cultural and spiritual terms, by *Conscious Evolution* Marimba Ani's *Yurugu* (*E2*), the "incomplete human" in Dogon and Kiswahili terms, awaiting east African, economic actualisation, via what we have termed *Yurugu-nomics* (*E3*). Thereby de-colonisation makes its economic way through Uganda in East Africa, whereby rural community leads and urban enterprise follows, in newly global guise. As such a marriage between southern community and eastern spirit is fostered through such an evolved *Kiswahili* enterprise (*E4*). We now turn to the path of reason in the African north.

North African Centre for Social Innovation: African Research – Inner Reason; African Innovation – Outer Macro Economics of Love/Micro Knowledge Creation

Inwardly Re-Searching via "Northern" Path of Reason: Theorizing, Critical Rationalism, Postmodernism, Socio-technical Design: Chapters 4, 13–15: N1–4

Via now *grounded theorising* method, to begin with, observations you undertake make sense when organized by some "conception", an organizing idea (N1). You apply hypotheses (theories) to bring some order to data, albeit that in African guise, a trivalent logic for the likes of Nigerian philosopher Chimakonam, as we shall see, replaces "north-western" binary logic, as an African version of *critical rationalism* (N2). Thirdly, and now via *Postmodernist* critique (N3), also resonant with de-coloniality, you pursue multiple discourses, or worldviews, focusing on meanings as multiple and shifting. You construct your own unfolding meaning, using language purposefully as a means of cultural representation, reviewing history as potentially transformative. Finally, by way of rationally based action research, Afrocentric in Asante's African diasporic guise, as we will see, you apply "African soul" (N4) in adopting a problem-solving orientation. Thereby your research is inevitably linked to action and geared towards social betterment. You thus use a co-generative approach to *Socio-Technical Design*, acting as a "friendly outsider".

Outwardly Innovating via "Northern" Economics of Love: Research Academy, Knowledge Creation, Economics of Love: Sekem in Egypt – ICS 3

Sekem in Egypt has built on its own vital force – Sekem meaning "vitality of the sun" – and on indigenous, ancient Egyptian *maat*, that is the local force of balance and harmony (*N1*), thereafter further co-evolved through the Islamic connotation of balance and integration, of, if you like, the three peoples of the book (*N2*). Such a local, Arabic, global Islamic idea assumes emancipatory navigational proportions when, via Rudolf Steiner's anthroposophy, building on prior Egyptian hermetic grounds, is turned into newly global associative economics (*N3*), whereby economics is based on fraternity, politics on equality and culture on liberty. Ultimately, and now assuming fourfold proportions, based on nature, a well as culture, polity and economy, Ibrahim and then Helmy Abouleish, as co-founders of Sekem, have turned to the Economics of Love (*N4*) that binds all these forces together.

West African Laboratory: African Research – Inner Realisation; African Innovation – Outer Macro Communitalism/ Micro Sustainable Development

Navigating Communitalism: Nature Power: Pax Herbals/Nigeria

<u>*Inwardly Re-Searching via "Western" Path of Realization*: Survey Method, Empirical Methodology, Critical Realism, Action Research: Chapters 4, 17–19</u>

Starting out with case study, *survey* if not also *experimental* method (W1), as a researcher, and research institution, you are able to ask good questions, you are a good listener and not trapped by your own ideologies and preconceptions, albeit that in an Afrocentric guise, as such, your African soul force will shine through. You are adaptable so that newly encountered situations can be seen as opportunities, whereby you are also unbiased by preconceived notions, and are responsive to contradictory evidence. Secondly, and methodologically, in the search for *empirically* based truth you seek after the "positive facts", again though seeking out those truths that bear upon the reality of Africa (W2).

Subsequently, by way of "western" research critique, now by way of *critical realism,* you are indeed critical of the status quo, now becoming involved with a stratified or layered, as opposed to merely surface, empirical reality, embodied in what philosopher Roy Bhaskar has termed Met-Reality (W3). You view such a layered perspective on reality as fallible, knowing that there is an interpretive as well as an empirical side to the research critique at hand, critical realism. Finally, by way of now *action research*, you begin transformatively, with appreciative inquiry, especially herein of an Afrocentric worldview (W4) challenging power relations. You diverge and also converge, undertaking social research for social change. As such knowing how is more important than knowing that, and finally action research, for you, incorporates action learning.

<u>*Outwardly Innovating via "Western" Communitalism: Socio-Technical Laboratory, Sustainable Development, Communitalism: Pax Herbals: ICS 4*</u>

In the *West* African case of PaxHerbals as a socio-technical laboratory, one of us (Anselm Adodo) started out by listening to nature *(W1)*, thereby tapping into what he terms *nature power*. Further to such, and from an empirical perspective, his observations and analysis of nature led him to uncover what he termed its *healing radiance (W2)*. Drawing subsequently on the layered character of such meta-reality, Pax Herbals tapped into the *generative mechanisms (W3)* of nature and community to come up with, both clinically and communally, the herbal medicines that became PaxHerbals reason for being. The overall means whereby such nature and community were transformed, through cycles of reflection and of action, in turn, into technology and economy was *communitalism (W4)*, thereby drawing, in soulful Africological guise, on Pax Natura, Pax Spiritus, Pax Scientia and Pax Economica altogether.

3.4. Crisis of Representation: Integral Research/ Innovation in Context

3.4.1. Academic Research and Social Innovation

Now you have a bird's eye view of the four levels, almost as if you had cast your eyes upon all of them, in the course of a picturesque journey. As we have mentioned before the research-and-innovation process is a non-linear one, and you are likely to move back and forth between levels, while cycling and re-cycling across each of the elements within each level, as well as connecting such roots of your research with the underlying soils, the mainstem of your research-and-innovation tree, the branches and ultimate fruits: healing the planet, promoting peaceful co-evolution, building up an open society, and creating economic opportunity.

Moreover, and more specifically in our African context, we are seeking not only to pursue research integrally, drawing on the four corners of the continent, if not also of the worlds at large, but we are also seeking to establish an alternative to "western" capitalism, that is "southern" communitalism, in the process, as well as to the conventional university, our communiversity, in the process. Indeed, and also as such, we are seeking to broaden out so called "African Studies", from its conventional base in the humanities, and to a lesser extent in anthropology, sociology and political science, to incorporate economics and management in such African guise. We now want, by way of conclusion to this chapter, to locate our integral approach to research and innovation in the larger research landscape.

3.4.2. Four Research Moments

Norman Denzin and Yvonne Lincoln (1994, 2003), based respectively at the Universities of Illinois and Texas in the United States, are probably the pre-eminent authorities on "qualitative research" in the world. For them there have been, historically speaking, seven critical moments in the recent development of such. However, the last three of these moments appear so recent, and thereby tenuous, that they hardly seem worth taking seriously. It is the first four such moments, which are critical for our purposes:

(1) *Positivist-quantitative Paradigm:* The traditional quantitative period is associated with the foundational "positivist" paradigm, which still exercises a strong empirical influence to this day, and in which basic research methods, quantitative and qualitative, still predominate.

(2) *Modernist quantitative-qualitative Era:* The modernist quantitative-qualitative conventional era comes second: the quantitative "positivist" orientation is now split between the former empirical and the latter rational approach, the one being inductive and the other deductive; at the same time the newly "interpretivist" approach becomes clearly distinguishable in its own right. It is at this point that Husserl heralds the phenomenological "Crisis in European Sciences", and joins hands with the prior hermeneutic influence to make their qualitative stand on research methodology.

(3) *Interpretative qualitative Perspectives:* In the "blurred genres" contemporary era (our level 3), new, interpretative and qualitative perspectives are vigorously taken up. Such includes, for Denzin and Lincoln, not only hermeneutics and phenomenology, but also structuralism, semiotics, cultural studies, and for us feminism, critical theory, postmodernism (discursive) and critical realism (stratified), as duly reformative.

(4) *Crisis of Representation:* In the fourth era, the so-called *crisis of representation* emerges. It becomes apparent that only a very small part of the world, geographically and philosophically, is represented in the overall methodological story. For us this is of critical import, not so much regarding research in and of itself, whereby there are few African variations on a predominantly Euro-American, but in dealing with research-and-innovation.
Thereby, drawing on our Pan-African examples of "communitalism", in its different worldly guises, Nhakanomics, Yurugu-nomics, the Economics of Love and generic Communitalism, we are able to overcome the "crisis of representation", with a view to social innovation, as such, which extends beyond academe, into communiversity, enterprise and economy at large. As such, in the social sciences which is our port of call, we overcome the divide between research (science) and innovation (technology) while also drawing, at least to some degree, on impulses from "south" and "north", "east" and "west".

Transcending this crisis of representation, our Integral Research and Innovation evolves a co-creative approach that is ultimately transformative, thereby resolving the crisis through its cultural spread. We are now ready to conclude this chapter.

3.4.3. Which Path Is for You?

In contrast to the traditional research approach, our integral one, on the one, inner directed, research side, requires you to take account of the full range of methods and methodologies, critiques and actions, to some degree or another, though you will inevitably specialize, possibly with an African pre-emphasis on the "southern" relational path. On the other, outer directed, innovation side, you need to focus on a relevant, prospectively African form of economy and enterprise. Both inner and outer directed rhythms or trajectories, then, follow our GENE-tic course, in both local African and global – worldly/wise – terms.

The choice for a particular research path is made based on the individual and societal background and context of the researcher, and the research academy. It is important that the research path is authentic to yourself and your cultural context. Moreover, and specifically in the African context in which our overall orientation is set, our focus on the *relational*, if not also *renewal*, takes pride of place over, but does not exclude, the paths of reason and realisation.

Each path ultimately reaches into the fourth action centred or transformative level, and the strong co-creative nature and scope of it (just listen to the rhythm of terms like e.g. participatory action research and cooperative inquiry) enables each of you who decided for one of the paths to ultimately encompass its full trajectory, analytically and transformatively. Furthermore, and of critical importance, your individual research needs to be located in an overall communiversity context, communally, transformationally, academically and laboratory-wise. For whereas in. the natural sciences there is a well work tradition of collective research, and thereby technological innovation, in the social sciences, research is conventionally individualised, for us to tragically limiting effect, especially given the nature and scope of the issues faced, socially and economically, in the world today.

Integral Research and Innovation in Africa
The Inner and Outer Directed Journey

Level 4	Action Research	&	Transformation for Innovation
Level 3	Research Critique	&	Emancipation for Innovation
Level 2	Research Methodology	&	Innovation Foundation
Level 1	Research Method	&	Origination of Innovation
	Analytical Research Trajectory	&	*Transformative Innovation Trajectory*

In the next chapter we enter the first prospectively integral level of research method (analytical) and innovation (transformative). "Method" – the first level – will tell you more about yourself then you had thought before – and indeed, the entire integral process introduced in this book is ultimately a journey to progressively heightened energy and consciousness – and far more exciting then the traditional "dry and boring reputation" of research in the social sciences has ever promised.

3.5. References

Adodo A (2017) *Integral Community Enterprise in Africa: Communitalism as an Alternative to Capitalism* Abingdon. Routledge

Denzin Y and **Lincoln** Y (eds) (1994) *Handbook of Qualitative Research.* London. Sage

Denzin Y and **Lincoln** Y (eds) (2003) *Landscape of Qualitative Research.* 2nd Edition. London. Sage

Heron J (1997) *Cooperative Inquiry.* London. Sage

Lessem R and **Schieffer** A (2009) *Transformation Management: Toward the Integral Enterprise.* Abingdon. Routledge

Lessem R and **Schieffer** A (2010) *Integral Economics: Releasing the Economic Genius of your Society.* Abingdon. Routledge

Mandela N (1994) *The Long Walk to Freedom.* New York. Abacus

Chapter 4 Originating Integral Research in African South. Feel Local, Intuit Local-Global, Think Newly Global, Act Global-Local

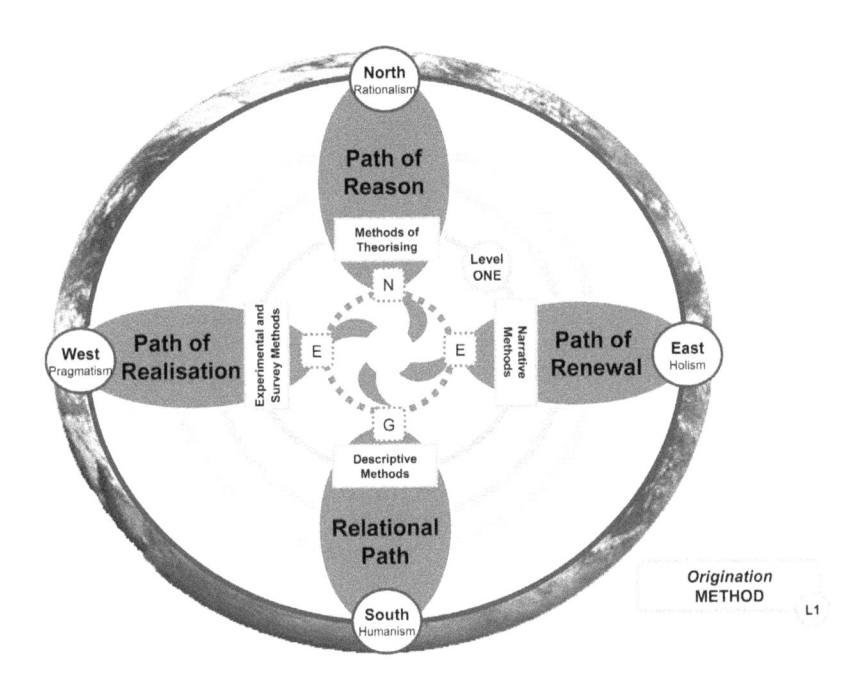

Figure 4.1: *Overview Chapter 4 – Method*

The dot in the middle of the ellipse is the person with the fertilized egg, the oak tree within the acorn, the universe within a dimensionless point, the potential prior to its manifestation. The ellipse then symbolizes the feminine aspect, the matrix of creation. In the last stage of creation, the lines of motion added the arms of the cross symbolize the movement of life from birth to death to rebirth, and the movement of human consciousness. Now the stationary cross has been transformed into a dynamic one.

Clyde Ford (2000)   *The Hero with an African Face:*

The Mythic Wisdom of Traditional Africa.

Summary: Originating Integral Research and Innovation

- ***Originating** Integral **Research and Innovation**:* We start with integral method (analytical research) and origination (transformative innovation). We introduce, as such, the research methods, grounding, processually, our integral research academy, and means of originating innovation, for both learning community and socioeconomic laboratory, with the transformation journey in between. We illustrate why "method matters", alongside origination, in grounding for a successful research-and-innovation.

- *Integral **Human Modes**:* Overall human integrity is comprised of four modes: *being, becoming, knowing, doing*. Directly linked to them are four integral methods, that constitute the source of origination for our four paths: descriptive methods (relational) and human *being* for the southern path; narrative methods (renewal) and *becoming* for the eastern path; methods of theorising (reason) and *knowing* for the northern; and experimental (realisation) and survey methods – *doing* – for the western path.

- **Being:** *Descriptive*: Context: "Southern" description requires you to engage with yourself and another *being* similar to the way in which an artist, or an empathetic counsellor might do. Being "scientific" in that descriptive sense involves opening yourself up to a world, without pride or prejudice, premise or preconception, being in touch with its natural and communal origins. This we regard of especially importance in the African "south", illustrated by our *Integral Kumusha* in Zimbabwe, indeed the communiversity realm of our learning community, all too often by-passed by conventionally "north-western" approaches to research and technological innovation. Being African, finally for us, is centred in such *African healing wisdom.*

- **Becoming:** *Narrative*: Process: Whereas description is overwhelmingly concerned with locational space and place, in "eastern" narrative methods you are more concerned with historical time, that is with *becoming,* and with "consciousness raising". Here you become a "Narrator" of the "stories we are", drawing upon the specific technique of "storytelling". In originating renewal you become familiar, actually and prospectively, with connecting past, present and future, entering our transformation journey, as illustrated by the *Good African Coffee Story* in East Africa, altogether embodied on our approach to societal re-GENE-ration.

- **Knowing:** *Grounded Theory* – Substance: From narrative methods we enter the mode of *knowing*. This – in research terms – is the world of theory building. Here we draw on Glazer, Strauss and Corbin's grounded theory, whereby theory is generated inductively from data. In originating the path of reason, moreover, you establish, conceptually and abstractly, hypotheses as to the causes of the particular issues or events in which you are working, the realm of our research academy, as illustrated by the case of Sekem's *Economics of Love* in Egypt in North Africa, as a variation on our Communitalist (as opposed to Capitalist and Socialist) theme.

- **Doing:** *Case Study* – Form: We finally introduce the fourth and by far the most prolific of the research building blocks, that is case study and survey methods and experimentation, the realm of our commiversity laboratory. Your ability to ask relevant questions, to be an impartial observer, and to adapt to circumstances, all applies here. Moreover, and in terms of origination, your ability to practically design and conduct relevant experiments, is all important, thereby serving to close the "method cycle" of describing, narrating, theorising, and ultimately experimenting, *doing*, as finally illustrated by Paxherbals in Nigeria in West Africa as a Socio-Technical Laboratory, set in the overall context of our Communiversity.

- Altogether, integrally, we initiate the grounding and origination of our inner directed research method (S1, E1, N1, W1) for all four African worlds, and the corresponding outer directed, *origination* of *innovation (S1, E1, N1, W1)*, which will be followed by methodology/*emergence*, critique/*emancipation* and ultimately action research/*transformation* applied to each of our four African worlds.

4.1. Introduction: Origins of Your Research-and-Innovation

4.1.1. Method: The Building Blocks of Research Matter

Process, Substance, Form and Context

Having introduced (Chapters 1–3) the *process* of integral research and innovation as a whole, set alongside the *substance* of communitalism and the *form* of the communiversity, altogether centred in the healing wisdom of Africa, as *context*, we turn specifically to the origination (grounding) of integral research and innovation. Thereafter, by way of emergent foundation, emancipatory navigation and transformative effect, we shall revisit each of the four paths of research and innovation in turn. Why then do we recast research method as a source of origination, with a view to innovation, as opposed to a technique for data processing, as it is more conventionally conceived? Let us take you almost two decades back to make the case.

Seeing the Southern Light Covered Over by the Western Dark

In the autumn of 2005, perhaps anticipating where we are now in relation to Africa and its diaspora, almost two decades later, we established our transformation programme on the African continent, in conjunction with CIDA (Community and Individual Development Association), South Africa's newest and seemingly most innovative university. Several of the participants from CIDA on our masters programme were tutors at the university, many of them recent graduates. What astounded us was that in their "research proposal" for their first transformation project on our part-time masters, every student followed the same basic "western" approach to research method, as a crudely conceived, or indeed copied, "technique" for data collection, questionnaires, and the like, each of which pointed towards specific kinds of empirical data. After that awful experience one of us (Ronnie Lessem) began to see the light.

First, the very fact that these otherwise highly creative students who were doing amazing things in their local communities, some even as potential social innovators, indeed promoting learning communities through their so called "extranet" activities, started with such an arid approach to individual research, to which they were obviously paying mere lip service, meant that we had to try all the more to help them evolve their own approach by building on their home African "southern" grounds.

Origination Lay Not in the Erudite Methodologies But Formative Methods

It then dawned upon us, that, potentially if not actually, *such individual research origination lay not in the erudite methodologies, but in the formative research method.* However, such methods would need to be newly connected with the grounds of especially their African individual and communal being, prior to their becoming, knowing and doing, if they were to assume such an originating purpose. Indeed CIDA – Community and Individual Development Association – must have been called such. CIDA that is, for a reason.

Focused on "Western" Doing, to the Exclusion of Their "Southern" Selves

The trouble was, that the students focused on using exclusively survey (and partly experimental) methods, while totally ignoring descriptive, narrative and theorising approaches. Further, they were totally oblivious, in this research context, to the grounds of their own "southern" (relational) being. In other words, they were all *focused on "western" doing, largely to the exclusion of "northern" knowing, "eastern" becoming as well as, most especially, to their "southern" selves.* In that respect they were out of touch with their local grounds, or origins. Their very *being* was out of touch with the very soil in which they intended to plant their social innovation tree.

4.1.2. Method: Activating the Vital Force of the GENE

In terms of our GENE (see previous chapter), our South African students were aiming to be effective, while lacking appropriate individual and communal grounding, emergence and, to a large extent, navigation. Indeed there was no explicit approach to communal learning, nor any purpose built research academy, and concept of African economics and enterprise to support their "southern" African cause. This way, the "southern" GENE-ius of these would-be-social-innovators was circumvented by a "western" by-pass. First, for us then, the grounds for social innovation – if not a fully fledged communiversity to go with it – needed to be prepared, and that's where our recast method (our level 1), as origination, comes in play.

Research method, and the origination of innovation, as we are going to show, does not only provide the analytic grounding of each of the four research-to-innovation paths, it also plays an initially transformative role, when recast in – herein in the African "south" especially – experiential (descriptive) terms, if not also in terms of imaginative (narrative), conceptual (theorising) and practical (experimental) learning.

4.1.3. Analytical Method and Transformative Origination

Start Your Research by Connecting with Your Individual/Societal Creative Source

As an integral researcher, in our explicitly contextualised guise, *you start your research by connecting with the creative source of your self and community*, organization and society. Here, as close as possible to yourself (to home), you find the original seed (or the origin) for, ideally in a "southern" context, your communal research and learning. You review, most especially descriptively, if not also narratively, theoretically, or indeed case study wise, your own personal and collective centre, before entering a particular research path that is altogether authentic for you, your community, your institution and your society. For one of us, Anselm Adodo (2012), in his book on *Nature Power*, evidently centred in the healing wisdom of Africa:

> In 1997, I started a small herbal garden. From the herbs that grew in the garden, I prepared some herbal mixtures for malaria, coughs and other common ailments. My office was a bamboo tent. Six months later, I was able to construct a 3-room wooden shaft with a loan of $200. A young man from the village, John Okoh, came to join me. The herbal remedies we prepared were based on local medical knowledge. The villagers who took the cough syrups and malaria medicine came back with very

positive results. Before long, the news had spread round the village, which comprises Christians, Muslims and traditional religion practitioners in a balanced proportion. The 3-room clinic was called PAX herbal centre.

Transformation Starts with Origination Grounded Through Research Method

Alternately, as a transformative practitioner, ultimately seeking to promote, with others, a social innovation, you build communally on experiential, culturally and spiritually on imaginative, scientifically on conceptual or politically/economically on practical learning grounds, in order to ultimately transform the herein African world around you, in south or east, north or west, Africa. While you will need to build a foundation, and to foster emancipation, before ultimately *bringing about transformation, it all starts with origination, grounded through research method.*

That is why we call the first level of integral research and innovation "origination" closely aligned with method. It is through method – describing or narrating, theorising or surveying – that you experience, most directly, which path is most authentic to you, your nature and culture, your communal being.

Origination Is Then Linked to the Soil and the Origins of a Person/Culture/Society

Origination, for us then, so different from conventionally arid "survey methods", is then linked to soil and the origins of a person/culture/society, embodied in your nature, art, religion, music, dance. Origination (as level 1) however not only alludes to the starting point of the social innovation journey, and thereby also to communal learning; the success of such a journey is also dependent on your capacity to connect with and activate the origins and originality of your particular individual and social as well as cultural context. Where then do we go from here, method/origination wise?

4.1.4. Integral Method, Origination and Culture

Description to Experimentation

Overall then, we would argue that:

- a southern circular mode would be best embodied in rich *description*
- an eastern spiralling mode would be best represented by unfolding *narrative*
- a northern linear mode would be best embodied in intricate *theorizing*
- a western point mode would be best represented in survey and *experimentation.*

Another strong reason, why we place research method at the beginning of the research to innovation journey, in the same way as we position communal learning at the base of our communiversity, and community building at the base of

Introduction: Origins of Your Research-and-Innovation   107

communitalism, is that this basic level allows you to get in initial touch with self- and-society more concretely than the immersion in philosophically based research methodology could ever do.

Being, Becoming, Knowing and Doing

Indeed, each passionate quest or re-search, for us, must be intimately connected with your personal as well as your societal, life story, and that of your immediate community, within your immediate learning community or without, and the mode of being or becoming, knowing or doing, which comes most naturally to you. In the same way, moreover, and transformatively speaking, it is critical to be in touch with, to feel, the local origins of your self, your community, your organisation or society. Moreover, such brings us back (see Figure 4.2. below) to the basic modes of being (descriptive), becoming (narrative), knowing (theorising) and doing (experimenting).

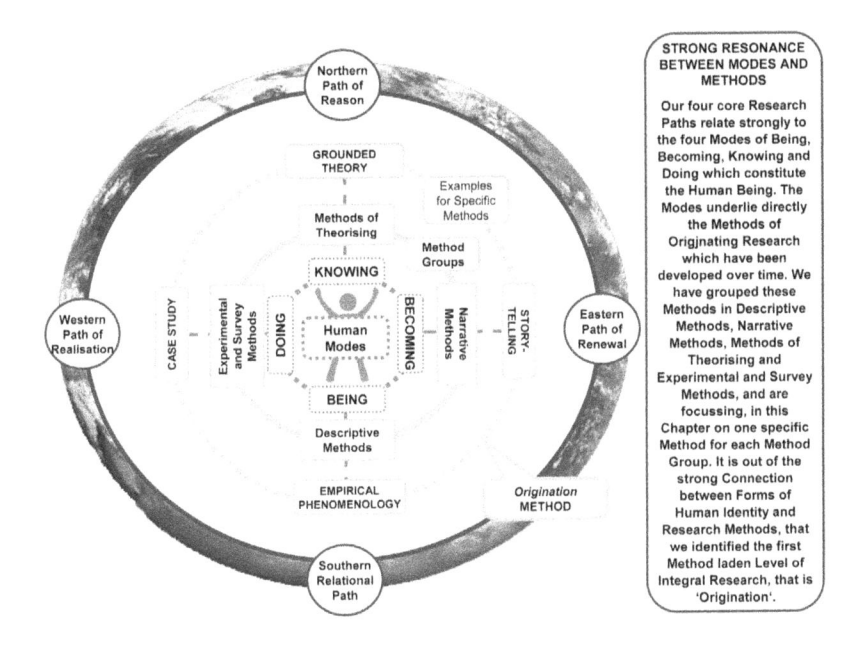

STRONG RESONANCE BETWEEN MODES AND METHODS

Our four core Research Paths relate strongly to the four Modes of Being, Becoming, Knowing and Doing which constitute the Human Being. The Modes underlie directly the Methods of Originating Research which have been developed over time. We have grouped these Methods in Descriptive Methods, Narrative Methods, Methods of Theorising and Experimental and Survey Methods, and are focussing, in this Chapter on one specific Method for each Method Group. It is out of the strong Connection between Forms of Human Identity and Research Methods, that we identified the first Method laden Level of Integral Research, that is 'Origination'.

Figure 4.2: *Human and Research Foundations – Following the same Rhythm*

4.1.5. Integral Method and Human Integrity

We realized then that, back to the CIDA story and onto our experiences in Africa, MENA, Asia, Europe and America, whether we were dealing with undergraduates or management practitioners, masters or doctoral students, researchers or consultants, we had to start with their all round human integrity. The equivalent to what we term a "western" (predominantly American) "survey" or "experimental" method, which our students at CIDA had reacted to mechanically, is "southern" *descriptive* method, more literary or visual art than scientific or technical as such. The overall relational path (see previous chapter), then, of which description-origination is the grounding, emerges out of the humanistic, if not also more-than-human naturalistic, mode of *being*. Ironically, our African students were psychologically much closer to such a descriptive life world, naturally and communally, and yet academically, in their conventional university setting, notwithstanding CIDA, disconnected from such.

We now delve into each method analytically, and means of origination transformatively in turn, starting with the underlying human, and more-then-human mode, of being and becoming, knowing and doing, before focusing, integrally, on analytical method and transformative origins.

4.2. Being: Originating Relationally via Descriptive Method: Kumusha Community-and-Enterprise in Southern Africa

4.2.1. Southern African Descriptive Orientation: The Learning Community

We turn then to each of the four methods underlying origination in turn, as well as to the orientation to learning in each instance, followed by a relevant exerpt from each southern and eastern, northern and western African illustrative case. Starting out with such a "southern" mode of *being*, we find that identity, to begin with, is originally rooted in the "life world" of or indeed circle or "life cycle" of local people, as much for the Bedouin or the Bantu as for the Belgians or the Burmese.

Within such close-knit community, it is love and engagement, with the fellow human, and more-than-human (plant and animal nature), that counts most. Such an indigenous world is lodged in nature, in community, and all too often in religion (from "re-ligere" meaning linking back). We refer to this circle of origination as "southern", because of the profound sense of identity of such communal people, though it is to be found all over the world, because of its deep roots in mankind's place of origin, where nature and religion continue to exercise a major influence.

> **The Spell of the Sensuous – David Abram (1997)**
>
> **Example of More-than-Human Being**
>
> *The living world – this ambiguous realm that we experience in anger and joy, in grief and in love – is both the soil in which all our sciences are rooted and the rich humus into which their results ultimately return, whether as nutrients or poisons. In contrast to the apparently unlimited, global character of the technologically mediated world, the sensuous world – the world of our direct, unmediated interactions – is always local. The sensuous world is the particular ground on which we walk, the air we breathe. Human persons, too, are shaped by the places they inhabit, both individually and collectively.*

Therein lie the very grounds of our being. This is the home or "oikos" of our vital, individual, organizational and societal existence. In terms of Integral Research method and origination, this is an intimately descriptive arena. We turn from such being to experiential learning.

4.2.2. Experiential Learning: Relational Origination and Contextualisation

Experiential learning, then, as notably identified by American educational and organisational psychologist David Kolb (1983), underlies our relational origination, and contextualisation, building thereby on concrete experience.

Individual people and whole societies, learn and develop more effectively when they are enjoying themselves and what they are doing; when they are satisfying some felt need or interest, and are emotionally involved in what has personal and societal relevance to them; when they feel good about the whole idea of learning and development as well as the exercise of their learning competence; when they feel confident, secure and in a low threat, co-operative, non-competitive position. We now turn from learning to descriptive method of origination, and from such a research method (and orientation to learning and knowledge creation) to the descriptive technique: empirical phenomenology. We now turn from origination, the grounds for transformation, underlying social innovation, to description, as method and building block for the analytically based, relational path to research.

4.2.3. Rich Description: Empirical Phenomenology as Relational Method

The specific analytical method that has been developed, for rich description, is termed *"empirical phenomenology"*, by American phenomenologist Clark Moutsakas (1994): to *produce an exhaustive description of the phenomena of everyday experience*. Such description, along the relational research path, underlies a phenomenological methodology, as we shall see, a feminist critique, and ultimately participatory action research, as well as the "southern" orientation to community building (micro) and communitalism (macro).

The challenge you face in preparing to *ground* such descriptive origination, is to focus on an issue *that has both social meaning and personal significance. The desire for origination grows out of an intense interest in a particular area.* But what exactly means "immersion" for you as an Integral Researcher and innovator (see Table below)

Table 4.2.3. *Descriptive Methods and Origination*

Towards an Original Description through Empirical Phenomenology

- You seek to reveal fully the Essences and Origins of communal Experience.
- Engage your total Self as Participant, in a State of Passionate Involvement.
- You do not seek to predict or to determine causal Relationships.
- You rather illuminate them through careful, comprehensive Descriptions, vivid and accurate Renderings of Experience, rather than Measurements or Ratings.

4.2.4. Descriptive Research Method and Social Innovation: Integral Kumusha

We now conclude our humanistic orientation to this originative and integral, descriptive method, as the source of origin of the "southern" African relational path, and to the process for evoking it through empirical phenomenology, as altogether illustrated by Daud Shumba and Christina Taranikhe's (Lessem et al 2019) *Integral Kumusha*. If you choose to engage fully in the southern relational path, individually or collectively, a deep understanding of phenomenology would be the next foundational step, involving immersion in a particular "life world". For them (see also Table 4.2.4. below):

> The Integral Kumusha builds upon a natural-cultural African homestead (musha), adding technology and enterprise thereby leading to a unique natural-cultural-technological-economic entity which is an alternative to the western corporate – technologically and economically based – firm, bereft of nature and culture. This newly integral business approach is unique in that it focuses on the availability of water (natural) supplied by boreholes and solar energy (natural) throughout the whole year for domestic use and also for farming using the drip irrigation system (technological). As such, economic activities such as horticulture, general farming, poultry and growing of fruit trees such as mangoes, citrus, etc take place grounded in nature within the Buhera community-and-culture.
>
> From these activities, the entity produces vegetables, fruits, chicken, eggs which it sells to the community and beyond. The Integral Kumusha has led to the emergence of

a new business which I have termed, in my own specific case, Vakamusha (grounded in naturally based Vaka Concrete) which serves to ground nature and community in technology and enterprise. This has allowed a new form of business which embraces nature and culture of the rural people.

Table 4.2.4. *"Southern" African Relational Path of Social Research to Innovation: Descriptive to Participatory;* Kumusha to Vakamusha

Southern Grounding Method and *Origination*	Southern Emergence Methodology and *Foundation*	Southern Navigation Critique and *Emancipation*	Southern Effect Action and *Transformation*
Descriptive Methods (S1)	Phenomenological Methodology (S2)	Feminist Critique (S3)	Participatory Action Research (S4)
Kumusha (S1)	*Integral Kumusha (S2)*	*Nhaka-Nomics (S3)*	*Vaka-Musha (S4)*

The symbolic lettering as above, and in all the tables that follow distinguish integral research from contextualised *innovation*, each in GENE-tic stages 1-4/ *1-4*. We now turn from being to becoming, from descriptive to narrative method.

4.3. Becoming: Origins of Renewal in Narrative: The Good African Coffee Story in East Africa

4.3.1. East African Narrative Orientation: The Transformation Journey

We now turn from being to becoming, and the unfolding of meaning, or consciousness, in our individual and communal lives, in a particular cultural and societal – most especially now *East* African – context. As such we turn to narrative method, analytically, and to originating the path of renewal, transformatively, thereby, and altogether, actualising "the stories we are". The most immediate application of such "stories we are", in now *East* Africa, in Uganda, as we more fully shall see (Chapter 12), is to Andrew Rugisara's (2014) *Good Africa Coffee Story.*

Such narrative method then serves to ground renewal, which subsequently emerges interpretively, is navigated via critical theory, and cooperative inquiry leads to finally transformative effect, thereby also constituting the "eastern" edge of generic communitalism, that is conscious evolution enterprise-wise and Yurugu-nomics East African economy wise, invariably centred in Africa's healing wisdom. We now engage your imagination, necessary for an unfolding narrative.

4.3.2. Engage Your Imagination

Underlying such narrative method, from a transformative perspective, and as also revealed by renowned English research philosopher John Heron (Yunus 2003), further to the experiential in his four modes of knowing, imagination, is a pre-conceptual form of learning orientation that is prior to explicit verbal and intellectual understanding. It is often represented in visual and colourful forms, as indeed we saw in Chapter 2, that relate to the meaning of the images portrayed, as well as rich and textured, metaphorically laden narrative. It can also be shown in mobile and dramatic form.

Such narrative, moreover, can be dynamically elaborated through the imaginative use of metaphor and analogy. Where possible and relevant, the visual and metaphorical representation tells a story, also giving a coherent, global overview of the subject matter, so that the basic "patterning" (Heron 1994) of its central concepts and principles stand out. For us, the best guide to such is William Randall, a Canadian Professor of English Literature, who has developed a particular method of uncovering *The Stories we Are*, in his essay on self-creation. Through his work we now turn from imaginative origination, generally, on the path of renewal, with a view to social innovation, to narrative method, specifically, and analytically, as part and parcel of integral research.

4.3.3. Narrative Method

The Stories We Are: Reality Itself Is Inherently Storied

For Canadian Professor of English literature, and developmental psychologist, William Randall (Lent 1997), the object of narrative method is not to survey (through pre-structured interviews or formalised questionnaires) or experiment, to hypothesize or to theorise. Rather, the aim is to uncover "the stories we are", individually, as well as, for us, organizationally and societally.

The *Stories We Are* imply, moreover, that your personal, institutional and societal stories are incomplete: that your individual and collective lives are still unfolding, mysteries yet unresolved, open books for whose endings you can but wait and see. This implies that each one of you, personally and collectively, is legendary. This could involve, for example in South Africa altogether societally, as well as the unfolding narrative of an individual researcher, that of the South African Truth and Reconciliation Commission (TRC) or of the country altogether. Such *reality itself – at least human reality – is inherently storied, that all events constitute one grand, unfolding story.* This is the story between the world and its Creator, understood as a "cosmic artist". Each event in your individual and institutional lives is therefore emergent and novel, charged actually or potentially with significance.

You Co-Author Your Story in Partnership with Some Authoritative Agent

Your author-ity, with respect to your unfolding story, lies somewhere in between you and it. *You co-author your story in partnership with some authoritative agent, whether nature, society, fate, God, ultimate reality, or whatever your philosophical propensities lead you to call it.* You are in a position to reconstruct – not so much the events or idea within your research and development story – but the plots whereby you make them into your own. A new plot means a new story, and a new story leads to a new construction.

Thus, over the course of originating your path of renewal you critique the old plots by which your story has previously been lived and told, and experiment with new ones, and you thereby assume authority over your work and your life, together with a cast of co-creators. Naturally people and communities vary in that respect. *Some are passive in the matter of self-creation; others active.* Some are less inclined to compose their own life-plot than to adopt one of the packaged ones proffered them by their family or clan, profession or culture, religion or cult, industry or society. Others reject such patterns passionately, preferring to do it their way, in stages.

In summary then, and in narrative terms:

Table 4.3.3. *Narrative Method Towards an Original Narrative Through The Stories We Are*

- Your *individual and communal* Stories are still *unfolding*.
- The narrative Mode leads to gripping Drama and to *creative Origination*.
- You are tieing together *Potentials and Possibilities* of your respective Beginnings.
- A Plot *shaped by* many of the *larger Stories* in which it is set.

4.3.4. Narrative Research Method and Social Innovation: Good African Story

We now conclude narrative method, research-wise, and the process of origination, applied to self, organisational or societal renewal, innovation wise. Typical for the path of renewal, overall then, is a thorough understanding of the "stories we are", and the capacity to engage in an ongoing dialogical process of revealing or "unfolding" meaning. Such, altogether communiversity wise, if not also communitalism wise, in this case her related to Yurugu-nomics, and *The Good African Coffee Story*, is critical underpinning for an individual or a collective transformation journey. Hence, our symbol for the path of renewal is the Spiral. A continuous (spiralling) process, on the path of renewal, will lead you, on the one hand, analytically as a thought leader, from narrative method to hermeneutics, critical theory and ultimately cooperative inquiry.

Table 4.3.4. *East African Social Research and Innovation: Path of Renewal Narrative to Cooperative: Good African Coffee Story to Kiswahili Enterprise*

Eastern Grounding Method and Origination	Eastern Emergent Methodology & Foundation	Eastern Navigational Critique and Emancipation	Eastern Effective Action and Transformation
Narrative Methods (E1)	Hermeneutics/ Interpretive (E2)	Critical Theory (E3)	Co-operative Inquiry (E4)
The Good African Coffee Story (E1)	Yurugu (E2)	Yurugu-nomics (E3)	Kiswahili Enterprise (E4)

In proceeding from research to innovation then, Andrew Rugisara's (2014), in his *Good African Coffee Story* narrates the following:

> Kabale is a hilly, border town, with a scenic and rugged terrain and home to the Bagika people. The cool evenings and meandering hills have led it to being nicknamed the Switzerland of Uganda and it is the place to which Rugisara traces his own roots. On 29 July his Good Coffee Brand opened their first field office in Kasese town and appointed their first community liaison officer with the responsibility for organising the farmers into producer organisations. By the end of the year he had made several trips to Kasese to assess their field efforts in the round and essentially to encourage their farmers, get feedback, and energise the team. They began to organise the farmers into groups, by reaching out to the communities directly and inviting them to attend meetings which they held at local trading centres in each sub-county.
>
> Eventually Good Coffee identified some community leaders before whom they presented their model, established a dialogue and line of communication, and then appealed to them to promote the model in the community. At the same time I shared his frustration at Africans being seen as nothing more than beggars, as incapable, poor and helpless. Such a view could be changed, but it would require them to produce quality coffees consistently. And this was why farmer training was critical. With their help, he told them, he was determined to make a change. The project would only work if they did it together.

We now turn from originating being and becoming to that of knowing, that is to the pursuit of truth (originating the path of reason), before we finally come to doing, originating the path of realisation.

4.4. Knowing: Originating Reason/Grounded Theory Method: Sekem and the Economics of Love in North Africa

4.4.1. Orientation to Grounded Theory Underlying the Research Academy

The purposeful navigation that we seek to ultimately establish, in pursuit of the truth then, represents the knowing consolidation of the prior process of becoming, building in turn on prior being. As such, transformatively, the fully-fledged new concept, is established out of the prior descriptive and narrative. The first step to be taken, as such, by way of now so called "grounded theory", as we shall see, noting that theory is thereby grounded, is to codify knowledge, thereby establishing such a northern version of an original storyline.

In the Sekem case what will follow as such a "fourfold" integral enterprise constituted of its nature, culture, polity and economy, its grounded theory will culminate in its so called "economy of love", following form its prior "being" (Sekem meaning "vitality of the sun"), and becoming, thereby restoring the desert earth. Sekem moreover, has established alongside a University for Sustainable Development, albeit that such a university falls outside of our communiversity arena.

We now turn from such to specifically conceptual learning, as a source of knowing origination, along the path of reason, with a view to social innovation in North Africa. Thereafter, we shall focus on the specific research technique "grounded theory".

4.4.2. Engage in Conceptual Learning

In knowledge creating, transformative terms, for the renowned Japanese organisational sociologists, and authors of *The Knowledge Creating Company*, Nonaka and Takeuchi (2008), we now approach the realm of knowledge combination, or of explicit knowledge. Therein for them lies the process of theorising underlying knowing. In other words, this is the conceptual realm of *statements, made in words or numbers, theories or mental models, which yield the explicit intellectual, conceptual content of the material to be learnt.*

Hitherto this has been regarded as the central and only medium of learning if not also research, and the policy base for development. In our integral scheme of things it is only one of four building blocks, to research and innovation, and tends to become alienated and desiccated if made the sole medium. In fact for Afro-French Benin based philosopher, Paulin Hountondji (2002), reflecting on the significance of theory building (see also Chapter 10):

> A standard feature of economic activity in colonial territories was the practical absence of industry. An equally standard feature of scientific activity was a howling absence of theoretical work. Just as there were no colonial factories, there were no

colonial laboratories or think tanks. Now generally speaking advances in all branches of knowledge, whether they belong to the natural sciences, the social sciences or the humanities, necessarily begin in laboratories, broadly defined as venues for the systematic processing of intellectual and scientific knowledge. In fact, the two forms of extraction – material and intellectual – are not discrete realities but two sides of the same coin .. accumulation on a grand scale.

We now turn, more particularly, from transformative learning, knowledge creation and social innovation, to analytically based research, along the path of reason.

4.4.3. Grounded Theory

Grounded Theory as the Origination of the Path of Reason

We finally, and analytically by way of method based (analytical) origination (transformative) on the path of reason, turn to grounded theory, as perhaps the best-known approach to systematically developing theory, from the bottom up as it were. Its American founders, Glazer and Strauss (Glaser 2000), were both social scientists, the one (Glazer) a social psychologist and statistician, and the other (Strauss) a social anthropologist and sociologist. *Grounded theory is a comparative method*, as is our own Four World approach. For the constant comparison of many groups draws attention to their many similarities and differences. Considering such leads to the generation of abstract categories and their properties, like our paths of reason or renewal, which, since they emerge from the data, will be an important part of an explanatory theory.

Lower level categories emerge rather quickly during the early phases of data collection. Higher level, overriding and integrating conceptualisations – and the properties that elaborate them – tend to come later during coding and analysis. A theory then, for them as for us, should never just be put together, abstracted from the underlying grounds, nor should a formal theory be applied unless we are sure it will fit the data, and the context. The possible use of a formal model of integration can be determined only after a substantive model has sufficiently emerged. The truly emergent integrating framework, which encompasses the fullest possible diversity of categories and properties, becomes an open-ended scheme. In working towards such it is critical that collection, coding and analysis of data are done together.

Strauss and Corbin (1997) then turn in great detail to what they term "coding". The particular focus of grounded theory, and its real strength (albeit that such *coding* imposes enormous demands on you as a researcher) is such "coding procedures". There are *three types of coding procedures: open, axial and selective*. Coding represents the operations by which data are broken down, conceptualised, and put back together in new ways, whereby theories are built from data, the very process that Hountondji (see above) has lamented as seldom taking place in Africa.

Open Coding: Establishing Categories

Open coding firstly pertains to the naming and categorising of phenomena. During open coding the data are broken down into discrete parts, closely examined, compared for similarities and dissimilarities. Through this process your own assumptions about phenomena are questioned or explored, leading to new discoveries. In our own case, for example, early in our qualitative research, we established the codes "southern" and "northern", "eastern" and "western", to describe different societal orientations.

Table 4.4.3.1. *Open Coding: Establishing Categories and Subcategories*

- *Break Data into Parts*, compare for Similarities/Dissimilarities, give each a Name.
- *Concepts are then identified* and developed as Properties and Dimensions.
- Two analytical Procedures prevail: *Making Comparisons and asking Questions.*

Axial Coding: Identify Sub-Categories and Underlying Conditions

We now turn from such open coding to so-called "axial" coding. Open coding allows you to identify overall categories, their properties and dimensions. So, for example, so called "westerners", for us, were identified by us as practical, empirical, individualistic and pragmatic. Axial coding puts those data back together in new ways by making connections between a category and its subcategories. Individualism, to take our example further, then incorporates masculinity, atomisation, competitiveness and assertiveness. In such axial coding, moreover, your focus is on specifying the underlying conditions that gave rise to a category, and sub-category: in terms of the context in which it is embedded, the action/interactional strategies by which it is handled, managed, carried out; and, finally, the consequences of these strategies.

Table 4.4.3.2. *Axial Coding: Identifying Intervening Conditions*

- Identify *causal Conditions* – Events or Incidents that led to the Occurrence
- Identify *intervening Conditions* – the constraining and enabling Conditions.
- *Recognize Consequences* – Outcomes of Actions and Interactions.

Selective Coding: Storyline, Core Category, Subsidiary Categories

We now finally turn from open and axial, to so-called "selective" coding, which in fact becomes key to our "northern" African grounding on the path of reason. You now have categories and sub-categories worked out in terms of their salient properties, dimensions and associated relationships, giving the categories richness and density. You should also have begun to note possible relationships between major categories along the lines of their properties and dimensions.

The question is how do you take these – in a rough form, in your diagrams and memos – systematically forward and turn them into an overall picture of reality that is conceptual, comprehensible? For Strauss and Corbin (Abouleish 2005) there are ten steps, which we have distilled down to four, whereby such "selective coding" is accomplished:

Table 4.4.3.3. *Selective Coding: Rationally Based Storyline*

Step 1:	*A Storyline* – a descriptive Story about the central Phenomenon under study
Step 2:	Description to Conceptualisation – *uncovering the Core Category.*
Step 3:	Relate subsidiary *Categories* around the core Category of an overall Story.
Step 4:	Revisit Story, *re-arranging the Categories* and Subcategories accordingly

4.4.4. Grounded Theory and Social Innovation: Economics of Love

Typical then for the path of reason is a thorough understanding of the positivist facts of life; it requires the ability to reason and to build strong, in our northern case indigenous-exogenous theories, which are able to drive out formerly existing weaker exogenous ones. You strive to uncover patterns and to codify knowledge. The symbol for the systematic path of reason is a Line of reasoning, exemplified in the Sekem case, for its founder Ibrahim Abouleish (2005) in Egypt, and his son Helmy Abouleish.

Table 4.4.4. *Sekem's North African Social Research and Innovation Path of Reason – Grounded Theory STD/Maat to Integral Enterprise*

Northern Grounding Method and Origination	Northern Emergent Methodology & Foundation	Northern Navigational Critique and Emancipation	Northern Effective Action and Transformation
Grounded Theory (N1)	Critical Rationalism (N2)	Post-Modernism (N3)	Socio/Technical Design – STD (N4)
Maat (N1)	*Anthrop-osophy (N2)*	*Economics of Love (N3)*	*Fourfold Integral Enterprise (N4)*

My wish then had been to build a community for people of all walks of life. It had to be built, for cultural reasons, on the borders of civil society. To begin with there was just a two-man team, a Bedouin villager and himself. Mohamed was a local villager who came to him when he was walking around the local area, put his hand on his shoulder, and said, "I am with you". There was no infrastructure, no energy, nothing. The two of them began the reclamation and greening of the land, and people started coming. It was clear to me by that time, in the late seventies, that the implementation of his dream was a life's task, culminating in

Economy of Love standing for ...

holistic farming, production and processing. We make different sectors and compounds of an economical and societal system work together within an associative way.

Economy of Love striving to ...

make our economics harmoniously correlate with society and nature. We want to work towards a sustainable development where every human being can unfold his and her individual potential; where mankind lives together in social forms reflecting human dignity; and where all economic activity is transparently conducted in accordance with ecological and ethical principle.

Overall then, and analytically as a researcher, individually, and as a research academy, institutionally, along the linear, and indeed cross-linear path of reason, you start out by theorising, continue with critical – involving falsification of hypotheses – rationalism, evolve towards the multiple perspectives contained within postmodernism, and end up with the development of a socio-technical design, where you engage in the evolution of democratic processes. Transformatively, as a social innovator, and within such a centre for social innovation, you make your assumptions transparent, engage in continuous improvement, build up and on complexity and discontinuity, and evolve democratic structures and processes.

We now turn from being, becoming and knowing to doing, and from, on the one research hand, description, narrative and theorising to survey and experimentation, and on the other, innovation-oriented hand, from experiential and imaginative, to conceptual and now practical learning.

4.5. Doing: Origins of Case Study/Experimental Method: Pax Herbals and Communitalism in West Africa

4.5.1. Exercising Capability: Towards Self Realisation

The ultimate realm of doing, following upon being, becoming and knowing, represents the practical culmination of the grounding and origination, methodwise, of our research, and innovation, journey, or indeed journeys, along now the path of realisation. The term "excellence", as a popular depiction of such ultimate realisation, in fact immortalised in management circles initially in the 1980s by Tom Peters and Bob Waterman (2015) *In Search of Excellence,* has in fact evolved from the Greek "arête", which originally stood for virtue. This was ultimately bound up with the notion of the fulfilment of, or fitness for, purpose or function: the act of living up to one's full potential, thereby being the best you can be.

Such "excellence", specifically then, involves purposefully incorporating all three other worlds into your own. In fact we might identify such an overall aesthetic, in living and learning, with beauty. Such a path of practical realisation, as you enter into a unique world of your own, makes for a kind of "global integrity" which is, at the same time, still connected with your local ground. Each one path or world, ultimately then, is incomplete and imbalanced in itself and needs the other three to become fully operational. We now turn from practical realization, in general, to the origination of such a path of realization, through practically based learning by doing.

4.5.2. Engage with Practical Learning

Practice, ultimately, can be physical embodied, interactive, written, graphic, spoken, or alternatively danced or sung, as we saw in, for example in 2011, in Tahir Square in Egypt. Alternatively, and collectively, it can involve extensive collaboration in peer groups, in which much co-operative and self-directed learning goes on.

The End of Poverty – Jeffrey Sachs (2005)

Survey and Case Study with a view to Experimentation

For Jeffrey Sachs, the Columbia University academic economist closely involved with both the World Bank and also the U.N. Millennium Development Goals, cites empirically identifiable reasons why some countries fail to materially thrive. Of the world's population of 6.3 billion, roughly 5 billion have reached at least the first rung of economic development. In actual economies, for Sachs, a rise in gross domestic product is typically the result of four factors simultaneously at work: saving and capital accumulation, increasing specialization and trade, technological advance and greater natural resources.

The key problem for the poorest countries is that poverty itself can be a trap. When poverty is very extreme, the poor do not have the ability – by themselves – to get out of the mess. Even if such a notion of a "poverty trap" is the right diagnosis, it does not explain why some countries are trapped and others not. The answer, for Sachs, lies in the frequently overlooked, and easily visible, problems of physical geography. What then are the measurable goals that the world community has set to alleviate poverty and suffering around the world?

- *Eradicate extreme Hunger and Poverty:* Halve, between 1990 and 2015, the proportion of people on one dollar a day; and halve the people that suffer from hunger

> - *Achieve universal primary Education:* Ensure that by 2015 children everywhere will be able to complete a full course of primary schooling
>
> - *Promote Gender Equality and empower Women:* Eliminate gender inequality in primary and secondary education by 2005, and for all levels of education, by 2015
>
> - *Reduce Child Mortality:* Reduce by two thirds, between 1990 and 2015
>
> - *Improve maternal Health:* Reduce by three quarters between 1990 and 2015, maternal mortality
>
> - *Combat HIV/AIDS, Malaria & other Diseases:* Begin to reverse, by 2015, the spread of HIV/AIDS, as well as malaria and other diseases
>
> - *Ensure environmental Sustainability:* Integrate the principles sustainable development into country policies; halve proportion of people without access to drinking water by 2015
>
> - *Develop a global Partnership for Development:* Commit to good governance, development and poverty reduction; address special needs of developing countries; deal comprehensively with debt problems; provide access to essential drugs, in co-operation with drug companies in co-operation with private sector, make available benefits of new technologies.

Overall then such practical activity is fit for purpose (beauty), based on prior conceptual discrimination (truth), drawn from inspiring material and ideas (meaning), building on emotional arousal emotional (love).

In knowledge creating terms, this is the realm of internalisation, that is moving from explicit to tacit knowledge. In terms of research method this is the realm, for us, of case study method. Along the path of realisation, from an originally transformative perspective, it involves serving to address practical problems, organisationally or societally (see below) as identifiable according to concrete evidence (Denscombe 2003). We now turn more specifically to experimentation, and to survey method, including, ultimately for our "west" African, original purposes, *case study method.*

4.5.3. Case Study Method

The case study method, then, is a more feasible, and versatile means of conducting empirically based, qualitative research. Of course, such a method is likely to incorporate survey elements, like interviewing, as part of a more integral empirical whole. Such a case study method has in fact only secured intensive coverage from one, inevitably American, Robert Yin (2018). For Yin, the doyen of case study-based approach to empirical research, such a study is an empirical inquiry that investigates a contemporary phenomenon within its real life context, especially when the boundaries between phenomenon and context are not clearly evident.

In other words, you would use the case study method because you deliberately wanted to cover contextual conditions, believing that they might be highly pertinent to your phenomenon of study. An experiment, by way of contrast, deliberately divorces a phenomenon from its context, so that attention can be focussed on a few "controlled" variables. A history, in comparison, does deal with the entangled situation between phenomenon and context, but usually with non-contemporary events.

For case study analysis three points related to research design are important:

- Study Questions: in terms of "who, what, where, how and why"
- *Study Propositions:* each proposition directs attention to something that should be examined in the scope of a study e.g. "organizations collaborate because they derive mutual benefits". At the same time, in the context of an exploratory case study, there may be no such definitive propositions, but, in their stead, an overall statement of purpose – like "I want to uncover the constituents of 'quality control' that can be identified with Islamic principles and practices" – together with criteria for success.
- *Unit of Analysis:* once the general definition of the case has been established, clarifications regarding the unit of analysis become important. If the unit is a small group, for example, those within must be distinguished from those without (the context). Moreover, boundaries of time and place are all important.

For Yin then, the demands of a case study on a person's intellect, ego and emotions are far greater than those of any other research strategy. This is because the data collection procedures are not routine. So what are the desired skills?

Such are illustrated below in Table 4.5.3.

Table 4.5.3. *Experimental and Survey Methods Towards an Original Case Study*

- You are able to ask *good Questions* – and to interpret the Answers.
- You are a good Listener – *not trapped by your own Ideologies* and Preconceptions.
- *You are adaptable* so that new Situations can be seen as Opportunities.
- You are *unbiased by preconceived Notions*, responsive to contradictory Evidence.

Intentional action is at the pinnacle of the supportive pyramid comprising being, becoming, knowing, and doing. It actualizes all these dimensions, bringing them to an integrated focal point. . Undertaken by a learning or knowledge creating community, for us embodied in the Four Worlds, it becomes a concerted and congruent set of behaviours that is honed through cyclical integration of all four modes, and includes a centred integration, as a necessary condition of its continuing practice.

Practice as such, then, as the outcome of an inquiry, fulfils all other modes. It fulfils them because it involves them all, integrates them, gives them human purpose, imbuing them with intentionality, and completes them by manifesting them. Furthermore, it *celebrates* them by showing the reality that they articulate manifests an ultimate effect. It is a declaration by concerted doing, as illustrated below by Pax Herbals (Adodo 2017) in West Africa, in harnessing *Communitalism*.

4.5.4. Case Study Method/Social Innovation: Communiversity/Communitalism

Practically speaking then, in terms ultimately of "west" African research and innovation, you serve to originate your path of realisation, individually or collectively, by compiling a factually, empirically based, case study, such as that of Paxherbals in Nigeria, an exerpt from such as we shall see, a case of Communitalism.

Table 4.5.4. *"Western" African Social Research and Innovation Path of Realisation: Case Study to Action Research/Nature Power to Pax Herbals*

Method and Origination	Methodology & Foundation	Critique and Emancipation	Action and Transformation
Case Study Method (W1)	Empiricism (W2)	Critical Realism (W3)	Action Research (W4)
Nature Power (W1)	Healing Radiance (W2)	Communitalism (W3)	Pax Herbals (W4)

For one of us, Anselm Adodo, as founder of Pax Herbals built on nature power:

> There are two approaches to herbal medicine practice, namely the clinic-oriented approach and community-oriented approach. In a clinic-oriented approach, emphasis is placed on scientific identification, conservation and use of medicinal plants. Laboratory research and screening are done to determine the chemical composition and biological activities of plants. Great interest is shown in quality control of raw materials and finished products, and development of methods for large scale production of labelled herbal drugs. The herbal drugs are labelled and packaged in the same way as modern drugs and distributed through similar channels, that is, through recognized health officials in hospitals, health centres or pharmaceutical supply chains. Huge sums of money are invested both by the government, private companies and non-governmental organizations to promote further research in herbal medicine. Minimal interest is shown in the socio-cultural use of the plants.
>
> In the community-oriented approach, the emphasis is on the crude and local production of herbs used for common illnesses. Knowledge of the medicinal uses of herbs is spread to promote self-reliance. Information is freely given on disease prevention

and origin of diseases. This approach aims at applying simple but effective herbal remedies to common illnesses. The target is the local community. No interest is shown in mass production of drugs for transportation to other parts of the country or exportation to other countries. The cultural context of the plants used is taken into account, and local perception of health and healing often takes precedence over modern diagnostic technology. Simple Herbal recipes are used for the treatment of such illnesses as coughs, colds, malaria, typhoid. The two approaches analysed above are two extremes. There was a need to harmonize these two extremes to complement each other. PAXHERBALS was established in 1996. It was registered as a private liability company, in 2002, as a Catholic research centre for scientific identification, conservation, utilization and development of African medicinal plants.

We are now ready to conclude.

4.6. Conclusion: Grounding One or Other Path Methodically

4.6.1. Grounding Research Method/Origination of *Innovation* in Africa

The Grounding of the four African southern, south-eastern, south-northern and south-western paths in for example Zimbabwe, Uganda, Egypt and Nigeria respectively, serve, for you, individually or collectively, as academic or practitioner, thought leader or social innovator, learning community, transformation journey, research academy or socio-economic laboratory, as the first steps (S,E,N,W – 1/S, E, N, W – 1) along the social research/innovation paths, integrally in Africa, through respectively the:

- relational path: via Description (southern research method – S1), exemplified, innovation-wise, by our *Kumusha* in Zimbabwe in Southern Africa (originating southern innovation – *S1*),
- renewal path: via Narrative (eastern research method – E1), exemplified innovation wise by our *Good African Coffee Story* in Uganda in East Africa (origination eastern innovation – *E1*),
- path of reason: via Grounded Theory (northern research method – N1), exemplified innovation wise by *Sekem/Maat* in Egypt in North Africa (originating northern innovation – *N1*)) and
- realisation path: via Case Study (western research method – W1), exemplified innovation by *Nature Power/Paxherbals* in Nigeria in West Africa (originating western innovation – *W1*).

This (1) will be followed, as we shall see, research-wise, by methodology, critique and action research (2,3,4) in each African worldly case (south – S, east – E, north – N and west – W), and innovation-wise, by emergent foundation, emancipatory navigation and transformative effect, again in each African worldly instance (Zimbabwe, Uganda, Egypt, Nigeria)

4.6.2. There Is More to Sustainable Development Than Meets the Western Eye

As illustrated by us, research method is more than a technique. It serves as what we term the inner directed integral research basis for originating outer directed innovation, the latter for us economy and enterprise wise in Africa, south, east, north and west. Whereas economically, and overall Communitalism-wise, his results in Nhakanomics (southern Africa), Yurugu-nomics (east Africa), the Economics of Love (north Africa) and generic Communitalism west Africa, in enterprise terms the equivalent is community building, while in integral university terms such is embodie din our communiversity.

As we can see, in such an all round pan-African context, there is much more to sustainable development than meets the conventional "western" – SDG – eye. We now turn to the emergent foundation of the "southern" African relational path, following descriptive origination as we have reviewed here. Such "southern" descriptive method (S1), research-wise, and relational origination, innovation-wise ($S1$), constitutes the original, natural grounding for what is transculturally and methodologically to follow, as our phenomenological, relational foundation.

In the chapters that follow, true to our ultimate aspiration to promote societal re-GENE-ration, from the ground up, we shall pursue the sequence: feel local – grounding and origination; intuit local/global – emergent foundation; think newly global – emancipatory navigation; and act global/local – transformative effect. This runs integrally counter to the conventional approach to thinking global-acting local, whereby the proverbial global "west" leads and the local "rest" follow.

4.7. References

Abouleish I (2005) *Sekem: A Sustainable Community in the Egyptian Desert.* Edinburgh. Floris Publications

Abram D (1997) *The Spell of the Sensuous.* New York. Bantam

Adodo A (2012) *Nature Power: A Christian Approach to Herbal Medicine. New Edition.* Edo State. Benedictine Publications

Adodo A (2017) *Integral Community Enterprise in Africa. Communitalism as an Alternative to Capitalism.* Abingdon. Routledge.

Denscombe M (2003) *The Good Research Guide.* Buckingham. Open University Press

Ford C (2000) *The Hero with an African Face: The Mythic Wisdom of Traditional Africa.* New York. Bantam

Glaser B (2000) *Discovery of Grounded Theory: Strategies for Qualitative Research.* New York. Aldine Transaction. First Edition

Heron J (1994) *Feeling and Personhood.* London. Routledge

Hountondji P (2002) *The Struggle for Meaning.* Buckingham. Open University Press

Kolb D (1983) *Experiential Learning: Experience as the Source of Learning and Development.* New York. Pearson FT Press

Lent J (1997) *The Patterning Instinct: A Cultural History of Humanity's Search for Meaning.* Buffalo, NY. Prometheus Press

Lessem R, **Mawere** M and **Taranhike** D (2019) *Integral Kumusha.* Mazvingo. Africa Talent Publishers

Moutsakas C (1994) *Phenomelogical Research Methods.* New York. Sage

Nonaka I and **Takeuchi** H (2008) *The Knowledge Creating Company.* Oxford. Oxford University Press

Peters T and **Waterman** R (2015) *In Search of Excellence: Lessons from America's Best Run Companies.* New York. Profile Books

Randall W (2018) *The Stories We Are: An Essay on Self-Creation.* Toronto. Toronto University Press. P 203

Rugasira A (2014) *A Good African Story: How a Small Company Built a Global Coffee Brand.* London. Vintage Books

Sachs J (2005) *The End of Poverty: We Can Make It in Our Lifetime.* New York. Penguin Books

Strauss A and **Corbin** J (1997) *Grounded Theory in Practice.* New York. Sage

Yin R (2018) *Case Study Research and Applications – Design and Methods.* New York. Sage

Yunus M (2003) *Banker for the Poor: The Story of the Grameen Bank.* New York. Aurum Press

Part 2 The Relational Path Out of *Southern* Africa: Towards Nhakanomics

Chapter 5 From Descriptive Methods (S1) to *Southern* Phenomenology (S2). Engage with Your Local-Global Southern Life World

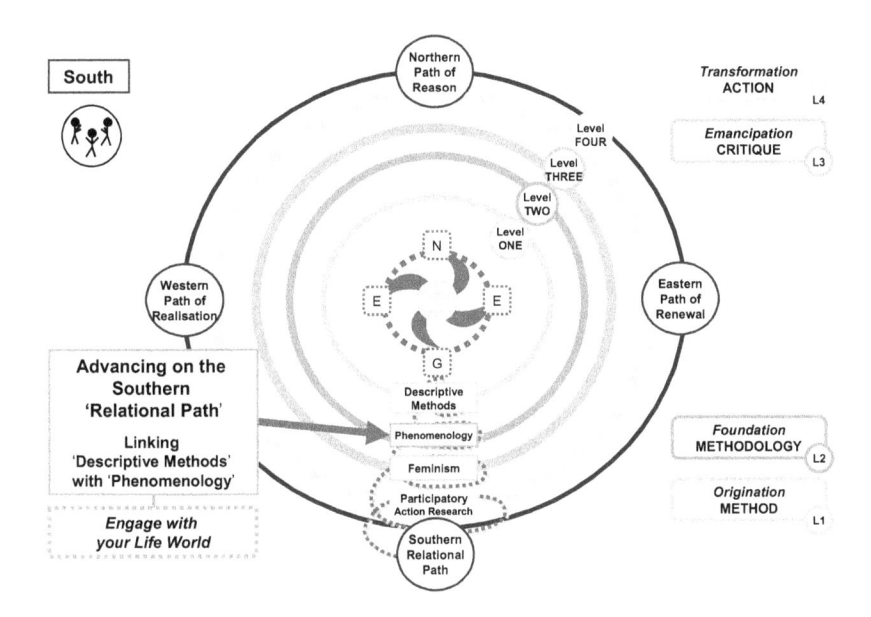

Figure 5.1: *Overview Chapter 5 – Level 1 / South*

Nature is the foundation of indigenous life. Without nature, concepts of community, purpose and healing would be meaningless. In other words, every tree, plant, hill, mountain, rock, and each thing that was here before us emanates or vibrates as a subtle energy that has healing power whether we know it or not. Nature is the textbook for those who care to study it and storehouse of remedies for human ills.

Patrice Some   (1999)   *The Healing Wisdom of Africa*

Summary: Southern Phenomenology

- Advancing firstly on the southern relational path, we now turn from research method to research methodology, and from social origination to social foundation. In the process, and unlike the conventional wisdom think global act local, we feel local, intuit local-global, think newly global and act global-local.

- A core claim of phenomenology is that explanations are not to be imposed before the phenomena have been understood from within, so that Husserl, the Moravian "father of phenomenology", as for Steve Biko, the father of Black Consciousness, sees this methodology also as putting the study of culture or "spirit" on a proper scientific footing.

- Husserl saw the life world ("Lebenswelt") as the universal framework, for us foundation, of human endeavour. For him, there is not one single life world, but a set of overlapping worlds, beginning from the world, which is the "home-world", and extending to other world farther away, the worlds of other cultures. As a social innovator you fully enter into, and engage with, such worlds.

- Husserl criticizes traditional empiricism for naively dictating that all judgments be legitimised by the "senses", instead of realising that many different forms of intuition underlie our judgments and our reasoning process. We overcome the subject-object divide only by finding a deeper meaning within subjectivity itself, in ourselves, and through empathizing with others

- For German 20th century philosopher Heidegger, the great threat to human existence is that thinking has become a kind of technical information processing. This leads to a fundamental homelessness and rootlessness, in both thought and action.

- Instead of Husserl's phenomenology being our global port of call, having felt Black Consciousness, *Africa-wise*, and intuiting radical consciousness, detachment, doubt, and empiricism, as well as bridging the ancient and modern *worlds-wide*, we turn newly globally to Ingold's Livelihood, Dwelling and Enskillment in. *southern* guise

- From this perspective knowledge ceases to be a mirroring, passive affair and becomes a process whereby we insert ourselves actively in the given setting of our lives. Hence, we need to accept the responsibility that as knowers (thought leaders), and doers (social innovators), change the potential and actual course of the world.

- Finally, we turn to the global-local *Keynotes* of our integral approach to Phenomenology, that is engaging with our *Life World, Inner Self, Natural/ Cultural History*, altogether *Beyond Positivism*.

5.1. Orientation to Phenomenology

5.1.1. Research to *Innovation*: Core Text to Case *Story*

Descriptive, Phenomenological, Feminist, PAR

We now turn on our relational southern research path from method to methodology, in this case from descriptive methods (S1) to phenomenology (S2). We also focus on the southern path of innovation, in Africa, from relational origins in a *kumusha* (see Table 5.1.1. below), locally, to its emergent foundation, via now an *integral kumusha*, engaging with a southern African, specifically Zimbabwean, *life world*(s) as a whole. However, such a fully innovative turn will only materialize in the Taranhikes' Integral Case Story (ICS1) to follow: Kumusha to Vakamusha.

In this chapter, we make our radical departure from the conventional wisdom of "thinking global-acting local", which we will then follow throughout the rest of this first volume on integral research and innovation. For thereby, and in such a conventional case, "north- western" approaches, in this case to phenomenology, globally so to speak, predominate over local adaptations of such, which then assume inferior status.

Table 5.1.1. *"Southern" African Relational Path of Research to Innovation: Descriptive to Participatory via PHENOMENOLOGY; Kumusha to Vakamusha*

Southern Grounding Method and Origination	Southern Emergence Methodology and Foundation	Southern Navigation Critique and Emancipation	Southern Effect Action and Transformation
Descriptive Methods (S1)	Phenomen-ological Method-ology (S2)	Feminist Critique (S3)	Participatory Action Research (S4)
Kumusha (S1)	Integral Kumusha (S2)	Nhaka-Nomics (S3)	Vaka-Musha (S4)

Instead, and following in the footsteps of John Heron's (1994) *Feeling and Personhood*, as well as our (Lessem and Schieffer 2009) own integral rhythm, we *feel local* (experiential-origination), *intuit local-global* (imaginal-foundation), *think "newly global"* (conceptual-emancipation) and *act global-local* (practical-transformation). So the local "south" takes a lead, as it were, and the "rest" follow.

Phenomenology: Local African, Local/Global Worlds-Wide, Newly Global Southern, Global-Local Relational Keynotes

Specifically then for each methodology and foundation, critique and emancipation, action research and transformation, that respectively follows, in this case phenomenologically, we shall incorporate, systematically, and further to an introduction to the inevitably Eurocentric orientation:

- a local *African* natural and communal orientation to phenomenology (5.2)
- a local-global orientation to phenomenology *Worlds-Wide* (5.3)
- a "newly global" *Southern* scientific, phenomenological orientation (5.3)
- a global-local expression of the four *Keynotes* of phenomenology (5.4)

Thereafter, in our supplementary chapter ICS (Integral Case Study) 1, we provide an overall, African *Relational Integral Case*, turning from social, inner-directed research, to outer directed economic and enterprise *innovation*.

5.1.2. Southern African Research to Innovation: S2fita

In this chapter then, the emphasis will be on phenomenology, as an inner directed, African social research methodology (S2) – from thereby feeling local to acting globally-locally – albeit with reference to outer directed economic and enterprise innovation, in Southern Africa. In ICS1 then, our first integral case story on our *Integral Kumusha*, the emphasis will be on economic and enterprise innovation (*S1 – S4*) as signalled in the Table 5.1.1. above.

We start then with our introduction to phenomenology, generically, before we come to *feel local* (S2f) in Southern Africa, more specifically, indeed integrally. For us, moreover, Phenomenology (S2i) provides the very African local-global Intuited foundation for a relational approach to inner directed social research, and outer directed economic and enterprise innovation to follow. However, it is necessary firstly to retrace steps, thereby originally Feeling local in Africa.

In fact, integral research-wise, we shall be undertaking such in every worldly case that follows, with a view to coming up with a "newly global" fully Thought through (S2t) African critique, of classically local-global methodologies, in this case phenomenology, for which we need prior local grounding. Ultimately then, thereby Acting (S2a) globally-locally, as will be fully spelt out in our Southern African case story, ICS, we have the integral Southern Foundation: S2fita.

So first, by way of introduction, we provide an overall, invariably Eurocentric, introduction to phenomenology, before we "get serious", re-GENE-ratively so to speak, with our relational methodology, starting by feeling local.

5.1.2. Historical Evolution of European Phenomenology

The Crisis of the European Sciences

From a phenomenological, overtly European perspective, all too often in the social sciences, when researchers refer to conducting themselves "scientifically", they have in mind an exclusively empirical, for us "western" foundational model of research. Interestingly enough, and originally as such, the typical Harvard case study, to which one of us (Ronnie Lessem) was prolifically exposed hitherto, notwithstanding his Southern African origins, sets that "western" stage It is worth noting, that Edmund Husserl (2012), radically parted company from such in the 1930s, but Harvard Business School since has not caught up with him!

Phenomenology then was initially developed, in Central Europe, by Edmund Husserl, a Moravian mathematician and philosopher. His work broke away from the purely positivist orientation of the science and philosophy of his day, globally, giving weight to subjective experience as the source of all of our knowledge of objective phenomena. This was not unlike, half a century later, as we shall see, in the then apartheid South Africa, in the 1970s, the phenomenological approach taken by Steve Biko's in his "Black Consciousness".

Husserl was born in 1859 into a Jewish family in Prostějov (Prossnitz), Moravia, Czech Republic (then part of the Austrian Empire). He was a disciple of the Czech philosopher and psychologist Franz Brentano, who influenced him greatly. Husserl felt that the objectivism of science, in the same way thereafter as the world of the white European, for Biko, influenced black consciousness, and thereby, in each case, precluded an adequate apprehension of the world. He presented various philosophical conceptualizations and techniques designed to locate the sources or essences of reality in the human consciousness.

In *The Crisis of the European Sciences* (Moran 2012), just like for Biko the "crisis of Eurocentric consciousness", as we shall see, Husserl for the first time attempts a historical overview of the development of western philosophy and science, emphasizing the challenges presented by their increasingly empirical and naturalistic orientation. Husserl, as indeed was subsequently the case for Biko, declares that mental and spiritual reality possess their own reality independent of any physical basis, and that a science of the spirit ("Geisteswissenschaft"), that we now liken to *Black Consciousness*, must be established on as scientific a foundation as the natural sciences have managed. For Husserl (1970):

> It is my conviction that intentional phenomenology has for the first time made spirit as spirit the field of systematic scientific experience, thus effecting a total transformation of the task of knowledge.

How Phenomenology Operates

Phenomenology operates rather differently from the former way social science was conducted. While it is a theoretical orientation, it does not generate deductions from propositions that can be empirically tested. It operates more on a sociological level, demonstrating its premises through descriptive analyses of the procedures of self, situational, and social constitution. Through its demonstrations, audiences apprehend the means by which phenomena, originating in human consciousness, come to be experienced as features of the world. Interestingly enough, and as we shall soon see, phenomenology has since developed in the 20th century, as a radical

European alternative to the positivist status quo, methodologically, while the same has now applied to "Black Consciousness" becoming such a *research* methodological perspective.

What does this suggest, generally, regarding humanity and sociology? Phenomenology advances the notion that humans are creative agents in the construction of social worlds. It is from their consciousness that all being emerges. Biko would undoubtedly agree. The alternative to their consciously creative work is meaninglessness and chaos: a world of dumb puppets (dumb blacks!), in which one is disconnected from the other, and where life is formless. This is the nightmare of phenomenology. Its practitioners fear that positivist sociologists actually theorize about such a world. We now turn "south".

5.2. Local African Phenomenology: Feel Local: S2f

5.2.1. Feel Local, Intuit Local-Global, Think Newly Global, Act Global-Local

Starting out then with a local "feel" for southern Africa, firstly, we ground ourselves in so called *ubuntu*, in both Zimbabwe and South Africa specifically, before turning to *humanity's search for* home in Nigeria, more generally. Thereafter we will intuit "locally-globally", now turning *phenomenologically* "worlds-wide", from south to east, north, west and centre.

Thirdly, and now "newly globally", we turn to British renegade anthropologist Tim Ingold's *Livelihood, Dwelling and Enskillment* whereby he newly conceptualises phenomenology in natural and communal guise. Fourthly then we reveal ways and means of acting phenomenologically, through its four global-local *Keynotes*. In thereby feeling local, intuiting locally-globally, thinking newly-globally and acting globally-locally we overturn the conventional mantra "think global-act local", thereby aiming to transform local identity into global integrity. Finally as such, in conclusion, we will outline the overall relational path, and case story, of which phenomenology is a methodological foundation., altogether and also aligned with the grounding of our communiversity as a *kumusha* laden learning community, and indeed version of communitalism, as *nhakanomics*.

5.2.2. Radical Consciousness in the South: I Am Because You Are

Contextualizing Unhu/Hunhu in Zimbabwe

We begin then, initially feeling our local phenomenological way in Zimbabwe in Southern Africa. In the indigenous Shona language so called *Unhu/Hunhu* encapsulates all spheres of life for individuals and the collective alike, as mutually beneficial, undergirded by reciprocity and respect for human life and dignity. Ruby Magosvongwe (2016), as such, Professor and current chair of the Department of English at the University of Zimbabwe, as a student of literature, has investigated the relationship between land and nature, culture and social movements in Southern Africa, drawing in particular on African works of fiction.

> Unhu permeates, inspires, regulates, and radiates through well-planned social and political organization of a community's way of life. Unhu is the attention that human beings should accord one another. Hence the expression, "Hahungave Unhu ihwohwo" in Shona, or in Isindebele, "Kabusibo Ubuntu lobo" – that is not behaviour attributable to a normal or/and fully conscious human being.

Being munhu/human being entails sharing belongingness with others. Munhu is therefore not just the physiological and physical human form. Observing the cardinal values that encapsulate and promote harmony, for sustainable livelihoods and collective survival on the land, is paramount. Expressions like Uyu ndiye munhu/ Ane unhu/ Uhu ndihwo unhu chaihwo – *His whole being exudes and encapsulates the totality of humaneness in addition to being cultured* – socialized holistically to uphold the fundamentals of harmonious co-existence.

Hence Impliedly, civility, politeness, tsika/good manners, respect, and kindness are deeply embedded in the and inextricably interwoven with social engineering that is underscored by interdependency with the community. When someone remonstrates *Hausi unhu ihwohwo* – that is animal/wild conduct – it means ethically, conduct is unbefitting. The deciding voice rests with the consensus of the collective, guided by sanctity of human life as the harmonizing principle.

Unhu, Munhu, and More-then-Human Ivhu: Land, Soil and Connectivity

Land/*Ivhu*/soil, for Magosvongwe moroever, is very much at the centre of the Shona philosophy of Unhu, including what being munhu entails. In Zimbabwean indigenous Shona terms, belongingness has always been tied up with the land. This has been transposed into liberation discourses where black identity is tied up with the land/ivhu/soil, hence references to "children of the soil"/vana vevhu.

The concept/notion chimes in well with the Biblical origins of the human being/ munhu – from dust you came and unto dust you shall return. "We are all sons and daughters of the soil", because rukuvhute rwedu rwuri muivhu re Zimbabwe: *our umbilical codes are buried in the Zimbabwean soil*". For the indigenous Shona then, land is revered as covenantal. The Shona rituals at birth and death seal this covenant with the land. At different stages of their lives, rites of passage are conducted, and libations are poured onto the soil/ivhu/land, making land the profound unifier and rallying point for families and communities among the Shona.

Ivhu/the soil/land, moreover, is sacred in *southern* Africa. By extension, for Magoswongwe, Shona ethics deem human life sacred. *To belong then is divine, and destinies are intertwined with the land/soil/ivhu*. It naturally follows that Shona Unhu – ethics and ethos – are guided by land traditions, inscribed spirituality, and taboos. Land is therefore believed to dictate conduct and relational terms between humans and their environment and other creatures, both animate and inanimate. Land is a living force. It is an abode for the departed.

In other words, land inscribes checks and balances that govern ecological awareness and environmental conduct. Expectations and rules inscribed in the land traditions are unwritten but inscribed in people's psyches and moral obligations. Confessions such as zvinoyera/hazvviitwi/it is taboo/sacred emphasize the reverence for the land. Confessions of taboos evidence "acquired quality of humanity that is the characteristic of a fully developed person and the community with others that results". "Community with others" demands that munhu's self-awareness/unhu becomes self- censored as dictated by the maxims inscribed in the land/muvhu. This is how the Shonas become vanhu/human beings with unhu/moral ethics/philosophy. We now turn from Zimbabwe to South Africa, and from Magosvongwe to Steve Biko, from the sacredness oft he land to Black Consciousness.

Ubuntu to Black Consciousness and Negritude: I Feel Therefore I Am

The attitude of seeing people not as themselves but as agents for some particular function either to one's advantage or disadvantage is, for the late Steve Biko (1987), a key figure in South Africa's "Black Consciousness" movement foreign to the African. We are not, he says, a suspicious race:

> "We believe in the inherent goodness of man. We enjoy man for himself. We regard our living together not as an unfortunate mishap warranting endless competition amongst us but as a deliberate act of God to make us a community of brothers and sisters jointly involved in the quest for a composite answer to the varied problems of life. Hence in all we do we always place man first and therefore all our action is usually joint and community oriented."

Nothing then dramatizes the eagerness of the African to communicate with each other more than their love for song and rhythm. Music in the African culture features in all emotional states, for South Africa's Steve Biko as for Senegal's former philosopher-president, and originator of the concept of *Negritude*, Leopold Senghor (Thiam 2017):

> When we go to work we share the burdens and pleasures of the work we are doing through music. In other words, for Africans, music and rhythm are not luxuries but part and parcel of our way of communicating. Any suffering we experienced was made more real by song and rhythm. There is no doubt that the so-called "Negro spirituals" sung by black slaves in the States as they toiled under oppression were indicative of the African heritage. The major thing to note about our songs is that they were never songs for individuals. All African songs are group songs.

For Senghor (Thiam 2017) then, more specifically:

> *To know is to live – the Other's life – by identifying oneself with the object. To know is to be born in the Other, while dying oneself. It is to make love with the Other, it is to dance the Other: "I feel therefore I am".*

Biko adds that Africans, being a pre-scientific people, do not recognise any conceptual cleavage between the natural and the supernatural. They experience a situation rather than face a problem. By this is meant that they allow both the rational and the non-rational elements to make an impact upon them. Hence, any action they may take could be described more as a response of the total personality to the situation than the result of some mental exercise. As such Africans would obviously find it artificial to create special occasions for worship. Neither did they see it as logical to have a particular building in which all worship would be conducted.

> "We believed that God was always in communication with us and therefore merited attention everywhere and anywhere. In rejecting western values, therefore, we are rejecting those things that are not only foreign to us but that seek to destroy the most cherished of our beliefs – that the cornerstone of society is man himself – not just his welfare, not his material being, but just man himself with all his ramifications. We reject the power-based society of the westerners that seems to be ever concerned with perfecting their technological know how while losing out on their spiritual dimension. We believe that in the long run the special contribution from Africa will be in the field of human relationships. The great powers of the world may have done wonders in giving the world an industrial and military look. But the great gift still has to come from Africa – giving the world a human face."

That is not a million miles away from where Edmund Husserl (2012) was coming from, philosophically in entering wholeheartedly into the "life world" of self and other, even though he and Biko were far apart in place and time. Husserl states in such "ubuntu-like" terms:

> Personal life means living communalised as "I" and "we", within a community horizon, and this in communities of various forms – family, nation, supra-national community. It involves purposeful life, the term life in this context not having a physiological sense, but in the broadest sense creating culture in the unity of a historical development.

Most ubuntu thinkers in an African philosophical context formulate their views in terms of "a person is a person through other persons", or, "I am because you are". In this way human dignity gains a central place and seems to be related to both morality and nationality. There is no dualism in this position because rationality and morality are required from community life and do not follow from so-called universal categories or fixed ideologies. We now turn from Biko and Senghor, historically, to Bayo Akomolafe currently.

5.2.3. Humanity's Search for Home

Nigerian philosopher, now living between India and the United States, Bayo Akomolafe's (2017), in his recent book on *Humanity's Search for Home*, subtitled "Letters to my Daughter", written in semi-autobiographical terms:

I whispered to you (my daughter) your secret name, your Yoruba Oriki or life song, the name Maya. For me, beyond its multicultural significance and spiritual connotations, maya means you are vast; that the whole world. its many twinkle-twinkle-little-stars and the shadows between them, conspired in your emergence; and that – most importantly – I am indelibly marked by the small and seemingly insignificant promise I made you to find your own home. To topple regimes of knowing, petition water spirits, climb mountains, and be pierced by a thousand proboscises if only to inch closer to understanding what it would take to live peaceably in this world of dust, shadow and burning sun ..

But where to begin on this quest? What does a home mean in this world of shifting sands and eroding foundations? What good is home if it doesn't preserve you for a while longer than if you were without it? This story – running through these letters – is the series of assumptions about being human and about the world that is often called "modernity". Modernity is home to us. Our flag is planted deep in this planet, this uncouth carnival of churning matter we barely understand. Not for a want of trying. We are doing our best to encounter the wold and make sense of it by reducing it to utilitarian units or potential exploitation. We seek to meet the world by conquering it. We treat ourselves the same way – subjecting the "other" to the brute force of our colonial narratives, a legacy that runs in your veins.

But then this drive to mastery has spawned many dreadful things, and the focus of "Western" critical inquiry has shifted once more: rejecting the grounds upon which our cities and empires of selves are premised, we are moving our tents. Many have left their material belongings and the camp, and headed for the sea, roaming in desolate, postmodern waters – stricken with thirst but unable to drink the impossibly salty water. Awash in a heady place. Lost with no possibility of redemption. For now bot the modern and the postmodern are struggling against "nature" ... how it has become imperative to discipline it, to leave its logic behind, and float above its assumedly brute profligacy. Spirit above matter.

So here we are, our feet showered with gold dust and tattooed with the paeans of might valour. Our cargo area filled with open secrets and many spoils form cultures plundered. And yet we are exiled from home. There is no arriving. We know no welcoming shores. Just hovering at the lip of a final resolution, stuck in the frustrating middle. Our days and nights are like that: filled with a certain feeling that something is missing, that there is something yet to be done, that the world could be more beautiful, more just, more inviting to leaf and limb. More like home.

I write about pure beginnings, corrupted middles, and redeeming endings. Home evoked a notion of future reconciliation and of bravely slugging through the tangle of the ordinary in order to arrive intact at the unspoiled gates of the real. I wish I could offer you a story of arrival, a tale of the city in the horizons with which you could warm your weary bones made hard and brittle by cold, long pilgrimages. A map to teach you how to go. But I can't. The inside and the outside are not easily divided. There is no out "there"; there is only yearning, an aching, and in the struggle we change .. In my revised reading of the biblical story of creation, Good curses man, but only apparently. "Dust thou art, and unto dust thou shalt return". Once immortal, we all will not have to learn limits. We will have to make do with hints of ideals, the dust trail of essences we will never catch up with. But this is a difficult lesson to learn, because iot comes with the message that we are not unilaterally in control of our circumstances. "Dust .. gives lie to the human presumption of power and control".

Is it any wonder that those of us in the mechanical heart of modernity cannot tolerate dust's presence. In a sense, modernity offers the prospects of returning to heaven. The myth of modernity proposes a home in a world that is progressively conquered by scientific and technological advances. And science, purportedly apolitical and neutral, was in cahoots with the economic and cultural agendas that led to the exploitation of black, brown, and even white bodies. On account of our "primitive" ways (or lack of proximity to the ultimate truths of modernity) we – your mother, father, their mothers and fathers – were given a dishonourable place in nature. In the quest then to stand resolute against the sandstorm, to affirm our place in a bold stance of anthropcentricity, and ensure a home for posterity, we only accelerated and enhanced the felt disconnect between us and the world around us.

Onto Integral Kumusha

Taking on then from where Okomolafe has left off, in humanity search for home, the Taranhike's extend and enrich their home, ecologically and economically, as well as culturally and technologically, accordingly. For them (Lessem et al 2019):

> The evolution of the Integral Kumusha in general and Vakamusha in particular, is providing opportunities for conducting productive income generating projects through-out the whole year. This has given the rural people of Buhera employment opportunities within their own communities thereby earning a good living, enhancing their livelihoods and contributing towards alleviating poverty in the area. Unlike the western corporate firm, the Integral Kumusha/Vakamusha is not primarily focused purely at making huge profits but at profiting the community of Buhera. People in the area now have access to the products at affordable prices and even conduct business through barter trade which is familiar within rural settings. Through the income they earn from working at the Integral Kumusha/Vakamusha the people are now able to pay school fees for their children and buy other necessities from the shops at Murambinda Growth Point (Semi-Urban Centre). Members of the community are using the technologies such as concrete brick moulding to build their homes and people's lives are being transformed. In this way, at family level, people can create good legacy for their children and as a community, are now passing on great legacy of prosperity instead of poverty and dependency.

We now turn from feeling local in *unhu/ubuntu*, invoking Black consciousness, in search of home, altogether in Africa, we turn, locally-globally, worlds-wide onto Asia, Europe, the Anglo-Saxon world and to MENA (Middle East and North Africa), before evoking our newly global *Southern phenomenology*.

5.3. Intuited Local-Global Phenomenological Variations: S2i

5.3.1. Radical Detachment from the East: Encountering the Other

Having then "felt local", also in our "search for home", in the African "south", phenomenologically so to speak, we now turn, respectively, to the "east", the "north", the "west" and the centre, to co-evolve, thereby intuiting altogether "locally-globally". There is indeed an interesting resonance between phenomenology and Buddhism, that is involving self-detachment, alongside of self-interest (intentionality) and self-knowledge (rationality).

Caroline Brazier (2003), in her book on "Buddhist Psychology", makes the point that Buddhist psychology is sometimes described as a "non-self" psychology. The self is a defensive structure built in response to affliction. This is what is referred to in Buddhism as ignorance or "avidya". We ignore much that is going on around us and limit our behaviour and interest to things that relate to our self-view. In the process, we initially grasp for something we can hold on to that seems permanent; we call this "me" or self. The self is the fortress we create to protect ourselves from experiencing loss and impermanence. It is our greatest defence mechanism. It is also our prison. Keeping the fortress in place becomes our life project, and consumes large amounts of energy. This constituted, for the Buddha, greed and attachment.

So what has this all got to do with phenomenology? If Buddhist psychology is a psychology of addiction, then it is also a psychology of encounter. Encounter is the antidote to those addictive patterns that holds us trapped. By encountering the world beyond the walls of self, we break through to freedom. The path to health is in encountering that which is not self. In other words, we need to encounter that which is other. To break out of self-absorption we have to allow ourselves to be touched by something beyond ourselves. We now turn from Asia to Europe.

5.3.2. Radical Doubt in the North: Liberation from Limiting Thought Forms

Rudolph Steiner, an Austrian who lived at the turn of the last century, was a philosopher and educator, architect and agronomist, historian and musician, economist and political scientist, amongst other things. Because of the esoteric nature of some of his "anthroposophical" work he became disconnected from the philosophical and methodological mainstream. Andrew Welburn (Welburn 2004), a Fellow of New College, Oxford, has done us a real service by linking Rudolph Steiner's work into the phenomenological establishment.

Actually, Steiner was a leading exemplar of researcher and innovation in the social realm, and as we shall see (Chapter 16) Sekem in Egypt has applied, and indeed further evolved his orientation in a North African context, through the so called *Economics of Love*. For not only did Steiner conceive of "anthroposophy" as a philosophical movement, but, through it, he pioneered innovative approaches to art and architecture, medicine and agriculture, education and indeed economics, some of which – particularly in education (Waldorf Schools) and agriculture (biodynamic farming) – have spread throughout the world.

Steiner's idea of philosophy was as liberation from limiting forms of thought, rather than as a wagging moral finger or an intellectual programme. Such liberation enables us to grasp other possibilities, taking place in the thick of life, and coinciding with the freedom to see things anew. Such a concept of freedom is precisely one that may be embodied in the form of a building or a room, in a gesture or in a painting, or in a new approach to economics, for him based on fraternity rather than liberty. Scientific knowing is the way in which we can relate to the world through developing our inner activity. Scientific activity does not reveal our passivity before fixed facts of nature, but our own living process of knowledge, the free development of the self. For example, his concept of "associative" economics was based on what he reckoned to be the phenomenological and concrete "reality" of economic life, rather than the liberal and abstract "ideal" of it embodied in the "free market" approach.

The polarizations of the modern world, according to Steiner, were rooted in assumptions that reach back to the beginnings of the 19th century and indeed before then. The one side of the polarity, an idealistic philosophy, traced its origin back to Immanuel Kant. The other, an embodiment of a materialistic worldview, had come down from Jeremy Bentham and was influenced by J.S. Mill. There was apparently no middle way. Their clash in the 19th century pre-figures some of the terrible struggles subsequently enacted in the twentieth. The struggles above all were concerned with the value of the individual. For Steiner, neither dominant tradition assigns value to the individual as such. Idealist Kant held that moral imperatives come to us with blinding force as "categorical imperatives". The knowing individual has only the function of recognizing the necessary laws of existence. The realist Bentham felt that fulfilment lies in the value of the whole society, tribe or race.

Steiner, in contrast with realism and idealism, is closely aligned with the emerging phenomenology. Instead of a desperate search for objective foundations, knowledge might emerge from the growing and changing being of man, in a continually developing society. That would mean abandoning the notion of the impassive onlooker, and including the seeking, striving human self in the picture we form of the cognitive process. As such we arrive at a picture, which is neither the blank sheet of empiricism, nor the mind locked up in its own categories as for Kant. What we know of the world depends on the fact that we are part of the world and have been shaped by it, so that from the beginning our nature and organization become not a limit, but the actual key to the nature of the universe to which we belong and which brought us into being. We now turn from "south", "east" and "north" to "west".

5.3.3. Radical Empiricism in the "West": Born Out of Reason

Husserl, through his focus on individual freedom and intentionality, had something in common with "western" Locke and Hume, even though he rejected Locke's exclusive focus on objective reality. He also shared with the Anglo-Saxon empiricists an orientation towards the concrete and "real", as opposed to the ideal. This he termed the "life world", albeit that such was full of subjectivity as well as objectivity. At the same time Husserl was a rationalist, who drew inspiration from "northerner" Descartes, through the latter's sense of "radical doubt", although he disagreed with Descartes' separation of body and mind. In Husserl's (2012) words:

> ... the European world was born out of reason, that is, out of the spirit of philosophy. The European crisis should therefore not be interpreted as the failure of rationalism ... an impoverished rationalism has become entangled in "naturalism" and "objectivism".

We now turn, worlds-wide, to what we term the "centre", the MENA region as the home of the peoples of the book, focusing herein on Islam.

5.3.4. Centred Islamic Reconstruction: Bridge Between Ancient/Modern

We finally turn to the phenomenology of religion. In this case, we do so via the 20th century Pakistani poet-philosopher, Muhammad Iqbal (2000) and his "Reconstruction of the Islamic Religion". Interestingly enough, Iqbal positions Islam, as do Husserl and Steiner, phenomenologically, in between the ideal and the real, emphasizing the relatively concrete nature of Islam vis-à-vis classical Greek philosophy:

> The failure of Cartesian ontological and teleological arguments is that they look upon "thought" as an agency working on things from without. This creates an unbridgeable gap between the real and the ideal. It is, however, possible to take thought not as a principle that organizes its material from the outside, but as a potency, which is formative of the very being of its material. Thus regarded thought or idea is not akin to the original nature of things; it is their ultimate ground and constitutes the essence of their beings, inspiring their onward march to a self-determined end. But our present situation necessitates the dualism between thought and being.

Iqbal argues that the radical doubt, that Husserl evolved from Descartes, was anticipated by Islam in the 11th century. Iqbal sees Islam as a bridge between the ancient and modern worlds. As such, he also sees Islam as the origin of empirically based scientific method, as we know it today. For him:

> The Prophet of Islam seems to stand between the ancient and modern worlds. In so far as the source of his revelation is concerned, he belongs to the ancient world. At the same time the birth of Islam is the birth of the modern, inductive intellect. In Islam, prophecy reaches its perfection in discovering the need of its own abolition – in order to achieve full self-consciousness man must be thrown inductively back on his own resources. The abolition of the kingship and hereditary priesthood in Islam,

Intuited Local-Global Phenomenological Variations: S2i   143

the constant appeal to reason and experience in the Qur'an, and the emphasis that it lays on Nature and History as sources of human knowledge, are all different aspects of the same idea of finality. As such the Qur'an regards both "Anfus" (self) and "Afaq" (world) as sources of knowledge. Inner experience is one source of human knowledge; the external sources are Nature and History.

Ultimately, for Iqbal and for many Islamic scholars, Islam is rooted not only in concreteness, as opposed to abstraction, but also in a concept of "inner freedom" that anticipates not only phenomenology as a whole, but also and particularly existential phenomenology, as reflected in the work of Heidegger and Sartre:

> The Qur'an has no liking for abstract universals. It always fixes its gaze on the concrete, which the theory of relativity has only recently taught science to do. Omniscience, abstractly conceived, is merely a blind, capricious power without limits. The Qur'anic legend of the Fall has, in fact, nothing to do with the first appearance of man on the planet. Its purpose is rather to indicate man's rise from a primitive, instinctive state to the conscious possession of a free self, capable of doubt and disobedience. The Fall does not mean moral depravity; it is man's transition from simple consciousness to the first flash of self-consciousness, a kind of awakening from the dream of nature to a throb of causality in one's own being. Man's first act of disobedience was his first act of free choice. Freedom is thus a condition of goodness. But to permit the emergence of a finite ego who has the power to choose, after considering the relative values of several actions open to him, is to take a great risk. For freedom to choose good also involves its opposite.

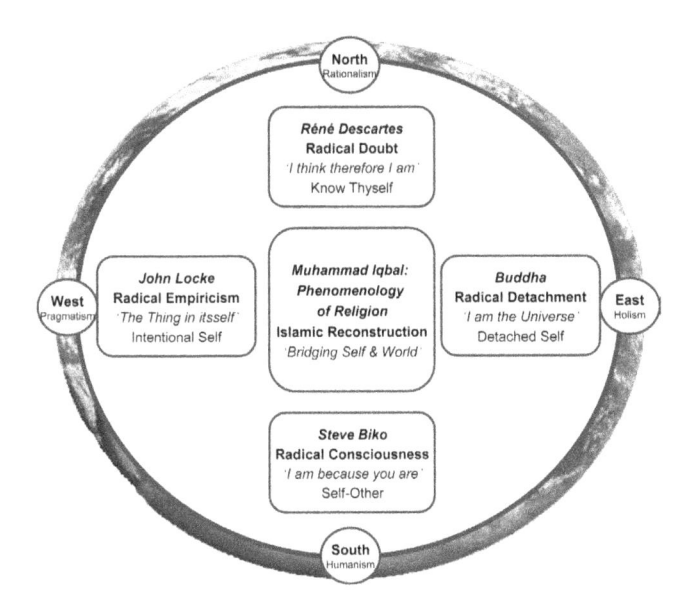

Figure 5.3.4: *A Phenomenal Field of Local-Global Force*

In that local-global guise, overall, (see Figure 5.3.4. above), we can see a link, phenomenologically, between Biko's *radical consciousness* in the *"ubuntu"* laden African "south", Brazier's *radical detachment* in the Asian "east"; Steiner's and Descartes *radical doubt* in the European "north", not to mention also the *radical empiricism* of Locke and Hume's "west", and finally with the *reconstruction of* Islam as bridge between the ancient the modern. All of such makes for a much-enriched phenomenological concept of "freedom" over the "western" conventionally "liberal" notion of such.

We now turn to a "newly global" approach to phenomenology, evoked by a renegade British anthropologist, who has based his findings on longstanding involvement with indigenous peoples in the Arctic. As such he serves to interlink (wo)man and nature, (wo)man and (wo)man, feeling and thought, and, above all, dwelling and making, like Okomolafe "in search of home". Altogether then, from what we would consider a "southern" *relational* perspective, albeit accommodating also other worlds, he comes up with what we consider to be a newly global southern, altogether phenomenological orientation towards community-and-ecology and skill-and-enterprise.

5.4. Newly Global Thought Through Southern Foundation: Livelihood, Dwelling, Enskilling: S2t

5.4.1. Anthropology Linking Nature and Humanity Via Phenomenology

Ecological Adaptations, Social Organization and Ethnic Politics

For Tim Ingold (2011) then, Emeritus Professor of Anthropology at the University of Aberdeen in Scotland, his seminal work was, as he himself recently relayed to us, *The Perception of the Environment: Essays on Livelihood, Dwelling and Skill*. His original doctoral work at the University of Cambridge in the 1970s was in fact conducted with the Skolt Saami indigenous peoples of north-eastern Finland, studying their ecological adaptations, social organization and ethnic politics.

In his contemporary work, more specifically, and for us now "newly globally" in our *Southern* guise, he links the themes of environmental perception and skilled practice, replacing traditional models of genetic and cultural transmission, founded upon the alliance of neo-Darwinian biology and cognitive science, with a relational approach. Such focuses on the growth of embodied skills of perception and action within social and environmental contexts of human development.

The Human as an Organism that "Feels" His/Her Way Through a World

Writing, overall, within the anthropological realm of phenomenology, Ingold explores the human as an organism that "feels" his/her way through a world that "is itself in motion", constantly creating and being changed by spaces and places as they are encountered. Concerned, moreover, about the widening gap between the arts and the humanities on the one hand, and natural sciences on the other, he was looking, already in the 1960s, for a discipline that would somehow close the gap, or enable us to rise above it, while remaining close to the realities of lived experience. Anthropology for him was that discipline.

Western Thought Separates "Two Worlds": Humanity and Nature

Yet he began to observe with mounting despair how it had become fractured along the very lines of the fission he thought he had overcome. These fractures seemed to derive from a single, underlying fault upon which the entire edifice of Western thought and science had been built – namely that which separates "two worlds" of humanity and nature: disciplines, on the one hand that deal with the human mind and its manifold linguistic, social and cultural products, and, on the other, with the structures and composition of the material world.

Social or cultural anthropologists would rather read the work of historians, linguists, philosophers and literary critics; biological or physical anthropologists prefer to talk to colleagues in the fields of biology or biomedicine.

Linking Ecological Psychology and Developmental Biology

There must be something wrong, Ingold reasoned, with a social or cultural anthropology that cannot countenance the fact that human beings are biological organisms that have evolved, and that undergo processes of growth and development, as other organisms do. But there must be something equally wrong with a biological anthropology that denies anything but a proximate role for agency, intentionality or imagination in the direction of human affairs

Identities and characteristics of persons as such are not bestowed on them in advance of their involvement with others but are condensations of histories of growth and maturation within fields of social relationships. Every person emerges as a locus of development within such a field, which is in turn carried forward and transformed through their actions. Understanding persons in this way, however, calls for a kind of "relational thinking". This would require nothing less than a radical, alternative biology. If every organism is seen not as an isolated entity but as a node in a network of relationships, we must rethink both the interdependence of organisms and their environments, as well as their evolution.

5.4.2. Relational Thinking as a Point of Departure

Organism-in-its-Environment, as Opposed to the Self Contained Individual

The characteristics of organisms, Ingold argues then, are not so much expressed as *generated* in the course of development, arising out of emergent properties of the fields of relationship set up through their presence and activity in a particular environment. Here then was the biology which would help to substantiate his view of the organism-person, undergoing growth and development in an environment furnished by the work and presence of others. It is a biology, however, that also resonates very closely with the principles of ecological psychology. Both approaches take as their point of departure the developing organism-in-its-environment, as opposed to the self contained individual confronting a world "out there".

Relational Thinking, Ecological Thinking and Developmental Systems

These parallels led Ingold to suggest that a combination of *"relational"* thinking in anthropology, *"ecological thinking"* on psychology and *"developmental systems"* thinking in biology would yield a powerful synthesis. Crucially such a synthesis would start from a conception of the human being made up of separable but complementary parts, such as body, mind, and culture, but rather as a singular locus of creative growth within a continually unfolding field of relationships.

Humans, he argues, are brought into existence as organism-persons- within a field that is inhabited by beings of manifold kinds, both human and non-human. Therefore relations among humans, which we are accustomed to call "social", are but a sub-set of ecological relations. This brings him onto the nub of what we consider to be his newly global, southern, relational argument, in overall phenomenological, foundational guise. Then we turn to the nub of his "newly global" *southern* thinking, building in prior local *unhu/ubuntu* and worlds-wide, local-global radical consciousness.

5.4.3. Newly Global *Southern* Phenomenology: Livelihood, Dwelling, Skill

Departure From Westernized Neo-Liberal Economics and Enterprise

Ingold's conceptual orientation, as such, is divided into three parts, which altogether serves to distinguish such from the conventional social sciences – in thereby *southern* newly global guise – especially, for us, from duly westernised neo-liberal economics and enterprise. Thereby in his:

- *first orientation*, towards *"livelihood"*, his concern is to find a way of comprehending *how human beings relate to their environments, in the tasks of making a living, that does not set up a polarity between the ecological and cognitive, natural and cultural domains.*
- the *second* part, on *"dwelling"*, explores the implications for our understanding of perception and cognition, architecture and built environment, local and global conceptions of environmental change, of mapping and what her terms, *crucially, wayfinding, not enterprise.*
- In the third part on *"skill"*, he focuses on practical enskillment, thereby overcoming the divide between works of human beings and non-human animals, and between art and technology.

Differentiates Between a "Building" and "Dwelling" Perspective

Starting then with livelihood, Ingold *differentiates between a "building" and "dwelling" perspective;* needless to say he favours the latter over the former. The essence of the building perspective is that *worlds are made before they are lived in*; or in other words, that acts of dwelling are preceded by acts of world-making. Human beings then inhabit the various houses of culture, pre-erected upon the universal ground of nature.

Among non-human animals, it is widely supposed, there can be no significant change in built form that is not bound to evolutionary changes in the essential form of the species. With human beings, by contrast, built form is free to vary independently of biological constraint, and to follow developmental pathways of its own, effectively decoupled form the process of evolution. To explode such a myth *requires nothing less than the dissolution of the dichotomy, which in modern scholarship separates the biological sciences from the humanities, between evolution and history, or between the temporal processes of nature and culture.*

Ingold's Dwelling Perspective: Akomolafe's Humanity in Search of Home

The German phenomenologist Martin Heidegger asks what it means to build and to dwell, and what the relation is between the two – between building and dwelling. He begins with what might be taken as a hegemonic view, as enshrined in the discourse on Western modernity. This is that building and dwelling are separable but complementary activities. He tackles the issue through an exercise in etymology. The current German word for the verb "to build", *bauen*, comes from the old English an High German *buan* meaning "to dwell". "I dwell, you dwell" is identical, for Ingold reflecting on the Sami peoples in the Arctic circle, to "I am, because you are", for Biko as for Magosvongwe in Southern Africa.

Yet *bauen* also means to preserve, to care for, to cultivate or to till. And then it also means to construct, to make something, to raise up an edifice. Both these modern senses of building – as cultivation and construction – are thus shown to be encompassed within the more fundamental sense of dwelling. In the course of time this sense has fallen into disuse, such that *bauen* has been used exclusively for cultivation and construction. Heidegger's concern is to regain the original perspective, so that we can once again understand how the activities of building – of cultivation and construction – belong to our dwelling in the world, to the way we are. Only if we are capable of dwelling, only then can we build, thereby echoing Bayo's search for home.

Philosophy of Freedom: Emergent Outcomes of Developmental Processes

What this means, for Heidegger as for Ingold, is that the forms people build, whether in the imagination or on the ground, arise within the current of their involved activity, in the specific relational contexts of their practical engagement with their surroundings. The forms of organisms, as such, are no more prefigured in their genes but are the emergent outcomes of environmentally situated developmental processes. For Steiner, analagously as such, there are no limits to the powers of human thought.

We can now see, by adopting a dwelling perspective, that it is possible to dissolve the orthodox dichotomies between evolution and history, between biology and culture. It is not necessary, then, to evoke one kind of naturally constructed hut, and another kind, of cultural history, to account for the transition from hut to skyscraper. For once history is recognized itself as an evolutionary process, the point of origin constituted by the intersection of evolutionary and historical continua disappears. Moroever, and in Iqbal's terms – see above – bridges are constructed between the ancient and the modern.

The House as Organism: Bridging the Ancient and the Modern

The form of a tree, according to Ingold, is no more given, as an immutable fact of nature, as per *ivhu,* than is the form of the house, as per *unhu,* as an imposition of one human mind in relation to another. Recall the many inhabitants of the tree: the fox, the owl, the squirrel, the ant, the beetle, among countless others. All, through their various activities of dwelling, have played their part in creating the conditions under which the tree, over the centuries, has grown to assume its particular form and proportions. And so too have human beings, in tending the tree's surroundings.

Building then is a process that is continually going on, for as long as people dwell in the environment. It does not begin with a pre-formed plan, and end there with a finished product. We may indeed describe the forms in our environment as instances of architecture, but for the most part we are not architects. For it is in the very process of dwelling that we build.

Radical Empiricism: Activity Embedded in a Social Relation Is a Task

To see an activity, in fact, embedded in a social relation is to regard *it,* in Ingold's terms, empirically so to speak, as a skill or a task. And of all the manifold tasks that make up the total current of activities in a community, there are none that can be set aside as belonging to a separate category of "work", nor is there any separate status of being a "worker". For work is life, and any distinctions one might make within the course of life would be not between work and non-work, but between different fields of activity, such as farming, cooking, weaving, and child-minding.

In Ancient Greece, for example, we do not find the idea of one great human function, work, encompassing all trades, but rather a plurality of different trades, each with their different technical operations and qualities required of the practitioners. If there was any overarching division, it was not between work and leisure, but between the spheres of making and doing, *poiesis* and *praxis*.

We now turn, globally-locally, to the *Keynotes* of phenomenology, as a whole, as the emergent foundation for our relational path and learning community, as well as our *southern* African grounds for Communitalism.

5.5. Acting Global-Local/S2a: Phenomenological *Keynotes*: Kumusha and Nhakanomics

5.5.1. Southern Relational Foundation

There are four global-local key tenets of phenomenology. These are, respectively, the following:

Phenomenology – Immersed in an African Lifeworld
Immersed in an *African Life World*: Kumusha
Concentrate on Illuminating the Natural-Cultural *"Inner Self"*.
Locate *Unique History* as an Episode in a larger Story
Go *Beyond Reductive* Positivism and naïve Empiricism.

5.5.2. Immerse Yourself in an African Life World: Kumusha

Phenomenology, for Biko as for Husserl, has as its exclusive concern experiences intuitively seizable in their essence, in the former case as revealed via Black Consciousness, not empirically perceived and treated as empirical facts. Further, it seeks to avoid all impositions placed on experience in advance, whether these are drawn from religious or cultural traditions, from everyday commonsense, or indeed from science itself. Explanations are not to be imposed before the phenomena have been understood from within. In the specific Zimbabwe case, by way of example, with which we are here concerned, thereby turning social research into innovation, enterprise-wise, the integral *kumusha* comes prominently into play. Such a kumusha turns the local, rural homestead into an *oikos*, so to speak, drawing on the ancient Greek model of household, ecology and economy, but in duly Southern African, *shona* Zimbabwean indigenous guise, thereby building on local *ukama* – relationships.

5.5.3. Illuminate the Natural/Cultural Nhaka Laden "Inner Self"

Husserl sees phenomenology as putting the study of culture or "spirit" on a proper scientific footing. In that guise, and locally-globally, for Biko and Magosvongwe as for Okomolafe (indigenous African) for Brazier (Buddhist Asian) as for Steiner (central European), for Locke and Hume (Anglo-Saxon) as for Iqbal (Islam), the same applies in their respective cultures. In that context your "life world" underlies your intentional experiences. They saw such a particular life world as the universal framework of human endeavor – including our scientific endeavours. It is the ultimate horizon of all human achievement. For the Taranhike's, as we shall see, what is key is to build on *nhaka*, that is indigenous for "legacy" – spiritually and materially as such.

5.5.4. Locate Your Unique Cultural History as an Episode in the Larger Story

Husserl's *Crisis of the European Sciences*, could for us, be reinterpreted as a *Crisis of the Sciences Worlds-wide*. Such a crisis for us, especially located in the African *South*, but with also a worlds-wide, local-global perspective, is an attempt to alert the world to the need for a "newly global" scientific and philosophical outlook, which has a local, African origination, and a truly worlds-wide foundation, thereby becoming also emancipatory, in southern guise. As such we need to purposefully feel local, intuit local-global, and think newly global in such *southern*, phenomenological guise, before applying our global-local keynotes. In the specific Zimbabwean case with which we are involved, via the Taranhike's, the marriage of culture and community with science and technology is something particular to a society which, while retaining its local identity has succeeded in co-evolving, at least in their case, a global integrity.

5.5.5. Go Beyond Reductive Positivism and naïve Empiricism

Science, for Husserl, comes from a very special theoretical attitude, one of detached playfulness and curiosity. Galileo, for example, had displaced our immediate forms of lived experience with forms of objects as dictated by these qualities. If the objects produced in this play are then uncritically asserted, without reference to their subjective intent, to be the real objects of our experience in the life world, then serious problems will arise. We all then have the potential to be a Galileo, to thereby revolutionize the activity with which we are engaged, because of our love for what we do, and our passion to be authentic.

For us, in Africa and the African diaspora, Galileo needs to be replaced by the likes of Bayo Akomalafe (2017), and his evocative *Wilds Beyond our Fences: Letters to My Daughter on Humanity's Search for Home*.

We are now ready to conclude.

5.6. Conclusion: Towards an Integral Kumusha in Zimbabwe

Emerging Phenomenological Southern Relational Nhakanomic Foundation

In conclusion then, we anticipate in such *southern* African, phenomenological guise, the *Integral Kumusha* we will meet in our first case story (ICS1), in

Zimbawe, whereby, via the Taranhikes, phenomenologically in this foundational case, we will:

- Immerse ourselves in their *unhu/ivhu* communal laden, local life worlds
- Concentrate on illuminating the natural-cultural *inner self* of "black consciousness" in Biko-like, local-global guise
- Locate the *unique cultural history* of their integral kumusha in the nely global story of livelihood, dwelling and enskillment that Ingold reveals
- Going *beyond reductive* positivism and naive empiricism in a now global-local light as revealed by the Taranhike's via *nhakanomics*.

Originally Grounded Descriptively in Southern Kumusha Guise

Moreover, such an emergent foundation, standing on the shoulders of Magosvongwe, Biko, Ingold and now the Taranhike's in particular, we will also build on prior descriptive grounds, whereby they:

- Seek to reveal the Essences and Origins of *human Experience.*
- Engage their total Selves as Participants, *passionately Involved*
- *Do not seek to predict* or to determine causal Relationships
- Illuminate these through *comprehensive Descriptions*, vivid and accurate Renderings of Experience, rather than Measurements or Ratings.

Along that relational way, research and innovation wise, moroever, we pave the further way toward communal learning, communiversity wise specifically, and an emergent foundation for community building enterprise wise, and communitalism economically, generally. We now turn from southern African descriptive method by way of original, relational grounding, and phenomenological methodology, by way of emergent relational foundation, to southern African feminism. Before we do that though, we will turn to our first case story, that is our Integral Kumusha.

Towards an Integral Kumusha in Southern Africa

Altogether then, and in conclusion, social research wise, in Table 5.6. below we summarise the integral phenomenological case, in Southern Africa, and in our first case story, our focus will be on Kumusha-like enterprise innovation to follow, thereby community building on the Southern African relational path.

Table 5.6. *Towards an Integral Kumusha in Southern Africa S2fita*

Feeling Local	Intuiting Local-Global	Thinking Newly Global	Acting Global-Local
Unhu/Ubuntu/ *Search for Home*	*Phenomenological* *Foundation*	*Livelihood,* *Dwelling,* *Enskillment*	*Integral Kumusha in* *Southern* *Africa*

5.7. References

Akomolafe B (2017) *These Wilds Beyond Our Fences: Letters to My Daughter on Humanity's Search for Home.* Berkeley, California. North Atlantic Books

Biko S (1987) *I Write What I Like.* London. Heinemann African Writers Series

Brazier C (2003) *A Buddhist Psychology.* London. Robinson Publishing

Heron J (1994) *Feeling and Personhood.* Abingdon. Routledge

Husserl E (1970) *The Crisis of the European Sciences.* Chicago. Northwestern University Press

Husserl E (2012) *Ideas: General Introduction to Pure Phenomenology.* Abingdon. Routledge Classics

Ingold T (2011) *The Perception of the Environment: Essays on Livelihood, Dwelling and Skill.* Abingdon. Routledge

Iqbal M (2000) *The Reconstruction of Religious Thought in Islam.* New Delhi. Kitab Bhavan

Lessem R and **Schieffer** A (2009) *Transformation Management: Toward the Integral Enterprise*

Lessem R, **Mawere** M and **Taranhike** D (2019) *Integral Kumusha.* Mazvingo. Africa Talent Publishers

Magosvongwe R (2016) Shona philosophy of Unhu/Hunhu and its Onomastics in Selected Fictional Narratives. *Journal of African Literature Association* 10 (2): 158–175

Moran D (2012) *Husserl's Crisis of the European Sciences.* Cambridge. Cambridge University Press

Some P (1999) *The Healing Wisdom of Africa.* New York. Jeremy Tarcher

Thiam C (2017) *Return to the Kingdom of Childhood.* Ohio. Ohio State University

Welburn C (2004) *Rudolf Steiner's Philosophy and the Crisis of Contemporary Thought.* Edinburgh. Floris Books

Chapter 6 From Phenomenology to Southern Feminism. Re-Inventing Africa

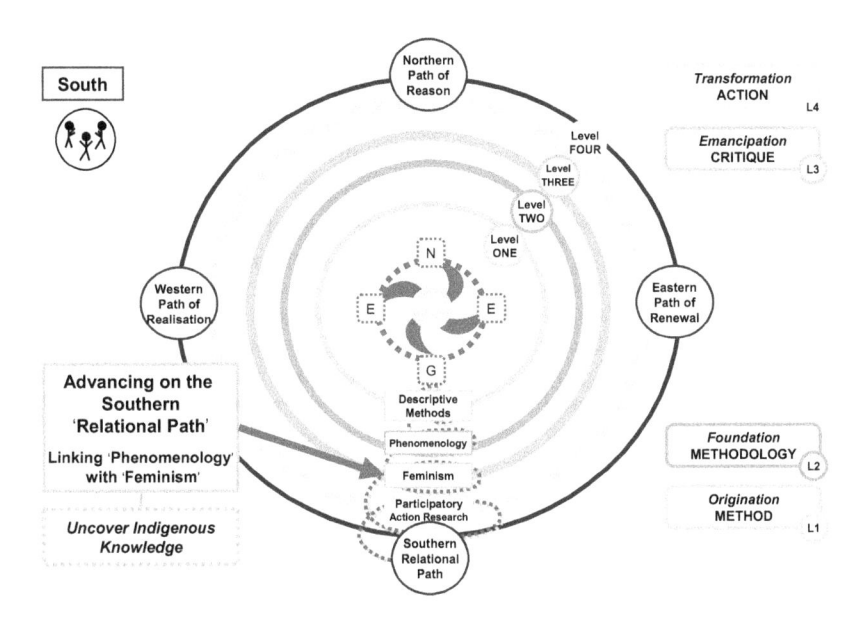

Figure 6.1: *Overview Chapter 6 – Level 3 / South*

Colonialism and capitalism transformed land and soil which form a source of life and a commons from which people draw sustenance, was converted into private property to be bought and sold and conquered; development, continued as colonialism's unfinished task. Sovereignty thus shifted from the soil and soil-linked communities to sovereignty of the nation-state. In this way organic communities gave way to slum dwellers or urban and industrial jungles. Devel-opment has converted soil from sacred mother into disposable object – to be ravaged for minerals that lie below, or drowned beneath gigantic reservoirs. The soil's children, too, have been made disposable: mines and dams leave behind wastelands and uprooted people.

Mies and Shiva (2014)   *Eco-Feminism*

Summary: Feminism in Africa and Worlds-wide: A Tool for Liberation

- Advancing the southern path, we are now entering its critical and emancipatory realm (level 3), where we meet feminism, and give expression to marginalised voices. Feminism, seemingly originating in Europe and America in the 1950s and 1960s, but which we have considered initially and alternatively in African guise, could be considered, as such, as a further, worldly-wise, development of Husserl's phenomenology, as poignantly illustrated by Nigerian American anthropologist Imi Imidiume through her *Re-inventing Africa.*

- Feminism emerged as an organized movement of social theories, moral philosophies, economic and political thought, all focused on the emancipation of women from a perceived subordination to men. With an increasingly broadening focus, feminism can now be regarded as a grassroots movement that does not only focus on gender issues, but seeks to cross boundaries based on social class, race, culture and religion, recently championing the cause of indigenous peoples. Its most thoroughgoing example locally-globally, worldwide, is in Rojava in Kurdish Northern Syria

- Feminist epistemology studies the ways in which gender does and ought to influence our conceptions of knowledge, the knowing subject, and practices of inquiry and justification. It identifies ways in which dominant conceptions and practices of knowledge systematically disadvantage women and other subordinated groups and strives to transform these conceptions and practices so that they serve the interests of these groups.

- The central concept of feminist epistemological analysis is that of a situated knower, and hence of situated knowledge: knowledge that reflects the particular perspectives of the subject. Further key tenets of the feminist emancipatory orientation is that it aims to create social change, whereby it sees knowledge as a tool for liberation (not domination), that it strives to represent, and express, human and natural diversity and sees itself as complementary to an androcentric perspective.

- For a newly global African approach to feminism, on the relational path to emancipation, we focus here on Ugandan-Swedish educationalist Catherine Hoppers' "Indigenous Knowledge Systems". For Hoppers, any dynamic knowledge system has to evolve through the continuance of traditional knowledge and contemporary innovations, and this should be pursued by individuals as well as communities. The present knowledge framework, however, lets knowledge flow in one direction only and excludes indigenous knowledge.

- Finally, and globally-locally, for transformative effect, we actively pursue four keynotes of feminism, in African relational guise, thereby *complementing androcentric* way, *inclusive of the person and of nature,* aiming for *social change,* drawing on *knowledge as a tool for liberation.*

6.1. Global Orientation to Feminism

6.1.1. Entering the Third Emancipatory Level of the Southern Relational Path

We now turn from the first and second to the third level of our Integral Research and *Innovation* relational path and re-GENE-rative trajectory, that is, research-wise, from descriptive methods and methodology ("phenomenology") to now critique ("feminism"), and, in a Southern African context innovation-wise, from origination (kumusha), and foundation (integral kumusha) to emancipation (nhakanomics). As we thereby progressively broaden and deepen our research and innovation base, so feminism can be identified with an ever wider range of marginalised people and beliefs, as well as specifically with an emancipatory form of community building/ communitalist Southern African enterprise and economy. As as been specifically illustrated moreover, in a Zimbabwean context (see opening case story below), we thereby advance from *kumusha* micro wise to *nhakanomics* macro wise.

Table 6.1.1. *"Southern" African Relational Path of Social Research to Innovation: Descriptive to Participatory via FEMINISM Kumusha to Nhakanomics*

Southern Grounding Method and Origination	Southern Emergence Methodology and Foundation	Southern Navigation Critique and *Emancipation*	Southern Effect Action and *Transformation*
Descriptive Methods (S1)	Phenomen-ological Method-ology (S2)	Feminist Critique (S3)	Participatory Action Research (S4)
Kumusha (S1)	Integral Kumusha (S2)	Nhaka-Nomics (S3)	Vaka-Musha (S4)

If then you engage in feminism, in African guise, you build on prior (S1) descriptive method and relational origination (see Table 6.1.1.). As such you have (at our first level) grounded your research in a richly descriptive approach to a both problematic and propitious life world, and rooted your prospective innovation in an initial response to both of such. Subsequently (S2), you drew on phenomenology as a distinct methodology, and engaged with a particular life world, accordingly. You deepen and broaden your involvement with an individual and communal, organisational and societal phenomenon, and began to purposefully seek to transform the troubled context therein, centred in the healing wisdom of Africa.

As such you have covered the first two levels of the southern relational path of your research, and innovation, project.

6.1.2. Emancipatory: Feminism, Critical Theory, Postmodern, Critical Realism

However, as a "would be social innovator", most especially set within the kind of African research academy, and communiversity, to which we have alluded, our Centre for Integral research and Societal Re-GENE-ration (SRRC), you will need, in particular, to span the third emancipatory level (S3), as you now move into critical terrain. The major critical methodologies, and emancipatory orientations, are:

Table 6.1.2. *Critical Emancipatory Methodologies (Level 3 of Integral Research in Africa and the Diaspora)*

Relational Critique and Emancipatory Path: Southern Africa	Engaging in Feminism, Giving Voice to the Marginalised	Focus of this Chapter
Renewal based Critique and Emancipatory Path:: East Africa	Building on Critical Theory, Liberating the Oppressed	
Reason based Critique and Emancipatory Path: North Africa	Taking on Postmodernism, Embracing Discontinuity & Complexity	
Realisation based Critique and Emancipatory Path: West Africa	Acommodating Critical Realism, Challenging the Prevailing System	

The trajectory we assume in this section is the third level of the relational path, now engaging with feminism, and giving voice to the marginalised, most especially for us in the global South. Let us first retrace steps to what feminism is all about, by way of orientation, before we turn specifically to Africa, where we "feel local" form the outset, before intuiting local-global, making our way, critically and vitally, towards a newly global, rooted in the global South, before identifying global-local Keynotes.

6.1.3. Origins of Feminism as an Emancipatory Movement and Methodology

Josephine Donovan (2000) identifies early *Liberal Feminism*, albeit for us in "western" guise, as a daughter of the Enlightenment. Thinkers like Mary Wollstonecraft and Sarah Grimké provided an 'image of a woman as a rational, responsible agent; one who is able, if given a chance to take care of herself, to further her own possibilities. These early thinkers shared a belief in a combination of relationality and rationality; a belief that both genders are ontologically the same; the belief that critical thinking is an effective way to transform society; the view that an individual is an isolated entity who operates as a rational independent agent.

Those were the early thinkers, with Africa out of the picture. Feminism can now be described as an organized movement of social theories, moral philosophies, economic and political thought, all focused on the liberation of women from a perceived subordination to men. Many feminists are concerned with practices and social, political, economic inequalities that discriminate against women. Some have argued that gendered and sexed identities, even "man" and "woman", are socially constructed.

6.1.4. Feminism's Many Forms: Social to Scientific and Technological

Several subtypes of feminist *ideology* have developed in the late 20th century, primarily in Europe and America. Early feminists and primary feminist movements are often called the first-wave feminists, and feminists after about *1960* the second-wave feminists. More recently, some younger feminists have identified themselves as *third-wave feminists*, although the second-wave feminists are still active.

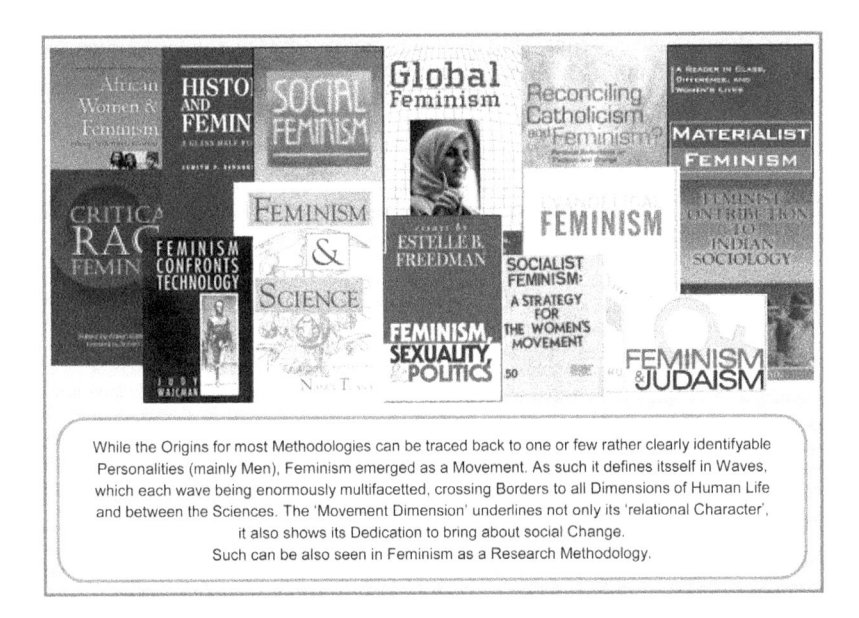

Figure 6.1.3: *Multifacetted Feminism*

6.1.4. In Feminism the Natural and Social Worlds are Socially Reconstructed

Feminism then, emerging in Europe and America in the 1950s and 1960s, could be considered as a further, reformative development of Husserl's phenomenology. Both methodologies take "personal experience" as a starting point. However, some researchers claim, that in phenomenology, the experience is more important than the external happening that is experienced. A phenomenologist gets therefore sometimes criticized as idealist, where the internal experience is the matter of contemplation. Feminism, on the other hand, focuses on what happens external to the impacted entity: it can hence be called a more realistic position than phenomenology.

The ontological claims of feminism are that both the natural and social worlds are socially constructed, and that these worlds are constructed differently by people who, in different locations, have different life experiences, for example men and women. Feminist epistemology, moreover, substitutes women's experiences for men's. Conventional dualisms such as fact/value, objective/subjective, reason/emotion, and the separation of the knower and the known are rejected as part of androcentric epistemology.

6.1.5. What is Wrong with Conventional Science?

Feminism, for us from a "north-western" perspective, has provided a collection of themes about what is wrong with conventional science, and what kind of social science will overcome such, that can be summed up in the following way:

Table 6.1.5. *Feminism – Core Themes*

Metabolism of Subject and Field	Deals with the Problem of Objectivity, proposing the Notion of "Dynamic Objectivity" or of the "Metabolism of Subject and Field" as if they are one Organism
New Materialism	Deals with the "New Materialism" in which Knowledge is to be grounded in personal Experience
Socio-Historical Location	Deals with the Problem of the socio-historical Location of the Researcher
Reflexive Nature of Social Enquiry	Deals with the reflexive Nature of Social Enquiry, whereby the Researcher needs to reflect, continually, on him or herself
Social Sciences as new Paradigm	Proposes that the Social Sciences, not Physics, should be the Paradigm for all Sciences
Nature is active and complex	Deals with the Recognition that Nature is active and complex, adopting an Ecological or Open Systems Approach
Knowledge for Liberation	Knowledge should be used as a Tool for Liberation not Domination

6.1.6. Feminism as an Epochal Shift

Feminism , in the final analysis by way of global orientation, has also gained power and influence by being more closely aligned with the environmental movement, as American anthropologist David Abram's (1997) *Spell of the Sensuous* (see Chapter 4) has indicated. As described by the American social philosopher Richard Tarnas (1991), in his *Passion of the Western Mind*, feminism heralds a complete ground-shift in our societal consciousness. Feminism for him is the most important movement of our times.

> Man now faces the existential crisis of being a solitary ego thrown into an ultimately unknowable universe. And he faces the psychological and biological crisis of living in a world that has come to be shaped in such a way that it precisely matches his world view – in a man made environment that is increasingly mechanistic, atomized, soulless, and self destructive. The crisis of modern man is an essentially masculine crisis, and I believe that the resolution is already now occurring in the tremendous emergence of the feminine in our culture: visible not only in the rise of feminism, the growing empowerment of women, and the widespread opening up to feminine values by both men and women, but also in the increasing sense of unity with the planet and all forms of nature on it, in the increasing awareness of the ecological, in the growing embrace of the human community, in the accelerating collapse of long standing ideological and political barriers separating the world's peoples, in the deepening recognition of the value and necessity of partnership, pluralism and the interplay of many perspectives.

We now turn from our global (Euro-American) orientation to Feminism to locating it, thereby to begin with, feeling locally, in the African continent, with a view, thereafter, having intuited locally globally, to think newly globally out of Africa prior to ultimately acting globally-locally. All of such, moreover, provides the inner directed, integral research orientation for the innovation to follow (see especially our Southern African case story above). We start then with Imi Amadiumi, with her local feel, thereby re-inventing Africa in that feminist light.

6.2. Feel Local: Grounding/Originating Feminism in Africa: S3f

6.2.1. Reinventing Africa: Matriarchy, Religion and Culture

The African Origin of Civilisation: Myth or Reality

Nigerian born social anthropologist and poet Ifi Amadiume (1997), based at Dartmouth College, New Hampshire in America, in her seminal work on *Reinventing Africa: Matrarchy, Religion and Culture* implies in her critique of Senegalese philosopher Cheikh Anto Diop's (1987) renowned macro history – *The African Origin of Civilisation: Myth or Reality* – that he ignored the base, that is the very foundations of the socio-political systems he described.

He placed emphasis on the kings and queens and not the people: he looked at cities and not villages; he focused more on centralized systems and not what he called the clan systems – in short, African communities. Yet every conceivable African political system had communities at its base. What, for her, are the social forms of organization of these communities? This she reckons seems to be a subject given least importance by "typically male" African academics.

Pre-Colonial Africa: No Transition from Matriarchy to Patriarchy

Yet Diop in fact postulated, from the outset, four cradles or histories of kinship and gender: Africa as the agricultural matriarchal south, Europe as the nomadic patriarchal north, the Mediterranean basin as the middle belt where matriarchy preceded patriarchy, and Western Asia as the zone of confluence. However, in all the so called scientific comparative reconstructions by nineteenth century theorists, African data were left out. It is significant that it is such African data that effectively overturned theories of a general evolution of kinship. For in pre-colonial Africa there was no transition from matriarchy to patriarchy.

Diop characterized the Aryan Greek and Roman cultures of Europe as idealizing the patriarchal family, war, violence and conquest. Guilt, original sin and individualism pervaded their moral ethics. The historical experience of African women was different, since they had relative structural power in all institutions of social organization. In piecing together, then, the "shattered diamond", in order to reconstruct Africa, men are constructing masculinist history contrary to social facts. This is the crux of the difference between Amadiume's and Diop's formulation of African matriarchy.

Diop said there was a harmonious dualism between men and women. Amadiume, on the contrary, argues that there were two contesting systems, the balance tilting and changing all the time. However, men and women were able to cross gender boundaries.

6.2.2. Mkpuke, Matricentric unit and Obi, Male-Focused Ancestral House

Compassion/Love/Peace – "Umunne"; Competition/Valor/Force – "Umunna"

The ideology of gender upon which her work was based then had its basis in the binary opposition between the mkpuke, the female mother-focused matricentric unit and the obi, the male-focused ancestral house. They formed interrelating systems representing different values such as compassion/love/peace in the ideology of "umunne", the spirit of common motherhood, and competitiveness/ valor/force in the ideology of "Umunna", common fatherhood. Interestingly enough we find such a combination represented by Christina and Daud Shumba (the *shumba* totem meaning lion) in the *Integral Kumusha* case story above.

The Nnobi social structure, the *mkpuke*, as an autonomous household-based unit, is reproduced in the wider political order in which the whole of Nnubi are bound as children of a common mother – the goddess Idemili, the deity worshipped by all Nnobi. Administratively and in political decision making, the human representatives of the goddesses are the arch matriarchs, the *Ekwe* titled women, leaders of the marketplaces and the Women's Council, a formal political organization of all women of Nnobi, which includes men. Unfortunately, such a society-wide political/economic model has not been adopted in Zimbabwe.

A Common Humanity, "Mmadu", Opposed to the European Concept of Man

The *Ekwe* system formed a political matriarchal system in binary opposition to the patriarchal one. Both systems are in a dialectical relationship. A bridge between these systems is achieved through a third classificatory social system: a non-gendered one, using a universalistic term for *a common humanity, "mmadu"*, human being, as opposed to the European concept of man. Such a matricentric structure, for Amadiume, moreover, is present in all West African societies. In Nnobi mythology specifically, the goddess Idemli is culture, while the male deity Aho-bi-na-agu lives in the wild.

The Matricentric Unit of Production Has Been Invisible in African Studies

The most important production unit for her – the matricentric unit, the basic structure of African society and common to all African social structures – has been invisible in the theoretical formulations of African Studies. Yet the moral values which this system generated constitute the basis of affective relationships so needed as an alternative to the present political structure of violence underlying, for Amadiume, all the current problems of Africa. She consequently proposes that gender be given a central place in social inquiry and critical analysis, whereby anthropology, with its hitherto racial overtones, change into a combination of social history and sociology of history.

6.2.3. The Dual-Sex Character of Political Systems Is Uniquely African

A Characteristic Uniquely African as a Form of Self-Rule

In fact, for Amadiume, there are two unique and specific contributions that African women have made to world history and civilization. The first is matriarchy as a fundamental ideological and social base on which African kinship and wider social and moral systems rest. The second is directly related to this matriarchal factor. This is the dual-sex character of political systems, a characteristic uniquely African as a form of self-rule, that is sovereignty or autonomy, as the ultimate goal of social groups, African women achieved this autonomy via their social institutions of women's organizations and councils.

A Woman's Power Was Based on Her Central Economic Role

Africans were basically agriculturalists. The woman was the agriculturalist while the man was the hunter. In Africa, therefore, a woman's power was based on her very important and central economic role. The moral ideals of the system encouraged the matriarchal family, peace and justice, goodness and optimism, and social collectivism. The economic role of women, moreover, was not confined to the household and wider-kin corporate units. They managed and controlled a very extensive market network where they were selling and buying.

6.2.4. Markets' Basic Need to Exchange, Redistribute, Socialize

Described as Subsistence, Communal, and Redistribution Economies

These women's marketplaces were also social places where outings were held after life-cycle ceremonies involving birth, marriage, and death. Markets and marketing were not governed by pure profit values, but the basic need to exchange, redistribute and socialize. That is why traditional African systems were not capitalist economies. They have been variously described as subsistence, communal, and redistribution economies, for us thereby "communalist" rather than capitalist or socialist. The most women would gain from being wealthy was the right to belong to prestigious associations, such as titles societies, and leadership of the various women's organizations including the Women's Council.

These Women's Councils constituted the leadership of women's autonomous government to which all women of specific villages belonged. In most cases, these women leaders were crowned queens by women themselves. If they abused their power or authority, women themselves removed them. These queens reigned inside the marketplace, which they kept in order. At the same time, they were simply titled women. In fact, there were two governments, that of men and women, which were supposed to respect each other's opinions. But for general matters everyone met at the village open assembly. Every human being had the right, there, to voice an opinion.

The Majority of African Societies Were Anti-Centralist, Non-State Systems

The majority of African societies, for Amadiume as such, were anti-centralist, non-state systems. However, in the seventeenth and eighteenth centuries, these were undergoing tremendous changes as a result of pressures from slave mercenary armies and slave merchants. Protected by no military strong kings and armies, they suffered continuous raiding. In the eyes of the colonialists, and slave traders, women were not considered as sacred.

African Sisterhood Compared with European Feminism

Economically Successful Women Titled "Ekwe" Aligned with Goddess Idemili

In fact, hitherto for Amadiume, the women had a socio-economic base from which they could accumulate wealth. They could also transform material wealth into prestigious titles and political power. For example, economically successful women could be aligned with the Goddess Idemili to take her title of "Ekwe". In this system spirit possession is not an articulation of powerless-ness resulting from invasion by alien spirits but a direct call to leadership.

All social and cultural activities, moreover, linked such women with surrounding communities, forming a regional system. Through the rotating periodic markets, shared ceremonies, marriages, organizations, trade and other cultural activities, women enjoyed a very extensive communication network which men did not. This is also true of most Igbo societies, which is why women could be mobilized across several communities.

Given such a history of the prominence of women in African social structures, such as women's institutions around the marketplace, it is not surprising that women's historical struggles have centred on two issues. They are: autonomy, that is women's self government, which has brought about the conflict between women's organizations and male control of these, and women's struggle to retain control over the marketplace, the spinal chord of the subsistence economy.

African Women's Fundamental Concern with Self-Organization and Economy

African women, therefore, have been concerned with the fundamental social issues of the self-organization and the economy. The evidence points to a simple explanation for this perpetual concern. It is the fact that there was an alternative system: a matriarchal system which was in opposition to the patriarchal one, even though both systems were in cooperation with each other in a shared social space. This matriarchy was both a social and an economic, ideological system. It is not the direct opposite to patriarchy.

African Women Do Not Understand Sisterhood Individualistically

African women do not understand sisterhood individualistically, as the European women. Female solidarity in the African context is fundamentally associated with the culture of matriarchy and the ideology of motherhood, whereas motherhood has negative connotations in Western feminist concepts. For African women, matriarchy was a means of institutional and ideological empowerment. Instead of dictating to African women on so called conservation and development, Western women would do well to concentrate their efforts on deconstructing history and the dialectic of racism and imperialism, the very historical link and divide between themselves and us Africans.

In fact, as we shall now see, it is almost as if in Rojava in Kurdish Northern Syria, that is Western Kurdistan, now in MENA – the Middle East and North Africa – has taken on from where Amadiume in West Africa has left off, albeit some centuries later. As such, and specifically in the context of our relational path to research and innovation, locally-globally, worlds-wide, Kurdish *jinealoji* (women's knowing), as we shall see, becomes a beacon of new knowledge and value creating light. Although as such we part physically from the continent of Africa, existentially we continue to evolve in an integrally "southern" light.

6.3. Intuit Local Global: Emergent Art of Freedom: S2i

6.3.1. The Kurdish Liberation Struggle

Havin Guneser (2021), writing in her *The Art of Freedom: A Brief History of the Kurdish Liberation Struggle,* is a long-time follower of, and spokesperson for, the work of the leading Kurdish philosopher and activist Abdullah Ocalan (2023) in general theory and specific Rojava practice.

The revolution in Kurdish Rojava, in Northern Syria, for her, was not a spontaneous miracle, but the result of forty years of organizing. The "vision of free life", and the organizational structures to support it, was originally established in pre-revolutionary Syria, and has thereafter been an ongoing struggle to realize. By the time Assad's army retreated from the northeast in 2012, the region was already organized in decentralised democratic committees – as an alternative to the nation-state. This system is now described as democratic confederalism. Where did such all come from?

6.3.2. Bookchin, Braudel, Wallerstein, Frank, and Emancipatory Tradition

Democratic Modernity the Outcome of Kurdish Revolutionary Politics

In fact in worlds-wide dialogue with the works of Russian-American social ecologist Murray Bookchin (2023), French macro-historian Fernand Braudel (Wallerstein 2004) and U.S based world systems analyst Immanuel Wallerstein (Braudel 1995), as well as Dutch development economist Andre Gunder Frank (Ghosh 2019), exogenously, combined with the emancipatory aspects of the Kurdish tradition, indigenously, Ocalan (2007) has developed his critique of capitalist modernity. Under the guise now of so-called "*democratic modernity*", this is *the* outcome also, as indicated above, *of a forty year experience of Kurdish revolutionary politics.*

In Rojava Academies and Learning Communities Are Everywhere

Kurdish revolutionaries over that period have proposed a synthesis of spontaneity and consciousness, insisting that we need to build the fact of the future in the present and organize in a way that by its very nature prefigures the democratic society. For Havin, moreover, education is central to any such revolutionary project, and in Rojava academies and universities are everywhere. If then Rojava is a revolution of life, education is seen as the revolution's most privileged aspect.

Educational practices are not limited to formal spaces, however. Rather people are educated in the street markets, meetings councils and committees, for us, altogether, as learning communities, activating Community, Awakening jineolojical consciousness, instigating Research and innovation, altogether Embodied in confederal as well as democratic developments.

Autonomous Cantons: Democracy Without a State

Revolutionaries then in Rojava have created a democratic nation, an autonomous region where Kurds, Arabs, Turkmen, Assyrians, Armenians, and Christians have instituted a nonethnic collective political structure of autonomous cantons run by councils, committees, and assemblies, a democracy without a state, altogether, for us, engaged in. an ongoing transformation journey, from Calling to Contribution, in their particular Context through variegated processes of Co-creation.

6.3.3. Critique/Self Critique: Democratic Modernity

Nation-States Imposed Everywhere

For Havin then, the quest for freedom that started on the basis of something very physical and very identifiable, the oppression, colonisation and annihilation of Kurdish people, moved on from there to become a quest for freedom in general and a questioning of the very meaning of life, for us from original communal Grounding to Emergent transcultural foundation, with oppression invariably in between, with a view to Emancipatory, scientific Navigation (jinealoji) toward transformational economic Effect, thereby transcending capitalism.

In fact, in the Middle East for her, the former state structures, which were empires that were not based on one nation or one ethnic identity but were autonomous structures of different tribes or ethnic groups, were deemed to be backward. The new then nation-states, an important pillar of the capitalist system, began to be imposed everywhere. For us then, rather than building locally-globally on the trans-cultural, emergent foundations of such empires, towards a "newly global", for Ocalan as for Bookchin, "confederal" society, in the MENA region, "globalised" states were unliterally imposed.

The very attempt at nation-building meant that various peoples who did not fit the single ethnicity of a nation-state, were eliminated, so that an overarching identity could be built. Because then the Middle East has a far-reaching tradition of different peoples developing as distinct and established communities, the making of nation-states therein has been, for Guneser, much bloodier. In fact the whole world order is constituted of nations and states, so for example, as a victim of genocide, you can't go to the UN because it is a United Nation-States.

Although then the early years of the Turkish Republic included Kurdish representatives in the Turkish Grand Assembly, the republic quickly moved to suppress the Kurdish identity and to enforce a capitalist nation-state based on a single culture/ethnicity/ religion and language. Such states then both colonised other people and their own. For Ocalan, meanwhile, the task was to recover and interpret the knowledge and truth of the Kurdish people, while the Kurdish freedom movement had been grasping how to live a meaningful life.

Democratic Civilisation and Democratic Modernity as the Integral Truth

From 1999 to 2005 then, Ocalan broke with the idea of a Kurdish state completely. We tend to think of world history in a very linear way. For example, we only look at the struggle of the working class under capitalism, he says, so we don't see the struggle of the colonised people or tribes and clans being sucked into classical civilization as just as important. What Ocalan has tried to do with his theory of democratic civilisation and democratic modernity is to bring all this together as the integral truth, the whole truth. Where has this specifically led?

6.3.4. Jineoloji: Science of Women and Life

Divorce From a Five Thousand Year Patriarchal Tradition

According to Havin Guneser as such, in the beginning, Kurdish women joined the guerrilla forces because of sexism they faced within the feudal tribal structures, for us locally, as well as the fury they felt in the face of the colonialist oppression of the Kurds at the hands of the Turkish state, globally as it were. In 1993, for the first time, autonomous women's units were formed. The subsequent development of their role in self-defence increased their self-confidence, leading to enormous ideological, political and social transformations. In 1995 the YAJK Woman's Association of Kurdistan was formed.

This reaction against the enslavement of women was not just about women. All of this was also connected with stealing surplus product, our ultimately transformative, or in this case, deformative, effect, beginning with women, the result of the overturning of morals – our moral core – had been installed in the matriarchal age. There was talk of an eternal divorce, a divorce from a five thousand year patriarchal tradition, both psychologically and culturally. In 2000 the women broadened their perspective and founded the Party of the Free Women. One can define the period between 1993 and 2003 as a transition period, accompanied by the attempt to establish an alternative to capitalist modernity.

Ideological Slavery, Use of Force, Seizure of Economy From Her

Ocalan determined that women's slavery had been perpetuated at three levels over five thousand years. First there was the construction of ideological slavery, then the use of force, and finally the economy was seized from her, for us, by way of an altogether repressive GENE, stamping out our natural and communal Grounding, inhibiting an Emergent matriarchal culture in the process, and preventing transformative economic Effect due to the by-passing of emancipatory, scientific thereby "newly global". Kurdish Navigation.

Without understanding how masculinity was socially formed, for Ocalan, you cannot analyse the institution of the state and therefore will not accurately define the culture of war and power related to statehood. The seizure of the economy, meanwhile, can be set against the ancient Greek notion of *oikonomia* or management of the home, very much belittled nowadays. To put it simply, for Ocalan, capitalism and the nation state are the monopoly of the tyrannical and exploitative male.

"Democratic Civilisation" Is Constantly Being Exploited

His main thesis therefore is that before patriarchy and state civilisation there was another system in which the position of women in society was very different. Indeed society was matriarchal and had very different principles for sustaining itself, namely sharing and solidarity. Now this "democratic civilisation" has not disappeared but is constantly being exploited and narrowed by patriarchy and by the state. The historical struggle then over the past five thousand years has been between the two, the former constituted of pre-state nomadic villages and agricultural communities.

Thus for him if women's enslavement is not overcome no other form of enslavement can be overcome. Initially, along with women, the wise elders played a positive role in a society that was not based on accumulation and ownership. They ensured communal security and the governance of society. But when voluntary dependence is transformed into authority and usefulness into self interest, it gives way to the instrument of force. An hierarchical and authoritarian structure is essential for a patriarchal society.

Democratic Confederalism, Knowledge For All, Moral and Political Society

Alternately then, for the Kurdish freedom movements:

- The proposal of *democratic confederalism* is not an alternative state but an alternative to the state
- Centred on democracy, women's freedom, and an *ecological society*
- Developing an ideology based on *moral and political society* grounded in solidarity
- Making *knowledge available to all* to prevent a monopoly over knowledge.

Abdullah Ocalan and the Kurdish freedom movement then are not just intellectuals. They are not studying history for the sake of it. Nor are they only operating from a woman's point of view or a class point of view or a people's point of view. For Guneser it is all integral, more of a whole cloth. The idea is not only to problematize capitalism or patriarchy in general but to find a way to surpass them. The key to such, from our integral perspective, and thereby as a "newly global" means of emancipatory, scientific navigation, is so called jineoloji.

Jineoloji: Moral and Political Society, with Women as Its Fulcrum

The middle class, thereby supporting capitalism, views history from the point of view of the state, especially the nation-state. Marxism, for Ocalan – for us the young, not the nature, Marx – alternatively focused on class. His starting point was the moral and political society, with women as its fulcrum. Ocalan called such democratic civilisation. He unites the stories of all the world's oppressed and colonised. Its form today is democratic modernity as opposed to capitalist modernity.

This is why the Kurdish women's freedom movement increasingly involved the concept of *xwebun*, which means "yourself", drawing upon *xwe-parastin*, which means "self defence" and other forms of *xwe* (self). These terms were first introduced by Ocalan, more specifically and indeed especially importantly, alongside *jineoloji*, the latter – women "jin" and knowledge – "loji" born out of feminism, and the struggle for social liberation.

Jineoloji, our "newly global" Kurdish (in MENA feminist terms) means of emancipatory, scientific navigation, is then defined as the science of women, the science of life, the science of how to live together. It is in fact the social science that Kurdish women's revolution rests upon. As such, for Ocalan, there is a need to link philosophy and science. But women's perspectives must develop without interrupting the connections between meaning, life, society and women. Thus jineoloji becomes the science of democratic modernity, thereby involving the reconstruction of science, its reconnection with society, and its dedication to animate, protect and defend, most especially for us MENA, society.

Freedom in Moments of Creation, Liberation, and Life

In the story of the formation of women's identity, for Guneser in fact, there is a connection between quantum (quantum science) and chaos (chaos theory) moments and jineoloji. Ocalan's purpose is to analyse the freedom hidden in moments of creation, liberation, and life, as we see in Rojava, and to contribute to building democratic modernity. It is the ability to create scientific, philosophical, and activist vehicles to express women's potential, in alliance with other forces of democratic modernity.

For this re-creation they have declared: "In the Middle East where many of the first inventions of social life emerged with women's justice, the women's spindle turns once again today to braid jineoloji", providing an ethical point of departure for social science.

In terms of methodology, one of the important critiques advanced by proponents of jineoloji targets rationalism, positivism and the subject-object distinction. What they criticize about narrowly based rationalism is that analytical intelligence and rational thought are not sufficient. Over time, moreover, and with philosophy playing a particular role, rationality came to be defined as male, irrationality attributed to women and colonial peoples. In fact analytical intelligence, for Guneser, was devoid of moral values and empathy.

Jineoloji also critiques positivism for its idea that problems can be resolved, exclusively, mathematically or empirically. Finally, rather than a distinction between subject and object, which lends itself to the creation of hierarchies, the two need to be unified. In the absence of such, typically, the objects become the barbarians, the peoples, and the women excluded from power, or, like nature, they serve "objectively" as a resource.

We Need a Vision of Life and Living That Is Different to That of Capitalism

Every imaginable theoretical infrastructure for Ocalan, like the conventional, ivory tower, conventionally "westernised university", for us, was developed to distance society from the possibility of producing and constructing knowledge for itself. The scientific-technical rationale of domination of nature and society turned science into ideology with positivism as its religion. Several dichotomies are necessary to perpetuate such control, including body/soul, black/white, alive/dead, god/subject, and for us subject/object, individual/community, local/global, north/south, east/west. Therefore we see the gradual development of patriarchal, class, and racial hegemony.

At the same time, jineoloji questions the meaning of life and explores how to live. First of all we need a vision of life and living that is different to that of capitalism. Where capitalism has been successful, for Ocalan, is that, whereas in the past people who were poor would revolt, today they hope to win the lottery, and occupy the place of the oppressor. Guneser now turns to a brief history of jineoloji, for us locally grounded in community, emerging locally-globally and trans-culturally, navigated newly globally Kurdish-wise through such jineolojical science, with a view to transformative political and economic effect.

Jineoloji Integrated into Freedom Movement's Educational Endeavours

In 2015 there was the first conference to establish how the Kurdish freedom movement envisaged jineoloji, laying the basis for its community laden establishment. Then a book introducing it was prepared. The next step was to make sure that jineoloji was integrated into all the freedom movement's educational endeavours. In Northern Kurdistan a jineoloji research academy, journal and research groups was established, and the space for its development and implementation was made available in Rojava.

A Jineoloji Faculty at Rojava University and also a jineoloji academy was then set up in Rojava. Women's research centres were established in three locations in Northern Syria. A woman-and-children only village was established in Jinwar, as for us a socio-economic laboratory. Everyone in Rojava was given an education in jineoloji. A jineoloji committee and academy examined all school books and engaged in dialogue to correct any religionist, positivist, sexist or nationalist mindset. There was also special education for those in positions of responsibility – teachers, self-defence units, healthcare workers, those involved with the economy and in the administration of justice. Overall, in working to overcome the distortion of science, women's roles and contributions as founders, maintainers and developers of society, in order to develop the meaning of social life, was enhanced, for us promoting a transformation journey in each case.

Jin Jiyan Azadi: Women, Life, Freedom – Collective Learning

For Havin, all this involved collective learning, collective discussion, collective moving together, for us communal learning. You could have, for example, three hundred people from civil society coming together at a school. There would be discussion and critique. This would be taped and sent to Kurdish homes. Families – women, men and children – would watch. The problems of the revolution would be discussed. Tools, institutions, organisations that could cause these problems would be reviewed. The process would be repeated across different Kurdish societies.

For her this is what sets the Kurdish freedom movement apart: the fact that the approach rests on, for us emancipatory feminism. In Kurdish the root of the world life is *Jin*, which also means woman, while it also means alive. And that is why they say *Jin Jiyan Azadi* whereby "Azadi" means freedom. Moreover, the Sumerian word from freedom. *Amargi*, also means "returning to mother": women, life, freedom, whereby for us emancipatory navigation is grounded naturally and communally.

6.3.5. Democratic Confederalism and Democratic Nation

"Moral and Political Society", Ecological Industry, Democratic Confederalism

Ocalan then has been looking, overall, at what the foundation of capitalist modernity is, building on three pillars: the first he calls "capitalist society", here meaning the mindset of competition and profit-seeking. The second is industrialism and the third is the nation state as we know it. He then builds democratic modernity on the three contrasting pillars. The first he calls "moral and political society", our moral core, placing women at the centre. Rather than industrialism, Ocalan's second pillar is ecological industry. The third pillar is democratic confederalism rather than the nation-state.

Furthermore, it is important to recognize that the state, for Ocalan, tries to implant law instead of morality, and instead of politics the state established a bureaucratic administration. Moreover, were we to orient industry and technology in a way that benefited moral and political society that would make our lives much easier. However, the pursuit of profit and accumulation only for certain elites increases oppression. Democratic confederalism is then proposed by him for the whole of the Middle East.

Represent People Rather Than Nation-States

The idea here is neither to overemphasize ethnic identities nor to ignore them. In fact, Ocalan proposes a World Confederation of Democratic nations to replace the UN, which currently represents nation-states rather than people. Indeed, for him, defining the nation on the basis of a single ethnic group has created a graveyard of cultures. Ocalan calls this "society/cide", which, for us, Putin is now conducting. Rather, various groups and cultural entities should have political formations that allow them to express themselves. The way to reinvigorate a society is to *organize all those who have been excluded*. Democratic autonomy, as such, opening up space for different segments of society, aims for direct involvement of people both politically and economically.

Kurds then are indigenous to the Mesopotamia area. The empires therein were not based on a dominant ethnicity. Therefore there were a lot of different autonomous peoples living within those former states. Kurds were one of the people in those empires. When the nation-state was introduced in the Middle East it was actually as destructive as it had been anywhere else, because it based the state on a single language, a single ethnicity, a dominant religion. *There was nowhere now for the Kurds to go because the world system was based now on nation-states.*

It Is Possible to Build One's Own Modernity

In general, and in the final analysis, the Kurdish freedom movement believes that there is a relationship among all living beings in the universe; they influence one another and so there is a relationship encompassing all things. Therefore, absolute independence is not something that is possible for anything. This is also true in terms of social history. The Kurdish movement for democracy and freedom is not focused on establishing a separate state in any part of Kurdistan, but rather areas where democracy and freedom prevails. A long while ago Ocalan said that the 21st century would be the century when people's desire for a free life is secured. It is possible to build one's own modernity.

Rojava University, for Guneser then, as of now (November 2023) is between moments. It is both a traditional university and a radical alternative educational institute, represented by the Mesopotamia Academy, which offers a radical alternative education. For us it provides a seminal example of a MENA based communiversity, with jineoloji, as we have seen, as a unique source of "newly global", scientific emancipation, promoted by a resident research academy.

We now turn from having re-invented the continent of Africa, locally via Amadiume, onto Rojava in MENA, locally-globally world-swide, now "newly globally" back in South Africa, onto Indigenous Knowledge Systems writ large.

6.4. Think Newly Global: Emancipatory Navigation: IKS – S3t

6.4.1. Indigenous Knowledge: An Integral Part of Culture

Applied Governance in Science, Knowledge, Systems and Innovation

For Ugandan born Swedish bred founder of todays' UNESCO based *Global Institute for Applied Governance in Science, Knowledge and Systems Innovation*, located in Uganda (also home to our second *Good African Coffee Story*), Professor Catherine Hoppers (2002), a feminist, social activist and international educator and researcher, any dynamic knowledge system has to evolve through the continuance of traditional knowledge and contemporary innovations, both technological and social, and this should be pursued by individuals as well as communities. Indeed such is clearly evident in the extensively abovementioned *jinealoji* case.

The aim is to connect creative people engaged in generating local solutions that are authentic and accountable, thus facilitating people-to-people learning. Knowledge for her as such then is a universal heritage and a universal resource. It is diverse and varied. The acquisition of western knowledge has been and still is invaluable to all, but, on its own, it has been, for Hoppers, incapable of responding adequately in the face of massive and intensifying disparities, and rapid depletion of the earth's natural resources. In that context a return to indigenous knowledge, albeit cast in contemporary light, is all-important.

Indigenous Knowledge Systems in a Newly Global Africa

By way of definition, the word indigenous refers to the root, something natural or innate. It is an integral part of culture. The ideal of knowledge as espoused within this framework, for instance, is not just about woven baskets, handicraft for tourists or traditional dances. Rather it is about excavating the technologies behind these practices and artefacts, recasting the potentialities they represent in a context of democratic, equitable participation for community, national and global development in real time.

The issue of indigenous knowledge systems posits profound challenges to contemporary practice, including:

- knowledge generation and legitimation processes, such as the type of knowledge being generated in scientific institutions, as well as in corporate research laboratories
- the social and economic survival of "resource rich but economically poor" local communities

- the need to explore deeper the interface between epistemology, diversity and democracy
- the need to facilitate the active re-appropriation and authentication of IKSs into current, living research work
- subjecting to direct interrogation the discourses behind the semantic shift that turned the illiterate from someone ignorant of the alphabet to an absolute illiterate
- realising the fundamental intolerance of modern science towards the legitimacy of folk or ethnic knowledge, coupled with our inability to develop an ecologically coded society
- moving the frontiers of discourse and understanding in the sciences as a whole, opening new moral and cognitive spaces within which constructive dialogue and engagement for sustainable development can take place
- finally developing a clearer sense of the ethical and judicial domain within which science works, and to begin to understand the political economy of "othering".

Indigenous knowledge systems are characterized by their embeddedness in the cultural web and history of a people, consisting of tangible and intangible aspects that:

- have exchange value and that, with support, can be transformed into enterprises or industries
- perpetuate social, cultural, scientific, philosophical and technological knowledge that can provide the basis for an integrated and inclusive knowledge framework
- It is in turn the re-appropriation of this heritage that may provide new clues and directions as to the visions of human society, human relations, sustainable development, poverty reduction and scientific development, all of which cannot be resolved using the existing ethos of the western framework alone.

6.4.2. Towards a Holistic Knowledge Framework: Culture and Science

Builds Strongly on the Female Dimension of Relating, Integrating, Caring, Love

The focus on IKSs, for Hoppers (2002) then, then aims at fostering understanding of the interface between culture and science, culture and technology, sustainable human development, and the comprehensive development of human, material and scientific resources, in a manner that gives cognisance to the wisdom and authenticity of traditional practices, institutions and knowledges. Moreover, it will provide a new basis for the generation of knowledge and a new consciousness in protecting intellectual property and other rights of those who have been ignored or taken for granted for so long.

Hoppers goes in her work beyond the gender issue of feminism. By proposing a holistic knowledge framework, builds strongly on the female dimension of relating, integrating, caring and love. For her, the challenge of creating an integrated and holistic knowledge framework for societal progress and development is not only real but also urgent, seeking to make whole that which was partial, incomplete, in large measure stunted and therefore also stunting. A dialogic search for integration is incompatible with legacies in which one group consistently deposits ideas into others. Dialogue cannot exist in the absence of profound love of the world and of people. The search therefore is for a framework that will affirm, not deny, the integrity of all human beings; a framework that by underscoring the notion of "agential citizenry" can posit people not as perpetual victims or pawns, but as knowing subjects, irrespective of the knowledge frameworks within which they are located.

A Profound Cultural Imbalance Has Resulted in the Systems We See Around Us

As governments seek to transform their societies and empower local communities, the challenge becomes one of how to "operationalise empowerment" itself in a context where diverse knowledges are barely tolerated and exist only in sufferance and subjective deference to a mainstream, essentially western form of knowledge. All in all, for Hoppers, a profound cultural imbalance has resulted in the systems of academic, political and economic institutions we see around us.

6.4.3. A Return to the Social

The Development of Knowledge and the Transformation of Societies

Instead the contingence of the social and the historical, as well as the affirmation of the multiplicity of worlds and forms of life, need to be recognised and affirmed. De-centred understanding of knowledge systems and other forms of universal conscience are emerging outside the exclusivist frameworks of western modernity. The total effect of these trends is to bring to bear a forceful return of philosophy to the social sciences, and to the evolution of emergent "open" non-linear and flowing spaces of information. Such is the strength of the new demands that it would appear that the legitimacy of the social sciences no longer rests in the obligation to produce objective knowledge alone, but also in the identification of a nexus between the development of knowledge and the transformation of societies.

Rural people's knowledge and modern scientific knowledge can be seen complementary in their strengths and weaknesses. Combined they can achieve what neither would alone. But for this complementarity to occur, outside professionals have to step in with humility down off their pedestals, and sit down, listen and learn. The present framework in which knowledge flows in one direction only – downwards – is not only disempowering but also demeaning.

The Aboriginal Significance of the Relational, Feminine

Hopper's focus on indigenous knowledge, and the marginalised status of indigenous peoples, and their respective knowledge systems, brings us directly to the following case: the hitherto downtrodden, and knowledge-wise unrecognized Australian aborigines. Often coined as "the world's oldest people", their concept of relationality included their own and other communities, the ancestors, the landscape and animals. Their story – though commonly not very well known – is a remarkable proof for the significance of the relational, feminine dimension for the building of a sustainable community and society, in tune with human nature and with nature in large, and offering a new-old sustainable route for mainstream "western" society to follow.

6.4.4. The Task for an Indigenous Academy

Knowledge Is an Integral Part of Social and Ecological Values

In the concluding part of Hoppers' (2002) book, the Australian aboriginal academics Fatnowna and Pickett then go on to describe what would be involved in setting up an "indigenous academy". For if unqualified, knowledge systems materialise, objectify, and marginalize, within an indigenous worldview, knowledge is an integral part of social and ecological values, with a sense of sacredness timelessly permeating all existence. The opening of indigenous wisdoms has coincided with an opening of indigenous systems to each other, an opening within the West to its own old-world wisdom, and a growing opening to the depths of Eastern and Southern cultures.

Connecting the Wisdoms Developed in Different Ways, in Different Places

Each reinforces and enriches the other, and the honeymoon distraction with rationality and scientific method in the West begins to be re-balanced. Integrating indigenous knowledge systems necessarily situates within this broad context, this global dynamic of seeking and connecting the wisdoms developed in different ways, in different places, at different times and through different experiences; looking across, yet also preserving this diversity. All speak of the nature of humanity, and how we might understand and conduct ourselves appropriately in the larger scheme of things.

Re-Inwarding of High-Tech Societies; Strengthening of "Cultures of Depth".

The world, for Fatnowna and Pickett, is set for a "whole system transition", involving the re-inwarding of high-tech societies, coincident with the strengthening of "cultures of depth". Following, for them, the tragic intervention of colonialism, this offers a path forward in a creative symbiosis, whereby each adds to the other while preserving its own individual cultural style and difference. The making of truth is not only a scientific process, it is also a method that encapsulates holistic well-being through the journey of self-discovery through one's cultural process.

With growing awareness of the astounding "layer upon layer" of the complexities of life, we are conscious that we have only ever gained access to very small bits of existing information, and even less to the inordinately interdetermining relatedness of it all. Despite the incredible advances in technology, we are conscious of our amazing but small place in the grand scale of things. The sense of humility, responsibility and respect for the natural world is in tension with the confidence of technological progress, just as the right of the human species to dominate nature and exploit the environment is in tension with a rights perspective beyond the human-centric.

Humanity is now left in a cusp of high information, control and action, but still without the development of relevant, new, appropriate systems of knowledge and responsibility from this that will guide its safe and effective use for just and equable quality of survival. The loss of a sense of embeddedness in and a co-nurturance and a responsibility for nature, and the assumption of control over and commodified exploitation of the natural world, including other people, results in a profound tension between indigenous and non-indigenous people.

Connection Back with the Western Culture Itself to Pre-scientific Knowledges

In broad historical context Richard Tarnas (Eisler), in his book on the *Passion of the Western Mind* as we have seen, sees this as the age of re-integration, a remaking of connections, following the long period of differentiation during the Western scientific tradition. The essential issues no longer primarily concern technical advancement, invention, competition and expansion, but questions of "living" purpose in a "living reality". Coinciding with this is the reconnection with the indigenous world-views, and connection back with the Western culture itself to pre-scientific knowledges of its cultural origins. As Western and indigenous societies together, though, we cannot expect a mere return to the past, but we can build on the past. For the Taranhike's (2019)

> *I am driven by the passion to see my children, grandchildren, my community and future generations living a much better life than my current life as a result of me and everyone else building a solid foundation upon which they can accelerate their development in harmony with the entire ecosystem. It is my burning desire for each generation to have a long term vision of the future and to preserve what they inherit from their predecessors or ancestors and use that as the foundation for their development by blending with exogenous knowledge and practices thereby accelerating their development in harmony with nature. Therefore, each generation must ask itself the question "what nhaka are we building for future generations in order for them to recognise and realise fully their GENEius as individuals, as communities and societies?"*

We now turn finally to the global-local keynotes of relational African effect, in duly feminist, altogether emancipatory guise.

6.5. Act Global-Local: Keynotes of African Liberation: S3a

6.5.1. Feminist Research Complements the Androcentric (Masculine) Perspective

Something that sets feminist research apart from other approaches to social inquiry is its ontological claim that the reality depicted by much of social science knowledge is incomplete and fundamentally distorted. The world described by many studies of human and organizational behaviour is dominated by an *androcentric* worldview: that means that it communicates the male experience and is based on male assumptions and perspectives. Females – their experience, assumptions, and perspectives – often have been excluded as subjects of study, as researchers, and as interpreters of results.

The *androcentric* perspective in and of itself is not a problem when the researcher acknowledges that women are missing in the study and, thus, in the interpretation of results. The problem is significant, however, when androcentric research is described as representative of the universe under study and when findings are presented as universally true. Many feminist researchers propose that social science dominated by theories and concepts emerging solely from a male consciousness may be irrelevant for the female experience and inadequate for explaining female behaviour.

At the most basic level, then, feminist research simply attempts to incorporate into social reality the female perspective. Further, feminist criticism of established research often stems from a distrust of the power and perspective of *androcentrism* in research and society, not from a rejection of traditional methods of inquiry. As such, some argue that *feminism* is rather a perspective than a method in itself. In fact, in the Taranhike's case as we shall see, it is Christina Taranhike who is playing the lead role in the kumusha, locally in Buhera, if not newly globally in the world at large.

African Global-Local Feminist Keynotes
Feminist Research for complements the androcentric perspective, *re-inventing Africa*.
As a Researcher you as a Person are included and so is Nature in Ubuntu/*Unhu* guise
You aim to Create Social and Economic Change in Africa via *Communitalism/* Nhakanomics
You see Knowledge as a Tool for *African* Liberation not Domination

6.5.2. As a Researcher You as a Person and Nature are Included in *Unhu* Guise

Feminism is seen as a science in which no rigid boundary separates the subject of knowledge (the knower) and the natural object of that knowledge. In contrast to much of mainstream research, which generally seeks to attain value neutrality, femism proposes often a "metabolism of subject and field", seeing researcher and researched as one organism. Feminist researchers will often integrate personal experiences into their research. Personal experiences are not perceived as tainting the methods and results of research. Rather, many feminists view it as serving to validate their research. Feminist researchers may use these personal experiences to inform their research questions, to guide their involvement in the research process.

However, while the subjective-objective relational character of the research becomes more distinct, the close relationship this establishes between the researcher and the subject of the research has also led to ongoing discussion in the feminist research community about how to walk that fine line and work out the tension between objectivity and subjectivity. Feminism moreover can be understood as a science where the subject/object split is not used to legitimise the domination of nature. Nature itself is conceptualised as active rather than passive, a dynamic complex totality requiring human cooperation and understanding rather than a dead mechanism, requiring only manipulation and control.

That links with US Cultural Anthropologist Riane Eisler's recent work on *The Real Wealth of Nations* (20), where she proposes a new caring economics that takes into account the full spectrum of economic activities – from the life sustaining activities of the household to the life enriching activities of carers and communities, to the life supporting processss of nature. Eisler demonstrates how our values are distorted by the economic double standard that devalues anything stereotypically associated with women and feminity; reveals how current economic models are based on a deep-seated culture of domination; and shows how human needs would be better served by economic models based on caring. From that perspective, the extension of the Zimbabwean kumusha into an integral kumusha, spanning nature and culture, technology and economy, brings such homely "caring" into a broader light.

6.5.3. You Aim to Create Social Change via Communitalism/ Nhaklanomics

At the heart of much feminist research, and prospective innovation as such, is the goal, even the obligation, of bringing about change in the condition of women. Even those feminists who don't directly speak of change in the condition of women have social change at the foundation of their goals as researchers. By and large, the international feminist community is committed to the dual vision of research as firstly benefiting the welfare of women and secondly furthering social science knowledge.. Whether a researcher recommends explicit policy recommendations or less overtly offers social implications of his or her findings, this focus on creating social change appears to be a theme across much of feminist thought.

The key then, in our Southern African kumusha case, to turning *nhaka* (legacy) into *nhakanomics* – a variation on the theme of communitalism – is the co-evolution of nature and culture, on the one hand, with technology and enterprise, on the other. Such co-evolution, moreover, has not only been articulated in theory, via Daud Shumba Taranhike's' (2019) PhD thesis, but also, and more significantly *innovation* wise in practice. As such, he not only has developed a micro version of such, in Buhera, but is now spreading the integral model, across Southern Africa, in the guise of a prospective nhakanomics writ large.

6.5.4. You See Knowledge as a Tool for Liberation Not Domination

Feminism takes a close look at language, gender and power. Language is the medium in which we conduct our social lives and create our symbolic existence; gender is the fundamental dichotomous figure of thought characterising our public as well as private lives; power entangles all of us in its constantly reinvented ruses and snares, which some scientists regard as the fine-grained structure that holds society together. The feminists add the gender dimension to considering the impact of power relations. They regard gender relations as problematic since they are associated with conditions of dominance, inequality, stress and conflict and argue that gender relations are socially constructed, which means they are not given by nature, nor are they inevitable; rather they are the result of socio-cultural and historical conditions and can be radically altered by human action.

From an emancipatory and transformative perspective, there are again three major movements associated with feminism. First, the movement to champion, and *give voice to marginalised peoples,* starting out with women themselves but, evolving over the past half century in particular, to involve a wide range of marginalised peoples. Second, a specifically *eco-feminist movement* identified with nature, ecology and the environment, thereby linking up with the overall environmental movement in itself. Third, and as illustrated here, in the context of integral research and social innovation, a *specific link with indigenous knowledge,* or so called alternative source of knowledge, outside of the scientific mainstream.

6.6. Conclusion: African Origination to Emancipation

6.6.1. Originally Grounded Descriptively in Southern Kumusha Guise

In our Chapter 4, standing on the shoulders of Magosvongwe, Biko, Ingold and the Taranhike's in particular, the latter initially built on prior descriptive grounds, whereby they:

- Seek to reveal the Essences and Origins of *human Experience*.
- Engage their total Selves as Participants, *passionately Involved*
- *Do not seek to predict* or to determine causal Relationships
- Illuminate these through *comprehensive Descriptions*, vivid and accurate Renderings of Experience, rather than Measurements or Ratings.

Emerging Phenomenological Southern Relational Nhakanomic Foundation

Subsequently in thereby *southern* African, phenomenological emergent relational guise, the Taranhike's:

- Immerse ourselves in their *unhu/ivhu* communal laden, local life worlds
- Concentrate on illuminating the natural-cultural *inner self* of "black consciousness" in Biko-like, local-global guise
- Locate the *unique cultural history* of their integral kumusha in the nely global story of livelihood, dwelling and enskillment that Ingold reveals
- Going *beyond reductive* positivism and naive empiricism in a now global-local light as revealed by the Taranhike's via *nhakanomics*.

Emancipatory Feminist Southern Relational Nhakanomic Navigation

Now thirdly, and building on what has come originally and foundationally before, by way of natural and cultural grounding and emergence, such now nhakanomic navigation, so called, building on societal legacy:

- Complements an androcentric perspective, *re-inventing* Africa
- Includes self and nature as an African in your social *unhu* laden research
- Aiming to create social and economic, *communitalist* change
- Seeing knowledge as a tool for *African* liberation *not* domination

Along that relational way, research and innovation wise, moroever, we pave the further way toward communal learning, communiversity wise specifically, and an emergent foundation for community buiding enterprise wise, and communitalism economically, generally. We now turn from southern African descriptive method by way of original, relational grounding, and phenomenological methodology, by way of emergent relational foundation, onto herein southern African feminism, to finally, on the African relational path, to transformative Participatory Action. Research, as illustrated below in the Kumusha laden case.

Integral Kumusha to Nhakanomics in Southern Africa: S2fita

As such, Feeling local, *kumusha*-wise, intuiting local-global, in *integral kumusha* terms, thinking newly global, now from an overall *nhakanomic* perspective, with a view to acting global-local as a community based *vakamusha* as opposed to a corporate enterprise, constitutes the overall hallmark of our Southern African innovation, building on the relational research path that came before.

Table 6.6. *Integral Kumusha to Nhakanomics in Southern Africa S3fita*

Feeling Local	Intuiting Local-Global	Thinking Newly Global	Acting Global-Local
Re-inventing Africa	*Feminist Foundation*	*Indigenous Knowledge Systems*	*Create Social Change through Nhakanomics*

We now turn from emancipatory feminism, in southern African guise, and the Nhakanomics that goes with it (see ICS1 for further elaboration) to participatory action research, and the Vakamusha *innovation* that has accompanied it.

6.7. References

Abram D (1997) *The Spell of the Sensous*. New York. Bantam

Amadiume I (1997) *Reinventing Africa: Matriarchy, Culture and Religion*. London. Zed Books

Bookchin M (2023) *The Philsophy of Social Ecology. Essays on Dilaetical Materialism*. Chicago. California. AK Press

Braudel F (1995) *A History of Civilisations*. London. Penguin Books

Diop C (1987) *The African Origin of Civilisation: Myth or Reality*. Chicago. Lawrence Hill Press

Donavan J (2000) *Feminist Theory: The Intellectual Tradition*. London. Continuum Books

Eisler R (2008) *The Real Wealth of Nations: Creating a Caring Economics*. ReadHowYouWant

Ghosh B (2019) *Dependency Theory Revisited*. Abingdon. Routledge Classics

Guneser H (2021) *The Art of Freedom: A Brief History of the Kurdish Liberation Struggle*. Oakland, California. PM Press

Hoppers C (ed) (2002) *Indigenous Knowledge Systems*. Cape Town. New Africa Books

Lessem R and Schieffer A (2010) *Integral Research and Innovation. Transformting Enterprise and Society*. Abingdon. Routledge

Lessem R, **Mawere** M and **Taranhike** D (2019) *Integral Kumusha*. Mazvingo. Africa Talent Publishers.

Mies and Shiva V (2014) *Ecofeminism*. London. Zed Books

Ocalan A (2007) *The Roots of Civilisation*. London. Pluto Press

Ocalan A (2023) *Beyond State, Power and Violence*. Oakland, CA. PM Books

Riane Eisler (2008) The Real Wealth of Nations. Creating Caring Economics. New York. McGraw Hill

Tarnas R (1991) *The Passion of the Western Mind*. New York. Ballantyne

Wallerstein I (2004) *World Systems Analysis: An Introduction*. North Carolina. Duke University Press

Chapter 7 From Feminism to Participatory Action Research in Africa and the Global South. Ujaama in Tanzania to Six S's in the Sahel

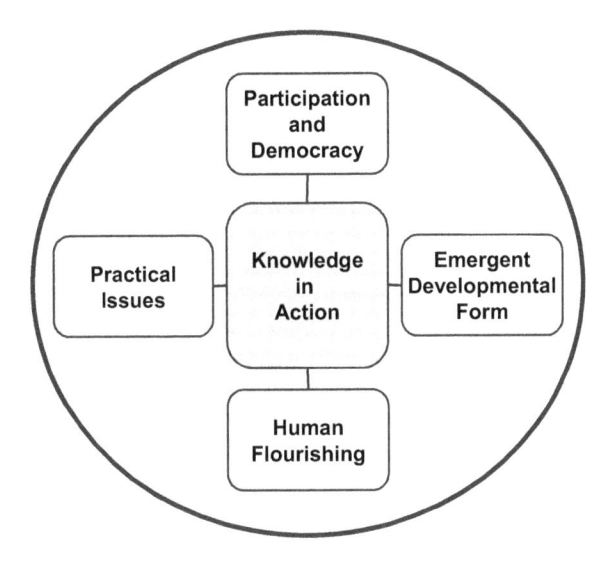

Figure 7.1: *Knowledge in Action*

Unlike Marxist theory, cultural revitalization theory does not focus on social classes, but, rather, on deliberate, organized, conscious efforts by members of society to construct a more satisfying culture. Such revitalization may be based on mass, ethnic, charismatic or revolutionary movements. For people embracing cultural revival theory, the research agenda may focus on the unique contributions of different people, that is elements in their knowledge, values, ideologies and experiences that promote social justice.

Dan Selener (Dewey 2009)   Participation Action Research for Social Change

Summary: Relational Transformation in Africa – Participatory Action Research
• Action and transformation come together at the fourth level of our Integral Research and Innovation in Africa – starting out with community development, through so-called participatory action research. Researcher and innovator now combine forces, following upon the original description, phenomenological foundation, and feminist emancipation, on the relational path.
• Participatory a as a branch of action – research, is unique in its "southern" origins, most specifically in Latin America, Africa and the Indian sub-continent, starting out with President Nyerere in Tanzania, orchestrator of Ujaama (familyhood), thereafter with Columbia's Fals Borda, Ecuador's Daniel Selener, and Bangladesh's MD Rahman being its leading lights.
• In place of the phenomenological life world or the Germanic "Lebenswelt", and Steve Biko's Black Consciousness in Southern Africa, Manuel Fals Borda cites the Spanish "vivencia" in Latin America in the global South, as a focal point for dialogic research and innovation, oriented toward such questions as "Why is there poverty?" or "Why is there oppression and dependence?".
• Grassroots representatives participate, feeling locally, as a reference group in the action-research processes, thereby "popularising science", transforming the researcher/researched relationship, and pursuing autonomy and identity in the course of exercising people's own countervailing power.
• The action centred journey for Bangaldeshi academic and social activist M.D. Rahman, now locally-globally, brings out the dynamic interrelationship between the development of people's consciousness, on the one hand, and the necessary control over the society's resources, and social, economic and political institutions, on the other, as such serving to bring about social innovation.
• Newly globally in the Sahel in Africa, though in partnership with the Swiss Development Agency in Europe, in such an Afro-European co-creation, the most prominent example of PAR is introduced: the monumental efforts of the Six S movement in Burkina Faso, albeit that the movement has faded away in recent times for lack of ongoing institutionalisation.
• Finally, the global-local keynotes of PAR, in Africa, as a transformative culmination of the relational path, are that it is aimed at the exploited, the poor, the oppressed, the marginal; it creates awareness of the people's own resources; it involves the full and active participation of the community; the ultimate Goal is the radical transformation of social reality.

7.1. Orientation to Participatory Action Research (PAR)

7.1.1. Introducing Action Research as a Whole

We now turn, inner directed research-wise, from our relational origination in Africa, in descriptive methods, naturally and communally, and our emergent foundation, phenomenologically and trans-culturally, onto our social scientific emancipatory navigation. in feminist guise, onto now our transformative effect, in terms of participatory action research (PAR). Similarly, in outer directed innovation guise, we turn from kumusha and integral kumusha to nhakanomics and vakamusha, as in the Table 7.1.1. below, as more fully articulated below in our opening case story.

Table 7.1.1. *"Southern" African Relational Path of Social Research to Innovation: Descriptive to Participatory; PAR: Kumusha to Vakamusha*

Southern Grounding Method and Origination	Southern Emergence Methodology and Foundation	Southern Navigation Critique and Emancipation	Southern Effect Action and Transformation
Descriptive Methods (S1)	Phenomenological Methodology (S2)	Feminist Critique (S3)	Participatory Action Research (S4)
Kumusha (S1)	Integral Kumusha (S2)	Nhaka-Nomics (S3)	Vaka-Musha (S4)

The "global", that is Euro-American, founding fathers of generic "action research", from which PAR has more recently evolved out of Africa, are the American pragmatic philosopher and educator, John Dewey (Lessem and Schieffer 2010), and the Jewish refugee from Nazi Germany, the social psychologist Kurt Lewin (2005) – in the middle of the last century. Action research – for one of its contemporary co-creators Peter Reason (Freire 2017) at the University of Bath in England, together with a follower of his, Hilary Bradbury based in California – is:

> ...a participatory, democratic process concerned with developing practical knowing in the pursuit of worthwhile human purposes, grounded in a participatory worldview which is believed to be emerging at this historical moment. It seeks to bring together action and reflection, theory and practice, in participation with others, in the pursuit of practical solutions to issues of pressing concern to people, and more generally the flourishing of individual persons and their communities.

However, as we will see, so called *participatory action research,* emerging out of Africa, represents a significant departure from its American and European roots, planting if you like, a new PAR-tree, through two if not three primary instigators.

7.1.2. Analytically Oriented PAR

A Problem Is Defined, Analysed and Solved by the Community

For Columbian born renegade academic sociologist, Orlando Fals Borda (Mandela 1994), ultimately based at the University of British Columbia in Canada, learning to interact and organize with PAR is based on the orientation toward experience proposed by the Spanish philosopher Jose Ortega y Gasset (Luther King 1991) in his *Revolt of the Masses.*

Through the actual experience of something, for him, we intuitively apprehend its essence; we feel, enjoy and understand it as a reality, and we thereby place our own being in a wider, more fulfiling context. In PAR such an experience, called "vivencia" (akin to life world and aligned to learning with head and heart) in Spanish, and popularized in South America, is complemented by another idea, that of authentic commitment. In that context both internal and external animators, or agents of change, have the shared goals.

A dialectical tension, then, is created between an academic orientation combined with a practical one, bringing together academic and popular knowledge in shared problem solving. Through participation a subject/subject relationship replaces the hitherto asymmetrical subject/object researcher/researched relationships; thereby it is attuned to feminism. The general concept of authentic participation as defined here is rooted in cultural traditions of the common people and in their real history referring to core values that have survived the destructive impact of foreign invasions. Such resistant values are based on mutual aid, the communal use of the land, forest and water, the extended family and other old social practices, the endogenous experiences of the common people.

Historical Experience Calls for Rethinking the Meaning of People's Liberation

For Fals Borda, moreover, action and knowledge go hand in hand. Historical experience calls for rethinking the meaning of people's liberation. The dominant view of such liberation has been preoccupied with the need for changing the oppressive structures of relations in material production – certainly a necessary task. But, and this is the distinctive view of PAR, domination of elites is also rooted in control over social power to determine what is useful knowledge. In fact, existence of the gap in knowledge relations can offset the advantages of reducing the gap in relations of physical production.

People then cannot be liberated by a consciousness and knowledge other than their own. It is therefore essential that people develop their own indigenous consciousness-raising and knowledge generation, and this requires the social power to assert this. The scientific character or objectivity of knowledge rests on its social verifiability, and this depends on consensus as to the method of verification. All scientific knowledge is relative to the paradigm to which it belongs, and the verification system to which it is submitted. An immediate objective of PAR is to return to the all too often poor and deprived people the control over their own verification systems. We now turn from Fals Borda to Rahman, from South America to Asia.

7.3.2. People's Self Development and Transformation: M.D. Rahman

Integrating Education with Life Processes

Like many other of his compatriots, MD Rahman (Gandhi 2001) had been inspired by popular mobilizations for social reconstruction and development in Bangladesh after its independence in 1971. He saw a breakthrough in the development status of the country to be possible only through a national mobilization for popular initiatives; on smaller scale, such initiatives were demonstrating their potential for solving people's problems and for creating a spirit of personal sacrifice for collective outcomes, challenging the premises of received economics and development thinking which were pushing the country towards humiliating dependence on external assistance rather than indicating a viable path for social progress.

As a teacher, Rahman had been stimulated by demands from sections of Bangladesh's student community for radical reform to integrate educational processes with processes of life. Yet most of the popular initiatives in the country faded, died or were repressed as reactionary forces gradually consolidated their hold on society's commanding structures. Joining the ILO (International Labour Organization) in 1977, Rahman was able to pursue the same interest, linking up with significant trends in the grassroots movements in several countries and jointly reflecting on their approaches, experiences and visions; initiating methodological experiments in field "animation" work (see below) and in the sensitization of animators; linking with intellectual trends; working with popular movements; and in synthesizing and conceptualizing from the ongoing experiences.

In his contribution to the faculty seminars, he raised as a basic problem in the transition to socialism the question of a "consciousness gap" between revolutionary intellectuals who generally provide leadership in socialist transition, and the masses. Socialism would be alienating if this consciousness gap could not be closed. This problem remained one of his central concerns throughout his explorations of participatory or people's self-development, and in his prolific engagement with the NGO movement, leading to prospective social innovation.

We now start our PAR based distinctively African journey by now *Feeling Local*, albeit that the "local" in this case spread from East Africa to indigenous Canada to Columbia and Bangladesh, in the global South, only skirted Africa in the process.

7.2. Feel Local: Originating PAR in Ujaama in Africa: S4f

7.2.1. The Beginning of the Story Can Be Traced to Nyerere

In 1975, a young Canadian adult educator named Budd Hall (Reason and Bradbury 2004), at that time temporarily based in Sussex, U.K., compiled a special issue of the journal Convergence on the topic of participatory research. Beyond Hall's expectations, this issue sparked a international network of educators, academics and activists interested in this area, the "International Participatory Research Network", which would grow stronger and larger over the next decades.

The beginning of this story can be traced to Tanzania, where Hall worked from 1970 to 1974. At that time, under the leadership of President Julius Nyerere (Pradervand 1990), Tanzania had launched his social and economic experiment in what was known as "ujamaa socialism". In Tanzania, Hall (who would later become Chair of Adult Education and Community Development at OISE/University of Toronto and Dean of Education at the University of Victoria) had the fortune of learning from many inspiring adult educators. Among them were Finland's Marja Liisa Swantz (Selener 1997), Brazil's Paulo Freire (Fals Borda 1991), and the Tanzanian President himself Julius Nyerere, out of Africa as indicated above, probably the only adult educator in the world who became president of a country. That said, and ironically enough, there was no direct link between ujamaa, largely imposed top-down, and bottom-up PAR, which may be one of then reasons why the former ultimately failed.

7.2.2. Potential of Research to Promote Transformative Learning

Hall meanwhile became acquainted with approaches to education based on the principles of self-reliance, active participation, and dialogue. He also became interested in the potential of research to promote transformative learning, local development and progressive social change, and in research models that departed from the traditional positivist approach to social research based on the natural sciences. In 1974/1975 Budd Hall was a visiting fellow at the Institute of Development Studies at the University of Sussex, where he met people from many other countries who were thinking along similar lines to him and his Tanzanian colleagues, seeking a connection between education, research, politics and action.

From his experiences in Tanzania and England, Hall noticed that many educators, researchers and activists from different countries were exploring similar paths through independent avenues, in most cases without being aware of related work done by others. At that time they did not constitute yet a community or even a loose network. Moreover, their approaches did not have yet an encompassing name that would capture its essence. The major impetus for the development of a network (and later an international community) came from that special journal of "Convergence" edited by Hall in 1975. In naming the theme of the issue, Hall labelled this approach "participatory research".

That term was used because it seemed to be the best common description of the various approaches that were described within the issue. While Hall had begun to learn about the long traditions in Europe of action research, and Maria Liisa Swantz had been using "participant research" to describe this approach for several years, the choice of the term "participatory research" was simply made as a descriptive term for a collection of varied approaches which shared a participatory ethos.

7.2.3. PAR Struck a Cord Among Adult Educators and Community Developers

The topic of participatory research struck a cord among adult educators and community development practitioners around the world, and soon after its publication, all the copies of the issue were sold out, a first in the history of Convergence. Moreover, requests for copies were sent from all regions of the world, and a comment in Hall's article inviting people to exchange information on the topic provided the needed driving force to create a community of practice. This massive response made Hall realize that many people in the world were actively pursuing alternative research avenues that were ignored by most universities, and that these people needed some spaces to establish connections among them in order to share their experiences. That issue of "Convergence", and the active networking of Hall, helped to generate those spaces, which in turn helped to consolidate a vibrant tradition in the field of adult education that would grow year after year for the decades to come. It seems that the time was ripe for an international network on participatory research, but a catalyst was needed.

A few months later, another important catalyst for the development of an international participatory research network came forth when the First World Assembly of the International Council for Adult Education, was held in Dar es Salaam, Tanzania, in 1976. Again, Hall played a key role, acting as Conference Secretary. One of the recommendations of the Dar es Salaam conference was that "adult educators should be given the opportunity to learn about and share their experiences in participatory research." The following year, a conference on action research took place in Cartagena, Colombia. Interestingly enough, the coordinator of this conference, was the Colombian sociologist Orlando Fals Borda, who has since become a leading light in the PAR movement. He was working on the same alternative approach to social research but without being aware of the international initiatives that took place in the previous years.

Orlando Fals Borda and his colleagues were using the term "action research", a concept that had been used in the 1940s by Kurt Lewin, as indicated above. Lewin argued that research that produced nothing but books was not sufficient, and that a new type of research for social practice was needed. Thus, he called for "a type of action research on the conditions and effects of various forms of social action, and research leading to social action". At the 1977 Cartagena conference the concept of "action research" used by Fals Borda met the concept of "participatory research" coined by Hall, and the concept of *"participatory action research"* was later born, indeed originally out of Africa. The term was used for the first time by Orlando Fals Borda to name a new paradigm in social research. Several decades later, the concept became popularized, worlds-wide, for us locally-globally and known by as PAR.

We now turn from Africa, locally, to Columbia and Bangladesh, locally-globally.

7.3. Intuit PAR Locally Globally: People's Self Development: S4i

7.3.1. Participatory Action Research and Knowledge Creation: Fals Borda

Doing Research With and For People

Building up people's self-awareness, for Fals Borda, has been an ever-present preoccupation of participatory action researchers – an extremely important task in order for their actions to be effective if they want to avoid the betrayal of ideals. For this purpose he places the interplay between explicit and implicit science – or between Cartesian and popular knowledge – as a fact, which has to be taken into account since it involves dialectical encounters, which are inevitably part of day-to-day living. His central concern has been to direct this interplay to allow the common people to have sufficient control over the generation of new knowledge, thereby "remaking science" for the benefit of the masses victimized by power.

The developing world, he says, of course, is too small for this tremendous task: the victims of poverty constitute the majority of the earth's inhabitants and the effort has many detractors. But a hopeful methodological start has been made with participatory action research. In adopting a marginal and even subversive role, following the likes of Gandhi (Rahman 1993), Luther King (Nyerere 1968) and Mandela (Swantz 1985), PAR is not denying the merits of science; without the scientific bearings they would have felt as if moving in a void. Ways of building connections between different scientific traditions are then sought while doing research with and for people, and not on them, duly combining the role of activist and researcher.

Fals Borda asserted, at the same time, that PAR applied rigor and responsibility in observation-inference or in carefully handling data just as positivists do. But it has had to remake other aspects of their scholarship so as to relate it to ordinary people's way of interpreting reality. In a similar manner it had to discover and apply its half hidden science – "people's knowledge" – for the people's benefit. For this purpose, a series of procedures have been developed in which theory and practice, conventional learning and implicit knowledge could be combined in special *vivencias*.

From Life World to Vicencia

The reconstruction of knowledge for the purpose of furthering social progress and increasing people's self awareness with PAR *vivencias* takes dialogue as its point of insertion in the social process. It is dialogic research, oriented to the social situation in which people live. PAR starts by asking such questions as "Why is there poverty?" or "Why is there oppression and dependence?". As such the grassroots representatives should be able to participate as reference group in the action research process from the very beginning that is from the moment it is decided what the subject of research will be. And they should be involved at every step in the process.

Popular Science, Transformed Interpersonal Relationship, Countervailing Power

Popular knowledge does not come as isolated facts known by specific individuals, but as packets of cultural data generated by social groups. PAR as an autonomous collective investigation is quite different from the detached individual observer undertaking his or her doctoral thesis, advancing science or gaining personal prestige or financial gain. The task now becomes a communal in which social validation of knowledge is obtained not only by confronting previous ideas but also through the people's own processes of verification.

Three theoretical elements – not usually included in dominant paradigms, are included:

- the ontological possibility of *a real popular science*
- the existential possibility of *transforming the researcher/researched relationship*
- the need of autonomy and identity in *exercising people's own countervailing power.*

People's science does have its own endogenous processes; it is formally constructed on its own terms, with its own practical rationality and empirical systematization and its own way of institutionalizing, accumulating and transmitting knowledge. As such, the wisdom of the sage and the know how of the scientist converge and intermingle, as recognized during the lifetimes of Descartes, Kant and Galileo themselves. By giving importance to both, a more useful and complete knowledge for social change can be produced. Emancipatory collective knowledge and popular science become tools then in the quest for justice, and this is the answer to the perennial question "knowledge for what?".

The second element, transformation of the researcher/researched liaison leads to an interpretation of participation that is indeed demanding, whereby both parties seek the mutual goal of advancing knowledge in pursuit of justice. They interact, collaborate, reflect and report in collectivities on an equal footing, each one offering in the relationship what he or she knows best. In other words, a meeting of diverse scientific traditions takes place, resulting in an enriched overall knowledge, which is more effective in the struggle for justice and the achievement of social progress and peace.

The third element – autonomy and identity in collective research – rests on the observation that progressive social movements cherish and fight for their culture and personality to the last, for their lives depend on it. Stimulating autonomous movements and defending the articulation of local life is a worthy goal for PAR researchers, involving both stripping down the oppressor's power and understanding how to internalize one's own. It also includes the power to speak in the context of establishing a "knowledge democracy".

If the 18th century in Europe, then, has been called "the Enlightenment" for its collective efforts to revamp science and philosophy, the 21st century may be expected to be the "Century of Awakening". The common peoples are already awakening to their rights and possibilities for action. They are also responding to the call of their own voices – hitherto half muted – to honour their dignity and the meaning of their own history.

Action, Knowledge and Animation

Stimulation of the poor and deprived, for Fals Borda, to undertake self-reliant initiatives requires two essential steps. The first is the development of an awareness about the reality in which they live. In particular, they need to understand that poverty and deprivation are the result of specific social forces rather than an outcome of some inherent deficiency on their part or even "fate". Second, based on such critical awareness, they need to gain confidence in their collective abilities to bring about positive changes in their life situations and organize themselves for that purpose.

A stimulation of this sort implies a specific mode of interaction with the people, the essence of which could be summarized as the break-up of the classical dichotomy between "subject" and "object" (manipulation and dominance) and its replacement by a humanistic mode of equal relation between two subjects (animation and facilitation). The essential difference between the latter approach and that typically undertaken by a political party or conventional development practitioner is:

- *Starting from where people are* – their perceptions, knowledge, experiences and rhythm of work and thoughts, as opposed to preconceived agendas
- *Stimulating people (animation) to undertake self-analysis of their life situations,* and helping them to derive from such self inquiry into the political-economic-cultural environment an intellectual base for initiating changes
- *Assisting people to organize themselves* into People's Organizations (PO's) which are non-hierarchical in structure and democratic in operations
- *Facilitating the actions for change,* with the external catalyst paving the way for internal self-reliance
- Stimulating the People's Organizations to *carry out regular self-reviews,* to assess and learn from success and failure

Creation of Sensitized Agents: A cadre of such sensitized agents will have undergone a process of rigorous learning based on exposure to concrete experience and self-reflection rather than formal training. Potential such persons have generally originated from:

- *socially conscious and active segments of the middle class* who have had practical experience in such social activities
- those who had begin to critically reflect on their earlier roles and were *looking for more relevant or fulfilling roles for society*

Specifically then:

- the starting point is a *collective reflection* on the experiences such people already have in working with communities, including self criticism and unlearning
- *exposure to concrete field experiences*, living among selected communities to gather socio-economic information through informal discussions
- through interaction with groups in the community, the learner seeks to stimulate them to *identify issues of common concern*, collect and analyse information on such, to enrich their understanding of their life situations
- while engaged in such fieldwork, meeting regularly as a group amongst themselves as a *collective learning* exercise
- *identify* those individuals within a community who possess potential *skills in animation*, and assist them in improving their skills.

We now turn from participatory action research and Fals Borda's knowledge creation to Rahman's *people's self-development*, and indeed transformation.

7.3.2. Rahman's People's Self Development

Organizing the Rural Poor

According to Rahman, organizing the rural poor, for an NGO, can have several different objectives:

> *Economic Uplift:* This means raising the incomes of the poor, giving them greater stability of income, and some social security or insurance against unforeseen situations, old age, and so on. If this is the only or the principal objective, external delivery of such can be in the form of credit, technology and expertise. But emphasis on external delivery contradicts with the other objectives.
> *Human Development:* Creativity is the distinctive human quality, for Rahman, and the human development objective aims to develop creative people. Creation is the product of thinking and action that is *participation*. This consists of investigation, reflection, decision-making and application of decision: reflection upon action gives men and women the sense of creation, of having developed as human beings. Human development is a process of *self*-development – outsiders cannot develop the rural poor. Outsiders can have a role, however, in stimulating and assisting development.
> *Achieving social and economic Rights:* The means of elimination of economic and social oppression, and achieving equity in the use of public resources, implies the exercise of collective power of the poor, and often implies *struggle*. The role of outsiders is to help develop a consciousness amongst the poor of short-run failures as a learning process upon which subsequent strategy is to be built.

The above three objectives, moreover, become complementary if they are pursued together. This implies care to pursue the economic uplift objective through primary reliance on the people's own resources and creativity, and channeling their organized efforts towards obtaining their rightful share of normal public resources. In all this, the emphasis must always be on stimulating people's reflection and analysis, assisted but not dominated by external knowledge and intervention. In this way, people's consciousness will keep advancing.

Macro-social Transformation: The above three objectives can be considered to be "locally progressive" if they are pursued together, that is progressive at a micro level. Their contribution to macro social transformation can be positive, if such micro work spreads on a broad enough scale. Since the great bulk of the flow of external resources is controlled by external forces, interested (according to Rahman) in dominating and exploiting the country rather than in its self-determination and development, a self-reliant development effort is an absolutely necessary element for the country to shape its own destiny and stand up with pride. Self-reliance at the national level cannot be achieved without self-reliance at the grassroots levels – in fact at all levels. This by itself requires primary reliance on people's own effort and creativity rather than on external deliveries.

However, successful social transformation, which includes social innovation, is much more than the mere act of formal transfer of political power: it requires a social psychology, culture and capability of self-reliant economic and social effort. A corollary of self-reliant people's effort is reliance on people's own knowledge. There is no self-reliant way of development without primary reliance on people's resources including their own knowledge, and professional knowledge must play a complementary but not dominating role in such *development*. With this perspective in view, work with the poor which seeks to develop their creativity primarily through their own collective effort, giving emphasis to both the people's self reliant thinking and acting through which collective action and consciousness both keep advancing, would be creating positive assets for the task of social transformation.

Take Action in Small Groups

Overall then, from an NGO perspective:

- The chosen objectives and their rationale should be discussed with the target groups; they should be asked to *reflect why development effort in the country has been a failure,* notwithstanding so-called "learned" men being in charge
- The people should be asked to deliberate *what they want to do in this overall context,* and how the NGO can help them
- The people should have the opportunity to discuss all of such, and *take action in small groups*
- The *people must periodically evaluate their own experience* and review their progress collectively, draw lessons from success and failure, formulate a future course of action based on past experience, and formulate advice on how to achieve agreed objectives. They should be encouraged to document, store, and

disseminate their ongoing experience for progressive advancement of their collective knowledge based on their collective effort.
- In areas where there is a past history of collective effort by the poor, this *history should be collected and discussed, and lessons drawn* from them as a guide to current effort.

We now turn from our local-global analysis of PAR, through the eyes and activities of Columbia's Fals Borda and Bangladesh's M.D. Rahman, to its, for us, "newly global" expression, through the so called Six S's, building on what had come locally-globally, foundationally worlds-wide, and locally before, originally out of Africa.

7.4. Emancipatory Navigation: Newly Global Social Innovation: S4t

7.4.1 Social Innovation Through Six S's

Local Knowledge, Development Expertise and Flexible Funding

What, then, is the significance of PAR as a macro-level social transformation, born, newly globally, as a purposeful partnership between Africa (the Sahel) and Europe (Switzerland)? Possibly the largest such PAR movement, of all time, was the so-called Six S's ("Se Servir de la Saison Sèche en Savane et au Sahel"), which in English means "using the dry season in the Savannah and the Sahel". Originally located in Burkino Faso, it subsequently covered about two-thirds of the country's villages, according to Swiss developmental economist, Pierre Pradervand (Ortega y Gasset 1994) as well as those of adjacent West African countries.

Six S's was then founded in 1976 and emerged out of the confluence of three forces, Bernard Ouedragao, Pierre Pradervand and the Swiss Development Corporation (DDA). While the first contributed his intimate knowledge of village conditions, and the second, a French development specialist, the idea of flexible funding, the third – through its Director, Marcel Heimo – was prepared to back a "barefoot" development of an unorthodox nature.

Bernard Lédéa Ouédraogo to begin with then, a core initiator of the Six S movement, was born in Upper Volta (now Burkina Faso) in 1930. Ouédraogo then became a teacher and school director before he then turned to agriculture, where his talents as a trainer led him to the top echelons of the civil service. But he found he was unable to help the farmers and village groups whom he was supposed to be training, so he left to find out why. Studying in France, he obtained a doctorate from the Sorbonne, in the Social Sciences of Development, in 1977.

Work with the Naam Structures: The Result Was an Initiative Unique in Africa

His first question, while he was undertaking his doctorate, was whether anything existed in the traditional society of the Mossi (Burkina's largest ethnic group) that resembled village groups. "We undertook a thorough study of village social organization – the people's thinking and their social and economic structures – and we discovered that the Naam group, a traditional village body composed of young people, had the most highly developed cooperative characteristics. We decided we would attempt to work with the Naam structures."

The result was an initiative unique in Africa. Despite a lot of problems, the Naam groups prospered. By 1978 there were over 2,500 groups in Yatenga province with 160,000 members. Twenty years later this had risen to 6,480 groups all over Burkina Faso and adjoining countries – almost half of them women's groups – with a membership of 300,000. The transformation of the traditional Naam groups into modern social structures was a brilliant piece of practical sociology by Ouédraogo.

At an acceptance speech, whenOuédraogo received the Right Livelihood Award in 1990, he referred to their principle of "developing without damaging" which aims at accomplishing economical, social and cultural changes, but without rejecting African values. Their (villages drawn from Senegal, Mali, Niger, Togo, Mauritania, Burkina Faso, Gambia and Guinea Bissau) point of departure was the traditional environment and they aimed at creating first an internal dynamic movement and then an external one. They also encouraged the target groups to contribute with themselves as they are (that is, their own nature), their knowledge and their way of living (that is, their own culture), their know-how (that is, the technology they master) and, finally, their ambitions (that is, their aspirations and aims in society).

Reasons for Their Success: Motivation Generated from Within The Group

Ouédraogo gives four reasons for their success: dynamic local leadership and activity; maintenance of traditional values; proscription of any sort of social, ethnic, political or religious discrimination; and training and motivation generated from within the group. The activities of the Naam groups are as broad as life itself. They grow, build, manufacture, trade. As of 1999, they had created 235 cereal banks, 115 mills, 22 dams and about 300 wells. In addition they have established 17 credit banks and constructed six cellars in Yatenga for preserving the 1,000 tons of potatoes they grow each year.

The Naam groups were helped with aid funds from French, Swiss, Dutch and German agencies, but they generated their own incomes as well. While Naam is a people's movement, Six S is a non-governmental organization. It was dedicated to removing three obstacles to peasant mobilisation: the lack of technical know how for coping with drought and desertification; the lack of negotiating skills to deal with government and aid agencies, and the lack of funds to implement small projects.

7.4.2. A Federation of Peasant Organizations from Nine Sahel Countries

Consciousness Is an Organic Part of One's Social Existence

More recently, Six S has undergone some restructuring. In the mid-1990s, Ouédraogo was elected Mayor of his hometown, Ouahigouya. Despite the success of Six S hitherto, by then he was doubtful of its future prospects: "The danger for many Africans is that the erosion of our ways by the aggressive ways of others, our own values by foreign values, will destroy our sense of responsibility for solving our communities' problems."

There is no assured method of transferring commitment to succeeding generations who have not lived through the struggles from which commitment is sociohistorically born. Such a pursuit becomes a happy hunting ground for self-seekers. And genuine accountability to the people is not merely a matter of formal institutional structures, but also, and critically, of people's self-awareness and the confidence to assert such in the affairs of society. The crisis of the left – and for that matter of the right as well – ultimately boils down to this dissociation between the productive forces and the leadership of concerned societies. With such dissociation prevailing, the need is to generate social processes, which would promote the possibility of organic leadership. PAR attempts, as has been demonstrated in the Burkina Faso case, just that.

Six-S then in the final analysis, for Pradervand, emerged as a result of three obstacles that prevented farmers getting together:

> The first obstacle was the lack of know-how. The farmers simply did not have the knowledge to face the unprecedented challenges of the drought situation. The second was the lack of "negotiators". By that I mean farmers capable of negotiating projects with both local administration and village elders. The third was the lack of funds to implement small projects.

The Breakthrough of Flexible Funding Run By the Farmers Themselves

What in fact made Six-S unique – apart from the fact that it is run by farmers themselves and the naam groups on which they historically drew – was its system of flexible funding. Funds were made available without knowledge of the projects for which they will be used, the zones making use of these at their discretion, taking into account the overall direction of the funds, the financial management thereof, and the cash generating potential of the projects. To begin with a zone receives modest funds, which were increased as it demonstrated its ability to manage funds, and then the funds would tail off once the zone was able to attract outside donors.

There were three stages identified then, in such funding and development: first, to help the farmers organize themselves – to build a network, find grass-roots communicators, master elementary concepts of management, lay the groundwork for literacy training. Only at the second stage, once the ability to save, manage, and to carry out dialogue internally and externally, was project finance offered. These first two stages could easily take 6–10 years. By the time the third stage was reached, they could then become autonomous.

An Ongoing University for Farmers Learning From Each Other

Six-S, moreover, was in fact an ongoing university for farmers learning from each other. It was a place where peasant organizations share differing philosophies with one point in common: self reliance. Six-S only helped those who had already shown they are capable of organizing themselves. The educational association formed taught farmers the basic elements of planning, evaluation and accounting, including what is called "accounts in the sunlight", that is transparency.

Sambo Gundo was a Six-S coordinator (*chef de zone*), or "animateur", in Mali:

> Communicators are selected by village groups and have various tasks. They transmit information from the grass-roots to the leaders and vice versa. They pass on technical information. They conduct literacy courses. Above all they stress the importance of self reliance and the "Six-S spirit", which forms the basis for all our action: help only those who help themselves.

In Sambo's own home village of Manaco:

> Our first project was a local paper in our own language. Development starts with the communication of ideas, for example on better ways to cultivate your fields, on how to create new sources of income, or how to save money. Money is something we spend and nothing remains, but ideas remain. We can use them to create our own means and tools for development. In my village, for centuries, farmers have organized themselves in groups called "walde", from the age of six until death. In these groups he undertakes social, cultural and agricultural activities. It is through these groups that we developed a new use of money, to fund productive activities, rather than to purely fund our festivals.

The first project the farmers undertook was building a literacy centre. The other activities were started: opening tracks through the bush between villages, purchasing a grain mill for the women, reforestation projects, and so on. In describing his role as coordinator, Samba said:

> One day I'll go to a village to check the construction work, Another day I'll receive a delegation from another village. Then I'll visit the communal fields and discuss a reforestation project. Next I'll meet the village chide and hold discussions with the elders. You listen to their different points if view on a project and try to reconcile them. I also make contact with the local state administration, and then with merchants to purchase materials. This process can take months. There are also training session to organize and reports to write. Finally, as coordinator, he is responsible for the overall health of the village.

The Transformation of Sexual Roles

Furthermore, possibly the most important impact of the village groups, for Pradervand, had been the transformation of relations between the sexes. In Africa's rural areas, women were unquestionably the more dynamic of the two sexes, perhaps accounted for by the historic developments to which Amadiume has alluded (see previous chapter). Liberating the creative potential of these women could be the most critical factor in rural development. For Ramata Sawadogo, a grass-roots communicator from Ouahigouya, in Burkina Faso:

> Before the village groups started to have an impact, women were forgotten, set aside. Their role was to have children and to care for the family, the sheep and the visiting guests. A woman could not choose her husband. The husband's father decided everything. Women worked like beats of burden.

For Marcelline Ruanda, from Konguossi, Burkina Faso:

> With the Naam groups women have become like sisters. Now there are no more racial, ethnic or caste distinctions. There is a real sisterhood now.

How then has the Six S's subsequently evolved?

The Six S's in Retrospect

Sad to say, in the new millennium, the Six S's project as a whole began to fade, because the three key protagonists were no longer involved. This is often the fate of such projects in the global South, which do not become fully institutionalised, even though, in the latter part of the last century, it had become the most prominent PAR based project in the world, and hence warranted our newly global status as such.

7.5. Act Global-Local: Transformative Effect: PAR Keynotes: S4a

7.5.1. PAR Is Aimed at the Exploited, the Poor, the Oppressed, the Marginal

We now return finally to Fals Borda and to MD Rahman and to the global-local Keynotes (see below) of Participatory Action Research. Stimulation of the poor and deprived, firstly as such, to undertake self-reliant initiatives, requires two essential steps. The first is the development of an awareness about the reality in which they live. In particular, they need to understand that poverty and deprivation are the result of specific social forces rather than an outcome of some inherent deficiency on their part or even "fate". Second, based on such critical awareness, they need to gain confidence in their collective abilities to bring about positive changes in their life situations and organize themselves for that purpose. To the extent, then, that

Nhakanomics (see our first 'southern' case story below) in Zimbabwe draws on the full legacy of rural community, like Buhera, that its natural and cultural heritage, thereby co-evolved technologically and economically, so people hitherto marginalized are bestowed new livelihoods.

PAR – Transforming the Southern African Social Reality – Keynotes
Nhakanomics is aimed at the Exploited, the Poor, the Oppressed, the Marginal.
Kumusha creates Awareness of the People's own Resources in Africa
Vakamusha involves the full and active Participation of the Community.
Goal of Integral Kumusha is radical Transformation of social Reality in Africa.

7.5.2. PAR Creates Awareness of the People's Own Resources

A typical PAR program, secondly then, stimulates direct self-analysis by the landless, and in this southern African case, also, by those living in homesteads with economic potential. In many places this had led to intense and sustained pressure-group action to confront social injustice and resist oppression by rural elites. In another areas, confrontational activity to resist such oppression had been particularly intense for several years and had led to many forms of harassment, both of the landless leaders and NGO workers. The kind of self analysis undertaken included:

- What was their experience?
- What did they learn themselves from this?
- What would they, with their past experience, advise the landless in other villages who might want to get organized?
- What was the relation of their present activities with past ones?
- Would they like to document their story, draw its lessons more systematically after thorough discussion in the base of the organization, and
- Disseminate them so that fellow landless in other villages would not need to start from zero and could benefit from their experience?

In the Zimbabwean kumusha case, Daud Shumba is especially active on radio and television, spreading the wors, while also actively networking in his own community, locally, in Zimbabwean nationally, and on Southern African regionally.

7.5.3. PAR Involves the Full and Active Participation of the Community

Overall and thirdly, in PAR, there is a break-up of the classical dichotomy between "subject" and "object" (manipulation and dominance), between in our Zimbabwe case community and enterprise, and its replacement by a humanistic mode of equal relation between two subjects (animation and facilitation). The essential difference between the latter approach and that typically undertaken by a political party or conventional development practitioner, in moving from analysis to transformation, is:

- *Starting from where people are* – their perceptions, knowledge, experiences and rhythm of work and thoughts, as opposed to preconceived agendas
- *Stimulating people (animation)* to undertake self-analysis of their life situations, and helping them to derive from such self inquiry into the political-economic-cultural environment an intellectual base for initiating changes
- *Assisting people to organize themselves* into People's Organizations (PO's) which are non-hierarchical in structure and democratic in operations
- *Facilitating the actions for change*, with the external catalyst paving the way for internal self-reliance
- Stimulating People's Organizations to *carry out regular self-reviews*, to assess and learn from success and failure.

What then is the ultimate goal of all of such?

7.5.4. Goal of Integral Kumusha the Radical Transformation of Social Reality

For Fals Borda finally, as for the Taranhike's, those involved in PAR start with the thesis that science does not have absolute or pure value but is simply a useful form of knowledge for specific purposes and based on relative truths. Any science as a cultural product carries those biases and values, which scientists hold as a group. It therefore favors those who produce and control it. A people's science may hence serve as a corrective. To that extent, Daud Shumba's engineering background has been abundantly deployed to good social and economic effect in developing water resources, harnessing renewable energy and engaging with organic agriculture. Overall, and in that guise, he has drawn on natural, cultural and scientific legacies form both near and afar.

Table 7.5.4. *People's Science: Collective Research, Recovery of History, Valuing Folk Culture, Producing and Diffusing Knowledge*

Collective Research	Obtained from Groups through Dialogue, Discussion, Argument and Consensus in the Investigation of Social Realities
Critical Recovery of History	To discover, selectively through collective Memory, those Elements of the Past which have proved useful in the Increase of Conscientization, using popular Stories and oral Traditions "fleshed out"
Valuing and Applying Folk Culture	Account is taken of Art, Music, Drama, Sports, Story-Telling and other Expressions related to Human Sentiment and Imagination
Production and Diffusion of new Knowledge	Different Levels of Communication are developed for People ranging from pre-literate to intellectual, using Image, Sound, Painting, Mime, Photograph, Theatre, Poetry, Music, Puppetry and Exhibitions. The Groups involved include Cooperatives, Trade Unions, Cultural Centres and so on

Ideally, in the process, the grassroots are able to participate in the research-and-innovation process from the beginning: that is from the moment it is decided what the subject of the research should be, to the time it is completed. Its essence is the proposition that more is to be gained by using the affective logic of the heart than the cold-headed analyses that come from laboratories.

We are now ready to conclude.

7.5. Conclusion

7.6.1. PAR in Retrospect

Reflecting on "What Is Development?"

People's collective self-development initiatives, for Fals Borda, not only point to a way out of the development impasse. They also suggest the need for reflection on the very notion of "development". For a long time, development has been associated with the mechanistic notion of the development of physical assets and increasing the flow of economic and social goods and services. Much of the activities articulated here are developmental, but questions remain as to whether the process of people mobilizing themselves is a means of "development" or an end in itself.

Africa in particular, for him writing in the 1990s, is indeed showing evidence of vibrant and assertive people's self development efforts in rural areas, which are in the frontier of such efforts anywhere and from which inspiration can be gleaned and much learned. Genuine people-oriented activists seldom come from the professional classes. However people with a powerful societal vision, conception, intellectual ability and methodological skill for translating conception into practice are needed to provide some guidance and perspective for such initiatives, and for these to spread widely with some coherence. People seem to be ready to respond to such "animation".

Must this be left to spontaneous historical emergence, or can some method of "schooling" be devised to promote a greater concern among a nation's potential intellectual leaders to work *with* and not *upon* the people, so that the "other Africa" could develop faster?

Praxis and the Recovery of History and Culture

Participative action research, in conclusion, has demonstrated in concrete cases its ability to further the progress of the grassroots rather then the vested interests of dominant groups. As such, the rediscovery of cultural roots is an essential element in any effort to improve depressed communities.

The more important practical challenge PAR faces, for Fals Borda, is the need of common people to articulate in social movements, along with new knowledge, the necessary political struggles for justice and progress. As such we are discovering once more the pertinence of participatory action research to the transformation of our societies into a more satisfactory and less violent world.

7.6.2. Walking the Relational Path in Southern Africa

Originally Grounded Descriptively in the Southern Kumusha Guise

We are now in a position to apply the relational path as a whole in Southern Africa, as we shall see in more detail, in our next chapter and opening case story. As such we start, descriptively, standing on the formidable shoulders of Magosvongwe, Biko, Ingold and the Taranhike's in particular, whereby they:

- Seek to reveal the Essences and Origins of *human Experience*.
- Engage their total Selves as Participants, *passionately Involved*
- *Do not seek to predict* or to determine causal Relationships
- Illuminate these through *comprehensive Descriptions*, vivid and accurate Renderings of Experience, rather than Measurements or Ratings.

Emerging Phenomenological Southern Relational Nhakanomic Foundation

Subsequently in thereby *southern* African, phenomenological emergent relational guise, the Taranhike's:

- Immerse themselves in their *unhu/ivhu* communal laden, local life worlds
- Concentrate on illuminating the natural-cultural *inner self* of "black consciousness" in Biko-like, local-global guise

- Locate the *unique cultural history* of their integral kumusha in the nely global story of livelihood, dwelling and enskillment that Ingold reveals
- Going *beyond reductive* positivism and naive empiricism in a now global-local light as revealed by the Taranhike's via *nhakanomics*.

Emancipatory Feminist Southern Relational Nhakanomic Navigation

Now thirdly, and building on what has come originally and foundationally before, by way of natural and cultural grounding and emergence, such now nhakanomic navigation, so called, building on societal legacy:

- Complements an androcentric perspective *reinventing Africa*
- Includes self and nature as African in your social research in *unhu* guise
- Aiming to create social and economic change through *communitalism*
- Seeing knowledge as a tool for *African* liberation not domination.

Effecting Transformative Feminist Southern Relational Nhakanomics

Ultimately then, in transformative terms, thereby applying Participatory Action Research to the development of Nhakanomics in rural Zimbabwe, PAR:

- Is *aimed at the Exploited*, the Poor, the Oppressed, the Marginal
- *Creates Awareness* of the People's own Resources
- Involves the full and *active Participation* of the Community
- Has the ultimate Goal as the *radical Transformation* of social Reality.

Along that relational path, research and innovation wise, moroever, we pave the further way toward communal learning, communiversity wise specifically, and an emergent foundation for community buiding enterprise wise, and communitalism economically, generally. We turn to the actualisation of the relational path, in the chapter that follows, after which we turn south-east, to the path of renewal, starting with natural/communal grounding and origination via narrative method.

7.6.3. Integral Kumusha to Nhakanomics in Southern Africa: S2fita

Participatory action research in the final analysis, as the transformative effect of our southern relational path, builds on all that has come before, that is the original descriptive, kumusha case story; the unhu based life world of the shona peoples in Zimbabwe; the feminist impulse that Christina Taranhike brings to bear upon would-be nhakanomics; and finally the transformation of a business corporation into a community based enterprise, vakamusha, in the overall process, for Amadiume, reinventing Africa. Moreover, as can be seen in Table 7.1.1. at the outset of this chapter, the dual analytical-research/transformative-innovation rhythm serves to reinforces the overall, developmental effect.

Table 7.6.3. *Integral Kumusha to Nhakanomics in Southern Africa S2fita*

Feeling Local	Intuiting Local-Global	Thinking Newly Global	Acting Global-Local
Re-inventing Africa	*Feminist Foundation*	*Indigenous Knowledge Systems*	*Create Social Change through Nhakanomics*

We now turn from the relational path in Southern Africa to the renewal path in East Africa, and thereby from community building to conscious evolution, and from communitalism in southern African Nhakanomic guise to such in east African guise, that is what we have termed Yurugu-nomics.

7.7. References

Dewey J (2009) *Art as Experience.* Exeter. Pedigree Books

Lessem R and **Schieffer** A (2010) *Integral Research and Innovation: Transforming Enterprise and Society.* Abingdon. Routledge

Lewin K (2005) *Principles of Topological Psychology.* Connecticut. Martino Fine

Freire P (2017) *Pedagogy of the Oppressed.* London. Penguin Modern Classics

Mandela N (1994) *The Long Walk to Freedom.* New York. Abacus

Luther King M (1991) *Testament of Hope: The Essential Writings and Speeches.* New York. Harper Collins

Gandhi M K (2001) *An Autobiography: A Story of My Experiments with the Truth.* London. Penguin Classics

Reason P and **Bradbury** H (2004) *Handbook of Action Research.* London. Sage

Pradervand P (1990) *Listening to Africa: Developing Africa from the Grassroots.* New York. Praeger

Selener D. (1997) *Participation Action Research for Social Change.* Ithaca, New York. Cornell University

Fals Borda O (ed) (1991) *Action and knowledge.* New York. Apex Publishing

Rahman M D (1993) *People's Self-Development.* London. Zed Books

Nyerere J (1968) *Ujamaa: Essays on Socialism.* Oxford. Oxford University Press

Swantz M (1985) *Women in Development: A Creative Role Denied – The Case of Tanzania.* New York. Palgrave Macmillan

Jose Ortega y Gasset (1994) *The Revolt of the Masses.* New York. W.W. Norton

ICS 1: Integral Case Story: Integral Kumusha/Nhakanomics
This story was contributed by Dr Daud Taranhike, founder of the Integral Kumusha in Buhera, Zimbabwe.
Integral Path of "Southern" African Renewal: Learning Community

Introduction

The Integral Kumusha case story details the evolution of a social innovation which emerged from a PhD research journey by Daud Taranhike with the Trans4m Centre for Integral Development in France in conjunction with the Da Vinci Institute for Technology Innovation Management of South Africa. In this chapter, Taranhike shares the reasons and rationale for embarking on this research journey, the research path he followed demonstrating the research method and methodology that were used and the key research outcomes or the research evolution cycle, including its impact and contribution to the body of knowledge and also towards rural development and total wellbeing.

What is intriguing about the Integral Kumusha case story is the fact that the concepts and models that emerged are novel, and they are contributing towards enhancing the lives and livelihoods of rural folks. This is a radical departure from traditional and conventional research where the research focuses on producing literature and theories that are stored in libraries. In the conventional research, the research recommendations are for further research to be undertaken with the same self-serving approach thereby creating a vicious cycle of writing theses that are seldomly used in real life. In this particular case, and as is the practice with other social research innovations, the emphasis is on implementing the findings in order to validate the outcomes through the application of the concepts and models in solving particular challenges or problems that exist in life. Hence, the PhD thesis becomes part of the operating manual to facilitate a continuous learning process. As such, this case story will be sharing some new developments that have happened as a result of the work being carried out on the ground, which continues to provide feedback on the research innovation.

Background of the research

According to the Zimbabwe National Statistics Agency (2011/12) in 2012, more than 70 % of the Zimbabwe population live in rural areas and the majority, approximately

65 %, live in abject poverty. This was the immediate result of colonisation, whereupon the black majority were displaced from their land and were driven into what was called the native reserves while the fertile land was allocated to the minority white farmers. These native reserves or the Tribal Trust Lands (TTLs) were mainly in ecological regions 4 and 5 which are semi-arid and arid, with very poor sandy soils, where crops yields are extremely low. According to the research conducted by Dr Ephreim Whingwiri the founder of Zimbabwe Earthworm Farms, more than 70 % of the soil in the rural area is sandy and very infertile (lacking humus and carbon) with very low crop yielding capacity. This also has resulted in people in rural areas experiencing hunger and failing to be food and nutrition self-sufficient. As a result, the rural communities are marginalised and most productive people desert these areas in search of employment and better life in urban areas. The rural to urban migration continues to be a big problem even with over four decades after Zimbabwe gained its independence from Britain.

The people who remain in these rural areas survive through supplements and support of food handouts from non-governmental organisations (NGOs), government and other social and civic organisations. As part of the rural development and support, the government, through various initiatives such as the Presidential Input Scheme, provides seed and fertilisers to help the people become self-sufficient. However, this has not achieved the desired objective, forcing the civic organisation to provide additional food to the people to avoid starvation and related diseases. While this assistance by government and other organisations provides huge relief against hunger among these rural folks, it is creating the unintended dependency attitude. This is a typical example of the proverbial saying of giving man fish instead of teaching him how to fish. This is one of the reasons the Zimbabwean economy is in constant deficit: the government spends huge amounts of money looking after people who should be looking after themselves and contributing towards economic development and growth. Consequently, the majority of rural people are marginalised and have no voice in national socio-economic development issues and programmes.

It is against this background that Daud Shumba Taranhike and his partner and wife Christina, sought to find ways of empowering the ordinary rural people in order to eradicate poverty, hunger and marginalisation. As an important consideration in addressing these challenges, they focused on how the people can be capacitated and empowered to identify the potentials, gifts and possibilities within their communities and how to unlock them in order to enhance their lives and livelihoods. This is a great paradigm shift for the ordinary people who have been used to receiving support for a very long time. This cannot happen by just lecturing to the people and expecting them to change their ways. The giant change process involved developing a practical model that demonstrates the transformation towards self-sufficiency and moving rural communities and society from poverty to prosperity (P2P).

The research established that a number of initiatives have been implemented to support rural development and growth, yet very little has been achieved in addressing poverty and hunger within rural communities (Scoones 2015). One of the main reasons for these initiatives' failure is that they lacked contextualisation, that is, a cultural and traditional way of life that holistically takes into account nature, culture, technology, and enterprise. In most cases, the interventions are designed and developed at the top and prescribed to the people at the grassroots with little or no real consultations involved. Hence, the programmes are divorced from the people's way of life, and the concerned people have no ownership of the overall programmes.

Therefore, rural transformation is such an important issue that cannot be used for political expedience nor for benefiting organisations which masquerade as donors, whereby the bulk of the funding is spent on purchasing expensive vehicles and supporting the lives of the project managers or coordinators while very little filters down to the common people. The Taranhike's, through their research and regeneration, sought an approach that would ensure genuine rural transformation with a re-imagined authentic African lifestyle and not the cosmetic approach that maintains the state quo. It is unattainable to accept that these rural people, who are the majority of the population, should continue in poverty and be marginalised. This understanding and appreciation justified the importance of this research innovation.

It emerged during the research journey and transformation that the regeneration of rural communities should take a holistic and integrated approach that incorporates nature, culture, technology and enterprise. In pursuing this approach, starting with the homestead (musha) was important. In the rural areas, the homestead is readily available to everyone. So, it became so critical that focus be directed on the musha. It also became quite apparent that the original economy in ancient times was built on the household trade of oikos (Rima 2001) in Greece. The power of the home has always been appreciated, but very little thought and effort has been devoted towards unlocking this huge potential and possibility that exists in rural areas and can be a game changer in rural transformation. Therefore, the research focused on how to transform the rural homestead (kumusha) into a viable socio-economic entity. Hence kumusha ceases to be just a place for people to be buried but a place to create value and a great legacy (nhaka) for future generations.

Research Questions

The above research background and information triggered a number of questions which Taranhike sought to pursue and be answered as part of the research process as well as his transformation journey. Some of the major questions that needed attention were as follows;

1. Why would the people in the rural areas fail to be food self-sufficient as they used to be in the past, with the majority of them being dependent on food handouts from the government, donors, and other well-wishers?

2. How can the rural folks be empowered and helped to enhance their lives and livelihoods by focusing primarily on the potentials, gifts and possibilities inherently available within their communities, which are the land and their homesteads?
3. Can a new economic framework that resonates with the African society anchored upon the indigenous African traditional cultural practices blend with exogenous knowledge rather than relying mainly on the alien capitalist economic model?
4. How can the existing socio-economic and learning models be changed to ensure continuous improvement and sustainability for every community member, and that helps create a great legacy for future generations?

The above four questions became the bedrock of the research journey to establish solutions and operating models that would empower rural people to transform from poverty to prosperity and create vibrant local and national regenerative economies that benefit all its citizens. Based on this desire, Taranhike also sought to establish transferable models that could be implemented beyond Zimbabwe's boundaries but within the Southern African Region, the African continent, and the Global South in general. The rationale for developing alternative models to those inherited from the colonial era was to ensure total emancipation of the people from the colonial mentality and ensure authentic and genuine systems that can help these formerly colonised and marginalised people take charge of their lives and their future (Ndlovu-Gatsheni 2018). There is a great need to change the current situation where the majority of the people who are the grassroots continue to be poor while a few elite and former colonialists are rich and control the economy. This will ensure that political independence is of real value and meaningful to the ordinary people.

Research Approach and Research to Innovation Journey

The Four Worlds approach (Lessem and Schieffer 2010) uses the metaphorical and physical approach to denote the strengths and potentials of different parts of the world as divided into four worlds together with the GENE rhythm as follows:

South: The Relational Realm

The South emphasises the local Grounding (G) in nature and community. This is the starting point of the research cycle and denotes the traditional rural homestead (Kumusha) in this particular research evolution. For the rural area, the homestead is the most valuable asset people own and most people even if they migrate to the urban areas, kumusha remains their main home and are connected with their ancestors and tradition. In traditional African Shona culture, the baby's umbilical cord is buried in the soil, giving the strong connection and bond between nature and humanity. This is where communal learning within the Communiversity approach (Lessem et al 2019).

East: The Inspirational Realm

The East is the local global Emergence (E) in culture and spirituality. This is the second part of the research cycle: the evolved homestead into what this research calls the Integral Kumusha. The evolution ensures development to new horizons as a build-up to the local context in the global arena. This is so fundamental because this helps people to be exposed to new practices without losing their own originality. This shift is very important and it put people in a dynamic evolutionary path rather than remaining static. The PhD research programme provides for development Communiversity wise. It is important to realise that development must be intentionally designed to achieve the desired objectives.

North: The Knowledge Realm

The North focuses on knowledge co-creation, leading to a new global Navigating (N) science and technology. In this research evolution, this denotes the Nhakanomics which is a new economic model that is anchored upon African heritage which is an Ubuntu based economic framework which helps people to create an economy that ensures integrality and legacy (nhaka) in the Shona language. This provides a new form of economy that is genuinely African and offers an alternative to capitalism which is alien to Africa. In the Communiversity guise, this is the Academy that the Integral Kumusha is working to establish as the Nhakanomics Transformation and Research Academy.

West: The Action Realm

The West emphasises entrepreneurship which is the global local Effecting (E) of enterprise and economy. For our research to innovation evolution, this is Vakamusha an enterprise that is home-based which helps in the creation of a vibrant village or community economy. This is the epitome of this research process that ensures an integral and holistic development bringing economic value to the people within the rural community. Vakamusha has been registered as Integral Kumusha Private Limited which is the socio-economic laboratory where the new ideas, models and thoughts are tested and implemented.

The Four World and the GENE approach was supported by the CARE AND 4Cs process that make the research process complete. The CARE provided the practical aspect of the research journey which involved Community Engagement (C) with the Inner and Outer Call, Awakening the Integral Consciousness (A) together with the research Context, Institutionalised Research (R) with knowledge Co-Creation and Embodiment (E) of the research and its Contribution. Thereby providing the double helix coil that reinforced the research process (Schieffer and Lessem 2014).

The Research Process Towards Restoring, Preserving, Enhancing and Creating Legacy

The research process followed the Eastern path of renewal. In the origination phase, the researcher had to clearly define his calling which in this case was to restore, preserve, enhance and create a great legacy for future generations. At the same time, the researcher engaged the Buhera rural community in Zimbabwe and shared the calling and challenges or problems which needed attention. In this case, the main challenges were poverty, hunger and marginalisation of this rural community which are also prevalent and similar to other rural communities throughout Zimbabwe if not throughout Africa and the countries of the Global South. During this phase, the narrative method was used since it was the most appropriate given the power of storytelling withing the African people.

The Origination Phase

It was during the origination phase that the traditional rural homestead was identified as the most critical asset and resource that was at everyone's disposal and could be transformed to enhance people's lives, livelihoods and wellbeing. It was established that every person within the village had a homestead and a piece of land to support their families. However, people did not value this resource as such and would not consider it an opportunity to transform their lives and livelihoods. It also became clearly evident that the community could also engage into communal learning without having to be subjected to the formal schooling system and still generate important knowledge required for transforming their lives. Through the Nhaka circles which were similar to the Study Circles which were employed in Sweden to raise political awareness, the community could build tremendous knowledge both indigenous and exogenous, for their salvation against poverty, hunger and marginalisation. So Kumusha became the key focus in solving these problems.

The Foundation Phase

The second phase in the research journey was the Foundation stage, where the researcher took adequate time to understand the research Context. To fully understand and appreciate the research context, it was important to explore the key historical developments and milestones and the cultural background and norms that influenced the African social construct, especially in rural areas. To do this well, the researcher used the Hermeneutics methodology with its powerful way of digging into history while at the same time providing an effective interpretation of the key phenomena that influenced life and livelihoods (Serequeberhan, 1994). The major highlight of this phase was the effects and impact of colonisation on black people and how they viewed themselves in terms of self-esteem and confidence.

Some cultural practices also contributed to the predicament of the majority of black people where anything that was a mystery was associated with the spiritual world with very little or no research being conducted to establish the exact knowledge and position. The researcher raised the people's consciousness towards the Integral Development approach and the conviction that the solutions to the problems that beset this rural community would be generated from within the community and by the people themselves. In this way, the solutions to the problems of hunger, poverty, and marginalisation would be original, authentic, and genuine. It also became important and clear that there was a need for a paradigm shift in order to facilitate real development. This research journey provided the much-needed opportunity to facilitate the shift to a new level of thinking and re-imagining the future within the rural set-up. The evolution of research in this phase resulted in the emergence of the Integral Kumusha concept and model.

The Integral Kumusha concept model brought into play the origin of household trade called oikos. The power and importance of household trade has, over the years, helped the common people to conduct trade among themselves and ensure an effective economic activity within a community. In the research that was carried out by German Sociologists and feminists (Bennholdt-Thomsem & Mies, 1999) in Bangladesh, household economic activities helped the marginalised women to subsist and enhance their lives. The research results also confirmed that this approach can be expanded to other countries and areas that transform the lives of the grassroots people and to other areas of the economy. in this research, the traditional homestead was developed to become socially and economically viable. This was a departure from the common belief that the rural homestead was of no real significance apart from burying the dead and keeping records of the ancestors. It could be used to generate wealth and create a great legacy for future generations in a manner that had never been thought possible before.

The Emancipation Phase

In the third phase of the research to innovation journey, which is the Emancipation phase, the researcher engaged with critical theory. In this process, the Feminist approach was used because of its applicability to grassroots issues (Bennholdt-Thomsem and Mies 1999). The feminist approach though it was originally focusing on advancing the rights of women, it has developed to cater for the common people hence it became very applicable to this research. A lot of literature was reviewed in order to establish and create new knowledge that is relevant to the issues confronting rural people and their livelihoods.

It was during the emancipation phase that new ideas and knowledge was generated. One of the major breakthroughs of this process was the emergence of the concept of Nhakanomics. This novel concept was a further evolution, now also in a macro guise of the Integral Kumusha concept, which became the obvious alternative of the Western pre-emphasis on the abstract market-based, if not increasingly neoliberal economy, because of the renewed grounding in nature and culture with a technology and enterprise reach. This provided a holistic and integral rural entity that would ensure food self-sufficiency at a household level while bringing economic activity within the community. This is unlike the Corporate Firm, which emphasises technology and enterprise bereft of nature and culture (Taranhike 2019).

The Integral Kumusha became the foundation upon which the Nhakanomics concept was built by taking the idea to a societal or national level where the economic framework or model can be tailor-made to the African traditional way of building inheritance or legacy (Dhaka) (World Bank 2007). It became apparent that the capitalist model has failed to deliver for almost all African countries. This is confirmed by the economic crises that exist in African countries despite the countries gaining political independence. As such, in the same way, the Integral Kumusha evolved and also challenged the notion that Capitalism continues to be considered a universal and one-size-fits-all economic model. There is rather an understanding that each society should have an economic approach that suits its needs. In Zimbabwe and in the Southern African region for Taranhike and his immediate associates, Nhakanomics has emerged as the economic model that resonates with the way African people develop and create inheritance and legacy. The model is built on Ubuntu heritage based approach that is grounded in relationships (ukama) and the culture of stewardship (Utariri), with emphasis on teamwork (nhimbe) and wealth creation (upfumi). These are the key ingredients that make up a holistic approach to creating a great legacy. Our African heritage has never been considered seriously in the economic development of Africa and its countries, yet this has been the mainstay of the African way of creating a legacy for future generations.

The beauty of Nhakanomics, unlike the emphasis on capitalism and neo-liberal economic systems, which stress national Gross Domestic Product (GDP) and other metrics, focuses on the critical and sometimes overlooked aspects that improve the quality of life and well-being of people. The special aspects such as having quality time with family and friends, the ability to rest and regenerate energy and sharpening the minds and collaboration are far better indicators of a progressive economy than an insatiable appetite for profits and an unending desire for continuous growth as what capitalism drives. In Zimbabwe, for example, the current economy is considered to be growing at an average of 3 % GDP, but the majority of people's lives do not show that life is improving (Heron 1996). So, to continue burying our heads in the sand and pretend that the current economic system is delivering is just insanity of indescribable proportions. Hence, Nhakanomics is ushering in a new economic paradigm that is not controlled or directed by the Multi-National Finance Institutions such as the World Bank and the International Monetary Fund (IMF), which prescribe economic recipes that would not deliver for the common man and ensure the so-called poor yet very rich countries continue to be indebted and captured.

During this third phase of the research, knowledge co-creation can be reinforced by developing a research academy that collaborates with other researchers and research institutes in creating new knowledge and ideas for use and consumption by the present and future generations. Through research and development, we can ensure sustainability and the creation of valuable knowledge for effective transformation and regeneration. In summary, the third phase helped in the evolution and emergence of three key research outcomes: the Integral Kumusha, Nhakanomics and the Inside-Out Communiversity (see below). All these innovations are closely related and are interdependent in our quest to eradicate poverty, hunger, and marginalisation at the household, national, regional, and continental levels.

The Integral Kumusha helps rural people transform towards self-sufficiency and move from poverty to prosperity starting at a household level, impacting the community and national economies regeneratively. This new practice and model brings consciousness among people that they do not have to despise their rural homesteads for urban life. At a national level and beyond, Nhakanomics also helps African people to seek and develop an economic model and practice that is not alien and perfectly suits and addresses our own real economic challenges, not those being described and dictated upon us by the so-called developed countries that have little or no appreciation of our way of life. The Communiversity concept and practice, as we shall also see in the case of Pax Herbal in Nigeria, brings everyone into the learning and transformation process. Learning and development cease to become a preserve for those who attend formal classroom education. The educational curriculum being followed in formal schools does not adequately address the real current and future issues that confront our communities and societies.

The Transformation Phase

The fourth and final phase of the research was the Transformation phase which used Cooperative Inquiry (CI) which is part of Action Research as advocated by Heron (Heron and Reason 2001) in P. Reason & H. Bradbury (eds) *Handbook of Action Research: Participative Inquiry and Practice* (179–188, 2001). The process allowed many views to be generated and in the process validated through an iterative process that refined and synthesised the different views and ideas that were generated thereby coming up with valid outcomes that resample the people and also with special and insightful breakthroughs that enriched the research findings. This way of research with people is far much better than trying to research on people and then drawing `conclusions without the involvement of the concerned people.

This knowledge Co-creation process was so vital because the people needed a methodology whereby they could participate freely while they expressed their views in an environment where they felt secure and never looked down upon. Every individual who participated in this process did it voluntarily and were free to disengage should they feel they were not benefiting from the process or that they were not being appreciated. The principal researcher, Taranhike in this particular case, facilitated the process and ensured that every individual's right and privacy were protected. Interestingly, none of the people who participated in this Cooperative Inquiry opted out and they all were actively and enthusiastically engaged throughout the entire process.

As a result of the Co-operative Inquiry process, the research evolution produced Vakamusha as the entity which was later registered as the Integral Kumusha Private Limited, an integral rural business. At the same time from the Communiversity perspective, Vakamusha became the Socio-economic laboratory which can be used to test, apply and validate the new knowledge and ideas that would have been generated at the research academy. This social economic entity provides an opportunity to create and regenerate the local economy while at the same time support continuous research and development in a practical and realistic way that enhances lives and livelihoods.

Developing the Integral Kumusha in the Perceived Poor District of Buhera

The Integral Kumusha is located in Mukoto Village in Buhera District of Manicaland Province in Zimbabwe. This overall innovation, arising from the Integral research above, also continuing after the PhD program, was developed by Dr Daud Taranhike together with his wife Mrs Christina Taranhike as the Co-Founders using the Integral Kumusha concept which emerged from the research process as a prototype to demonstrate and validate the results of the research findings and outcomes. Buhera is in ecological region 4/5 which receives very limited rainfall, and it is considered the poorest district in Manicaland province. This is the reason why there are many NGOs in Buhera yet very little has been achieved in terms of enhancing the lives and livelihoods of people in Buhera. This is the same place where Professor Ronnie Lessem's father Abe and his uncle Jack lived and operated their business venture where they traded grain from the same community with different merchandise from their store. The place was popularly known as Kwa Jack. It contributed significantly to the economic activity in the area and enhanced the people's livelihoods. Although Kwa Jack is no longer operational, the buildings and infrastructure is still standing which serves as reminder of the once vibrant business enterprise and was the precursor to the Integral Kumusha.

The Rationale of Transforming a Traditional Homestead into Integral Kumusha

The traditional homestead was set up by Daud Taranhike's late parents and he inherited it upon the passing on of his parents. There are three main reasons why Taranhike embarked on this transformation journey. Firstly, his father had allocated the homestead to Daud while he was still alive and had instructed that the homestead should not be allowed to perish. The original traditional homestead was an inheritance, and hence, he attached so much value to it. The second reason is that Daud wanted to implement the concepts that emerged from the research and would want to contribute towards the eradication of poverty and hunger in Buhera. Buhera is prone to droughts and long dry spells which often result in poor yields and insufficient food for the households in this area. The aim of developing the Integral Kumusha in this area was to ensure food self-sufficiency and dismantle the people's dependency syndrome on handouts by government, NGOs and other donors and civil society. The third reason for Daud to engage in this transformation journey was to allow the young generation to create wealth and value in this often-considered barren land where he grew up. This transformation would serve as a demonstration that it is possible to live a transformed life even in this marginalised remote area. It was important to demonstrate practically rather than preach theories that have not been tried and tested. The picture below shows the original traditional homestead that was inherited from Taranhike's parents.

The Transformation to a National Model Rural Homestead

In order to ensure that the project was effectively managed, Christina, now popularly known as Mai Chimuti, relocated from Harare, where she was managing the King Lion Motorways family public passenger business, to the Buhera district. In order to make sure that the project received adequate attention, Taranhike brought in his other business enterprises to be part of this research development agenda while following the Integral Development Approach. In Figure 2 below he shows how the different entities were deployed in line with their nature of business operations.

Vaka Concrete, which is a concrete brick and pavers manufacturer, represented the grounding in local nature and communities. The company uses quarry dust as its key raw material from nature to construct houses and build communities. The Buhera Community represented culture and spirituality. This is where the African traditional values are practised, with traditional leaders being the custodians of our African heritage and culture. High Performance Capabilities Africa (HPCA), an engineering consulting company denoted the science and technology part of the integral development. King Lion Motorways as the business involved in public passenger transport with its payline "Connect People with Places" represented enterprise and economy. the movement of people, especially across the Zimbabwean borders, facilitated trade among people and countries, thereby creating wealth for individuals and promoting economic activities in different communities and societies. By combining all the four entities, helped in the creation of a great legacy (nhaka) which was the researcher's inner calling

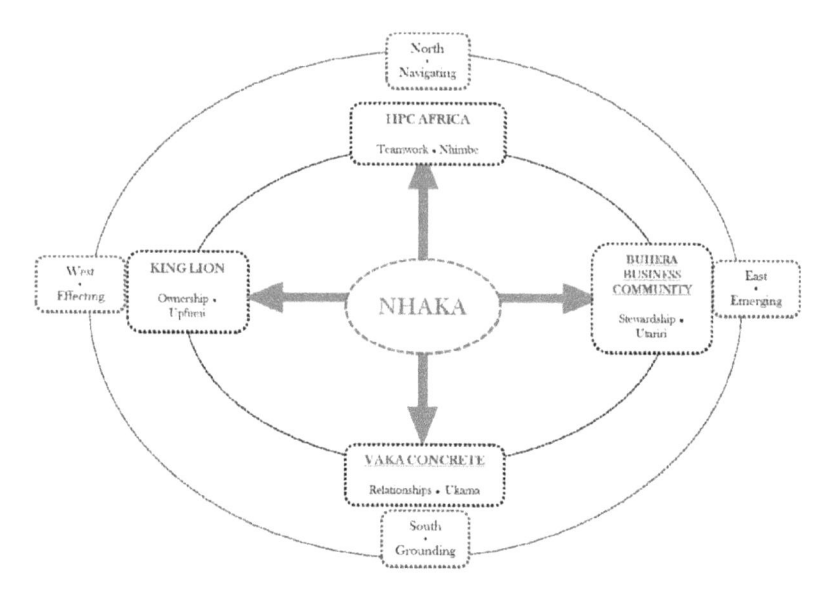

Figure 1 *Creating an Integral Ecosystem*

Honouring Our Ancestors by Creating a Special Garden of Remembrance

The first project that was embarked on was the creation of a special garden of remembrance for our departed family heroes and heroines. This was done as part of honouring our parents who had worked so tirelessly to establish the traditional homestead and also looking after us to be who we are today. They deserved a special recognition. This entailed erecting tombstones on the graves of our loved ones and protecting the place and planting lawn, trees for shade and flowers that would make the place beautiful and attractive. The practice of erecting tombstones was not common in the place but has now become an in thing which many families are doing the same for the loved ones.

Water Harvesting as the Primary Activity Towards Self-Sufficiency

The traditional homestead depended primarily on dry land agriculture using rainwater during the rain season. This approach made rural people to be productivity for five months during the summer season and the rest of the year they would be idle. In Buhera where water is a scarce resource especially during the dry months of the year, it was indeed necessary to embark on water harvesting in order to support agricultural activities during the dry season. To this end, the development focused on harvesting rainwater and also underground water into storage tank for future use. As a result of active water harvesting, water availability improved to support drip irrigation and horticultural activities. It was important to use drip irrigation system in order to conserve the available water and make production throughout the whole year possible. In this way, transformation towards self-sufficiency became a reality.

In order to ensure that there is adequate water throughout the year at the Integral Kumusha, a four hundred and fifty thousand (450,000) litre water reservoir was constructed and commissioned. Water is harvested from under ground using solar powered water pumps and is stored in this giant tank until it is required during the dry season. This has made it possible for the Integral Kumusha to be productive throughout the whole year unlike the scenario which is common in rural areas where people are only product during the five summer months and the rest of the year they will be idle.

Security of the Premises Became of Paramount Importance

It was important to provide security of the place in the form of perimeter fencing and building infrastructure including road access. The security of the people and fields made it possible to establish orchards and to protect trees and vegetation around the new look homestead. The operational activities and infrastructure development at the place were supervised by Christina who was on site daily. The picture below shows the new look homestead, which is the Integral Kumusha.

The Integral Kumusha has now been established and is operational with Mai Chimuti (Christina Taranhike) now engaged into regenerative activities that include regenerative agriculture based primarily on organic farming, land and soil regeneration and creating a regenerative local economy within the community. The regenerative economy is the basis for upscaling to Eco-Rural Industrialisation, Rural Tourism and the establishment of the Nhakanomics Transformation and Research Academy as part of the Inside-Out Communiversity!

Mai Chimuti Redefining Rural Livelihood and Total Wellbeing of the People

Christina Taranhike commonly known as Mai Chimuti as the Co-Founder of the Integral Kumusha imitative spent more than two decades working in various roles within the hospitality industry. She also spent more than four years managing a thriving public passenger family business. During her time as the Operations Director for King Lion Motorways, she worked closely with schools within her rural community with the aim of improving learning and sporting standards among the schools by sponsoring the Taranhike Trophy and various learning and teaching competitions among students and teachers. She also supported various building and development projects at schools within the community. It was during this time that it became evidently clear that the community had huge problems relating to food insufficiency, marginalisation and poverty of unexplainable proportion. Touched by this plight, she together with her husband Daud embarked on a transformative journey towards food self-sufficiency and socio-economic transformation and regeneration. Hence the idea of the Integral Kumusha was mooted as social innovation that empowers rural folks especially the vulnerable, that is women and the youth in order to achieve rural socio-economic transformation and development emerged during the social innovation research journey described in the section above.

Contextualising her role within the community – Mai Chimuti identity.

As she embarked on the Integral Kumusha journey, it was very important for her to fully identify with the women within her community. This is how she adopted the name "Mai Chimuti" as a way of identifying with the marginalised rural women who are often perceived as insignificant in the same way as Chimuti (stick) is neglected yet it such a vital part of the rural life and livelihoods. The stick has various roles and functions at home without which it would be extremely difficult to have some form of decency in a rural setting. Mai Chimuti naturally grew to become very popular and she has now adopted it as her brand name!

Integral Kumusha Transformation Journey – Support from local leadership

Mai Chimuti shared her dream with the Mukoto Village Head Mr Mahachi and Mbuya Mahachi who fully supported the initiative during its inception in early 2017. Members of the community were also engaged as part of the community engagement process. The whole idea was to develop a prototype based on the integral development approach and the social innovation research process which would be expanded and replicated as rural development model within the community and other rural communities within Zimbabwe and beyond.

Vakamusha Registered as Integral Kumusha Private Limited

Vakamusha was registered as the Integral Kumusha Private Limited in 2022 which made it a first legal entity established and registered in a rural village set up. As part of the development, a logo for the Integral Kumusha was designed which depicted the following important features;

A rural homestead as part of the ecological system with particular emphasis on the land which is shown by the black curved line representing the earth. This part of the logo emphasises the local Grounding in nature and community with the huts showing the African traditional values and way of life. The letter "I" with a women's head signifies the role of the woman in the home and also the enormous indigenous knowledge that is within the local community which can be tapped through communal learning that drive cultural development and advancement. The words Integral Kumusha Private Limited bringing in the local enterprise thrust with Mai Chimuti as the trading brand name. The Integral Kumusha Logo which has just been explained is shown in Figure 4 below.

Applying the Integral Approach to the Integral Kumusha Model

In order to align the Integral Kumusha initiative to the Integral Development Approach, time has been taken to explain how the model fits into the approach based on the research outcomes and the current reality in Zimbabwe and rural context. The Integral Kumusha (IK) is a home grown socio-economic innovation, aimed at eradicating hunger, poverty and marginalisation within the rural communities anchored on achieving self-sufficiency for each homestead as the basis of development and transformation. It is a well-known fact that the current national self-sufficiency stands at 45 % (NDS1, 2021). To achieve the target of >95 %, it was imperative to implement an initiative that takes a holistic approach, hence the adoption of the integral development approach.

The Centre and Local Grounding are the Ubuntu and Agro-based Activities

Therefore, the Integral Kumusha has a centrifugal force which is Ubuntu and simply put "I am because we are!" As such we are grounded in our local community and in nature. This grounding is what makes us Africans who greatly value our land. That's why the fight for freedom placed land as the key priority. And for the IK, the key assets at our disposal are land and homestead (musha). This is what makes our operations agro-based with emphasis on our traditional crops as the starting point rather than developing other alternative crops and forms of agriculture. To this end, the IK projects include dry land farming of crops such as zviyo, mhunga, mapfunde, nzungu, nyimo, and now cassava as part of the crop portfolio. In the drip irrigation area, horticulture is carried out with high value crops such as ginger, turmeric and garlic and vegetables being the major crops. Fruit trees such as mangoes, citrus and avocados are now part of the horticulture project.

We also harvest and harness value from our nature such as water harvesting, solar harness, conservation of the environment including both indigenous and exotic species. Animal husbandry is part of our key activities thus having mixed free ranching poultry of chicken, guinea fowls, geese, peacocks, rabbits, goats, sheep, cattle and bees. Fruit tree growing is paramount and this is promoted by planting and nurturing different types of fruit tress both indigenous and exotic varieties.

Local Global Emergence in Culture and Spirituality

The second integral dimension is the emergence of local global culture and spirituality. Our African tradition and cultural values are so important in our development. The pursuit of cultural development lays the basis for the advancement of the IK. The IK is promoting rural eco-tourism and showcasing our traditional cultural lifestyle as depicted in our traditional meals, dances, music, languages, and other traditional practices. The IK has the African posture while at the same time exhibiting the developmental aspect that takes us forward as a people while maintain our African identity.

Navigating the Newly Global Knowledge Creation in Science and Technology

In order to ensure that our development is sustainable, we ensure continuous improvement by navigating newly global science and technology by blending indigenous and exogenous knowledge. It is a pity that in formal education, indigenous knowledge has been ignored and relegated to the dust bin yet there is great wisdom for living. In this knowledge realm, we exploit new knowledge and practices to ensure availability of water through boreholes and to effectively conserve this precious liquid through drip irrigation which is dependent solely on gravity, thereby demonstrating the application of science and technology in a practical way. The availability of water makes it possible for the IK to conduct its agricultural activities and processes throughout the year rather than depending only on rainwater. The IK processes most of its produce to finished products such as upfu hwemhunga, rukweza, mapfunde, dovi, and different beverages. In order to accelerate rural eco-industrialisation, the IK is constructing a processing plant which will ensure that most products are manufactured locally thereby creating employment and accelerating rural development and transformation.

Effecting the Global Local Enterprise and Regenerative Economy

The fourth and final integral dimension is the global local effecting of the transformation process into making the IK an enterprise which contributes positively towards the national economic development. This is the business aspect of this innovation which is managed and marketed under the "Mai Chimuti" Brand. So, the IK generates its own revenue and funds its own activities in order to ensure sustainability. The marketing is done in all forms including digital marketing since the IK has access to the internet through the Community Network WIFI being supported by our local partners, Vision Internet. The Integral Kumusha model is shown in Figure 4 below.

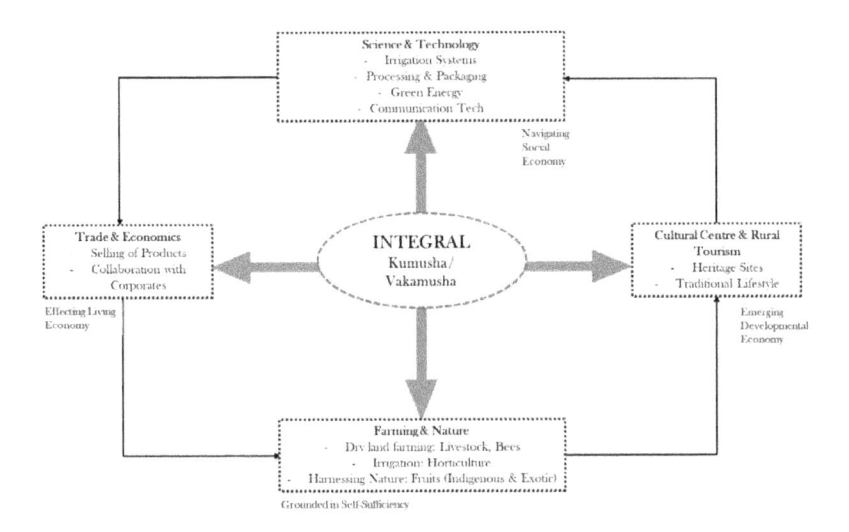

Figure 2 *The Evolved Integral Kumusha Model*

The Impact and Contribution of the Integral Kumusha

In line with its vision of enhancing rural livelihoods and total wellbeing, the IK has made significant impact and contribution within the community, the nation and within our region and continent. Some of the achievements to date include;

1. Employment Creation
   The people within this community are being employed in different areas where they earn money and enhance their lives. At peak, the IK employs more than 60 people per day especially the women and the youth. The activities at the Integral Kumusha has facilitated the creation of local regenerative village economy which is benefiting many rural folks.
2. Bridging the Divides and Change the Migration Path
   The Integral Kumusha has helped in bridging the rural/urban, poor/rich, tradition/modernity, public/private, gender and the digital divides. As a result, more and more people are realising that there is immense value in transforming their traditional homesteads into viable economic enterprises thereby changing the migration path from rural to urban and people are now trooping back to kumusha including those in the diaspora.
3. Skills Provision
   Through its Look, Learn and Action programme, the IK provides skills in different agricultural activities and new ways of farming including organic manure production, conservation and regenerative agriculture, etc.

4. Socio-economic Empowerment
   Various projects are conducted involving members of the community such as the Mee Mee Goat Project which started with only 6 members but has now grown to 30 members. The Integral Kumusha is promoting family social stability by ensuring that spouses stay together as they can be gainfully employed at the IK without having to migrate to urban areas or even to the diaspora. The IK is indeed an economic and a socially viable entity thereby eradicating poverty and hunger while enhancing total wellbeing of the rural people.
5. Education for Life and Communal Learning
   The IK provide an opportunity for students to learn and conduct research. This year two university students (one PhD student and One MPhil Students) from Great Zimbabwe University conducted their research at the IK with the support of Mai Chimuti and her team.
   The Inside-Out Local Communiversity is providing the much needed learning opportunities within the community and also helping students within the community to learn what they would have otherwise done just in theory.S
6. Facilitation of Creation of other Integral Kumusha Initiatives
   Mai Chimuti has helped to influence many people to set up their own integral kumusha initiatives and transform their livelihoods and their communities. Many people are appreciating the value of their traditional homesteads and the opportunity to transform these homesteads by incorporating nature, culture, technology and enterprise. Some of the examples include the following;
   - Chief Rwizi from Mhondoro, Mashonaland West who came with 48 people to learn from the IK and have now set up such projects in their community.
   - Chief Makumbe who is the paramount chief of our area and is fully supportive of this innovation.
   - Edmore Dzirove, Chief Chitsunge, Buhera who has set his own Integral Kumusha project
   - George Machanja Mrehwa District who has set up his PaShumba Integral Homestead.
   - Modreck Maeresera of Bedza Village, Buhera Central who has also established his Integral Kumusha.
   - Mathew Chidhindi of Mombeyarara, Buhera North who has also established his Integral Kumusha project.
   - Honourable William Mutomba, MP Buhera North, our local Member of Parliament who has also established his Integral Kumusha project using the IK Model.
7. Possibility of Spreading into SADC
   There has been inquiries for the IK to offer support and assistance to organisations within the SADC Region such as Integral Initiatives in Zambia, South Africa, Lesotho, Namibia and Botswana.

8. Research and Development
   Universities such as Catholic University, Midlands State University, Great Zimbabwe University and also the Marondera Horticulture Research Centre in conjunction with the Ginger, Garlic and Turmeric Association have conducted demonstration and research plots to establish better methods and varieties of different crops.
9. Planetary Regeneration Course
   The IK together with the Home for Humanity conducted a 10 month course across all continents with 88 participants on Planetary Regeneration and creation of a new Earth civilisation that is just, equitable, inclusive and peaceful. The IK hosted the graduation ceremony for the ten (10) participants from Zimbabwe and Zambia.
10. The Integral Kumusha was launched as the Exemplary Home for Humanity by the Home for Humanity in France and the Homes for Humanity Global Movement on 18 April 2021. This special launch coincided with Zimbabwe Independence Day which made particularly important.
11. The Integral Kumusha was commissioned as the National Model Rural Homestead dubbed the "SMART INTEGRAL KUMUSHA" by the Minister of Information Communication and Technology, Postal and Courier Services Dr Jenfan Muswere on 21 December 2021. This function was attended by Ministry Directors, local Traditional, Political and Administrative Leaders.
12. Mai Chimuti was among the global panellist for the Women Earth Innovators that was conducted on 9 June 2023. This follows her recognition as the first recipient of "The Woman of the Earth Award" presented to her by the Home for Humanity and Homes for Humanity Global Movement 19 October 2022.
13. Mai Chimuti was awarded the Manicaland Province Agric4SHE First prize by the First Lady Dr Auxilia Mnangagwa who came and presented the award to her on 27 June 2023 where more than ten thousand (10,000) people attended the function. This achievement confirmed the Integral Kumusha and the Mai Chimuti as the National Model Homestead and Brand.
14. Mai Chimuti and the Integral Kumusha impact received more attention as Christina was awarded three accolades by the Zimbabwe Chamber of Commerce at a special function that was held at the Holiday Inn Hotel in Mutare on 8 December 2023. She was awarded the Woman in Agriculture Award, the Manufacturing Award and the Special Recognition Award which made her the most outstand awards winner at the function.

The above contributions are just a few of the many achievements that Mai Chimuti has achieved through the IK initiative. The IK is contributing immensely to the eradication of poverty, hunger and marginalisation of rural areas. Therefore, the IK is contributing positively towards self-sufficiency and the creation of local rural regenerative economies with a national, regional and continental reach. Given the tremendous progress recorded so far, the IK is now seeking external funding to accelerate the total emancipation of the African people and allow them to take charge of their socio-economic development in an authentic African regenerative manner, that is the Nhakanomics way.

Opportunities in the Future

1. The IK Model can be made the vehicle for rural development and transformation through its activities and especially the development of Eco-Industrial sites in every community thereby enhancing lives, livelihoods and total wellbeing of people in rural communities. This initiative has significant value and contribution towards national socio-economic development as it will lift more that 70 % of the Zimbabwean population that live in rural areas to become prosperous. Therefore, the IK thrust is to move rural people and the entire society from poverty to prosperity (P2P) in a way that resonates with the African people within their cultural and traditional set up.
2. There is a great opportunity to develop the Integral Kumusha into the first Rural University Campus that addresses real challenges and provides practical solutions. This will be the only institution with this focus and will change the rural socio-economic and education landscape in Zimbabwe and Africa in general. The current university structure and system needs total overhaul and alignment to meet the needs of the community and society. This can only be possible by bringing systems change and not adjusting the existing system which is archaic and obsolete.
3. The Integral Kumusha is currently putting the final touches to ensure that the Inside-Out Communiversity which emerged at the central part of the Integral Kumusha is fully operationalised. A lot of work and gone in this initiative and the three aspects (Communal et al and the IK as the Socio-economic Laboratory) now in place. The remaining part is the Academy which will be part of the Nhakanomics Transformation and Research Academy. So, far close relationships with the Great Zimbabwe University and the Catholic University of Zimbabwe have been established and on 24 November 2023, the first graduation of the combined institutions (IK, GZU and CUZ) was held at the Integral Kumusha with Professor Ranga Zinyemba – Vice Chancellor of CUZ being the Guest of Honour. What is now left is the formalisation of this partnership in the form of Memorandum of Agreement which should happen in 2024.

Opportunities for Collaboration Cooperation with Econet Wireless Zimbabwe Ltd

The Integral Kumusha has been engaging with Econet Management Team in order to improve relationships and collaboration between the two organisations. The Econet Management Team has shown willingness to support the Integral Kumusha in its transformation agenda given the impact and contribution to rural communities and the society at large. Partnerships with Corporate Organisations will help accelerate the regenerative initiative currently under way. below are some of the prospective benefits from the Econet partnership.

1. Improved and effective mobile telephone network system
   Wards 31 and 7 experience serious network problems. There is an opportunity for Econet Wireless to develop and or improve its network infrastructure such as installation of the repeater to enhance network performance. This will assist more than 20,000 people within the Integral Kumusha vicinity automatically increase Econet business and improved livelihoods through effective communication of business and social issues within and beyond the area in line with the Econet's drive towards re-imagining rural communities.
2. Knowledge creation and Human Resource & Leadership Development
   There is opportunity for Econet to support knowledge creation through sponsoring research and development projects to ensure continuous improvement and development.
   Econet can participate in human and leadership development through its Higher Life Foundation by supporting and sponsoring high potential young leaders in rural communities who can carry the development agenda forward. This ensures succession in leadership and sustainable socio-economic development.
3. Promoting the use of the Renewable Energy and creation of Smart Villages
   Since the Integral Kumusha has demonstrated the effectiveness of using solar energy in rural community, Econet through its Solar Energy Project can build a solar plant while the Integral Kumusha provide the space. This initiative can transform the community in terms of provision of energy and while contributing to curbing the negative effects of climate change. Provision of energy will translate in increased use of technology to enhance lives and livelihoods thereby creating smart villages and promoting smart agriculture.

Assistance Needed by the Integral Kumusha for It to Realise the Great Vision

The IK would need the following support it to achieve its vision as described above. The Integral is just looking at two key areas where it needs support;

1. Provision of Electrical Power Supply – Solar Farm for its Agro-Processing Plant
   The Integral Kumusha urgently and desperately need electrical power supply to drive its equipment and machinery at its processing plant. Currently, the IK is off grid and relies solely on solar energy but this has no capacity to drive heavy machinery which it wants to instal for its manufacturing plant. This can be a dedicated power line just like the one at Shawa Mine and Dorowa Mine to ensure uninterrupted production. This facility is the first of its kind in Buhera District and has potential to create employment for people in this area and curb rural/urban migration. The main thrust of the Integral Kumusha is promote use of renewal energy and as such, going into the future, it would be good for

reliable solar farm to be constructed on site that will reduce carbon emission into the atmosphere. The advancement in solar technology makes this initiative a possibility that would need to be supported.
2. Soft Loan or Grant for the Development of the Nhakanomics Transformation and Research Centre
The IK can be viewed as a micro integral rural enterprise which is an alternative of the Western Capitalistic Corporate Firm with its grounding in nature and culture with a technology and enterprise reach unlike the Corporate Firm that focuses on technology and enterprise yet bereft of nature and culture. This can be extrapolated at a macro level to support the development of the Nhakanomics approach which is an alternative to Capitalism and neo liberal economic system. This will help the Zimbabwe, Africa and the Global South to transform their economic systems and abandon the Western Capitalistic Approach being driven by the World Bank and The International Monetary Fund with no success at all to African economies. Africa needs an economic system that resonates with its own culture and traditional practices blend with exogenous knowledge which is where the Nhakanomics Transformation and Research Centre comes in. The soft loan or grant advanced to Mai Chimuti and the IK will be repaid from the revenue generated from the IK and the Nhakanomics Transformation and Research Centre.

Integral Kumusha Major Projects for the Future

As part of its development plan, the Integral Kumusha has lined up key major project as follows;

1. Commissioning of the new Manufacturing and Eco-Rural Industrial Hub
2. Launching of the Rural Satellite University Campus.
3. Launching of the Nhakanomics Learning and Transformation Centre & Inside-Out Communiversity Commissioning.
4. Conference and Accommodate facilities for visitors, students and researchers.

Conclusion: Kumusha, Communitalism, Nhakanomics

Common Future to African Future

We end then by comparing and contrasting the vision of *Our Common Future*, underlying "sustainable development", as per the UN's environmental commission:

> We come to see that a new development path is required, one that sustains human progress not just in a few places for a few years, but for the entire planet into the distant future. Technology and social organisation can be both managed and improved to make way for a new era of economic growth. Equity would be aided by political systems that secure effective citizen participation in decision making and by greater democracy in international decision-making.

With a vision of African *Integral Kumusha* as our grounding and origination, whereby, *chivanhu* developmentally follows:

> The African community comprises plants, animals, human beings, the spirit and the ancestors. Every plant has a reason for existing. Plants grow for a particular purpose. Every plant is a manifestation of the energy field which is the universe. Nature Power is inviting our continent to come down to earth so as to regain our health. The earth is the primary source of our creativity, intelligence, and humanness. The wisdom of the ancients is there in the molecules of the air around us, waiting to be tapped when we are open enough to perceive them. It is left for human beings to open nature's book of Wisdom and learn and use them. It is only this knowledge which will bring permanent healing to our sick and wounded cosmos, and set us free. Such knowledge is our African destiny. We are vibrating and creating our energy fields. Each creature has their own energy field. Holiness is a state of union with God, with oneself and with others: your fellow human beings as well as plants, animals, and indeed the whole of creation.

Nature Power, Communitalism and Nhakanomics

Enter Nhaka-nomics

In fact, we ask, in our mind's eye, Taranhike as co-creator of what he has termed *Nhaka-nomics* (Nhaka standing for "Legacy" in his African language) on our behalf. So here is the connection between where we have travelled so far and the constituents of such "Nhaka-nomics".

Relationships: Ukama

The African community comprises plants, animals, human beings, the spirit and the ancestors. Every plant has a reason for existing. Plants grow for a particular purpose.

Stewardship: Utariri

Nature Power is inviting our continent to come down to earth so as to regain our health. The earth is the primary source of our creativity, intelligence, and humanness.

Teamwork: Nhimbe

The wisdom of the ancients is there in the molecules of the air around us, waiting to be tapped when we are open enough to perceive them. It is left for human beings to open nature's book of Wisdom and learn and use them. It is only this knowledge which will bring permanent healing to our sick and wounded cosmos, and set us free.

Co-Ownership: Upfumi

We are vibrating and creating our energy fields. Each creature has their own energy field. Holiness is a state of union with God, with oneself and with others: your fellow human beings as well as plants, animals, and indeed the whole of creation.

The above constituent parts is being expanded and development in line with the regenerative Nhakanomics Transformation and Research Academy working in collaboration with other researchers and research institutions.

Psychology Is for Back-Room Boys

It is important in conclusion to provide more insight about Professor Ronnie-Samanyanga Lessem because of his enormous contribution to the Zimbabwean and African regenerative efforts. He was Taranhike's PhD supervisor and played a pivotal role in the research process and the research outcome. It is in that sense that sustainable development takes on a new African guise, starting out with natural and communal *kumusha* as origination, further evolved through a culturally and spiritually based *chivanhu*-like foundation, scientifically and technologically followed by *nhaka-nomics* by way of emancipation. Of course, this far away from where Zimbabwe's Cambridge University educated, London School of Economics based, WITS Business School oriented, Finance Minister, Mthuli Ncube is allegedly coming from, though he too was probably born and bred in a village like Buhera. In fact, Samanyanga can't resist revisiting his own life story at this point when, at the tender age of 17, when he was at school in what was then Southern Rhodesia, he resolved that he wanted to study *Industrial Psychology*.

So, his business oriented father, Abe Lessem, duly forgetting his proximate Buhera-heritage, immediately took him off to see the then English born, white Minister of Finance, Sir Cyril Hatty, who proclaimed that "psychology is for back-room boys". In fact, and in the very same guise, Buhera, the very source of "southern" subsistence, had been relegated to the back room of the Rhodesian economy. The rest, as they say, is history, which is why we are now seeking re-GENE-ration, to "make and remake African history".

Fast forward thereby some six decades, and we turn back to the same Cambridge University where Ncube was educated, but this time to a heterodox economist there, a longstanding friend and colleague of Samanyanga's, Tony Lawson, who has just sent his latest paper to him, and this is what he says:

> What is wrong with modern economics? The clear answer is that it is mostly simply irrelevant. It has been becoming increasingly so for about seventy to eighty years now. Its formulations, in the main, are patently and repeatedly unrealistic, and so able to provide little or no explanatory insight or understanding of the world in which we live.. But little can improve at any level until we discard the widely-worn methodological blinkers which encourage the view that mathematical modelling is everywhere automatically relevant, even essential, so that paying explicit attention to matters of ontology is unnecessary.

Needless to say, Ncube's Oxbridge background is in mathematical economics and finance, and there lies the rub. For his countryman, Sabelo Ndlovu-Gatsheni in his recent book on *Epistemic Freedom in Africa:*

> Decolonisation is a process of conducting research in such a way that the worldviews of those who have suffered a long history of oppression and marginalisation are given space to communicate from their frames of reference. It is a process that involves "researching back" to question how disciplines – psychology, education, history, anthropology, sociology and economics, or science – through an ideology of Othering have described and theorised about the colonised Other, and refused to let the colonised Other name and know their frame of reference.

In implementing Integral Kumusha in Buhera, each of the three business enterprises has had a critical role to play in order to purposefully create a new concept that transforms the rural home into an economic entity that promotes livelihood within an African indigenous context. Therefore, the Integral Kumusha constitutes an indigenous Zimbabwean enterprise as opposed to the western exogenous form of corporation. The Integral Kumusha is built upon the four pillars of creating nhaka for future generations. The four pillars of nhaka are located within the integral approach together with the three business enterprises and the Buhera community. We now proceed from business enterprise to social anthropology, and back again.

Mai Chimuti Leading the Transformation Journey

Mai Chimuti has spearheaded rural transformation and development through the Integral Kumusha and has demonstrated that this model works and is contributing immensely to the community, the nation, the region and beyond. Mai Chimuti using an integral approach in her approach and she has realised huge benefits and great impact and contributions to the community. There are huge potentials and possibilities to accelerate rural development and national socio-economic transformation through the Integral Kumusha and the Nhakanomics concepts and models. For the dreams to be realised, Mai Chimuti requires support in terms of electrical power and funding to take this initiative to new levels.

References

Bennholdt-Thomsem V and Mies M (1999) *The Subsistence Perspective: Beyond the Globalzed Economy.* London. Zed Books.

Heron J (1996) *Co-operative Inquiry: Research into the human condition.* London. Sage.

Heron J and Reason P (2001) The Practice of Co-operative Inquiry: Research with Rather Than on People. in P. Reason & H. Bradbury (eds) *Handbook of Action Research: Participative Inquiry and Practice 179–188.* London. Sage.

Lessem R and Schieffer A (2010) *Integral Economics: Releasing the Economic Genius of Your Society.* Abingdon. Routledge.

Lessem R, Adodo A and Bradley T (2019) *The Idea of the Communiversity.* Manchester. Beacon Books and Media Ltd.

Ndlovu-Gatsheni S (2018) *Epistemic Freedom in Africa: Deprovincialisation and Decolonisation.* Abingdon. Routledge.

Rima I (2001) *Development of Economic Analysis.* London. Routledge.

Schieffer A and Lessem R (2014) *Integral Development: Realising the Transformative Potential of Individuals, Organisations, and Societies.* Abingdon. Routledge.

Scoones I (2015) *Sustainable Livelihoods and Rural Development.* Rugby, UK. Practical Action Publishing Ltd.

Taranhike D (2019) *Integral Kumusha Leading to Nhakanomics.* PhD Thesis. Unpublished.

World Bank (2007) *World Development Report 2008.* Washington, DC. Agriculture development.

Zimbabwe National Statistical Agency (2011/12) *Poverty and Poverty Datum Line Analysis in Zimbabwe.* Harare. Government Printing Office.

Part 3 The Renewal Path Out of South-*East* Africa: Towards Yurugu-nomics

Chapter 8 Narrative Methods to African Hermeneutic Methodological Foundation Tradition/Modernity Fusing South-Eastern Horizons

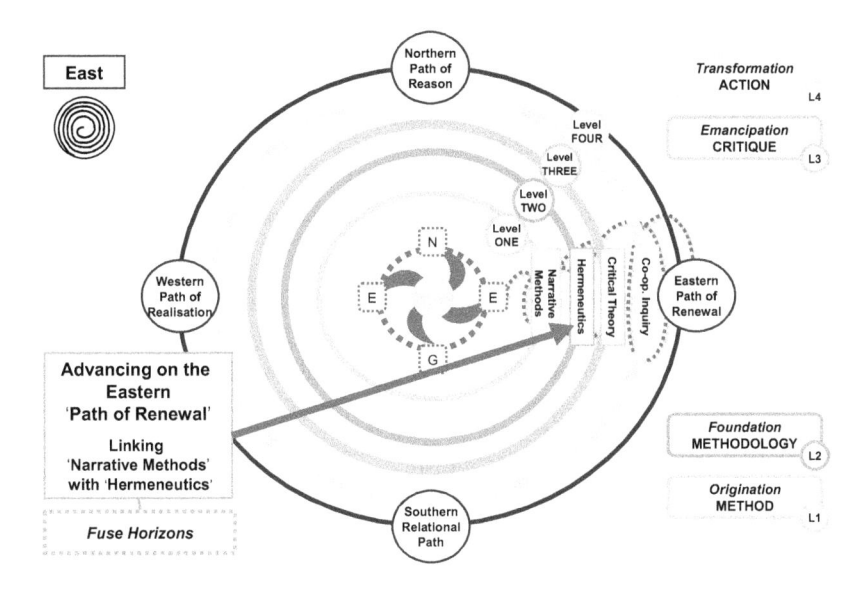

Figure 8.1: *Overview Chapter 8 – Level 2 / South-East*

Narrative inquiry, if practiced within the Islamic perspective, can illuminate the soul and awaken the inner self, giving us the courage to create and reconstruct our personal experiences, to go beyond the pain and the hurt, and transform such into higher qualities of acceptance, understanding, and submission to God's will. Narrative inquiry can be the first step on the long, spiritual journey, where we are in continual dialogue with our inner self, God and the "other". Any inquiry, regarded from an Islamic perspective, ought to be multileveled and multi-dimensional. Researchers have to be open and flexible, therefore, to operate within different inquiry methods so as to be able to capture the complexity of the phenomena. Whereas phenomenology deals with personal, subjective experiences, hermeneutics interprets the larger social context in which individual meaning is embedded.

Zara al Zeera (2001) Wholeness and Holiness in Education

> **Summary: Hermeneutics: Emergent Foundation of African Renewal Path**
>
> - Turning from the African south we now turn to the south-eastern research path of renewal, building on prior narrative methods, and originating "stories we are". Therein you engaged, individually and collectively, in narrating your own story and that of your life world and society.
>
> - European (interpretive) and analytically oriented hermeneutics, in the 20th century, came to be seen as perhaps *the* methodology of the social sciences. Its aim has been not to conform and extend universalized experiences to attain knowledge of a law, or indeed society, but to understand how this particular person, people, or state has become what they are.
>
> - In feeling local, as such, naturally and communally, originally and turning now to East Africa, we begin with the notion of "destiny", not only in spiritual, but also in cultural and historical, terms, which underlies Eritrean American philosopher Tsenay Serequeberhan's African hermeneutics
>
> - To further such, locally globally, we turn to a more explicitly transformative turn, reinforced by African American anthropologist Marimba Ani's Kiswahili concept of Yurugu, meaning an "incomplete person" in both the Swahili and Dogon languages. She goes onto uncover both actual fission and prospective fusion in the Afro-European encounter.
>
> - People and things exist then only within a certain political and moral context, and they are not understandable outside of it. This is where hermeneutics differs from phenomenology. Individuals and their context form a dialogical, interpenetrating unit. You then bring your own cultural frame of reference into the picture, which continually and unavoidably frames and shapes the process.
>
> - African hermeneutics as we have seen then has a more transformative edge to it than the Eurocentric version. The fruitful tension tradition and modernity, now newly globally, when properly cultivated, constitutes that edge. Hermeneutics, here, has also the role of reconnecting a people with its own source. Such a "return" is not a return to tradition or stasis. Rather, we are engaged in the past affirmation, present and future role, of our historicity.
>
> - Finally, and globally locally, we apply the Keynotes of hermeneutics to the path of renewal, individually and collectively, *understanding how your world is constructed*, while *giving the other a voice*, evolving form the *interpretive to the transformative*, and *reconnecting with your source*.

8.1. Orientation to Hermeneutics

8.1.1. Narrative to Cooperative/Good African Story to Kiswahili Enterprise

We now turn from the relational research path, aligned with the kumusha and nhakanomic laden path of southern African innovation, and the learning community lying in between, to the research path of renewal. Such is accompanied innovation-wise by Uganda's (Rugasira 2014) *Good African Coffee Story* in *east* Africa, aligned with conscious evolution and Yurugu-nomics, as we shall see, and an associated transformation journey, in our communiversity terms.

After our initial orientation then to the path of renewal, we start, as was the case in Southern Africa, by feeling local, via Congolese philosopher Okonda Okolo (Bell 2002), and his concept of *Destiny*. Thereafter Eritrean-American philosopher Tsenay Serequeberhan (1999, 2002), intuits locally-globally via both his *Hermeneutic Philosophy for Africa* and also his following work on *Our Heritage: The Past and in the Present of African and African-American Existence*. Then, by way of thinking newly globally, we turn to Ghanean philosopher Kwame Gyekye's (2002) *Philosophical Reflections on the African Experience* via his masterly *Tradition and Modernity*. Finally, and globally-locally, we turn to the Keynotes of interpretive hermeneutics, as the emergent and trans-cultural foundation of the path of renewal.

Such an emergent, interpretive foundation though, on the relational research path, following narrative origination, merely sets us on the way, ultimately illustrated by the *Good African Coffee Story*, to innovation. It is only later, in Chapters 9 and 10, as we turn to critical theory and cooperative inquiry, research-wise, and to so called Yurugu-nomics and the Kiswahili enterprise, innovation wise, that the transformation journey in *East* Africa will be fully accomplished (see Table 8.1.1. below)

Table 8.1.1. *East African Social Research and Innovation: Path of Renewal Narrative to Cooperative via HEREMENEUTICS/Yurugu: Good African Coffee Story to Kiswahili Enterprise*

Eastern Grounding Method and Origination	Eastern Emergent Methodology & Foundation	Eastern Navigational Critique and Emancipation	Eastern Effective Action and Transformation
Narrative Methods (E1)	Hermeneutics/ Interpretive (E2)	Critical Theory (E3)	Co-operative Inquiry (E4)
The Good African Coffee Story (E1)	*Yurugu (E2)*	*Yurugu- nomics (E3)*	*Kiswahili Enterprise (E4)*

We now turn to our overall orientation to hermeneutic methodology as the emergent foundation on the path of renewal, and briefly to so called Kiswahili *Yurugu*, innovation-wise, that accompanies it. Building as such upon the narrative method, and storyline, that formed the origins of your relational path, and the accompany *Good African Story*, we carry interpretively on. But let us first retrace steps and understand hermeneutics' own global story, in brief, within Europe, by way of orientation, before we turn formatively, and locally, as we did in the "southern" case, to feel Africa.

8.1.2. Global Origins of Hermeneutics

Understand Your Point of View in Relation to Another's

Hermeneutics may be generally described as the interpretation of places, of people, of texts. Essentially, it involves cultivating the ability to understand things from somebody else's point of view, and to appreciate the cultural and social forces that may have influenced their outlook. Further to such, for us on the path of renewal with an added, especially African touch, as we shall see, is a transformative orientation. Such is then picked up, innovation wise, as an emergent foundation by the notion of Yurugu and subsequently, as emancipatory navigation, by Yurugunomics, as the east African variation on a communitalism theme.

In contemporary usage, hermeneutics often refers to the interpretation of biblical texts. In fact, it was Rabbi Ishmael Ben Elisha (90 to 135 AD) of the Amoraic era of Judaism who interpreted laws from the Torah through 13 hermeneutic principles. This was the first known appearance of hermeneutics in the world. In the last two centuries of the modern era, the scope of hermeneutics has expanded to include the investigation and interpretation not only of textual and artistic works, but of human behaviour generally, including language and patterns of speech, social institutions, and ritual behaviours (such as religious ceremonies, political rallies, football matches, rock concerts, etc.). Hermeneutics interprets or inquires into the meaning and import of these phenomena, through understanding the point of view contained within your "inner life", in relation to another's, spiritually, psychologically and culturally.

> The word 'Hermeneutics' is a Term derived from 'Ερμηνεύς', the Greek Word for Iinterpreter. This is related to the Name of the Greek God Hermes in his Role as the Interpreter of the Messages of the Gods. Hermes was believed to play Tricks on those he was supposed to give Messages to, often changing the Messages and influencing the Interpretation thereof. The Greek Word thus has the basic Meaning of 'one who makes the Meaning clear'.

Figure 8.1.2: *Origins of the Hermeneutic Term*

Hermeneutics in the western world then, as a general science of textual interpretation, can then be traced back to two sources. One source was the ancient Greek rhetoricians' study of literature, which came to fruition in Alexandria. The other source has been the Midrashic and Patristic traditions of biblical exegesis,

Modern Hermeneutics: From Schleiermacher to Dilthey

Modern hermeneutics, moreover, started in the 19th century with the German philosopher Friedrich Schleiermacher (1996). He explored the nature of understanding in relation not just to the problem of deciphering sacred texts, but to all human texts and modes of communication. Schleiermacher said that every problem of interpretation is a problem of understanding. He even defined hermeneutics as the art of avoiding misunderstanding.

Understanding does not simply come from reading the text, but involves knowledge of the historical context of the text and the psychology of the author. The German 19th century philosopher Wilhelm Dilthey (2019) broadened hermeneutics even more by relating interpretation to all historical descriptions. For Dilthey, understanding is not a process of reconstructing the state of mind of the author, but one of articulating what is expressed in the work, that is specifically by placing it in its historical context.

... to Heidegger and Gadamer

Since Dilthey, the discipline of hermeneutics has detached itself from this central task and broadened its spectrum to all texts, including multimedia and to understanding the bases of meaning. In the 20th century, Martin Heidegger's (2006) philosophical hermeneutics shifted the focus from interpretation to so-called "existential" understanding, thus in a sense more authentic, way of being in the world than simply as a way of knowing.

Hans-Georg Gadamer's (1989) hermeneutics – as we can see all the modern interpretive philosophers were German – is a development of that of his teacher, Heidegger. He describes the process of interpreting a text as the fusion of one's own horizon with the horizon of the text. He defines "horizon" as "the totality of all that can be realised or thought about by a person at a given time in history and in a particular culture."

Fusing Horizons

Gadamer's philosophical project, as explained in his opus magnus opus "*Truth and Method*", was to elaborate on the concept of "philosophical hermeneutics", which Heidegger initiated but never dealt with at length. Gadamer's goal was to uncover the nature of human understanding. In his book Gadamer argued that "truth" and "method" were at odds with one another. He was critical of two approaches to the human sciences. On the one hand, he was critical of modern approaches to humanities that modeled themselves on the natural sciences (and thus on rigorous scientific methods). On the other hand, he took issue with the traditional German approach to the humanities, represented for instance by Friedrich Schleiermacher and Wilhelm Dilthey, which believed that correctly interpreting a text meant recovering the original intention of the author who wrote it.

In contrast to both of these positions, Gadamer argued that people have a "historically effected consciousness" ("wirkungsgeschichtliches Bewußtsein") and that they are embedded in the particular history and culture that shaped them.

> In fact history does not belong to us; but we belong to it. Long before we understand ourselves through the process of self-examination, we understand ourselves in a self-evident way in the family, society and state in which we live. The focus of subjectivity is a distorting mirror. The self-awareness of the individual is only a flickering in the closed circuits of historical life. That is why the prejudices of the individual, far more than his judgments, constitute the historical reality of his being.

Thus, interpreting a text involves a "fusion of horizons" where the scholar finds the ways that the text's history articulates with their own background. To that extent it is concerned with our overall search for meaning, and significance. So far then, and clearly in our overall orientation, the pre-emphasis has been on European hermeneutics. We now turn from our overall orientation as such, largely developed in our modern era by German, European philosophers, to its African origins, thereby feeling local in such African nature and community, thereafter most especially and locally-globally in an *east* African, both in an Eritrean-American context, and also then Swahili-East African one.

8.2. Feel Local: Nzonzi: E2f

8.2.1. "Nzonzi" As a Leader with an Aesthetically Laden "Mastery of Speech"

African and Afro-American philosophers lend a somewhat more transformative edge to "narrative" interpretive method and to "hermeneutic" constructivist methodology than their more purely interpretive European counterparts. For Afro-American philosopher Richard Bell (2002), to begin with, in his "Understanding African Philosophy":

> ... we share in forming and expressing our particular life worlds through stories or narratives. It is through such narratives that we see both the uses and the abuses of power and human identity ... Out of our liberation struggles come the poetry, the stories, the telling of Africa's suffering and indignity. From the cries of injustice, the memory and narration, come a new and broader sense of justice and the hope of the transformation of communal values to engage modernity.

We immediately see the different "critical emancipatory" tone when compared, for example, with that of Germany's Gadamer. For the Congolese philosopher Ernest Wamba-di-Wamba, as cited by Bell, for example, *the "Nzonzi" was a special kind of leader with an aesthetically laden* "mastery of the clarification of speech", but at the same time a concern whereby he or she:

> ... must know how to listen attentively and tirelessly; to pick up the essence of each spoken word, to observe every look, every gesture, every silence, to grasp their respective significance, and to counter unjust positions, while reinforcing just ones ...

8.2.2. Drawing upon Local Tradition and Destiny: Okolo to Abouleish

Another Congolese philosopher Okonda Okolo (Bell 2002) proposes a hermeneutical interpretation of two notions of fundamental importance in Africa – tradition and destiny. In western anthropology a culture based on tradition is frequently portrayed as one devoid of change. Destiny is portrayed as encouraging determinism, and thereby inhibiting the development of individual initiative. For *Okolo:*

> .. tradition in Africa is constantly interpreted and reinterpreted – and therefore always changing – by different individuals in different historical contexts. Tradition therefore does not inhibit invention or change, creation or transformation. Destiny, from the vantage point of African hermeneutics, is not a symbol of determinism, but involves a people's "vision of the world".

For Sekem's founder, and author of *Sekem: Cultivating a Sustainable Community in the Desert*, Ibrahim Abouleish (2005) in Egypt, whom we shall be meeting up with much more fully in Chapter 15 as a culmination of the African North:

> I carry a vision deep within myself: in the midst of sand and desert I see myself standing as a well drawing water. Carefully I plant trees, herbs and flowers and wet their roots with the precious drops. The cool well water attracts human beings and animals to refresh and quicken themselves. Trees give shade, the land turns green, fragrant flowers bloom, insects, birds and butterflies show their devotion to God, the creator, as if they were citing the first Sura of the Koran. The human, perceiving the hidden praise of God, care for and see all that is created as a reflection of paradise on earth. For me this idea of an oasis in the middle of a hostile environment is like an image of the resurrection at dawn, after a long journey through the nightly desert. I saw it in front of me like a model before the actual work in the desert started. And yet in reality I desired even more: I wanted the whole world to develop.

As such it represents the history of a people – and of Ibrahim Abouleish himself – their past, present and future and whatever sense of identity they can create and recreate for themselves. We now turn locally-globally to a transformative hermeneutics developed by Eritrean American philosopher based at Morgan State University in the U.S., Tsenay Serebequerhan.

8.3. Local Global Transformative Hermeneutics: E2i

8.3.1. Hermeneutics of African Philosophy

The Critical Edge of Transformative Hermeneutics

In his book on the *Hermeneutics of African Philosophy*, Serequeberhan (1999) is, on the one hand, radically open to that which is preserved in his own Eritrean cultural heritage. On the other hand, he is critical of tradition to the extent that the cultural elements, which have been preserved in it, have ossified and are a concrete hindrance to the requirements of contemporary, or modern existence. This fruitful tension between esteem and criticism, tradition and modernity, when properly cultivated, constitutes the critical edge of his transformative hermeneutics, the foundation, as such, for our path of renewal.

This emergent transformation is in that guise a grasping and exploring of grounding concerns, aimed at the enhancement, emergence, and ultimate transformation of an individual's, or a society's, own lived actuality. In Africa's specific political and historical context (this could equally apply to Latin America, and parts of Asia and the now especially the Middle East), the concerns of contemporary philosophy are focused on the possibility of overcoming the misery and political impotence of the continent's post-colonial situation.

Hermeneutics in such a context has more of a critical, emancipatory and transformative edge to it than it does in the European one. Postcolonial Africa then poses the challenge of self-transformation and the concrete actualisation of its alleged "independence". It does so in view of the suffering millions that have been victimized by the lived actuality as opposed to the hoped for ideality of an "independent" Africa. This is the case for Latin America and the Arab world as well.

Turning Over a New Leaf and Working Out New Concepts

For Serequeberhan, *it is in this painful gap between ideality and actuality that the hermeneutic philosophy finds its source and the locus of its concerns*, engaged, in the words of the late Franz Fanon (2001) – the extraordinary Martiniquan psychiatrist and philosopher – in *"turning over a new leaf and working out new concepts"*. As such, Africa and other societies in transition including the former communist countries of Eastern Europe, China and India, and now the Arab world, need to reinvent themselves to transform themselves, rather than "be developed" by others. In so doing, the review of an individual's, an institution's or a society's own narrative and destiny, is matched by hermeneutical re-invention. This is patently not what is happening in China and Eastern Europe today, neither of which actually draws on their combined tradition and destiny, in the sense, for example, to which Okolo alludes.

In other words, the social innovator should not passively adhere to what is given by that tradition. Rather the relation to tradition is an open-ended encounter, between self and other, past and present, in which what is explicitly preserved and implicitly betrayed by tradition is revealed. For example, China would engage with its Taoist, Confucian and Buddhist past, with a view to renewing it, in a purposeful and open-ended way, as Egypt might to, in relation to its ancient, Greco-Roman, Coptic and Islamic heritage. Historically "being there" – a person, organization or community – always becomes what it is by projecting itself out of its past, its lived inheritance. Its "destiny" is thus always what comes out of itself, out of the prospects of its history and the possibilities of its generation. For contemporary Africans, what impels them to such is precisely the estranged actuality of the continent's present deriving from the colonial experience, the specific particularity of Africa's history.

As Okolo (Bell 2002) points out:

> Our hermeneutical situation is that of the formerly colonized, the oppressed, that of the underdeveloped, struggling for more justice and equality. Here we affirm the methodological pre-eminence of praxis on hermeneutics, praxis understood in the sense of an action tending toward the qualitative transformation of life.

This applies as much for Ibrahim Abouleish in Egypt as we have seen, as it does for Okolo in the Congo or for Serequeberhan in Eritrea or Fanon in Algeria.

Fractured Split and Fusion of Horizons

Insofar, as the anti-colonial struggle then, for Serequerberhan, is aimed at overcoming colonialism and neo-colonialism, it is an attempt to end the fissure in African existence between exogenous dominance and indigenous tradition. It is in the hope of overcoming this split through a positive union that the counter-force of the colonised acquires a political form and becomes a project for a possible freedom.

In fact, liberation movements in Africa or in Latin America, in Asia as in the Middle East, are born out of the "fusion of horizons" of two broad segments of society, the urban and the rural. Each manifests in itself what the other does not have and is estranged from. The westernised urbanised native is acquainted with the "global" world beyond the colony or neo-colony and the struggles of other peoples. The rural non-westernised native, on the other hand, is steeped in the broken "local" heritage of his own particular past. In the fusion of these two fractured urban and rural "worlds" the possibility of African, or indeed of Brazilian or Indonesian freedom is concretized or made tangible in the form of specific historical movements. In like manner, in a neo-colonial context, it is when the globalised native puts at the local people's disposal the intellectual and technical capital that he or she snatched, that the dialectic force and counter-force is transcended in the reconstitution of a new ethos.

This lived self-formation then, of a fusion of horizons, becomes the practice of freedom. This is the hermeneutical response to the emergent question: what are the people of Africa, or the Middle or Far East, trying to free themselves from and what are they trying to become? This brings us from Serequeberhan onto the work of the renowned British African historian and freedom fighter, with Amilcar Cabral as we shall see, in the Portuguese colony Guinea Bissau, Basil Davidson

The Liberation Struggle: Reclaiming or Discarding History

In his *Africa in Modern History* the eminent historian on Africa, Basil Davidson (2001), notes that the African countries that achieved independence in the late 1950s and early 1960s were, paradoxically, wedded to colonial attitudes and values. Old inequalities from the precolonial heritage were enlarged by the new inequalities of the colonial heritage. In contradistinction to the above, starting from the 1970s, a more radically democratic conception of liberation took root. In concrete and practical terms, the new liberation movements emerged out of the contrast between the miserable situation of post-colonial Africa and the empty status of "political" independence. They were grounded on the lived and stark comparison between unfulfilled ideals and unforgiving realities. In so emerging, in differing ways and out of the lived exigencies of differing African histories and specific contexts, such becoming served to articulate a notion of liberation as a process of reclaiming history. Such a dialectical notion draws as much on critical theory (Chapter 9) as it does on hermeneutics.

Davidson points in this context to the theoretical perspective of Guinea-Bissau's Amilcar Cabral (1973). The political parties initially formed in that country, after independence, were of and from the urban centre. Their point of reference was European theory and practice. Their basic objective was to transfer power from Europeans to Africans. In the process they were susceptible to the rationality of the coloniser. So, on the one hand, they were the mediating link between colonialism and neo-colonialism; on the other, they abstractly formulated the possibility of African freedom. In the process they suspected indigenous culture as being worthless. It was those who were closest to Europe who became leaders of the pack, and the political parties formed totally disregarded the rural native or indeed the "Lumpenproletariat", that is the coolie labour that inhabited the shantytowns.

The Urban-Rural Dynamic Fusion

The urban parties were not inserted in the lived needs and concerns that move and define the life of the rural native. And yet, for Serequeberhan, in the meeting between those who come from the towns as globalised natives and local country dwellers as peasant or nomads, is the dynamic locus, out of which unfolds self-emancipation.

This approach is instead of a situation where the cities remain the centres of European mimicry and the interior is frozen, mummified and held back in stasis as the enclave of "ethnic cultures", that is as wildlife preserves, and ethnic "cultural" exhibitions yielding foreign exchange. The politics and economics that emanate from the centre are then geared towards Europe, cash crops complemented by Parliamentary "procedures" or socialist edicts of a one-party state.

Cabral's Return to Source in Guinea Bissau

Therefore, for Cabral, there is a need to return to source. Only when a rooting in history becomes a lived actuality at the grassroots level, through the establishment of local mass political institutions of people's power – peoples' assemblies, village associations and so forth – in which popular democracy is implemented, only in such a context is "the practice of freedom" possible. The struggle secures the support of the mass to the extent that it concretely involves the common folk at all levels, and in doing so helps them metamorphose themselves from inert, a-historical beings absent from history into active and emergent protagonists of their own existence.

This process of becoming, then, does not come out of formal proclamations. It occurs out of cohabiting the same historical, political, and existential space. It occurs by osmosis and diffusion. It is in this concrete sense that the struggle at a fundamental level necessitates the radical reformation of traditional society. Colonialism "globally" petrifies the subjugated culture. This is the "local" state of affairs that needs to be overcome. To date the African liberation struggle has failed in its promise, for Serequeberhan, to reclaim the historicity of African existence.

Such a *"return" is a cultural and political recovery of the oppressed historic possibilities in the existence of the colonised.* The turning toward the "native mass" is the first moment in the fusion of the rural and the urban. The westernised urban natives who join the anti-colonial eruption do so by rejecting their assimilation and successfully indigenise themselves into the historicity of their people. It is the moment of a historical and existential decision, at which point the *assimilado* begins the cultural and historical metamorphosis that will positively re-immerse him or herself into the local historicity of the indigenous folk. *The "return" is not a return to tradition or stasis.* We are not engaged in an antiquarian quest for an already existing authentic past tradition. Rather, we are engaged in the affirmation by the exogenised native of the historicity of the rural indigenous mass. For Cabral (1973):

> Urban working classes discover at the grassroots the richness of their cultural values – philosophical, political, artistic, social and moral – and realise, not without astonishment, the richness of spirit, the capacity for reasoned discussion, the facility for understanding, on the part of population groups who were yesterday forgotten.

The "Return" to Source Is a Two-Way Dialectic

European values and skills are thus absorbed, in management as in agriculture, in development as in ecology, into a new synthesis, through this hermeneutic fusion of horizons, of self and other, of tradition and modernity, of indigenous and exogenous. This is possible because in embracing indigenous historicity the westernized native purges himself of the Eurocentric frame that structures his consciousness. *The "return" to source is thus a two-way dialectic.* In this dialectic, European culture/history is recognized as a particular and specific disclosure of existence, aspects of which are retained or rejected in terms of the lived historicity and practical requirements of the history being reclaimed. The ossified African past – embodied in the rural native – is thus not preserved intact, but is cut and cast to fit the historic requirements of the struggle. For Cabral (1973):

> ... the practice of democracy, of criticism and self-criticism, the increasing responsibility of peoples for the direction of their lives, literacy work, creation of schools and health services, training of cadres from peasant and worker backgrounds, and many other achievements ...

Overall then, for him (1973) "... the objectives must be at least the following: development of a popular culture and of all positive indigenous values; development of a national culture based on the history and achievements of the struggle itself; constant promotion of the political and moral awareness of the people to the cause of independence, justice, progress; *development of a scientific and technological culture based on a critical assimilation of man's achievement in science, art and literature*".

We now turn to Serequeberhan's more recent work on *Our Heritage*.

8.3.2. Our Heritage: Past and Present of African/African-American Existence

African Heritage and Effective History

For Gadamer, according to Serequeberhan (2002), the horizon of the past out of which all human life lives, and which exists in the form of tradition, that is heritage, is always in motion. It is not historical consciousness that first sets the surrounding horizon in motion. But in this motion becomes aware of itself. In its lived existence, each generation sees for itself its own-most possibilities out of the concerns of its own horizon. For the "motion" of a heritage becomes aware of itself only in concrete individuals and as the horizon of their lives self awareness. For it is in the living and thinking of those who embrace it that a heritage – an "effective history" – in terms of *nhaka*-nomics in our previous chapter – becomes aware of itself.

The "colonised in refusal" – in the very act of refusal – radically changes the directionality of his or her horizon of life possibilities, as indeed the Taranhike's have done. In this choice he (Daud Shumba) or she (Christina) becomes open to the "effects" of a different "effective history". In refusing such a person negates his or her self understanding within the colonial horizon. The struggle that arises institutes, culled and cultivated out of the "effective history" that is actualising it, a heritage in formation. It creates, or makes out of itself, a new ethos – a tradition or heritage – of the daily life that constitutes the struggle. Fanon (2021) writes, then, that we need to "make a new skin, develop a new thinking, try to put afoot a new human being".

For a heritage, as Gadamer tells us, is not transmitted by nature because of the inertia of what once existed; it must be sustained, affirmed and embraced, to maintain itself in and as the present. What Fanon (2021) calls for is not a cultural-historical egoism, but an other-directed openness, not "an already established interpretation of nature, history, world and the ground of the world". It is an open-ended project of a humanity that finds itself engaged in joint struggles.

Universe or Multiverse

We are, for Serequeberhan, at the close of the 20th century, at a point in time when the dominance of the *uni*verse of European singularity is being encompassed or engulfed by the *multi*verse of our shared humanity. The central concern for the practice of philosophy focused on the formerly colonised world should be directed at helping to create a situation in which the enduring residue of our colonial part is systematically overcome. Indeed our communiversity has been conceived in such a multiverse-laden light.

In the last decade of the 20th century we are, at a formal level, beyond the constricting confines of colonialism. And yet every aspect of existence in the formerly colonised world, and in Africa specifically, is still, in essential and fundamental ways, determined and controlled by our former colonisers. This is not to allocate blame but to locate specifically the source of our present predicament, not only as it pertains to our economic and political dependence on the West, but also as it pertains to our dependence and subordinate position in the realm of thinking and in questions of knowledge. For Fanon (2021) we must invent, we must discover.

To invent, the Latin *invenire,* here means to come upon ourselves, to discover ourselves; for once "old" Europe is left behind – once we see "European-style development" for what it is – we are then left to our own generic human identity. But to heed Fanon requires that we destructure the metaphysical constraints – universalism – that have held us, and hold us, captive. We now turn, on the one hand to Ghanean philosopher Kwame Gyekye's *Tradition and Modernity*, and on the other, to African American Marimbia Ami's *Yurugu: An African Centred Critique of European Thought,* in both cases turning from intuiting local-global, to thinking newly globally, thereby fully inventing our thereby newly global, African selves.

8.4. Newly Global Navigation: Tradition/Modernity; Yurugu:E2t

8.4.1. Tradition and Modernity in Africa

Evolving Viable and Appropriate Democratic Political Institutions

Kwame Gyekye (1997), one of a significant band of contemporary Ghanean philosophers, setting the stage of tradition and modernity in Africa, raises the kind of questions which are very much of a newly global, specifically African concern, in relation to philosophy and transformation on the continent. Among the issues on which philosophical attention could be brought to bear are the following problems of:

- inculcating political morality to deal a death blow to corruption
- dealing with traditional moral standards crumbling in wake of social change
- evolving appropriate, credible, viable ideologies for African nations today
- hammering out a new modernity on the anvil of the African people's experience of the past and vision of the future
- nation-building – of integrating and wielding together several ethnic groups into a large cohesive political community
- *evolving viable and appropriate democratic political institutions* that will be impervious to violent disruptions by a military, tyrannical or corrupt leader

Indeed all of such could well also apply, newly globally as such, to counties like Russia and Iran, by way of prominent examples, today.

Choosing an Appropriate Communalist Ideology

<u>Choosing an Appropriate and Effective Ideology</u>

Because of the dynamic relationship between politics and economics, unstable and corrupt politics, in the long run, usually begets bad economics. Hence it is not surprising, for Gyekye, that African nations have fared, for him, disastrously in the post-colonial era. Despite the constant infusion of capital and other forms of assistance from the developed nations of the world and other international organisations, Africa is in a deep development crisis. The causes, for him, are legion.

Choosing an appropriate and effective ideology, firstly, has been a besetting problem. The ideology pursued by a very large majority of African political leaders on attainment of political independence was socialism, though they preferred to refer to it as "Africa Socialism" because they regarded it as having an African ancestry. The pursuit of socialism was aggressive and unrelenting, but with disastrous consequences that, over time, led some African leaders to change ideological choice or direction. Thus it can be said that African nations in the post-colonial era have been groping through an ideological labyrinth. Philosophical insights such as his own, for Gyekye, might serve as an Ariadne's thread through the labyrinth.

It would be correct to say that no human culture has remained pure since its creation, free from external influences. But the most important thing is what to do with the ideas, concepts and institutions that come from different cultures. This is especially when, as in Africa, these are foisted on it, without its having, or being given, the opportunity to select or adopt what it considers desirable or worth its while, and adapt it to suit its own circumstances.

Difference between Communalism or Communitalism and Marxism

On regaining the political independence of their nations, African political leaders, in search of ideologies to guide their policies and actions in matters of the development of their societies, had the options of pursuing capitalism – the free enterprise economic system, and socialism – the system of public ownership of the means of production and distribution. The ideological system chosen by all but a few was socialism. But they preferred to call it "African socialism" to invest it with, for Gyekye, a spurious patina of African ancestry and justification. Their main argument was that socialism was foreshadowed in traditional African thought and practice.

However, communalism, similar to our communitalism – albeit that we have identified four integral versions of such – in Africa is essentially a socio-ethical doctrine and not a narrowly economic one, whereas Marxist socialism had a much more strongly economic, if not latterly, for us, ecological, emphasis. Also the modern conception of state ownership is different from the traditional conception of communitarian ownership. For example, traditional ownership of the land includes the rights of an individual to use the land but not to own it. There is no room for such in state ownership. In fact the traditional economic culture exhibited features of both "socialist" and capitalist methods in managing economic life. We now turn more fully to tradition and modernity.

Revitalise Tradition: Internal Criticism/Appropriate Worthwhile Exogenous Ideas

The traditional, for Gyekye, is depicted by sociologists and anthropologists as rural, agrarian, pre-scientific, resistant to change and innovation and bound by perception to its past. By contrast, the modern is characterised as scientific, innovative, future oriented, culturally dynamic, and industrial and urbanised. It is the alleged contrast that grounds the polarity between the traditional and the modern.

The contrast, for him however, is based on some false assumptions. Historical inquiries would show that even though the societies characterised as "traditional" have a large proportion of beliefs and practices inherited from the past, they nevertheless experience varieties of changes over time. The refinement or abandonment of a tradition and the need to revitalise it by adding on new elements are the consequence of two main factors: internal criticism of the tradition undertaken from time to time and the appropriation of worthwhile exogenous ideas, values and practices. The causal factors of cultural change, or transformations of tradition, are therefore internally and externally induced.

It would be a safe assumption to make, then, that those cultural values and practices that evolve into tradition were, at the time of their creation, grounded in some historical circumstances, some conceptions of society, social relations, certain metaphysical ideas, and other kinds of beliefs and practices. That is to say the beliefs, practices and institutions are inevitably grounded in some conceptions. But the conceptions themselves, from the point of view of subsequent generations, may not have been rationally enough grounded. So they might discover them to be simply false, inconsistent, or morally unacceptable, as inadequate to the realities of the times.

Continuity and Change in Indigenous Culture

The Adaptive Capacity of Indigenous Culture

Some critics, then, may see tradition, or an element of it, as a drag on the kind of progress they envisage for their societies. Thus they see it as dysfunctional. Others may see it as discordant with a new set of cultural values that a new generation is bent on establishing. Yet others may see it as simply morally unacceptable. They may see it as not cohering with other parts of the tradition. Finally, still others may see the whole metaphysical base of the society as no longer convincing or credible. Criticism may be aimed at merely refining a tradition to bring it into more harmony with contemporary trends, or at abandoning a tradition altogether because it is seen as totally out of tune with the contemporary cultural ethos.

Changes may be brought about, primarily, through exogenous causal factors. These come into play in the wake of encounters between an indigenous cultural tradition and an alien one. No tradition can claim to be pure, in the sense of having developed purely on its own terms, in total isolation from other cultural influences. In one way, elements of an alien cultural tradition can be voluntarily assimilated by adaptation by an indigenous tradition; in another, alien cultural traditions may be said to have been foisted upon the indigenous culture. In the history and evolution of cultures the former has been the more common and effective mode of diffusion.

The success in moulding and appropriating the elements of an alien culture is determined by the adaptive capacity of the indigenous one. It is the exercise of such which will make the adopted elements of the alien tradition meaningful and understandable to the practitioners of the indigenous tradition, establish a real basis for genuine commitment and attachment to the appropriate elements of the alien tradition, and enable the users of the indigenous tradition to build on, and thus to contribute to the advancement of the received elements of the alien tradition. In the absence of an adaptive capacity, the indigenous tradition may absorb the alien tradition without fully appreciating the real implications of the absorption.

Imposition Deprives the Indigenous Culture of Opportunities to Appraise and Select

An indigenous cultural tradition, however, can also come into possession of alien elements by having them foisted upon them by alien practitioners. The imposition deprives the indigenous culture of opportunities to appraise and select such elements of the encountered tradition as it would consider worth appropriating. This will have a damaging effect, then, on self perceptions and self understandings of the recipients of the tradition. Second, the circumstances would be such that it could not be predicted how along the tradition will endure in its new cultural environment.

Third, the users will find themselves absorbed only in the outward frills of the alien tradition; but, not only that, they would also find themselves confused in the pursuit of the practices and institutions imposed. A particular cultural creation, overall then, will have two faces: a particular face, confined to its local origin, and a potentially universal one, for us *newly global,* when it transcends the borders of the environment that created it.

Drawing on the Legacy of the Past in the Present

There is a significant Akan proverb that states the need to evaluate a cultural past:

> "A person cutting a path does not know that the path he has cleared behind him is crooked". The path refers to the whole corpus of values and practices pursued in the past. The proverb implies that later generations are supposed to take a critical look, with a view to eliminating the "crooked" or inelegant aspects of the past.

The growth of human culture, its capacity to avoid decadence and dysfunction and to adapt itself to new situations and demands, its capacity to constitute itself into a credible and viable framework for human fulfilment – all this is due, surely, to the reinterpretation and critical evaluation of cultural tradition as it moves through history. Such a critical reinterpretation will not only leads to refinement, if not the expunging of cultural features which inhibit development, but also to an affirmation of the positive features of a traditional culture, altogether with a view to revitalisation and renewal. What, then, about modernity?

On the Notion of Modernity: Embedded in Western Cultural Values

Modernity, for Gekye, can be defined as the ideas, principles and ideals covering a whole range of activities that have underpinned Western life and thought since the 17th century. Modernity was and is culture dependent, although this should not inhibit the appreciation of the notion, and the exploitation of its practical implications. While it cannot be denied that "modernity" is indigenous to Europe, some exogenous non-European cultural inventions or institutions were appropriated by it along the way, and thereafter uniquely developed by it.

In view of the need and desire of human society to advance its material existence, it would be expected that Europe's modernity, and even more so now America's, would serve as a model in other countries. But the important question is, for Gyekye, is it possible to assume Western models of science and technology and the capitalist economic system without taking into account cultural values of Western modernity in tandem? This question may be answered yes and no. There is a very close link, for example, between capitalism and democracy, individual freedom (distinguished from unbridled individualism) and human rights.

Modernity, whatever else it entails, certainly involves transition to a new era: the transition is born partly on the wings of the elegant or worthwhile features of a cultural tradition, and partly through the production of new ideas and the invention of new techniques that have far reaching consequences. The latter may involve whatever can usually and suitably be appropriated and adapted from outside a given culture in addition to what can be acquired from within the culture itself by way of the exercise of the indigenous intellectual, evaluative and adaptive capacities. The former will require the abandonment of negative features of a culture as well as the maintenance – albeit through refinement – of what Gyekye calls the positive features. The creation of modernity in Africa will be a function of both methods of transition. It will also inevitably involve science and technology. Gyekye now turns to individualism and communalism.

African Humanism May Embody Individualism and Communalism

In the pre-modern era of Western cultural development, humanism and communitarianism were philosophical and ideological allies; in the modern era, however, one of them was dropped, to be replaced by individualism. The replacement implies that individualism and communitarianism were held by Locke and others as incompatible doctrines, a position still maintained today by some, but by no means all, Western liberal thinkers.

Yet, for Gyekye, there are no logical tensions in interpreting humanism as implying either individualism or communitarianism. For in insuring the wellbeing of every member of society, the communitarian arrangement, may be said to have an edge over the individualist framework. A consideration of the intrinsic moral worth, capacities and self development of the individual human being, however, requires a more individualistic orientation. In creating African modernity, then, a social and political theory should be evolved that such as will integrate the values of individuality and community.

For the African the human being is held as possessing a speck of God. This is what is called the soul. This theomorphic perception of humanity constitutes all human beings into one universal family of humankind – a family fragmented into a multiplicity of peoples and cultures. The common membership of one universal human family should, it is held, constitute a legitimate basis for the idea of universal human brotherhood. Thus part of the African view of humanity is to recognize all persons, irrespective of their racial or ethnic backgrounds, as brothers, socially and economically, of not also politically.

Cultural Borrowing That Follows the Contours of Cultural Encounters

The many sided nature of the African cultural heritage, in fact, is not peculiar to the African experience: it is an aspect of the historical phenomenon of cultural borrowing that follows the contours of cultural encounters. As long as people from different cultures appreciate what is good in each, according to Gyekye, and know what would be conducive to the fulfilment of their own goals, cultural borrowing will continue to be a lever of human progress. But what is borrowed needs to enrich, rather than confuse or deracinate, another culture. Wisdom and adaptive capacity needs to be profoundly exercised in the pursuit of modernity, a pursuit that requires an innovative ethos. African modernity must be a self-created one, if it is to be realistic and meaningful, sensitive and enduring, and self sustaining.

Modernity is a stage, a significant stage in the civilisational trajectory of mankind. It behoves mankind, while it is inebriated by its sophisticated achievements – especially in its scientific and technological achievements made possible by modernity – to create and maintain values consistent with its conceptions of what human beings, and their societies, ought to be. Modernity is created for humanity, and not humanity for modernity. The essence of our humanity – of which our intrinsic sociality is a natural part – should not be jettisoned in the transition to modernity. For in the final analysis, the pursuit of such values is always a matter of rational or moral choice that human beings are free to make. We now turn from tradition and modernity in general to Yurugu in particular, lodged in Swahili, African culture, whuch, for us, straddles both African heremenutics and, also as we shall see (Chapter 9) critical theory.

8.4.2. Yurugu as Emancipatory Navigation

Asili Means "Beginning", "Origin", "Source", "Nature"

African American anthropologist Marimba Ani (2000), based at Hunter College in the U.S, in her seminal work on *Yurugu: An African Centred Critique of European Thought* introduces the concept of *asili*, a Kiswahli word that *means "beginning", "origin", "source", "nature", "essence" or "fundamental principle"*. It can also be taken to mean "seed" and "germ", that is the source or initiating principle.

It refers, as such, to the explanatory principle of a culture, the germinal principle or essence. The *asili* is like a template that carries within it the pattern or archetypal model for cultural development. We might say the DNA or "logic" of a culture, that forges a people into an ideological unit. It is not an idea, but a force, an energy, for us a source or grounding of societal re-GENE-ration.

Utamawazo Meaning the "Thought" as Determined by Culture

Ani has borrowed other Kiswahili terms to denote *utamaduni* or "civilisation", or indeed "culture"; *wazo* meaning "thought" and *roho* meaning "spirit-life". She then creates the concept of *utamawazo* to mean *"thought"* as determined by culture, and *utamaroho* as "the spirit-life of a culture", or the collective personality of its members. Whereas "utamawazo" is self conscious, *utamaroho* remains unconscious. Both originate from the meta-conscious *asili*. We speak of *utamaroho* as we might speak of temperament, character or emotional response. *Utamaroho* is not individual but societal and collective.

Utamaroho Focuses on the Uniqueness of a Particular Culture

Utamaroho does not categorize the ethoses of cultures into types, but as inseparable from *asili*; it focuses on the uniqueness of a particular culture with respect to its emotional rather than cognitive patterns. While the character of a culture's *utamawazoi* is expressed most obviously in literature, philosophy and academic discourse, and pedagogy, *utamaroho* becomes more evident in aesthetic expression whether visual, aural or kinaesthetic. At the same time *utamaroho* is the inspirational source from which *utamawazo* derives its form as "forms of thought". *Utamawazo* (thought), *utamaroho* (spirit life) and *asili* (seed) influence, reinforce and build on each other in a circular process. This circular process and synthesis is culture itself.

The *asili* is the seed, the origin, but once in existence the *utamaroho* is the vitality of the culture. The *asili* compels the culture to fulfil itself, but it does so through the form of its *utamawazo* ans the life of its *utamaroho*. The *utamaroho* of a people is a force made powerful through its collectiveness. The unique character of the culture – its accomplishments, limitations, brilliance, institutions and posture vis a vis other cultures – are spirited by its *utamaroho*.

But such a life force must be continually regenerated by the institutions, creations and patterns of thought and behaviour in which it is reflected. The axiological aspects of the culture will be related to its *utamaroho*, which significantly accounts for motivation in a collective sense. The *aslili* is the seed that produces a force. The force is the *utamaroho* of a people. It is the collective personalisation of the *asili* and represents the possibility of its continued existence. The *utamawazo* is the thought modality in which the people's life must function in order for them to create and to accept a culture that is consistent with the originating *asili*. Neither the character of the European *utumaroho* not its *utamawazo* can change unless the *asili* changes. Understood this way, the culture is the unfolding of principles already implied in the originating process.

The First World Refers to the Descendants of Africa and Its Diaspora

As cultural traditions go, the "West" is, after all for Ami, quite young and biologically or racially Europeans are "the new boys on the block". Critiques of such European culture suffer from the common malady of representing such as a universal stage in human development. Africans must therefore become "modern", and as such "European", before they can even deal with them. As the argument goes "every culture becomes European as it becomes more modern", so there is only one valid culture. Ani then begins with the assumption that European-ness is not inevitable. At the same time she refers to the *"First world" to refer to the descendants of the oldest civilisation: Africa and its diaspora.*

It is in that overall guise, turning to our *Good African Story* in such *Yurugu* light that, in Rugisara's (2014) own words:

> Sharing and caring for the community is something that is intrinsic to the African way of life; an unofficial welfare system in the absence of a public sector that delivers effective community support to extended family members and many others. His ambition with Good African was to entrench this commitment to the community as a fundamental element of his business model as opposed to just being something they could do once that had plenty of money to throw around. He therefore sought to recognize their coffee growers, their employees, their shareholders and the environment as their business shareholders – their quadruple bottom line.

Needless to say, he is not as well steeped in Kiswahili cosmology as Marimba Ani is, but the two in combination, research and innovation wise, make a power, for us newly global emancipatory connection, which will be furthered in our next chapter.

Now it is time to reconnect with source, in hermeneutic guise, thereby articulating the global-local keynotes of African hermeneutics (see Table 8.5.1).

8.5. Global Local Renewal – Reconnect with Source: Keynotes:E2a

8.5.1. Understand How the African World Is "Constructed"

Hermeneutics is perhaps the most pre-eminent, conventionally "interpretive" qualitative methodology. So called qualitative research, as such, is a process of a careful, anaytically based inquiry into the social world, indeed worlds, with a view to newly understand them, and produce knowledge that becomes practically useful.

The primary aim of such an interpretive approach is to develop an understanding of how the world is *"constructed"*. The notion of the world being constructed implies that it is complex, layered, and can be viewed from different perspectives. We construct the world through talk, action, systems of meaning, rituals and institutions that have been created, as well as through the ways in which the world is physically and materially shaped. Hermeneutic research seeks to uncover historical and cultural horizons of meaning, that is, if you like, interactive story lines, through which a world is mutually experienced.

Table 8.5.1. *Hermeneutics – East African Renewal Foundation – Keynotes*

Understand how the African World is "constructed".
Give "the Other" a Voice: Multi-culturalism – South Africa's Rainbow Nation
Evolve from European Interpretive to African Transformative.
Reconnect with the African Asili Source.

Parallel to such, moreover, transformationally and innovation wise, in an east African context, we have combined our focus on Gyekye's tradition and modernity with that of Ani's Yurugu, sewing the seed (asili) for re-GENE-ration and renewal. Such, then, is aligned with our Good African Coffee Story (see East African case story 2).

8.5.2. Give "The Other" a Voice: Towards Multi-Culturalism

The pursuit of interpretive understanding, secondly, serves to expand your awareness of any field, including such social disciplines as anthropology, economics, management, social work, or psychotherapy, within particular contexts. Such research may cover the historical development of a field, or serve to establish a bridge between one field and another, either in terms of disciplines or in terms of cultures. Hermeneutics is therefore, as such, "tradition-informed understanding". As a result, it is especially suited for a transcultural orientation, and for a grounding of self and organization in a particular place and time.

Multi-culturalists, in the above vein, focus on understanding and living with cultural and social difference. However such a pursuit poses an epistemic (knowledge based) problem: if others live within their own framework and we live within ours, how can we understand them? That is where hermeneutics comes in. As such, for the interpretively included, the basic question of the philosophy of social science today ought not to be whether social science is "scientific". Rather, it ought to be whether understanding others – particularly others who are different – is possible, and if so, what does such understanding involve? This brings in, in aspiration of not in reality, Nelson Mandela's (1994) idea of South Africa as a "Rainbow Nation".

In fact we will see, in Uganda, the dramatic consequences, in our *Good African Coffee Case* of "not giving the other a voice" in between the African and Asian populations, in the one black African case not given enough of an economic voice, by the insular Asian business community, and in the other case, regarding the Asian citizenry, not given enough of a civil voice, with ugly consequences.

8.5.3. Evolve from European Interpretive to African Transformative

For Serequeberhan, as we have seen thirdly, Africa's core hermeneutic philosopher, it is in the painful gap between ideality and actuality that the African hermeneutic philosophy finds its source and the locus of its concerns. As such, Africa and other societies in transition including the ex communist countries of Eastern Europe, China and India need to re-invent themselves to transform themselves, rather than *"be developed" by others*. In so doing, the review of an individual's, an institution's or a society's own narrative and destiny, is matched by hermeneutical re-invention or re-construction. Both the focus on tradition and modernity, generally, and on Yurugu specifically, the latter implicitly if not explicitly, in the *Good African Story*, has led the transformative way in Rugisara's (2014) case:

> The negative branding of Africa is not a recent phenomenon but has its roots in Africa's long history of exploitation by foreign powers. It is evident in the justifications for slavery and colonial domination and is rooted in the image of African primitiveness and the urgent need to be brought into modernity. The enduring nature of this misinterpretation can be seen in the absence of African voices in the contemporary development debate. The popular champions for Africa tend to be white male Europeans or Americans who are celebrities, academics, policy experts, politicians or philanthropists. In that light of so called "The White Man's Burden" Africa seemingly needs these others to champion its recovery and development, with western "civilisation" representing the "standard" model for development. Thus the solutions promoted are unquestionably Western in concept, design and application.

In the view of the late Edward Said (1994), the renowned Palestinian-American literary theorist, the presentation of "otherness" by the colonialist or the colonised was a justification for power and domination of the oppressed. In fact as a child growing up in Uganda Rugisara found little in school or in the community that celebrated his history. If there was any of such, it was restricted to legend and folklore and was never documented or systematically taught. Much of what was taught began with colonialism. Many such thinkers and respected African scholars, such as Ali Mazrui, Leopold Senghor, Aime Cesaire, Kwame Nkrumah, Julius Nyerere, Mahmoud Mamdani, Wole Soyinka, Valentin Mudimbe, Amilcar Cabral, Frantz Fanon and Walter Rodney, though, opened his mind to the reality that there was an Africa with a history far richer and deeper, more complex and worth celebrating than what was marketed as *"official history"*.

A critical pillar of the Good African model became the advocacy that Africans had to become the solution to their own problems. The notion that a Ugandan company could advocate for a business relationship that considered farmer empowerment, in relation to such, as a key goal, was, even for the famers themselves, initially not believable, as they initially and seemingly claimed that Good African belonged to a "white person".

8.5.4. Reconnect with Your Individual and Collective Asili Source

Humans, finally for Serequeberhan again then, do not have a pure, fundamental human nature that is transhistorical and transcultural; you are incomplete and therefore unable to adequately function unless embedded in a specific cultural matrix. Hence, the cultural matrix "completes" humans, the Yurugu then, by definition for the Swahili as for the Dogon, being an "incomplete person". In that guise, for us, in East Africa, the "south" without the "east", and vice versa, both culturally and spiritually was well as technologically and economically, is an "incomplete person and society".

The material objects we create, the ideas we hold, and actions we take are therefore shaped in a fundamental way by the social framework in which we are raised. These cultural artefacts are not only the reflection or expression of an era, they are the immediate stuff of daily life. Your taskthen as a would-be social innovator, as evidently in the Rugisara case (2014), is to interpret the multitudinous and conflicting ways in which various worlds are constructed and human meanings developed, and co-create something new, and worthwhile, out of all of these, emerging together.

> For sustainable empowerment, farmers need to be linked to the formal financial markets by literacy training creating savings and credit knowhow through the intermediation of savings and credit cooperatives. Farmers need to move up the value chain by engaging in some form of value-added processing at source. The Fairtrade movement has been largely preoccupied with celebrating African producers for their small-scale and rural idyll, as through this is really worth celebrating. Only then by increasing farm sizes, through land consolidation and communal farming, where technologies can be applied across bigger tracts of land generating efficiency and economies of scale, can output and productivity increase. Good African has encouraged farmers to consolidate their land rather than managing very small plots of land. In the final analysis, transformation begins when we change social structures and relationship frameworks among the economic actors in the community.

Ultimately as such, you should not passively adhere to what is given by tradition and convention. Rather the relation to the tradition is an open-ended encounter, between self and other, past and present, whereby what you choose to preserve, and discard, of tradition, is revealed. Historically – a person, organization or community – always becomes what it is by projecting itself out of its past, its lived inheritance.

Your "destiny" is therefore always what comes out of yourself, individually and collectively, that is the prospects of your history and the possibilities of your generation. As such, in many countries, a "return" to history is a cultural and political recovery of the oppressed historic possibilities in the existence, for Serequeberhan, of the colonised. However, the "return" is not meant to be a return to tradition or stasis. You as a social innovator are not engaged in an antiquarian quest for an already existing authentic past tradition. Rather, yor are engaged in the affirmation of who you both are, and could be, as you engage, simultaneously and interactively, woth tradition and modernity. We are now ready to conclude.

8.6. Conclusion

8.6.1. Originate Local Renewal Path: Narrative Method/Trans4mation Journey

In Chapter 4, under the guise of *narrative* method, we originated the "eastern" path of renewal, to be represented, practically in our second case story by the *Good African Coffee Story* in Uganda, in East Africa. As such

- Your individual and communal Stories are still unfolding.
- The narrative Mode leads to gripping Drama and to creative Origination
- You tie together Potentials and Possibilities of your respective Beginnings
- A Plot shaped by many of the larger Strategy-Stories in which it is set.

8.6.2. Found Local-Global Renewal Path: Interpretive Methodology/Trans4mation

In this Chapter 8, we took a further step, from communal grounding to cultural emergence, from local origination to local-global foundation, interpretively as such:

- Sought to understand how our African world was Constructed
- Gave other cultures and communities a voice, likended to a "rainbow nation"
- Evolved from the Eurocentric interpretive to the Afrocentric transformative
- Reconnected with our particular African source: asili.

Thereby, and furthermore, our transformation journey proceeded from calling to context, and commmunitalism advanced from a nhakanomic towards a yurugunomic perspective that now drew transformatively on effective history. We now turn from African hermeneutics to African critical theory, along the research path of renewal, adding, in the process, more fuel to the transformative fire.

8.6.3. Toward a Good African Coffee Story in East Africa: E2fita

In the final analysis, as we shall see (ICS2) *The Good African Coffee Story* takes us a good deal of the way in turning the interpretive into the transformative, in African hermeneutic guise (see Table 8.6.3. below).

Table 8.6.3. *A Good African Coffee Story in East Africa E2fita*

Feeling Local	*Intuiting Local-Global*	*Thinking Newly Global*	*Acting Global-Local*
Good African Coffee Story	**Yurugu**	*Yurugu-nomics*	*Kiswahili Enterprise*

However, from a *Yurugu* perspective, the interweaving, true to the Kaswhili language, of the "east" and the "south", in cultural and spiritual terms, is incomplete. We now turn from hermeneutics, interpretively and transformatively, to critical theory.

8.7. References

Abouleish I (2005) *Sekem: A Sustainable Community in the Egyptian Desert.* Edinburgh. Floris Publications

Ani M (2000) *Yurugu: An African Centred Critique of European Thought.* New Jersey. Africa World Press

Bell R (2002) *Understanding African Philosophy.* Abingdon. Routledge

Cabral A (1973) *Return to the Source: Selected Speeches.* New York. Monthly Review Press

Davidson B (2001) *Africa in Modern History.* London. Weidenfield and Nicholson

Dilthey W (2019) *William Dilthey: Selected Works.* New Jersey. Princeton University Press

Fanon F (2001) *The Wretched of the Earth.* London. Penguin Modern Classics

Fanon F (2021) *Black Skin White Masks.* London. Penguin Modern Classics

Gadamer HG (1989) *Truth and Method.* London. Sheed and Ward

Gyekye K (2002) *Tradition and Modernity: Philosophical Reflections on the African Experience.* Oxford. Oxford University Press

Heidegger M (2006) *Being and Time.* Bern, Switzerland. Peter Lang Publishing

Mandela N (1994) *The Long Walk to Freedom.* New York. Abacus

Rugasira A (2014) *A Good African Story: How a Small Company Built a Global Coffee Brand.* London. Vintage Books

Said E (1994) *Culture and Imperialism.* New York. Vintage

Schleiermacher F (1996) *Schleiermacher on Religion.* Cambridge. Cambridge University Press

Serequeberhan T (1999) *Hermeneutic Philosophy for Africa.* Abingdon. Routledge

Serequeberhan T (2002) *Our Heritage: The Past and in the Present of African and African-American Existence.* Lanham, MA. Rowan & Littlefield

Zara **al Zeera** (2001) *Wholeness and Holiness in Education: An Islam Perspective.* Leicester. International Institute of Islamic Thought

Chapter 9 From Hermeneutics to African Critical Theory Towards Yurugu-Nomics. Develop a Dialectical Argument

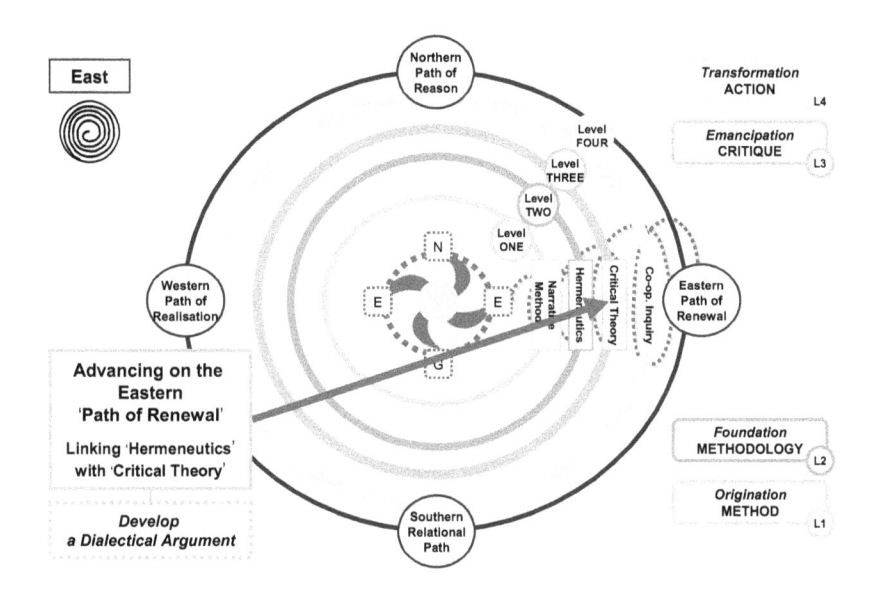

Figure 9.1: *Overview Chapter 9 – Level 3 / East*

When we live our lives with the authenticity demanded by the practice of teaching that is also learning, and learning that is also teaching, we are participating in a total experience that is simultaneously directive, political, ideological, gnostic, pedagogical, aesthetic, and ethical. In this experience the beautiful, the decent, and the serious form a circle with hands joined. At the same time, in the context of true learning, the learners will be engaged in a continuous transformation through which they become authentic subjects of the construction and reconstruction of what is taught, side by side with the teacher, who is equally subject to the same process ... I believe that all educational practice requires the existence of 'subjects' who, while teaching, learn. And who in learning also teach. The reciprocal learning between teachers and students is what gives educational practice its gnostic character. It is a practice that involves the use of methods, techniques, materials; in its directive character, it implies dreams, ideas, objectives – the political nature of education.

Paulo Freire (2001)   *Pedagogy of the Oppressed*

Summary: Eurocentric to Afrocentric Critical Theory

- We now turn from hermeneutics to critical theory, both with strong German philosophical links, in Europe and more especially then in Africa. European Critical theory, in sociology and philosophy, was a label used by the predominantly German Jewish Frankfurt School. As a term critical theory describes their collective work *oriented toward radical social change.*

- For their core thinkers, Max Horkheimer, Theodor Adorno, Herbert Marcuse, Jurgen Habermas and Erich Fromm, three aspects of their approach stand out: critical social theory should be *directed at society in its historical specificity;* critical theory should improve understanding of society by *integrating all the major social sciences*, including economics, sociology, history, political science, anthropology, and psychology. Thirdly, critical theory anticipated "postmodernity" in its *orientation to a post-capitalist, post-industrial, but non-communist world.*

- Turning to Africa, in feeling local, in an East African context, political scientist Ali Mazrui's seminal work on *The Africans' Triple Heritage: Indigenous, Christian, Islamic* is supplemented by African humanist Ngugi Wa Thiong'o (both of the above being of Kenyan origin based in the U.S), the latter in pursuit of an *African Renaissance,* drawing especially South Africa's *Long Walk to Freedom*

- Locally-globally moreover, in the African path of renewal, in more recent guise, the search for a de-colonial African episteme, is accompanied by the development, and articulation, of *theories from the south* which now prospectively inform the north, rather than vice versa

- Newly globally, we draw on the unique work of African American, of Kiswahili African heritage, Marimba Ani, also drawing on Dogon cosmology, on so called *Yurugu,* signalling the incompleteness of Eurocentric *north-western* "modern being", and the African *south-eastern* potential to complete what is thereby missing, centred in the healing wisdom of Africa, as such

- Engaging in critical theory related research, globally-locally finally, includes the rooting of the researcher in *concrete experience,* that the research issue arises out of *problems of everyday life.* Further such research needs to be strongly critical in orientation, *uncover power relations,* while *analysing the suffering of people,* and *focusing on promoting "liberation".*

9.1. Orientation to Critical Theory

Origins and Meaning of European Critical Theory

Critical theory, historically, has taken on from where hermeneutics left off. Both born and bred in Germany, hermeneutics originated in the late 19th century, and critical theory in the early 20th, herein also reconstructed such in African de-colonial guise. Whereas hermeneutics emerged out of tradition, that is through the interpretation of religious texts, critical theory heralded, at one and the same time, modernity and postmodernity, as opposed to modernisation. In Africa then as we shall see (see Table 9.1.1), in the latter part of the 20th century, in fact following developments in Latin America, *de-coloniality* entered the world scene, especially in the Global South, as the continents' visible equivalent of European instigated critical theory.

Table 9.1.1. *East African Social Research and Innovation: Path of Renewal* Narrative to Cooperative via CRITICAL THEORY/Yurugu-nomics: Good African Coffee Story to Kiswahili Enterprise

Eastern Grounding Method and Origination	Eastern Emergent Methodology & Foundation	Eastern Navigational Critique and Emancipation	Eastern Effective Action and Transformation
Narrative Methods (E1)	Hermeneutics/ Interpretive (E2)	Critical Theory/De-coloniality (E3)	Co-operative Inquiry (E4)
The Good African Coffee Story (E1)	*Yurugu (E2)*	*Yurugu-nomics (E3)*	*Kiswahili Enterprise (E4)*

Furthermore, anticipating such, especially in southern and east Africa, the African Renaissance movement emerged, notably via Kenyan novelist, poet, and activist Ngugi Wa Thiong'o, as will be revealed later, but then soon sadly disappeared from visible sight. Finally, and unbeknownst to most, African American – originally East African Kiswahili – Marimba Ani's extraordinary work on so-called *Yurugu*, as already intimated in the last chapter, has blazed a newly global African critical trail on the path of renewal.

Critical theory in Europe then was a label used by the so called Frankfurt School in the 1930s. The "school" consisted of members of the Institute for Social Research of the University of Frankfurt in Germany, including their intellectual and social network. As a term "critical theory" describes their collective work oriented toward radical social change. "Critical theory" was for the first time introduced by one of the Frankfurt School's founding members, Max Horkheimer (2013). He defined it as a social theory oriented toward critiquing and changing society as a whole, in contrast to traditional theory oriented only to understanding or explaining it. Horkheimer characterized critical theory as a radical, emancipatory form of Marxian theory. As such he critiqued both the model of science put forward by logical positivism and what he and his colleagues saw as the covert positivism and authoritarianism of orthodox Marxism and communism.s

The Term "Critique": Routed in Kant and Marx

The choice of the term "critical theory" was also partly influenced by its wanting to sound less politically controversial than "Marxism". However, in an intellectual context defined by dogmatic positivism on the one hand and "scientific socialism" on the other, critical theory meant to rehabilitate both, through its philosophically critical approach and revolutionary orientation.

Furthermore, critical theorists were explicitly connecting with the 18th century "critical philosophy" ("Critique of Pure Reason") of Immanuel Kant (2007). For Kant the term "critique" meant philosophical reflection on the limits of claims made for certain kinds of knowledge, a direct connection between such critique and the emphasis on moral autonomy. We now turn to the core, European critical thinkers.

Core Thinkers – Core Concepts

Philosophers Max Horkheimer, Theodor Adorno and Herbert Marcuse (Held 1980), all of them German and Jewish, became the most prominent thinkers of the Frankfurt School at its early stage, with Jürgen Habermas (Morrow and Torres 2002), also German but not in his case Jewish, being the best known representative of the second generation. However, there are many other notable, first generation figures in critical theory, who are globally acclaimed, among them psychoanalyst Erich Fromm, literary critic Walter Benjamin, as well as the one non-European outlier, Brazilian pedagogue Paulo Freire (2001).

For all of these critical thinkers three aspects of their approach stand out. *Firstly* critical social theory should be directed at *society in its historical specificity* (that is how it came to be configured at a specific point in time). Secondly, critical theory should improve understanding of society by integrating all the major social sciences, including economics, sociology, history, political science, anthropology, and psychology. Thirdly, it anticipated "postmodernity" in its orientation toward a post-capitalist, post-industrial, but non-communist world. Interestingly enough, virtually all of the critical theorists were Jewish, and victims – hence their familiarity with what it means to be oppressed – from Nazi Germany.

Political Activism: Marcuse and Habermas

Herbert Marcuse (2002) then, also escaping as a Jew from Nazi Germany, emigrated to the United States of America. Marcuse's critiques of capitalist society resonated with the concerns of the leftist student movement in the 1960s. Because of his willingness to speak at student protests, Marcuse soon became known as "the father of the New Left", a term he disliked and rejected. Many radical scholars and activists, however, were influenced by him. Marcuse argued that genuine tolerance does not tolerate support for repression, since doing so ensures that marginalized voices will remain unheard. He characterized tolerance of repressive speech as "inauthentic". Instead, he advocated a discriminating tolerance that does not allow repressive intolerance to be voiced.

In the 1960s, Habermas's critical theory conceptualized knowledge in terms that enabled human beings to emancipate themselves from forms of domination through self-reflection. As such he considered "psychoanalysis", including the psychology of the unconscious mind, as the paradigm of critical knowledge. This expanded considerably the scope of what counted as critical theory within the social sciences, European critical theory, thereby, being philosophically oriented, whereas the African version, as we shall see, was more spiritually, culturally and politically oriented.

We now turn from Europe and North America to Africa and to South America, where the African Renaissance and the overall De-colonial movement takes the place of critical theory, in our "south-eastern" context. As we shall see moreover, our *Good African Coffee Story* has such a critical theoretic connection, if not also with de-coloniality, the African Renaissance and indeed Yurugu-nomics, as we shall reveal, albeit that overall, from our perspective, such an economic, if not also political, as well as a scientific-technological, orientation, has been missing from de-coloniality.

9.2. Feel Local African: Grounding Critical Theory in Africa: E3f

9.2.1. The Compact Between Africa and the Twentieth Century Is All Wrong

The renowned, recently late Kenyan American, east African philosopher, based for most of his academic life in the U.S, Ali Mazrui (1986), wrote his seminal work on *The Africans* in the 1980s, which subsequently became a film series watched by millions. Mazrui started out by proclaiming:

> .. the compact between Africa and the twentieth century is all wrong. It involves an attempt to "modernize" without consulting cultural continuities, an attempt to start the process of "dis-Africanizing" Africa.

If the Jews of the Diaspora, he goes on to say (reflecting for us on the above German-Jewish critical theorists themselves), had scrambled to change their culture as fast as Africans recently seemed to be doing, the miracle of Jewish identity could not have lasted the two or three additional millennia in the wilderness. For Mazrui (1986) then:

> The crisis of efficiency on the continent is symptomatic of the failure of transplanted organs of the state and of the economy. Indigenous African culture is putting up a fight. It is as if the indigenous ancestors have been roused from the dead, disapproving of what seems like an informal pact between the rulers of independent Africa (the inheritors of the colonial order) and the West – a pact which continues to allow the West to dominate Africa.

9.2.2. Something Torn and New: Towards an African Renaissance

Planting European Memory in Africa

For Mazrui's Kenyan colleague, the renowned Ngugi Wa Thiong'o (2009), currently Professor of Comparative Literature at the University of California, Irvine, the African landscape is blanketed with European memories of places like, in South Africa, Port Elizabeth, East London, or Grahamstown. Moreover, Lake East Africa, the main source of the Nile and hence the base of one of the world's civilizations, becomes Lake Victoria. However, to the Luo people of Kenya, this lake in East Africa was known as Namlolowe. So after the planting of European memory, the identity of the place becomes that of Europe.

My Soul Has Gone Deep, Like the Rivers

Though his language may die, for Ngugi, the diasporic African's memory of Africa does not itself turn into a corpse. His spirit begins to sing, and out of it comes the great freedom spirituals, whose force of beauty and imagery of hope and deliverance still make freedom sing everywhere in the world. The spiritual is an aesthetic of resistance. Out of that tradition of African-American and African-Caribbean speech, which produced the spiritual, came the blues, jazz, and calypso, as well as reggae and hip-hop.

For Afro-American 20th-century poet Langton Hughes, the rivers he has known – rivers ancient as the world and older than the flow of blood in human veins, rivers that symbolise the depth of history and self-renewal of his inheritance – include the Nile, the Congo, and the Mississippi. My soul, he proclaims, has gone deep like the rivers. Ngugi then turns to Negritude, thereby feeling African, or indeed diasporan African at that.

Onto Negritude: Senghor, Cesaire, and Damas

Negritude was then born of the interactions between diasporic and continental Africans in the streets and classrooms of Paris in between the world wars, symbolised by the trio of Leopold Senghor (Thiam 2014) from Senegal, Aime Cesaire (2000) from Martinique, and Leon Damas (Rabaka 2015) from Guinea. Cesaire says that his discovery of negritude proceeded from his realisation that though he was French and bore the marks of French customs and had been branded by Cartesian philosophy and French rhetoric, if he broke with all that and plumbed the depths of his unconscious, what he would find was fundamentally black. "I felt that beneath the social being would be found a profound being, over whom all sorts of ancestral layers had been posited." His plunge into Africa was a way of emancipating his black consciousness.

Black Consciousness and the African Renaissance

For Ngugi, then, as such (writing in 2009), the African renaissance seems to be an idea whose time has come. It is interesting, in that context, that Marx and Engels, in their "German ideology," describe the entire process of the production of a language in terms of "the language of real life." In the same text, they describe language as practical consciousness. That is why we must ask: Is an African renaissance possible when we keepers of memory have to work outside our own linguistic memory? Ultimately, however, renaissance, as rebirth and flowering, can spring only from the wealth of imagination of the people – and above all, from Africa's keepers of memory.

Rugisara (2014) is, in fact, cited in the last chapter, and as such:

> The negative branding of Africa is not a recent phenomenon but has its roots in Africa's long history of exploitation by foreign powers. It is evident in the justifications for slavery and colonial dominance and is rooted in the image of African primitiveness and the urgent need to bring it into modernity. The enduring nature of this misinterpretation can be seen in the absence of African voices in the contemporary development debate. The popular champions of Africa tend to be white male Europeans or Americans who are celebrities, academics, policy experts, politicians, or philanthropists.

How might such materialise, especially now that, in the third decade of the 21st century, the African Renaissance seems to have disappeared from view? For an answer, we turn to now local-global Zimbabwean political scientist Sabelo Ndlovu Gatsheni (2018) as Chair of Epistemologies of the Global South at Bayreuth University in Germany, a local-global African vantage point if ever there was one, via his recent *decolonial* work on *Epistemic Freedom in Africa*.

9.3. Intuit Local-Global Emergence: African Cultural Renewal

9.3.1. Epistemic Freedom in Africa

The African Academy Has Remained a Site of the Inculcation of Western Knowledge

For Ndlovu Gatsheni, African intellectual productions today have not yet assumed dominance in the field of global knowledge in the way that, for example, Marx and the Critical Theorists have done so. The African Academy has remained a site of inculcation of Western knowledge, values, ways of knowing, and worldviews that are often taught as universal values and scientific *knowledge*. The first generation of African intellectuals, then, were the first to occupy academic positions at the time of political independence. Many of them became ardent supporters of African nationalism and uncritical supporters of political independence. The second generation comprised scholars that were produced in the heyday of Marxism. The third-generation imbibed neoliberal, postcolonial, and postmodern thought.

Shifting the "geography of reason," he goes on to say, means a number of decolonial moves. In the first place, it challenges the imperial/colonial historiographical tendency of making European and North American historical experiences the template for measuring other historical experiences and that Europe and North America are the only repositories of rational thinking. In the second place, it challenges the Hegelian idea of an Africa that existed outside the geographical reach of reason. In the third place, shifting the geography of reason challenges the old Cartesian view of knowledge as an individual possession and restores the situatedness of knowledge in communities and civilizations. He then turns specifically to de-colonisation.

Five Decolonial Imperatives: Starting with the Role of the University

What Ngugi wa Thiong'o, cited above, understood as "colonisation of the mind" has direct implications for struggles for epistemic freedom. How can people with colonised minds even think of freeing themselves from the colonial invasion of their mental universe? This reality makes the decolonisation of the 21st century, which is confronting coloniality within the domain of knowledge, very complex and difficult.

Five broad imperatives, for Ndlovu-Gatsheni, dictate what is defined as the decolonisation of the 21st century. They flesh out its key contours as a necessary ethical, epistemic, and political movement. The first is that the key site and flashpoint of current decolonial studies is the university. The second imperative is that this decolonisation is misunderstood by the beneficiaries of the status quo, who are not even familiar with the extensive literature on such. The third imperative is that there are those, even amongst scholars, who misbelieve that decolonisation struggles belong to the past. The fourth imperative is the genuine need for clarity on concepts, theories, and ideas cascading from the field of decolonisation if we are to implement sustainable decolonial change.

The fifth imperative is that sites of colonisation such as Latin America, Asia, the Caribbean, Africa, and the African diaspora need to continue to generate concepts as they grapple with the consequences of the colonial experience.

Epistemological Decolonisation and Circulation of Knowledge

What is emerging, then, is the importance of epistemic freedom as the foundation of other freedoms. It has the potential to create the new political consciousness and economic thought necessary for creating African futures.

Table 9.3.1. *Dimensions of Epistemic Decolonisation*

Dimension of Colonisation	Elements of De-colonisation
1. Provincializing Europe while de-provincializing Africa	This entails two moves: restoration of Africa as a legitimate epistemic site of knowledge and taking seriously African knowledge as a departure point without necessarily throwing away knowledge from the North and West
2. Africanization of knowledge	This entails reassertion of African identity and re-founding of knowledge in African cultures and values.
3. Adding/including African knowledge into existing knowledge	This is a poor form of decolonisation adding new items to the existing canon.
4. De-colonial critical engagement with existing knowledge	This entails deep questioning of "received" knowledge and critical engagement with the politics of knowledge production and dissemination
5. Democratizing Knowledge ecologies	This entails Opening up the academy to a plurality of Knowledge, including subjugated ones, to achieve cognitive justice.

Unless African people extricate themselves from epistemic coloniality, for Ndlovu-Gatsheni, the "political kingdom" will be presided over by political leaders suffering from what Steve Biko understood as imposed inferiority complexes. Epistemic freedom (see table above) is necessary for building decolonial consciousness and decolonial pedagogy. Indeed, for us, while Ndlovu-Gatsheni, in fact a Zimbabwean, has dealt brilliantly, indeed critically, with the substance of African knowledge, he has not considered in any detail the process of research and innovation, nor the form of the university or community.

This brings us, locally and globally in an African context, onto so-called *Theories of the South,* as identified by the South African anthropologists now based at Harvard's School of African Studies, John and Jean Comaroff (2012), originally South African but now based in the Department of African Studies at Harvard University.

9.3.2. Theory from the South: Euro-America is Evolving Towards Africa

The Global South Affords Privileged Insight into the Workings of the World

In their seminal work on *Theory from the South: Or, How Euro-America is Evolving Towards Africa,* the Comaroffs as anthropologists maintain that the modern world has *posited itself as the wellspring of universal learning, thereby of science and philosophy,* regarding the non/West – variously known as the ancient world, the Orient, the primitive world, the third world, the underdeveloped world, the developing world, and now the global south – primarily as a place of parochial wisdom, of antiquarian traditions.

This "south," in other words, is treated less as a source of knowledge than as a reservoir of raw facts: of the historical, natural, and ethnographic minutiae from which Euro/modernity might fashion its testable theories and transcendent truths, its axioms and certitudes, its premises, postulates, and principles. It does so then, just as it has capitalised on non-Western "raw materials" – human and physical, moral and medical, cultural and agricultural – by ostensibly adding value and refinement to them.

But what if, as the Comaroffs say, we invert that order of things? What if we subvert the epistemological scaffolding on which it is erected? What if we posit that, in the present moment, it is the global south that affords privileged insight into the workings of the world at large? They then take Africa as their "newly global" point of departure, ultimately extending to the global order at large. Their argument is in two parts, as follows:.

A Unique Civilization Founded on Precious Creations of Its Own

Firstly, the Comaroffs contrast modernity against modernization, advocating the former against the latter. Like its European counterpart, modernity in Africa entailed a re-genesis, for us, a re-generation, a consciousness of new possibilities, and a rupture with the past, congealed into "tradition," which was in itself a modern construct. Sometimes the process has been strikingly self-conscious, as with the New Africa Movement in South Africa early last century (Ngugi wa Thiong'o 2009) in the time of Pixley ka Isaka Seme, who famously insisted on *"The Regeneration of Africa"* that the continent cannot be compared with Europe since it had its own genius, about to "march to the future's golden door.".

Being part of a new order of things, "it was entering a higher, more complex existence, a unique civilization founded on precious creations of its own, creations alike spiritual, moral, humanistic, and eternal.".

Modernity as Regenerative versus Modernization as Degenerative

Modernity, as such, refers to an orientation to being in the world, to the concept of the person as a self-actualizing subject, and to a vision of history as a progressive, man-made construction. It refers to an ideology of improvement through the accumulation of knowledge and technical skill, to the pursuit of justice through rational governance, and to a restless impulse towards innovation.

Modernization, like globalisation, in contrast, posits a strong normative teleology, a uni/linear trajectory towards the future – two to which all humanity might aspire, towardsss which all history ought to lead, and towardsss which all people seek to evolve. *African modernity,* as opposed to modernization, speaks to an endogenous history, one still actively being made – a history that is not running behind Euro-America, for the Comaroffs, but ahead of it.

This brings them to the second argument. Contrary to the received Euro/modernist narrative of the past two centuries, which has the global south tracking behind the curve of Universal History, always in deficit, always playing catch-up, there is good reason now to think the opposite: that, *given* the unpredictable, under-determined dialectic of capitalism and modernity in the here and now, it is the south that is often the first to feel the effects of world-historical forces, the south in which radically new assemblages of capital and labour are taking place, thus prefiguring the future of the global north.

While Euro-America and the south are caught up in the *same* all-embracing world-historical processes, it is in the latter that the effects of these processes tend most graphically to manifest themselves: where industrial manufacture opens up ever more cost-efficient sites for itself, where highly flexible, informal economies have long thrived. Which is why, for the Comaroffs, in the dialectics of contemporary world history, the north appears to be "evolving" southward, the latter heralding "history-in-the-making." They then go on to review such theories from the south, starting with the nature of the work itself.

Work as Relational: Making of Self and Others

Is then the "autonomous person" a European invention and, as such, "the end of history," something to which non-occidentals are inexorably drawn as they cast off their primordial differences? Is it, in other words, a universal feature of modernity-in-the-making, a construct in the upper case? Or is it merely a lower-case, local euro-construct? *For the Southern Tswana* in Botswana, for example, that the Comaroffs (1997) have extensively researched within South Africa, *go dira,* in the vernacular, means "to make" or "to do" or "to cause to happen.".

Work, in short, is the positive, relational aspect of human social activity – the making of oneself and others in the course of everyday life. Not only are social beings made and remade, fort the tswana, by *tiro,* but the product of such, namely personhood, was inseparable from the process of production itself. An individual then not only produced himself but also produced his entitlement to be a social person. That was their "southern" version, so to speak, of western entrepreneurship or even leadership.

Problematizing the Liberal Constitution

Secondly, for the Comaroffs, the generic citizen of post-colonial South Africa may not be the rights-bearing individual inscribed in the country's new Constitution – typically urban and cosmopolitan – but, in contrast, ethnopolitics and traditional leadership speak the language of subjects and collective beings. What then happens when a liberal democracy encounters a polity of difference that it cannot embrace ethically or ideologically within its commonwealth? This, to be sure, is occurring more and more across the world in the new millennium.

In postcolonies, which are endemically heterogeneous, citizenship always exists in an immanent tension with what the Comaroffs term "politicism/culturalism.". It is on this terrain that the modernist sense of ideology gives way to ID-ology. While they have paid particular attention to South Africa, this applies, for them, increasingly to the nation-state form in general. Why? Because one of the social effects of neo-liberal capitalism is to make polities ever more diverse, such policies are likely to run up against the limits of liberal citizenship. Which is why the post-colony, for them, is so often a harbinger of history.

Herein lies the paradox of the liberal modernist state in post-colonial, post-ethnic times. In an epoch in which cultural rights have come increasingly to substitute for political and economic enfranchisement, no government can afford to ignore the passions that inflame such collective action. In this respect, dramatic acts like witch-burning in Africa are merely an extreme instance of the challenge posed everywhere to the sovereignty of the state. In fact, the South African Bill of Rights has been lauded precisely because it does seem to acknowledge, within limits, the entitlement of persons bound by culture, religion, and language governed by their own customs.

Reflections on the Post-colony: Imagined Communities of Difference

The modernist notion, thirdly, was an imagined community defined by its cultural homogeneity. The European polity, after Westphalia, was always a work in progress; never a singular, finished article, it evinced a great deal of variation across time and space. Further, for all the idea that it was composed of rights-bearing persons equal before the law, it excluded many from its politics and the commonweal and was typically inhospitable to difference.

Whether or not the nation-state is alive and well, ailing, or metamorphosing, the Comaroffs prefer an alternative. The received notion of polities based on homogeneity is rapidly giving way to imagined communities of difference, or

ID-ology. For most post-colonial states, moreover, the policy of difference is not new. Heterogeneity has been there since the beginning. Born of long histories of colonisation, these polities typically entered a new world order with legacies of ethnic diversity invented or exacerbated by imperial governance. In their wake, the colonists tended to leave behind them not just an absence of infrastructure but also a heritage of fractious differences.

Though such theories of the south then reveal a new local-global configuration of the world, potentially, if not yet fully, neither the Comaroffs nor Gatsheni-Ndlovu in southern Africa, nor Mazrui nor Ngugi from east Africa, have provided an overarching, for us, *newly global*, theory as such, especially one that can lead to such an African form of economy. For this, we now turn to the extraordinary, though all too little known, work of the African American Marimba Ani. Based on the Swahili, East African notion of so-called *Yurugu*, first cited by us in the last African hermeneutic chapter, which we now re-view, somewhat speculatively, together with Rugisara's *Good African Coffee Story*, in our so-called *Yurugu-nomic* light,.

9.4. Think Newly Global: Emancipatory Yurugu-nomics: E3t

9.4.1. Grounding in Asili

Africa's Triple Asili Heritage: Indigenous, Christian, and Muslim

Yurugu and the Good African Coffee Story

Marimba Ani (2000), then (born Donna Richards), as we saw in Chapter 8 above, has drawn uniquely on her Kiswahili, East African heritage. Specifically as such, firstly, Asili, as we have seen, is the logos of a culture, within which its various aspects cohere. It is the developmental germ or seed of such. It is the cultural essence, the ideological core, and the matrix of a cultural entity that must be identified in order to make sense of the collective relations of its members. What remains to be developed and is currently missing, however, from our Good African Coffee Story to come, is the economic expression of this cultural seed.

Good African Christian Values: Love, Respect, Humility, and Generosity

Indeed, what follows from Rugisara (Rugisara, 2014)) is as close as the *African Story* socially and economically gets, in the guise of, for him, so-called *Good African Values:*

> Good African strives to adhere to Christian values rooted in the biblical principles of love, respect, humility, and generosity. They believe that if they conduct their business according to these principles, they can create genuine and sustainable community transformation. They also believe that they are here on earth for a purpose greater

than their own subjective and individual needs – a purpose that recognises that they are all inheritors of this earth and that they all share one destiny. If they sow kindness, love, and respect, they shall reap the fruits of what they sow – a kinder, more gentle, and more respectful world. They aim to be a blessing in the lives of those with whom they do business. Their prayer is to be known as making a contribution to improving the living conditions of the communities where they work.

Indeed, Rugisara, as such, does centre his *good African* coffee story, at least in part, as can be seen from the above, in the healing wisdom of Africa, healing the earth and the world, so to speak.

Compared to Sekem's Islamic Heritage in Egypt

What we can see in such is well endowed with the one exogenous element of Marzrui's triple heritage, the Christian one, but not explicitly to the other Islamic exogenous element nor, overall, to the indigenous African one. In fact, as we shall find by way of example in the African north, Ibrahim Abouleish planted such an Islamic seed in Sekem, which, incidentally, indigenously in ancient Egypt, means the *vitality of the sun*. For Abouleish (2005) then, in his own *asili* terms:

> I carry a vision deep within myself: in the midst of sand and desert, I see myself standing as a well, drawing water. Carefully, I plant trees, herbs, and flowers and wet their roots with the precious drops. The cool well water attracts human beings and animals to refresh and quicken themselves. Trees give shade, the land turns green, fragrant flowers bloom, and insects, birds, and butterflies show their devotion to God, the creator, as if they were citing the first Sura of the Koran. The human, perceiving the hidden praise of God, cares for and sees all that is created as a reflection of paradise on earth. For me, this idea of an oasis in the middle of a hostile environment is like an image of the resurrection at dawn, after a long journey through the nightly desert. I saw it in front of me, like a model, before the actual work in the desert started. And yet, in reality, I desired even more: I wanted the whole world to develop.

Paxherbals' Indigenous Yoruba Nigerian Heritage

However, for one of us (Anselm Adodo), turning now to his African, indigenous heritage, underlying Pax Herbals, as we shall see, by way of *Nature Power* (Adodo 2017):

> The African Universe is a world of relationships, of interactions between the living and the dead, between the natural and the supernatural. A community is not just a place where human beings dwell. The African community comprises plants, animals, human beings, the spirit, and the ancestors. Trees are more than trees; the sky is more than we see. There is more to plants and animals than we can see with our eyes. Everything in the universe is a language of life and an expression of life. Therefore, they are sacred and holy.

Such indigeneity is absent from the *asili* of the good African coffee story.

9.4.2. Asili Grounding, Emergent Utamaroho, and Utamawazo Navigation

Asili as Beginning, Origin, Source, Nature, Essence, and Fundamental Principle

Ani elaborates further, then, on the concept of *asili*, meaning in Kiswahili "beginning," "origin," "source," "nature," "essence," or "fundamental principle." It can also be taken to mean "seed" and "germ," which is the source or initiating principle. It refers, as such, to the explanatory principle of a culture, the germinal principle, or essence. The *asili* is like a template that carries within it the pattern or archetypal model for cultural development. We might say the DNA or "logic" of a culture forges a people into an ideological unit, perhaps analogous to our genes.

From Asili to Utamaroho and Utamawazo

She then, as we saw in our previous chapter, creates the concept of *utamawazo* to mean "thought" as determined by culture and *utamaroho* as "the spirit-life of a culture," or the collective personality of its members. Whereas "utamawazo" is self-conscious, *utamaroho* remains unconscious. Both originate from the meta-conscious *asili*. We speak of *utamaroho* as we might speak of temperament, character, or emotional response. *Utamaroho* is not individual but collective.

The *aslili* moreover for Ani is the seed that produces a force. The force is the *utamaroho* of a people. It is the collective personalisation of the *asili* and represents the possibility of its continued existence. Whereas *utamaroho* is the vital force of a culture, utamawazo is culturally structured thought. It is the way in which cognition is determined by a cultural Asili. It is the way in which the thoughts of the members of a culture must be patterned if the Asili is to be fulfilled.

For us, then, such *asili* can be linked to our natural grounding, *utamaroho* to our cultural emergence, and *utamawazo* to scientific navigation. What is missing from Ani is the ultimate, political and economic, transformative effect. This is what Rugisara (2014), specifically, provides in his *Good African Story*:

> We see the rural economy as a place with huge potential and rich social capital – land, labour, and knowledge – in which they have made three principal interventions: knowledge transfer (agronomy training), technology provision (hand pulpers, improved crop varieties), and institutional capacity building (savings and credit cooperatives and producer groups).

Europe's political imperialistic success, for Ani, and we would add economic success, can be accredited not so much to superior military might as to the weapon of culture: the former ensures more immediate control but requires continual physical force for the maintenance of power, while the latter succeeds in long-lasting dominance that enlists the cooperation of its victims. The secret Europeans discovered early in their history is that culture carries rules for thinking and that if you could impose your culture on your victims, then you could limit the creativity of their vision. To be truly liberated, then, Africans must come to know the nature of European thought and behaviour.

For Andrew Rugisara (2014) as such:

> The presentation of "otherness" by the colonialist or the colonised was a justification for the power and dominance of the oppressed. In fact, as a child growing up in Uganda, I found little in school or in the community that celebrated his history. If there was any such, it was restricted to legend and folklore and was never documented or systematically taught. Much of what was taught began with colonialism.

9.4.3. Utamazowo: Cultural Structuring of Thought – European versus African

For the Europeans, Through Separation, We Achieve "Objectification"

Ani then goes on, in her Kiswahili version of critical theory, to critique prevailing Eurocentric thought. For the Europeans, our north bereft of south, she says then, the need to control and have power over others ascended to a position of priority. It became an obsession, always struggling to negate whatever humanism existed in the culture because of the asili. In order to know something, for Plato, we must be dealing with "objects." By eliminating or gaining control of our emotions, we become aware of ourselves as thinking subjects, distinct from the contemplated object. Through this separation, we achieve *"objectification."*

As such, and in the Good African Coffee Story (Rugisara 2014) again:

> A critical pillar of the Good African model became the advocacy that Africans had to become the solution to their own problems. The notion that a Ugandan company could advocate for a business relationship that considered farmer empowerment as a key goal was, even for the famers themselves, initially not believable, as they initially and seemingly claimed that Good African belonged to a "white person."

Linear Eurocentric versus Circular Afrocentric Time

For Ani, the illusion created of the isolated self becomes embodied in twentieth-century European and American society. Painful isolation and alienation either incapacitate participants in the culture or make them extremely efficient competitors and technocrats. The soul becomes identified with "cold calculation." The sensation of controlling others becomes emotionally satisfying. The world is understood as having so many objects that can be manipulated by the knower.

For the African, our south, conversely, the circle or sphere adds dimension to the line as it envelops it. The sphere is multidimensional and curved. Sacred time, as such, is not "past" because it is not part of a linear construct. The ancestors live in the present, and the future is in us.

The Asili Seed of European Culture Dictates the Development of Structures

The asili seed of the European culture, again in our north, Ani goes on to say, prefigures, then dictates, the development of structures, institutions, and arrangements that facilitate the achievement of power over others. The *"asili"* forces its own self-realisation through the cognitive structure of self-realisation, through:

dichotomization: all realities are split into two parts, separating self and other, followed by splitting reason from emotion and intellect from nature.

> Dichotomization splits all realities into two parts, separating self and other, and further divides reason from emotion and intellect from nature.
>
> - *The self knows itself through confrontation, as it separates from the other, encompassing the natural and affective aspects of the self.*
> - *Hierarchical segmentation:* the effect is to eliminate the possibility of an organic or sympathetic relationship, establishing grounds for the dominance of the "superior" over that which is perceived to be "inferior."
> - *Analytical thought tears apart realities to know them.*
> - *Objectification:* an autonomous self is identified with "pure thought" made possible by a cognitive emphasis on "absolutism" and "abstraction." The self, as an emotionless mind, creates the proper "objects" of knowledge through an act of controlling that which is phenomenally inferior to it.
> - *Absolutism/abstractification* mandates the universalization and reification of truths, using epistemology as a power tool.
> - *Rationalism/scientism:* extreme rationalism is the attempt to explain all reality for purposes of control; scientism, as such, is the merger of religion and rationality. Here, the European God becomes the great scientist.
> - *authoritative/literate:* the written symbol becomes the authoritative utterance as a lineal modality, alienating the knowing self from its affective environment.
> - *Desacralization:* viewing the universe as material reality only, to be acted upon by a "superior" mind.

9.4.4. Cultural Alternatives to Yurugu

That Is Our Destiny. To End Destruction – Utterly

For Ani, then, in the Yurugu conclusion, for those of us who are African, our salvation (redemption) lies in our ancientness and connectedness – not in a romanticised glorification of the past, but in a return to the centre in which all contradictions are resolved and from which the spiral of development can continue with clarity. From the centre, ikons are retrieved in our image, which will allow us to tap the energy of the collective conscious will of our people.

That is our destiny: to end destruction utterly.
To begin the highest, the profoundest work of creation, the work
that is inseparable from our way, inseparable from the way.

Substantia Nigra: African Origin of Biological Psychiatry

In that guise, Ani cites the work of a student of ancient Africa, Richard King (2012), Professor of Global Philsophy at SOAS (the School of African and Oriental Studies in the UK). In his *African Origin of Biological Psychiatry*, in the symbols and sacred texts of ancient Africa, that is, Kemet (Egypt), he finds evidence of the scientific study of human consciousness.

The pineal gland, placed in the middle of the forehead, indicated *substantia Nigra*, or the black substance of the middle brain. This, he says, they knew to be the key to "inner vision," the closest to what we now call "intuition." The pineal gland secretes melatonin (Greek *melas* stands for "black"). While the growth of plants is directed towards sunlight, in human beings it is towards higher consciousness. Melanin, as such, is related to high states of consciousness, or "spiritual light." King argues that blackness, or carbon, is life and is therefore divine. Ancient Africans understood that the Kemites, as we see in Chapter 11, were people of the black earth, and the Greeks developed the word chemistry and the Arabs alchemy.

> Blackness, the universal solvent of all, was seen as the one reality from which spun the threads of the loom of life. All colours, all vibratory energies, were but a shade of black; black was the colour of the night sky, primaeval ocean of outer space, birthplace and womb of the planets, stars, and galaxies of the universe; black holes were found at the centre of our galaxy; black was the colour of carbon, the key element found in all living matter; carbon atoms linked to form black melanin, the first chemical that could capture light and reproduce itself, the chemical key to life.

In King's view, the comparative lack of melanin, combined with the demands of harsh living conditions, cut off the unconscious as a source of knowledge. This would account for a materialist worldview and an emphasis on technology. The fear of the unconscious was projected onto the fear of others. Blackness was the spiritual realm to which Europeans had little access. This served to explain the patriarchal nature of European consciousness, as the matriarchal principle, for Jung, is the key to spiritual consciousness.

In "progress" theory, moreover, human origins (Africa) represent a state of ignorance (darkness). Being outside of the natural order, then, the European made *himself* the order. Nature became the object, and alienation from nature was reconstructed as being natural. This perception served to defend the European's alienated consciousness, the phenomenal gap, a fabricated reality in which the value of being "white" is exaggerated. Hence, for Ani as for King, the African version of critical theory, most especially the *east* African version as in her case, is infused with a southern spirituality, and indeed for us, a nature power and healing wisdom that are missing from the European equivalent.

Towards Yurugu-nomics

In the final analysis, though, notwithstanding Ani's brilliant Kiswahili, east African insights, where she has truly aligned south and east, communality and spirituality, thereby critical of the north and west, her *yurugu* still leaves much to the economic imagination. To complete the Yurugu-nomic story, therefore, at least to some further degree, we will need to turn to our *Good African Coffee* case story at the end of this south-eastern section. In this chapter, though, we conclude with our keynotes.

9.5. Global-Local Tran4mative Keynotes of African Renewal: E3a

9.5.1. It Arises Out of the Problems of Everyday Life

Critical theory, as we have seen, arises out of the problems of everyday life, and is constructed with an eye towards solving them. It offers a way out of an untenable situation. For Brazil's Paulo Freire for example, cited at the outset, to be literate is to be able to name one's experience as part of what it means to "read" the world and to begin to understand the political nature of the limits and possibilities that make up the larger society. Language is the "real stuff" of culture, and constitutes both a terrain of domination and a field of possibility. Critical literacy is both a narrative for agency as well as a referent for critique.

Literacy then becomes synonymous with an attempt to rescue history and experience. It means developing the theoretical and practical conditions through which human beings can locate themselves in their own histories, and in doing so make themselves present as agents in the struggle to expand the possibilities of human life and freedom. For Rugisara, in an East African context, it is economic literacy that counts, born out of the problems that his rural communities faced in Uganda.

Table 9.5.1. *Critical Theory – African Keynotes*

It arises out of the Problems of everyday communal Life.
African Critical Theory is strongly emancipatory in Yurugu-nomic Orientation.
Critical Theory uncovers Power Relations.
You analyse specifically the Suffering of African People.

9.5.2. African Critical Theory Is Emancipatory in Its Yurugu-nomic Orientation

Critical theory secondly is based on an emancipatory interest in achieving rational autonomy of action freed from domination. This orientation includes the conviction that the search for the truth must be tolerant of ambiguity and pluralism. Statements about society cannot be impartial. Rather they tend to confirm or challenge existing social institutions and establish modes of thought. According to the German Frankfurt School, social science should strive to develop an independent and critical stance vis-a-vis these institutions and modes of thought, and should call attention to the contradictions in the way society functions. The inherent restrictions and irrationalities that inform modern capitalist societies should be among the major subjects of research. From this perspective, the social sciences are doing the business world, today, a disservice by helping it to enhance its "bottom line" performance.

As such, and in our East African context, the Pursuit of Yurugu-nomics needs to build on the seed – *asili* – of Swahili culture, redefining an *utamaroho*, or civilisation, that is essentially in imbalance, and restructuring *utamawazo* that is Eurocentric into also Afrocentric thought patterns.

9.5.3. Critical Theory Uncovers Power Relations

Uncovering hidden power relations, thirdly, critical theory engages in the critical interpretation of unconscious processes, ideologies, power relations, and other expressions of dominance of one group of interests over others. There are four types of mechanisms of hegemony identified that form a culture of silence:

(1) "conquest", involving relations of domination and subordination;
(2) "divide and rule", rather than seeing the totality;
(3) "manipulation" through communicative distortions;
(4) "cultural invasion", imposing a view of the world that deprives subordinate groups of any sense of alternative possibilities.

In the East African case this has specifically been revealed by Rugisara in his *Good African Coffee Story* whereby, as we shall see, he continually relied on well
  meaning individuals, be they supermarket executives or leading commodity brokers,
  whose very European institutions, and their surrounding forces, acted against him.

9.5.4. You Analyse Specifically the Suffering of People

Finally critical theory names the people for whom it is directed; it analyses their suffering; it offers enlightenment to them about what their real needs and wants are. One of the first kinds of knowledge indispensable to the person who arrives in a ghetto, or in a place marked by our betrayal of the right "to be" is the kind of knowledge that becomes solidarity, becomes a "being with". In that context, the future is seen as something not inexorable but as something that is constructed by people engaged together in life, in history. It is knowledge that sees history as possibility, not as determined. The world is not finished. It is always in the process of becoming.

The subjectivity with which you dialectically relate to the world, your role in the world, is not restricted to a process of only observing what happens, but it also involves intervention as a subject of what happens in the world. Your role in the world is not simply that of someone who registers what occurs but of someone who has an input into what happens, as equally subject and object in the historical process. In the context of history, culture and politics you register events not so as to adapt yourself to them but so as to change them. For Rugisara (2014) as such:

> In my heart, I was not put on this earth just to pursue his own selfish ends but to contribute to the lives of others, as his Christian faith and biblical teachings commanded. My genuine belief was that if we conduct our business according to these principles, sustainable community transformation will follow, and we shall reap the rewards: a kinder, more gentle, and more respectful world.

9.6. Conclusion

9.6.1. Habermas, Ani, Freire

In concluding this chapter on critical theory, from a dialectical and also developmental viewpoint, we can see, that the perspectives from the developed and the developing worlds are somewhat different. While both have strongly sociopolitical overtones, they are more overtly so in the latter case, and, furthermore, as highlighted *"newly globally"* by Ani in the East African case, the spiritual as well as cultural dimension comes especially to the fore. While Habermas, for example, is an academic with strong political views as well as epistemological perspectives, Ani has a strongly anthropological as well as metaphysical orientation. Interestingly enough Brazil's Paulo Freire (2001) occupies a position in between:

> One of the first kinds of knowledge indispensable to the person who arrives in a ghetto, or in a place marked by our betrayal of the right "to be" is the kind of knowledge that becomes solidarity, becomes a "being with". In that context, the future is seen as something not inexorable but as something that is constructed by people engaged together in life, in history. It is the knowledge that sees history as a possibility, not as determined. The world is not finished. It is always in the process of becoming. The subjectivity with which I dialectically relate to the world, my role in the world, is not restricted to a process of only observing what happens, but it also involves my intervention as a subject of what happens in the world. My role in the world is not simply that of someone who registers what occurs but of someone who has an input into what happens. I am equally subject and object in the historical process. In the context of history, culture and politics I register events not so as to adapt myself to them but so as to change them.

9.6.2. Originate Local Renewal Path: Narrative Method/ Trans4mation Journey

In Chapter 4, under the guise of *narrative* method, we originated the "eastern" path of renewal, to be represented, practically in Chapter 11, by the *Good African Coffee Story* in Uganda, in East Africa. As such

- Your individual and communal Stories are still unfolding.
- The narrative Mode leads to gripping Drama and to creative Origination
- You tie together Potentials and Possibilities of your respective Beginnings
- A Plot shaped by many of the larger Strategy-Stories in which it is set.

9.6.3. Found Local-Global Renewal Path: Interpretive Methodology/Trans4mation

In Chapter 8, we took a further step, from communal grounding to cultural emergence, from local origination to local-global foundation, interpretively as such:

- Sought to understand how our African world was Constructed
- Gave other cultures and communities a voice
- Evolved from the interpretive to the transformative
- Reconnected with our particular African source.

9.6.4. Newly Global Renewal Path: Critical Theory/Trans4mation Journey

Finally, and in emancipatory guise, in this chapter on African critical theory/yurugu, to further our navigation along the road to renewal, your research and innovation:

- arises out of the problems of everyday life
- your critical theory was strongly emancipatory in orientation.
- critical theory uncovers power relations.
- you analyse specifically the suffering of people.

Thereby, and ultimately, your transformation journey proceeded from calling to context, and commmunitalism advanced though a good African story that now drew transformatively on effective history, centred in the healing wisdom of Africa, in the Yurugu case overcoming Eurocentic incompleteness in Ani's terms. We now turn from African critical to African cooperative inquiry along the research path of renewal, adding, in the process, more fuel to the transformative fire.

9.6.4. Toward Yurugu-nomics in East Africa: E3fita

In the final analysis, *Yurugu-nomics,* even if only, economically a gleam now in the East African eye, it takes us some of the way towards critically outgrowing the Eurocentric, capitalist model, in African critical theoretic guise (see Table 9.6.4. below), ti be further uncovered via *The Good African Coffee Story* (see case story 2). The transformation journey towards Yurugu-comics, though that is, toward completeness, integral in our terms, remains a work in progress, to be furthered through our Centre for Integral Research and Societal Re-GENE-ration.

Table 9.6.4. *A Good African Coffee Story in East Africa E2fita*

Feeling Local	**Intuiting Local-Global**	Thinking Newly Global	Acting Global-Local
Good African Coffee Story	**Yurugu**	Yurugu-nomics	Kiswahili Enterprise

We now turn from emancipatory navigation to transformative effect, from critical theory/yurugu-nomics to cooperative inquiry/Dogon-Kiswahili enterprise, now drawing on the African Dogon peoples for their pre-modern ways of knowing pre-forming contemporary English research philosopher John Heron's transmodern modes of knowing. Thereafter, and as our south-east African culmination, we shall turn to the *Good African* case story.

9.7. References

Abouleish I (2005) *Sekem: A Sustainable Community in the Egyptian Desert.* Edinburgh. Floris Publications

Adodo A (2017) *Integral Community Enterprise in Africa: Communitalism as an Alternative to Capitalism.* Abingdon. Routledge

Ani M (2000) *Yurugu: An African Centred Critique of European Thought.* New Jersey. Africa World Press

Cesaire A (2000) *Discourse on Colonialism.* New York. Monthly Review Press

Comaroff Jean and **Comaroff** John (1997) *Revelation and Revolution: Dialectics of Modernity on a Southern African Frontier.* Chicago. University of Chicago Press

Comaroff Jean and **Comaroff** John (2012) *Theory from the South: Or, How Euro-America is Evolving Toward Africa.* London. Routledge

Freire P (2001) *Pedagogy of the Oppressed.* London. Continuum Publishing

Held M (1980) *Introduction to Critical Theory.* London. Routledge

Horkheimer M (2013) *Eclipse of Reason.* Cambridge, Mass. MIT Press

Kant I (2007) *The Critique of Pure Reason.* London. Penguin Classics

King R (2012) *African Origin of Biological Psychiatry.* Createspace Independent Publishing

Marcuse H (2002) *One Dimensional Man: Studies in the Ideology of Advanced Industrialized Societies.* Abingdon. Routledge Classics

Mazrui A (1986) *The Africans – A Triple Heritage*. London. Guild Publishing

Morrow R and **Torres** C (2002) *Reading Freire and Habermas. Critical Pedagogy and Transformative Social Change*. New York. Teachers College Press

Ndlovu-Gatsheni S (2018) *Epistemic Freedom in Africa: Deprovincialisation and Decolonisation*. Abingdon. Routledge

Ngugi wa Thiong'o (2009) *Something Torn and New: An African Renaissance*. New York. Basic Books

Rabaka R (2015) *The Negritude Movement and the Evolution of an Insurgent Idea*. Washington, DC. Lexington Books

Rugasira A (2014) *A Good African Story: How a Small Company Built a Global Coffee Brand*. London. Vintage Books

Thiam C (2014) *Return to the Kingdom of Childhood: Re-Envisioning the Legacy and Philosophical Relevance of Negritude*. Ohio. Ohio State University

Chapter 10 From Critical Theory to Co-Operative Inquiry in Africa AMP, MSET, CIDA: Integral PHD, Green Zimbabwe and Beyond

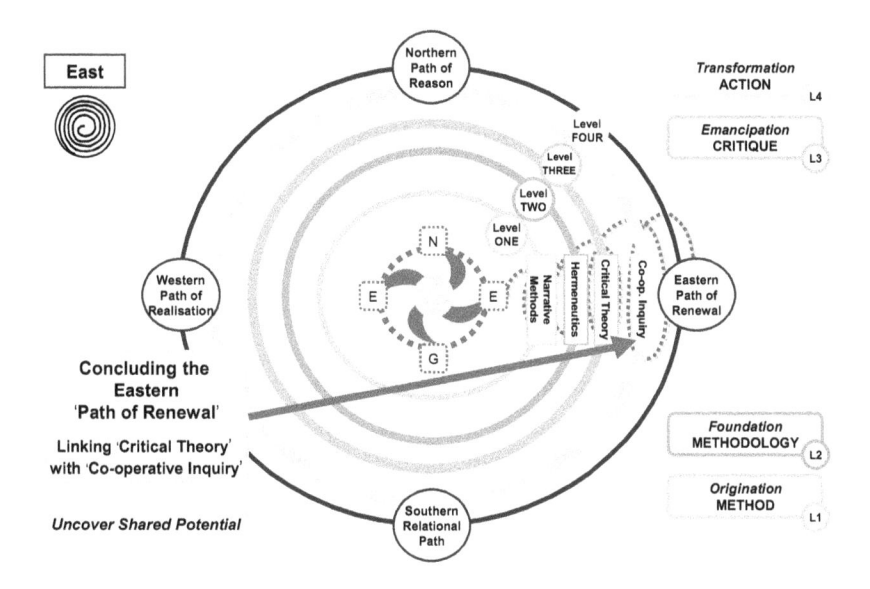

Figure 10.1: *Overview Chapter 10 – Level 4 / East*

Kongo civilization records the turning of the cosmogenic ground in the compact symbology of an ideogram. Known as the yowa, this cross predates the intrusion of Christianity into central Africa. The cycle of man's life consists of rising, beginning, birth or re-growth; ascendancy, maturity, responsibility; handing on, death, transformation; existence in another world, eventual rebirth.

Clyde Ford (2000)   *The Hero with an African Face*

Summary: Co-operative Inquiry/Integral Enterprise and Economy

- Co-operative inquiry, invented mainly by UK action researchers John Heron and Peter Reason, takes on from where narrative methods, interpretive methodology (hermeneutics), and critical theory leave off, giving rise to an ultimately transformative and integral approach, in our African context of Integral Green Zimbabwe, releasing the GENE-ius of economy/enterprise within, drawing on our Integral Development programs that came before
- Such an approach to co-operative research is both politically integral and epistemologically transformative, in that it involves co-researchers working individually and institutionally together, as fellow subjects rather than as researcher/subject and researched/object, and encompasses experiential, imaginative, conceptual and practical ways of knowing.
- These four ways of indigenous-exogenous knowing or modes of consciousness include altogether the southern humanistic (experiential) and the eastern holistic (imaginative), the northern rational (conceptual) and western pragmatic (practical) dimension, drawing on Dogon cosmology
- As such, and re-GENE-ratively now in Africa by way of social innovation, Yurug-nomics (south-east Africa) builds on Nhakanomics (southern Africa) leading to the Economics of Love (north Africa) onto Communitalism (west Africa)
- Overall, the guiding objectives of co-operative inquiry are: *political flourishing* in individual and social life which includes a process of *social participation* where there is a balance between autonomy, co-operation and hierarchy; *epistemic flourishing* in individual and social life which includes a growing participative awareness of social contexts; and a *conscious indwelling and resonsonance with the cultural life of the planet,* centred in the healing wisdom of Africa.
- More specifically, the keynotes of cooperative inquiry and an integral economy lie within a politically oriented, participative process; a knowledge oriented economic process involving experiential (community building), imaginal (conscious evolution), conceptual (knowledge creation) and practical (sustainable development) domains; alternation between analysis and transformation; and validity reflected in goodness, trustworthiness and authenticity.

10.1. Orientation to Co-operative Inquiry: CI

10.1.1. Beyond Yurugu-nomics

In the previous chapter, we were exposed to Marimba Ani's *Yurugu* – the incomplete Eurocentric human – a notion she retrieved from the Dogon peoples of West Africa, before she focused on Swahili epistemology, in the east of the African continent. In this next chapter oriented now towards our eastern transformative effect, we initially centre ourselves in Dogon cosmology, thereafter turning to what we (Mamukwa et al 2014) have termed *Integral Green Zimbabwe*, taking on from where Yurugu-nomics has hitherto left off, in terms of societal re-GENE-ration, following integral research.

In between cosmology and economy, though, as the main methodological focus of this chapter, thereby intuiting locally-globally, we will turn to John Heron's world renowned, so called *Cooperative Inquiry*, our "eastern" version of action research, on the research path of eastern renewal. Newly globally, moreover, we focus on Integral Green Zimbabwe, before turning globally-locally to integral/cooperative keynotes. At the same time, on the East African innovation path, we will turn to the Good African story, by way of culmination, via Yurugu/nomics towards now both the Kiswahili enterprise (see Table 10.1.1. below), as a community based enterprise. We start then with our overall orientation to cooperative inquiry.

Table 10.1.1. *East African Social Research and Innovation: Path of Renewal* Narrative Method to COOPERATIVE INQUIRY/Community Based Enterprise: Good African Coffee Story to Kiswahili Enterprise

Eastern Grounding Method and Origination	Eastern Emergent Methodology & Foundation	Eastern Navigational Critique and Emancipation	Eastern Effective Action and Transformation
Narrative Methods (E1)	Hermeneutics/ Interpretive (E2)	Critical Theory (E3)	Co-operative Inquiry (E4)
The Good African Coffee Story (E1)	*Yurugu (E2)*	*Yurugu-nomics (E3)*	*Kiswahili Enterprise (E4)*

10.1.2. Co-operative Inquiry (CI) in an Action Research Context

A Changing East-West Paradigm Also Turning South

John Heron, while an educator and psychologist at the University of Surrey in the 1970s, together with his close colleague Peter Reason hitherto at the University of

Bath, were the two leading co-creators of action research in Britain. Later, Reason and Bradbury, in their *Handbook of Action Research* (Heron 1997), took on, from where Heron and Reason had left off. For them, the idea of a paradigm in science can be transferred to the worldview of a whole culture, as is the case for Ani and the Swahili, and to the notion that the western worldview may be in evolutionary transition, for them via the "east". This work of ours, overall, in Africa, in such overall "southern" footsteps.

Research in the west, hitherto for them, has been associated with a so-called "positivist" worldview, a view that, also for Ani, sees science as separate from everyday life and the researcher as a subject within a world of separate objects. This is part of a worldview, as we also saw cited by Marimba Ani, based on the metaphor of linear progress, absolute truth and rational planning. Seeking objective truth, this positivist, competitive, modern worldview makes no connection between knowledge and power. In fact Bradbury today practices collaborative living with her family and is involved in various cooperative communities in her adopted home of Portland, Oregon, being also a senior practitioner in Japan's *Eastern* Soto Zen tradition.

For Bradbury, Reason and Heron, then, a "westernised" positivist view has outlived its usefulness. Indeed for contemporary critical theorist Habermas, whom we met in our previous chapter, such western "modernism is dead". Against such a historical backdrop, what does action research generally, and CI specifically, stand for today, set in the transpersonal and even spiritual "eastern" context of this chapter?

Contemporary Action Research: Towards a Participatory Worldview

The emergent worldview that action research espouses, indeed resonating well with Yurugu that has critically come before, is described by Reason and Bradbury as systemic, holistic, relational, feminine, and experiential, but its defining characteristic is that it is participatory and developmental; our world does not consist of separate things but of relationships which we co-author. As you can see, and in our overall integral context, such a perspective has distinctly "eastern" holistic connotations.

John Heron, who just recently died at the age of ninety four, was a pioneer in the creation of participatory research methodologies in the social sciences. As such, he was the founder and director of the Human Potential Research Project at the University of Surrey in England from 1970 to 1977, the first university-based centre for humanistic and so-called "transpersonal" psychology and education in Europe. He was Assistant Director of the British Postgraduate Medical Federation at the University of London from 1977 to 1985, in charge of an innovative programme of personal and professional development for hospital doctors and GPs, including a co-operative inquiry into whole-person medicine, out of which the British Holistic Medical Association was formed. Later, from 1990 to 2000, he became the director of the International Centre for Co-operative Inquiry in Tuscany in Italy, where radical forms of spiritual inquiry were developed. Most recently, he had been co-director of the South Pacific Centre for Human Inquiry in Auckland, New Zealand. He was truly as such a local-global, trans-national, public intellectual operator.

Cooperative Inquiry: A Sacred Science

Within the context of co-operative inquiry, for him. human persons are linked in a generative web of communion with other humans and the rest of creation. Human persons do not stand separate from the cosmos; we evolved with it and are an expression of its intelligent and creative force, in the Yurugu case hitherto in the African east. As we are part of the whole we are necessarily actors within it, which leads us to consider the fundamental importance of the practical. All ways of knowing, then, support our skilful being-in-the-world from moment to moment, our ability to act intelligently in support of worthwhile purposes. Hence, human inquiry is necessarily practical, and any participatory form of inquiry is, for Reason, Bradbury and Heron, as it is for one of us (Anselm Adodo – see previous chapter) a "sacred science". It is a kind of knowledge, moreover, that one has only from within a social and (in this "transpersonal" case) within a spiritual situation.

Such a participatory worldview is at the same time a political statement as well as a theory of knowledge. Just as the classical Cartesian worldview emerged out of the political situation of the time, and found its expression in science and technology, so a participatory worldview implies democratic, peer relationships as the political form of inquiry. The political dimension affirms people's right to have a say in decisions that affect them and which claim to generate knowledge about them. It asserts the importance of liberating the muted voices of those held down by class structure and neo-colonialism, by poverty, sexism, racism and homophobia.

Healing and Whole Making in Africa and Worlds-wide

A participative worldview invites us to inquire into what we mean by flourishing and into the meaning and purpose of our endeavours. As the contemporary philosopher and priest Thomas Berry (Reason and Bradbury 2005) has written: "What is the 'great work' of humanity in our time, and how are our individual human projects aligned with it?" For him, sacred experience, like sacred science, is based on reverence, in awe and love for creation.

Given the condition of our times, a primary purpose of human inquiry is not so much to search for the truth but to heal. For Reason and Bradbury (Berry 2000) then:

> To heal means to make whole: we can only understand our world as a whole if we are part of it; as soon as we attempt to stand outside, we divide and separate. In contrast, making whole necessarily implies participation: the individual is restored to a circle or community and the human community to the context of the wider natural world.

> To make whole also means to make holy: a participatory worldview restores meaning and mystery to human experience, so that the world is experienced as a sacred place.

Such is entirely resonant, then, with the *healing wisdom of Africa*, as highlighted by Burkina Faso's Malidoma Some (1997), in which CIRSRE is overall centred:

> Indigenous people see the physical world as a reflection of a more complex, subtler, and more lasting yet invisible entity called energy. It is as if we are the shadows of a vibrant and endlessly resourceful intelligence dynamically involved in a process of continuous self-creation .. The history of humankind is plagued by this psychic disease that has caused much pain and disappointment in the world, as we still see today. Methods of healing, then, must take into account the energetic or spiritual condition that is in turmoil, thereby affecting the physical condition.

As we have seen, co-operative inquiry and its creator John Heron have been born and bred in the "west". However, Heron is certainly an unusual "westerner", in that he has been heavily exposed to the "north", "south", and, most particularly, the "east".

Self-Generating Culture Promoting a Research Community

In the latter respect he has been influenced by critical theory in the overtly political and critical emancipatory stance he takes towards both research and also education. The self-generating culture he has sought to promote is a research community whose members are in a continuous process of co-operative participation, learning and development. Its forms are consciously adopted, periodically reviewed and altered in the light of experience, reflection and ever-deepening vision. Its participants continually recreate themselves and their work through cycles of collaborative inquiry in living and working together.

At the same time co-operative inquiry has affinities with the more conventionally recognized approach to action research as well as experiential learning, that arose originally from the work of the social scientist Kurt Lewin (Reason and Bradbury 2005), and was duly espoused by the critical theorists, whereby:

For Lewin Collaborative Participation Is Theoretical, Practical and Political

> "In action research, all actors involved in the research process are equal participants, and must be involved in every stage of the research process ... Collaborative participation in theoretical, practical and political discourse is a hallmark of action research and the action researcher."

In similar guise, in pursuit of *The Good African Story* (Rugasira (2014):

> .. the Good Africa team had hopes that were not tied to material comfort but on a richer fellowship that could only be born out of a struggle for something bigger than individual needs at the time. This commitment was also not due to Andrew Rugisara's

persuasiveness or logic of argument but rather because they recognized the value of their labor and sacrifice and how important it was for the thousands of farmers they worked with.

We now turn from our overall, methodological orientation to cooperative inquiry, with its east-west leanings, now moreover retracing African steps, to thereby feeling local in our particular African context, indeed geographically lodged in the African west bit cosmologically in the *east*, with a view to transformative economic effect on the path of African renewal, thereby grounded in Dogon cosmology/local feel.

10.2. Feel Local: Dogon Grounding/Bummo, Yala, Tomu, Toy: E4f

10.2.1. Deconstructing & Reconstructing Knowledge and Value in Africa

In our (Adodo and Lessem 2021) recent book on *Afrikology: Deconstructing and Reconstructing Knowledge and Value in Africa*, we prominently cited the Dogon people as a source of primordial wisdom in Africa. Furthermore, and in doing our research for that book, we came across the remarkable body of work on so called *African Creation Energy* by Ghanean African-American Osiadan Borebore Oboadee (2010).

He makes the point, from the outset, that the word "Africa" comes from the Afro-Asiatic word "Afar" meaning "dust", which represents the "Earth". The etymology of the Word "Creation" comes from the word "Crescent", which represents the "Moon" and the word "Energy" represent the "Sun", which is the primary source of energy in the planet. The letters used to abbreviate his research institute "African Creation Energy", A.C.E, moreover, not only spell the English ACE, meaning "First" or "Primary" or "Original", but also represent the three fundamental geometric shapes of the Triangle (A), the Circle (C), and the Square (E), combining to form the ancient Alchemic symbol of the "squared circle".

Utilizing African Creation Energy, Osiadan Borebore Oboadee has used the "Squared Circle" as a metaphor and symbol to represent the unification of dualities necessary to bring about the birth and creation of a new paradigm. This brings us, as we shall see, onto the four-fold cosmology of the Dogon which, for us, runs prior – hence local feel – to locally-globally intuited (east-west) cooperative inquiry, which as we shall see, newly globally in turn, leads onto our Integral Green Zimbabwe. Moreover, as we highlighted in Chapter 2, according to Some (1997) in his *African Healing Wisdom*:

> In Dagara cosmology, the image and structure of the circle, or wheel, organizes perceptions of the world. The indigenous tendency therefore is to perceive all of life within the context of this cycle, or integrating cosmology. The medicine wheel of the Dagara, as for the native American, is a symbolic representation of the relationships

between the five elements of the cosmos ... Earth, is the centre and touches all the other elements. Water in the East is adjacent to Fire in the South. Mineral lies in the North, and Nature in the West.

10.2.2. The Dogon as a Cosmological Cycle of African Primordial Entry

Dogon Cosmology Encompasses a Rich Set of Archetypal Symbols

Further to such, the remarkable American software engineer and cosmologist, Laird Scranton (2002), for his hobby, as it were, has extensively studied the Dogon, amongst several other primordial peoples, in fact geographically adjacent to Some's Dagara peoples. For him, they constitute an ideal promordial point of entry, because the Dogon are remotely located, effectively distanced from corrupting outside influences, whereby their cosmology encompasses a rich set of archetypal symbols, myths, themes and practices, and their tribal ethic emphasizes purity of language and preservation of original traditions and themes. Moreover their traditions embrace a set of practices that have significance for at least three religious traditions: those of ancient Egypt, of Buddhism and of Judaism.

Perhaps more importantly, Dogon cosmological beliefs were carefully documented by a team of French researchers over three decades. This team was so dedicated to its subject that its lead anthropologist, Marcel Griaule (1965), succeeded in gaining both initiated status within the Dogon esoteric tradition and honourary citizenship in the tribe itself. This emerged out of his longstanding *Conversations with Ogotomelli: An Introduction to Dogon Religious Ideas,* Ogotomelli thereby being a Dogon African sage.

The Dogon, for Scranton then, are a modern-day African tribal people who live along the cliffs of the Bandiagara escarpment, south of the Sahara Desert, near Timbuktu and not far from the Niger river in Mali, West Africa. The tribe consists of approximately 100,000 people in 700 villages. Highly suggestive of an ancient lineage for the Dogon people are their religious rituals and practices which in key ways mirror those of Ancient Egypt, on the one hand, and those of Judaism on the other. Furthermore, the Dogon myths, for Scranton, are expressed in words and symbols that are shared with the Amazigh, the tribes of hunters who lived in Egypt prior to the beginning of the First Egyptian dynasty. Perhaps most significantly, indeed surprisingly, Dogon mythology is documented in tribal drawings that often take the same shape as the ancient pictograms used in Egyptian hieroglyphic writing.

Some of course will think it absurd to suggest that the people of 3400 BC were learning theories of advanced science at a time when they hardly had mastered the skills of stone masonry. What is believable, for Scranton though, is that the structures of civilized knowledge were presented to mankind in a form that would orient us towards a larger understanding of the sciences, which is then our immediate êast African concern, cosmologically here. Indeed hints about the origins of the universe, the composition of matter, and the reproductive processes of life, as Oboadee has also intimated, were incorporated into this framework.

Surface and Deep Story

The oldest such creation stories centre then on a surprisingly constant set of themes. Firstly, if we look at the themes that appear in the Dogon religion, we find that they can be grouped into two distinct storylines, which Scranton calls the surface story and the deep story. In other words, the universe actually consists of two creations, one we can see and one that we cannot. Interestingly enough we will find a further expression of such as we turn south-*west* to aboriginal Australia, on one hand, and west-*east* to Anglo-Indian philosopher Roy Bhaskar and critical realism on another (Chapter 15).

The same pattern can be seen in the dominant Egyptian creation traditions of Heliopolis and Hermeopolis, as we shall also see later (Chapter 13). The surface story line included some or all of the following: first, a self created god emerges from the waters of chaos. The Dogon called such Amma, and the Egyptians Amen (Atum). This self-formed god/goddess creates four sets of masculine-feminine pairs. In Heliopolis these eight, overall, constituted the so called Ogdoad: Shu and Tefnet, Geb and Nut, Isis and Osiris, Seth and Nephythis. For us (Lessem et al 2013) such a "surface story" is constituted of the "topsoil" (inclinations) and "subsoil" (institutions) of a society.

The deep story includes more intimate details, for us drawn "topographically" from a societal "bedrock" (ideologies) and core (images).

Typically the unformed universe, for the Dogon, is described as an egg that contains all of the seeds, or signs of the world, like the *asili* in the Swahili case (see last chapter). In some cultures these signs are represented as the letters of the alphabet, but in others they are simply identified as the seeds of the world to come. Implied throughout are a basic set of principles.

The Four Quantum Forces

Further examining the Dogon symbols – which will implicitly form the local underpinning for Heron's four local-global modes of knowing (see next section) – we see how they relate to quantum physics. Scranton then notes that the four creative stages constituted of *bummo, yala, tonu and toy*, in turn, within Dogon cosmology (see below), for him have a bearing on quantum physics. This is specifically in relation to the four types of force-carrying particles the renowned quantum physicist Stephen Hawking (Griaule and Dieterlen 1986), described in his *Brief History of Time*, as also cited by one of us (Anselm Adodo) earlier in his *Nature Power* (Hawking 2015):

> .. The first category is the gravitational force. The force is universal, that is every particle feels the force of gravity, according to its mass or energy .. our Grounding:

the next category is <u>electromagnetic force,</u> which interacts with electrically charged particles like electrons .. The electromagnetic attraction between negatively charged particles and positively charged protons in the nucleus causes the electrons to orbit the nucleus of the atom .. our **Emergence;** the third category is the <u>weak nuclear force</u> .. exhibiting a property known as spontaneous symmetry breaking. This means that what appear to be a number of completely different particles at owe energies are in fact found to be all the same particle, only in different states ..our **Navigation;** the fourth category is <u>the strong nuclear force</u>, which holds the quarks together in the proton and neutron, within the nucleus of the atom .. our **Effect.**

The gravitation is so weak and undetectable as to be a seed (bummo – grounding – *experiential*). The electromagnetic force defines the outline of the object (yala – emerging – *imaginal*). The weak nuclear force at states of high energy refines the component particles (tonu – navigating – *conceptual*) and the strong nuclear force binds or draws the atoms together (toy – effecting – *practical*). The underpinnings, as was also subsequently revealed by Griaule's disciple, French anthropologist Germaine Dieterlen (Adodo 2021) Africa-locally. We will then relate such to Heron's cooperative inquiry, worldwide – locally/globally. We first turn to contemporary string theory in physics.

Dogon Quantum Forces Parallel to Contemporary String Theory in Physics

String theory came to the forefront of scientific thought in the early 1980s, whereby particles were conceived as vibrating, oscillating, dancing filaments. Just as the strings of string theory, as such, are thought to give rise to the four quantum forces, so the Dogon tell us that the spider gives birth to four seeds, or *sene na,* which as wes shall see underlie both Heron's fouu modes of knowing, in his Cooperative Inquiry, and our own GENE (ius). For Scranton (2002) then:

> The four branches of the "sene na" in which the spider was working will bear fruit .. The first seed caught by the sense was that of the "mono", a word meaning "to bring together" .. the second sene "gommuzo" or "bumpy"; the third sene "benu" or "stocky"; and sene "urio" – its "head". The four "sene" contained the four elements – sene na (water); sene gommuzo (air); senne benu (fire) and sene urio (earth).

We now turn to Cooperative Inquiry, localy-globally, and thereafter to our own recognition of GENE-ius, as we call it, newly globally via Zimbabwe, before articulating the global-local keynotes arising on this African, *eastern* path of renewal, which altogether build up to Uganda's *Good African Story.*

10.3. Intuit Locally-Globally on the Path of Renewal via Cooperative Inquiry: Experiential, Imaginal, Conceptual, Practical: E4i

10.3.1. Cooperative Inquiry Is Political and Epistemic

As we have previously intimated, while the originator of Cooperative Inquiry (CI), John Heron, was English, during the course of his life he migrated, physically, from the UK onto Italy and finally to New Zealand, on each occasion for prolonged periods. Moreover, psychologically and spiritually, he was very influenced by the "east", as well as the "north" and "west", in our terms, though not by the "south", whereby we have provided that missing dimension.

The co-operative paradigm has two wings, for Heron (1997), that is political (value based) and epistemic (knowledge based). In local-global terms then, while the former has strongly "north-western" connotations, the latter is explicitly influenced by the "east", and implicitly – thereby drawing on original Dogon cosmology – by our "south". *Co-operative* inquiry, distinctively speaking, does research with other people, who are invited to be full co-inquirers with the initiating researcher. They become involved in operational decision-making and are then committed to this kind of research design in principle, both politically and epistemologically. We can see already the resonance with critical theory, if not also with feminism, if not also centring itself again in the healing wisdom of Africa. For Some (1997):

> At the opposite end from healing is the illness of not being able to accept or even tolerate those who are different from us. Worse, this inability encourages suspicion, fear, and resentment. Thus it is an illness of the collective psyche when different cultures don't understand one another.

The political wing of the participative paradigm then is formed by a theory of value, oriented, for Heron, to being values, which holds that:

- *human flourishing is intrinsically worthwhile;* it is construed as a process of social participation in which there is a mutually enabling balance within and between people, of autonomy, hierarchy and co-operation, and is conceived as interdependent with the flourishing of the planetary system.
- *what is valuable as a means to this end is participative decision making,* through which people speak on behalf of the wider ecosystem of which they are a part, including the way that integral research is conducted within our research community.

We now turn more fully to Heron's epistemic wing, which is also elaborated further upon in his two books on *Feeling and Personhood* (Heron 1994) and also (Heron 2006) *Participatory Spirituality: A Farewell to Authoritarian Religion.*

10.3.2. The Epistemic Perspective: Ways of Knowing

Four Inquiry Outcomes: Experiential to Practical

For Heron, there are at least four main kinds of cooperative inquiry outcomes, corresponding to his four modes of inquiry, or of knowing:

- Transformations of personal being, *experientially* for you as a researcher, through engagement with the focus and process of the inquiry: our original **G**rounding and local feel
- Presentations of insight about the research inquiry, through expressive, *imaginative* modes such as participating in drama, providing significant patterns in our realities: our **E**mergent foundation intuited locally-globally
- *Propositional* reports which are informative about your research inquiry domain, *conceptualising* what has been researched, through your research activity: our emancipatory newly global **N**avigation
- *Practical* skills you exercise, which are connected with transformative action within the inquiry domain, on the one hand, or are connected with various kinds of participative knowing and collaboration on the other:: our global-local transformative **E**ffect

Inquiry Outcomes as an Up-Hierarchy

There are two important features of this fourfold epistemology. Firstly, there is a pyramid of support or grounding. Experience of a presence, experientially, is the ground of having presentational, or imaginal, knowledge of significant patterns of imagery. Both these together are the ground of propositions about it. Experiential knowing is the ground of fourfold knowledge, intentional action the consummation of it, and imaginative as well as propositional, or conceptual knowing mediates between them. Because of their relatively autonomous form, each of these can function in a limited way without the other three, except for practical knowing.

As we can see then, Heron's modes of knowing also underlie our GENE-tic architecture, throughout, though we apply such to a society as a whole, *feeling* locally (experiential), *intuited* locally-globally (imaginal), *thinking* newly globally (conceptual) and *acting* globally-locally (practical), arguably centred in healing if not also, for us, overall re-GENE-ration.

There is a fundamental asymmetry in the epistemological pyramid. Thus you can experience a phenomenon with little or no presentational (imaginal) data about it, as with audio-visual images, in the absence of the people being filmed, without propositional information about them, and without acting in relation to them. However, you cannot take intentional action in direct relation to something without having some conceptual information about it, without some presentational/imaginal data, and without meeting/experiencing it.

Intentional action, at the apex of the supportive pyramid of fourfold knowing, consummates it and brings it to an integrated focal point. Undertaken by a group of co-inquirers, it becomes a concerted and congruent set of behaviours that is honed through cyclical integration of all four modes and includes that integration as a necessary condition of its continuing practice. "Practice as consummation", in that context, is a way of saying two things.

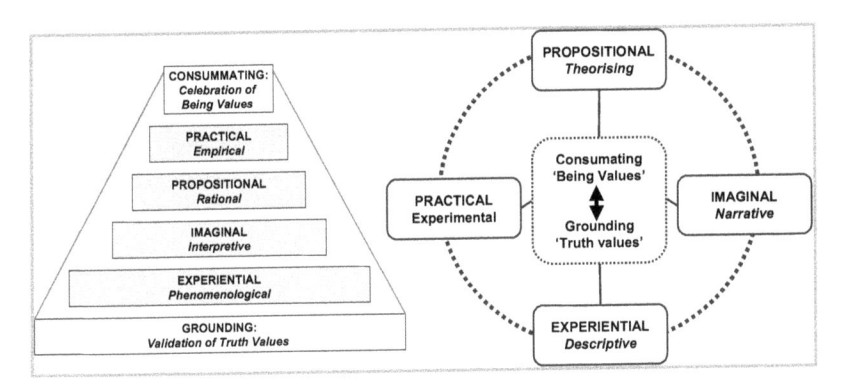

Figure 10.3.2: *Bipolar Convergence (Pyramid) and Bipolar Congruence as a dialectical Process (Cycle)*

Interestingly enough then, while Heron's typology is well known in social research circles, it has never been applied, as we are attempting to do here, to societal re-GENE-ration or indeed social innovation.

Grounding and Consummation: Experiential/Bummo to Practical/Toy

What is below, then, grounds and validates what is above, and what is above consummates, celebrates and shows forth what is below, for us communally as well as individually. The same (see above) applied to the fourfold Dogon cosmology, as for Some's Dagara: experiential-*bummo*-fire, imaginal-*yala*-water, conceptual-*tonu*-mineral, practical-*toy*-nature, altogether centred, for Some, in the earth element which as we shall see below applied to our integral approach to economics and society.

Whether it is illustrated as a pyramid form or a four worldly circular process form (see Figure 10.3.2 above), the following is important: At one pole it is the congruence between the four modes of knowing as their building on each other, and originally on experiential knowing, for us feeling local, naturally and communally, unrestricted and integral lived experience that makes their expressions valid. At the other pole is their congruence as being consummated in and through excellent and concerted practice, our acting global-local, economically and enterprise-wise, the apex of the pyramid that fulfils them and shows them forth. This crowns their world with the value of human flourishing. Valid outcomes alone are not enough. They need to be self-transcending and metamorphose into exuberant outcomes.

10.3.3. Validity You Seek Is Goodness, Trustworthiness and Authenticity

Most unusually in fact, for Heron, altogether though his Cooperative Inquiry, research validity, becomes a matter of quality or goodness or trustworthiness, far removed from the more usual quantitatively based measures of validity. He further proposes some of such "authenticity criteria".

What then arises, newly globally out of Africa for us, duly building on local Dogon if not also Dagara grounds (origination) and Heron's local-global methodology (foundation), now leads on to newly global (emancipation), social science, and to economy, as our means of African emancipatory navigation? This takes us onto Integral Green Zimbabwe.

Table 10.3.3. *Authenticity Criteria in Co-operative Inquiry*

Informants have equal Access to the Inquiry Process, being involved from the Outset in the salient Questions and how to answer them.	⟹	*Fairness*
Informants have enlarged their personal View of their Culture.	⟹	*Ontological Authenticity*
Informants have improved Understanding of the Views of others in the Culture.	⟹	*Educative Authenticity*
Informants have been stimulated and empowered to act to reshape their Culture on the Basis of expanded Awareness.	⟹	*Catalytical & Tactical Authenticity*

10.4. Newly Global Navigation: Integral Green Zimbabwe

10.4.1. An Invitation to Transformation

Integral Green Zimbabwe in Retrospect: Integral Kumusha and Nhakanomics

<u>The AMP, MSET, CIDA and our PhD in Integral Development</u>

Our overall focus on what we came to term *Integral Green Zimbabwe* (Mamukwa et al 2014), which in recent times has given rise, via the Taranhike's, to their Integral Kumusha and to Nhakanomics (see our opening Southern African Case Story), originally emerged out of our Masters in Social and Economic Transformation (MSET) run by Transform in conjunction with CIDA (Community and Individual Development Association) in South Africa. This MSET program, developed in the new millennium, arose, in turn, out of our prior African Management Project (AMP), that evolved (Christie et al 1993) in the 1990s out of a partnership between

Wits Graduate Business School, the South African business community, and our own integral worlds. All of such in turn, in the second decade of the new millennium, led onto our Trans4m/Da Vinci Institute PhD in Integral Development, from which Daud Shumba Taranhike graduated, as we saw (Chapter 3) altogether leading onto to Integral Green Zimbabwe in turn.

CIDA to Missed GSALT (Global School for African Leadership and Transformation)

CIDA in itself, was a unique institution that promoted Communal learning, and Individual transformation journeys, as well as being a socio-economic laboratory in and of itself, in Developmental Association with the corporate world, though the research academy we sought to create – GSALT (Global School for African Leadership and Transformation) ultimately failed to materialise. This indeed has been our repeated experience, worlds-wide, which is why we are now engaged intellectually with the development of SRRC. Moreover CIDA itself failed to endure as a community based academy, largely because the route to transformation it pursued, philosophically, was Far Eastern rather than Southern African, and its business curriculum was western rather than grounded in southern soils.

Starting with Rapoko: The Grass That Turns to Gold

In fact, the unfolding story of Zimbabwean Integral Green Economy began arguably seven decades ago, as one of us, Ronnie Lessem, was born and bred in Zimbabwe, and became conscious, over time, culturally as well as economically, of his African roots. And though he left the country as a young man to research the wider world, "as a son of the soil" he regularly returned to his "southern" African world of local origin, always keen to make his local-global contribution to the renewal of his African economy and society, penultimately "newly globally".

More precisely, though, the story of *Integral Green Zimbabwe* began in 2004, when Chidara Muchineripi and Steve Kada (2012) from Zimbabwe joined our South African based Masters Program on Social and Economic Transformation, at CIDA, and were thereby first exposed to the *Integral Worlds* approach, and in particular to *Integral Research*. As is the case for all our programs, so was also this one designed to support researchers in addressing the most burning issues in their respective communities and economies, drawing on the unique natural and cultural gifts therein. For Muchineripi, the son of a rural chief in Chinyika in Zimbabwe's Gutu province, and for Kada, a then Human Resources Manager of a Harare based food processing company, that burning issue was that their people, at home, were starving; their unique gifts were their particular "green" potential, lodged in their miracle crop *rapoko,* for a villager (Some 1997) as such:

> "The grass that turns into gold
> The grass that gives people their livelihood
> The grass that is fed to people and their livestock

The grass that connects the Chinyika people with the ancestral spirits
The grass that acts as a medium between the people and the spirits
The grass that has value beyond money
The grass that makes and gives life to people
The grass that derives its life from the soil but also gives back to the soil the green nutrients that nourishes the soil
The grass whose seed grain lives forever
The grass that pervades through every aspect of the Chinyika people's lives
The grass that makes delicious food and drinks
The grass that is used to celebrate success and to talk to the ancestral spirits
The grass that gives the human body everything it needs.
The grass that makes and gives life to people, the grass that turns to gold the magical grass."

At that time, early on in the new millennium, much of rural Zimbabwe faced severe food shortages. The country, once coined the breadbasket of Africa, could not feed their own people any longer. Through their combined masters project based research and development, pursuing the relational path, Muchineripi and Kada developed a multi-stakeholder approach to food security, including community, private sector and public sector. Building on our integral models and processes that underpinned the ("integral") program, drawing on wisdom, embedded in local ("green") nature and community, and including various sectors and stakeholders of society ("integral green society"), they brought food security to initially 5000 villagers.

A key vehicle for such was the process of Cooperative Inquiry they pursued, together with communal others, drawing on the four modes of knowing.

Business Training to Integral Development

Joining subsequently our international *PhD Program on Integral Development*, Muchineripi and Kada expanded this project – employing integral research as a means and Integral Economics as an end – and built up a new approach to a self-sufficient economy in Chinyika and the surrounding communities. Today, over 300.000 rural villagers benefit from this initiative, enjoying food security and sustainable livelihoods. This almost miraculous Chinyika case provided the foundation of our newly emerging Integral Green Society and Economy in Zimbabwe.

The majority of our researchers have since built on this foundation. Interestingly enough the Zimbabwean agriculturalist who sponsored our MSET program, as Regional Director of Kellogs Foundation in Southern Africa, Mandivamba Rukuni, and a graduate of our subsequent PhD program, Permanent Secretary in the ICT Ministry, Dr Sam Kundishora, have now both joined hands with Daud Shumba Taranhike, via his integral kumusha.

The next part of this story is no less remarkable. While concluding his own PhD-driven integral development in Chinyika, Muchineripi began to transform BTD, his Harare based Business Training and Development company, into a hosting platform for a local version of our *PhD Program on Integral Development*. Again, the design and execution came largely from our Geneva based *Trans4m Centre for Integral Development*, while accreditation was provided by the Da Vinci Institute in South Africa, originally co-founded by Nelson Mandela, a developmentally oriented Mode 2 University, oriented toward knowledge production rather than academic knowledge – Mode 1 – per se.

Together, Da Vinci Institute in South Africa (co-founded by Nelson Mandela in the 1990s), BTD and Trans4m, refined the PHD into an ever more potent individual and institutional research-and-development program and process, supporting participants to effect integral development on the ground, while simultaneously building up centre of integral development – the latter being very much still work in progress. Again, what has never been constituted in relation to such, as yet, is an integral research academy – GSALT's failure revisited.

10.4.2. What Do We Mean by Integral "Green" Society and Economy?

Originally and Cosmologically Linked with the Soul of Africa

Travelling the Earth, though, we discovered, that the pledge for "green" has many different cultural undertones. For example, while for the European mind "green" often refers to issues like "cradle to cradle", "clean technology", "no waste", "no pollution" and "reduced consumption", for many Africans "green" rather refers to their relationship to their rural homes, their farms, to cattle and game, to the healing power of nature and to ancestors being buried in their natural home grounds, to finger millet or rapoko as we have seen in the Chinyika case. For Some (1997) then again, as equally for one of us (Anselm Adodo):

> Nature is the foundation of indigenous life. Without nature, concepts of community, purpose and healing would be meaningless. In other words, every tree, plant, hill, mountain, rock, and each thing that was here before us emanates or vibrates as a subtle energy that has healing power whether we know it or not. Nature is the textbook for those who care to study it, the storehouse of remedies for human ills.

Invariably in our integral approach, therefore and thereby as such, we start out by feeling local. Building on such, an integral green society that we were seeking to co-evolve in Southern Africa through our integral approach to research and development, promotes an inclusive image containing all sectors of society, jointly contributing to a healthy, dynamic balance of that society – in relationship to other societies and to the world as a whole. Such public, private, civic and environmental sectors represent themselves, on a societal level, in terms of the underlying dimensions, originally and cosmologically linked with the soul of Africa, as illustrated in the Dogon case.

Translated into an Economic Moral African Core

What was then crucial for us, in the context of an African path of renewal, aimed ultimately at societal and economic, contextualised and ultimately transformative "green" effect, in emancipatory guise, is that we feel local (the grass that turns to gold), intuit local-global (via cooperative inquiry), thereby thinking newly globally, in integral green southern African terms, more generally in a overall African context:

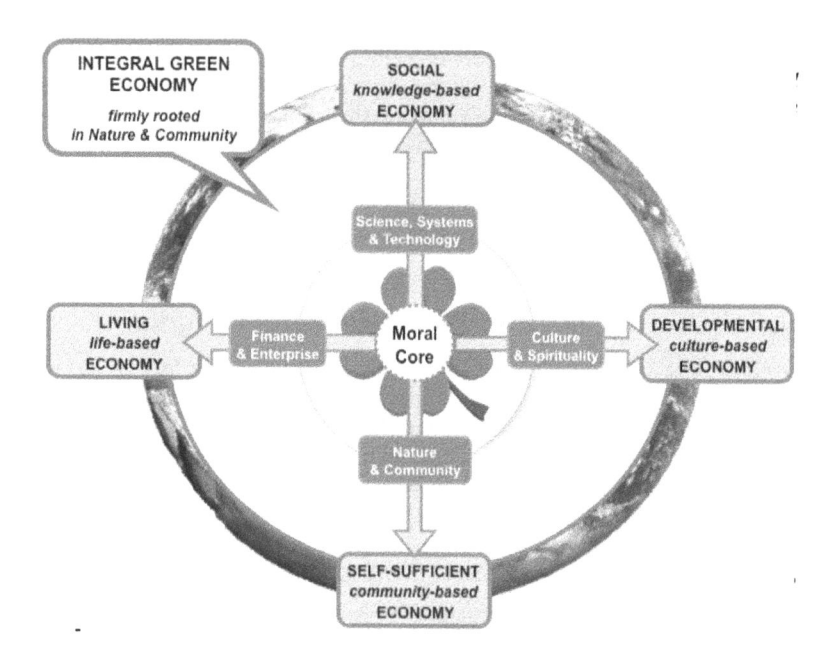

Figure 10.4.2: *Integral Green Economy – An Overview*

- being grounded *cosmologically* in Africa, to give it local feel
- emerges integrally, and *methodologically* locally-globally, intuited, and in combination, experientially, imaginatively, conceptually and practically
- navigates newly globally, as we (Lessem et al 2012) have articulated in our *Integral Economics,* now Grounded naturally (experiential-*bummo*), Emerging culturally (imaginatively – *yala*), Navigating scientifically (conceptually-*tonu*) and Effected economically (practical-*toy*).
- such economic and enterprise effecting, ultimately, pursued cooperatively and co/creatively, politically and epistemically, analytically and transformatively, to good, trustworthy and authentic effect.
- ultimately centred in African healing wisdom, whereby cooperative inquiry, politically and epistemologically translates in *Integral Green Zimbabwe.*

Nhakanomics, Yurugu-nomics, Economics of Love, Communitalism

The Integral Economics model has its starting point in its healing centre, in the moral core of such an Africam society. In our own research we uncovered how vital it is that the outer economic expression of a society is in resonance with its inner moral core. We additionally maintained that a society, like Zimbabwe in this case, needs to build up, substantively, communitalism-wise, by encompassing "southern" *experiential/bummo* oriented nature-based, kumusha laded nhakanomics before its focuses on the other "eastern", "northern" and "western" economic functions.

Subsequently culture-based *imaginative/yala* oriented yurugu-nomics (ensuring that the economy is aligned with the cultural evolution the society), is where a south-eastern African impulse comes in a knowledge-based *conceptual*/tonu based economy of love (aligning its socio-economic structures with technology-driven knowledge systems) and a *practical/toy* based life-based commuinitalism (reconnecting finance and economic performance measurement to natural and human wellbeing).

We now turn to the final, transformative keynotes of CI, starting with its political nature and scope.

10.5. The Keynotes of CI – Transformative African Effect: E4a

10.5.1. You Engage in a Politically Oriented, Participative Form of Inquiry

For Heron, as for us, the reasons for political participation, for transformative economic and societal effect, are:

- persons have *a right to participate in research* – or educational – *design*, the purpose of which is to formulate knowledge about, and through them
- this gives them the opportunity to *identify and express their own preferences and values in the design*, in association with the other members of their research and development community
- it *empowers them to flourish* as fully human persons in the social research and innovation, and to be represented in its communal and institutional conclusion
- it *avoids their being disempowered*, oppressed and misrepresented by a conventional university's implicit, and inevitably "western" laden values in any unilateral research design.

Table 10.5.1. *African Co-operative Inquiry – Keynotes*

You engage in a politically oriented Process, in a participative Form of Inquiry.
You are involved in a knowledge-oriented Process – epistemic in African Nature
You alternate between informative Research and transformative Regeneration
Validity Integral Green Zimbabwe seeks: Goodness, Trustworthiness, Authenticity.

We now summarise each keynote in turn.

10.5.2. A Knowledge-oriented Process – Epistemic in African Nature

Formed by Truth Values

The epistemic wing of cooperative inquiry, formed by truth-values, is:

- *an ontology that affirms a mind-shaped reality which is subjective-objective*: it is subjective because it is only known through the form that the mind gives it; and it is objective because the mind, individually and societally – in our case here an African integral mindset – interpenetrates the given cosmos it shapes
- *an epistemology that asserts the participative relation between the knower and the known*, again societally as well as individually, where the known is also a knower
- *a methodology that commands the validation of outcomes through the congruence of practical, conceptual, imaginal and empathetic forms of knowing* amongst co-operative knowers, individually and communally, organisationally and societally, in south and east, north and west, Africa, and cultivation of skills that deepen these.

Multiple Ways of Knowing

Co-operative inquiry, for us centred in African healing wisdom, and further evolved through an integral research, from grounding (experiential) to effect (practical), as we have seen, is ultimately geared towards social innovation, or indeed societal re-GENE-ration. The four ways of knowing are, duly aligned with Dogon if not also Dagara African cosmology:

- Practical Knowledge/*Toy:* evident in exercising skill, and closely aligned with the empirical, and with the path of realisation, builds upon the experimental, the real
- Propositional or Conceptual Knowledge/*Tony:* closely linked with theory, builds on hypothesis formation, and upon multiple discourses
- Presentational or Imaginal Knowledge/*Yala:* which can be identified with interpretive approaches, evident in the intuitive grasp of the significance of patterns, builds upon the narrative and dialectical

- Experiential (empathetic) Knowledge/*Bummo:* closely aligned with phenomenology, and evident in meeting and feeling the presence of some energy, person, place, process or thing.

As a result, for Heron:

- *experiential* knowing lies at the base of a "knowledge pyramid", comprising your lived "being-in-the-world", aligned with originally local, communal *Grounds*
- *imaginal* knowing, underlying your interpretive research as it locally-globally trans-culturally *Emerges,* foundationally, which
- supports *propositional* or *conceptual* knowledge, your social scientific concepts, newly globally in terms of emancipatory *Navigation*
- upholds *practical* knowing, the exercise of your practical, globally-locally, to realise a transformative economic herein African effect.

10.5.3. You Engage in an Alternating Informative and Transformative Inquiry

Uniquely in co-operative inquiry – when compared and contrasted with other research methodologies – there are two distinct forms of inquiry, the first being "informative":

Informative Inquiry: Research

- participation in nature: molecules to galactic clusters
- participation in art: sculpture to song
- participation in intra-psychic life: sensations to ecstasies
- participation in interpersonal relations: one to one to large groups
- participation in forms of culture: environment, economics, politics, education
- participation in altered states of consciousness: ESP to cosmic consciousness

The second form covers transformative inquiries or research that have a practical or skill based outcome. This form is more in line with action research generally, and also with our kind of integral research and innovation project.

Transformative Inquiry: Innovation

- transformation of the social and economic structure, organization development, economic and political transformation, liberation of the disempowered
- transformation of the environment: ecology to architecture
- transformation of education: birth to death, self directed learning
- transform professionalism: creating a culture of competence, de-professionalisation
- transformation of personhood: personal growth skills, interpersonal skills
- transformation of lifestyle: intimacy and domicile to occupation and recreation in our case in a specific African context, feeling local, intuiting local-globally, thinking newly globally, and acting globally-locally, altogether integrally.

10.5.4. Validity and Co-operative Inquiry

Validity in General

For Heron finally, the outcomes of co-operative inquiry are valid only if they are well grounded in all four modes – practical, conceptual, imaginal, experiential, whereby, for us, communally based Nhakanomics in Southern African (Kumusha in Zimbabwe), a culturally based Yurugu-nomics in East Africa (Good African Coffee Story in Uganda), knowledge based Economics of Love in North Africa (Sekem in Egypt), and life based Communitalism in West Africa (PaxHerbals in Nigeria), altogether in Africa subsumed by a cooperative essence. While practice – economy if not also polity – is the primary societal outcome, it is validated by being grounded on criteria of sound practice: so-called "executive", "technical", "psycho-social" and "value" criteria. This can be compared and contrasted with the more narrowly circumscribed validity criteria in quantitative research, as indicated below.

Validity in Quantitative Research

Traditional positivist research assumes there is one objective reality, just like the neo-liberal economy today that seemingly conquers all; hence, the world is empirically perceived by the senses, which is the same for all observers independent of what they think about it. Research findings are sound if they are accurate, if they match this reality and measure it correctly. This is so-called internal validity and it appeals to a simple correspondence, or dictionary theory of truth: truth is in conformity with the facts, as if facts are empirically, independent of us and waiting to be confirmed.

This in turn dictates criteria for an acceptable methodology. The research must be designed so that its findings are generalizable – so-called external validity – hence, for example, the importance of randomised sampling. It must be designed so that it can be replicated by others with similar results thus establishing the reliability of its findings, their consistency or stability. And it must be designed so that it is free of your bias and distortion, thus ensuring the objectivity of the findings.

The collapse of such overt positivism, for Heron, with the advent of phenomenological, interpretive, and critical emancipatory orientations, has led to the collapse of the necessarily objective fact, if not also the preoccupation economically with the GNP . The well-established counter-positivist view is that every statement of fact is theory, or perspective, laden. It is, for Heron, an interpretation of reality.

Participative Reality

Rejecting outright positivism, Heron's transactional or participative view of reality is seen as subjective-objective, an intermarriage between the creative, construing human mind and what is externally given. In the same guise, for us, the African mind interacts with the world at large, local-globally, with a view to a newly global synthesis arising. Participative reality is neither wholly subjective nor objective, neither wholly dependent on your mind nor independent of it. It is always subjective-objective, inseparable from the creative, participative, engaged activity of your mind but never reducible to it, always transcending it.

Truth and Reality

"Valid" then becomes a perfectly healthy word, and in a generic overall sense – applied to the expression of the diverse modes of being, becoming, knowing and doing – simply means sound, well founded, well grounded. "True" is a closely related, and also healthy word as long as it is stripped of any necessary association with objective fact, or indeed, for us, measure of economic growth. What is important about it, once the notion of independent fact is taken out of it, is that it implies some validating relationship with reality, sometimes today referred to as the "real economy", as opposed to the speculative, financial economy, other than the mistaken notion of correspondence. Heron uses it then in the generic sense of "articulating reality", meaning a combination of revealing and shaping. Further he proposes that "true" is applied not just to propositions but also to the forms of expression of the other three modes. He speaks of four "types" of validity, which we have somewhat speculatively aligned with the *Dogon* cosmology. So we can say that:

* interpersonal encounter (experiential being) involves a true meeting of minds;
* a piece of music (imaginal becoming) is true to heartfelt experience; and
* your knowledge of a text (propositional/conceptual knowing) is accurate
* a person's action (practical doing) is true to his or her principles.

"True" and its validating Relation with Reality Set in a *Dogon* Cosmological Context		
True Experiential Encounters	⟹	Humanistic Validity/*Bummo*
Truly Imaginative Presentations	⟹	Holistic Validity/*Yala*
True Statements	⟹	Rational Validity/*Tonu*
Truly Practical Actions	⟹	Empirical Validity/*Toy*

What makes a subjective-objective reality a reality, for Heron, is a congruence between the four modes, our integrality. By means of cycles of inquiry, the four ways are brought successively and repeatedly to bear upon each other. Ultimately, though, and this is where Heron remains true to his Anglo-Saxon heritage, the outcome of practical knowing, albeit built upon the other three, is the most critical. Reality, in terms of each of the four modes, can then be understood by the Dogon and indeed the shona in Zimbabwe, as revealed by the Taranikhe's (Lessem et al 2012) as follows:

- experiential/*bummo*/ukama (relationship): reality is the lived experience of the mutual co-determination of person and world.
- imaginal/<u>utariri</u> (stewardship) reality is significant form and pattern, in perceptual and other imaging, that interconnects analogically and metaphorically the whole network of other significant forms and patterns
- conceptual/*tonu*/<u>nhimbe</u> (teamwork): reality is combined reference of concepts
- practical/*toy*/<u>upfama</u> (co-ownership): reality is excellent practice and its affects.

The Validation of Practice

Practice as the culminating mode has a self-validating criterion internal to it, which is the knack of knowing how to perform it, according to:

Executive Criteria:

* Can you execute the practice?
* Can you do it elegantly, with style and grace?

Technical Criteria:

* Does the practice have the effects claimed for it?
* Is this form of practice the most effective?

Psycho-Social Criteria:

- Is the practice relatively free of social pathology – free of distortions caused by personal distress?
- Is the practice relatively free of organizational pathology – the distortion of restrictive and rigid norms and values?

Intentional Criteria:

- Is the practice intentional, not merely ad hoc or reactive?
- Do the inquirers give evidence of creatively sustaining congruence among the components of their practice – its motives, guiding purpose and values, strategy and norms, actual behaviour and effects?

Value Criteria:

- Does the practice contribute to personal and social transformation as to your view of an intrinsically worthwhile way of life for human beings?
- Does the practice support your view of basic human rights?

For any given practice some will be more relevant than others. The value criteria, though, are indispensable for any transformative inquiry. We are now ready to conclude.

10.6. Conclusion

10.6.1. The Political Perspective: Participation "with" People

Beyond the Academic Status Quo

Research in the human sciences, for Heron, conventionally speaking as we have so often seen, is very much an academic pursuit, based in and originating from the kind of universities that are committed to the intellect as the controlling force in individual and social life, and to the pre-eminence of propositional or conceptual knowledge, a set of intellectual statements published in systematic form.

Faculty, as such, unilaterally make decisions on behalf of students. They decide what the students should learn, how and when, and assess such according to their own criteria. Academics, as has also been our experience in the various institutions with which we have been involved, do not need to acquire the kind of emotional and interpersonal competence to empower students to learn more holistically, and participate in educational decisions to enable them to become progressively more self-determining. Moreover, and especially for us, focus is on the individual rather than community, on analysis over and above transformation, on technological and social, normally "north-western" content bereft of natural and cultural "south-eastern" context, and, as Heron affirms, on theory not practice.

For Heron moreover, this model of "authoritarian" control, which has strongly Eurocentric "Yurugu" connotations is transferred from teaching to research. The same kind of authority is exercised over the research subjects, as has taken place amongst teaching their students. While we consider, then, that the 18 year old has the right to vote, he or she has no right to participate in educational decision-making.

We consider that a person has the choice whether to take part in a research program, but has no right to have a say in what it is about. As such, people are surveyed, but not enabled, case studies are drawn up, but the cases in point are not emancipated as a result, as one of us (Ronnie Lessem) so prolifically experienced while analysing such cases as. a student at Harvard Business School. As well as universities sustaining a model of seemingly authoritarian intellectual control of students, in education and as subjects in research, they are also, as Heron has said, biased in favour of propositional, conceptual knowledge, invariably also, in the fields of economics and management, drawing on European and American sources. Such involve intellectual statements, verbal and numeric, that can be suitably examined, and conceptually organized, so as not to infringe on rules of logic and evidence. This one-dimensional approach to "knowing" offends a fundamental principle of systemic logic, that the conceptual part is interdependent with the experiential, imaginal and practical whole.

Beyond Research "on" People

Co-operative inquiry, hence, favours, as we do, research "with" over research "for" people. It is a form of participative, person-centred inquiry, which does research with people and not on them or about them. What then are the defining features of such?

Table 10.6.1.1. *Research with People – Defining Features*

All the Subjects are involved in Decisions about Content and Method of Research.
There is an intentional Interplay between Reflection and Making Sense, on the one Hand, and Experience and Action on the other.
There is shared explicit Attention to the Validity of the Inquiry.
It is both informative about and transformative of the Issues at hand.

What does this imply, epistemologically and politically?

Table 10.6.1.2. *Research with People – Core Implications*

Propositions about Human Experience that are the Outcome of the Research are of questionable Validity if they are not grounded in your Experience as a Researcher, and for us in your community and society being researched.
The most rigorous Way to do this is for you to ground the Statements directly in your experience as a Co-subject: this involves a deep kind of participative Knowing, individually and societally.
The Human Condition is one of shared and dialogic Embodiment; you can only operate through the full Range of your Sensibilities, in a Relation of reciprocal Dialogue, and for us equally a full range of worlds-wide societal perspectives .
This enables you as a Researcher, and a community or society being researched upon, to come to know not only the external Forms (individual and collective) but also the inner Apprehension of these.

and Innovation

In conclusion, co-operative inquiry, as well as participative action research, are humanistic and holistic approaches to research-and-innovation, albeit that they are generally integral in nature and scope. Co-operative inquiry is actually a halfway house between social research and innovation, information and transformation. For whereas Heron does focus on both, he is still recognized as part of the academic research community.

Actually, Denzin and Lincoln (2017), in their "Handbook of Qualitative Research", are great supporters of his approach. Although Heron was influenced by the east, he remains true to his Anglo-Saxon pragmatic colors, with practicality as his hallmark. In fact one of the distinguishing features of co-operative inquiry is that, in itself, and through its for modes of "knowing" – or, as we would describe such, being (experiential) and becoming (imaginal), knowing (conceptual) and doing (practical) – Heron encompasses all four of our worlds, albeit, for us, his major orientation is towards the path of renewal, that is toward co-evolution.

10.6.2. From Academic Analysis to Transformation Journey

We hence come to the end of the eastern path of renewal by revisiting once more the four levels along the research-to-innovation trajectory that you have, by now, progressively built upon. Through such, overall, you engage in a transformation journey, on an individual and communal, organizational and societal level, supporting conscious evolution (the eastern function of an enterprise or community) and, on a societal level, co-evolving the "eastern" form of communitalism, as we shall see thereby ultimately promoting a *Good African Story*.

Table 10.6.2. *South-Eastern Path of African Renewal Transformation Journey*

Narrative *Origination:* **Good African Story**	*Each* event in the Grounding of Self, Organization and Society is novel; no Struggle, no Story; no Trouble, no Tale. The overall Plot in each Case unfolds with a View to continuing Development of the *Good African Coffee Story*
Interpretation *Foundation:* *Yurugu*	Through a Fusion of Horizons between Tradition and Modernity, indigenous and exogenous, you *imaginatively re-conceive* of your World in *Yurugu light of incompleteness*
Critique *Emancipation;* *Yurugu-nomics*	Such understanding and co-evolving of Reality is dialogic and dialectical – via History, Psychology, and Spirituality – *promoting* De-colonial Consciousness, and thereby a Yurugu-nomics that completes the African story
Co-operation *Transformation:* **Integral Green Zimbabwe**	Effectively engaging Co-Researchers as fellow Subjects, you *consciously evolve* Self/Others via experiential/*bummo,* imaginative/*yala,* conceptual/*tonu,* and practical/*toy* laden Modes underlying Integral Green Zimbabwe

What does that more specifically mean?

10.6.3. The Integral Path of "Eastern" African Renewal as a Whole

Originate Local Renewal Path: Narrative Method/Trans4mation Journey

In Chapter 4, under the guise of *narrative* method, we originated the "eastern" path of renewal, to be represented, practically in Chapter 11, by the *Good African Coffee Story* in Uganda, in East Africa. As such

- Your individual and communal Stories are still unfolding.
- The narrative Mode leads to gripping Drama and to creative Origination

- You tie together Potentials and Possibilities of your respective Beginnings
- A Plot shaped by many of the larger Strategy-Stories in which it is set.

Found Local-Global Renewal Path: Interpretive Methodology/ Trans4mation

In Chapter 8, we took a further step, from communal grounding to cultural emergence, from local origination to local-global foundation, interpretively as such:

- Sought to understand how our African world was Constructed
- Gave other cultures and communities a voice
- Evolved from the interpretive to the transformative
- Reconnected with our particular African source.

Newly Global Renewal Path: Critical Theory/Trans4mation Journey

Thereafter, and in emancipatory guise, in this chapter on African critical theory/ yurugu, to further our navigation along the road to renewal, your research and innovation:

- arises out of the problems of everyday life
- your critical theory was strongly emancipatory in orientation
- critical theory uncovers power relations
- you analyse specifically the suffering of people.

Act Globally-Locally via Dogon Cosmology/Cooperative Inquiry/ Integral Economy

Finally, turning from East Africa back to Southern Africa, through the pursuit of cooperative inquiry:

- engaging in a political oriented, participative research/innovation process
- involved in a knowledge oriented process, seeking African epistemic freedom
- alternating between analysis and transformation in Integral Green Zimbabwe
- seeking research validity via goodness, trustworthiness, and authenticity

Thereby, and ultimately, your transformation journey proceeded from calling to context, and commmunitalism advanced though a good African story that now drew transformatively on effective history, is actualised through a form of cooperative inquiry that is, on the one hand, grounded in African cosmology, and, on the other, leads to an integral, green African economy and society. We will now illustrate how this unfolds through the *Good African Coffee Story*.

Table 10.6.3. *Good African Coffee to Integral Green Zimbabwe: E4fita*

Feeling Local	Intuiting Local-Global	Thinking Newly Global	Acting Global-Local
Dogon Fourfold Grounding	*Cooperative Inquiry*	*Integral Green Zimbabwe*	*Good African Coffee Story*

Thereafter we turn to our overall orientation to so called "Critical Rationalism" in "northern" guise, to "feeling local" via so called *Ezumezu*.

10.7. References

Adodo A (2021) *Nature Power: Natural Medicine in Tropical Africa*. Tennessee. CMD Publishing

Adodo A and Lessem R (2021) *Africology: Deconstructing and Reconstructing Knowledge and Value in Africa*. Manchester. Beacon Academic

Berry T (2000) *The Great Work: Our Way into the Future*. New York. Crown Publications

Christie P, **Lessem** R and **Mbigi** L (1993) *African Management: Philosophies, Concepts and Applications*. Johannesburg. Knowledge Resources

Denzin N and **Lincoln** Y (2017) *The SAGE Handbook of Qualitative Research*. Fifth Edition. New York. Sage

Ford C (2000) *The Hero with an African Face: Mythic Wisdom of Traditional Africa*. New York. Bantam

Griaule M (1965) *Conversations with Ogotomelli: An Introduction to Dogon Religious Ideas*. Oxford. Oxford University Press

Griaule M and **Dieterlen** G (1986) *The Pale Fox*. Baltimore. African World Books

Hawking S (2015) *A Brief History of Time*. New York. Bantam

Heron J (1994) *Feeling and Personhood*. Abingdon. Routledge

Heron J (1997) *Cooperative Inquiry*. London. Sage

Heron J (2006) *Participatory Spirituality: A Farewell to Authoritarian Religion*. New York. Lulu Press

Lessem R and **Schieffer** A (2010) *Integral Economics: Releasing the Economic Genius of Your Society*. Farnham: Gower.

Lessem R et al (2013) *Integral Dynamics: Cultural Dynamics of Political Economy*. Abingdon. Routledge

Lessem R, **Muchineripi** P and **Kada** S (2012) *Integral Community*. Abingdon. Routledge

Mamukwa E, Lessem R and Schieffer A (2014) *Integral Green Zimbabwe. An African Phoenix Rising.* Abingdon. Routledge

Mandela N (1994) *The Long Walk to Freedom.* New York. Abacus

Osiadan Borebore **Oboadee** (2010) *African Creation Energy: The Science of Sciences and the Science in Sciences.* www.AfricanCreationEnergy.com

Reason P and Bradbury H (2005) *Handbook of Action Research.* New York. Sage

Rugasira A (2014) *A Good African Story: How a Small Company Built a Global Coffee Brand.* London. Vintage Books

Scranton L (2002) *The Science of the Dogon: Decoding the African Mystery Tradition.* Rochester. Vermont. Inner Traditions

Some M P (1997) *The Healing Wisdom of Africa.* New York. Jeremy Tarcher

Taranhike D (2020) *Integral Kumusha.* Johannesburg. Da Vinci. PhD Thesis

ICS2: Integral Case Story 2: The Good African Coffee Story
Integral Path of "East" African Renewal: Transformation Journey

Introduction
Integral Research and Innovation

We now turn to our second integral case story, that of the Good Africa Coffee Company, based in Uganda, in East Africa, whereby we focus on, and indeed ultimately critique, its Transformation Journey, towards and East African Communitalism overall, that is both an inner directed and an outer directed, one, thereby drawing upon the full set of Keynotes from the African path of renewal:

Originate Local Renewal Path: Narrative Method/Unfolding Story

- Your individual and communal *stories are still unfolding.*
- Leads to gripping *drama and to creative origination*
- You/it tie/s together *potentials and possibilities of your/its beginnings*
- A plot is *shaped by* many of the *larger stories* in which it is set.

Local-Global Renewal Path Foundation: Interpretive Methodology/Effective History

- You seek to understand *how your African world was constructed*
- You *give other cultures and communities a voice*
- You evolve from the *interpretive to the transformative*
- Reconnecting with a particular *African natural and cultural source.*

Newly Global Renewal Path: Critical Theory/Asili Laden Orientation

- Arising out of the *problems of everyday life leading to an African Renaissance*
- Critical theory has a *strongly emancipatory Asili laden* orientation
- The Theory of the South leads to the *de-colonial overturning of power relations*
- Analyses specifically the *suffering* of people.

Act Globally-Locally via Cooperative Inquiry/Integral Economy

- You engage in a political oriented, *participative pursuit of an integral economy*
- Involved in a knowledge oriented process, *seeking African epistemic freedom*
- You alternate individually and societally between *analysis and transformation*
- You seek research validity via *goodness, trustworthiness, and authenticity.*

As though with any good story, we will not be following all of these keynotes sequentially, but we aim to cover a select number of them in iterative fashion. Thereby, and ultimately, the *Good African Coffee Story*, as a transformation journey proceeds from calling to context, whereby commmunitalism is advanced or otherwise, drawing on effective history, actualised through a form of cooperative inquiry that is grounded in *East* African cosmology, and leads, potentially if not altogether actually, to an "east" African form of communitalism.

The Good African Mission

Local, Local-Global and Global-Local

Andrew Rugasira (2014), the founder of what became *Good African Coffee*, grew up in Uganda, studied Law and Economics as an undergraduate at the University of London, and later completed a Masters in African Studies at Oxford. In 2003 he founded the first African-owned coffee brand to be stocked in UK and US retailers. Indeed, and as we shall now see, Rugasira in East Africa, as a social innovator, like Taranhike in Southern Africa before him, and Abouleish in North Africa as well as Adodo in West Africa that come after him, is both intellectual and enterprising. Thereby also feeling local, while operating locally-globally, if not quite "newly globally", as we shall see, his "Good African Coffee Story" does now have a global-local ring to it.

Good African Origination: Vision, Mission and Values

On the Good Africa Coffee website (https://www.devex.com/organizations/good-african-coffee-44483) we now see the following overview:

Good African Origination: Use Trade to Bring About Sustainable Development

In 2003, Ugandan entrepreneur Andrew Rugasira had an idea; he believed that *it was time for Africans to process and market their own products globally and use trade as a means to bring about the sustainable development so desperately needed by the farmers and communities.* That same year Andrew and a small team of dedicated colleagues travelled to western Uganda, a region that once produced quality coffees, but had over the years suffered from poor farming practices and low prices. Seeing the potential, the Good African team began organizing the farmers into producer groups. The team then embarked on an intensive program of best practices training for the farmers to produce quality Arabica coffees that would ensure a better return on their harvest. Today, they are proud to say that more than 14,000 farmers have joined their network of suppliers.

For decades Africans have produced what they do not consume and consumed what they do not produce. With few exceptions, processing and value addition has historically taken place outside Africa. Processing the coffee in Uganda where it is grown allows the company to retain a greater proportion of the value addition thereby *enabling the Company to better support the farmers and empower their communities.*

Good African Vision
To be a leading African agribusiness producing quality products for the global market and using trade to bring about sustainable community development.

Good African Mission
- To sell the finest African agro products bought direct from the growers at prices that ensure they make a profitable return on their harvest.
- To operate their company on a sustainable financial basis within a framework of commercial best practices that places community empowerment at the heart of their business.
- To create value for their farmers and their communities by investing a guaranteed portion of their profits in sustainable projects.
- To train their farmers in agricultural best practices, and enable them to improve their crop quality and overall farm productivity.

Good African Values
Good African strives to adhere to Christian values rooted in the biblical principles of Love, Respect, Humility and Generosity. They believe that if they conduct their business according to these principles they can create genuine and sustainable community transformation. They also believe that they are here on earth for a purpose greater than their own subjective and individual needs; a purpose that recognizes that they all are inheritors of this earth and that they all share one destiny. If they sow kindness, love, and respect, they shall reap the fruits of what they sow – a kinder, more gentle and respectful world. They aim to be a blessing in the lives of those with whom they do and share business. Their prayer is to be known as having made a contribution to improving the living conditions of the communities where they work.

Critical Theory Has a Strongly Emancipatory Asili Laden Orientation

As a Devout Christian: Building a Social Enterprise

In the *The Good African Story* that Rugasira wrote in 2014 then, about the founding and development of their community based enterprise, he started, as a devout Christian – in the same overtly religious guise as Adodo (Yoruba and Benedictine), Abouleish (Muslim and anthroposophist), if not also Taranhike (building on indigenous and exogenous *nhaka* or "legacy") – with a quote from Corinthians:

> Now finish the work, so that your eager willingness to do it may be matched by your completion of it, according to your means (Corinthians 8:11)

To that extend what "seeded" his vision – *asili* – was an exogenous, Christian mission, rather than an indigenous one. What no Ugandan coffee company had done before, according to Rugasira, was to place a branded coffee product on supermarket shelves in South Africa, the UK, and ultimately also the US. This became his mission and has been his journey since. Under the "trade not aid" banner, aligned with his Christian beliefs, as above, and a profit share commitment to their farmers, he, together with his wife, developed the building blocks for what he termed a "social enterprise" in Uganda.

He Was Put on this Earth to Contribute to the Lives of Others

Rugasira then turns specifically to agriculture. At the time of his writing (2014) 64 % of Africans were employed in agriculture. Agriculture then is two to four times more effective than other sectors in reducing poverty, as well as being a powerful stimulus to growth in non-agricultural sectors. He goes on to say that, in his heart, he was not put on this earth just to pursue his own selfish ends, but to contribute to the lives of others, as his Christian faith and biblical teachings commanded. His genuine belief was that if we conduct our business according to these principles, sustainable community transformation will follow, and we shall reap the rewards: a kinder, more gentle and respectful world.

He introduced programmes that would invest in the areas of coffee agronomy support that would improve crop quality, post-harvest handling, productivity and environmental stewardship, and institutional capacity-building through financial literacy training and the development of Savings and Credit Cooperatives for the farmers. His challenge, though, was could an African social enterprise that aspired to empower the rural community develop a profitable, global brand?

A Knowledge Oriented Process, Seeking African Epistemic Freedom

Non-Africans Dominate the Production and Articulation of Knowledge on Africa

He decided, in fact, to write his *Good African Coffee Story* because, for us with the exception of the likes of Adodo, Abouleish and Koopman cited by us here, few African entrepreneurs document their experiences. Like many other subjects on the continent, African enterprise remains largely unpublished. The result is that non-Africans continue to dominate the production and articulation of knowledge on Africa. By default they are given privileged status, called "experts" or "analysts" or even "specialists"; they are perceived as credible and institutional voices, who understand the continent even better than its inhabitants. Feeding into this architecture, for Rugisara, is the constant flow of negative narratives that define most of the news coverage on Africa.

These narratives have then been cemented into a widely accepted construct of a desperate, violent continent. While, admittedly for him, Africa's leaders have generously fed this perspective through prodigious misrule, greed and brutality, many more complex and dynamic factors are simply ignored or purposefully overlooked. Because most knowledge published in Africa comes from the West, intellectual capital and power invariably has been transferred to Western institutions. This has led to a debilitating asymmetry. Africa's contribution to independent research is pitiful. For example, not one of the continent's business titans has published a memoir on the reasons for their success, whereby future African entrepreneurs are denied such inspiration.

The Theory of the South Leads to the De-colonial Overturning of Power Relations

Africans Consume What They Do Not Produce, and Produce What They Do Not Consume

In fact the persistence of the "bad African story" derives, for Rugisara, from deep-seated prejudices which underpinned and informed much of the colonial experience and lingers on today, which makes doing business in the West without being stereotyped very difficult. Indeed the largest barrier facing African exporters is limited access to high-value markets in the advanced economies, rooted in the nature of these markets. Markets are dominated by large firms with huge financial resources, advanced technologies and complex supply chains and capital structures. there is also very limited processing taking place in Africa, meaning that a significant portion of the value of African commodities is surrendered to the economies of the West. *For decades Africans have consumed what they do not produce, and produced what they do not consume.*

The critical issue is one of power. The truth is that most ACP countries (African and Caribbean) are former colonies negotiating from very weak psychological, economic and political positions. In fact such non-tariff issues are much more pernicious, for Rugisara, because they are hidden and difficult to quantify. In the majority of cases his brand would have to compete with other coffee brands that have significant advantages: access to capital, technology and skilled labour for the processing of products, and better logistics and supply chain infrastructures.

His outlook has undeniably been shaped by the political and economic history of his country and the African continent and it is for that reason that he begins his story through the critical themes: logistics, markets and access to capital, but especially African politics.

You Seek to Understand How Your African World was Constructed

The Private Sector Being Constrained by Extractive and Repressive Regimes

Witnessing state failure and its ramifications on his family in Uganda led Rugisara to question, at an early age, why an African regime would become the worst enemy of the people. Growing up he saw state failure and warlordism in Somalia, Liberia and Sierra Leone in the 1990s, and an almost permanent state of war in parts of east and central Africa, where he lived, as well as the lethality of the civil wars in the 1970s and 1980s in southern African states, including the former Rhodesia and in Namibia. As a businessmen he was aware that the private sector could not become the engine for economic growth when it was being constrained by dysfunctional, corrupt, extractive and repressive regimes.

There has been much progress in Africa, he says, since the 1990s, but many states on the continent remain blighted by structural weaknesses and complex problems that are not only rooted in their history but also in how they have evolved since independence. The coups in Mali and Guinea Bissau in 2012 reminded us that the fragility of these states is not only a historical issue – it is very much a contemporary one.

Neocolonialism: Continued Colonial Control of the Former Colonies Via the Economy

Independence in many former colonies, in fact, ushered in what Kwame Nkrumah, the pan Africanist who led Ghana to independence in 1957, termed *neocolonialism: the continued colonial control of the former colonies through the economy, cultural forces and other means in lieu of direct political and military control*. After independence a pattern of dependency and extractive linkages in the newly independent states became increasingly apparent. Newly independent African states were fertile ground for superpower contestations and these superpowers very much influenced the decolonisation process. As the anti-colonial struggle gathered momentum they were increasingly inspired by either the Soviet Union or the American worldview of modernism, leaving many African countries in a constant state of civil conflict. The Cold War in fact made a military elite dominant and ushered in the militarisation of politics. By 1974 there was not a single democracy in mainland Africa.

Colonialism Exploited Africa's Resources Rather Than Build Up Its Institutional Capacity

For Acemoglu and Robinson, professors of economics at MIT and Harvard in *Why Nations Fail: The Origins of Power*, extractive states suppress personal and economic freedoms, distinguishing incentives for innovation and wealth-creating activities. A small elite group tends to control the pipeline of extraction, keeping the bulk of the population insecure, suppressed and poor, and without protection for their human and property rights. For example, by independence in the 1960s, the Congo was characterised by entrenched backwardness and an extractive model that was in many ways, for Rugisara, a modern version of the 14th century Kongo. European colonialism compounded the problem by focusing on plundering and exploiting Africa's natural resources rather then building up its institutional capacity.

Much of 19th century Africa was in fact militarised and many of the great kingdoms and powerful warlords on the continent rose and fell with the slave trade. The Atlantic slave trade had a very significant impact on the social and political institutions in Africa. African states organized themselves around such predatory activity instead of providing protection and welfare for its citizens. Trading in ivory, moreover, became the monopoly of kings and rulers and was a major cause of inter-state wars. The colonial order, for Rugisara then, was brutal and oppressive and many of its extractive features have survived o this day. The promotion, by the colonial powers, of the native chief, led to the syndrome of the African "big man", finding expression today in the personalised rule of many African leaders, a relationship for Rugisara that has endured today, in his native Uganda, between the chief and the peasant.

The External Orientation of Colony as the Imperial "Gate"

This promoted personalised rule and negated institutional autonomy in political and economic affairs. In Uganda, for example, the colonial chief-peasant nexus has found modern expression in the executive-local government relationship. The external orientation of the colony, meanwhile, focused attention on the "gate" – the interface between the local and imperial economies. The African elites who took over at independence used patronage, corruption, coercion and scapegoating of opponents to reinforce their control of resources that flowed through the gate. Thereafter, predatory elites, following in such colonial footsteps. became the new political actors in Africa.

Meanwhile the post-colonial political alignments were based on ethnicity, religion and other social factors. It also meant that the state failed to integrate society, regulate social relationships, or use resources in a purposeful way. All energies were deployed in the pursuit of power. While the colonial state had ruled by fear rather than affection, it became a major challenge, in the context of a multi-ethnic and multi-religious society, for the post-colonial ruler to exact the same compliance without using similar coercive methods. Whereas in Western democratic societies, for Rugisara, the people own the state, in effect seeing the ruler as their servant, in most African nations, for him, the ruler owns the state. Institution building, in fact, requires sacrificing personal ambition for the collective good.

Africans Inevitably Followed the Developmental Path of Western States

Ugandan nationalist leaders, for example and in fact, made their transition to power in only a few years; they did not, as such, have the timeframe required to build sustainable national constituencies. Opportunistic alliances, when the country gained independence in 1962, were cobbled together to achieve power. The subsequent political crisis of 1966, which led to the abrogation of the constitution, and the abolition of the Bagandan monarchy, sowed the seeds of the notorious Idi Amin's coup.

Also the use of the European concept of the state as the ideal against which African institutions should be measured, led to a Eurocentric premise of analysis, according to Rugisara, which posited that Africans are bound to follow the developmental path of western states, failing to take into account the unique and diverse political experiences of the African continent. Modern states in Europe and North America have indeed developed modern order, education, healthcare and welfare services, but they have at the same time spent vast sums on the military and weaponry, as we see with Russia and the NATO countries today.

Regimes Assume Power with the Same Mindset They Had as Guerrilla Movements

That said, in addition, most of the African regimes that have captured power through guerrilla wars exhibit peculiar ways in which power is distributed and maintained. The regimes assume power with the same traits, outlook and mindset that they had as guerrilla movements. They are secretive and concentrate decision making among very few people. Protective of their comrades, for Rugisara, they place a huge premium on loyalty, sometimes over efficiency. This tends to breed sycophancy and compliance rather than independent mindedness and efficiency, discouraging long term investment and making doing business unpredictable. Huge potential, he maintains, exists on the African continent, though, in retracing his own family's steps as we shall now see, he illustrates specifically in Uganda, what has, recently and historically, got in the way.

A Major Socio-Economic Cleavage Created by a Distorted Colonial Capitalism in Uganda

In 1973, Andrew's father started a manufacturing plant to produce chalk for Ugandan schools. The factory marked an important milestone for Uganda's emerging indigenous capitalist class. He has always tried to understand, in fact, why the majority of capital in Uganda is concentrated in the hands of a few expatriate companies and mainly in the Asian business community.

Then on August 5, 1972, Idi Amin, as President of Uganda, announced that he was giving Asians living in the country ninety days to leave. The Ugandan economy, he claimed, needed to be returned to the Africans. Thirty five years later, in April 2007, Kampala expected a day of riots in response to the current President Musevene's proposed donation of a portion of the Mabira forest outside the capital to an Indian sugar baron. The events of April 12 then illustrate the fact that the Asian question was still very much alive and will continue to define the business landscape of Uganda's future.

The original Asian expulsion was a consequence of a major socio-economic cleavage created by the distorted capitalism established in colonial Uganda which privileged the Asian minority and disadvantaged the majority Africans. A racialised division of labour was established, and an economic system where

Asians dominated the processing and export sector, and the majority of import trade. Secondly, the hardening of African attitudes towards the Asians was a result of their increased dominance of the trading and commercial sectors. Attempts at Africanisation then followed a haphazard path after independence.

The exodus of Asians in the 1970s destroyed trading networks and productive capacity and a loss of skill sets in the economy but the gap then created ushered in several pioneer African entrepreneurs. This nascent business class managed to navigate the political insecurity of the day to become Uganda's indigenous capitalist class. However, and overall, Asia's economic dominance in the marketplace was replaced, politically, by the repression of Africans in the wider society. Africanisation as such was an ideal but, for Rugisara, never a reality.

The Burden of History: Modernising Influence or Distorted Form of Capitalism

What then was the overall impact, for him, of the colonial project in Uganda? There are two lines of argument. The first, imperial argument, assumed that colonialism was a modernising impact on the country by fostering development in a backward and traditional society. The impact here assumed was transformational, installing new values, monetizing the developing markets, and creating new venues for capital accumulation.

The second, and opposing argument is that colonialism introduced a distorted form of capitalism aimed at supporting colonial interests in metropolitan Europe. It was a system that privileged expatriate capital and discriminated against indigenous Africans. The type of racialised division of labour created an economy with mutually exclusive modern and traditional sectors. The modern sector was served by the Europeans and Asians while the traditional sector was served by Asian imports and technical skills. The supply of goods provided by Africans was restricted to cash crop production.

Cotton and Coffee: Examples of Plantation Economics

The pattern of development was completely unlike that of early capitalist Europe. In Britain, for example, the evolution of capitalism produced an indigenous class that was firmly anchored in the country's social structure and culture. In Uganda, external dominance meant that the commanding heights of the new economy were occupied ad controlled by external groups – the Europeans at the top followed by Indians. The Indian class, moreover, operated under the protective umbrella of the colonial state, and it shared no common cultural heritage with the African masses. Colonialism, overall then, did not facilitate the structural change required for sophisticated economic activity, and kickstart the move to processing.

When Good African Coffee set up its coffee roasting and packing facility in Kampala in 2009, it was immediately exposed to production systems, operational etiquette and global packaging standards that inhibited their development from otherwise mere exporters of raw coffee, as was the case for fellow Ugandans.

It was in fact cotton historically, for Rugisara, that linked Ugandan production to British manufacturing industries and effectively stratified the relationship between the African cash crop producer and expatriate capital, a pattern of development akin to a plantation economy as experienced in the European economies of the West Indies, where sugarcane production as first carried out by African enslaved labour and later by Indian indentured labour. Colonial arguments that African communities were backward and caught up in "traditional" beliefs and lacking in "achievement orientation" circulated to justify the structure.

The Seeds of Bitterness: Key to Unlocking the Future Potential of Africa

The economic privileging of Asian capital, meanwhile, and the economic disenfranchisement of the indigenous Ugandans brought about a racialised division into economic spheres creating a traditional and a modern economy. The traditional economy had very little impact on trade in the economy and was characterized as peasant, non-monetised, working with rudimentary inputs such as hoes to produce a small array of crops and crafts. The Indians and the Europeans between them provided the skills required by the modern economy and received a disproportionate high return. This pattern of development continued, as we shall see, with the advent of Ugandan independence.

A "Common Man's Charter" Did Not Build in a Coherent Actionable Program

It was in October, 1962, that Uganda gained its independence from Britain. Milton Obote became the first executive Prime Minister and King Muteesa the ceremonial head of state. It was a tense relationship. Obote's ostensible "move to the Left" in the form of *a "Common Man's Charter"* gave a hint as to the nationalization strategy of his government but did not build in an actionable coherent program.

By 1969 there was strong evidence of a deteriorating balance of payments position, and by 1971 Obote had been ousted in a military coup. Amin's coup emerged out of factional interests in the Ugandan army. A brutal series of arrests and murders then ensued. The subsequent expulsion of Indians was followed by the transfer of Asian assets into Uganda hands, as part of so called Africanisation, which included 5655 firms, factories, ranches and agricultural estates. More than 500 businesses were personally distributed to army officers and their friends. The economy in the post-expulsion period deteriorated fast. Huge scarcities led to the growth of a black market – *magendo* – which soon accounted for two thirds of the monetary GDP and became the dominant mode of production. *Magendo* create its own class structure with a few *mafuta mingi* – so wealthy they were "dripping with oil".

The Current Economic Situation Is a Continuation of the Historic Economic Distortions

The current economic situation in Uganda, according to Rugasira, reflects a continuation of the historic economic distortions, with 14 out of the top 25 companies being foreign multinationals. Post-independence politics not only failed to reverse the colonial distortions; it cemented them with brutal dictatorships, corruption and abuse of human rights. The issues involved are deep and complex but need to be explored, as they hold the key to unlocking the future potential of Africa. We now turn more specifically to the "Good African Story".

The Good African Story: Tie Together Potentials and Possibilities of Your Beginnings

Africans Are One of the Most Resilient and Creative Business People in the World

Rugasira then reveals his bewilderment when he hears policy experts talk about Africa's need for more entrepreneurs to develop a strong private sector that can boost economic growth. The problem is definitely not a lack of entrepreneurs – not if you have ever driven through the bustling streets of Lagos or downtown Nairobi or witnessed the thousands of entrepreneurs in Kampala's suburbs who bring their wares to you whether you are in your vehicle, home or office. Indeed for him Africans are one of the most resilient, innovative and creative business people in the world.

To navigate poor and decaying road networks, maddeningly corrupt and inefficient bureaucracies, government regulations that frustrate and hinder business operations, a lack of reliable electricity or water, all of such demand ingenuity, agility and determination. He doubts that Western entrepreneurs operating in such an environment could last long. Such extraordinary competencies enabling such African entrepreneurs to adapt and navigate these very challenging environments must be recognized, appreciated and motivated, he says, instead of being trampled upon by the arrogant rhetoric of "experts" who harp on about the need to unlock Africa's private sector. The African private sector, for him, is already unlocked. It is just waiting for an "enabling environment". What about Uganda then?

Producers of What It Does Not Consume and Consumers of What It Does Not Produce

After Ethiopia, Uganda is the second home of coffee. Whilst the variety of coffee originating from Ethiopia is the milder arabica, in Uganda, like many parts of Africa's equatorial rain forests, the robusta variety of coffee is indigenous. The coffee there is essentially grown by small-scale farmers on smallholdings, with up to a million farmers engaged in production. In fact almost five million Ugandans depend in some way or another on coffee earnings. Historically, almost 90 % of the country's export earnings have come from coffee, a typical example of the mono-crop dependency in Africa. Indeed between 1994 and 2001, however, coffee earnings dropped to less than a quarter of their original value. This is a sad testimony, for Rugisara, of Uganda being producers of what it does not consume, and consumers of what it does not produce. He then set out to address this imbalance.

A plot Is Shaped by Many of the Larger Stories in which It Is Set

Good Coffee Brand Appointed Their First Community Liaison Officer

Kabale is a hilly, border town, with a scenic and rugged terrain and home to the Bagika people. The cool evenings and meandering hills have led it to being nicknamed the Switzerland of Uganda and it is the place to which Rugisara traces his own roots. On 29 July his Good Coffee Brand opened their first field office in Kasese town and appointed their first community liaison officer with the responsibility for organising the farmers into producer organisations.

By the end of the year he had made several trips to Kasese to assess their field efforts in the round and essentially to encourage their farmers, get feedback, and energise the team. They began to organise the farmers into groups, by reaching out to the communities directly and inviting them to attend meetings which they held at local trading centres in each sub-county.

Determined to Make a Change – The Project Would Only Work If They Did It Together

Eventually Good Coffee identified some community leaders before whom they presented their model, established a dialogue and line of communication, and then appealed to them to promote the model in the community. At the same time Rugisara shared his frustration at Africans being seen as nothing more than beggars, as incapable, poor and helpless. Such a view could be changed, but it would require them to produce quality coffees consistently. And this was why farmer training was critical. With their help, he told them, he was determined to make a change. The project would only work if they did it together.

Soon they had registered and trained forty-four producer organisations, and helped them organise elections for their leaders. The farmer groups elected a chairperson. Vice chairman, treasurer, and both male and also female trainers. Then they assembled the hand pulpers to remove the pulp on the ripe coffee cherries and distributed them to the established producer organisations. There was tremendous joy when Mzee Bwambale, a member of the Nyakabingo producer organisation, became their first farmer to deliver coffee to their stores. Their first coffee consignment thereafter was loaded and taken to Kampala to the Cooperative Union for dehusking, cleaning and bagging.

After their first buying season, they continued to recruit farmers in producer organisations in other sub-counties. Field trips continued using locally hired vehicles and *boda-bodas*, that is local motor bikes, and it would be a year before they acquired their own pick up truck. Then in June 2005 they launched their coffees in Waitrose, the first African owned brand to sell direct into British stores. In January 2006 they acquired their first field office computer dedicated to their MIS, developed by systems developer Tharcisse Maniraho. The system captured coffee deliveries by farmer, location, producer organisation and gender. He brought system and procedure, and wise council to younger team members.

Savings and Credit Cooperatives Owned, Operated and Managed by Farmers

Between seasons, through, farmers seldom met. The company only had five active field officers and one sub-country coordinator for over 14,000 farmers in seventeen sub-counties. This remained a big challenge. They therefore tried to increase communication amongst farmers, through pooling savings via the *Savings and Credit Cooperatives* (SACCO's) Rugisara helped set them up. He supported these SACCO's with financial literacy training, financial manuals and book-keeping. By 2010 seventeen of them were operating boosting the farmers' saving culture and providing micro loans to those in need. The SACCO's were not only owned by the farmers but operated and managed by them.

Logistical Difficulties and Poor Infrastructure Frustrate Trade Between African Countries

Meanwhile, while logistical difficulties and poor infrastructure frustrated trade between African countries, they also undermined, as Rugisara was now experiencing, the capabilities of African exporters to competitively deliver goods and services to the global market. He then spent most of 2004 and 2005 trying to break into the South African and UK markets and experiencing many barriers that he had not anticipated – barriers that demanded perseverance and adaptability from African entrepreneurs.

Leads to Gripping Drama and to Creative Origination

Good Coffee Became The First Ugandan Brand to Be Sold in South Africa

That said, on March 9, 2004, the Good Coffee Brand became the first Ugandan brand to be sold in South Africa to Shoprite Checkers, the leading supermarket chain, who agreed to retail the company's roast and ground coffees. Their three inaugural coffee products – "Prestige", "Gold" and "Classic" – were branded under the "Rwenzon Finest Coffee" label, in fact the company's original name before it became Good African Coffee in 2005, The roasting and packing of the coffee was done in Cape Town in South Africa. What then began a year before as a conversation with the Shoprite Checkers founder and CEO, Whitey Basson, in a discussion with Rugisara in the back of his car from Entebbe airport in Uganda to Kampala, was now a reality.

Key Pillars Being Empowerment of the Producer Community and Processing in Uganda

In fact the Good Africa coffees could never have entered the South African market had it not been for Rugisara's relationship with Basson. Social and commercial networks are indeed critical. In mid 2003 in fact he had met with Basson, for whom he had facilitated a meeting with Uganda's President Musevini. Rugisara took the opportunity to outline his vision for working with small-scale farmers, developing a coffee brand built on a philosophy of trade as opposed to aid. Moreover its key pillars were empowerment of the producer community and their owning the value-addition processing in Uganda. With Shoprite behind them they could build up a truly African-owned and distributed brand. Rugasira did not have coffee industry experience but what he did have was marketing and brand-building capabilities, and he was sure that a brand with a high social mission would be an attractive commercial proposition.

Between August 2003 and the launch in March 2004, he worked with various service providers – brand designers, PR and marketing companies – as the project began to gain momentum. However, and following the launch in 2004, it became clear, after several months trading, that unless they could inject more capital into the business, to market and promote the brand – capital they did not have – their presence in South Africa would be very difficult. So sixteen months after the launch they decided to withdraw, and rather focus on the UK, a bigger market, and one Rugasira had some familiarity with, having studied in the UK.

Development Is a Partnership Not An Imposition

They began planning for their UK launch in early 2005, Baroness Lynda Chalker, hitherto Minister for Overseas Development under then Prime Minister John Major, agreeing to host a reception for them. When people received an invite from the said Baronness it tended to have more impact than one from the desk of Andrew Rugasira, CEO of Good African Coffee. At the event Andrew had much to say: the billions of dollars that Africa had received in foreign aid after the Second World War had done more to stifle creativity amongst the continent's entrepreneurs, creating a chronic dependency, than to foster sustainable economic growth. Recipient countries than had to adopt policy prescriptions designed by experts thousands of miles away. This had undermined the sovereignty of African governments. Most Africans are fed up with lectures, double standards and paternalism from African "specialists", reinforcing the image of Africa as the "white man's burden".

For Rugasira as such, development is a partnership not an imposition, but African leaders, for him, need to shape up too. They continue to mortgage the future of their children through destructive systems of misrule that foster corruption, create conflict and undermine democracy and good governance. But the time had come, in 2006, for Good African Coffee to build on its prior Waitrose experience in the UK.

If Sainsbury Lists Good Coffee It Will Be Helping Africans Help Themselves

On a cold January morning Rugasira walked into the London headquarters of J. Sainsbury, the UK's second biggest supermarket, for a first meeting with their coffee buyers. He began a presentation he had made a dozen times. The continent had received over one trillion dollars over the last five decades with very little to show for it except chronic dependency on handouts, a stifling of the entrepreneurial spirit of its people and the perpetuation of the image of Africa as a basket case. If Sainsbury lists Good Coffee it will be helping Africans help themselves in the most sustainable way possible. The meeting ended with a commitment that the Sainsbury buyers would come back to Rugisara, which they subsequently did, but to no good avail.

Breaking Decades of Unequal, Unjust and Unfair Trading Systems in the US

Meanwhile Rugasira was also determined to see Good Coffee make its mark in the U.S. In May 2000, the U.S. Congress passed trade support legislation to assist the economies in sub-Saharan Africa to access the lucrative US markets. However, set against such as non-tariff barriers, unprocessed primary commodities, typically agricultural products, have always been imported into the U.S., processed in the environment of cheap capital and huge agricultural subsidies and then either consumed or re-exported as finished products. So African processed and branded products trying to get into the US markets are not only breaking decades of unequal, unjust and unfair trading systems, but even with their best efforts they will always be trying to catch up with more advanced product manufacturing and delivery systems.

Forging a Partnership Between Afro American Church Community and Coffee Business

Mitigating trade asymmetries then is a complex matter that goes beyond market access legislation; it must address historical distortions that undermine the market access of African countries. Between April 2004 and March 2011 Rugasira made eleven trips to the U.S. seeking to establish a presence in the North American market.

In 2004 he had travelled to Los Angeles to meet Charles Blake, one of the leading African American church ministers, a man with considerable social and political clout. He told Rugisara how he had always hoped that African Americans could be for Africa what Jewish Americans were for Israel, with their economic partnerships and cultural links. He envisioned a powerful relationship, especially given their African-American shared history, despite the fracture of the slave trade. They agreed that they would try and forge a partnership between his church community and the coffee business. Finally, in 2011, after seven years of a growing relationship, as we shall see, a partnership was thereby secured.

Meanwhile, in 2005, Bishop Blake recommended that part of building up a U.S. trading relationship involved strengthening Good Coffee's social networks. He proposed Rugasira go to Boston to meet Reverend Charles Rivers 111, who would assist him in making some helpful connections on the East Coast. He had a well established reputation as one of the most effective inner-city community organisers in the country. The Reverend, in turn, suggested Andrew and his wife Jackie go and meet Professor Louis Gates of Harvard University, a leading American literary critic and head of WEB Dubois Institute for African and American Research, who had good contacts in corporate America. Rivers thought it was important for the Rugasira's to share their "trade not aid" vision with Gates. These trips to America also exposed Andrew to the American marketplace – its complexity culture, business etiquette and knowledge; it was a valuable and necessary investment to make. But no immediate breakthrough, into the North American market, was in prospect.

Arising out of the Problems of Everyday Life Leading to an African Renaissance

Disconnect Between Good African Coffee Model and Prevailing Funding Agencies

Indeed, and with a view now to such, accessing affordable and patient capital for Good African Coffee had been Rugasira's biggest challenge since inception. Venture capital and other such long term credit are in short supply in Africa, and where and when available, infrastructure projects and established forms are preferred to agribusiness. Almost all capital available in the banking sector is short term. Yet the sector with the highest impact on economic growth, the agriculture one, needs capital with long term horizons. The financial sector in Uganda then like in many sub-Saharan countries, is still underdeveloped, only 4 % of bank credit going to agriculture. Between 2003 and 2008 Rugasira met with over two dozen financial institutions in Uganda and several outside the country in an effort to raise capital. There seemed to be a real disconnect between the excitement over the Good African Coffee Model and his ability to close in on any fundraising.

Organic Certification, Financial Literacy, and SACCO's to Build Sustainable Business

The investments they were making in Kasese included providing farmers with inputs, training on harvesting and washing their coffee cherries, organic certification, financial literacy training, and start-up costs for SACCO's. These investments could not be entirely funded by internal sources, and yet to build a solid and sustainable business they needed to get the above Kasese supply side right – and from day one. Upon this solid foundation they could build their commercial activities. Another challenge lay in trying to build the supply side of the business; activating the demand side by investing in brand-building activities.

Responsibility of Government in Africa to Create Capital Where Markets Have Failed

Indeed Robert Wade, a leading economist at the London School of Economics, has pointed out the hypocrisy of western policy recommendations in his seminal book Governing the Market. Wade argues that none of the industrialised economies of Europe and America ever subjected their nascent industries and firms to the vagaries of the free market. Instead they had a very deliberate industrial-assistance policy. A fairer treatment of the early stages of development would instead emphasize the responsibility of government in Africa to create capital where the markets have clearly failed to provide it.

Of course it is critical that this is done within clear frameworks of public-private partnerships or within strategic industry guidelines that provide sector-wide support, as opposed to individuals on the basis of cronyism. This is unlike what happened in many African countries which under structural adjustment were forced to swallow the bitter pill of adjustment and then hope for recovery.

Hopes That Were Not Tied to Material Comfort But on a Richer Fellowship

Meanwhile the Good Africa team themselves had hopes that were not tied to material comfort but on a richer fellowship that could only be born out of a struggle for something bigger than individual needs at the time. This commitment was also not due to Andrew's persuasiveness or logic of argument but rather because they recognized the value of their labour and sacrifice and how important it was for the thousands of farmers they worked with.

One of the ironies of Good African was how the external perception of the brand tended to be positive – that it was a business making great strides in the marketplace, but this conflicted with the fragility of its financial situation. There was also concern that their model seemed to favour social impact over commercial return.

KCL Understood Their Business Model and Appreciated Its Value to the Community

In 2006 though, Rugisara developed the partnership that would help Good Coffee address its working capital needs for buying green coffee. This strategic relationship was with Kyagalanyi Coffee Limited (KCL), a local subsidiary of Volacafe, Switzerland, one of the largest coffee-trading companies in the world. He met KCL's chief executive, David Berry, in 2005, together with the head of finance, Robert Whitwam, and Gabriel Artunduaga, the production manager. They all subsequently became a critical source of support for the Good Coffee operations. When Rugisara met Berry, he was excited to find someone who was not only a leading coffee trader with enormous experience at the commodity level, but who also understood their business model and appreciated their value to the community. He was responsive to the challenges Good Coffee faced and quickly leveraged his company's resources in support. KCL essentially became the financing arm of green coffee operation. They also rented a warehouse next door to their plant where Rugisara eventually set up a roasting factory in Kampala. Both David and his division head from Switzerland, Peter Moser, became important supporters of Good African Coffee within the Volcafe group.

The President's Approval Spoke of His Belief in the Importance of Value-Addition

Meanwhile in December, 2006, Good Coffee held an awards ceremony in the Catholic Gardens of Kasese town to recognize the best farmers, and farmers' groups, by quality and volume over the year. Uganda's Ministers of Agriculture, Finance and Defence were all in attendance, and Dr Ezra Suruma, as Finance Minister, would become a major supporter thereafter. In fact Rugisara subsequently approached him for a loan to purchase roasting and packaging equipment. Dr Suruma wrote to the President seeking his approval for the transaction. Three months later the reply came back giving the project a green light. The president's approval as not just a vital endorsement, it spoke of his belief in the importance of value-addition in the Ugandan coffee sector.

Pitfalls of Economic Prosperity Without Values: Stage Play to Governance Structures

Over 2000 farmers trekked down the mountains to attend the function. They put on a play with a strong message about transformation in the community and the pitfalls of economic prosperity without values. In fact, eleven years later, and following such, Good Coffee embarked on a programme of strengthening the governance structures of their farmer groups, as it Rugisara explored the idea of them becoming shareholders. He thereby developed a plan for bringing the farmers into the shareholding structure of the company.

Meanwhile in March, 2009, the roasting factory, for which the equipment had now been secured, was launched in Kampala, and the President was the guest of honour. Given the extent to which he had been championing the case of value addition it seemed only right. In fact the launch of the factory represented a significant milestone for Good Coffee. For too long African economies have exported unprocessed raw materials, meaning the developed countries that carry out the processing keep the lion's share of the added value.

Capturing the Full Value Addition: Empowering Farmers and Communities Sustainably

The roasting plant in Uganda then not only addressed Good Coffee's commitment to capturing the full value addition of its exports but also enabled it to employ local staff and to empower its farmers and communities in a meaningful and sustainable way. As gratifying, though, as this all was, 2011 was spent trying to source more capital for market expansion and opportunities within the U.S. if not also UK markets.

You Evolve from Interpretive to Transformative

Give Us the Opportunity to Help Our People and Ourselves

In fact Rugasira's initial attempts, in 2004, to secure a commitment from Sainsbury's, in the UK, to purchasing Good Coffee, had come to naught. So a year later he decided to approach its then Managing Director, Justin King, directly. This is an extract of the the e-mail he wrote to him:

> As the only African exporter of coffee to the UK, I naturally want to have our Good African Coffees on the shelves of J. Sainsbury. However, given Sainsbury's commitment to fairer trade with African suppliers I am increasingly surprised by how difficult that is proving .. At home we have a saying that if you give a person a fish you feed them for a day but if you teach them to fish you feed them for life. I hope you will consider our product listing in your supermarkets and give us the opportunity to help our people and ourselves.

A reply from Justin King's PA indeed arrived a couple of weeks later and it carried encouraging news: Sainsbury's were planning an autumn launch of three lines of coffee, including one exclusive to their stores, whereby Good Coffee would become stocked in 200 of their supermarkets, from September 2006, the first Africa-owned coffee to be sold in them. The same year Tesco supermarkets agreed to retail Good Coffee, and thereafter became a big supporter. All this was a long way from Rugisara's initial coffee trip to Britain in April 2004.

What Began as a Dream Back in 2004 Was Now a Reality

Rugasira's break in the U.S. meanwhile came in August 2009, when he was invited to speak at the annual Global Leadership Summit, organised by the Willow Creek Community Church in Barrington, Illinois. Willow is the mega church pastored by Bill Hybels, a prolific author, renowned Bible teacher, thought leader and mentor to many CEO's. Rugisara spoke on his personal theme of Trade for Africa and the Good African case study. The day after the speech he was approached by Jerry Kehe, whose father had founded Kehe Distributors in 1956, with today retail distribution centres around the whole country. Indeed Kehe since 2001 has been employee owned by its 4000 person staff. Jerry then advanced the capital that Good Coffee needed to launch in the U.S. and online sales began in March 2011.

What began as a dream back in 2004 was now a reality, and with it came new challenges and opportunities, celebrations and frustrations, but, ultimately, the proof was there – it could be done. Many others then on the African continent could do the same. But how they might do about it was another matter.

Reconnecting with a Particular African Natural and Cultural Source

Commitment to Community as a Fundamental Element of Good African's Business Model

Sharing and caring for the community, Rugasira maintains, is something that is intrinsic to the African way of life; an unofficial welfare system in the absence of a public sector that delivers effective community support to extended family members and many others. His ambition with Good African was to entrench this commitment to the community as a fundamental element of his business model as opposed to just being something they could do once that had plenty of money to throw around. He therefore sought to recognize their coffee growers, their employees, their shareholders and the environment as their business shareholders – their quadruple bottom line.

To Draw Attention to African Farmers as the Real Engine for Transformation

In 2005 they had already unveiled their new coffee packaging with two of their key values placed prominently on the front of the packaging: "African Needs Trade Not Aid" and "50 % profit shared". In fact they were the first African brand that openly communicated their core values on the packaging of their products, to draw attention to the argument that African farmers are the real engine for transformation, thereby effectively re-imaging rural.

"Getting our heart right", as such for Rugisara, was the first step on which they could build their profit-share commitment, aligning their values to their aspirations and securing the commitment to deliver on them. And the key issue, for him, was to put the stake in the ground very early on. Another objective was to confront the image of Africa as a "basket case". For many Africa is characterised as a place full of conflict and violence, poverty and disease. *A good place to start was to brand their* coffee with a positive name and attributes that are lacking in the narrative of Africa, emphasizing commitment to the community and transformation through trade and not handouts.

You Give Other Cultures and Communities a Voice

Negative Branding of Africa Rooted in African Primitiveness in Need of Modernity

The negative branding of Africa is not a recent phenomenon but has its roots in Africa's long history of exploitation by foreign powers. It is evident in the justifications for slavery and colonial domination and is rooted in the image of African primitiveness and the urgent need to be brought into modernity. The enduring nature of this misinterpretation can be seen in the absence of African voices in the contemporary development debate. The popular champions for Africa tend to be white male Europeans or Americans who are celebrities, academics, policy experts, politicians or philanthropists.

In that light of "The White Man's Burden" Africa seemingly needs these others to champion its recovery and development, with western "civilisation" representing the "standard" model for development. Thus the solutions promoted are unquestionably Western in concept, design and application. In the view of the late Edward Said, the renowned Palestinian-American literary theorist, the presentation of "otherness" by the colonialist or the colonised was a justification for power and domination of the oppressed. In fact as a child growing up in Uganda Rugisara found little in school or in the community that celebrated his history. If there was any of such, it was restricted to legend and folklore and was never documented or systematically taught. Much of what was taught began with colonialism.

There Was An Africa with a History Far Richer, Deeper, Complex and Worth Celebrating

Many such thinkers and respected African scholars, such as Ali Mazrui, Leopold Senghor, Aime Cesaire, Kwame Nkrumah, Julius Nyerere, Mahmoud Mamdani, Wole Soyinka, Valentin Mudimbe, Amilcar Cabral, Frantz Fanon and Walter Rodney, though, opened his mind to the reality that *there was an Africa with a history far richer and deeper, more complex and worth celebrating than what was marketed as "official history"*.

A critical pillar of the Good African model became the advocacy that Africans had to become the solution to their own problems. The notion that a Ugandan company could advocate for a business relationship that considered farmer empowerment, in relation to such, as a key goal, was, even for the famers themselves, initially not believable, as they initially and seemingly claimed that Good African belonged to a "white person".

You seek Goodness, Trustworthiness, and Authenticity

Knowledge Transfer, Technology Provision and Institutional Capacity Building

Indeed as *Good African* they *see the rural economy as a place with huge potential and rich social capital* – land, labour and knowledge – *in which they have made three principal interventions: knowledge transfer (agronomy training), technology provision (hand pulpers, improved crop varieties) and institutional capacity building (savings and credit cooperatives and producer groups)*. The results have been a tremendously improved quality of harvest and a growth in volumes of coffee delivered from 7 tons delivered in 2004, supplied by several hundred farmers, to 430 tons supplied by over 7,000 farmers in 2011. A key element of their business model is that as much of the value addition was carried out at source, as possible. The launch of their coffee factory in Kampala in 2009 was therefore a major milestone.

The Foundation Would Best Serve the Community Initiatives in a Focused Way

In 2011 Good African took the decision to separate their community activities from the business operations by setting up the Good African Foundation. *They felt that the foundation would best serve the community initiatives in a focused way* while the business did the work of selling the coffee. This would mean that the profit share commitment from the business would go direct to the foundation that then carries out the two principal activities of farmer agronomy training and SACCO training and strengthening. The foundation then allows for more specialised interventions to be carried out, like business development skills training, that hitherto, Good African had lacked the resources to carry out. In fact such foundational activities also served to distinguish the Afrocentric Good African model from Fairtrade.

Fairtrade Structural Dynamics Keeping Third World Producer Countries Poor

In thereby comparing and contrasting the Good African model with *Fairtrade*, Rugisara felt that the latter is a European-based social movement shaped by student activism and political consciousness of the 1960s. It became especially popular, moreover, during the crisis of low coffee prices in the 1990s with Fairtrade's strong advocacy for better prices for poor farmers in producer nations. The sales for their products in Europe have since grown tremendously. Indeed in the UK roast and ground Fairtrade coffees sold through retail outlets have increase exponentially over the past 15 years. However, underpinning the advocacy for the improvement of third world living conditions *is a western model of trade that entrenches the commercial interests of the advanced economies without altering the structural dynamics keeping third world producer countries poor and advanced economies rich.*

Fairtrade then, for Rugisara, is overly generous about their value, being not far removed from the old charity model, which encourages consumers to pay a few extra cents for products with the in-built assumption that transformation of the producer communities will happen as a result. But Fairtrade, he says, has an inbuilt distortion of its own. With Fairtrade, the distortion is in the nature of the markets themselves; they are neither free not fair, for subsidies, tariffs and non-tariff barriers define the environment for producers from Africa. *Fairtrade then presents a false panacea to this systemic problem by paying a few extra cents for a pound of coffee, as a Eurocentric model for compassionate consumption that defines Africa as deserving of western generosity, diverting attention from structural issues.*

Empowerment and Community Transformation Requires More Than Just Better Prices

Coffee farmers in Africa are poor not just because the world commodity prices have been low, but fundamentally because these farmers operate at the bottom of the coffee value chain, have limited crop diversification and limited access to farm inputs and other appropriate technologies. They face these structural impediments every day and Fairtrade, for Rugisara, does not even begin to address them. *Empowerment and community transformation requires more than just better prices for third world growers, they necessitate linking farmers to African processors, who then adds value and supply the global marketplace with value-added products.* Most Fairtrade products are sold in the retail outlets of developed countries and are processed in those countries, very little value-addition taking place in the producer countries.

For sustainable empowerment, farmers need to be linked to the formal financial markets by literacy training creating savings and credit knowhow through the intermediation of savings and credit cooperatives. *Farmers need to move up the value chain by engaging in some form of value-added processing at source.* For Rugasira the Fairtrade movement has been largely preoccupied with celebrating African producers for their small-scale and rural idyll, as through this is really worth celebrating.

You Alternate Individually and Societally Between Analysis and Transformation

Transformation Begins When We Change Social Structures and Relationship Frameworks

Only then by increasing farm sizes, through land consolidation and communal farming, where technologies can be applied across bigger tracts of land generating efficiency and economies of scale, can output and productivity increase. Good African has encouraged farmers to consolidate their land rather than managing very small plots of land.

In the final analysis, *transformation begins when we change social structures and relationship frameworks among the economic actors in the community.*

Conclusion

Whither East Africa?

As we altogether reflect on the path of *East* African renewal, in the light of the Goof African Story, we find most of the Keynotes have been covered. However, what stand out is that the newly global emancipatory navigation falls somewhat short, especially regarding:

- You seek to understand *how your African world was constructed*
- You *give other cultures and communities a voice*
- Critical theory has a *strongly emancipatory Asili laden* orientation
- The Theory of the South leads to the *de-colonial overturning of power relations*

In other words, and in our overall terms of an *East* African communitalism, there is insufficient emphasis on the *fusion of horizons* between "east" and "south". Both literally and symbolically the Asian Ugandan, our "east" in the "south" has been a troubled relationship from the outset. In *Yurugu* terms specifically, the human has remained incomplete, in that the fusion of horizons has been ill begotten. While the Kiswahili language is unique in Africa for its fusion of African-ness and indeed Arab-ness, not to mention also the adjacent India on the "east" coast of Africa, spiritually as well as economically, this dimension is largely lost from the *Good* African Story.

Pervasive Yurugu

In fact the "incomplete human", alluded to by Marimba Ani, in her version of critical theory attached to European-ness, is this case pertains to the incomplete East African in two respects. Firstly there is a lack of fusion between African and Asian, culturally-and-economically; secondly the African in himself, is more evidently, exogenously Christian than indigenously Ugandan. In terms of the "Theory of the South" promoted by the Comaroffs in Chapter 9, the prospects and potential of contemporary African polity in dealing with diversity, in this case specifically between "east" Asian and "southern" African is by passed in this "good" story, leaving Communitalism in that dynamically harmonic guise, humanly incomplete.

Incomplete Transformation

In other words, whereas the overall transformation journey with which Rugisara has been engaged has been a remarkable one, in terms of the establishment of an authentically communal enterprise, the fusion of horizons, hermeneutically as such, both between indigenous and exogenous African, and also between African and

Asian, has been lacking, most especially in the latter *East* African case. Indeed, that is not helped by the fact that, in political terms, the African model of governance, throughout the continent, as Rugisara and Gyekye before him (see Chapter 8) has not realised the potential revealed in Comaroff's "Theory of the South".

Integral African Communitalism

South versus East

Integrally speaking then, for Africa as a whole, what this *Good African Story* serves to reveal, both by its presence and its absence, is that, on the one hand, Africa needs its east and its west, its north and of course especially its south, in thereby fusing horizons, so that a *Communitalism* as whole can be co-evolved. In this Ugandan instance the fusion of "south", our natural and communal and "east", our cultural and spiritual, on the one hand, is especially called for, so as to constitute an integrally "good" African story.

South versus North and West

On the other hand, what is also especially evident in this case, is that the fusion of "south" and "north-west" remains in complete. Time and again, Rugisara found himself having to struggle with northern and western, technologically and economically oriented institutions that were and are ill fitted for southern natural and communal purposes. It was only through the intervention of exceptionally well meaning individuals, in British supermarkets, European commodity markets, and American churches that he was able to break through; the institutions they represented remained communally economically ill fitting.

What Is Missing in the Unfolding Story of Communitalism

What is revealed, overall then, in this Good but also "not so good" African story, is that the marriage African communal experience, Asian cultural imagination, European social theory/methodology, and American style praxis, in Heron's CI terms, is somewhat missing in action. Indeed Rugisara points to the poor publication record of his fellow Africans, which led him indeed to write and publish his own story, so he could think though, for us in prospectively "newly global" guise, *Good Africa*. As such for us, what remains unfinished business, for the African Communtalism we seek here, is a marriage between Marimba Ani and Andrew Rugisara, to consummate the *East* African story. Moreover, and in the final, integral analysis, there is a need to amalgamate "south", that is the Integral Kumusha and indeed Nhakanomics, in Southern Africa, with this Good African Coffee Story in the African "east", thereafter connecting with the African "north" and "west", Communitalism wise.

Indeed, and to the extent that such a macro societal mission is incomplete, such cases as the Good African Coffee Story, for all its formidable achievements hitherto, is on fragile micro ground, and in fact, in the third decade of the new millennium has seemingly met its demise. In fact, not unlike Cashbuild in South Africa as we shall see (Chapter 16 below), if there is no overall macro economic and societal infrastructure to meet an Afrocentric micro enterprise, half way, problems are likely to arise, all the more reason for an integrally evolved communitalism to make its way across the continent.

We now turn to *North* Africa, both metaphorically and also literally, starting with a "northerly" philosophical-scientific west Africa, and ending economically-enterprise wise in Egypt, North Africa, duly and indeed "newly globally" connected, also now culturally and philosophically, with the European "north", as we shall ultimately see.

Reference

Rugasira A (2014) *A Good African Story: How a Small Company Built a Global Coffee Brand.* London. Vintage Books

Part 4 Path of Reason Out of South-*North* Africa: Towards the Economics of Love

Chapter 11 Grounded Theory to Critical Rationalist African Foundation: Towards the Economy of Love. Build up a Theoretical Perspective

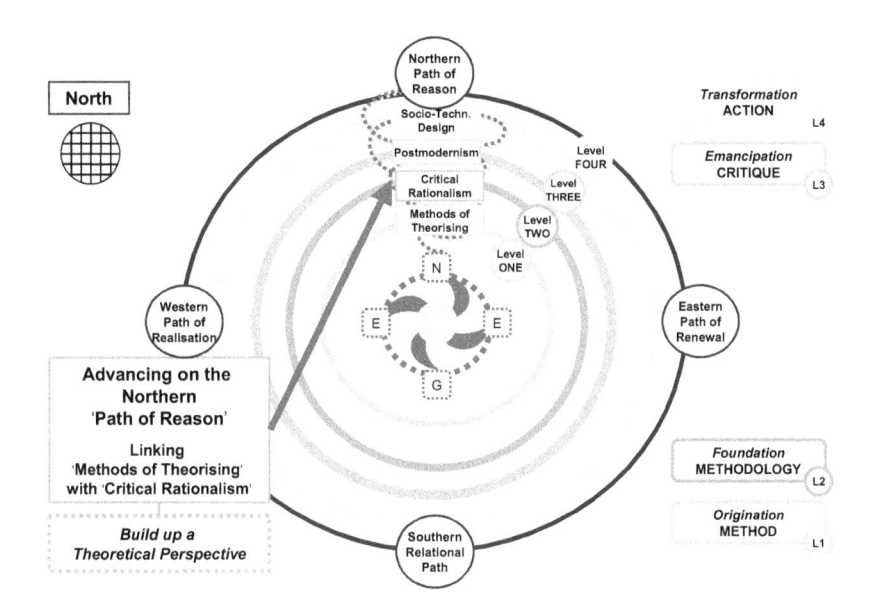

Figure 11.1: *Overview Chapter 11 – Level 2 / North*

Within a complementary ontology truth is sought in the comprehensiveness of its interrelatedness and in the complementary multidimensional nature of its expression. What this means is that all forms of human accomplishment can be thought of and articulated within the context of all the actors and factors that enter into their genesis and expression. The same can be said of human failures. Here all human beings, as aspects of missing links of reality, are mutually dependent and serve each other with a view to articulating meaning, and upholding their being. Where this has not been imbibed, differences will be pursued as ends in themselves, inducing bifurcation into human consciousness.

Innocent Asouzu (2007) Ibuanyidanda.: A New Complementary Ontology

Summary: Critical Rationalism in African Guise

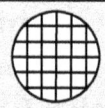

- Having built up your capacity to theorise, and to thereby develop theories from the data you have gathered, we now turn to critical rationalism as a means of consolidating upon such theoretical origination, drawing primarily on the work of Jonathan Chimakonam and Paulin Hountondji, in Africa, duly aligned with that of Karl Popper in Europe

- Chimakonam, in feeling local, draws on "Okwu" as an Igbo-African concept, the Igbo being one of the three major Nigerian ethnic groups, forming the raw material from which words are constituted. The Igbo term for word is mkupuruokwu meaning the first fruit of okwu

- In Popper's theory of knowledge, hypotheses, theories or conjectures precede all observation. Analytically based concepts, emerging out of your experience and imagination, serve to evolve your original research question into a set of testable hypotheses, with a view to a social innovation.

- Popper was also the leading advocate of an "open society". For him, an open society is one in which critical thinking and discussion can flourish; the society is open to improvement. The key to progress towards such is the recognition of your fallibility.

- From Popper we turn locally-globally to the Beninois-French philosopher Paulin Hountondji, who is considered to be the pre-eminent rationalist amongst African "professional" (as opposed to "ethno") philosophers, urging Africa onto its own theorizing and industrializing

- Modern science, hitherto, was introduced by the coloniser in the overseas territories in the form of an impoverished science, deprived of the theory-building activity that makes it more integral. This, in fact, was a side-affect of the same colonisers' launch of so-called "modern", rational and pragmatic economies in these territories, devoid of holistic and humanistic underpinnings.

- Chimakonam unveils his prototype of African logic, for us newly global, on the African path of reason. The synonym for the word logic in Igbo (a West African language) is *ngho* which means dynamic or flexible reasoning: *itu ngho* therefore becomes an expression for *"to do flexible or dynamic reasoning"*

- For Sekem there is nothing more powerful than the invisible net of life, which connects people with their hearts. Its fabric is woven deeper than our understanding, and long before we first shake a hand we have moved along its threads.

- What is needed, in developing societies, is to help their people including their educated elite, to capitalise and master the existing indigenous knowledge, and develop new knowledge in a continual process of uninterrupted creativity, while applying the findings in a systematic and responsible way to improve their own quality of life.
- To further such, globally-locally, on the African path to reason, we need to go beyond empirical science, deriving theories from tentative conjectures built on Ezumezu, formulate strategies emerging out of African philosophy, working toward an integrative African society.

11.1. Orientation to Critical Rationalism as a Rational Foundation

11.1.1. Introduction the African Path of Reason

South-North African Social Research and Innovation

We now turn, research wise, from the Southern African relational path and the south-East African path of renewal to the south-North African path of reason. Innovation-wise, moreover, we turn from the Integral Kumusha in Zimbabwe via Nhakanomics, the Good African Coffee Story in Uganda via Yurugu-nomics, and now Sekem in Egypt via The Economics of Love. First then, generally, we want to introduce the research path of reason as a whole, as illustrated in the Table 11.1.1. below, together with the north African path of innovation, Thereafter specifically, in this chapter, we turn to critical rationalism in itself – feeling local, intuiting local-global, thinking newly global and acting globally-locally.

Table 11.1.1. <u>North African Social Research and Innovation: Path of Reason</u> *Grounded Theory to SOCIO-TECHNICAL DESIGN/Maat to Integral Enterprise Sekem and the Economics of Love*

Northern Grounding Method and Origination	Northern Emergent Methodology & Foundation	Northern Navigational Critique and Emancipation	Northern Effective Action and Transformation
Grounded Theory (N1)	Critical Rationalism (N2)	Post Modernism (N3)	Socio-Technical Design (N4)
Sekem (N1)	Integrativity (N2)	Transient Workspaces (N3)	Economics of Love (N4)

Ibrahim Abouleish Became a Public Intellectual, Ultimately on a Worldwide Stage

Ibrahim Abouleish, the founder of Sekem in Egypt had a PhD in Engineering and Pharmacology, and worked in leading positions in pharmacological research, in Austria, before he returned in his midlife to Egypt, the land of his birth. In Egypt, while establishing Sekem in the 1970s, he also became a public intellectual, ultimately on a worldwide stage, ultimately establishing such intellectual credentials in his (2005) seminal work of *Sekem: A Sustainable Community in the Egyptian Desert*. In that book he describes already in his childhood:

> One of my uncles, also named Mohammad, was a university professor and had a huge library in his house. None of my friends could understand what drew me to him, and led me to engage in deep discussions with him. Sometimes Mohammad would give me a book out of his library, and one day I came across Goethe's Young Werther written in Arabic. I avidly absorbed this work, which made me want to get to know more about the German people and their writers. Art and science, economic life, citizens' rights – I deeply admired them all these European attributes.

So from an early stage of his life Abouleish was establishing his intellectual credentials, befitting the historical positioning of Egypt as "the cross-roads of civilization".

I Will Bring Together the Men and Women of Higher Learning From the Village

Moreover, in his youth, and on the even of his departure from Egypt to study in Austria, he wrote a latter to his father, to say, upon his return to his country and indeed his home village, Mashtul, he (2005) would become actively engaged in building up his community's and his society's physical and intellectual infrastructure:

> I will build factories where the people can work, different work than they are used to from farming. I will build workshops for women and girls, where they can make clothes and carpets and household goods and everything that the people need. I know that transport and communication is very important, so I will get the roads tarred and plant trees to right and left of it. I will build a large theatre on your grounds, where renowned artists can give performances for the people of my village. I will build a hospital near the main road and schools for children. I will bring together the men and women of higher learning form the village to help establish the idea, so that the village of Mashtul can become a shining centre in Egypt ..

Inner Changes and Outer Learning

Then during Abouleish's (2005) studies, at university in Austria, he would immediately establish himself, not only within and across the sciences and the humanities, but also across the east and the west, if not also the north, though less so in the south.

> Technical chemistry consisted of many different subjects, each one of which would have been an entire subject of its own. I was inspired by everything. I noticed my fellow students, whom I came to teach, had a completely different approach to understanding from my own. They learnt everything by heart. I wondered how one could learn a subject by heart without understanding it properly.
>
> During my studies, in fact, I noticed inner changes taking place within me. I became thoroughly involved with European culture, getting to know its music, studying its poetry and philosophy. Somebody looking into my soul would have seen anything "Egyptian" left completely behind, so I could absorb everything new. Because of my childhood and adolescent grounding, though, in Egyptian culture, I could not leave such entirely behind. I now existed in two worlds, both of which were essentially different: the oriental, spiritual stream I was born into and the European, which I felt was my chosen course. But I was neither Egyptian nor European.

Weaving a Net of Life, Which Connects People with Their Hearts

As such he (2005) was setting the integral stage for a path of what would ultimately become, as we shall later see, newly global reason, for what Sekem now terms *The Economics of Love*, albeit standing on the shoulders of one particular intellectual giant, Austrian polymath Rudolf Steiner, if not also, in Egyptian guise, the grounding of *maat (*balance). In fact in the new millennium, some three decades after Sekem's founding, Aboleish had this to say, anticipating the economics of love to fully follow another two decades later, with his on Helmy Aboulesh then taking the lead:

> My vision now has a new, further level; to found a "council of the future of the world" together with other institutions striving towards developing a better world. This council would not be an abstract term, but carry a concrete message into the world: there is nothing more powerful than the invisible net of life, which connects people with their hearts. Its fabric is woven deeper than our understanding, and long before we first shake a hand we have moved along its threads.

We will return more fully to Sekem specifically and to the Economics of Love generally in Chapter 15 on *Socio-Technical Design*, on the northern path of reason, but first we need to focus on the path's emergent foundation, critical rationalism for which we turn, first by way of overall orientation, to Karl Popper.

Popper's Logic of Scientific Discovery

The doyen of such rationality is the late Anglo-Austrian philosopher and leading advocate of "open society", Karl Popper (2002), in fact a central European neighbor of Moravia's Husserl, whom we met in Chapter 5. Interestingly enough, Paulin Hountondji, whom we shall soon meet, locally-globally in our integral context, was a student of Husserl's, but deliberately put our "southern", phenomenology on the "back burner" until he had pursued his rational and professional philosophical, our "northern", course, that he felt his continent required of him.

Karl Popper, in fact, was born in Vienna (then in Austria-Hungary) in 1902 to middle-class parents of Jewish origins, who had both converted to Christianity. Popper received a Lutheran upbringing and was educated at the University of Vienna. His father was a bibliophile who was rumored to have 10,000 volumes in his library at home. Popper took a PhD in philosophy in 1928. In 1934 he published his (2014) first book, "The Logic of Scientific Discovery", in which he criticized the inductive, empirically laden approach to scientific method, and the logical positivism that underlay it. At the same time he put forth his theory of potential falsifiability being the criterion for what should be considered science.

In 1937, the rise of Nazism led Popper to emigrate to New Zealand, where he became a lecturer in philosophy at Canterbury University College New Zealand (at Christchurch). In 1946, he moved to England to become reader in logic and scientific method at the London School of Economics, where he was appointed professor in 1949. He was president of the Aristotelian Society from 1958 to 1959, altogether providing excellent credentials for our embodiment of "northern" rationalism.

Popper's Philosophy of Science: Critical Rationalism

Popper coined the term "critical rationalism" to describe his philosophy. The term indicates his rejection of classical empiricism. Popper belived that scientific theories are universal in nature, and can be tested only indirectly, by reference to their implications. He also held that scientific theory, and human knowledge generally, is irreducibly conjectural or hypothetical, and is generated by the creative imagination in order to solve problems that have arisen in specific historico-cultural settings.

Popper's account, moreover, of the logical asymmetry between verification and falsifiability lies at the heart of his philosophy of science. It also inspired him to take falsifiability as his criterion of demarcation between what is and is not genuinely scientific: a theory should be considered scientific if and only if it is falsifiable. This led him to attack the claims of both psychoanalysis and contemporary Marxism to scientific status, on the basis that the theories enshrined by them are not falsifiable.

For Popper, it is in the interplay between the tentative theories (conjectures) and error elimination (refutation) that scientific knowledge advances toward greater and greater problems; in a process very much akin to the interplay between genetic variation and natural selection. Where does "truth" fit into all this? As early as 1934 Popper wrote of the search for truth as *"one of the strongest motives for scientific discovery"*.

Drawing Closer to the truth More Important Than the Question of Who is Right

When Popper, then, speaks of reason or "critical rationalism", what he means is that is that we can *learn* through criticism of our mistakes and errors, especially though criticism by others, not by simply taking over another's opinions, but by gladly allowing others to criticize our ideas and by gladly criticizing the ideas of others. The emphasis, for Popper, is on *critical discussion*. The genuine rationalist does not think that he or anyone else is in possession of the truth; nor does he think that mere criticism as such helps us to achieve the new ideas. But he does think that, in the sphere of ideas, only critical discussion can help us sort the wheat from the chaff. For the rationalist knows he owes his ideas to other people. As such our drawing closer to the truth is more important than the question of who is right.

The Enlightenment thinker then, the true rationalist for Popper, never wants to talk anyone into anything. He does not even want to convince: all the time he is aware that he may be wrong. Above all, he values the intellectual independence of others too highly to want to convince them in important matters. He seeks not to convince but to arouse. Free opinion formation is precious to him: not only because this brings us closer to the truth but also because he respects free opinion formation as such.

We now turn to the African counterparts to Popper, Nigerian philosopher Chumakonam and Beninois philosopher Hountondji, as well as the South African anthropologists John and Jean Commaroff, as we shall see, starting by feeling local, then turning local-global, and thereafter newly global, on the northern African research path of reason. We also need to bear in mind that *north* is used metaphorically here rather than literally and geographically, although the path of innovation – via Sekem – literally comes from Africa's geographical north, that is, out of Egypt, the ancient cross-roads of civilisations.

11.2. Feel Local: Ground Path of Reason Naturally in Okwu: N2f

11.2.1. The Pervasive Influence of Greek European Logos

So we turn from grounded theory (N1) specifically, as outlined in Chapter 4, to its fully-fledged, rational foundation (N2), critical rationalism, outlined in this chapter. Firstly as invariably the case in all our paths, we start by *feeling local* in Africa through Nigerian philosopher Jonathan Chimakonam's so called Okwu bearing fruit in African logic. Thereafter, and thereby intuiting locally-globally we turn to Africa's probably most notable contemporary professional philosopher, also having pursued his doctoral studies in France, since then based in Benin, Paulin Hountondji.

For our *newly global* approach to research, overall, we turn back to the work of Chimakonam, now based on his so called *Ezemezu* logic, co-evolved uniquely with the African Calibar University School of Philosophy, again in Nigeria. Finally, and with a view to *acting globally-locally* we reveal the overall Keynotes of critical rationalism, the research path of African reason, and emancipatory scientific naviation of innovation.

Jonathan Chimakonam Okeke (Hountondji 2002) is the youngest, prominent representative of Nigeria's Calibar School of Philosophy from which we shall hear more later in the chapter, though he is now based at the University of Pretoria in South Africa. The purpose of the study of African philosophy, for him then, has to be narrowed down to the use of reason in resolving social, political, economic and environmental challenges facing the continent as well as the management of interaction with other peoples. Moreover, it is the lot of philosophy, as the French postmodern philosopher Jacques Derrida had observed, to honour its debts and duties to the cultural settings in which its questions arise. That sets the stage, in his terms, for our *feeling local*.

To begin with for Chimakonam as such, logos, he says, is a Greco-European concept for word, speech or reason and from this concept logic was derived. There is probably no other concept in the entire history of Western philosophy that has been instrumentalized and perhaps as abused, according to him, as logos has been. It has been identified as God, as son of God, as soul, as mind, as logic, as being, as life, as word, as speech and as reason. By *logomania*, therefore, he means the mindless adoption of the Greco-European logos by epistemologies of the south in their cultural and philosophical particulars.

11.2.2. Okwu as Unbranded Index for Thought

Logos is ontologically branded then as such, and has dragged reason off course in its journey into so called African philosophy. Here Chimakonan offers in its place an unbranded entity called "okwu", for us grounding. Okwu thus is an Igbo-African concept – the Igbo being one of the three major Nigerian ethnic groups – forming the raw material from which words are constituted. The Igbo term for word is *mkupuruokwu* meaning the first, for us emergent fruit of okwu. It is the very ancestor of word, raw and shapeless. For Chimakonam (2019):

> Like animals and plants the world's languages are the result of a long "natural history" which began with a single first language spoken in Africa.

11.2.3. African Philosophy and the Question of Method

It should be observed, for Chimakonam then, that the modern research framework whether in the sciences or philosophy is a Western particular elevated to an absolute stance. The western advance in knowledge, which has come to be treated in modernity not just as a model but as *the* model, for all humanity, is an indication of an unchallenged hegemony, for him, and not an accurate depiction of human intellectual history. Post-modernism in fact, as we shall see in the next chapter, is an outcry against the systematic domination and silencing of other cultures.

Specifically then the classical Greek Platonic and Aristotelean framework, for him, lies at the foundation of philosophy. It then blossomed in modern times in the work of French philosopher Rene Descartes and German philosopher Immanuel Kant in the 17th and 18th centuries. Modernism is simply a continuation of that tradition. The same applies, for us, to the "modern" nation state, market based or planned economy, and business corporation, altogether conceived of in the modern "north-west". African philosophy in fact, then, began to find proper direction (in the creation of original ideas) theoretically, for Chimakonam, in the early 1990s.

11.2.4. The Need for Villagisation of Knowledge

The need for what he then terms "villagisation of knowledge" arises for four reasons. Firstly there is no knowledge perspective that is absolute and comprehensive and as a result suffices for all places and times, which is why we have identified four overall social research paths: southern *relational*, eastern *renewal*, northern *reason* and western *realisation*. Secondly true justice demands the accommodation of all knowledge perspectives, whereby we have added a research trajectory from origination (grounding) to transformation (effect). Thirdly *we cannot have social and economic justice,* as Ndlovu-Gatsheni has also intimated in the last chapter, without epistemic justice. Fourthly the villagisation of knowledge entails the accommodation of different perspectives, as the last frontier in the battle to dethrone Plato's and Aristotle's European hegemony.

We now turn from Chimakonam to his West African Beninois (originally form Code D'Ivoire) the renowned Afro-French philosopher Paulin Hountondji.

11.3. Intuit Local-Global in Africa: Professional Philosophy

11.3.1. Ethno, Sage, Statesman and Professional African Philosophers

We now turn from feeling local, Africa-wise, on the path of reason, in Nigeria, to adjacent Benin, that is now locally-globally to the Beninois-French philosopher Paulin Hountondji. As now Director of the Centre for Advanced African Studies on Porto Novo in Benin, he previously also served as a Benin government minister. In fact Hountondji is as renowned amongst the older generation of African philosophers as Chimakonam is amongst the newer ones.

Indeed Kenyan African philosopher now based at the University of Louisville, D.A. Masolo (1994), in his *African Philosophy in Search of Identity*, identifies four kinds of African philosopher: the ethno-philosopher (Malidoma Some), the sage philosopher (like Ogotomelli of the Dogon peoples), the professional philosopher, and the statesman philosopher (Kwame Nkrumah, Julius Nyerere, Leopold Senghor). Hountondji is the most prominent representative of the so called African professional philosophers. We now turn to his work.

11.3.2. Europe and Africa in Philosophical Perspective

In this now local-global context, the present debate on the question of African philosophy, for Hountondji (1983), can be seen to form part of a comprehensive process of reflection by the African intelligentsia upon its historical being. As such it represents a significant moment in the intellectual response of Africans to the challenge of Western civilisation.

Hegel's philosophy of history, Hountondji maintains as such, remains the most exalted statement of European self affirmation in opposition to other races, the most elaborate rationalization of European ethno-centricism. It provides a powerful philosophical base for the chorus of denigration of the non-white races which buoyed up the European colonial adventure. The high point of such denigration was attained in the work of French anthropologist Levi-Bruhl, who devoted his career to demonstrating the "primitive mentality" of the non-Western peoples. On the one hand, for Levi-Bruhl, there were the Western societies that had emerged from the Mediterranean civilisation, within which developed rationalist philosophy and positive science, and on the other hand, "primitive" societies ruled by a mentality to which the Western mode of thought was alien. Such societies, so he argued, were "pre-logical".

11.3.3. To Gain Our African Soul We Must Lose It

In fact, for Hountondji, African philosophical literature sometimes rests on a confusion between the popular (ideological) and strict (theoretical) use of the word philosophy. According to the first meaning, philosophy is any kind of wisdom, intended to govern the daily practices of a people; in the second sense philosophy is a discipline, like mathematics, with its own exigencies and rules – Hountondji, as an African rationalist, albeit also as such a universalist, of course favours the latter.

As such he reckons that ethno-philosophers have wasted their time with ready-constituted thought – whether for example Dogon or Dagara or Yoruba or indeed Egyptian – to justify themselves in European eyes. Instead, African philosophers should have thrown themselves into the fray, in order to confront today's and tomorrow's problems. In a completely sterile withdrawal, Hountondji laments, Africa goes on vindicating its cultures instead of transforming them. He who must gain his soul must lose it. By dint of trying to defend our cultures, he says, we have mummified them. We have betrayed our original cultures by showing them off for external consumption.

Motivated by the genuine need for an African philosophy, ethno-philosophical predecessors have wrongly believed, according to Hountondji, that it lies in the past, needing only to be exhumed and then brandished like a miraculous weapon in the astonished face of the colonialist European. They have not seen that African philosophy, like science or culture in general, is before us, and must be created, albeit embracing, in the process, the heritage of the past. Philosophy, for him (Hountondji 2002) needs to be active, not passive, an open system rather than a closed on:

> .. we want the relentless questioning, the untiring dialectic that accidentally produces systems and then projects them towards horizons of fresh truths African philosophers who think in terms of Plato and Marx and then transcend such are producing authentic African work.

The real problem is not to talk about Africa but to talk amongst Africans. Europe is what she is today because she transformed the heritage of other peoples, including the ancient Egyptians. Africa must liberate its thoughts from a previous ghetto, open up a breach in its closed space of its collectivist fantasies, so that theoretical issues will surge in, to be shared first of all with our immediate brothers, thus to steep them in the melting pot of African science. The real problem is to liberate the theoretical creativity of African peoples; everything else, including science, as opposed to religion, will come afterwards.

11.3.4. Philosophy and Its Successive Revolutions

Philosophy therefore for Hountondji, as for Popper as we have seen above, is firstly a history and not merely a system, and essentially as such an open process, a restless unfinished quest, not closed knowledge; second, this history does not move forward by continuous evolution but by leaps and bounds, by successive revolutions, and consequently follows a dialectical path; thirdly, and as such, African philosophy may currently be going through a decisive mutation, its outcome depending on contemporary philosophers, indeed like Chimakonam, today.

No philosophical doctrine, then, can be regarded as *the truth*. The absolute is contained in the relative of an open-ended process. In other words, truth is the process where we look for propositions more adequate than others. Truth lies in a journey, that takes into account all prior doctrines, and then outdoes them. Traditional African systems of thought, limited for Hountondji as such, are not in themselves such a journey. There is no philosophy, moreover, that would be an implicit system of propositions or beliefs to which all individuals of a society, past, present and future, would subscribe. Every great philosophy, moreover, is a rebirth, a radical questioning. But the break occurs after the event, though a kind of recursion that is essential to all philosophy, as a necessary moment in the history of philosophy, a turning, a renascence, a revolution, a mutation taking place within history and not a suppression coming in from the outside. Every great philosophy, to establish itself, must ravage the existing theoretical space.

Nor is African civilisation a closed system. It is the unfinished history of a similarly contradictory debate. We now turn, more specifically, to Hountondji's perspective on science, which he contextualised in terms of a "struggle for meaning", revisiting, as such, his prior connection with Husserl's phenomenology, albeit in rational guise.

11.3.5. Hountondji's Struggle for Meaning

In Husserl's Hierarchy of Cultural Practices, Science Occupied the Highest Rung

For the European creator of phenomenology Edmund Husserl, as we saw in Chapter 5, in the hierarchy of cultural practices, science occupied the highest rung. To him, no other form of thought, way of life, vocation, art or religion, appears nobler. This is not, Hountondji emphasizes, scientism: science is not valued for itself, but for its human significance and meaning for life. It is subordinated, like any other cultural production, to ethics; its exceptional value – far from its technical accomplishments – is that it is the bearer of norms and generative values. In our terms, and for Hountondji (2002) as such, it emerges out of a particular and formative "life-world", is subsequently re-formed through exposure to other such worlds, and thereafter bears new values and norms.

Science, for Husserl then, can either be defined pragmatically, as an experimental montage, a body of regulated material practices, or psychologically, as a linkage of acts of cognition. Husserl mentions the first only to annex it immediately to the second; instruments and apparatuses will never be anything but extrinsic tools linked to a unity of acts of thought. Hountondji's doctoral research, when he was based in France, actually built on Husserl's philosophy. In fact he deliberately held such phenomenological research back, in an African context, until he had deepened and extended his critical and dialectical, rationally based analysis, believing that such was required first.

Impoverished Science and Detached Philosophy in Africa

Overall and as such, philosophy, for Hountondji as for us, must bring about the transformation of the world. In Africa, as everywhere else, theory has meaning only if it is organized and subordinated to practice, that it derives its legitimacy in relation to other practices. The myth of white supremacy, in that respect, cannot be dealt with by attachment to a counter myth. A simplistic comparison between a stereotyped "north" and "south" then, will not do, without due consideration of the interactions between the two, not to mention, in our context, the "east" and the "west".

The problem for Africa today (Hountondji 1997), which is all too evident for us in its business schools, is that Africa has to a large extent internalised the discourse of its former masters in its research and educational activities, including, as we have already seen, their denigrating views on African ways of life and thought. At the same time he warns against the opposite danger, that of closing off its heritage without any critical approach, without any attempt to update and renew the intellectual legacy, in a way that allows a higher degree of rationality, and a steadier march towards efficiency and self-reliance. Things have to be considered afresh, therefore, at an equal distance from cultural alienation, which takes up the colonial masters' prejudices and any self-denigration, both of which results in a kind of intellectual self-imprisonment.

In the process of scientific investigation as understood in our times, the decisive stage is neither the collection of data that, in a way, starts the whole process, nor the application of theoretical findings to practical issues, which is the final stage. The decisive stage is what comes between them – the interpretation of raw information, the theoretical processing of the data collected, and the production of those particular utterances which we call scientific statements.

For Hountonji, *the one essential shortcoming of scientific activity in the colonies was the lack of the intermediate stage. We missed the central operation of theory building*. We only had the first and the third stages of the process: first the data collection, the feverish gathering of all supposedly useful information, and second a partial, occasional and limited application of the research outcomes to some local issues. The medium stage then took place in the so called "mother country". Thus science in the colonies was characterised by a theoretical vacuum – the lack of those intellectual and experimental procedures that, being at the heart of the entire enterprise, depended on infrastructure that existed only in the ruling countries.

This theoretical vacuum was substantially the same as the industrial vacuum, as highlighted by Rugisara in his *Good African Story* hitherto, that characterised economic activity.

Deprived of Theory Building/Deprived of African Economic Theory

Therefore modern science was introduced by the coloniser in the overseas territories in the form of an impoverished science, *deprived of an inner element, the theory-building activity that makes science. This, in fact, was a side-affect of the same colonisers' launch of so-called modern economies in these territories.* The theoretical emptiness of scientific activity in the colony derives from the very nature of peripheral capitalism – a mode of production based on the search for surplus, as in Europe, but deprived of the industrial activism, the will to transform, the creativity and inventiveness, the sense of initiative and propensity to risk, that makes capitalism productive in the coloniser's own country.

Moreover, as a consequence of what Hountonji terms "extroversion", local scholars tend to address issues that are primarily of interest to the Western public, specialising in the study of their own natural and social environment. The problem, however, is that this orientation indulges too often in some kind of imprisonment into the particular. In order to give a proper account of the peculiarities of our culture, we first need to be aware of what is universal about them. We need, therefore, to take that minimum theoretical distance that allows one to put things into perspective.

What is needed in Africa today is not just to apply traditional knowledge in agriculture or medicine, while continuing to import from the West technologies that are poorly understood and mastered by the local users. What is needed, instead, is to help the people and their elite to capitalise and master the existing knowledge, whether indigenous or not, and develop new knowledge in a continual process of uninterrupted creativity, while applying the findings in a systematic and responsible way to improve their own quality of life.

Instead, for Hountondji, we have been serving as learned informants, for a theory-building activity located overseas and entirely controlled by the people there. Africa needs to invent ways in which knowledge can be better shared by the North and South in all its phases, be it the phase of production, accumulation and capitalisation, or of application. It needs to develop an ambitious strategy of knowledge appropriation that will allow Africans to freely and critically take up anything that can be useful for us in the intellectual heritage now available in the world.

The Liberation of the Future

The illusion of timelessness, moreover, that is associated with any reductive reading of African civilizations, the tendency to mummify them, to empty them of their history, evolution, diversity, and of their creative tensions, is therefore questioned by Hountondji. What is demanded, instead, is the internal dynamism of African cultures, the pluralism of beliefs transmitted by them. Individual speech must then be liberated, and a multiplicity of speeches then released, and related to each other. African thought must be released from its local confines, and related for instance, as Nkrumah has done at least in part, to Plato or Aristotle, or Marx.

The great issue at stake, therefore, in Hountondji's critique of ethno-philosophy, is the liberation of the future. For the African intellectual, the burden of having to conform, on pain of repudiating his identity, to a system of thought that had been worked out in advance, had to be lifted. It had to be demonstrated that the freedom of the individual, at a conceptual level, could not be restricted in advance. The horizon of possibilities had to be opened. In short, the over-determination of the concept of Africa is an obstacle to the freedom of Africans.

For the same reason the notion of philosophy had to be re-examined, to describe a history not a system, a discipline in which results matter more than reasoning, whose goals is to go beyond the results to achieve better ones. To liberate the future required a disentanglement from the collective "us". To liberate the future, the past has first to be liberated by restoring movement, contradiction and dynamism to it, in the same sense as Nkrumah conceived of, but did not apply. Real pluralism does not only consist in affirming, against the West's cultural hegemony, a plurality of cultures, but recognizing the complexity, diversity, tensions, contradictions, internal dynamics of each world, and seeing in that a source of richness.

The African philosopher, finally as such, should not be required to reflect on Africa alone. Hountondji's critique of ethno-centricism leads to a de-territorialisation of cultural values. At a stroke this approach makes it possible for Africa to claim to be universal, for us local-global. He deplores Africa's exclusion from science, and its remaining on the margins of the global production of knowledge, and he argues for constructing a new space of theoretical construction. Hountondji as such seeks to de-marginalise Africa, to place it firmly at the centre of its own history in a pluralized world, whose unity needs to be periodically re-negotiated.

The reinsertion of thought in the real movement of history should enhance both a recognition of the specificity of works of speculative thought and their relationship to the social, political and economic context of different periods. It should finally find a pluralist vision of philosophy and African culture by sweeping away unanimist prejudice. We now return, in this case newly globally in our terms, to Chimakonam.

11.4. Think Newly Globally in Africa: Ezumezu: N2t

11.4.1. Philosophical Reason Is Leaving the West

Western Philosophers Have Built a City of God for Themselves

For more than 2000 years for Chimakonam then, since the Golden Age of Greek philosophy, for him, Western philosophers have abandoned the world, and took flight at the top of mount Olympus where they built a city of God for themselves, talking to themselves alone. In their isolated city, they dreamt of the universal dream exported from their cultural particular for all of humanity. Instead Chikamonan thinks of finding new conversations sister traditions from the south and east, as per African, Indian or Chinese, instead of courting and aged northwestern bride, as we are seeking to do through our integral research, also adding innovation tot he societally regenerative whole.

Philosophical reason, he says, is therefore leaving the West and making its way into various cultures in the south. For hedged up in the, for us globalised, digitised, marketized, mountain top, within the bulwarks erected by Plato and Aristotle, there is no more room for the next big idea to emerge. Yet there are now exciting conversations going on in the south, while the Western philosopher, and for us also political scientist, economist and management scientist, is out in the cold obsessed with his logos. In the south we are unveiling new concepts, ideas and opening new vistas for thought, philosophically for us if not yet economically.

Villages Hold Conversations with Philosophers and Non-Philosophers Alike

Chimakonan ultimately advocates the disbanding of the philosophical city on which *philsophicitizens* maintain their exclusion from those othered (on the basis of a superior-inferior dichotomy) and reconstituting such as philosophical villages. There philosophers of varied persuasions in their different – for us also political, economic and managerial – villages emerge and hold conversations with philosophers and non-philosophers alike. This brings us onto his Igbo (Chimakonam himself is of Igbo heritage) based, Ezumezu.

11.4.2. Ezumezu as a Philosophy of Logic

Ngho: To Do Flexible or Dynamic Reasoning

Here Chimakonam wants to show that logic is central to how African philosophers interpret the world and relate to reality within it as against the position of those who think otherwise. He then unveils his prototype of African logic, for us newly global, on the African path of reason.

The synonym for the word logic in Igbo (a West African language) is *ngho* which means dynamic or flexible reasoning: *itu ngho* therefore becomes an expression for *"to do flexible or dynamic reasoning"* or simply to do logic. African ontology thereby holds that reality could be interpreted from three perspectives: the physical, the non-physical, and the combination of the two. The third of these values is referred to as *ezemezu*, where the true polar values (both truth and falsity) complement each other, as well adding the element of context dependence. Ezemezu then is an Ibo word meaning "the collective, the aggregate, the totality of all that is most viable, potent and powerful".

Western Logic Systematised Out of the Native Thought System of Aristotle

As then the structure of a thought system varies from culture to culture, so does the structure of logic born out of them, and thereafter, for us, the overall structure of research and innovation, as well as the polity, economy and management to follow, if not also the overall university within which such knowledge is disseminated and further evolved.

The Western logic was systematised out of the native thought system of the West, specifically that of Aristotle. The question then is what is African logic therefore that would attract a different answer from, say, Indian or Chinese logic. To formulate an African logic Chimakonan had to accurately map an African system of thought. He traced the various stages of development of metaphysics which he called the theory of the ontological quadrant.

The Structure of Metaphysics Developed Across Four Stages

His theory, like ours, holds that the structure of metaphysics developed across four stages of human thinking leading to the emergence of logic, and for us also, ultimately, praxis. In the first stage, which can be aligned with our local and original, communal grounding, metaphysics was dormant, whereby *superstitions and religious concerns were all pervasive* (though Griaule and Scranton – see Chapter 10 – would beg to differ). In the *second* stage, our local-global, emergent cultural foundation, metaphysics begins to offer critical explanations of phenomena. The *third* stage, our newly global, emancipatory scientific navigation represents the purest development of metaphysics into science, and *it is here that the diversities of cultures manifest* with regard to how a people look at reality, on the one hand bivalent (our north-western), on the other hand trivalent (our south-western). *The fourth stage is where metaphysics births logic*, the stage, which for us, as for John Heron, also and ultimately involves praxis.

The Complementary Nature of Ezumezu Logic

There are then for Chimakonan three systems that have been formulated in African logic tradition, namely: *Complementary Logic* developed by Innocent Asouzu (2007), *Harmonious Monism* worked out by Chris Ijiomah (Chimakonam 2014), and Ezumezu logic formulated by Chimakonam himself, all of which can be aligned, in one way another, with our Integral Worlds. All three are members of the Calabar School of Philosophy. Chimakonan conceives of African philosophy elementarily as a deconstructive and reconstructive discourse that is conversational from the background of an African thought system opening new vistas, creating new concepts and sustaining the conversation.

The complementary mode (ezu-mezu) is a distinct value in itself where the other two standard values – ezu and izu – converge and complement. It is also a tentative mode whereby it disintegrates by means of a conversational mechanism called a creative struggle to re-instate each truth value in their contextual modes. As such the values T (True) and F (False) are insufficient in themselves in that one affirms and does not negate; while the other negates but does not confirm, hence forming an emergent foundation together in our terms. It is in the complementing value C that they both achieve sufficiency, or what we term emancipatory navigation.

11.4.3. Ezumezu as Methodology

Plato and Aristotle: Casting Their Shadows over Far Reaches of the World

The success story and reputation of Western philosophy, for Chimakonan, besides being intimidating, is ironically enough for him well deserved. Behind this success story are two towering giant shadows of *Plato and Aristotle*, the former yielding epistemological and metaphysical batons of essentialism and the latter wielding metaphysical and ultimately logical batons of relativism. Together these wardens of Hellenistic civilisation are now casting their shadows over far reaches of the world.

At the foundation of this Hellenistic influence is methodology. Indeed, no tradition of philosophy today can be regarded as truly different from the Western tradition if it subscribes to the dichotomous, essentialist and divisive epistemic metaphysical visions propelled by the logic of non-contradiction, and the excluded middle, whereby for us the thereby composite global-local precludes the complementary local-global.

Nwa-nsa Proposes; Nwa-nju Opposes; Nwa-zugbe Creative Struggle

Chimakonan then identifies, in Igbo terms, three main pillars of thought, namely nwa-nsa, nwa-nju and nwa-izugbe in African philosophy, which together form a triangle of Ezumezu methodology. He conceives as *nwa-nsa as a peripheral agent or variable that proposes; nwa-nju as one that opposes; and nwa-zugbe as a product of creative struggle between the two.* These three pillars are at the tips of the triangle and are *connected together by a line of relationship that could be called nmeko* characterised by contestations, protestations and conversations, that brings together the three pillars. It is a logical relationship that follows two patterns, arumaristics and ohakaristics. For us, in similar terms, the local, and the local-global is followed by a *nmeko*-like newly global.

Arumaristics is when the peripheries move towards the centre for a logical relationship of inclusion in complementary guise, and *ohakaristics* is when the centre moves towards the peripheries to promote integration, also between peripheries and their contexts.

Nmeko as Creative Struggle – Contestation, Protestation and Conversation

The method of conversational thinking in African philosophy demonstrates the encounter or relationships of variables as arumaristic. A disjunctive motion is slowed down by what can be called a "concessional bridge" – defined as a mechanism for determining when complementation has taken place. At the other end a conjunctive motion begins to bring opposed, our four worldly, variables into a relationship at what can be called a "complementary – our integral – turn". This overall process is known as *creative struggle or nmeko* – a relationship of contestation, protestation and conversation.

This moreover gives birth to new questions and with it new concepts. Every question is supposed to open new vistas for thought and elevate the discourse to a higher level. Thus the ultimate goal of the conversational method is the sustenance of the conversation and not the final resolution of the questions. What this implies is that while methods such as dialogue and polylogue, following from Hegel-like dialectics, are open to the unity of opposed variable in a synthesis, conversational thinking which rides on the crest of arumaristics regards synthesis as anathema.

Nwa-izugbi then is not a synthesis but a phase in ever unfolding outcomes of a creative struggle. Indeed, for us, "newly global" emancipatory, scientific navigation, as such an interim synthesis, merely paves the way for a global-local, transformative economic effect which is invariably periodic and intermittent, rather than ultimately conclusive, as falsely built into the "equilibrium" of supply and demand, or indeed perfect competition, in economics. Chimakonan then turns to the significance of context in African philosophy.

Context-Dependence of Value (CdV) Making Truth in African Logic Dynamic

The principle of Context dependence of Value, for Chimakonam moreover, states that credible value judgments are ones based on contexts. Esemezu as methodical consideration begins from the premise that realities are sorted in terms of nwa-nsa and nwa-nju. Though independent, they exist in a network of interrelation in which the ideas of difference and equality are inherent and not isolated units. Thereby the notion of truth in African logic is dynamic; what is asserted to be true at one point of history turns out to be false at another time when circumstanced change. So truth manifests from context to context from which they are able to exercise a form of intercommunication or solidarity. What does this more specifically mean?

The Centrality of the Concept of Nmeko: Truth, Solidarity and Regeneration

Nmeko in fact, for Chimakonam, an Igbo word that roughly translates to relationship is central to theorisations in African philosophy and studies. It has a taproot in African logic where it marshals different types of logical relationships. Nigerian philosopher Chris Ijomah defines African logic as the science of relationships among realities. With this concept of relationship South African/American philosopher Thaddeus Metz (2021) is able to go beyond the bar set by Kant's Categorical Imperative to formulate a possible ethical theory inspired by sub-Saharan worldviews.

For Chimakonan, as such, no properly formulated system or methodology in African philosophy and studies, including for us polity, economics and management, will be worth its name and function without nmeko occupying a central role, in the context of:

1. The Axiom of *Truth*: *no variable is viable without a context*
2. The Axiom of *Solidarity*: *each variable needs to interact with others*
3. The Axiom of *Re-generation*: *when variables interact new ones are produced – new ideas produced via creative encounter with older ones.*

Interestingly enough then, for Chimakonam as for ourselves, the axiom of regneration is the culminating one.

11.4.4. Ezumezu and Integrality

The Law of Njikoka and Integrativity: Nothing Stands Alone

Njikoka moreover in Igbo, for Chimakonam, maintains that because things exist in a network every existence forms a necessary link of reality and nothing stands alone. This is not a form of synthesis because everything in the network retains its identity despite being in a relationship with other things, similar to our integral worlds. Arumaristics meanwhile is different from Marxist and Hegelian dialectics because thesis and antithesis are not contradictories, for Chimakonan, but sub-contraries and as such do not yield a synthesis in Ezumezu logic.

Integrativity, aligned with our integral, is a near equivalence of the Igbo concept Njikoka which means universal value or meaning is derived from variables when they come together. In the law of Njikoka the individuals are not subsumed or lost in the group because they are autonomous, but they come together to create a more powerful centre. In that context, for example, the variable A is said to be true only on the company of other variables. This is the law that upholds the ohakaristic as a reasoning procedure. It also resonates, as we shall see in Chapter 13, with Sekem, whereby nature, culture, society and economy are interwined, with its integral enterprise, rather than focus being on the bottom line.

Law of Nmekoka: Enhanced Individual Identity Within the Group

The term complementarity, in fact, comes nearest to explaining, according to Chimakonan, the concept of Nmekoka. The difference between the law of Nmekoka and that of Njikoka is that while the former centres on the enhanced group power of identity made possible by the combination of individual identities, our integrality, the latter focuses on the *enhanced individual identity within the group*, our four worlds.

Law of Onana–Eti/The Included Middle: Our Integral

If we then say as the traditional law of excluded middle posits that either a thing is or is not, for Chikanonam the possibility exists of a thing being and not being at the same time. Thus, as disjunction polarises and bifurcates in mutually exclusive absolute difference, conjunction unifies and centralises in mutually exclusive relative difference. Included middle therefore becomes a term which closely interprets the Igbo concept *Onana-etiti* which means *"between others, that which comes to the middle".*

Ezemezu logic then admits of modes of interpretation of variables mainly contextual, complementary, contingent or integrated, in both its overall ontological and specifically logical theses.

Ezumezu Ontology: A Network of Interdependent Relationships

Ezumezu, in the final analysis for Chimakonam, has two prominent theses then, namely the ontological thesis and the logical thesis. It is from the spectra of these two that the methods of African philosophy can be understood, as can be our own approach to integral research and innovation, integral economics and enterprise, as well as our networked communiversity which serves to bring together learning community, individual transformation journey, societally based research academy and socioeconomic laboratory, organizationally. Briefly the ontological thesis states that:

Realities exist not only as independent units at the periphery of the circle of existents but also as entities capable of coming together towards the centre of the circle, in a network of interdependent relationships. Just like our communiversity.

11.5. Effect of Integrative African Society – Globally/Locally: N2a

11.5.1. Empirical Science Has Nothing Absolute About It

We now turn, finally, to the global-local effects of critical rationalism, aligned on the one hand with critical rationalism in the "north-west", but on the other hand building on the alternative "southern-northern" logic that we have now seen emerging, locally-globally, as well as ultimately "newly globally" from Africa.

Table 11.5.1. *Critical Rationalism – Keynotes– Rational Foundation*

Empirical Science has nothing absolute about it.
You Derive Theories from Tentative Conjectures built on Ezumezu
Formulate an overall Deductive Strategy based on African Philosophy
Strong Theory drives out the Weak – Towards an Integrative African Society

The empirical basis of science, for Popper, as we have also seen now in African guise from Chimakonam, has nothing absolute about it. Science does not rest on solid bedrock. The underlying idea of this theory of knowledge, from Popper's perspective, is that problems and attempts to solve them through hypotheses, theories or conjectures precede all observation. From Chimakonam's perspective, an African form of logic is of the essence, albeit set in relation to, rather than inferior, to other culturally contextualised logics.

11.5.2. Derive Theories from Tentative Conjectures Built on Ezumezu

Theories can only be tentative conjectures about the world, for Popper as again for Chimakonam, which are ultimately unverifiable by empirical evidence. Their discovery involves imaginative leaps, which are the forerunners of scientific activity. The process whereby predictive and thereby testable hypotheses are deduced from theoretical conjectures and subjected to confrontation with a cognitively accessible world is the distinctive attribute of a critically rational science, of theory, which has not yet been disproved. Moreover, such hypothesis are subject to continual revision, as a result of ongoing questioning and disputation.

For Chimakonam, this method of conversational thinking in African philosophy demonstrates the encounter or relationships of variables as arumaristic. A disjunctive motion is slowed down by what can be called a "concessional bridge" – defined as a mechanism for determining when complementation has taken place. At the other end a conjunctive motion begins to bring opposed, our four worldly, variables into a relationship at what can be called a "complementary – our integral – turn".

This overall process is known as *creative struggle or nmeko – a relationship of contestation, protestation and conversation.*

11.5.3. Formulate an Overall Deductive Strategy

Deductive strategy can be summarized, for Popper, as:

- Begin by putting forward a tentative idea, a conjecture, a hypothesis or set of hypotheses that form a theory.
- With the help of other previously accepted hypotheses, or by specifying conditions under which the hypotheses are expected to hold, deduce a conclusion, or a number of conclusions.
- Examine the conclusions and the logic behind them; compare this argument with existing theories to see if it constitutes an advance in understanding; if so
- Test the conclusion by gathering appropriate data; make the necessary observations or conduct the necessary experiments.
- If the test fails – if the data are not consistent with the conclusion – the "theory" must be false; the original conjecture must be rejected.
- If the conclusion passes the test, because the data are consistent with it, the "theory" is temporarily supported; it is corroborated, not proved to be true.

A deductive theory consists of a set of hypotheses or propositions, which are arranged in such a way that from some of the propositions all other propositions follow. Such a theory has the form of a logical argument that leads to certain conclusions. For Hountondji, on the other hand, what is critical is that such a deductive strategy should be formulated, and as such theorized, within Africa, rather than imported from Europe or America. Moreover, African itself should be engaged with the prior theorizing, and thereby also industrializing, and producing, rather than merely data processing, and thereby consuming.

11.5.4. Open Integrative Society – Strong Theory Drives Out the Weak

Science can only ever be piecemeal and incomplete. Social engineering, as a result, should involve "piecemeal tinkering", which, combined with critical analysis is the main way to achieve practical results in the social as well as natural sciences. In essence, such falsification leads to what Popper termed epistemological Darwinism where the strong theories drive out the weak.

> ... finding theories, which are better approximations to the truth is what the scientist aims at ... This involves the growth of the content of our theories, the growth of our knowledge of the world.

For Chimakonam in Africa, on the other hand, it is not epistemological Darwinism that prevails but, on the other hand, realities exist not only as independent units at the periphery of the circle of existents but also as entities capable of coming together towards the centre of the circle, in a network of interdependent relationships. We are now ready to conclude.

11.6. Conclusion

11.6.1. Impoverished Science and Detached Philosophy

The problem for Africa and many other transition countries today – which is all too evident in their business schools and universities – is that they have to a large extent internalised the discourse of their former masters in their research and educational activities, including their denigrating views on African (or Arab or Latino) ways of life and thought. At the same time Hountondji warns against the opposite danger, that of closing off Africa's or Islam's heritage without any critical approach, without any attempt to update and renew the intellectual legacy, in a way that allows a higher degree of rationality, and a steadier march towards efficiency and self-reliance. Things have to be considered afresh, at an equal distance from cultural alienation, which takes up the colonial masters' prejudices and any self-denigration, both of which results in a kind of intellectual self-imprisonment. Most transitional societies cultures are caught in between such closed traditions and a westernised modernity.

Hence, in the process of scientific investigation in today's social sciences, the decisive stage is neither the collection of data, as fieldwork that so often starts the whole process off, nor the application of theoretical findings to practical issues, which is all too often the final stage. The decisive stage is what comes between them – the interpretation of raw information, the theoretical processing of the data collected, and the production of those particular utterances which we call scientific statements, or indeed theory building. For Hountondji, *the one essential shortcoming of scientific activity in the colonies was the lack of the intermediate stage. He claims, that the former colonies missed the central operation of theory building, then as now.* They only had, and still have, the first and the third stages of the process:

- Stage 1: data collection, the feverish gathering supposedly useful information, and
- Stage 2: intermediate theory building took place in the so-called "mother country"
- Stage 3: partial, and limited application of the research outcomes to local issues.

Thus science in the former colonies was, and indeed still is, characterised by a theoretical vacuum – the lack of those intellectual and experimental procedures that, being at the heart of the entire enterprise, depended on infrastructure that existed only in the ruling countries. This theoretical vacuum (stage 2) was substantially the same as the industrial vacuum that used to, and still does, characterise economic activity. Universities today fall into the same trap, where the west and north lead, and the south and east follow; however, we are determined, with you, to get out of there.

11.6.2. Towards African Reappropriation

Science is not reducible to one single methodology, that is the empirically based collection of information, and empirical observation, any more than it can be confused with a technical object that is only its technical by-product. *Science is an activity, for Hountondji, whose goal it is to produce true statements. Such an activity was seriously lacking in the dominated territories. The colonies lacked laboratories as they lacked factories.* Once this theoretical void – the equivalent of an industrial void – is acknowledged, you get a fairer picture of development. Decolonisation did not put an end to this, with the former colonies as huge reservoirs of facts and raw data, and second, as testing fields for the results of metropolitan inventions. The system has quite simply become more refined. The research institutions at the periphery are mere annexes of the mother institutions at the centre.

The theoretical demand like the economic one comes from the centre. In Africa, no effort was made to formulate new and original questions. To answer the questions of others seemed to be the continent's destiny. The international division of scientific labour freed Africa from thinking. To develop it had to apply the inventions of others, still the case today; social innovations like the Truth and Reconciliation Commission in South Africa are a notable exception. The four weaknesses that Hountondji has detected, that prevent African scientific practices from serving its peoples, are:

- financial dependence vis-à-vis the outside world,
- institutional dependence on the research centres of the north,
- primacy of north-south vertical scientific exchanges over south-south ones,
- intellectual subordination to the questions and expectations of the west.

What we need, he says as a critical rationalist, is a "radical appropriation of theory".

11.6.3. African Southern Periphery Cut off from the Northern Centre

Theory then, from a peripheral perspective, is always physically distant. The best universities, the best business schools, the best businesses, the best laboratories, the greatest libraries, the most credible publishing houses, the best researchers, are massively located in industrialised countries. The result is that the African or Arab or Chinese researcher in search of the sacred fire – the material and intellectual tools of knowledge – must move elsewhere. Just as integration into the world capitalist markets had resulted in the destruction of the equilibrium mechanisms of subsistence economies, without giving rise to industrial development in the periphery, so integration into world scientific research resulted in arresting the development of pre-existing forms of knowledge, all the while pushing the periphery into subaltern roles in relation to the global process of knowledge creation.

Research wise, the periphery is shut off by the local and the particular, which becomes their research domain, at the expense of theory. Abstract universalism of course, as in the natural sciences, is no better, for it eliminates an essential question, that of the collective appropriation of the universal both as project and result. The African historian must be as interested in the process of industrialisation in Japan as in the slave trade. Studying Japan or Finland or Ireland gives one an understanding, through contrast, of one's own society. As soon as it is produced, African knowledge is "stolen" and integrated into the world system of knowledge administered from abroad.

To put an end to extraversion, to break with a marginalisation that constantly siphons the results of their research, peripheral researchers need to be involved in what Thomas Kuhn called "extraordinary" science (Kuhn 2012), to maintain a critical relationship with the paradigms in each discipline, and to raise new problems that are linked to the preoccupations of their societies. The researcher at the periphery has to go back to the paradigms themselves, and challenge them, developing his or her own basic research, promoting invention in all its forms. There is a great need for a sociology of science to be developed at the periphery.

11.6.4. Participating in the Construction of the Future

To participate in the construction of our future, in Africa as in the Middle East, in Latin America as in South-East Asia, *we need a double movement, a critical appropriation of the scientific and technological heritage available globally, and, at the same time, a re-appropriation of indigenous local knowledge.* In fact, the knowledge produced in the north has been produced over centuries. Rationality is therefore not appropriated in advance. It is still to be built. Hence the immense responsibility of contemporary generations: that of *contributing together in a spirit of solidarity and sharing to the building of the common edifice, so that the germs of irrationality and progressively of ignorance and poverty will be eliminated* forever from the planet earth. How, in our integral terms, is this to be achieved?

11.6.5. Rationally Based Integral Research and Innovation in Africa

Grounding and Origination in Grounded Theory on the Path of Reason

We start out then with grounded theory, with:

- A storyline – a descriptive story about core phenomenon under study
- Describing and then conceptualising – uncovering the core category.
- Relating subsidiary categories around the core category of overall story
- Revisiting the story, re-arranging categories, subcategories accordingly.

Emergent Foundation is Ezemezu on the Path of African Philosophy and Reason

Thereafter, in turning to an African path of professional philosophy and reason

- Empirical Science has nothing absolute about it.
- You Derive Theories from tentative conjectures built on Ezumezu
- Formulate an overall Deductive Strategy based on African Philosophy
- Strong Theory drives out the Weak – Towards an Integrative African Society

University to Communiversity/Capitalism to Communitalism

Further to such, and ultimately on the path of African reason, turning hereafter to postmodernism and socio-technical design, altogether in African guise, we seek to establish a research academy, communiversity wise, that can institutionally serve to pursue our "northern" African cause, and develop the rational arm of communitalism, underpinned by Ezemezu, and professional philosophy, to promote knowledge creation, micro-wise, and a knowledge based social economy, macro-wise.

Critical Rationalism Out of Africa: N2fita

In concluding this chapter on critical rationalism in north African guise, metaphorically in the "north" rather than literally, in fact with strong geographical connections with *west* Africa, we are also able to connecting such research path of reason (okwu to Integrative African Society) with the northern innovation path of Sekem (maat to net of life).

Table 11.6.3. *Okwu to Integrative African Society/Maat to Net of Life: N2fita*

Feeling Local	Intuiting Local-Global	Thinking Newly Global	Acting Global-Local
Okwu	*Professional African Philosophy*	*Ezumezu*	*Integrative African Society*

We now turn from critical rationalism to post-modernism, out of Africa, thereby feeling local, intuiting local-global, thinking newly globally and finally acting globally-locally, in such a now post-modern guise.

11.7. References

Abouleish I (2005) *Sekem: A Sustainable Community in the Egyptian Desert.* Edinburgh. Floris Publications

Asouzu I (2007) *Ibuanyidanda..*Zurich. Lit Verlag

Chimakonam J (2019) *Ezumezu: A System of Logic for African Philosophy and Studies.* Bern. Springer

Chimakonam J (ed) (2014) *Atoulu Omalu: Unanswered Questions in Contemporary African Philosophy.* Lanham. University Press of America

Hountondji P (1983) *African Philosophy.* Indianapolis. Indiana University Press

Hountondji P (2002) *The Struggle for Meaning.* Buckingham, UK. Open

Hountondji P (ed) (1997) *Endogenous Knowledge* Dakar. Codesria. Senegal

Hountondji P (2002) *T*

Kuhn T (2012) *The Structure of Scientific Revolutions. 50th Anniversary Edition.* Chicago. Chicago University Press

Masolo DA (1994) *African Philosophy in Search of Identity.* Bloomington, Indiana University Press.

Metz T (2021) *A Relational Moral Theory: African Ethics in and Beyond the Continent.* Oxford. Oxford University Press

Popper K (2002) *The Open Society and Its Enemies.* Abingdon. Routledge

Popper K (2014) *The Logic of Scientific Discovery.* Connecticut. Martino Fine University Press

Chapter 12 Southern-*Northern* African Post-Modernism: Theory of the South. Feel Local – Tswana Go Dira; Intuit Local/Global – Multiple Discourses; Newly Global Theory of the South; Global-Local Pre-Post Modern Africa

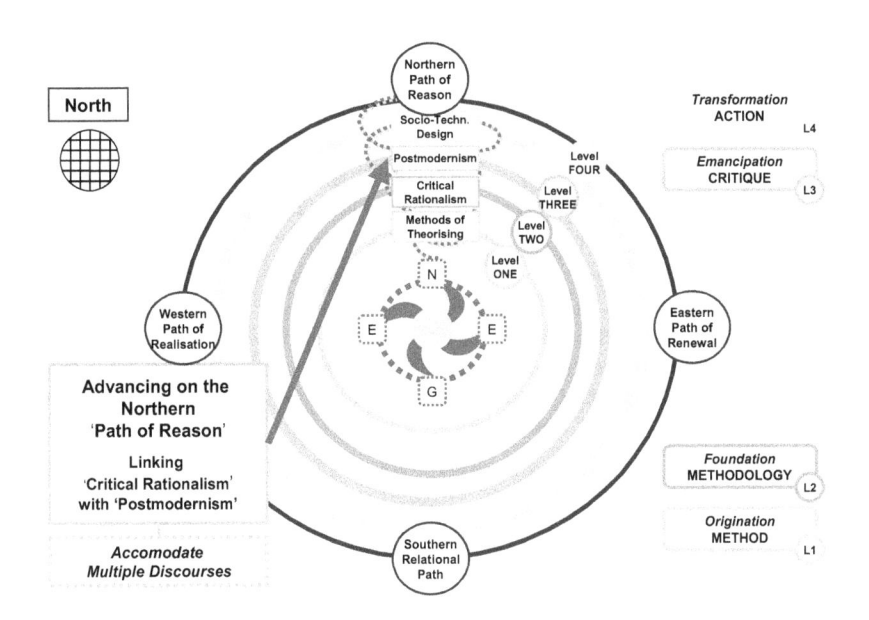

Figure 12.1: *Overview Chapter 12 – Level 3 / North*

> *Like many of the anglophone and francophone states of West and east Africa these are economically and ecologically diverse. Out of these diverse cultures, economies and ecologies, four European states – Britain, France, Portugal and Belgium – constructed the national geography of contemporary Africa. If the history of metropolitan Europe in the last century and a half has been a struggle to establish statehood for nationalities, Europe left Africa at independence with states looking for nations. Once the moment of cohesion against the British was over (a moment whose meaning was greatest for those in the cities*

who had the most experience of the colonizers), the symbolic register of national unity was faced with the reality of our differences.

Kwame Appiah (1992). *In My Father's House: Africa in the Philosophy of Culture.*

Summary: African Postmodernism

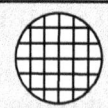

- You are now entering the third level of the northern path of reason. You have started out with the originating methods of theorising (most likely via grounded theory) and have then worked yourself through Karl Popper's modernist approach to critical rationalism, and Chimakonam's Ezumezu African equivalent. We now turn from modernity to postmodernity.

- While modernist critical rationalism has Anglo-Austrian roots in Europe, and was picked up by the so-called "professional philosophers" in an African context, postmodernism is strongly French in its original orientation, while in Africa we find a unique blend of the pre (local feel) and post-modern (intuited locally-globally) to give rise to Mavhunga's newly global transient world.

- While modernism and thereby critical rationalism is oriented towards uncovering an "objective truth", postmodernism argues that there are multiple truths, depending on the time and place, and that discontinuity rather than continuity is the order, or indeed disorder, of the postmodern day, giving rise in African to transient workspaces.

- The acknowledged European originators of postmodernism are primarily French philosophers, including Foucault and Derrida, while from Africa anthropologists such as the Comaroffs, who combine pre-modern and post-modern in trans-modern combination, today respectively based at Harvard and MIT in the U.S, are exemplars

- Such a postmodern or trans-modern reality, incorporating the emergence of multiple voices, has been turned, by American social philosopher Richard Tarnas, into the hallmark of our contemporary age. After postmodernism we shall come onto socio-technical design, and with that to the culminating social innovation along this northern research path.

- Keynotes of global-local African post modernism, ultimately, are inclusive of *multiple discourses, transient meanings and workplaces* that are multiple and shifting, *history that is transformative*, and, ultimately, a combined pre and post modern, *socially constructed meaning*.

12.1. Orientation to African Postmodernism

Integrativity and Transience at Sekem

Continuing on the path of reason, social research-wise, and towards the economics of love, social innovation-wise, via Sekem in North Africa, for Abouleish (2005):

> The intertwined natural and economic realms of activity within Sekem's group of companies begins on a practical level by healing the soil through the application of biodynamic farming methods. Through this method it has raw material at its disposal and is able to develop and manufacture natural medicine and a wide range of other products, adhering to the highest possible quality standards, which conform to the true needs of its consumers. In partnership with its friends and colleague in Europe and its local partners in trade, it strives to market its products, employing what it calls the "Economics of Love".

In other words, as we can see, the Sekem version of what is commonly today called a *circular economy*, ecologically-economically, is accompanied by a workplace in Egypt that is *transient* – see the Camaroffs below – in the specific sense that there is a fluidity between work and life, workplace and community, healing and productivity, as well as ecology and economy, if you like centred in Africa's healing wisdom.

Table 12.1.1. N*orth African Social Research and Innovation: Path of Reason: N3 Grounded Theory to Socio-Technical Design/Sekem to Economics of Love POST-MODERNISM/Transient Workspaces*

Northern Grounding Method and Origination	Northern Emergent Methodology & Foundation	Northern Navigational Critique and Emancipation	Northern Effective Action and Transformation
Grounded Theory (N1)	Critical Rationalism (N2)	Post Modernism (N3)	Socio-Technical Design (N4)
Sekem (N1)	Integrativity (N2)	Theory of the South (N3)	Economics of Love (N4)

In our integral terms, as such, nature and culture, technology and enterprise, are intertwined, if not also the interconnection between learning community and transformation journey, research academy and socio-economic laboratory, altogether in post-modern terms, as multiple discourses.

Modernism to Postmodernism via Multiple Discourses

We then turn as such, in this chapter, from critical rationalism to postmodernism, its more recent and better-known counterpart, ultimately in African guise whereby, as we shall see, pre-modern and post-modern interconnect. While critical rationalism had strong Anglo-Austrian roots, postmodernism is French in origin, and needs newly global evolution for our *southern-northern* purposes. While such a postmodern orientation toward the relativism of multiple discourses is a deliberate reaction against the modern notion of "absolute" truth, both of these "reasonable" research orientations are indeed "rational". Actually, the very fact that such French intellectuals as Foucault and Derrida have taken up the postmodern high ground, is a reflection of such ultra-rationality, in the African case combining pre and postmodernity. Moreover, and as we shall see, in alluding herein to the south-*north* of Africa, we view such "northern" rationality in metaphoric rather than necessarily literal/geographic terms.

In Africa then, we first return to South African anthropologists today based at Harvard School for African Studies, John and Jean Comaroff (1991), who, in their seminal work on *Revelation and Revolution*, take culture to be the space of signifying practice, Thereafter we turn via our own work (Lessem et al 2019), once again to the Comaroffs, now focusing on their *Theory from the South* as we shall see.

The evolution from so-called modernism to postmodernism, towards (in the late Peter Drucker's terms) the *Age of Discontinuity* (2017), and (for UK's management guru Charles Handy's) *The Age of Unreason* (1995), is perhaps the most distinctive overall movement of our times. For American social philosopher Richard Tarnas (2010), whom we first came across in Chapter 6, what we can see in the 21st century, and which he anticipated in his *Passion of the Western Mind*, was a postmodernity reflected:

> ... in the widespread call for and practice of open "conversation" between different understandings, different vocabularies, different cultural paradigms. Not only is the postmodern mind itself a maelstrom of unresolved diversity, but virtually every important element of the western intellectual past is now present and active in one form or another, contributing to the variety and confusion of the contemporary Zeitgeist. Moreover, these in turn have been joined, and affected by a multitude of cultural perspectives from outside the west, such as the Buddhist and Hindu mystical traditions; by underground cultural streams from within the west itself; and by indigenous and archaic perspectives antedating western civilization altogether – all gathering now on the intellectual stage as if for some kind of climactic synthesis.
>
> The postmodern collapse of meaning has been countered by an emerging awareness of the individual's self-responsibility and capacity for creative innovation and self-transformation in his or her existential and spiritual response to life. In virtually all contemporary disciplines it is recognized that the prestigious complexity, subtlety and multi-valence of reality far transcend the grasp of any one intellectual approach, and that only a committed openness to the interplay of many perspectives can meet the extra-ordinary challenges of the postmodern era.

Indeed what Tarnas describes, for him in postmodern terms, reflects a contemporary Egypt as a historic, civilisational cross-roads, whereby Abouleish (2005) brought to bear not only a crossover between the sciences and the humanities, between agriculture and human culture, between the orient and the occident, but also a prolific interchange between Islam in the Arab world and anthroposophy in the European one:

> I wanted to work through the Koran, using anthroposophy to achieve a deeper understanding. What sounds so easy in retrospect was attained gradually with great internal struggle

What then is more specifically is involved in such a postmodern, rational, firstly overall European orientation, before we turn to local African "feel" and integrally locally-globally, newly globally and globally-locally beyond?

Popper to Foucault – Acknowledging a Multiplicity of Discourses

The leading figure in post-modernism, the French philosopher Michel Foucault (2002) like his critically rational predecessor, Karl Popper, is very much in favor of discussion, but such discussion is not aimed at revealing or falsifying a single truth for Foucault, but rather at *acknowledging a multiplicity of discourses*. Foucault then was a French philosopher and historian. He held a chair at the Collège de France, giving it the title "History of Systems of Thought" and taught at the University of California, Berkeley, from 1975 until his death in 1984. He is known for his critical studies of various social institutions, most notably psychiatry, medicine, the human sciences, and the prison system, as well as his work on the history of sexuality. His work concerning power, the relationship between power and knowledge and "discourse" in relation to the history of western thought, has been widely discussed and applied.

We now turn from Europe to our African context, where the post-modern and the pre-modern combine forces, starting with anthropologists Jean and John Comaroff.

12.2. Feel Local on the Post Modern Path of *Go Dira* Laden Tswana-African Reason: N3f

12.2.1. A Lively Tswana World of Open Polities and Changing Societies

Pre-Modern and Post-Modern

For the originally South African, now Harvard based anthropologists, as we have seen (see Chapter 9) John and Jean Commaroffs (1991), the Tswana peoples of what is today Botswana, far from living in an unproductive desert, or hellish spiritual void, that is in the "dark" pre-historical abyss of contemporary European imaginings, these peoples appear to have inhabited a world of dynamic communities, *a lively world of open polities and changing societies.*

Their supposedly pre-modern chiefdoms were not islands unto themselves, nor did they suffer "closed predicaments". Quite the opposite: the Tswana, and others like them, were caught up in complex regional relations, subtle political and material processes, and vital cultural discourses with arguably post-modern charcteristics; in short, in processes that gave historical motion to the construction of economy and society – just as they did in Europe.

Regulated by Conventional Rules and Practices Yet Enigmatic, and Fluid

The most notable feature of "the ordinary life of a Bechuana community", it seems, was its dualistic quality: *structured, yet negotiable, regulated by conventional rules and practices yet enigmatic, fluid, and full of internal strifes. Even the law embodied by the ruler was impermanent.* A Setswana proverb, also uttered in initiation rituals, declared that "the law has an end, it can be left behind". Left behind is derived from *go ela*, which also meant to flow. As a corollary of such, personal identities and positions, relationships and rank, groups and alliances, appeared to be the object of ongoing work – *tiro* – the active fabrication and negotiation of everyday life.

12.2.2. Whenever a Community Moved, Its Forms Were Laid Out Anew

A Polity Capable of Great Variation over Space and Time

Not only, then, was a Southern Tswana *polity in the early nineteenth century capable of great variation over space and time,* but no single fold model could have grasped it in its entirety. Depending on their positions in the social division of labour, some would have perceived it from the "bottom up" or the periphery inward, others from the "top down" or the centre outward. Nonetheless, the dominant imagery of the period, inspired in the spatial autonomy of the community, portrayed society as an hierarchical order. According to the dominant Tswana worldview of the time then, the administrative hierarchy, with the chief-ship (*bogosi*) in the middle, was a necessary condition for the persistence of civil society (*botho* – socialised community); *whenever a community moved, its forms were laid out anew and the anatomy of the chiefdom was thereby recreated.*

There Radiated a Number of Pathways

The *motse*, as such, did not merely translate as a "town", but also connoted a "nucleus", the epicentre of the surrounding world. Circles and arcs, in fact, were the primary motifs in Tswana architecture. From the ruler's place to the fringe of the wild *there radiated a number of pathways,* the spines which moved people and products, cattle and commerce, along, the traffic of everyday life. Significantly moreover, the plural from of motse, that is *metse,* also meant water, a critical source of life, and the symbol of growth and transformation. Such water featured prominently in public ceremonies. And yet, at the same time, the Tswana world appears to have contained other centrifugal forces, that encouraged the disaggregation of the community.

12.2.3. The House and Beyond

Homestead as Loumo, the "Fruit of Her Womb"

In the early nineteenth century Tswana imagination, the quintessential domestic unit was a polygynous household, although such polygamy was the preserve of the rich and the powerful. Indeed, when the Non-Conformists tried to banish the "barbarism" of plural marriage, they had scant idea of what was at issue. For they were tampering with the invisible scaffolding of the socio-cultural order.

The cultural point also had an economic aspect: houses were the primary unit of production and property. Just as every wife had a hut and courtyard of her own, so each was allotted a field to till. Its yield was inalienably hers to use in nurturing her *loumo,* the "fruit of her womb". In addition, while a woman might also feed her spouse, her grain was kept in separate storage and could not be taken without permission. Cattle meanwhile, the most valued possession, were the preserve of males. Cultivation, the female preserve, was thereby less valued.

The social anatomy of the house, then, held the symbolic key to Tswana economy and society: its everyday social and productive processes, its discourses of property and power, its gender relations, and its division of labour. Women moved out seasonally to the fields, bringing back the harvest, while men moved daily inward to the chiefly courts. These movements retraced the flow of value that animated the chiefdom itself, spelling out the connection between the communal centre and domestic periphery.

A Structured Order of Relations and a Fluid Environment

Thus males could only enter the public arena as heads of households that produced their own subsistence, and surpluses, to pay tribute. In this they drew on the agricultural and domestic work of the females, whose labours subsidised the *morafe* (polity). Nevertheless it was the sovereign who was seen as the *fons et origo* of the productive process.

All this returns us to the dualistic nature of Tswana society – to the fact that, from within, it appeared ordered yet fluid. While individuated households were seen to be critical social units, the community was full of intrigue and sorcery. As such, social reality was shifting and enigmatic. *The social field, then, was at once a structured order of relations and a fluid environment in which persons and identities had to be socially constructed.*

12.2.4. Work and Social Being: Go *Dira* – To Make or To Do

From Cultivation, Cooking, and Family to
Politics, and Ritual Performance

In Setswana, *go dira*, as we have seen, has long meant "to make", "to do", or "to cause to happen". It includes a wide range of acts, *from cultivation, cooking, and creating a family to pastoralism, politics, and ritual performance*. It yields positive value in the form of persons things and relations, although it may be undone by sorcery and other malign forces. But *tiro* appears never to have been regarded as an abstract quality or a commodity to be exchanged. It cannot exist as alienable labour power. In short "work" was, and is, the creative process inherent in all human activity; it is expressed in the "building up" of self and others in the course of daily life.

An individual not only produces for himself, but actually produces his entitlement to be a social person. At the same time it seems clear that *tiro* (aligned with *itera* – the reflexive form "to make oneself"), connoted the effort to fashion an identity and to do "great works" by husbanding material assets and wealth in people. And it accorded with a particular notion of time (*lobaka*) which, far from being an abstract resource to be spent or wasted, was itself to be created as an integral part of the social world made by human action and interaction.

Building of Identities, Relations and Statuses an Active, Ongoing Process

The imagery is also tied to another familiar fact: that here as elsewhere in Africa, *the building of identities, relations and statuses was an active, ongoing process*. For example, a Tswana marriage was forged by a gradual, cumulative series of incidents and exchanges; marriages, like most relationships, are best described as having been processes of becoming, not states of being. The work of "building oneself up" and of creating social value was not easy, however. For it was always threatened by negative forces, driven by social conflicts within the social order itself. Not surprisingly, "great work" included the protection of one's own efforts, and those of one's dependents, from the ever present danger of being undone.

While both African and European cultures placed a great deal of weight on the active subject – the human being acting on the world – the two forms of individualism had fundamentally different ontological roots. The Tswana might have recognized something quite familiar in the Protestant notion of the self and its construction. But their own conceptions of personhood and the production of value were to remain quite distinct, individually and socially, even under the prolonged assault of the civilizing mission. Apart from all else, these conceptions were difficult to entangle from the social essence of material life; that is, from relations of production.

Relations of Production Centred on the Household

In contemporary Tswana society, for the Comaroffs moreover, *relations of production were centred on the household. Domestic units regularly cooperated with one another and exchanged labour and goods, but they worked hard to retain their own autonomy.* Within them activities were sharply differentiated by gender and generation, and were part of a more pervasive division of tasks in an economy, based on agriculture and pastoralism, supplemented by hunting and gathering. The labour of women, and youths, laid down the material base on which rested the transactions of male politics; moreover, by freeing adult males from the need to contribute to the physical production of the household, it allowed them to engage in the public domain.

12.2.5. Chiefs Fallible Human Beings Whose Authority Could Be Questioned

Cultivation Involved Dispersal, the Antithesis of Centralisation

Women, corn and bush foods represented a fragile, unstable culling of the wild; men, stock and game evoked the potent, stable domination of its forces. Cattle were the very embodiment of reliability and control over nature. They were the pliable symbolic vehicles through which men formed and reformed their world of social and spiritual relations.

By its very nature, *cultivation involved dispersal, and, therefore, was the very antithesis of centralisation.* In a world where the unit of production was socially individuated – and its independence culturally valued – the tension between chiefly control and household autonomy hovered close to the surface.

While in Office "Kings" Had Constantly to Prove Themselves

Despite this, *chiefs were taken to be fallible human beings whose authority could be questioned and in certain circumstances spurned.* Even their succession, although phrased in terms of immutable genealogical status, was open to negotiation – and was on many occasions contested. A thoroughgoing distinction was made, then, between the chief and the chief-ship. The latter defined a context and conventional stock of resources that enabled the former to construct himself as ruler. *While in office "kings" had constantly to prove themselves.*

12.2.6. Worldview, Ritual and the Life of the Spirit

The Wild Provided Ingredients for Healing; The Town, the Apex of Civil Society

The social and productive arrangements of the period also entailed a classification of beings and forces, things and actions, space and time; in short a worldview. The wild provided the vital ingredients for both healing and sorcery, and, most important, was the habitat of "bush" people. The town, on the other hand, was the apex of civil society and its achievements. It was the domain of free citizens, especially persons of wealth and worth.

The indigenous cosmos was populated by a panoply of beings who interacted with living persons, beings with the capacity to affect the material and social circumstances of others for good or ill. These spirit forces ranged from the familial ancestors of the household through the royal dead, to the supreme being – *modimo* – located in the "far distance". The subtle yet vital force of the ancestors was to be overlooked or misunderstood by most missionaries. The Europeans all too often likened such deceased beings – *badimo* – to demons.

At the Very Edge of the Cosmos Was the Realm of the Supreme Being

Yet such "badimo" were guarantors of civil society and centralised political authority, standing in contrast to the *medimo* left unburied in the wild. The opposition between these spirit forces was critical. *At the very edge of the cosmos – beyond space and time itself – was the realm of the supreme being.* Modimo was said to be "above where the clouds float and the lightening flashes" and "in the west where the sun sets and the streams flow". This is not "heaven", but merely the inconceivable fringes of the world.

As we shall now see, when we turn from the local, pre-modern Tswana path of reason to the post-modern, local-global path that Foucault followed – he lived and worked in France and U.S., in Sweden, Poland and Germany, in Tunis and Iran over the course of his adult life – we can see a connection between if you like, the pre-modern Tswana laden world portrayed by the Comaroffs (1991), and the post-modern one portrayed by Foucault absent from the modern mind.

12.3. Intuit Local-Global Postmodern: Force of Discontinuity: N3t

12.3.1. Foucault's New Order of Things

Doubted the Possibility of Creating Totalities

The high priest of postmodernism, as we have seen, is the late Michel Foucault. For him, in the history of ideas, that is of thought in general and of the sciences in particular, the same mutation has broken up the long series formed by the progress of consciousness, or the teleology of reason, or the evolution of human thought. It has *questioned the themes of convergence and culmination; it has doubted the possibility of creating totalities.* It has led to the individualisation of different series juxtaposed upon one another, for us locally-globally overlapping and intersecting, without being able to reduce them to a linear schema.

Thus in place of the continuous chronology of reason there have appeared periods that are sometimes very brief, distinct from one another, irreducible to a single law.

These periods bear a kind of history peculiar to each one, and thereby cannot be reduced to the general model of a consciousness that acquires, progresses, and remembers. It has now become one of the basic elements of historical analysis. As such *the historian is trying to discover the limits of a process, the point of inflexion of a curve*, the boundaries of an oscillation, the threshold of a function, the instant at which a circular causality breaks down. One of the most essential features of the new postmodern approach to history, as we shall see below for Camaroffsin culture and economy, through their so-called "transient" workplaces in Africa, for Foucault in his *Archaeology of Knowledge* (Foucault 2002) then, is this *focus on the discontinuous*.

Globalisation Has Been Uniformly Thrust Upon the World

Pre-existing forms of continuity, all these syntheses that are accepted without question, must, for Foucault, remains in suspense. They must not be rejected definitively of course, but the tranquillity with which they are accepted must be disturbed; we must show that they do not come about by themselves but are always the result of a construction the rules of which must be known. In short, they require a theory, and this theory cannot be constructed unless the field of the facts of discourse are built up as such. So *globalisation, for example in this postmodern context, has been uniformly thrust upon the world, through the force of imposed capitalist circumstances, rather than naturally emerging out of the world's diversity.*

In placing yourself in whatever unities are already given, such as psychology or economics, business or management, you need to question by what right they can claim a field that specifies them in space and time; according to what laws they are formed; against the background of what contexts they stand out; and whether or not they are ultimately the surface effect of more firmly grounded unities. You accept the groupings that history suggests only to break them up and then to see whether they can be legitimately reformed.

12.3.2. Discursive Reality

Genealogy to GENE-ology

A postmodernist approach would then treat the constituent disciplines of ecology and economics, agriculture and human culture, for example for Sekem as we shall see, not as dealing with resources, connected to different aspects of reality, but as discourses, which socially construct and certify particular meaningful versions of reality. *The manager is constituted and reconstituted through historically and socially contingent discourses. Any management discipline would hence be seen as a particular historical and social mode of engagement that restricts what is thinkable, knowable and doable.* For Foucault, such so-called "genealogy", is the analysis of the conditions that make it possible for a particular discourse to develop, change and adapt. For us such a GENE-alogy involves our local original Grounding, local-global Emergent foundation, newly global emancipatory Navigation and global-local transformative Effect.

Power Resides Not in Individuals as Conscious Agents But in Discourses

In the construction and deconstruction of the taken-for-granteds that underlie a particular discipline or indeed society, including management in general, a key focus would be to analyse the socio-historical conditions that made it possible for a particular discourse to be developed and through which it might change. Moreover, *central to a postmodern analysis, as for critical theory, would be power. Such power is seen to reside not in individuals as conscious agents but in the discourses themselves.* For Foucault the exercise of power perpetually creates knowledge and, conversely, knowledge constantly induces effects of power. *The deployment of any discourse is seen as empowering those people with the power to speak while subordinating others who are the object of the knowledge and disciplines produced by the discourse.*

Research Methodology Is Part of a Power Structure

Research methodology is hence part of such a power structure, affecting the relationship between research student and supervisor, not to mention the relationship between the research subject and the people connected with it. Such an underlying power structure, in broader and much more poignant guise, underlies the relationship between fundamentalist Islam and the secular "west" in our day and age. We now turn to the Comaroff's *Theory of the South*.

12.4. Newly Global Theory of the South: Pre/Post-Modern Africa

12.4.1. Modern Core and Traditional Periphery

For Jean and John Comaroff (2012), in their more recent *Theory from the South, Western enlightenment thought has, from the first, posited itself as the wellspring of universal learning, of Science and Philosophy; concomitantly, it has regarded the non/West – variously known as the ancient world, the orient, the primitive world, the third world, the underdeveloped world, the developing world, and now the global south – primarily as a place of parochial wisdom,* of antiquarian traditions, of exotic ways ad means. Above all, of unprocessed data. This is then something that they, like we, strongly contest.

This "south", in other words for them, and in short, *is treated less as a source of knowledge than as a reservoir of raw fact: of the historical, natural and ethnographic minutiae from which Euro/modernity might fashion its testable theories and transcendent truths,* its axioms and certitudes, its premises, postulates and principles, just as it has capitalized on non-Western "raw materials" – human and physical, moral and medical, cultural and agricultural – by ostensibly adding value and refinement to them. But what if we invert that order of things? What if we subvert the epistemological scaffolding on which it is erected? *What if we posit that, in the present moment, it is the global south that affords privileged insight into the workings of the world at large?* In our own terms, what they might be sating is that "south" is providing the "grounding", as well as the "emergent" developments, for the world as a whole, upon and through which we will need to "navigate" our way in the future.

First, for the Comaroffs some background. Euro-American social theory has tended to treat modernity as if it were inseparable from the rise of Enlightenment reason. Not only is each taken to be a condition of the other's possibility, but together they are assumed to have animated a distinctively European mission to emancipate humankind from its uncivil prehistory, from a life driven by bare necessity. *Whether the Enlightenment is regarded as an epoch, as a free market, as Marx's capitalist mode of production, or as liberal humanism, the modern, as such, has its origins in the West. To the degree that, from a Western perspective, the global south is embraced by modernity at all, then, it is as an outside that requires translation, mutation, catch-up.*

European historicism therefore allows only one trajectory to non-Western societies if they are to be recognized as part of the grand human story: they must undergo a visible metamorphosis to Western capitalist modernity. More immediately though, despite decades of postcolonial critique the modernist social sciences, not excluding those of radical bent, tend still to by-pass the third world in writing the planetary history of the present. Even critical theorists take the driving engine of late capitalism to lie wholly in Euro-America.

Hyphenated in many respects, capitalist-modernity, for the Comaroffs, has realized itself, very unevenly, in the great aspirations of liberalism, via liberal democracy, the "free" market, civic rights and civil society, as well as the rule of law, the separation of the public form the private, the secular form the sacred. . But it has also *excluded* many populations from these things, especially those in colonial theaters who have been subjugated to its modes of extraction – or have been rendered disposable by virtue of having no value to extract, as always both a universal project and a host of specific, parochial emplacements. Here then, for them, is the point. *To the degree that the making of modernity has been a world-historical process, it can as well be narrated from its undersides as it can from its proclaimed centres.* But the Comaroffs seek to do more than just turn the story upside-down. What they suggest, in addition, is that *contemporary world-historical processes are disrupting received geographies of core and periphery, relocating southward – and of course eastward as well – some of the most innovative and energetic modes of producing value.* They then take Africa as their point of departure, ultimately however extending to the global order at large. Their argument is in two parts.

12.4.2. Afro/modernity, in Theory and Practice

The first argument is that modernity in the south is not adequately understood as a derivative, a callow copy, of the Euro-American "original". To the contrary, it demands to be apprehended in its own right. Modernity in Africa has a deep history, is polymorphous and mutating, partly in dialectical relationship with the global north, and partly with others of the same hemisphere.

Should then Afro/modernity be part of a universal enlightenment, of Christianity and civilization, of Shakespearean English and scientific reason – the very things presented to Africa as the epitome of Western culture? Should it choose only the good things of that civilization and discard the rest? Or should it combine the native and the alien, the traditional and the foreign, into something new and beautiful? In point of fact, for the Comaroffs, there has been a steady move from the first to the third, a process establishing similarities with something else while at the same time inventing something original. *Like its European counterpart, modernity in Africa entailed a re-genesis, a consciousness of new possibilities, and a rupture with the past, congealed into "tradition", which was in itself a modern construct.*

Sometimes the process has been strikingly self-conscious, as with the New Africa Movement in South Africa in the time of Pixley ka Isaka Seme (1905–6) who famously insisted in "*The Regeneration of Africa*", that the continent cannot be compared with Europe since it had its own genius, about to "march to the future's golden door". *Being part of a new order of things "it was entering a higher, complex existence, a unique civilization founded on precious creations of its own, creations alike spiritual, moral, humanistic and eternal".* Nor is it best labeled as an "alternative modernity", for it is, for the Comaroffs, a *vernacular*, just as Euro/modernity is a vernacular, wrought in an ongoing, geopolitically situated engagement with the unfolding history of the present. And like Euro/modernity it takes many forms.

Modernity, as such, refers to an orientation to being in the world, to a concept of the person as a self-actualizing subject, to a vision of history as a progressive, man-made construction, to an ideology of improvement through the accumulation of knowledge and technical skill, to the pursuit of justice through rational governance, to a restless impulse towards innovation. Modernization, in contrast, posits a strong normative teleology, a uni/linear trajectory toward the future – capitalist, socialist, fascists, African, whatever – two which all humanity might aspire, toward which all history ought to lead, toward which all people sought to evolve. *African modernity, as opposed to modernization, is both a singularity and a plurality that speaks to an endogenous history, one still actively being made, a history that is not running behind Euro-America, for the Comaroffs, but ahead of it.*

12.4.3. The Global South: Harbingers of Future-History

This brings them to the second argument. Contrary to the received Euro/modernist narrative of the past two centuries – which has the global south tracking behind the curve of Universal History, always in deficit, always playing catch-up, there is good reason now to think the opposite: that, given the unpredictable, underdetermined dialectic of capitalism-and-modernity in the here and now, it is the south that is often the first to feel the effects of world-historical forces, *the south in which radically new assemblages of capital and labor are taking place, thus to prefigure the future of the global north.*

While Euro-America and the south are caught up in the *same* all-embracing world-historical processes, it is in the latter that the effects of these processes tend most graphically to manifest themselves: where industrial manufacture opens up ever more cost-efficient sites for itself, where highly flexible, informal economies have long thrived. Which is why, for the Comaroffs, in the dialectics of contemporary world history, *the north appears to be "evolving" southward, the latter heralding "history-in-the-making".*

In recent decades, moreover, capital, with its stresses on flexibility, liquidity and deregulation, has yet again found untapped bounty in former colonies, where postcolonial states, anxious to garner disposable income and often in desperate need of "hard" foreign currency, bow to the tenets of *laissez-faire* at their most extreme. As a result it is increasingly the south where the practical workings of neo/liberalism are tried and tested. Today the north, of course, is now experiencing these practical workings itself as labor markets contract and employment is casualized, not to mention the ever-widening wealth gap within as well as between rich and poor communities and societies.

At the same time, same nation-states in the south, by virtue of having become economic powerhouses – India, Brazil, South Africa – evince features of the future Euro-America in other ways: for example, the seizure of the global initiative in biofuels in Brazil, the reach of the Indian auto industry in Britain, or the impact of the Hong Kong banking sector. Or, in another register, the emergence of South Africa, as a major force in the international mineral economy, as the America of Africa. Or, in yet another, in the rise of urbanism, Lagos in Nigeria has moved to the forefront of globalizing modernity.

In large part, of course, it is its undersides that are worked out first in the south, where much of the working class of the world is dispersed. Moreover, the post-colonies have remained dependent and debt-strapped, tending still to export their resources as raw materials and unskilled labor rather than an value-added commodities and competencies. Furthermore: (1) because large sectors of the populations have long worked in conditions designed to depress wages; (2) because market conditions in Africa have never been cushioned by regulation; (3) because governance has been frequently been based on kleptocrtic patronage, African polities have been especially hospitable to rapacious enterprise. It is precisely this mélange of its inherited colonial institutions and postcolonial availability to liberal development that make Ghana today, for example, a vanguard in the epoch of the market.

The US and Europe have colluded further in this by seeking to impose their future vision – infamously in the guise of structural adjustment – on Africa, Asia, Latin America, inadvertently giving early warning of what would lie in store for themselves. How was it then that the over-analysed Asian and Latin American financial crises, or the ill effects of structural adjustment in Africa, sounded no warning bells for the future of the global north? *Blinkered by our own narratives of Universal History, perhaps we have been unable to see the coming counter-revolution, the north going south.* Talk, even moral panic, about the imminent breakdown of order is to be heard in places as specific as Sweden and Denmark, and read, tellingly, in their socially conscious, creatively diagnostic crime fiction. Or at least,

Africa as imagined in Euro-America. Its reality, for the Comaroffs, is more complex. And not all darkness.

It is in fact here that their two theses converge: *first the ontological claim that Afro/modernity exists, in itself, not as a derivative of the Euro-original, meets the second assertion that, in the history of the present, the global south is running ahead of the global north,* prefiguring future-in-the-making. How then so?

12.4.4. Critical Estrangement Into Africa: Mapping the Fourfold V-Effect

Defamiliarising the Ordinary

The effort to make other – largely African – facts undermine established verities about the nature of the contemporary order of things is an enterprise that, perforce, juxtaposes social processes of different kinds, different temporalities, geographies, dimensions, riding the gaps between them. The Comaroffs identify such in terms of *critical estrangement,* what the playwright Bertold Brecht called *Verfremdung,* or the V-effect of defamiliarizing the ordinary, in fourfold guise, starting with personhood.

Firstly: On Southern Personhood, Difference and ID-ology

If the "autonomous person", firstly then, was indeed a European invention are these principles nurtured only by a relatively small fragile fraternity of freedom-loving societies, the Comaroffs ask, locked in combat with "civilizations", they say, ironically, driven by fundamentalist faiths, primordial passions, authoritarian constraints and communitarian impulses.

The enlightened individual, as both archetype and ideal-type, has served as the grounding of liberal society *ab initio,* notwithstanding the fact that, sociologically speaking, personhood within the north has varied widely, and certainly has not always conformed to this ideal type. But what of the claim that Africa, and other European elsewheres, lacked a concept of autonomous personhood? The Comaroffs then cite the case of the Southern Tswana peoples of South Africa, who have an elaborate theory about the nature of the self, including a qualified idea of "autonomous personhood", close to Durkheim's version "what makes a man a person is what he shares with other men", that is *Motho ke motho ka botho,* a person is a person by virtue of other people.

Baldly stated, by way of a "southern" example, *the Southern Tswana conception of the self that has survived into the postcolonial era seems to have foreshadowed recent shifts in Euro-American ideas of personhood.* Not only does their sense of the individual as a constant labor of becoming, of ethical self-construction, as such, call to mind the obsession with "personal growth" in various new wave movements in the north, but *it also conjures up the figure of the "entrepreneurial self" that French post-modernist philosopher Foucault associates with the rise of neo-liberalism: the self who has his own capital, while at the same time transcending it.*

Moreover, such can be aligned with the displacement from public life of ideology, the –ology of the Idea, by the ID-ology of communities of faith and culture.

Secondly: Taking up the Spaces Left by the Economic Deficit

The implications of economic liberation, secondly in fact, including the escalating mobility of people in search of incomes, the evolution of free-trade agreements, the growth of the global electronic commons, and the workings of supranational institutions – everywhere is altering the way in which Euro/modernist polities manage their sovereign integrity. *Like southern post-colonies, whose frontiers were breached and buttressed under the imperatives of structural adjustment, the north too is now faced with the paradox of frontiers at once open and closed.* Therein now, just as hitherto for example in South Africa, antipathy toward foreigners tends to flare into full-blooded xenophobia, fuelled by adverse economic conditions, especially rising unemployment. We may be forgiven then for thinking that the colonial and post-colonial societies of the south were not so much historical inversions of the northern metropole as templates of what, in a post-modern world, the north would become.

But what of the political *interiors* of the Euro/modernist nation-state, the public sphere so jealously protected by its nationalist citizens, especially in post-colonial and post-Soviet societies? In point of fact, *a very thin idea of "government by the people", one largely measured by the presence or absence of national elections, was being exported to the non-Western world*, often coercively, by the USA and its allies; freedom, went the mantra, inheres above all in the right to choose – one party or another, as per "multi-party democracy". It was accompanied by the equally insistent imposition of free market capitalism.

The global south in general, Africa in particular, is often said to be intrinsically – culturally or geographically – averse to such democracy. The sheer number of African dictatorships, kleptocracies, and "failed states" is the evidence given of such. Democracy, in fact, has now become a kind of fetish, for the Comaroffs, in much of the south. It is widely regarded, as it were, as an enchanted force, one that, if only it could be fully domesticated, not hijacked by those who seek to empower and enrich themselves, might solve real problems in the world.

What has indeed happened in Africa, epitomized by the Botswana case with which they are very familiar, *appears to have anticipated a gathering sense of discontent throughout Europe and America with its own democracies.* In fact, with the spread of neo-liberalism deep into the capillaries of public life, political parties have converged ideologically, with little of real principle to separate them. In addition, growing numbers of the "poor whites", and racially marked populations, feel themselves excluded from "northern" public life.

So everyday politics has migrated elsewhere. As in Botswana, with their "freedom squares", *African versions of "democracy" find their voice in civil society (witness recently Tahir Square in Egypt) to take up the space left by the democratic deficit.* Thus we see the assertive rise, or return, of the town hall meeting, the talk radio, faith-based associations and grassroots organizations. Alongside and behind them has lain the liberalization of the means of communication, and social technologies which create their own commons, and communities of consciousness.

Thirdly: The Commonweal in Recognition of Historic Rights

Meanwhile thirdly, truth commissions and insurgent law-fare may draw on jurisprudence and jurisdictions developed in Euro-America, but they have taken their modern shape, for the Comaroffs, in antipodean sites, first in Latin America and later in South Africa – thence to return to the north. The former Yugoslavia held a truth commission in 2002, for instance, as did Germany a decade earlier in relation to the former East. The latest is in Canada where one was convened to address the grievances of First People. In 1992 Pope Paul even apologized to Galileo for the churlish reaction of the Church to his insistence that the earth was not at the centre of the universe.

As nationhood becomes more heterodox in Euro/America, *as the politics of identity gather momentum, claims against the commonweal in recognition of historic rights denied, or violations suffered hitherto, challenge the sovereign narratives there too.*

Fourthly: Economics of Exclusion to the Politics of Life

Fourthly and finally, the avid espousal of free markets and private enterprise by those charged with bringing the post-colony into step with the new world may not have been inevitable. But few were able to imagine a national economy that did not accommodate itself to the neo-liberal turn. As a result, *the transition to democracy was accompanied by intensive downsizing, de-regulation, the casualization of labor, and with it, the steady disappearance of wage employment in its older forms – creating a void* into which rushed migrants from across the continent, many of them ready to toil at a deep discount.

Speculation of all kinds, at the same time, became rife, and so, too, was the swelling sense that one country or another had been opened up to malign forces, forces that yielded money without material effort. A rash of fraudulent get-rich schemes aimed at the affluent and the abject alike. Here was Marx's dread image of the ultimate achievement of capitalism: production without human workers, the final alienation, as it were, of the species being. Such jobless growth, as evidenced in the south, for example in South Africa or in Nigeria, anticipated fears in the north of the growing gap between the dazzling feats of finance and the "real" economy; of unrestrained speculation in domains formerly associated with sober investment (banks, mutual funds, pension schemes).

At issue was the credibility of a credo that deduced people across the planet into believing that they had entered an era when fortunes, fame and virtue might be made by gaming with the equity of everyday life, with dwellings, bodies, identities, commodities. All of these could be considered as assets, equipping even the most humble to think of themselves as entrepreneurs. In the last decades of the 20th century what was once pariah profiteering – unfettered speculation, gambling, retailing contagious assets – was deemed legitimate, even esteemed enterprise. Then the implosion hit. Yet at the same time, the limits of bare life, for the Comaroffs, breed their own positive possibilities, more visible in the south than in the north. This is illustrated by such citizen's movements as the Landless Workers' Movement in Brazil, the Urban Poor Consortium in Indonesia, even political parties like Evo Moraes' *Movemento al Soalismo*.

At the same time, AIDS had made visible the stark distinction between privilege and vulnerability that divide and unite the contemporary global order; distinctions, some would say, on which the order rests. In South Africa for example, AIDS policies, famously typified by the Treatment Action Campaign, made common cause with grassroots movements fighting for basic services, education and social equality. Here *collective action centred upon that Hannah Arendt has called "the condition of life itself". Such a popular politics of life drew on a diverse global archive, from Marx, Gandhi and Fanon, through the Book of Revelations, Black Consciousness, and the Zapatistas, to born-again faiths and human rights campaigns*.

As the contemporary capitalist world order – at once global and local and everything in between – catches all and sundry in its web, as its peripheries become vanguard and its centres mimic its peripheries, so the world is turned upside down. But it is often in quite perverse, counter-revolutionary ways. *For better and worse, the south seems to be tracking as the front end of history, there to challenge as to understand the world from its vantage, to make it*, as the South African Ministry of Higher Education has said, *an "active producer of social theory"*.

We now turn finally to the Keynotes of African pre/post-modernism.

12.5. Global-Local Active Keynotes/Pre-Post Modern Africa: N3a

12.5.1. Pursue Multiple Discourses

A "modern" approach to research and innovation, in conventionally, critical rational guise, sees useful knowledge as a hypothesis shaped (critical rational) or a mirror reflection (empirical) of things in the world. A postmodernist one, in contrast, involves constructing specific accounts of the world, through language and archive, discourse and culture, that form complex representations which have cultural significance. Reality then is not a solid, monolithic and self-contained but a fluid, unfolding discursive process, an "open universe", continually affected and moulded by a diversity of actions and beliefs. It is possibility that counts rather than fact.

You cannot regard reality as a removed spectator against a fixed object; rather you are always and necessarily engaged in reality's multiplicity of forms and perspectives, thereby at once transforming them while being transformed yourself.

In the Sekem case, for Abouleish, such multiple discourses spanned Egyptian, Islamic and anthroposophical realities altogether.

Table 12.5.1. *African Pre-Postmodernism – Keynotes*

Pursue multiple Discourses.
Focus on Meanings and African workplaces as multiple and shifting.
You socially construct Meaning in Premodern, Modern or Postmodern Guise
Review History as transformative.

12.5.2. Focus on Meanings and Workplaces as Multiple and Shifting

For the post-modernist, if not for the pre-modern Tswana or transient workplace as we have seen, point language is organized into discourses, or interpretative repertoires, thereby having an immense power to shape the way that people behave in the world. Specifically Foucault refers to the fact that, instead of studying the mind as if it were outside language, discourse analysts study spoken and written texts – that is conversations, debates, and discussions – where images of the mind are produced and transformed. Such a "discourse analysis" offers a social account of subjectivity by attending to the linguistic sources by which the socio-political, the organizational and managerial, realms, are produced and reproduced.

The overall implication is that meanings are multiple and shifting, rather than unitary and fixed, and the same applies, in Africa, to thereby, for the likes of Camaroffs, transient workplaces. At the same time such postmodernism or post-structural research involves a commitment to the socially constructed nature of reality; and a good way to examine such is through "discourse analysis". Indeed, conventional survey methods are flawed because they do not take into account the true variability of human thought and action, instead concentrating on the uniform, rational and classifiable. Finally, whereas modern attitudinal research sees language as an essentially colourless, transparent medium, unproblematically describing some underlying "real" entity, discourse analysis takes language, again like the workplace, as actively constructing, and constructed of, versions of the social world.

12.5.3. You Socially Construct Meaning in Premodern/ Postmodern Guise

For discourse analysts, all forms of social reality have a peculiarly human and socially constructed nature. They share an assumption that "knowledge of" can never be an objective fact, as all knowledge is produced, bounded and sustained by human beings and their constructions. This postmodernist constructivist and historicist commitment, for us in Africa also linking the pre-modern with the postmodern, thereby transcending the modern, leads to a heightened emphasis on the means through which human meanings and experience are manufactured, that is through discourses. Such "discourse" refers not only to observable linguistic activities, but also to the world of human signs, symbols, activities, texts that together comprise a particular worldview.

12.5.4. Review History as Transformative

An "archive" can be both a vehicle for research and also a stimulus for transformation, as, for example, in the new South Africa, in the 1990s. For the French-Algerian postmodernist and so-called "deconstructionist" philosopher, Jacques Derrida (2017):

> The archive draws us forward in taking us back. Every beginning gathers energies from antecedent endings. All forgetting of the past is also a forgetting of the future. A focus on history as narrative and history writing as a charged political act has made the thinking about archives no longer the pedestrian pre-occupation of flat-footed archivists. The archive is not a library of events but a system of evocations.

The Egyptian archive, for Sekem as such, reached back to the ancient idea of *maat*, mediated by Islam and as the middle way, onto the economics of love which balanced together nature and culture, society and economy in a new of life.

12.6. Conclusion

12.6.1. Epochal Transition

For American contemporary philosopher Richard Tarnas (2010), two antithetical impulses can thus be discerned in the contemporary intellectual situation, one pressing for a radical deconstruction and unmasking – of knowledge, beliefs, worldviews – and the other for a radical integration and reconciliation. The intellectual question, that looms over our time is whether it is indeed the entropic prelude to some kind of apocalyptic denouement of history; or whether it represents an epochal transition to another era altogether, bringing a new form of civilization and a new world view with principles and ideals fundamentally different from those that have impelled the modern world through its dramatic trajectory. It is our role, as social researchers and innovators in such a postmodern/pre-modern/transmodern and also value-laden context, to help promote such an epochal transition.

Grounding and Origination in Grounded Theory on the Path of Reason

We start out then with grounded theory, with:

- A storyline – a descriptive story about core phenomenon under study
- Describing and then conceptualising – uncovering the core category.

- Relating subsidiary categories around the core category of overall story
- Revisiting the story, re-arranging categories, subcategories accordingly.

Emergent Foundation Is Ezemezu on the Path of African Philosophy and Reason

Thereafter, in turning to an African path of professional philosophy and reason

- Empirical Science has nothing absolute about it.
- You Derive Theories from tentative conjectures built on Ezumezu
- Formulate an overall Deductive Strategy based on African Philosophy
- Strong Theory drives out the Weak – Towards an Integrative African Society

Emancipatory Navigation via Transient Workplaces on the Path of African Reason

Therafter, and now moving onto a pre-modern/post-modern path of African reason you, individually and collectively:

- Pursue Multiple Discourses via Theory from the South
- Focus on Meanings and African workplaces as multiple and shifting
- You socially construct Meaning in Premodern, Modern or Postmodern Guise
- Review History as transformative.

Pre-Post Modernism Out of Africa: N2fita

In concluding this chapter on post modernism in north African guise, metaphorically in the "north" rather than literally, we have connected with the pre-modern world of both the Tswana and the Vashona in Southern Africa, drawing on the so called *go dira*, to give us a local feel, and thereafter on the substantive indigenous knowledge underlying a post-modern *transient workplace*. Needless to say such a local-global interchange between pre and post-modern is easier said than done, in fact all too seldom done. Indeed, it is more likely to be anthropologists who make such links, as the Comaroffs and have done.

To that extent, as we shall see in the next chapter, the link between maat, and hermeticism from ancient Egypt, and the economics of love, in modern Sekem, remains a tenuous one.

Table 12.6.3. *Go Dira to Pre/Post Modern/Maat to Net of Life: N3fita*

Feeling Local	Intuiting Local-Global	Thinking Newly Global	Acting Global-Local
Go Dira	Post Modernism	Theory from The South	Pursue Pre-Post Modern Meaning

University to Communiversity/Capitalism to Communitalism

Further to such, and penultimately on the path of reason, turning hereafter to socio-technical design, altogether in African guise, we seek to establish a research academy with a view to aligning such with a socio-economic laboratory (on the path of realisation), building on a prior learning community (on the relational path), also aligned with transformation journeys (on the path of renewal) overall communiversity wise. All of such can institutionally serve to pursue our "northern" African cause, and develop the rational arm of communitalism, underpinned by Ezemezu and lodged in transient workplaces, to promote knowledge creation, micro-wise, and a knowledge based social economy, macro-wise.

We now turn from pre/post-modernism, out of Africa, to socio-technical design, thereby feeling local, intuiting local-global, thinking newly globally and finally acting globally-locally, in such a guise, focused now also geographically on the north of the African continent, that is in Egypt, hitherto cross-roads of civilisations.

12.7. References

Abouleish I (2005) *Sekem: A Sustainable Community on the Desert.* Edinburgh. Floris Publications

Appiah KA (1992) *In My Father's House: Africa in the Philosophy of Culture.* Oxford. Oxford University Press

Comaroff J and Comaroff JL (2012) *Theory from the South: Or, How Euro-America Is Evolving Toward Africa.* London: Routledge.

Comaroff John and Jean (1991) *Of Revelation and Revolution – Christianity, Colonialism & Consciousness in South Africa.* Chicago. University of Chicago Press

Derrida J (2017) *Archive Fever: A Freudian Impression,* Chicago. Chicago University Press

Drucker P (2017) *The Age of Discontinuity: Guidelines to Our Changing Society.* 2nd Edition, Abingdon. Routledge

Foucault M (2002) *The Archaeology of Knowledge.* Abingdon. Routledge Classics

Handy C (1995) *The Age of Unreason: New Thinking for a New World.* New York. Random House Business

Lessem R, Adodo A and Bradley T (2019) *The Idea of the Communiversity: Releasing the Natural, Cultural, Technological, and Economic Genus of Societies.* Manchester. Beacon Academic.

Tarnas R (2010) *Passion of the Western Mind: Understanding the Ideas That Have Changed our Worldview.* New York. Pimlico

Chapter 13 From Postmodernism to African Integral Design. Towards an Integral Enterprise

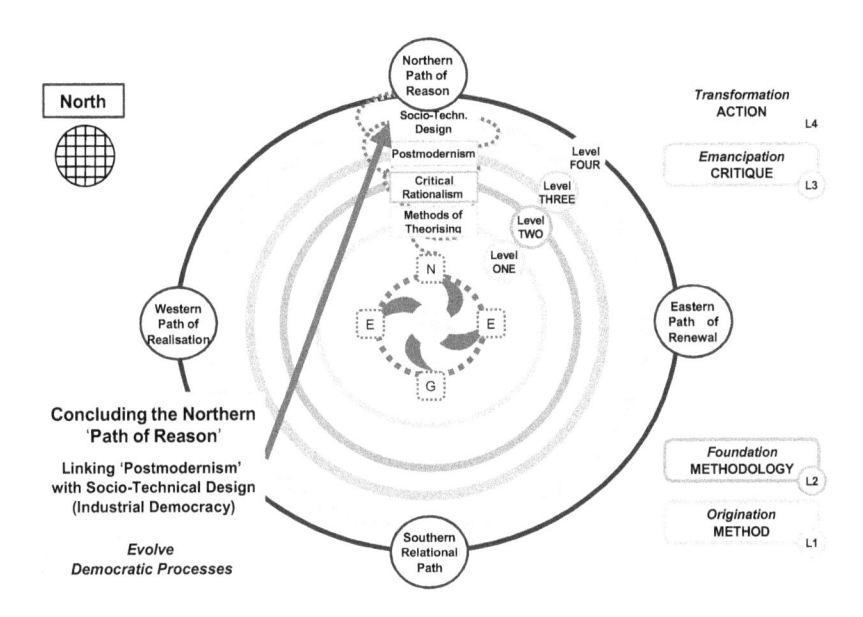

Figure 13.1: *Overview Chapter 13 – Level 4 / North*

The five elements, which make up five clans, together allow an entire village to form a cosmological wheel. The village can then balance itself by keeping the various elements in balance, that being its principal task. Such an elemental wheel exists in each person, moreover, just as it is present in each clan and community. Each person needs to keep the water of reconciliation flowing within the self, in order to calm the inner fires and live in harmony with others. Each person needs to nourish the ancestral fire within, so that one stays in touch with one's dreams and visions. Each person needs to be grounded in the earth, to be able to become a source of nourishment to the community. Each person needs to remember the knowledge stores in one's bones – to live out one's own unique genius. And each person needs to be real, as nature is real, keeping in touch with a sense of mystery and wonder, and helping to preserve the integrity of the natural world. To be out of balance in any of these areas is to invite sickness to come to dwell within.

Patrice Some (2003) *The Healing Wisdom of Africa:*
   Finding Life Purpose through Healing, Ritual and Community

Summary: African Socio-Technical Design

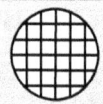

- Socio-Technical Design is the culmination of our northern research path of reason. It builds progressively on methods of theorising, critical rationalism and postmodernism, albeit altogether in now explicitly *south-north* African guise.

- The originators of such socio-technical design, from Europe and America, were Kurt Lewin and John Dewey, the one a social scientist and a refugee from Nazi Germany, the other an educator and philosopher, with a passion for democracy in both educational and political institutions, both with an overall leaning towards action oriented research.

- *Feeling local* in Africa, we immerse ourselves in the four-world cosmology of the Dogon and the Ancient Egyptian peoples, also aligned with the "four elements" – earth, water, air and fire – as embodied in a wide range of African cosmologies centred in the heling wisdom of Africa

- Locally globally we trace a path from Africa and MENA to Europe, whereby, grounded in *maat* and in Egyptian-Greek *hermeticism* we turn its their further Asian-European also *Islamic* evolution (the middle way) through *theosophy* and ultimately *anthroposophy*

- Newly globally, theoretically via Trans4m and its "four worlds" of economics and enterprise, underpinned by nature and culture, together with Sekem, practically, such an integral four world orientation is evolved out of anthroposophy's threefolding

- Our integral, *south-north* African transformative effect, evolved out of socio-technical design, is indeed an action research approach, which is both socio-politically and techno-economically integral and transformative. Why? Because it involves co-researchers working together, within democratic institutions, as fellow subjects rather than as researcher/subject and researched/object.

- It is integral insofar as the problem solving orientation, the pursuit of social betterment, altogether as a friendly outsider, is further evolved through our re-GENE-rative approach that builds on local grounding, communally, local-global emergence, transculturally, emancipatory, newly global navigation, scientifically, and transformative, global-local economic effect, our African keynotes.

13.1. Orientation to African Socio-Technical Design

13.1.1. Integral Design and the Economics of Love

We now turn to the final global-local stage of the northern research path of reason, via integral design, and innovative path, via the so called economic of love, altogether embodied in the evolution of Sekem in Egypt. What then, and overall for Ibrahim Abouleish (2005), writing on such in 2005, is our relationship with the natural, cultural, social and economic realms?

- We build our cultural, social and economic activities to invigorate each other
- We intend to restore the earth through implementing and developing biodynamic agriculture
- We want to provide products and services of the highest standards to meet the needs of the consumer

The intertwined natural and economic realms of activity within Sekem's group of companies begins on a practical level by healing the soil through the application of biodynamic farming methods. Through this method it has raw material at our disposal and is able to develop and manufacture natural medicine and a wide range of other products, adhering to the highest possible quality standards, which conform to the true needs of our consumers. In partnership with our friends and colleague in Europe and its local partners in trade, it strives to market its products, employing what it calls the "Economics of Love". In the long term we want to neutralize capital. This would mean that everything belonging to Sekem is not private property, but put into the services of Sekem. For this purpose we will establish a foundation into which we can transfer all Sekem's productions.

Table 13.1.1. <u>North African Social Research and Innovation: Path of Reason: N4</u> Grounded Theory to SOCIO-TECHNICAL DESIGN/Sekem to Economics of Love Socio-Technical/Integral Design

Northern Grounding Method and Origination	Northern Emergent Methodology S Foundation	Northern Navigational Critique and Emancipation	Northern Effective Action and Transformation
Grounded Theory (N1)	Critical Rationalism (N2)	Post Modernism (N3)	Integral Design (N4)
Sekem (N1)	Integrativity (N2)	Transient Workspaces (N3)	Economics of Love (N4)

Some seventeen years later this mission, of establishing a foundation, has indeed been accomplished. For us then, in pursuing our northern African path of research and innovation, we seek to turn, accumulatively, from Sekem and integrativity to transient work spaces and, ultimately, towards the integral design of the economics of love.

13.1.2. Building up Towards the African South-North

On the northern research path of African reason, from grounded theory to socio-technical design, now altogether to be reinforced by transformative effect of the path of innovation, you have now progressed through methods of theorising onto what we have termed "integral design", underlying, in the Sekem case – further elaborated in our third Sekem case story that follows this chapter – as we shall see, the economics of love. Such socio-technical design is an overall manifestation of action research, potentially though not necessarily also incorporating industrial democracy. Industrial democracy, or the communal like – in the Sekem case a Social Development Centre – promotes reflection about *designing* institutional *processes* that redefine the relationship between associated, learners and researchers (our learning community) towards a *greater degree of mutuality*.

Once again, though, one path overlaps to some extent with the others. In this culminating stage of the research path of reason, there is something of an overlap between realisability (west) and reasonability (north), as well as relationality (south) and renewal (east). In fact the two founding fathers of action research in general and of socio-technical design in particular were such typically rounded "north-western" characters. Between them, as such, Kurt Lewin and John Dewey, whom we already met in Chapter 10, spanned philosophy and psychology, biology and education. Moreover, when it comes to the path of African innovation, reasonwise, we shall here draw, geographically, from both South and also North Africa, for Value Sharing and the Economics of Love, in related turn.

13.1.2. Founders of Action Research in Euro-American Guise: Lewin and Dewey

Lewin's Experiential Learning, Group Dynamics and Action Research

Kurt Lewin's work had a profound impact on social psychology as well as on experiential learning, group dynamics and action research. He was born in 1890 in Prussia (now part of Poland) as one of four children in a middle class Jewish family. In 1909 Kurt Lewin entered the University of Freiburg to study medicine. He then transferred to the University of Munich to study biology. Around this time he became involved in the socialist movement. His particular concerns appear to have been the combating of anti-semitism, the democratization of German institutions, and the need to improve the position of women. Along with other students he organized and taught an adult education program for working class women and men. He was also, by implication, educationally and vocationally, concerned with healing, originally medically and subsequently socially.

His doctorate was undertaken at the University of Berlin where he developed an interest in the philosophy of science and encountered "gestalt psychology". In 1921 Kurt Lewin joined the Psychological Institute of the University of Berlin – where he was to lecture and offer seminars in both philosophy and psychology. His work became known in America and in 1930 when he was invited to spend six months as a visiting professor at Stanford. With the political position worsening in Germany, he and his family settled 1933 in the USA. Kurt Lewin was first to work at the Cornell School of Home Economics, and then at the University of Iowa (this was also the year when his (Lewin 2008) first collection of papers in English *A Dynamic Theory of Personality* was published).

The University of Iowa remained Kurt Lewin's base until 1944. There he continued to develop his interest in social processes. He also became involved in various applied research initiatives linked to the war effort. These included exploring the morale of the fighting troops, the psychological backdrop to warfare, and reorienting food consumption away from foods in short supply. His social commitments were also still strong – and he was much in demand as a speaker on minority and inter-group relations. He wanted to establish a centre to research group dynamics – and in 1944 this dream was realised with the founding of the Research Centre for Group Dynamics at MIT.

At the same time Kurt Lewin was also engaged in a project for the American Jewish Congress in New York – the Commission of Community Interrelations. It made use of Lewin's model of action research (research directed towards the solving of social problems) in a number of significant studies into religious and racial prejudice. It was also out of some of this work in 1946 with community leaders and group facilitators that the notion of "T" (for sensitivity) groups emerged. He and his associates were able to get funding from the Office of Naval Research to set up the National Training Laboratories in 1947 in Bethel, Maine. However, Lewin died of a heart attack in 1947, before the Laboratories were established.

John Dewey: Reflection and Experience, Community and Democracy

John Dewey (2008), the American philosopher on democracy and education, whose long life overlapped with that of Lewin, has made, arguably, the most significant contribution to the development of educational thinking in the 20th century. *Dewey's philosophical pragmatism, concern with interaction, reflection and experience, and interest in community and democracy,* were brought together to form a highly suggestive educative form. In many respects his work cannot be easily slotted into any one of the curriculum traditions that have dominated North American and UK schooling traditions over the last century.

John Dewey's significance for informal educators lies in a number of areas. First, his belief that education must engage with and enlarge experience has continued to be a significant strand in informal education practice. Second, and linked to this, Dewey's exploration of thinking and reflection – and the associated role of educators – has continued to be an inspiration.

We can see it at work, for example, in the models developed by e.g. Kurt Lewin and the organizational psychologist Donald Schön (1991) anticipating socio-technical design, at MIT. Third, his concern with interaction and environments for learning provides a continuing framework for practice. Last, his passion for democracy, for educating so that all may share in a common life, provides a strong rationale for practice in the settings in which informal educators work.

13.1.3. Kolb's Experiential Learning

Indeed, again based at MIT, David Kolb built on Schon's, and on Dewey's, prior work, also strongly inspired by C.G. Jung, but also by the Swiss developmental psychologist and philosopher Jean Piaget and the American psychologist Carl Rogers, one of the founders of humanistic psychology. Furthermore, the experimental orientation of Kolb's approach to learning was heavily influenced by the abovementioned fathers of Action Research, John Dewey and Kurt Lewin.

Table 13.1.3. *Kolb's Learning Stages* Compared with Jung's Psychological Types and the Gene-ius Rhythm of Integral Research and Innovation

Kolb's Learning Stages	The Psychological Types of Jung	The GENE-ius of Integral Research
① *Concrete Experience* (CE)	Feeling	Grounding
② *Reflective Observation (RO): Reflection on that Experience*	Intuiting	Emerging
③ *Abstract Conceptualisation (AC): Formation of abstract Concepts based on Experience*	Thinking	Navigating
④ *Active Experimentation (AE): Testing of new Concepts*	Sensing	Effecting

Kolb's model works on two levels, as he (1983) explains in *Experiential Learning*. The first level is represented by the learning cycle that includes four learning stages that, ideally, progressively build on each other. The Table above (in italics on the left hand side) introduces each of them – and illustrates also the corresponding steps in Jung's typology and in our own re-GENE-rative process.

Kolb argued that his learning stages are to be seen in circular or even spiralling form. The learner is supposed to engage with the full circle of experiencing (G), reflecting (E), thinking (N), and acting (E). Concrete experiences lead to observations and reflections. These reflections are then assimilated and translated into abstract concepts, which then inform a person's action, where the person actively tests and experiments. This fourth and final step, in turn, enables the creation of new experiences, which makes the cycle start all over and turns it into a spiral.

Indeed, and as we shall see, when we come to "feeling local" in Africa, his experiential learning model builds on primordial wisdom that has come before. Moreover, as we shall see, in turning to Egypt in North Africa to pursue the path of African reason, we shall build purposefully on prior feeling and intuition. This then is a North that builds on the prior East and South. We now retrace Egyptian steps.

13.2. Feel Local: African Path to Reason/Maat: N4f

13.2.1. Dogon to Egyptian Cosmology: Recognizing Genius

Grounded in Maat, *Emergent* Ahau, *Navigating via* Teni, *Effective* Tematu

For cosmologist Laird Scranton (2017), as first intimated above in Chapter 10, a concept of great importance to the earliest religions is the idea of the cardinal points of the Earth – south, east, north and west – which can be seen, for example, in the Great Pyramid of Egypt. For English Egyptologist Wallis Budge (1985) moreover, early last century, in his *Legends of the Egyptian Gods*, we find the ancient Egyptian equivalent of the creation of matter, known as "laying the foundations". As such, again duly aligned with our re-GENE-ration (Grounding to Effect), and the constituents of our communiversity (Learning Community to Socio-economic Laboratory):

- firstly the hieroglyphic counterpart of the Dogon word *bummo*, the act of conception, is *bu maa*, a synonym for **maat**, based on the roots word *maa*, which means to "perceive" – our **Grounding**: *learning community*
- secondly, the Egyptian counterpart of the Dogon *yala* is *ahau*, which means "delineation of posts or boundaries" – our **Emergence**: *trans4mation journey*
- thirdly, the Dogon *tonu*, an "approximation of what is to be created" is the Egyptian *teni*, meaning "to estimate" – our **Navigation**: *research academy*
- finally, the Dogon creational stage, *toy*, is *tematu*, which means in ancient Egyptian "complete", the same notion as the God Atum (to be complete), which for us is transformative **Effect**: *integral laboratory.*

Moreover, and as indicated at the outset of the chapter by Burkina Faso born sage, Malidoma Patrice Some, such a fourfold design, indeed even more pervasively lodged worlds-wide (see our Chapter 2 on integral cosmology), can be found in most African cultures, centred cosmologically in the healing wisdom of Africa, indeed for us anticipating Sekem, thereby healing the earth. We now turn specifically to Egypt.

Grounded in Southern Kemet

In fact the name *Egypt* was coined by Greek colonists in the 4th century CE, and it is a corruption of the name *Koptos*, itself a corruption of *Gebtu*. This was the name of the ancient area in the south of the country, probably existing as long ago as 3000 BCE. The name that was most commonly used by the ancient Egyptians themselves, however, was *Kemet*, whereby *the name, meaning "Blackness", stems from the inhabitants themselves, from the color of their skin.*

Thanks then to the precious cargo of knowledge *these Black settlers brought with them into the Nile Valley around 5000 BCE – astronomy, timekeeping, husbandry and perhaps even stone building.* For Rice then within a few centuries of their arrival, the place began to develop and flourish and eventually became a country with the most enlightened and creative civilization the world had ever known: the country we now call Egypt. As such the grounds of their learning were as much communal as they were individual, whether in relation to science, agriculture or construction.

13.2.2. Energy Patterns Out of Egypt in Africa

One Becomes Four

In fact rather than "polytheism" the religious outlook of the ancient world, according to Oxford philosopher and cultural historian Jeremy Naydler (2009), is better described as *henotheism*, "heno" meaning one in Greek. The henotheistic orientation is one in which the divine is conceived of as being fundamentally a unity, but a unity that reveals itself in a multiplicity of forms. *In the Heliopolitan creation myth*, upon which we shall elaborate below, *the original divine unity is referred to as Nun, visualised as a vast and infinite ocean within which every possibility of existence is contained, but in a state of potentiality.*

As such then, as the life-potential of Nun (One) is activated, something solid appears in the midst of the ocean of potentiality, and this is Atum (Two). Atum then comes into being out of the non-being of Nun and, in the very act of Atum's becoming, a third principle arises – Khepfer, the Becoming one. The completion of this first phase of Nun's self-manifestation is the unfolding of the light in the darkness of the infinite waters, imaged as the appearance of a "light-bird", which symbolizes the fourth aspect of Nun's self-unfoldment: Ra (Four). In this manner the *One "becomes" Four,* that is *Nun-Atum-Kheprer-Ra,* also reflected, as we shall see, in our integral worlds.

Gods, Nature and the Psyche

The gods moreover were experienced in and through nature this way: not as identified with natural phenomena but rather as underlying energy-patterns that a range of natural phenomena might express through their characteristic forms of modes of behaviour. Instead of regarding these inner experiences as belonging to oneself, the ancient attitude was that each human soul participated in a "psychic world" common to all. This indeed resonates with Swiss psychoanalyst Carl Jung's (1991) notion of a collective unconscious. We now turn, more concertedly, to the ancient Egyptian metaphysical, alongside its physical, landscape.

East and West, North and South

In ancient Egypt, for Naydler then, one is constantly impressed by the balance and interplay of the opposites: life and death, abundance and barrenness, light and dark, day and night, silence and solitude. Their landscape teaches the metaphysics of the equilibrium of the opposing principles. As such, the directions of east and west, north and south are never in doubt. Through the whole span of the Nile valley there is *an almost unbroken constancy in the northward flow of the river.*

This physical division of the country by the Great River is given symbolic meaning by the cosmic and divine event of *the daily birth of Ra in the **east***, his journey across the heavenly Nile (of which the earthly Nile is but an image), *and his senescence and descent into the realm of the dead beyond the desert cliffs of the **west***. East and west are therefore not just physical directions but also mythical and metaphysical orientations. The east has to be the side of rebirth, of new life, for every morning the whole country turns east as it awakens to the enlivening rays of the newborn sun.

But just as the country is divided into easterly and westerly realms, as much mythological and geographical, so it is also divided between the ***north***ern, low-lying expanse of the Delta, and the narrow Nile valley to the ***south***. Looking *southward,* one can have the sense of g*azing into another mysterious, metaphysical zone,* where geography again blends into mythography.

We now turn from ancient Egypt to the modern world, ultimately onto Sekem in modern Egypt, but first we connect with the local-global maat, hermeticism, Islam and anthroposophy on which Sekem, implicitly if not explicitly, drew.

13.3. Intuit Local-Global: Maat/Islam/Anthroposophy/EoL: N41

13.3.1. Local to Local/Global: Out of Maat – Truth, Justice and Balance

The Egypt Code

In his renowned if controversial book *The Egypt Code,* Egyptian born Belgian engineer and prolific author Robert Bauval (2007) proposed that the whole of Egypt has been developed as a kind of "kingdom of heaven" that was meant to function in harmony with the cycles and changes in the sky, including the four seasons and the four winds, like our "four worlds". Egypt thus became a cosmic land governed by cosmic law – a sort of astrological ten commandments – inscribed not on stone tablets but in the sky, as *maat,* for us as for Sekem, integral, as a balancing force.

Interestingly, moreover, "maat" was personified as a woman, a goddess with wings outstretched, wearing on her head "the feather of truth". *Egyptologists thereby define maat as being "truth, justice and balance"*. Bauval and his co-author, Egyptian born engineer author and politician Ahmed Osman (2002), in a subsequent book on *The Soul of Egypt* would also add that "maat" was the cosmic instrument by which all things serving the well-being of Egypt were regulated and maintained as they had been at the moment of creation.

From Maat to Islam as Middle Way

In Islam moreover, modern Egypt today being predominantly a Muslim country, the most significant indicator of man's nobility, besides righteousness, for leading Pakistani based, UK based Muslim public intellectual Ziauddin Sardar (1987), in his book on *The Future of Muslim Civilisation*, is the use of *moderation and balance* in his material dealings, reasoned pursuits and spiritual quests. It is by virtue of moderation that *order, proportions, refinement and beauty* are created. Sad to say, as we can see in and around the Islamic *umma* today, this potential is sedlom realised, through the fact that at the time of writing (December, 2023) the COP 28 talks are being hosted in Dubai, is a good sign.

These then are the principles that Islam, in prospect if not necessarily in reality, seeks to propagate in its synthesis of three basic aspects of civilization: materialism (pragmatism), rationalism, and mysticism (holism). By achieving an *organic synthesis* of these aspects, Islam, for Sardar, presents a composite picture of what human civilization ought to be. The fact that such an intrinsic Islamic orientation is all too seldom born out in practice may indeed be because the link, as in this Egyptian case, for example, between indigenous maat and exogenous Islam is seldom coherently made, in theory or in practice, nor indeed with the contemporary anthroposophy that follows, as we shall see in prospect.

13.3.2. Marriage of the Occident and the Orient

Maat, Islam and Anthroposophy

We now turn, locally globally, from Africa and MENA (Middle East and North Africa) to Europe, Egypt historically as such being cross-roads of civilisations. For founder of Sekem in Egypt, Ibrahim Abouleish, whom we have already met (see Chapter 8) while working still as an engineering and pharmacological researcher in Austria, on the eve of departure for Egypt, he (1987) declared:

> For my soul Austria was like a spiritual childhood garden. Now I hope the souls of Egyptian people can be revitalised by a garden in the desert. After establishing a farm as a healthy physical basis for soul and spiritual development, I will set up further things, following the example of human development: a kindergarten, a high school. vocational education, a hospital and various cultural institutions. My goal is the development of humans in a comprehensive sense. I want to pass on this richness of nature and spirit to Egypt, to sow the seeds I have been given.

More specifically moreover, for the Austrian polymath, and originator of anthroposophy, Rudolph Steiner (Shepherd 1954) whose thought and practice Abouleish and Sekem would subsequently closely follow:

> In acquiring higher consciousness man discovers that he is a fourfold being. In addition to the material substance of the physical body, he possesses three other elements of being, all inter-penetrating each other and the physical body, and each of them functioning according to the laws of its own level of existence.
>
> Alongside firstly the **physical** body, that which gives life and powers of growth, are secondly the **etheric**, formative forces. That which thirdly gives him consciousness and the capacity for feeling, also imposing control on the etheric life-forces is the **astral** body. Finally, at the centre of all is the immortal core of his being, his **ego**.
>
> It is only possible to advance to this ultimate stage of higher knowledge, that of intuition, after special moral preparation. The most essential requirement therein is one of complete humility and a sense of reverence toward the whole world of reality, and particularly towards one's fellow human beings.

So how then does one, indigenous *Maat* and the other, exogenous *anthroposophy*, follow one from the other, with *Islam*, if you like, lodged as middle way in between?

Hermeticism, Theosophy, and Anthroposophy

In Pursuit of the Middle Way: Between Poverty and Egyptology

For Bauval and Osman then, as for now Ibrahim's son, Helmy Abouleish, as current CEO of Sekem, taking forward his father's legacy together with Sekem others, Egypt today has a second chance to fulfil its destiny and hopefully find *maat* again, anew, that is through now *The Economics of Love*.

As such, *Egyptians need to be reminded of their ancestral origins rooted in its black and fertile "Kemet" soil,* for us its natural and communal "grounds", as is also the case for us in other parts of Africa). *Only once this fundamental truth is recognized and regarded with pride, will Egypt rise again* as the place where the world's soul manifested itself in a golden civilization that still awes and inspires us today.

Interestingly enough, casting our recent minds back to COP 27 in Sharm-el-Sheikh, there was no intimation of such, whatsoever. The world was too preoccupied with the "rich" ancient heritage of Tutenkamen's Egyptology on the one hand, and a poverty stricken modern Egypt on the other, to be able to see anything in between, albeit that Sekem itself made its best efforts to illustrate such a middle way.

Unveiling Isis via Theosophy: Rebirth of Hermetic Philosophy

Yet in Hermes' words, drawing on the Egyptian/Greek God Thoth-Hermes (Lachman 2015),

> And this will be the geniture of the world: a reformation of all good things and a restitution, most holy and most reverent, of nature itself, recorded in time.

Half a millennium further on Russian mystic Madame Blavatsky's (2002) first major work in her newly forged, so called "theosophy", was what she termed the massive *Isis Unveiled,* named after the ancient Egyptian goddess of fertility, healing and rebirth, which appeared in 1877 to great acclaim. *The New York World* called the book "an extremely readable and exhaustive essay" upon the paramount importance of re-establishing the ancient Egyptian-Greek Hermetic Philosophy.

Blavatsky argued, contrary to Darwin and his followers, the entire universe, from the smallest clod to the greatest galaxy, is involved in a long, continuous process of cosmic and spiritual evolution, the essential element of which is consciousness. and that all religions have emerged from a common, primal source, once again voicing the recurrent and ancient Egyptian-Greek Hermetic insight, and wishing that different faiths should abandon their fruitless squabbles and focus on the real work of getting mankind to step up the evolutionary ladder. It was indeed at that point that Rudolph Steiner left Theosophy, with which he had been previously aligned, to start his own anthroposophical movement, which Steiner termed a "spiritual science".

Spiritual Science: Ancient Wisdom, German Philosophy and Western Practicality

Why did anthroposophy so called, with which Abouleish would subsequently become aligned, part company from theosophy? Where Blavatsky looked philosophically toward the East, Rudolph Steiner, because of his practical orientation toward art and architecture, health and education, agriculture and economics, was also integrally oriented to the West, and *the Anthroposophy he developed after 1912 was a unique amalgam of ancient wisdom in Egypt (our south-north), German philosophy (our north-east) and Western practicality.*

While moreover he applied his Spiritual Science (Shepherd 1954) in relation to himself and to his fellow man, he believed, as did his contemporary Ibrahim Abouleish (Abouleish, 2005), *there is another relationship of the greatest importance* of which man has become almost unconscious in its spiritual significance. This is *the relationship to the world in which he lives, the Earth and the world of plant and animal.* While there is, in the hearts of most of us, an instinctive love of nature and animals, yet from a general economic point of view, man has come to look upon Earth and Nature as objects of exploitation for his wealth and comfort. Hence, remedially, the turn to the *economics of love* in the course of healing the earth.

As we shall see then, Helmy Abouleish, building also on kemet, the local soil of Egypt, and maat, combined with Islam, and anthroposophy building for him locally-globally, would come up with his *economics of love,* albeiy that the link between ancient tradition and contemporary modernity may not have been consciously evolved in this case.

13.2.3. Economics of Love/EoL

Biodynamic Agriculture: Earth as a Living Organism

Underlying such, moreover, also as an offshoot of anthroposophy, was biodynamic agriculture. The farm in fact, for Steiner as for Ibrahim Abouleish, has hitherto been treated like a factory, with the wide use of chemical fertilizers to secure increased production. Both pointed out these dangers and his principles of agriculture proceeded even further. *They saw the errors of modern scientific agriculture,* not so much in its methods as in its concepts, in *its failure to understand the spiritual relation between man and nature,* and to consider the influences emanating from the various extra-terrestrial bodies, in addition to the obvious influences of the sun.

The first principle that Abouleish therefore applied was that of which we have become unconscious, the reality of spirit-activity in relation to Nature. *The Earth,* for Steiner as then also for him, *is not a dead mineral substance in which living seed is planted, but it is a living organism, with its own life forces,* which, in the plants springing from its surface, rise up to meet the down-pouring of life- forces form the Cosmos. Just as in our own bodies, so in the Earth, the mineral substances are present in transmuted form, in living processes, and not as they are found in chemical analyses. In that form their potency is, not as substance, but as a life-force.

Sekem as a Vital Force/The Vitality of the Sun/Applied Healing Wisdom

This brings Steiner to a second principle, that *the primary factor in the nature of the Earth is not substance, but life, and that the aim, in replenishing the Earth, is to restore life-force,* as for us a European variation on the African theme of healing wisdom . This relation to life force, just like Sekem as indeed a vital force, explains the use of the word "Bio-Dynamic", is applied, in anthroposophy, to agriculture. In fact, the revitalisation of plant life, through appropriate composting, can have an effect on the thinking capacity of man, according to Steiner, assisting create and constructive via enhanced nutrition.

For those particular "etheric" formative forces, which are active in plant growth, are also closely associated with the etheric body of man. The aim of Bio-dynamic agriculture is so to develop the characteristic vital forces of plants that they are less vulnerable to disease and to pest infestation, and where attacked are ore capable of resistance. In short, *Steiner showed that in agriculture the farm is an organism, in which man, animal and pant should live in relationship to each other and to the Cosmos.*

In all this bio-dynamic agriculture is not indifferent to the need for economic efficiency, but rather than employ forced development for immediate profit, which may prove unsatisfactory in the long term, it seeks to reach the highest level of harmonious growth of man, animal and plant, in the right proportions. The relationship of Man to earth on which and by which he lives thereby becomes a conscious one. Ibrahim Abouleish, through founding Sekem, as a *Sustainable Community in the Egyptian Desert,* indeed drawing on, and duly evolving both his *feeling* local for maat and his "local global" anthroposophical emergent foundation, is aligned, for Abouleish, with Islam.

Islamic Stewardship of the Earth: Reconnecting with Kemet

For Ibrahim Abouleish then, as a committed Muslim, as well as a follower of anthroposophy, Allah says in Islam that the earth and the ground are only given to us to take care of. He alone owns the ground. It is the same with capital; we can only manage it for the good of the people. He says that whoever enters into trade works together with Allah and, following his principles, should give the proceeds to the poor. In the light of such *he considered the modern joint stock companies to be dysfunctional, as ist upholders act as if God's legacy was their own. The interest and the riches they receive are not their own achievement, because even intelligence and abilities are the gifts of Allah.*

The Qur'an relates, how Adam and Eve lived in paradise before satanic whispers led them to the forbidden tree and they were expelled. But the Qur'an promised to return the Garden of Eden to believers as a most beautiful reward for their devoutness – the god fearing will live forever in gardens. The greatest source of joy for people living in arid surroundings is green gardens, shady oases, flowers and trees. It also gave Ibrahim the greatest fulfilment to watch Sekem flourishing.

The final element then to be drawn into such a composite, economy of love, is Kemet itself, the "black earth" of the original Egypt, for Micheal Rice (Rice, 2003) as above *the economy of Egypt was rooted in the rich alluvial soil which the Nile river deposited along its banks when it flooded every year.*

Towards an "Economy of Love": Nature, Culture, Society, Economy

Overall, Sekem (https://www.sekem.com/en/economy/economy-of-love-fairtrade/) today declares, as we saw above., informed by anthroposophy, out of Africa/Kemet/Egypt, and by Islam, as well as Maat, out of Asia/Arabia:

- We *build our **cultural, social and economic** activities to invigorate each other.*
- We intend to *restore **nature** through* implementing and developing biodynamic agriculture.
- We want to *provide products and services of the highest standards* to meet the needs of the consumer.

The intertwined natural and economic realms of activity within Sekem's group of companies begin on a practical level, as we have seen, by healing the soil through the application of biodynamic farming methods. Through this method, it has raw material at its disposal and is able to develop and manufacture natural medicine and a wide range of other products. In partnership with its friends and colleagues in Europe and its local partners in trade, Sekem strives to market its products, now for Helmy Abouleish (Lessem and Schieffer 2009), newly globally:

Economy of Love stands for ...
holistic farming, production and processing. We make different sectors and compounds of an economical and societal system work together within an associative way.
Economy of Love strives to ...
make our economics harmoniously correlate with society and nature. We want to work towards a sustainable development where every human being can unfold his and her individual potential; where mankind lives together in social forms reflecting human dignity; and where all economic activity is

transparently conducted in accordance with ecological and ethical principle. We now turn from intuiting local global, trans-culturally, to thinking newly globally, scientifically.

13.4. Thinking a Newly Global Integral Worlds Design: N4t

13.4.1. Embodied in Sekem as an Integral Enterprise

When Sekem and Trans4m came together, in matter and in spirit, joining hands in Egypt, in North Africa, in the first decade of the new millennium, what we, that is both Abouleish and ourselves, immediately realized was that the *integral enterprise* that we (Lessem and Schieffer, 2009) Trans4m had conceived of in theory, with its fourfold integral design, was embodied in Sekem, practically.

Moreover, Abouleish himself in North Africa, as a follower of anthroposophy, as one of us too (Ronnie Lessem) in Southern Africa, had further evolved Rudolf Steiner's (Adodo 2017) *Threefold Commonwealth* (cultural, social, economic) into a fourfold, adding nature, a Kemet laden fourth-fold element to his threefolding. Interestingly enough such a four-world, integral design (see Figure 13.4.1.) echoed what had archetypally come before, naturally and culturally in Egypt as in Dogonland, but was newly conceived economically and enterprise-wise. We now turn more fully, to that *newly* global "four world" conception, very different from the conventional wisdom on what it is to be "global"!

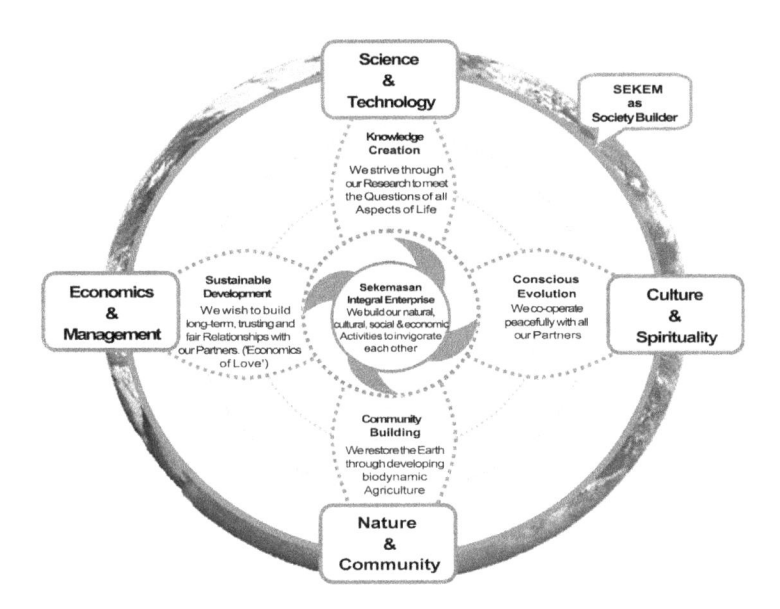

Figure 13.4.1: *Fourfold Sekem*

13.4.2. Managing in Four Worlds: Conceived Out of a Missing Africa

An Imbalanced World

As we now have become abundantly aware, our four worlds, in archetypal guise (see Chapter 2), underly most cultures, worlds-wide, and certainly within Africa, therein, for Some, characterising the elements of African healing wisdom.

However, and that said, within the worlds of economics and management with which we are primarily concerned, there is just one "western" world that predominates, today ever more so. Starting in the 1980s then, we set out to address that conundrum, also recognizing at the time, that with the rise of Japan as an economic power house in the "east" (now joined by the Pacific Tigers, China and India), alongside Europe in the "north" and the United States of America in the "west", Africa if not also Latin American in the "south", was getting left out in the economic cold.

It was then, as Africans, that we set out to redress this integral imbalance, at first in theory but then also in practice, as is illustrated by one of us as founder of Pax Herbals, as an African integral enterprise in Nigeria in West Africa, Anselm Adodo (Adodo, 2017)2000), also joining forces with Sekem in North Africa, as we have seen. We now reproduce, and somewhat update, part of the original article one of us,

Ronnie Lessem (Lessem, 2000)., wrote for the mainstream management *Long Range Planning* journal in the UK at the end of the last millennium (cited in *italics* below). Such then anticipated the conceptual work that followed, spanning research and innovation, economy and enterprise in the 21st century, as well as, ultimately, our communiversity.

No Ecology Can Thrive for Long When One Element is Rampant

The world of economics and business has become dominated by one cultural frame of reference – "north-western" – to the point that the hidden strengths of other cultures, even those of China and India which are pursuing a strongly "westernised" economic course today, are being ignored by individuals, organisations and societies, alike. Before the demise of communism there was at least an alternative approach, albeit one in opposition. Now, the post-modern age of the information society is almost universally capitalist and even in its latest manifestation, that of globalisation, it exploits difference (market and consumer segmentation) rather than differentiating and integrating between and within cultures and economies. No ecology, including the modern university, can thrive for long when one element, is rampant.

Towards a Communiversity Drawing on Four "Worlds"

We propose, then, a new structure of thought, or indeed socio-technical design, and interinstitutional agency, using four cultural archetypes or "worlds" (drawing on Jung's

personality types – feeling, intuiting, thinking, sensing) as a metaphor to both explain trans-cultural/trans-disciplinary differentiation in individual, organisational and societal approaches and to point the way towards their trans- personal/trans-formational integration. The resultant "four worlds" integral orientation, would also serve to dynamically promote societal re-GENE-ration, continuity and change, research and innovation, learning and development, and overall cultural transformation, through a new "genealogical combination" of community, journey, academy and laboratory.

Such a **communiversity** design, as we have already intimates, constitutes the re-GENE-rative *form*, underpinned by an integral *process* of social **research and innovation** realizing the *substance* of **community building and communitalism**, in one societal guise or another, in an African context of **healing wisdom**. We now return to action research in general, and socio/technical design per se.

13.5. Act Global-Local: Keynotes of Socio-Technical Design: N4a

13.5.1. You Adopt an Integrally Based Problem Solving Orientation

Participation and Democracy in the West

Action research, at least as conceived of in the Euro-American "north-west", focuses on solving real-life problems. The focus of such institutionally based action research, for Greenwood and Levin (Pateman 1970) in the U.S., is determined by what the organizational participants consider important, what affects their daily lives. The inquiry process is

thus linked to actions taken to provide a solution to the problem being examined. As such, the knowledge produced by the inquiry process must increase participants' control over their own situations, as well as being built on a critical understanding of the historical and political contexts within which the participants act. The participants must be able to use the knowledge that emerges, and this knowledge must support the enhancement of the participant' goals. In such action research insiders and outsiders join in a mutual learning process. The enabling mechanism for this is communication. New understandings are created through discourses between people engaged in the inquiry process.

The conventional social research community believes that credibility is created through generalizing and universalizing propositions, whereas action research believes that only knowledge generated and tested in practice is credible. Conventional social research assumes that only a community of similarly trained professionals is competent to decide issues of credibility, while action research places emphasis on the stakeholders' willingness to accept and act on the collectively arrived at acts and the defining characteristic of credibility.

Industrial democracy, moreover, in the "west", though more in theory than in practice, also began the first reflections about designing research processes that redefined the relationship between participants and researchers towards a much greater degree of mutuality. Carole Pateman, in her 1975 book on *Participation and Democracy* (1991), drew a genealogy from Rousseau's and Mill's thinking to the modern debate on democracy at the shop-floor level. Despite this, the strongly idealistic-democratic content of this first decade of the industrial democracy tradition was gradually replaced by pragmatic arguments. The rhetoric shifted towards empowerment, from participation as the key to democracy to participation as a means to motivate workers to shape a more effective and profitable organization. For Greenwood and Morten, empowerment with its hierarchical connotations is an inevitable step backward.

Table 13.5.1. *Integral South-North African Design – Keynotes*

You adopt a Integrally Based Problem solving Orientation.

Research and Innovation is geared towards social Betterment/Healing the Earth

You use a co-GENE-rative Approach to Organization/Societal Development.

You act in the South as a "friendly Outsider" out of the North.

Participation and Integrality in the South/North

In fact, for Albert Koopman (1991) in South Africa, from whom we shall hear much more in the next chapter, in turning the rurally based, retail building supplier Cashbuild, into a worker democracy, in the process drawing on *the divine will of Africa,* his integral design (see Figure 13.5.1. below) he came up with was somewhat different form that of such an industrial democracy in the "north-west", uniquely combining, democratically, southern communality with north-western enterprise, for us in integral guise.

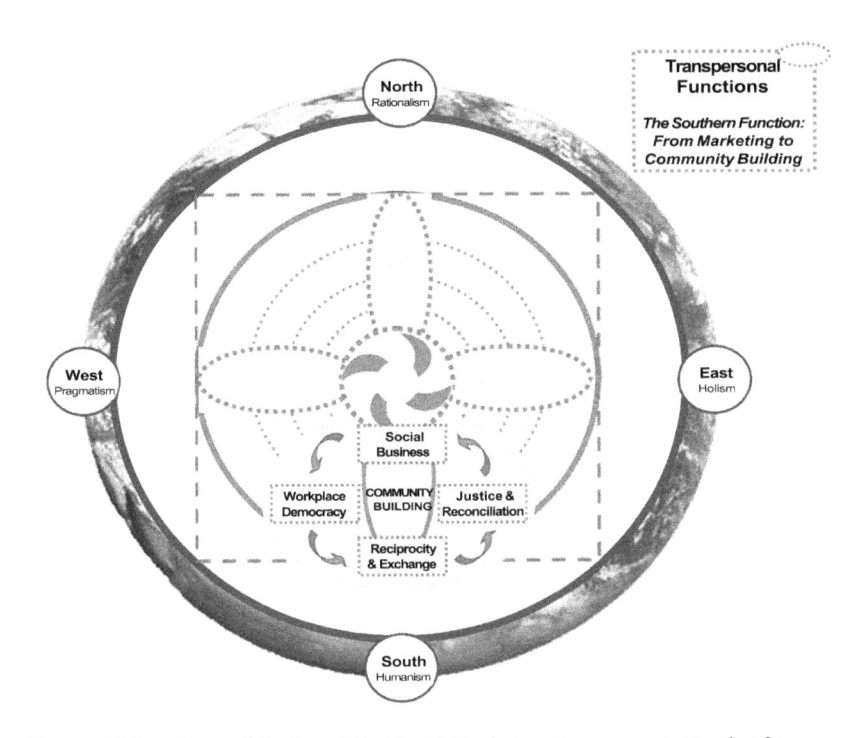

Figure 13.5.1: *Integral Design of Cashbuild Workplace Democracy in South Africa*

13.5.2. Geared Towards Social Betterment/Healing the Earth

Change as a Three-Stage Process

For the originator of action research, Kurt Lewin, as cited above, "nothing is as practical as a good theory", and "the best way to understand something is to try to change it". The social sciences themselves began as a form of engaged political economy, aimed at social betterment. Only as the social sciences, for him, were split out into the various existing conventional disciplines and subjected to harassment and purges because their social activism, offended the rich and powerful, did the social sciences become separated from action. Indeed, from our own experience in Africa, north or south, east or west, the management sciences, so to speak, are so influenced by the all pervasive American conventional wisdom, that the African "south" does not even get a scientific look in. Lewin then in America conceptualized change (see Table 13.5.2 A below) as a three-stage process:

Table 13.5.2A. *Change as a Three-Stage Process (Lewin)*

• Dismantling former Structures	⟹	Unfreezing
• Changing the Structures	⟹	Changing
• Locking them back into a permanent Structure	⟹	Freezing

Old and New Paradigms of Work Organization

Moreover, his work on group dynamics, identifying factors and forces important for development, conflict and co-operation in groups, led to the concept of so-called T- groups, or sensitivity training, which have a rich subsequent history. In summary, the new paradigm that he and his colleagues brought to work and organization is the following (see Table 13.5.2B below). For Greenwood and Levin though, *Lewin's specific orientation to managing change, related to unfreezing and re-freezing, is limiting. They argue in favour of action research as a continuous and participative learning process, not as a form of short-term intervention. For them, the change process has an open starting point and no absolute ending point* (see Table 13.5.2 B below).

Table 13.5.2B. *Old and New Paradigms of Work Organization*

Old Paradigm *Scientific Management*	⟷	New Paradigm *Socio-Technical Design*
The technological imperative Man as an Extension of the Machine Man as an expendable Spare Part Maximum Task Breakdown External Controls (Supervision) Tall Organization, Autocratic Competition Alienation		Joint Optimization Man as Complementary to the Machine Man as a Resource to be developed Optimum Task Grouping, Broad Skills Internal Controls (Self Regulation) Flat Organization, Participative Collaboration Commitment

Interdependence and Transformation in South Africa (ITISA)

For Koopman (Lessem et al 2012), by way of comparison, in setting up ITISA, in a consulting capacity, modelled on what he had achieved at Cashbuild:

> The underlying approach involves sharing value to add value. Most notably moreover, within ITISA's southern context – as differentiated from east, west and north – politics cannot be separated from economics. Therein lies the primal southern force of unity. "The three interrelated facets of society, namely authority, economy and

community, form an interdependent whole. If they are in open interaction with one another it is called a democracy". Whereas the AUTHORITY pole stands for the rationality of the "north", and the COMMUNITY pole for the humanism of the south, the ECONOMY represents a force of pragmatic integration. In business, Koopman maintains, the equivalent of the economy is creating and keeping customers through adequate performance. If, for whatever reasons, the relationship between "northern" authority (management and shareholders) and the "southern" community (employees and trade unions) breaks down, then the organisation's "western" economy (performance to create and keep customers) will suffer.

However, Lewin's work, even in South African where Koopman was based, remains a fundamental building block of what today is called action research oriented towards organizational change. He set the stage for knowledge production based on solving real-life problems. From the outset he created a new role for researchers, and redefined criteria for judging the quality of the inquiry process. It was Lewin who shifted the researcher's role from being a distant observer to involvement in concrete problem solving. The quality criteria he developed for judging a good theory focus on its ability to support practical problem solving in real-life situations.

13.5.3. You Use a Co-GENE-rative Approach to Organization Development

Co-Generative Process Between Insiders and Outsiders

Organizationally instigated action research, in the world at large, can be thought of as a process consisting of at least two analytically distinct phases. The first involves the clarification of an initial research question, whereas the second involves the initiation and continuation of a "social change and meaning construction process". Both culminate in the *creation of opportunities for learning and reflection in action* (see Figure 13.5.3), *within an co-generative process between insiders and outsiders.* Arguably, in the Sekem case, the Egyptians are the insiders and the German speaking peoples (the current CEO Helmy Abouleish is a mix of the two) the outsiders, and Islam, as an outgrowth of Jude-Christianity, occupying the middle ground.

```
                    ┌─────────────────────────────────┐
   Reflection  ↑    │ Creation of Opportunities for   │    Reflection
               │    │ Learning and Reflection in Action│      ↑
               │    ├─────────────────────────────────┤      │
               │    │  Solving Problems through Acting │      │
               │    ├─────────────────────────────────┤      │
   Insider     │    │  Communicative Action in Arenas │    Outsider
               │    ├─────────────────────────────────┤      │
                    │       Problem Definition         │
                    └─────────────────────────────────┘
```

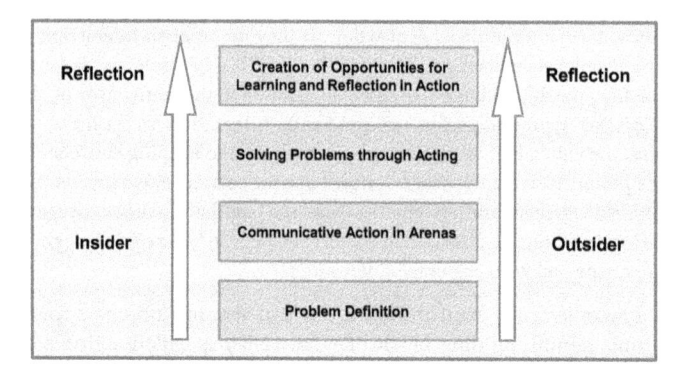

Figure 13.5.2: *A: Co-generative Approach to Organization Development*

It is integral, and thereby co-GENE-rative, insofar as the problem solving orientation, the pursuit of social betterment, altogether as a friendly outsider, is further evolved through an approach that builds on local Grounding, communally, local-global Emergence, transculturally, emancipatory, newly global Navigation, scientifically, and transformative, global-local economic Effect, our African keynotes. The approach we (Lessem et al. 32) adopted to such in the re-GENE-ration of Chinyika, in Zimbabwe, with one of us (Ronnie Lessem) as the "friendly outsider", and Muchiniripi (son of the local chief) and Kada (local Human Resource Director of Cairnes Foods) as the insiders, was that portrayed below (see Figure 13.5.3 B)

As such, and more generally, in North Africa societally as a whole, we have drawn locally on Maat, locally-globally and hermenetically on anthroposophy, newly globally on our four worlds, altogether embodied in an integral, organisational design that serves to actualise all of such in *northern* African guise.

COMMUNAL WEALTH GENERATION
Releasing the Economic Gene-ius of Chinyika
THE STORY SO FAR

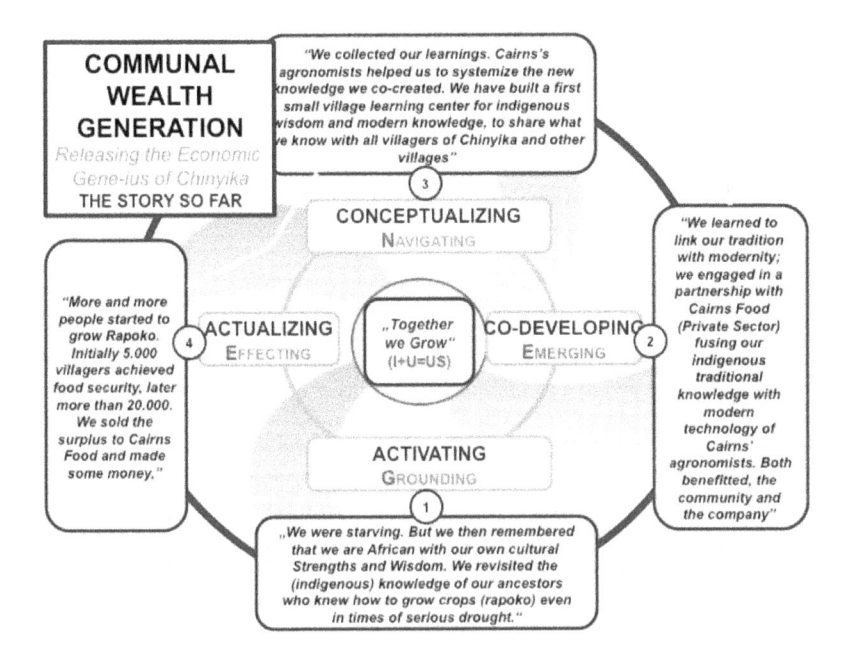

"We collected our learnings. Cairns's agronomists helped us to systemize the new knowledge we co-created. We have built a first small village learning center for indigenous wisdom and modern knowledge, to share what we know with all villagers of Chinyika and other villages"

(3) CONCEPTUALIZING — NAVIGATING

"We learned to link our tradition with modernity; we engaged in a partnership with Cairns Food (Private Sector) fusing our indigenous traditional knowledge with modern technology of Cairns' agronomists. Both benefitted, the community and the company"

"More and more people started to grow Rapoko. Initially 5.000 villagers achieved food security, later more than 20.000. We sold the surplus to Cairns Food and made some money."

(4) ACTUALIZING — EFFECTING

"Together we Grow" (I+U=US)

CO-DEVELOPING (2) — EMERGING

ACTIVATING — GROUNDING **(1)**

"We were starving. But we then remembered that we are African with our own cultural Strengths and Wisdom. We revisited the (indigenous) knowledge of our ancestors who knew how to grow crops (rapoko) even in times of serious drought."

Figure 13.5.3: *B: Communal Wealth Gene-ration at Chinyika – The Story so Far*

13.5.4. You Act as a "Friendly Re-GENE-rative Outsider"

Regeneratively as such, you know how, individually, organisationally or societally, to be a "friendly outsider". This role is vital in action research generally, as it was for Seem specifically – albeit that such is conventionally aimed at organisations, or, in the PAR case (see Chapter 7) on communities rather than whole societies – because the external perspective is a key element in opening up local group processes for change. But this outsider is "friendly" in a special sense. He or she must be able to reflect back to the local groups things about them, including criticism of their own perspectives, in a way that is experienced as supportive rather than negatively critical or domineering.

The friendly outsider must also be expert at opening up lines of discussion, a kind of good Socratic teacher. Often local organizations or groups are either stuck in positions that have hardened or they have become pessimistic about the possibilities for change. Flexibility and opportunities for change are pointed out to local people, along with encouragement in the form of moral support, and information from other cases, where similar problems existed but change turned out to be possible. Another key role of the friendly outsider is to make evident the tacit knowledge that guides local conduct. This can be in the form of critical reflections or supportive comments about local capabilities.

We are now ready to conclude this chapter and thereby the path of *northern* reason in an overall African context.

13.6. Conclusion

13.6.1. Horizontal and Vertical Social Innovation Needs to Take Place

Learning Community to Socio-Economic Laboratory

What are the implications for our integral research and innovation, on the path of reason in a southern-northern African context? As we can see, *social innovation is an institutional, as well as a communal and societal process.* Specifically, an academic establishment, or for us research academy like SRRC)(Societally Regenerative Research Centre)., hosting the research, needs to integrate it, thereby aligned with laboratory, community and individual transformation journeys, within its knowledge creating and community building orientation. As such, and as is well appreciated in the natural sciences, and technology – not in the social sciences as such – a university cannot go it alone when it comes to innovation. And indeed, in the social arena, each different natural and cultural context needs to be taken into account.

What is becoming ever more apparent moreover, as we move from the humanistic (PAR) – see Chapter 7 – towards the more rationally based approaches to building socio-technical systems and industrial democracies, and/or indeed integral enterprises, is that one requires the other, if a process of integral research, with a view to social innovation, is to take place. Furthermore, the development of such democratic and communal processes in the workplace, to accompany such evolving socio-technical systems, is likely to come to a halt if profounder shifts in the power balance, as the postmodernists would have called it, fail to come about.

In other words, the formative build up of new theories, for example ones dealing with enhanced participation, in the absence of a regenerative approach to building open systems within and around organizations will fall on stony ground. Further, on a societal level, without the development of new postmodern norms around the power and participation of hitherto marginalised (race, class, and gender based) groups, actions on a group or organizational level are likely to fail. The kind of democratic and participative vision that the likes of Dewey and Lewin – not to mention also the likes of Abouleish and Koopman in an African context – held will inevitably fail to materialise, unless horizontal and vertical social innovation takes place.

We now, ultimately, summarise the path of African reason, altogether, from grounded theory to critical rationalism, from post-modernism to socio-technical design, albeit suitably evolved in our *northern* African guise. Thereby rationalism is aligned with *ezemezu*, post-modernity with pre-modernity via *transient workplaces*, and socio- technical is transformed into more thoroughgoing *integral design,* ultimately, as illustrated in Table 13.6.3 also below, also aligned with the path of innovation.

13.6.2. Pursuing the Path of African Reason Altogether

Grounding and Origination in Grounded Theory on the Path of Reason

We started out then with grounded theory, with:

- A storyline – a descriptive story about core phenomenon under study
- Describing and then conceptualising – uncovering the core category.
- Relating subsidiary categories around the core category of overall story
- Revisiting the story, re-arranging categories, subcategories accordingly.

Emergent Foundation is Ezemezu on the Path
of African Philosophy and Reason

Thereafter, in turning to an African path of professional philosophy and reason

- Empirical Science has nothing absolute about it.
- You Derive Theories from conjectures built on Trivalent Ezumezu
- Formulate a Deductive Strategy based on Professional African Philosophy
- Strong Theory drives out the Weak – Towards an Integrative African Society

Emancipatory Navigation via Transient Workplaces
on the Path of African Reason

Therafter, and now moving onto a pre-modern/post-modern path of African reason you, individually and collectively:

- Pursue Multiple Discourses
- Focus on Meanings and African workplaces as multiple and shifting
- You socially construct Meaning in Premodern, Modern or Postmodern Guise
- Review History as transformative.

Transformative Effect via Integral Design on the Path of African Reason

- You adopt a Problem solving Orientation within an Integral Enterprise
- Research/Innovation is geared towards social Betterment/healing the Earth.
- You use a co-GENE-rative Approach to Organization/Societal Development.
- You act on the southern Inside as a "friendly northern Outsider".

Research to Innovation on the North African Path of Reason

In turning from research to innovation, in a Southern-Northern African context, situated at the cross-roads of civilization, for Egypt historically if not currently,

Sekem located in the north of the south, itself, has drawn on contributions worldwide, but most especially from Europe.

thereby, prospectively if not altogether actually, for us, transforming ancient maat into contemporary economics of love.

Table 13.6.2. *Go Dira to Pre/Post Modern/Maat to Net of Life: N3fita*

Feeling Local	Intuiting Local-Global	Thinking Newly Global	Acting Global-Local
Maat	Economics of Love	Integral Worlds Design	Co-GENE-rative Approach

University to Communiversity/Capitalism and Socialism to Communitalism

Penultimately on the path of reason, thereby adopting integral design, altogether in southern-northern African guise, we seek to establish a socio-economic laboratory aligned with a research academy, building on a prior learning community, also aligned with transformation journeys, overall communiversity wise. All of such can institutionally serve to pursue our "northern" African cause, and develop the rational arm of communitalism, underpinned by Ezemezu as well as professional African philosophy lodged in transient workplaces, to promote knowledge creation, micro-wise, and a knowledge based social economy, macro-wise. We now turn from the path of African reason, research and innovation wise, to the path of realisation.

The Miscontrued Un-Healing Wisdom of Africa/MENA/Worldswide

In the final analysis, moreover, as 2023 draws to an end, we cannot help pointing to the irony of a middle world, a MENA, wherein COP 28, with a view to healing the planet, is being held in UAE, at the very same time as the fighting goes relentlessly on in Israel-Palestine. Whereas the former is largely conceived of in technological, political terms, worldwide, and the latter in political and military terms, regionally speaking, for us the underlying issue, in MENA, in Africa, if not in our worlds at large is a metaphysical one.

In. other words, naturally and culturally, scientifically and economically, politically and economically, we are failing to consciously draw on the healing wisdom of Africa, together with is worlds-wide amplifications. Moreover, and for us, such "healing wisdom", needs to explicitly inform polity and economy as much as is does, more evidently, ecology and sociology. To that extent the likes of Sekem in Egypt, the Good African Coffee Story in Uganda, and our Integral Kumusha in Zimbabwe, and, as we shall see, Paxherbals in Nigeria, each have a huge role to play in relation to such healing and re-GENE-ration, albeit in a wider Communiversity form, and herein Pan-African context. We now turn to our third case story, on the more detailed history and evolution of Sekem.

13.7. References

Abouleish I (2005) *Sekem – A Sustainable Community in the Egyptian Desert.* Edinburgh. Floris Publications

Adodo A (2017) *Integral Community Enterprise in Africa: Communitalism as an Alternative to Capitalism.* Abingdon. Routledge

Bauval R (2007) *The Egypt Code.* New York. Arrow Books

Blavatsky H (2002) *Isis Unveiled Volumes 1 and 2.* Knutsford. Cambridge. A and D Publishing

Budge W (1985) *The Egyptian Book of the Dead.* Mineola. New York. Dover Publications

Dewey J (2008) *Experience and Education.* New York. Free Press

Greenwood D and **Levin** M (1998) *Introduction to Action Research: Social Research for Social Change.* New York. Sage

Jung C (2022) *Psychological Types.* Abingdon. Routledge Classics

Jung CG (1991) *Archetypes and Collective Unconscious.* Abingdon. Routledge

Kolb D (1983) *Experiential Learning: Experience as the Source of Learning and Development.* New York. Financial Times/Prentice Hall

Koopman A (1991) *Transcultural Management.* Chichester. Wiley-Blackwell.

Lachman G (2015) *The Secret Teachers of the Western World.* New York. Jeremy Tarcher. Penguin

Lessem R (2000) Managing in Four Worlds: Culture, Strategy and Transformation. *Long Range Planning.* Volume 34, Issue 1, February 2001, Pages 9–32

Lessem R and **Schieffer** A (2009) *Transformation Management: Toward the Integral Enterprise.* Abingdon. Routledge

Lessem R, **Muchineripi** P and **Kada** S (2012) *Integral Community: Social Commons to Political Economy.* Abingdon. Routledge

Lewin K (2008) *A Dynamic Theory of Personality.* Lewin Press

Naydler J (2009) *Future of Ancient World.* Rochester, Vermont. Inner Traditions

Osman A (2002) *Moses and Akhenaten: The Secret History of Egypt at the Time of Exodus.* Vermont. Bear and Company

Pateman C (1970) *Participation and Democratic Theory.* Cambridge. Cambridge University Press

Rice M (1997) *Egypt's Legacy: Archetypes of Western Civilization.* Abingdon. Routledge

Sardar Z (1987) *The Future of Muslim Civilisation.* London. Mansell

Schon D (1991) *The Reflective Practitioner: How Professionals Think in Action.* Abingdon. Routledge

Scranton L (2017) *Seeking the Primordial: Exploring Root Concepts of Cosmic Creation.* New York. Self Published

Shepherd AP (1954) *A Scientist of the Invisible.*

Some PM (2003) *The Healing Wisdom of Africa. Finding Life Purpose through Nature, Ritual and Community.* New York. Jeremy Tarcher Reprint Edition

Steiner R (2018) *Threefold Commonwealth.* Oxford. Franklin Classics

ICS3: Case Story 3: Africa South-North: Egypt
SEKEM: Economics of Love to Re-Gene-Rating Value

Contributed by Helmy Aboueish, CEO, and Max Boes-Abouleish, Chief Sustainability Officer, Sekem

Introduction

We open this third of our integral African case stories, now located in Egypt, in the African *north* of the so called Global *south* by revisiting and indeed regenerating the very notion of such a *Global South*. For us, in fact, such a notion merely reinforces the idea of *globalisation*, and as such a globalising *West*, in its altogether monolithic guise. Rather than such then, and in our particular focus on Africa, we distinguish between *southern, east, northern and west Africa*, each in particular, centred cosmologically in what Burkina Faso based, renowned African sage Malidoma Some has termed *The Healing Wisdom of Africa*.

As such, and in our first *southern* African case story based in rural, Zimbabwe related to our so called **integral kumusha,** we focused, via our social innovators, and kindred spirits, Christina and Daud Shumba Taranhike, on healing the divide between homestead (kumusha) and enterprise. In our second *south-east* African case, our focus was on Andrew Rugisara's **Good African Coffee Story** based locally in Uganda, extending globally, somewhat worlds-wide, healing the divide between enterprise and community. Herein, in this third case *southern-northern* case on **Sekem** in Egypt, as we shall see, we focus, through Ibramin, Helmy and Max Abouleish on healing the earth. Finally, in turning to *south-west* Africa, that is to our fourth and final story, we accompany our own **Paxherbals/Pax Africana**, the largest producer of phytomedicines in Africa, founded by one of us, Anselm Adodo, on its journey to heal Africa through what it terms nature power and healing radiance. How then does this resonate with current COP28 global south initiatives?

CATALYST 2030: Collaborating to Achieve the SDG's

For the South X Alliance Solutions From the Global South Exist

At the current COP 28 conference in Dubai (at the time of writing in December 2023), *the global south is projected as a victim of climate change and yet,* for the so called South X Alliance, including Sekem from Egypt and Ashoka as well as the

Skoll Foundation from the U.S, *solutions from the Global South exist*. These then need to be at the forefront, for them, at policy tables and in funding corridors. Climate change is no longer a fringe issue and with COP28 shaping up to cover critical aspects of commitments to climate change, the global south can't be left behind. The current design and architecture of climate financing and policy has not worked for these geographies.

Social Innovation is the Core of the Solution

According then to the South X Alliance (2023) as of December 3, 2023:

> We need a new way of thinking, financing, and supporting climate action. There is no Net Zero/Just Transition/Reversible Loss and Damage/Green Economy/ Zero Poverty/Locally-led adaptation – without people centred, evidence backed, Southern solutions by high impact social innovators, involving systemic change rather than one-off projects and initiatives that can scale and spur a cross-geographical revolution. Social innovation is the core of the solutio -- through this we can explore new alternatives to old, wicked problems.

The South X alliance is made up of like-minded stakeholders who have been rewriting the climate narrative, constituted of social innovators, funders, funder intermediaries, and policy experts. As such:

> We are dedicated individuals who are committing their time, energy, and resources towards the implementation of tried, tested, and effective solutions to combat climate change in the Global South. We work by applying community-centred approaches that create a bottom-up engagement for those most affected by the undesirable impacts of climate change. Climate change impacts the lives of people at local level, most severely in the global south, and we need to prioritize solutions, finance and capacity support not only to cope with climate impacts but to transform towards a resilient development.

Social Innovators the "Living Tissue" of Climate Change That Enable Scalable Solutions

Social innovators, they say, are based in the communities and understand the locally-led needs and opportunities. They are already addressing mitigation and adaptation strategies, however their voices are not being heard and their solutions are not being supported and replicated to the extent needed. *Social innovators are the "living tissue" of climate change that enable change and scalable solutions.*

To that extent, according tot he Alliance:

> We must work together to channel the voices of local changemakers and the solutions coming from the communities to the policy makers. We are calling on policy makers to enable the channel at COP to allow these voices to co-shape

strategies and policies, especially from the global south. We are calling for an environment of mutual learning and respect; to enable and prioritize the role of social innovators to access adaptation finance funds, mechanisms and instruments and to strengthen the delivery of private and public flows following the funding principles suggested by Catalyst 2030, launched at the World Economic Forum in 2020, inclusive of Ashoka, the Schwab and Skoll Foundations, and specifically prioritizing social innovators from the global south and the community driven solutions they deliver on the ground, ultimately responding to the UN founded SDG's (Sustainable Development Goals).

It is interesting to note, from the above, that whereas our re-GENE-rative case stories, of prominent social innovations, and innovators, in the four worlds in one African continent, are centred in different varieties of healing wisdom – *home versus enterprise* (south), *enterprise versus community* (east), *healing the earth* (north) and *healing Africa* (west) – catalyst 30, on behalf oft he *global south*, is centred in the UN's SDG's. What the two versions have in common is the focus on social innovators and social innovations, and the need for scaling up one-off innovations. However, where they profoundly differ is in the attention they give to a particular nature and culture, of a specific community and society, in the one hand, and to technology and economy oft he Global South in general, on the other. Ulimately, as we shall see, both perspectives are necessary if scaled up social innovation. is to ensue. We now turn to the Sekem case story specifically, and re-GENE-ratively, to illustrate the altogether integral point.

Sekem's Natural Grounding and Origination

Abouleish's Childhood Dream of Paradise in the Desert Earth

Drawing substantively from Ibrahim Abouleish's (2005) book on *Sekem – A Sustainable Community in the Egyptian Desert*, subsequently also amplified by his grandson and Sekem Sustain-ability Officer Max Abouleish-Boes, as wes shall later see, we start out in the former's childhood and youth:

> I carry a vision deep within myself: in the midst of sand and desert I see myself standing as a well drawing water. Carefully I plant trees, herbs and flowers and wet their roots with the precious drops. The cool well water attracts human beings and animals to refresh and quicken themselves. Trees give shade, the land turns green, fragrant flowers bloom, insects, birds and butterflies show their devotion to God, the creator, as if they were citing the first Sura of the Qu'ran. The human, perceiving the hidden praise of God, care for and see all that is created as a reflection of paradise on earth. For me this idea of an oasis in the middle of a hostile environment is like an image of the resurrection at dawn, after a long journey through the nightly desert. I saw it in front of me like a model before the actual work in the desert started. And yet in reality I desired even more: I wanted the whole world to develop.

Well Grounded in His Muslim Faith, and in the Relevant Sura from the Qu'ran

We can see then that, in his childhood Ibrahim was *well grounded in his Muslim faith, in general, and in the relevant sura from the Qu'ran, specifically*. Ramadan, in fact, was the time when his mother told Ibrahim all the stories about the Prophet. He listened reverently and in admiration to accounts of the Prophet's suffering and endurance, to how intelligently he answered questions, and to how much confidence Prophet Muhammad had in people's ability for freedom. The image of an admirable man was created in In Ibrahim's soul: very gentle and wise, very strong and resolute.

Abouleish's Young Adulthood Emergent Trans-cultural Foundation

Adopting Nature and Religion

Ibrahim Abouleish, in fact, was born into a typical, though well of, extended family in Egypt, with homes in both the city and countryside.

> My grandfather listened to all my childlike questions and found comprehensive answers for me, which were deeply satisfying. He sat down beside the bright white flower with the dancing butterfly, and took me on his knee. I leaned back against him, enjoying his gentleness. The butterfly opened its colourful wings, and flew from the white blossom up into the sky. We both followed its flight for a long time.

Alongside the Islamic faith, from a cultural perspective, it becomes apparent, from an early stage, that young Abouleish had a deep affinity for nature. He was also introduced, when very young, to business and to morality:

> I was nine when my father established a business and I started becoming interested in industry. Every day after school I changed my clothes and went to the factory. I was greeted by the smell of soapsuds boiling in huge vats. Shortly before establishing his business, in fact, there was a terrible attack in our local area, which was heavily populated by Jews. An ice-cream van was blown up by a bomb planted by extremists, just as the van was surrounded by children. So my father built his factory on the exact spot where the bomb had left its devastation to show that such things could never be tolerated.

Adolescence – Taking Note of Unmet Needs

The years between 1952 and 1956, when Ibrahim was in his late teens, were of great importance for the political future of Egypt, and were accompanied by unrest. In 1954 a Republic was founded by Abdul Nasser, after two years of unrest, during which we were given time off school to take part in demonstrations. He had a few close friends who were interested in social and cultural topics. They would go rowing on the Nile when they were off from school, and took many bicycling trips across the whole of Egypt. Such excursions tested his willpower and endurance.

He always spent the summer in the countryside, in his home in the village of Mashtul, in the Nile delta 50 miles from Cairo. He talked to the workers about their way of life, took note of their unmet needs, and brought back such things with him, on a next visit, of which they were in need.

Young Adulthood – Inner and Outer Development
The Village of Mashtul Becoming a Shining Centre in Egypt: Peace Be with You

One of his uncles, also named Mohammad, was a university professor and had a huge library in his house. None of his friends could understand what drew Ibrahim to him, and led the young man to engage in deep discussions with him. Sometimes Mohammad would give Ibrahim a book out of his library, and one day he came across Goethe's *Young Werther* written in Arabic. He avidly absorbed this work, which made him want to get to know more about the German people and their writers. Art and science, economic life, citizens' rights – he deeply admired them all these European attributes. The closer he got to finishing school, the more seriously he considered going to Germany to study at university. Having eventually convinced his parents to support him, and having a friend who had moved to Graz, in Austria, he applied and got accepted at university there. He wrote the following farewell to his father:

> Peace and greeting be with you .. When I get back, if God wills, I will go to Mashtul, the village I have always loved and where I spent the best time of my childhood. I will build factories where the people can work, different work than they are used to from farming. I will build workshops for women and girls, where they can make clothes and carpets and household goods and everything that the people need. I know that transport and communication is very important, so I will get the roads tarred and plant trees to right and left of it. I will build a large theatre on your grounds, where renowned artists can give performances for the people of my village. I will build a hospital near the main road and schools for children. I will bring together the men and women of higher learning form the village to help establish the idea, so that the village of Mashtul can become a shining centre in Egypt .. Peace be with you.

As it happened, while studying pharmacy and engineering in Austria – ultimately acquiring two PhD's before joining and Austrian pharmaceutical company, ultimately running its R and D department – and reaching out to another culture, Ibrahim fell in love with his Austrian wife to be Gudrun. Their two children to be would be of mixed Catholic and Muslim in their background, if not their faith.

Practising His Inner Faith: Realising Allah's Ninety Nine Qualities

When Ibrahim got to the university in Graz he joined the foreign visitors' club. During the early years, though, he felt quite lonely. So while he put a lot of energy into his studies of technical chemistry, the Qu'ran accompanied him through his daily meditations, the same ones he had undertaken throughout his childhood. While Islam is a monotheic religion, Allah has ninety nine different names which the Muslim can meditate upon.

> For one, "Allah is the patient one", so I practiced patience. Because of this, these were years of inner exercise, which had led me to believe, throughout my life, that I am a "practicing person". Through such inner exercises I tried to establish a relationship with Allah. I do not want to be known as a religious person, but as a striving, practising one. I had a goal, an ideal, Allah's ninety nine qualities. When a situation becomes unbelievably difficult for me I could see how small I was in relation to those names, which made things bearable. In fact, the names are divided into three sets of thirty-three, in terms of: the One (for example creator, wise, evolver, initiator), the Light (for instance watching, destroyer, expander, compassionate), and the Judge (for example strong, just, loving, forgiveness). To BE, meanwhile, is the highest ideal.

Ibrahim's approach to education, given that all that came in his life before, inwardly and outwardly, was very different form his fellow students. He felt reminded as such of the golden era of Islam and the flourishing culture in Egypt.

Where the Orient and the Occident Meet

Technical chemistry consisted of many different subjects, each one of which would have been an entire subject of its own. Abouleish was inspired by everything. He noticed that the students, whom he came to teach, had a completely different approach to understanding from his own. They learnt everything by heart. He wondered how one could learn a subject by heart without understanding it properly.

During his studies, moreover, Ibrahim noticed inner changes taking place within himself. He became thoroughly involved with European culture, getting to know its music, studying its poetry and philosophy. Somebody looking into his soul would have seen anything "Egyptian" left completely behind, so he could absorb everything new. Because of his childhood and adolescent grounding, though, in Egyptian culture, and in Islam, he could not leave such entirely behind. *He now existed in two worlds, both of which were essentially different: the oriental, spiritual stream he was born into and the European, which he felt was his chosen course. But he was neither Egyptian nor European.*

Ibrahim realized this particularly when he was experiencing art. For example he started hearing Handel's Messiah with Muslim ears as praise to Allah. *The two differing worlds within him gradually began to dissolve and merge into a third entity, so he was neither completely one nor the other.* What he experienced was not a cheap compromise, but an elevation, a real uniting of the two cultures within himself. But now he wanted more – he wanted to achieve this state of being a "third" state, in religion too, to transcend to a higher level of being. At the same time he felt reminded of the golden era of Islam and the flourishing culture in Egypt at the time.

Problems Underlying Arab-Isreali Conflict Cannot Be Solved by War, Only by Education

Shortly before the outbreak of the first Egyptian-Israeli was, Nasser asked Egyptian embassies to invite representative Egyptians from around the world to a conference in Alexandria. Ibrahim knew Sadat, Nasser's Deputy, from the days of his youth. One after the other people got up to speak in favour of war with Israel. After a short introduction he said "I am in favour of peace. Even the thought of war is harmful". He heard words like "traitor". So he told people that "(i)f Israel and Egypt keep the peace, then the money and energy saved from supporting the war could be used for establishing a functioning economy and a cultural life for both countries". After the conference Sadat took him aside and said: "What you said was excellent". Ever since, for Ibrahim, peaceful and indeed cocreative co-existence has been his vision. War is much easier then peace!

In 1972, still in Austria, Ibrahim was again asked to give a talk on the Egyptian-Israeli conflict. He tried to illuminate his inner thoughts on the subject:

> Without thinking, people let themselves be roused and sacrificed for emotions like national pride, dogmatisms and territorial claims. A justification for fighting can only come from a perception of complex connections. I don't believe my contemporary politicians in the Middle East have this thinking ability. The problems underlying this conflict cannot be solved by war, only by education. People need to be educated to understand that their lives do not depend on material objects, whether they can own a piece of land. Neither Nasser nor the Israelis are acting out of an overview of higher ideas, but out of their emotions. I would put, instead, all the money and energy into establishing schools infra structure and creating jobs. Cultural exchange and research should be promoted, not themes that can divide people.

Abouleish noticed a dignified old lady in the front row, listening intensely. She asked him whether he had heard of Rudolph Steiner. Her name was Martha Werth. Ibrahim said no.

Towards a Philosophy of Freedom: Anthroposophy and the Qu'ran

She then asked whether he would like to find out more, which he did. After that Ibrahim went to her house almost every second day. She gave him Steiner's (2001) *Philosophy of Freedom,* and asked him to read it. She then interrupted him after every paragraph and asked him to repeat it, in his own words. He began to experience the act of thinking through this enormous mental effort. He also began to develop a deep love towards this anthroposophy which has the Greek meaning of "the knowledge of the nature of man".

Through it he grasped a tiny part of the whole world, and humanity as well as nature were revealed to him in a new light. *He wanted to work though the Qu'ran, using anthroposophy to achieve a deeper understanding.* What sounds so easy in retrospect was attained gradually with great internal struggle, a daily observation of his relationship with Christianity, with which anthroposophy was closely aligned, and with European culture. Meanwhile his life had taken a new turn, with Martha Werth playing a major part in such.

Newly Global Midlife: Emancipatory Scientific Navigation Departure and Return

What Is Your Destiny?

"Wouldn't you like to come with me on a journey to Egypt?", Martha Werth asked Ibrahim one day. She wanted to know if he had come across ancient Egyptian cultures? So he decided to take the opportunity, and to go with her.

They started out in 1974, and visited Aswan, Luxor, Karnak and the Valley of the Kings. She gave him a new enthusiasm for ancient Egyptian art and mythology. Ibrahim was in fact shocked by the contrast between the greatness, wisdom and elevation shown thousands of years ago by the pharaohs, and modern Egypt. In the evenings he discussed his experiences and thoughts with Martha. She listened and asked him what he wanted to do? "What is your destiny?"

Biodynamic Agriculture Could Transform Egypt's Agriculture

On the return journey he thanked Allah that he did not live in Egypt, but in beautiful Austria with his wife and children, a son and a daughter, and his successful career, as now head of research for an Austrian pharmaceutical company. And yet *he could not forget the images and encounters he had experienced. Every morning he awoke and realized anew how the events of the journey had transformed him.* At the same time he continued to work with anthroposophy and became acquainted with its practical applications in many walks of life. The deeper he was able to penetrate into the matter, the more answers he received for his persistent questioning and inner restlessness.

He repeatedly found life-changing solutions suddenly presenting themselves to him after intense contemplation. *Biodynamic agriculture, which was a product of anthroposophy, particularly fascinated him.* One day Martha Werth told him about a lecture, being given locally, by a disciple of Steiner's, George Merckens, an advisor to biodynamic farms in Austria and Italy. At last he found a friend who understood that biodynamic farming could transform Egypt's agriculture.

He Developed a Vision of a Holistic Project Able to Bring About a Cultural Renewal

Ibrahim's subsequent Italian journey with him was an important step along the path toward his decision to return to Egypt. *He developed a vision of a holistic project able to bring about a cultural renewal.* As well as the farm it would need several economic projects, a school, and cultural projects as well as a hospital. His first priority was to educate people. Meanwhile he was certain that a cultural meeting between Egyptians and Europeans could become a healing force in this oppressed country. Most especially in fact the relationship between Germany and Egypt is a very strong one.

Farewell to Europe – I Could Liberate Egypt from its Misery

The Souls of Egyptian People Can Be Revitalised by a Garden in the Desert

Ibrahim then told his children the story of a man who decided to move to the desert with his children and who created a big garden there. Once he had painted the picture in great detail he suddenly asked: "And what would happen if we were that family? Spontaneously there were shouts of joy". His son was 16 and his daughter 14. His son would ride a motorbike across the desert and his daughter would ride horses. To Martha Werth he wrote a farewell letter:

> For my soul Austria was like a spiritual childhood garden. Now I hope the souls of Egyptian people can be revitalised by a garden in the desert. After establishing a farm as a healthy physical basis for soul and spiritual development, I will set up further things, following the example of human development: a kindergarten, a high school, vocational education, a hospital and various cultural institutions. My goal is the development of humans in a comprehensive sense. I want to pass on this richness of nature and spirit to Egypt, to sow the seeds I have been given.

See Things in a New Light, and Transform Them to a New and Higher Level

In another letter he wrote to a scientist friend, Dr Zwieauer in Vienna:

> My soul has begun to separate into two parts: an ambitious, successful part and a seeking questioning one, willing to see things in a new light, and to transform and elevate them to a new and higher level. I am consciously leaving the successful part behind me and am giving myself up to the questioning one. With this I am uniting my soul with its spiritual home and am liberating the rigidity of ambitiousness so I am open for new tasks, encounters and goals.

Ibrahim then was in the process of giving up a successful career as a scientific researcher in Austria to exchange it for an incredibly unpredictable future in Egypt. He was also in a state of sorrow for the loss of his chosen spiritual, European home. On his last journey through Egypt he had experienced a deep sense of hopelessness caused by the way of life of the country's population. This had deeply moved him, and his work with anthroposophy led him to sense a way in which he could liberate them from their misery.

His Inner Strength Had Grown Out of Years of Meditation on Allah's Qualities

Meanwhile his faith in God gave him *inner strength which had grown out of years of meditation on Allah's qualities in particular.* Ibrahim asked himself what the Koran meant by stating: "He is the representative". He felt this spiritual and soul emptiness as he travelled in Egypt, and he experienced himself as their representative. Because of this awareness he wanted to establish new social forms for the Egyptian people. The Quran goes on to say: "He is the initiator, the originator, the strong one". Ibrahim felt power in him for this new start, able to develop inner peace through his devotion to Allah and to this day he can still submerge himself in its depths.

Global-Local Maturity: Transformative Economic Effect – Sekem Entering and Cultivating Desert Country
The Prophet Says Every One of You Is a Shepherd

After arriving in Egypt Abouleish went to see the Ministry of Agriculture, and told them he was looking for a patch of desert, which he wanted to cultivate using organic methods. He -was shown a patch in Belbeis, near Cairo, where the quality of ground was very bad and water supply difficult, but he knew he wanted it. *If biodynamic farming could thrive in this wasteland, then it would be possible to transfer this model to easier environments.* So Ibrahim bought the land and moved over, leaving his family behind in Cairo. Most of the time he was alone, with only now and then a Bedouin with goats wandering over. They could not understand his idea, but they saw it develop before their eyes.

The Prophet says every one of you is a shepherd, and everyone is responsible for those under your protection. For those living with their feelings, like the Bedouins in the desert, a concrete step is to establish social forms. This starts with elementary principles: starting punctually, getting up and catching a bus. Since that time the morning circle with a select group of Sekemassociates has been invented, not only to start the day together but also to share a sense of unity and invariably to listen to a beautiful poem, or such a recitarion, to praise the beautifulness of nature and human beings. After Ibrahim had positioned the first roads and plotted the fields, the next task was to drill two wells. He himself did not know how to do this so he was in the lucky position of having to employ people. They terraced the entire ground together and dug canals for the water to flow to the fields.

Linking Nature and Culture, Society and Economy

Abouleish's wish, then, was to build a community for people of all walks of life. It had to be built, for cultural reasons, on the borders of civil society. To begin with there was just a two-man team, a Bedouin Mohamed and himself. Mohamed was a local villager who came to him when he was walking around the local area, put his hand on his shoulder, and said "I am with you". There was no infra-structure, no energy, nothing. The two of them began the reclamation and greening of the land, and people started coming. It was clear to Ibrahim by that time, in the late seventies, that the implementation of his dream was a life's task. In fact it would probably take many generations to progress.

Sekem as a Cultural as Well as Natural Initiative Had to Generate Capital

Because the whole initiative was, from the outset, a cultural as well as a natural one, Ibrahim had to generate capital. Such necessary cash flow started with the sale of the extract of a medicinal plant which was exported to the United States. Then Sekem moved on from there. To create the environment and microclimate people see today they had to plant 120,000 trees. The economic life of the initiative began at a practical level to "heal" the soil through biodynamic methods, in partnership with close friends and colleagues in Europe, and local partners in trade. *This associative way of doing business is one of the major success factors underlying the way in which the "mission impossible" of biodynamic agriculture in the desert has worked out.* What then are the overall implications for Sekem today, which employs some 2000 people and has close links with 300 other farms in Egypt?

The Sekem Group

Farming to Phyto-Pharmaceuticals

SEKEM aims to establish a blueprint for the healthy corporation of the 21st century. To begin with, as such, it was the first entity to apply biodynamic farming methods in Egypt. Its commitment to innovative development thereby led to the nationwide application of biodynamic methods to control pests and improve crop yields. SEKEM has since grown exponentially into a nationally renowned enterprise and market leader of organic products and phyto-pharmaceuticals, which are now also exported to Europe and other countries.

The SEKEM group that represents the economic branch of the initiative, includes a holding company with five main subsidiaries: SEKEM for Land Reclamation for farming and organic seedlings, fertilization and pest control; Isis for fresh fruits and vegetables as well as for organic foods and beverages (such as juice, dairy products, oils, spices and tea); Lotus for herbs and spices; NatureTex for organic cotton and textile children's clothes and home wear; and Atos for phyto-pharmaceutical products.

Smallholder Farmers in Its Network: Egyptian Biodynamic Association (EBDA)

Sekem has a highly unconventional business model that incorporates what are usually considered social and environmental externalities and in fact maintains this to be the basis for an increasing competitiveness in the future. While it is a profit-making enterprise, it does not aim for profit maximization. Through a profit- sharing methodology, it shares its returns with the smallholder farmers in its network *called the Egyptian Biodynamic Association (EBDA)*. Ten per cent of Sekem's profit go to the SEKEM Development Foundation (SDF) that has launched many community development initiatives to benefit communities . These include establishing different schools and a medical centre, celebrating culture and diversity, and promoting peace, cooperation and understanding between all human beings, and, as from 2012 as we shall see, a Heliopolis University for Sustainable Development.

Sekem Addressing Societal Challenges

The societal challenges of Egypt such as climate change, resource scarcity, population growth, extreme poverty, absence of food security– need innovative, problem-solving solutions. In that context it is important to realize that the Energy-Water-Food nexus represents a huge challenge for sustainable development in Egypt and agriculture is strongly related to that. Sustainable desert reclamation, that is healing the earth, plays a key role in addressing those challenges and therefore contributing to political stability and the related transition towards an authentic form of democracy. This is not only relevant for Egypt but for the whole region. It is within this context of food insecurity and social and environmental challenges that SEKEM represents a viable economic alternative, one that builds upon a praxis of sustainable agriculture that resonates strongly with Muslim insights and teachings, as we shall see, now encapsulated in what they term *the economics of love* .

Sekem as an Integral Enterprise

The Fourfold Structure of Sekem

SEKEM's model for sustainable development integrates different spheres of life to a holistic whole where all parts are at the same time independent and interconnected. As seen in the following figure (Lessem and Schieffer 2009) – see Figure C3.4.3. – the Sekem fourfold reads as follows:

- *Restoring Nature:* We restore the earth through developing biodynamic agriculture.
- *Peaceful Cooperation:* We co-operate peacefully with all interested parties.
- *Researching Life:* We strive through research to meet the questions of all aspects of life.
- *"Economics of Love":* We wish to build a long-term, trusting and fair relationship with our partners.
- *Integral Perspective:* We build our natural, cultural, social and economic activities to invigorate each other.

Now of course, since 2012 as we shall see, Heliopolis University for Sustainable Development has become a leading part of Cultural Development.

Strategy and Structure

Sekem is formed by three closely interrelated entities: the Sekem holding company, with eight constituent companies, each one responsible for an aspect of its business value proposition; the Sekem Development Foundation (SDF), responsible for all cultural aspects, and the Cooperative of Sekem Employees, responsible for human resource development.

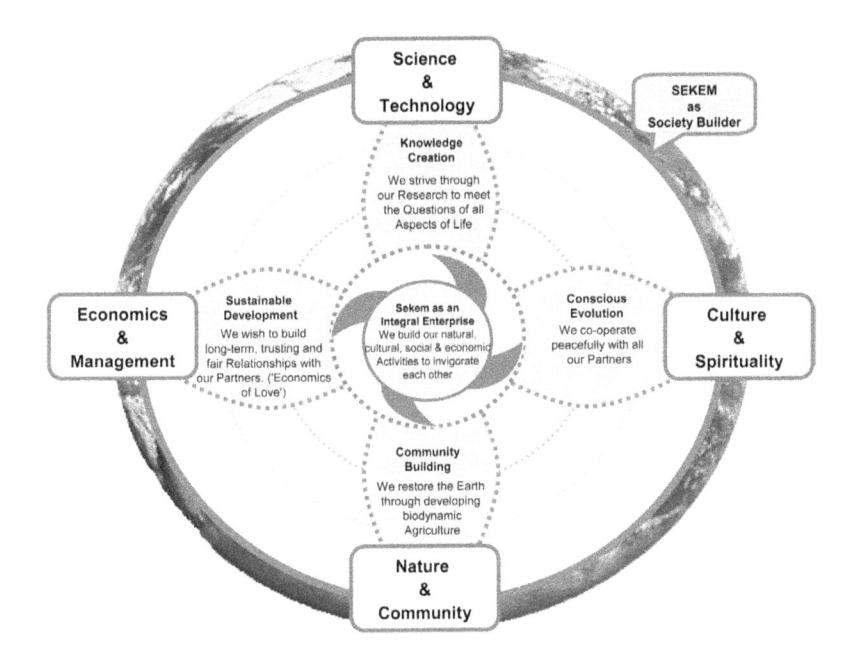

Figure 3.4.3: *Fourfold Sekem as an Integral Enterprise*

Working together they have produced a modern corporation based on innovative agricultural products and a responsibility towards society and environmental sustainability. The eight companies are Atos (phytopharmaceuticals and health products), Libra and Hator (fresh fruits, vegetables and herbs), Conytex (organic textiles), Isis (organic food), Lotus (organic herbs and spices), Mizan (organic seeds, plantlets and seedlings) and Salis (agricultural info, technology and services).

Sekem has grown exponentially in the past decade to become a national market leader in organic products and phytopharmaceuticals. It has established export links with European and U.S. customers and built up a strong local market, with 55 % of domestic sales. Its commitment to innovation, moreover, has led to the nation-wide development of biodynamic methods to control pests and improve crop yields. The company's most significant impact, locally though, has been through the Egyptian Biodynamic Association (EBDA), an NGO established in 1990 as a means of conducting R&D into biodynamic agriculture in Egypt and training farmers in its methods. In collaboration with the Ministry of Agriculture, Sekem deployed a new system of plant protection in cotton farming, which led to a ban if crop dusting throughout Egypt. By 2000, according to the UN and FAO reports, pesticide use in cotton fields had fallen by 90 %, annual yields having increased by over 30 %.

Heliopolis University for Sustainable Development

The next stage in Ibrahim Abouleish's life story, in fact his legacy phase, came to the surface early on in the new millennium when he began to conceive of a new kind of university for sustainable development that would serve to take the Sekem story further on, into society at large, both locally and globally. In fact it took seven years of unrelenting effort to turn the dream into a reality, and in October, 2012, Heliopolis University for Sustainable Development opened its doors to its first group of undergraduate students, in pharmacy, engineering, and business and economics, altogether underpinned by a core program in nature & community (grounding), arts (including culture) (emerging), science & innovation (navigating), and language, communication & enterprise (effecting).

All faculties were to be supported by a Social Innovation Centre with the role to promote integral development that is to enhance integration between the humanist core and specialised sciences, as well as to promote curriculum and faculty development. However, now a decade later, such has not yet materialised, because of the constraints of conventional academe. The intention of such a centre, when it ultimately materialises, is to engage in identifying and understanding burning societal needs and directing the research capacities of HU to find, implement and upscale solutions together with the Sekem initiative and other stakeholders from the society, to, in our terms, recognize and release GENE-ius.

The Economics of Love: EoL

What has then emerged, in the third decade of the new millennium, in partnership with Sekem's friends and colleagues in Europe and its local partners in trade, for Helmy Abouleish (SEKEM), who took over full charge of Sekem after the death of his father Ibrahim, is a new ethos and brand for the enterprise, an:

Economy of Love stands for

> *holistic farming, production and processing. We make different sectors and compounds of an economical and societal system work together within an associative way.*

Economy of Love strives to ...

> make our economics harmoniously correlate with society and nature. We want to work towards a sustainable development where every human being can unfold his and her individual potential; where mankind lives together in social forms reflecting human dignity; and where all economic activity is transparently conducted in accordance with ecological and ethical principle.

Maat, the Middle Way of Islam and EoL

As we can see from the above, Sekem's restoring of the earth, implicitly for us (though not explicitly) *centred in the healing wisdom of Africa,* while explicitly for its founder Ibrahim Abouleish *grounded in both ancient Egyptian Maat (balance) and the middle way of Islam,* has also explicitly *emerged through anthroposophy,* albeit bereft of its ancient Egyptian, hermetic antecedents, thereafter, together with us at Trans4m, newly globally *navigating its integral enterprise.* Ultimately moreover by way now of so called "EoL" (Economics of Love), as stated (SEKEM. Economy of Love) in October, 1922, in advance of Cop 27 held in Egypt, manifesting the *transformative effect* of Sekem's healing wisdom:

> Imagine agriculture of the future that helps in mitigation of climate change, promotes fairness and well-being of farmers and fosters affordable sustainable and healthy food. To make this dream come true, the Economy of Love has been working for the past few years on the creation of such a model, and now is putting a lot of effort into making it mainstream ... Economy of Love (EoL) is an ethical, sustainable and transparent certification standard that supports biodynamic farmers and brings a positive environmental impact by sequestering carbon and enhancing farms' biodiversity. EoL was developed under the Egyptian Biodynamic Association (EBDA) which strives for sustainable agriculture in Egypt.
>
> This year EoL acquired a license for certification of carbon credits projects among Egyptian farmers. This carbon credits certification scheme follows the same EoL values: transparency and the true cost accounting along the whole value chain. This step is expected to fundamentally shift the global agriculture and business sectors. To receive additional income from generation of carbon credits, farmers will need to

shift from conventional harmful agricultural practices to the sustainable ones, and thus contribute to the sequestration of CO2 and bring positive impact to the world.

SEKEM farm in Wahat El Bahariya was the first carbon farming project certified by EoL and thus played the role of a prototype. This project has shown great results and proved that regenerative agriculture under the EoL guidelines can contribute to climate change mitigation. By using biodynamic agricultural methods, desert land on the farm was revitalized, while complementary activities of carbon sequestration generated around 12 000 carbon credits in one year, bringing roughly 300 000 EUR of additional income to be reinvested into the expansion of the farm. Inspired by the pilot project's success, the EoL standard was introduced to 2100 smallholder farmers (members of EBDA), who are committed to the ecological regenerative practices and can benefit from the financial incentives through the carbon credits scheme. Currently, these farmers are in the process of verification and validation according to the EoL standards. A rough calculation says that this amount of farmers can help to sequester 84,000 tons of CO2 per year and this will bring invaluable climate positive impact.

The supremely ambitious vision of EoL is to convert 250,000 farmers towards sustainable agriculture practices by 2028. It will enhance the economic resilience of the farms, climate adaptability, and stimulate regenerative agriculture in Egypt. Besides, it will make a significant contribution to combat climate change with roughly 9.6 million tons of sequestered CO2 through farms' activities.

How then, overall, has Sekem arrived at this EoL point, and where might it go form here? More importantly, what are the overall lessons we can learn for social innovation generally, and regenerative value creation, so to peak, specifically?

Towards Social Innovation and Regenerative Value Creation African Healing Wisdom, Maat in Ancient Egypt, Anthroposophy and Islam

A Global-Local Socio-Technical design

In our previous chapter on *socio-technical design*, we illustrated how Sekem in Egypt has drawn, implicitly on the healing wisdom of Africa, and, at least to some degree, indigenously-exogenously on the ancient Egyptian concept of *maat* (justice and balance). More explicitly, moreover, Sekem has drawn prolifically on the so called *spiritual science of anthroposophy*, generally, and on biodynamic agriculture, specifically, albeit that such also draws on ancient Egyptian hermetic wisdom. Over and above all of such, naturally and culturally, Ibrahim Abouleish was a serious scientist and engineer, in more conventional terms, having two separate doctoral degrees in pharmacy and engineering respectively. All of such then underlay the social innovation that Sekem has become.

Yet there is, as we have already intimated, and will now articulate more fully, more to such than that, Abouleish was a profound devotee of Islam. Therein, in fact, and of great relevance to the MENA region, if not to the Islamic *umma* at large, a thereby global-local design that arises out of originally distinct local origins, that belie such a generalised notion as the *global South*. We start with Islam and nature.

Inner Depths of Islam and the Outer Reaches of Sekem: Fitra to Khalifa

Concept of Natural State (Fitra)

Allah's creation or the natural state (*fitra*), as revealed by Max Abouleish et al (2016), also aligned with the formidable work of contemporary environmentalist and water technologist Al Jayyousi on *Islam and Sustainable Development* (see below) in our previous work on *Integral Polity: Aligning Nature, Culture, Society and Economy*, can be referred to as the natural equilibrium or balance (*mizan*). Therein full harmony of nature, people and the built environment are given. In the agricultural context it is obvious that there is a divine force that creates live. Growing plants or raising animals is more than just transforming inputs into outputs. Ibrahim Abouleish has often explained this approach to religious people who initially distrusted SEKEM's approach to agriculture, quoting the Qur'an:

> 006: 095 It is Allah Who causeth the seed-grain and the date-stone to split and sprout. He causeth the living to issue from the dead, and He is the one to cause the dead to issue from the living. That is Allah: then how are ye deluded away from the truth? (SEKEM)

He has explained how the millions of micro-organisms work in the earth and has intimated how the living earth was connected to the heavens. Biodynamic farming with its composting process and its preparations is thereby adding vitality to the soil, acknowledging its context in the larger picture, and hence is related to a divine idea, also waiting for specific star constellations before planting can be interpreted as being inspired by Allah to act correctly:

> 016: 012 He has made subject to you the Night and the Day; the sun and the moon; and the stars are in subjection by His Command: verily in this are Signs for men who are wise.

To read then and understand Allah's signs in nature people needs wisdom and knowledge.

Concept of Knowledge (Ilm)

The first surah that Prophet Mohamed received from Allah started with the following imperative to all humans:

> 096: 001 Proclaim! (or read!) in the name of thy Lord and Cherisher, Who created-

It underlines the value of knowledge in Islam. But according to our close colleague Professor Odeh Jayyousi (Al-Jayyousi 2012), who head their Department of Technology and Innovation at the Gulf University in Bahrain, the English term "knowledge" falls short of expressing all the aspects of *ilm*. Knowledge in the western world means processed information while *ilm* is an all-embracing term covering theory, action and education. Another surah also illustrates that God wants people to gain knowledge:

> 002: 269 He granteth wisdom to whom He pleaseth; and he to whom wisdom is granted receiveth indeed a benefit overflowing; but none will grasp the Message but men of understanding.

Harmonizing human action to cosmic processes and recognizing that dealing with nature has a divine context is embedded in SEKEM's approach to agriculture. To grasp this, demands a high level of consciousness and human capacity. This is the reason why SEKEM puts so much emphasis on education and cultural life in general. Dance movement or painting do not directly transfer specific knowledge content but makes the human soul, for Abouleish, much more receptive and hence more open to nature and knowledge (*ilm*). The aim of conducting such artistic sessions with farmers and agricultural engineers and workers is – besides the positive effect on teamwork and group dynamics – to enable them to experience something new and to develop their sense for openness and curiosity. The objective is to transfer this experience to their work context and view their world in a different light. Islam refers to the process of consciousness development as a form of beauty and excellence (*ihsan*).

Concept of Excellence and Beauty (Ihsan)

Ihsan means excellence and inner beauty in the form of conscious evolution of individuals, organizations and society (*ummah*). It also entails continuous development, and value and knowledge creation for all humanity. This realization of beauty is embedded in the approach of SEKEM that wants to develop individuals, organizations and societies at large. Nature provides great inspiration for that. In SEKEM's vision statement it says:

> In nature, every organism is independent and at the same time systemically interconnected to other organisms. Inspired by ecological principles, representing the wisdom of nature and the universe, we continuously strive to gain and sustain a harmonious balance between (this polarity) and to integrate (it) into our development.

The development model of SEKEM is holistic and rooted in sustainable, now even regenerative, agriculture. Many challenges need to be overcome on the way towards excellence and it needs a lot of time and generations to see the fruits of this work. Most of the people who first heard about the ideas of Sekem before it bore fruit thought it was a mission impossible and organic desert greening can never succeed. However, it did and it still does, but only because of people who believe in it. It is that inner transformation that has to come before the outer transformation, the ability to see a vision and the will to bring a holistic and divine idea "down to earth" i.e. into reality. The importance of such lies on the way towards that vision and not in the final achievement, as per, for us, the SDG's!.

Concept of Justice (Adl)

Justice (*adl*) corresponds to cosmic, ecological and human justice as well as harmony with the universe. Therefore, ethical governance is the cornerstone for attaining and sustaining progress and thus a good life (*hayat tayebah*) or, in other words, sustainable development. Human brother- and sisterhood, regardless of faith, would be a hollow concept without socio-economic justice. There are no fewer than a hundred different expressions in the Quran embodying the notion of justice, placing justice nearest to piety.

> 004: 135. O ye who believe! Stand out firmly for justice, as witnesses To God, even as against Yourselves, or your parents, Or your kin, and whether It be (against) rich or poor: For God can best protect both. Follow not the lusts (of your hearts), lest ye Swerve, and if ye Distort (justice) or decline To do justice, verily God is well-acquainted with all that ye do.

The concept of *Adl* has different dimensions and can have different meanings. Next to the social justice, which basically means upholding the dignity and freedom of the individual, *Adl* stands also for economic justice that one can find as the fairtrade practice in the context of agriculture. Actually, all Sekem operations are conducted according to fairtrade principles even though the official logo does not occur on every product because of the expensive accreditation that is done only based on customer demand. All supplying farmers from Sekem get a price premium on their organic or biodynamic products and have long-term contracts with regulated pricing mechanisms which constitutes the basis for a fair relationship. In the Qu'ran there are passages describing this:

> 004: 049 O ye who believe! Eat not up your property among yourselves in vanities: But let there be amongst you Traffic and trade by mutual good-will: Nor kill (or destroy) yourselves: for verily Allah hath been to you Most Merciful!

Then there is also the principle of ecological justice, which refers back to the responsibility of humans towards the earth and nature. Islam teaches that species including plants and wildlife are in a state of prayer referring to the intrinsic value of nature and the ecosystem services. Praying in its wider meaning is about fulfilling a task in the bigger context of God's creation. Al-Jayyousi rightly pointed out that the harm of any species means that we are disrupting the symphony of life and silencing worshipers:

> 024: 041 Seest thou not that it is Allah Whose praises all beings in the heavens and on earth do celebrate, and the birds (of the air) with wings outspread? Each one knows its own (mode of) prayer and praise. And Allah knows well all that they do.

Concept of "Stewardship' of the Earth (Khalifa)

Ultimately, and for Sekem in an Islamic context, The human is viewed as a trustee or steward to ensure that all resources, physical and human, are utilized in a reasonable, equitable and sustainable manner to sustain and develop the natural state.

> 033: 072 We did indeed offer the Trust to the Heavens and the Earth and the Mountains; but they refused to undertake it, being afraid thereof: but man undertook it;- He was indeed unjust and foolish;

The application of chemical fertilizer and pesticides is harming the environment and destroying the fragile balance of the ecosystem. It represents a mechanistic worldview that does not realize the bigger context in which agriculture takes place. The perverse large-scale and destructive forms of "modern" agricultural systems do not consider ecological and ethical values. That is one of the reasons why SEKEM is convinced of its sustainable approach to organic and biodynamic agriculture that excludes chemical fertilizer and pesticides and the usage of GMO.

Stewardship (*Khalifa*), moreover, implies social equality and dignity of all human beings – regardless of skin color, social status, etc. – a cardinal element of the Islamic faith. Within such, the right attitude toward others is not "might is right," the struggle to serve one's own self-interest, or "the struggle to survive," but rather mutual cooperation, to develop the entire human potential. Secondly, resources are a trust *(amanah)*, provided by Allah, whereby the human being is not the primary owner, but is just a trustee *(amin)*. So resources are for the benefit of all, for the wellbeing not just for oneself and one's family, but for the community at large. This includes the whole web of life, from soil organisms to insects to birds to wildlife to plant life. This is explained in the Qu'ran as follows:

> 006: 038 There is not an animal (that lives) on the earth, nor a being that flies on its wings, but (forms part of) communities like you. Nothing have We omitted from the Book, and they (all) shall be gathered to their Lord in the end.

Acting responsibly in the interest of communities implies also that resources should not be wasted. This is also made clear several times in the Qu'ran, such as here:

> 007: 031 O children of Adam! Wear your beautiful apparel At every time and place Of prayer: eat and drink: But waste not by excess, For God loveth not the wasters.

Waste recycling is the underlying principle of composting in general. At Sekem organic waste produced by all Sekem firms and some additional green waste that comes from the surrounding farms is used to produce high quality compost that is applied on own fields and also for sale to external customers. This and many other practices of organic and biodynamic agriculture represent responsible human action and justice towards nature and society. Because justice is such an important cornerstone in the Islamic belief system it is presented below even though it is strongly connected to the principle of *Khalifa*.

We now finally compare and contrast the world of Sekem as a whole, as revealed in this case story, thereby drawing on its overall African and specifically Egyptian heritage, indigenously, its anthropophical and scientific reach, exogenously, and indeed Islam resting in between the two. This can then be compared and contrasted with the approach taken by its fellow travellers in the South X Alliance specifically, if not also Catalyt 2030 generally, on behalf of the so called *global* South, with its overall orientation toward the UN's SDG's.

Conclusion. Towards Regenerative Value Creation

Indigenous Healing Wisdom, Exogenous Anthroposophy and Islam in Between

In conclusion then, we have been introduced Sekem as a holistic development initiative based on the principles of organic and biodynamic agriculture. Islam is one main indigenous pillar of the cultural context of Sekem and, in significant part, its spiritual source of inspiration, building also on the more ancient indigenous wisdom that has come indigenously before. The other exogenous source of inspiration is European culture, philosophy and science. All together have been authentically integrated in the personality of Ibrahim Abouleish in particular if not also now Sekem in general.

Islam then offers a particular story of the origin of the universe and human beings which is embedded, in significant part, in Sekem's origin story. Humans are thereby trustees (*khalifa*) to ensure all resources are used in a sustainable manner, for us thereby also aligned, in terms of healing the earth, with the healing wisdom of Africa. Reading the Qu'ran informs the mind and soul that our natural and social capital are interconnected and interdependent. Sekem builds on that insight and provides a practical example of Islamic values in agriculture but also in building communities, developing humans and conducting what they have recently been calling regenerative value creation.

Conflict Arises Out of Inhibited Recognition and Release of GENEius

For us this is of especial significance, given the fact that COP28 is being held in in the UAE in MENA, in the heart of the Islamic Middle East, while at the same time Palestine and Israel are in dire conflict, which is affecting the whole region if not the whole of the world at large. While on the one hand (as of December, 2023) COP 28 is dealing with an emergency arising out of the conflict between man and nature, and the conflict in Israel/Palestine has arisen out of unreconciled human differences, both within each society and without, for us the two natural-ecological and socio-cultural issues are intimately connected.

In our integral, GENEtic terms, then, to the extent that any society fails to recognize and regenerate, nature and culture in harmony with its science and technology, polity and economy, conflict will arise, within and without. In other words, *to the extent that such a society is inhibited from recognizing and releasing its GENEius, which thereby can be likended to the gifts of mother nature being recklessly squandered, hell will break lose.*

Turning Towards Re-GENE-rative Value Creation

In other words, re-GENE-rative value creation, so to speak, ecologically and economically, is particular to one society or another, albeit in relation to others. Such involves, in principle through seldom in practice, local natural Grounding, local-global transcultural emergence, *newly* global scientific and humanistic navigation, and ultimately global-local economic, if not also political, Effect. Sekem then remains a rare regenerative case, as we have seen, when natural and cultural riches are equally brought to bear on itself and the world.

Little of such is in fact apparent in the South – X Alliance instance. Moreover, given the overall image of Islam in today's world, seldom for good and all too often for ill, the Sekem case story is especially significant: how alongside Africa's healing wisdom, Egypt's maat, central Europe's anthroposophy, as well as contemporary western science, it has profoundly underpinned the social innovation that Sekem, in our *south-north*, has become.

Social Innovation at Sekem in MENA/South X Alliance in the Global South

Towards and Integral Worlds Approach

In fact there is no hint, within the South X Alliance, not unlike the case of the Global South as a whole, of the particular natural and cultural, if not also scientific, underpinnings, as we have seen with Sekem in Egypt – and indeed for us with Paxherbals to come, in Nigeria, and our Integral Kumusha in Zimbabwe – of their social innovations, each in their particular societal contexts. That definitely does not mean, though, that there is no value to the South X Alliance proposition.

True to our integral perspective, what we term the "south-eastern" natural and cultural orientation that the Sekems of this world bring to bear, needs to underlie the technological and economic, if not also political, orientation of the South X Alliance. It is only when all such integral realms, for us, are aligned, that the GENE-ius of a particular society – what the alliance calls scaleability – can be realized. Moreover, and for us most specifically, the north (science and technology) and west (polity and economy) needs to build on the south (nature and community) and east (culture and spirituality), rather than vice versa.

Re-GENE-ration Has Gone Largely Unregnized, in Integral Terms

Sad to say such is much easier said than done. While the Sekem's of this world, in Egypt, like our Paxherbals, in Nigeria, have duly "scaled up" in and around their own societal terrain, they remain singular exceptions, even in their own societies, never mind in the wider world. The natural and the cultural south and east need the technological and economic north and west, just as much as the north-western latter need the south-eastern former. Co-evolving all of such, together, remains the noble, integral task at hand.

Sekem has made an invaluable start, but such value *re-GENE-ration has gone largely unregnized, at least in our integral terms,* and together with such GENEuine social innovation, which is why we have articulated this case story, standing on the ginat sholders of the three generations of the Aboueish's themselves. We now turn from the south-north to the south-west, from Egypt to Nigeria, in Africa.

References

Abouleish I (2005) *Sekem – A Sustainable Community in the Egyptian Desert.* Edinburgh. Floris Publications

Abouleish M ex **Lessem** R, **Aboleish** I, **Pogacnik** M and **Herman** L (2016) *Integral Polity: Aligning Nature, Culture, Society and Economy.* Abingdon. Routledge

Al-Jayyousi O (2012) *Islam and Sustainable Development: New Worldviews.* Abingdon. Routledge

Lessem R and **Schieffer** A (2009) *Transformation Management. Toward the Integral Enterprise.* Abingdon. Routledge

SEKEM. Economy of Love. https://sekem.com/en/economy-of-love-rethinking-agriculture-for-future/

SEKEM. https://www.sekem.com/en/economy/economy-of-love-fairtrade/

South X Allaince J (2023) *COP 28 Launch, December 3*

Steiner R (2001) *The Philosophy of Freedom: Basis for a Modern World Conception.* Forest Row. Sussex. Rudolf Steiner Press

Part 5 Realization Path Out of South-*West* Africa/Diaspora: Communitalism

Chapter 14 Case Study Method to African Empirical Foundation. Positivism to Naturalism

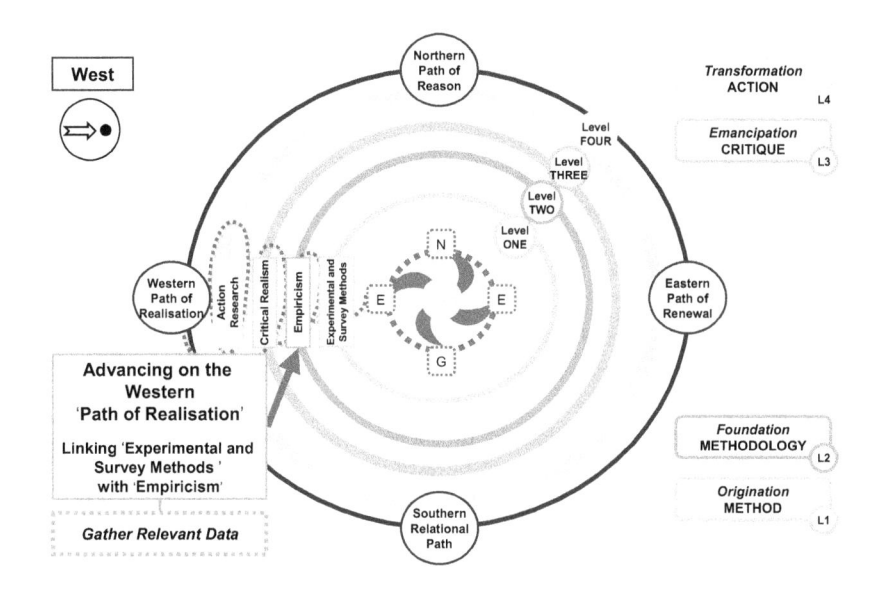

Figure 14.1: *Overview Chapter 14 – Level 2 / West*

> "I think it is fair to say that a case is really a distinct literary form. it is highly important that the case develop a great deal of interest on the part of the student. and then bring about the willing suspension of belief, that is the willingness to take at face value the situation the case presents, and become the person concerned with it. Then there must be plot, narrative structure, an issue that the student must discover for himself, a disguised problem, whereby the student is really putting himself in the shoes of a particular individual" ... The truth of the matter, though, is that HBS cases are not a distinct literary form. They are a mishmash of poorly written summaries of business situations, on top of which are piled page after page of tabular data, charts and graphs.
>
> Duff Macdonald (2017)   The Golden Passport: Harvard Business School, Limits of Capitalism and the Moral Failure of the MBA Elite.

> **Summary: Empiricism in South-*West* Africa**

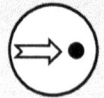

- We now turn from the south-north research path of reason and innovation laden economics of love to the *south*-western research path of realisation. Building lightly on the experiment and survey, as well as heavily on case study, we are move on to empirically analyse cause and effect, and build a south-western African foundation for the practically based transformation to follow.

- Empiricism is a theory of knowledge emphasizing the role of experience in the formation of ideas, while discounting the notion of innate ideas. Such empiricism is closely related to positivism, seeking after the "positive" facts, rather than relying on pure faith or indeed dogma.

- As such, and starting by feeling local, we follow the case of Cashbuild, in South Africa in the 1980s and 1980s, as Albert Koopman gradually transformed this rurally based, building supplies retailer into a workplace democracy, under the guise of value sharing

- Positivism, then locally-globally, broadens such a "south-western" empirical orientation into one that incorporates continental European, especially selective Austrian and French philosophical thought, of a structurally ordered universe made up of atomistic, discrete and observable events, typified by the economic marketplace.

- Newly globally furthermore, starting out in America with C.S. Pierce, William James and John Dewey, all such so called pragmatists extended such inductive thought. Now combined with deductive and also relationally based abductive thought, Australian contemporary research philosopher Norman Blaikie added retroductive thought to the above three thought forms. What emerges is a newly global inductive, deductive, retroductive, and abductive integral orientation

- Globally-locally in Africa then, and overall, the keynotes of such a *south-western* empirical orientation involve firstly the search for a *place bound truth*; secondly *securing positive facts* that are true to the indigenous worlds contained therein; whereby thirdly the data collected are then turned into *home grown theories*; whereby finally s *"closed system"* protects the integrity of place.

14.1 Overview of Empiricism as Foundation for the Realization Path

14.1.1. Empiricism in Context

An Integral West Builds on the Rest

For us the "west", in the African case the "south-west", is unlike what we see in the world at large. Thereby the west, economically at least, has dominated the rest. We now invoke *an integral west that builds on the rest*. In that guise, on the one research hand, the path of economic realisation needs to build on the naturally relational path, the path of cultural renewal, and that of scientific reason that come before. Similarly, in relation to the path of innovation, communitalism ultimately needs to build on nhakanomics, yurugu-nomics and the economics of love that precedes it.

Moreover, within the path of realisation itself (see Table 14.1.1. below, action research and learning needs to build on a particular case at hand, in this case our (Anselm Adodo) own case; and Pax Herbals as such lays the ground for nature power, healing radiance and communitalism, as an ultimately layered African reality.

Table 14.1.1. W*est African Social Research and Innovation: Path of Realisation Case Study to ACTION RESEARCH/Paxherbals to African Layered Reality Paxherbals and Communitalism*

Western Grounding Method and Origination	Western Emergent Methodology & Foundation	Western Navigational Critique and Emancipation	Western Effective Action and Transformation
Case Study (W1)	Empiricism (W2)	Critical Realism (W3)	Action Research and Learning (W4)
Pax Herbals (W1)	Nature Power/ Healing Radiance (W2)	Communitalism (W3)	African Layered Reality (W4)

Empiricism Has Been the Single Most Influential Force in Modern Science

Empiricism has certainly been the single most influential force in modern science. It is not only the core research orientation within the natural sciences, it has – until recently – also been the dominant paradigm in the social sciences. We have highlighted various times in our work the dangerous consequences of such a myopic approach, which excludes much more than it includes. However, such empiricism, within our Integral framework, remains the foundation of the western path of realisation; however, as we shall see, transcended in emancipatory guise by its methodological critique, in the form of critical realism (Chapter 15); and ultimately transformed by action research as a means, together with communitalist substance and communiversity form into "south-western" social innovation (Chapter 16).

What we need then to incorporate in such is an African south-*western* perspective, as we shall reveal, and to some extent seek to remedy, not least through our opening Cashbuild South African case in this chapter, also herein touching base with aboriginal Australia in the "*south*-west" as it were, and ultimately culminating with our West African case story, that of Paxherbals in Nigeria, which one of us (Anselm Adodo) originally founded.

A Dearth of Empirical Case Studies in the "South", If Not Also the "East"

Empiricism, as such a "western" foundation, builds on experimental and survey methods, by way of origination, as well as, especially in a management and economic context, on the renowned case study (see opening quote). Such one of us (Ronnie Lessem) was thoroughly immersed in, through his MBA studies at Harvard. Indeed, though business schools, worlds-wide, might be overly saturated with such predominantly "western" cases, *the dearth of such in the "south", if not also the "east" has continually alarmed us, leaving, if you like, a "big black empirical hole", foundationally speaking, which we are determined to fill, starting with the four case stories contained in this volume.*

Indeed later in this chapter we shall present such a south-western mini case, and thereafter, more fully, through Paxherbals case story. As such, and referring to Duff Macdonald's poignant comments, at the outset of this chapter, we attempt to get inside the African "individual skin", something your typical HBS case study, as opposed to a fully fledged case story, fails to do.

Such a western perspective, however, in isolation from the south and east, then, as we can see from the desolate state of today's social sciences dominated by neo-liberal economics, runs overall aground, which is why we allude to an "integral west"; moreover each research path, needs to move re-GENE-ratively through its originating method, foundational methodology, and emancipating critique, and transformative action research to have any chance, so we argue, to build up towards viable social innovation. Finally, to fully actualise such the research process needs to be aligned with African context(healing wisdom), substance (communitalism) and form (communiversity) altogether.

Feeling and Personhood: Experiential (Feel Local), Imaginal (Intuit Local-Global), Conceptual (Think Newly Global) and Practical (Global-Local)

Furthermore, and in each such successive case, there is a need to feel local, before intuiting local-global, thereafter thinking newly global, and acting ultimately globally-locally. For such an overall insight we are indebted to John. Heron's (1994), through his *Feeling and Personhood* (see Chapter 10) related four modes of knowing: *experiential (our feel local), imaginal (our intuit local-global), conceptual (our think newly global) and practical (our global-local)* in turn. Let us now turn first, as we have done for all four of our research paths, to an overview of western empiricism.

14.1.2. Empiricism: A Conceptual Overview

Empiricism Defined: Prioritising Sensing

Empiricism is a theory of knowledge emphasizing the role of sense-based experience in the formation of ideas, thereby aligned with Jung's (2022) sensing personality type, while discounting the other thinking, feeling and intuiting personality types, and their societal manifestations. In the philosophy of science, moreover, empiricism is focused, most especially, on such sense based experience gauged through deliberate experimental arrangements. In fact, as Paulin Hountondji (2002) has pointed out (see Chapter 12), in Africa we are invariably relegated to such a data gathering role (Jung's sensing), in the absence of deriving our own prior theories (Jung's intuiting/thinking).

Empiricism: The Etymology of the Term

The term "empiricism" has a dual etymology. It comes from the Greek word εμπειρισμός, the Latin translation of which is experientia, from which we derive the word experience. It also derives from a more specific classical Greek and Roman usage of empiric, referring to a physician whose skills derive from practical experience as opposed to instruction in theory. In fact, the term "empirical" was originally used to refer to certain ancient Greek practitioners of medicine who rejected adherence to the dogmatic doctrines of the day, preferring instead to rely on the observation of phenomena as perceived in experience.

English empiricism, as we shall see moreover, is closely related to European positivism, that is seeking after the "positive" facts, rather than relying on pure faith or indeed dogma. Positivism (Markie 2004) incorporates a "north-western" ontology of an ordered universe made up of atomistic, discrete and observable events, typified by the economic marketplace. Only that which can be physically observed, that is directly experienced by the senses, can be regarded as real. In such an epistemology, knowledge is seen to be derived from sensory experience by means of experimental or comparative analysis.

Scientific theories, in such an empirical light then, are regarded as law-like statements, specifying simple relations or constant conjunctions between phenomena. Value judgments and normative statements, as such, require a separation of objective "facts" and subjective "values"; furthermore "subjective" values are denied having the status of knowledge. The grounds for origination, therefore, are lodged entirely and objectively in the external world "out there", rather than in the internal and subjective world, that is in yourself, as researcher or as would-be social innovator. As a result, so-called objectively based case studies, survey methods, including questionnaires and structured interviews, incorporating also statistical controls, constitute the original qualitative as well as quantitative base for such.

Such scientific "method" with its conventional procedure of observation, experimentation, and verification, in fact emerged in Europe, mainly in Britain, in the 17th century. It was forged out of a "liberal" and reasoned Enlightenment reaction to the perceived dogmatism of religious orthodoxy in Europe. As such it was spearheaded by such British luminaries as English political scientists John Locke and David Hume, political economists Adam Smith in Scotland and John Stuart Mill in England, and English natural scientist Frances Bacon and Italy's Galileo Galilei. These kindred spirits were the early advocates of democracy, free markets and the pursuit of the objectively "scientific" truth. Ironically in their day, they were all radical thinkers, staking their liberal claims – often risking their lives – against the conservative status quo. All together, these positivists were responsible for three of the major social innovations of the past two to three hundred years: free markets and liberal democracy, and scientific method itself, in its classically "western" vein.

Empiricism and the Rise of Economics

Empiricism also gave rise to a new discipline called economics, detached as such form previous moral philosophy. The Scottish philosopher Adam Smith, who is depicted on the back of today's Bank of England £20 note, was probably the most pioneering thinker in this field. It was Smith's systematic studies of the historical development of industry and commerce in Europe that led to his famous 18th century treatises: *The Theory of Moral Sentiments* (Smith 2010), and *An Inquiry into the Nature and Causes of the Wealth of Nations* (Smith and Sutherland 2008). Smith's work helped to create the modern academic discipline of economics and provided one of the best-known intellectual rationales for free trade, capitalism, and libertarianism.

In the empirically laden process, of course, his later book on the wealth of nations, proceeded to eclipse the former, much less popular work. Smith libertarian ideas were taken forward by John Stuart Mill whose early economic philosophy was one of free markets. Mill's *Principles of Political Economy* (1848), first published in 1848, was one of the most widely read of all books on economics in the period. As Adam Smith's Wealth of Nations had during an earlier period, Mill's Principles dominated economics teaching, in England then, and today in the wider world.

We now depart from such "north-western" conventional wisdom, on empiricism, to feel local, in the "south-west". We turn thus to *Nature Power* that underlies Paxherbals, which one of us (Anselm Adodo) founded. Later on, in our fourth south-western case story we shall illustrate how an integral community enterprise altogether built in such in rural Nigeria

14.2. Feel Local African Realization – Nature Power: W2f

14.2.1. Before We Came the Plants Were Here

To Survive We Must Learn from Nature

We thereby, feeling local in West Africa, go back to African source, via Adodo's (2012) book on *Nature Power*. It was there, for him, where the African, relational grounds for the path of realisation lay, thereby combining our south and west, also cosmologically centred in the healing wisdom of Africa.

For him when God made men and women he gave them all they needed to be happy, to be whole, to be healthy. He gave us sunshine, water, air and earth. But due to our greed and selfishness we began to exploit the earth, abuse it, destroy it, and treat it with disrespect. The result is crisis: economic crisis, mental crisis, social crisis, political crisis, climatic crisis. We human beings are the youngest occupants of the planet. *Before we came, the plants were here; before we came, the animals we here; before we came the oceans, the forests and the mountains were here. To survive, we must learn from nature. To learn from her, we must respect her.*

Earth Is the Primary Source of our Creativity, Intelligence, and Humanness

Nature Power, for Adodo, *is inviting the world to come down to earth so as to regain our health. The earth is the primary source of our creativity, intelligence, and humanness. Before we set out to calculate, to create, to invent, to fabricate, the earth already was.* Today, faced with globalization, high-technology and a fast-paced modern lifestyle, we are often tempted to forget our link with the earth and therefore become DIS-EASED.

In the past we heard about physicians who provided health CARE to the sick. Our health, our life, our future in fact depends on the quality of the earth: soil, water, sunshine, forests and air. The rich, the poor, the sick, the healthy, black people, white people, we all breathe the same air. At the end of the day what we put into the earth will come back to us, either to purify us or poison us. The air we breathe is the same air inhaled by Jesus Christ, by the Blessed Virgin Mary, by Mohammed, and by the great scientists, philosophers and saints of the past.

The Wisdom of the Ancients Is There in the Molecules of the Air Around Us

Viewed from this perspective, we can now see how scientific our Africa ancestors were when they asserted that only a thin line separates the physical from the spiritual, spirit from matter, life from death. In fact for the African Creation Energy Group, that is for the Ghanean African American Osiadan Borebore Oboadee (African Creation Energy 2014):

> The historical origin of human life started on the African continent, so surely African mythology, magic and symbolism should begin any discussion on scientific principle. The origin of human invention, moreover, lies with nature. For example a plant that turns its leaves towards the sun to receive more sunlight is a form of technology. The Samara winged seed, from the maple and elm tree, that flies through the air has an aeronautical design similar to that of a helicopter propeller.

Indeed the wisdom of the ancients is there in the molecules of the air around us, waiting to be tapped when we are open enough to perceive them. Millions of men and women from all parts of the world are coming together to remind us that it is our human greed and selfishness, rather than nuclear bombs, that constitute the greatest threat to our human survival, to human health and peace. Humanity is sick, for Adodo, and needs to be administered the medicine of justice, fairness, concern for others and respect for our symbiotic cosmos. Adodo then turns specifically to the African Universe, as a world of human and more-than-human relationships.

14.2.2. The Natural Road to Wholeness

The African Universe as a World of Relationships

The African Universe is a world of relationships, of interactions between the living and the dead, between the natural and the supernatural. A community is not just a place where human beings dwell. *The African community comprises plants, animals, human beings, the spirit and the ancestors.* Trees are more than trees: the sky is more than we see. There is more to plants and animals than we see with our eyes. *Everything in the universe is a language of Life and an expression of Life. Therefore they are sacred and holy.*

The Third World: Our Problem Is the Lack of Love

We have only one problem, for Adodo, a lack of love. *Our problem is not the lack of power, or the lack of leadership, nor the lack of money. Our problem is the lack of love.* The fruits of this lack of love are divisions, strife and violence. Look around you. What do you see? Angry faced, hungry stomachs, broken families and warring nations. The image one gets is that of a people who are not at peace with themselves or with one another, and of countries which are either "developed" or "under-developed".

There is a tendency in our time to draw a sharp line between the "developed" and the "under-developed" people of the earth. The "developed" people are the people of Western Europe and Northern America. They are the world changers, with a high level of technological advancement and superior technical knowledge and skills. *The "underdeveloped" people are the people of Africa, Asia and Latin America. They are the passive receivers of technology and civilization; hence they are referred to as the third world.* Behind this division lies a false concept of western civilization as the ideal civilisation. A more viable concept, for Adodo, is that of "holiness".

Union with God, with Oneself, with Nature and with Others

Holiness is a state of union with God, with oneself and with others. Others include your fellow human beings as well as plants, animals, and indeed the whole of creation. When you discover that you are not just anybody or just a spirit, but a complete and whole person, then you will discover the meaning of holiness. The holy person is the one who has discovered the balance between the physical, the psychological and the spiritual.

When there is imbalance there is disease. For society says: be rich, have pleasure, obtain power, be famous, for these are the goals of life. The false conception of life, for Adodo, of all reality, is the root of all diseases. Having imbibed the mechanistic world view, which sees natural things as mere objects to be exploited and the human body as a mere object of pleasure, we eat what we like, drink anything that comes our way and live as we want. The result of this, for him, is disease. We are no longer at ease. We have lost touch with our origins.

14.2.3. The Healing Potency of Sound

The Primordial Sacred Sound by Which the World Came into Being

For the traditional African, the drum is the carrier of the word, the primordial sacred sound by which the world came into being. *The drum is to the traditional African as the Bible is to the Christian. The drum is the symbol of God's incarnation, of God present among us, of Logos.* It is the sacrament of the divine in the human, of spirit in matter, and the sacred in the profane. Sound for Africans is an emotive and creative force.

Music Permeates Your Being, You Are Nothing But Music

In the Yoruba language, for Adodo moreover, there is a clear distinction between the spoken word and potent speech. The former is called *oro*, common words used in conversation. The latter is called *ofo*. The Hebrew equivalent is dahbar, while the Greek is logos. *Ofo* refers to words that have the power of becoming an event in life simply being uttered. When an *ofo* is uttered it goes onto actualise itself. When sound is then organized into rhythm, you have music. Music is a powerful tool. No one can resist the lure of music.

Music permeates your being, you are nothing but music. The body is a living entity, and intelligent being with its own laws. The wisdom of the cosmos is reflected in the body, and the body is a musical composition. The different forms of sound, the human voice, sound of nature and the sound of music carry waves of energy which they impress on us. *It is only when we learn to be silent that we can hear the creative sound of creation restoring us to harmony, peace and contentment.* We now turn from our local, African feel for nature power, as the very foundation upon which Pax Herbals has built its economic realization, to a local-global approach to empiricism and to positivism.

In turning back to conventionally north-western empiricism, in and of itself, now locally-globally as it were, we review such local *English* empiricism, explicitly social scientifically, in the light of also "global" continental *European* positivism. In the process we shall immediately see the chasm between local African natural feel and the local global intuited local-global Anglo European empirical reality.

14.3. Intuiting Locally-Globally: Empiricism and Positivism: W2i

14.3.1. Classical Scientific Method: Empiricism and Positivism

For Open University based social scientist Mark Smith in the UK, overall then, in his Social Science in Question (Smith 2000), the success of the scientific "method" is specifically explained in terms of its ability to reveal the truth.

In order to achieve progress, as such, we should deploy our capacity for reason within the methodological rules of scientific method, in order to objectively and factually establish the truth of a situation and use this as a means of serving the needs of humanity. These were the roots of so-called "positivism", originally established in the seventeenth and eighteenth centuries to counteract "unscientific" dogma.. However, in more recent years, and now during the 20th century, the radical nature and scope of such original theorists has been dissipated, and they have come to represent the status quo, at least in "western" secular terms. Let us explore further the link between the empirical methods and the positivist philosophy underlying them, drawing upon the even more refined version of such empiricism, that is "logical positivism".

14.3.2. The Austrians' Logical Positivist Approach

Logical positivism placed an exceptional emphasis upon sensory perception and the role of observation in research as the foundation for knowledge. Scientific statements were seen as pictures or snapshots of the things they refer to. The more contemporary origins go back to England's Bertrand Russell but also to Austria's

Ludwig Wittgenstein subsequently promoted by the Vienna Circle from the 1920s. To each object, they maintained, corresponds a definite statement. For Austrian Rudolph Carnap, an influential member of the circle, this approach was identified as "physicalism". Indeed, logical positivism, a close ally of empiricism, is more associated with continental Europe, especially Austria and France, in our "north" than it is with Anglo-Saxon empiricism in the "west".

The logical positivist uses induction to collect observational data and build theories o explain the observations. Thus the method of induction involves two movements simultaneously: from the particular to the general, and from observed events to theoretical constructions. Such induction, with its focus on doing, can be compared with deduction (focus on knowing), retroduction (oriented towards becoming) and abduction (linked with being).

To summarize, the method of induction refers to a logical process of constructing knowledge about observed relationships between variables in particular instances. This can be taken as a basis for making universal generalizations in as yet unobserved, particular instances. The strength of induction lies in its appeal to data collected through human senses, rather than perceived intuitively, or conceived abstractly, as a means of validating propositions. The explanatory power of this approach is said to rest upon its predictive uses. However, such prediction tends to be restricted to "closed" systems.

14.3.3. Closed Systems Take Precedence over Open Systems

Typical of such a "closed" scientific orientation, especially in the 20th century, was the *use of mechanical and experimental metaphors*, along with a desire to emulate physics as the purest form of scientific activity. Indeed, experimental method was correlated with scientific method. Newton (1642–1727), for example, in his study of matter, motion and light, was developing the method of induction by using observations of particular conditions – experimenting with light through the use of prisms and pieces of white card – as a foundation for constructing a general theoretical account of light. Within such a closed system it is possible to:

* identify a limited number of variables
* observe their behaviour, the frequency of changes in one in relation to the other
* account for or avoid any interference from unexpected external forces.

The scientific experiment was Newton's way of artificially replicating the idea of a closed system, enabling researchers to isolate the objects they wish to investigate from all other objects, which would confuse the picture (see Table 14.3.3. below).

Table 14.3.3. *Closed and Open Systems*

	Closed Systems	Open Systems
Simplicity & Complexity	A limited Number of Variables is involved to increase the Possibility of Identifying and Predicting clear Relationships.	A "State of Complexity" is acknowledged as the Condition of one's Object of Analysis and the Relation between them.
External Boundary	Exclusion clauses ensure that the Mass of possible Influences are screened out (ceteris paribus).	Each Object can be Part of multiple Relationships and no Outcome can be predicted.
Intrinsic Properties	All Objects of Analysis are taken at face value so that the intrinsic Properties of an Object are not taken into Account.	It is recognised that all Objects have intrinsic Properties and Structures affecting Performance in different Conditions.

Identifying simple relations between discrete things would enable a scientist to understand and explain events beyond the experimental situation. The idea of such "closure" has been an important part of all scientific disciplines, which have sought to establish objective knowledge, including the social sciences. In psychology, for example, such experimental closure involves the physical separation of human beings from their normal context, and subjecting them to particular stimuli with a view to gauging their response.

Through theoretical closure, in econometric models for example, the economy is replicated as a series of variables and relationships through a computer programme, including growth measures, the money supply, manufacturing output, employment levels and prices. The relationships between the variables are conceived of in terms of the susceptibility of one variable to changes in the others. No model though, however elaborate, can mirror or replicate the uncertainties or complexities of the real economy. Furthermore, statistical closure involves a situation in which quantitative numerical data sets are processed to identify correlations, as for example with the study of voting behaviour.

As soon as the complexity of social life is acknowledged in social research, though, these techniques for simulating closure are problematised and the status of causal laws produced in this way is dramatically altered. This *problem is accentuated if it is accepted that social objects have an internal complexity and structure as a complex responsive open system* (see Table 14.3.3 above). Yet the traditional "quantitative" orientation, historically promoted by the physical sciences in the "west", has reinforced the "closed" nature of such a "positivist" epistemology. This applies as much to experimental research method, as it does to positivist research methodology.

14.3.4. France's August Comte and Positivist Epistemology in the Social Sciences

Such positivist approaches to the social sciences often exclusively claim the label of "scientific", for they assume things can be studied as hard facts, and the relationship between these facts established as solid, empirically based, scientific laws. For such positivists, these laws have the status of truth as social objects, and can be studied in much the same way as natural objects. Not surprisingly, *classical and neo-classical economics, with its belief in "market mechanisms" is heavily influenced by positivism.*

The most influential early positivist in the social sciences was the French sociologist Auguste Comte (1798–1857). He brought together the search for the truth with his faith in progress. To replace "divine truths", Comte looked to the natural sciences, calling his approach "social physics". Comte sought to identify the laws of social statics and social dynamics with a view to social engineering. The English utilitarian Jeremy Bentham, following in Comte's footsteps, characterized human beings as pleasure seeking or pain avoiding, based on their making rational choices. This approach treated aggregate bodies as the total of individual actors, with a view to gaining "the greatest good for the greatest number". The economy is thus an aggregate of individuals, firms and households; the political process is an aggregate of voters in elections and parties and pressure groups.

Needless to say, the *local* to which we have been alluding, in this Anglo-Saxon empirical case, alongside the *global*, continental European positivism in this case, are far removed from our "feeling local" in the African south-*west*. To retrieve this imbalance we now turn "newly globally" to research philosophers CS Pearce, William James and John Dewey historically in America, and then onto Norman Blaikie, currently in Australia. We start then with Pearce's pragmatism.

14.4. Newly Global Emancipatory Natural Realisation Path: W2t

14.4.1. Emerging Pragmatism: Inductive, Deductive and Abductive

For Peirce Evoked Directly Out of Peoples' Life Worlds

In the late 19th century and early 20th century several forms of pragmatic philosophy arose out of empiricism. The ideas of pragmatism developed mainly from discussions that took place while American philosopher Charles Sanders Peirce (1986) and psychologist William James (2000) were both at Harvard in the 1870s. James popularised the term "pragmatism", giving Peirce full credit for its patrimony. Along with its pragmatic theory of truth, this perspective integrated the basic insights of empirical (experience-based induction) and rational (concept-based deduction) thinking, but also, as we shall see, added a newly relational (abduction) touch.

Charles Peirce in fact, in the 19th and early 20th centuries, was highly influential in initially laying the groundwork for today's empirical scientific method. Although Peirce severely criticized many elements of Descartes' peculiar brand of rationalism, he did not reject rationalism outright. Indeed, he concurred with the main ideas of rationalism, most importantly the idea that rational concepts can be meaningful and the idea that these necessarily go beyond the data given by empirical observation. In later years he even emphasized the concept-driven side of the then ongoing debate between strict empiricism and strict rationalism, in part to counterbalance the excesses to which some of his colleagues had taken pragmatism under the "data-driven" strict-empiricist view.

To this, significantly for our "newly global" purposes, *Peirce added the concept of abductive reasoning, evoked directly out of peoples' life worlds,* which we have identified with our "southern" world. Peirce's approach presupposes that firstly the objects of knowledge are real things (see Freya Mathews' "love of matter" below), secondly the characters (properties) of real things do not depend on our perceptions of them, and thirdly everyone who has sufficient experience of real things will agree on the truth about them'. In his Harvard *Lectures on Pragmatism* (1903), Peirce then enumerated what he called the *"three contrary propositions of pragmatism" – inductive, deductive, and abductive –* saying that they "put the edge on the maxim of pragmatism".

Action Research Built on Theories of Pragmatism

The renowned US-American Social Philosopher and Educationalist John Dewey, as we have seen (see previous chapter on socio-technical design) who became one of the founding fathers of *"action research" built on such theories on pragmatism to form a theory known as instrumentalism. The role of sense experience in Dewey's theory is crucial,* in that he saw experience as unified totality of things through which everything else is interrelated. Dewey's basic thought, in accordance with empiricism was that reality is determined by past experience. Therefore, humans adapt their past experiences of things to perform experiments upon and test the pragmatic values of such experience. The value of such experience is measured by scientific instruments, and the results of such measurements generate ideas which serve as instruments for future experimentation.

We now turn from Peirce, James and Dewey in America, albeit an integral America and a "west" which is somewhat different from the conventional, empirical, Anglo-Saxon norm, the Australia.

14.4.2. Social to Natural Inquiry: Inductive, Deductive, Retroductive, Abductive

Approaches to Social Inquiry: Four Worlds of Research and Knowledge Creation

Norman Blaikie (2007), an Australian contemporary research philosopher, formerly based at the University of Science in Malaysia, published his *Approaches to Social Inquiry* in 1993, followed by a new version in 2007. In effect, and as we outlined (Figure 14.4.2 below) in our (Lessem and Schieffer 2010) original book on *Integral Research and Innovation,* building on Blaikie (highlighted below in capitals) also drawing on the work of Japanese organisational sociologists, Nonaka and Takeuchi (1995) in their *Knowledge Creating Company* (in italics below):

> In the same way as we have distinguished between "western" and "northern", "eastern" and "southern" worlds, Blaikie has identified INDUCTIVE and DEDUCTIVE, ABDUCTIVE and RETRODUCTIVE strategies. Interestingly enough, moreover, the Japanese industrial sociologists Ikijiro Nonaka and Hirotaka Takeuchi, have interwoven all four into a "knowledge creating spiral", organisation-ally comprised of Internalisation, Combination, Socialisation and Externalisation.

Figure 14.4.2. *Integral Worlds, Modes of Social Inquiry and Knowledge Creation*

	Northern DEDUCTION *Combination*	
Western INDUCTION *Internalisation*		Eastern RETRODUCTION *Externalisation*
	Southern ABDUCTION *Socialisation*	

What Blaikie has done, drawing on CS Pierce, is to add retroductive reasoning to his mentor's inductive, deductive and abductive approaches. For Blaikie (2007):

> Retroductive reasoning, according to the originator of the term CS Peirce, differs fundamentally from inductive and deductive logic. For it entails working back from observations to an explanation; once the explanatory idea has emerged it will be overwhelming and irresistible.

Towards and Integral Australia

The problem though that Blaikie leave us with is that he does not situate his fourfold approach to social inquiry in his own Australian context, so he leaves us, speculatively, to fill the contextual gap. We know of course that Australia is populated by immigrants from Britain (west), continental Europe (north) and now increasingly from Asia (east) and that its original, aboriginal population is, in our terms, southern. However, such integrality remains implicit rather than explicit in a country that is visibly "north-western" in its political and economic outlook.

Thereby, epistemologically, we would expect "western" induction and "northern" deduction to predominate. We now turn back to Africa, whereby one of us (Anselm Adodo) reveals how what he terms *healing radiance* in fact connects with our own integral worlds (see previous chapter) and with abduction, retroduction, deduction and induction in turn, thereby assuming newly global, now African proportions.

14.4.3. Revisiting Healing Radiance

The Four Natural Forces and the Integral Nature of Social Inquiry

One of us, Father Anselm begins this second work of his, originally cited above, by representing the four classes of natural forces, which we (Adodo 2003) might align with our own "four worlds", and constitute a keynote of both science and technology today. The *force of gravity,* firstly, aligns with our "south", and our *grounding* as such, and for Blaikie abduction. Like light and waves, material objects are subject to the law of energy and mass. This means that all things are attracted, pulled or drawn to each other. Since gravitation has no mass, it carries a long range force, which makes it very active over long distances.

Secondly, our "eastern" *electromagnetic force* results in the generation of, for us, *emergent* force, Blaikie's retroduction, through the action of electrically charged particles like electrons and quarks, resulting in the generation of a forcer stronger than gravity. This energy generation is caused by the mingling, or fusion, of some massless particles called photons, each one having both a positive and a negative charge.

Thirdly, we have our "northern" *weak nuclear force,* that for us *navigation,* and for Blaikie deduction. The photon plus three other particles combine to make up the weak nuclear force. The main characteristic of our "western" *strong nuclear force, finally* for Blaikie induction, is that it binds massless particles together, thereby having no colour of its own. To get a white quark, so to speak, the strong nuclear force combined red, blue and green quarks, *effectively* making up a proton or neutron, leading to a prolonged chain of reactions. Adodo then turns to the mystery of life, or more specifically the hidden life of plants.

Unlike Animals, Plants Manufacture the Chemicals They Need to Survive

Plants then, for him, are more independent than animals when it comes to the essentials of life. *Unlike animals, plants manufacture the essential chemicals they need to survive. Making use of the essential cosmic elements of sunlight, air, and water, plants manufacture all they need to grow and reproduce.* Plants manufacture carbohydrates, proteins, fats, hormones, vitamins and enzymes. These chemicals are called primary compounds. Animals, including human beings need these primary compounds to survive. Without plants to manufacture these compounds, animal and human life cannot be sustained. Each plant manufactures the precise amount of chemical it needs. Since animals depend on these chemicals, plants grow to make life possible.

Since moreover, for Adodo, plants are so important to animal and human existence, it is important that plants continue to grow and reproduce. In order to protect themselves against use and misuse, plants manufacture new sets of chemicals that can both positively or negatively affect or alter the biological state of animals and humans. These chemicals are called secondary compounds. There are as many as 100,000. The compounds serve as a defence mechanism for the plants to help them fight against infections with bacteria, viruses and fungi.

When acacia leaves are attacked by an animal, for example, they re-grow leaves that have a higher concentration of toxic compounds which will harm the animal which is foolish enough to come back for more. Plants are able to send warning signals to other plants when they are being attacked. Flowering plants send out nice fragrances not to pamper or please our senses but to attract pollinators, so that the cycle of life can continue. The amount of phytochemicals produced by each plant depends on the environment and soil condition. Some plants produce as many as 200 different phytochemicals. For example, the Apple tree contains as much as 150 compounds, 60–70 % of which are medicinal. *There is more concentration of useful compounds in the peels of fruits than in the fruits themselves.* The peel of a mango, for example, is richer in useful phytochemicals than the mango fruit itself, while the root of a pawpaw tree contains more active compounds than the trunk.

Every Day, Every Hour, New Species of Plant Are Created

There are more than 400,000 species of plants, according to Adodo, in this planet. Human beings in different continents use about 100,000 of these for medicinal purposes. Of these, only some 10,000 have been clinically analysed and thus recommended for human consumption.

The truth which science is discovering is that we have not yet begun to explore the deep mysteries of life. *Every day, every hour, new species of plant are created unnoticed to our human eyes.* To the untrained eye, plants remain what they are and there is nothing special about them. But the sensitive person knows there is more to them. Our universe, for Adodo, is composed of an energy field, a power that is invincible. This energy field vibrates at different frequencies. Plants grow and mature according to the energy field around them.

Every Plant Has a Reason for Existing

Every plant then has a reason for existing. Plants grow for a particular purpose. Every plant is a manifestation of the energy field which is the universe. Some plants exist to give nourishment to the earth. Some exist to give support to other plants. Some grow to regulate the exchange of oxygen and carbon dioxide between human beings and plants. Some give information about events.

For one who has eyes to see and ears to hear, Adodo goes on to say, plants speak many languages. They are mirrors reflecting the intensity and nature of the energy field of the environment where they grow. There are some plants that signal the coming of a drought. Some sprout to signal the coming of rain or an epidemic. On getting to a new place, experienced herbalists and mystics know the prevalent sickness and mood simply by observing the kinds of plants growing nearby. The types of plants growing in a particular place often reflect the need or problem of the place. Shortly before any epidemic or disease, the plant that has the antidote begins to sprout. For every sickness, disease or lack there is always a medicinal plant growing nearby. *It is left for human beings to open nature's book of Wisdom and learn and use them.*

Uncovering the Theory of Plant Signatures

In traditional African societies, and indeed in other parts of the world, people look at the colour and shape as well as the location of a plant to get an insight into its use and importance. *This is called the theory of signatures. They believe that plants grown in a specific area because there is a need for them.* Herbs that grow on mountains, for example, are believed to be good for the respiratory system. Herbs that grow in water are considered very medicinal, and also specifically for treating infertility. Herbs that grow close to the soil are considered good for circulatory and digestive problems.

The challenge for today's African thinkers is to sift out the fetish and the superstitious from our inherited deposits of knowledge without throwing away the truth. May the silent echoes of the eternal wisdom, for Adodo then, continue to resound through us. This brings him, overall, to the art of healing, for us and for him, in an African context, underlying sustainable development.

14.4.4. African Healing Wisdom to the Art of Healing

That Single Creative Force That Sustains the Cosmos

African Traditional Religions, for Adodo then, generally believe in the presence of mysterious forces controlling activities in the world. These forces manifest in terms of spirits. Africans believe that it is through the manipulation of sound that they link up with this force and use it. Hence great emphasis is placed on speech, incantations, singing and music, including also dance. Modern science has also come to accept the existence of this force that sustains the universe. Even though science, for Adodo, uses different terms, it explains the same reality. *What is the law of gravity, the electromagnetic force, the weak and strong nuclear forces, other than the effect of that single creative force that sustains the cosmos.*

We Are Vibrating and Creating Our Energy Fields

The universe, as we have seen then, for him, is vibrating at different intensities, creating an energy field. *We too are vibrating and creating our energy fields. Each creature has their own energy field,* making it clear that we are in a world that is alive with activities, charged with energies. Our energy fields, moreover, fluctuate according to our thought process, our psychological states and the influence of these thoughts on other people. Buildings, art works, paintings, machines, literary work, poems were all thoughts or ideas that were eventually materialised.

The electromagnetic energy spectrum then radiates through nature: the seas, mountains, plants, earth and rocks. By living close to the land and nature, we receive this energy into our own energy fields and so are energised. However, as we build more highways, manufacture steel cars, build bridges and make electronic gadgets, we become prone to hitherto unknown diseases. As human beings become more complicated and adopt a so-called modern, sophisticated mode of life, so also our illnesses become more complicated.

Adodo has been amazed at the huge number of infertile couples in our society today. Every day we are bombarded with electro-magnetic stresses. Radio-waves, micro-waves, telephone rays, all expose the organs of the body. The most dangerous, for him, are the rays of the mobile phone. It is not then surprising that the USA, which is the most technological nation in the world, also has the highest number of degenerative diseases.

At the Cost of Their Soul, Pulling Themselves Away from the Earth

Western man and woman, he then goes on to say, *has purchased materialism at the cost of their soul, pulling themselves away from the earth, from nature.* Humankind seems to have lost their conscience. The result is intense anger and bitterness: leading to violence and war. The millions of immigrants from the plundered poor countries who sit at the gates of the rich nations without being given access to their opulence remind them that there will be no peace unless there is equity and justice in the world.

We are living therefore, according to Adodo, in a sick world. A world polluted by greed, injustice, materialism, racial prejudice and wickedness. *Religion, which is meant to be an instrument of our re-union with the Divine also becomes an instrument of disunity and violence.* Perhaps, he says, the time has come for us to drop the Bible and the Koran an look each other in the face. For right there in the eyes of the poor, the sick, the abandoned, the weak, the rich earning their wage from the honest work of their hands there in their faces you will read the gospel of life, the Koran of the Just and Merciful Allah. What we have then is a lifeless religion, for religion without spirituality leads to death. Religion without spirituality leads to ignorance, bloody fanaticism, spiritual brainwashing and deceit. Religion without spirituality allows evil leaders to deceive and manipulate their subjects to their selfish advantage.

Knowledge Is Our Destiny

What Adodo then terms *Priestcraft* and *politicraft* pollute their victims with the poison of ignorance and religiosity, weaken their critical intellectual questioning and turn them into zombies. And while their blood is being drained they are busy thanking God and asking for God's blessing on their exploiters.

Science, in contrast, is only another word for knowledge. What knowledge? Knowledge of the deeper meaning of life. Knowledge of who we are, where we come from, and where we are going. Knowledge of the essence of religion, of spirituality. Knowledge of our inherent power to transform the world by love, not hatred; by gentleness not violence. *Knowledge of the true nature of power is nature power. It is only this knowledge which will bring permanent healing to our sick and wounded cosmos, and set us free. Such knowledge is our African destiny.*

Such a newly global destiny, we eprews here is in terms of *natural* realisation. We now finally turn to the keynotes of empiricism, albeit in our African light.

14.5. Empirical Keynotes on the African Path to Realisation: W2a

14.5.1. Search for Real Natural Truth

The search for truth, for Mark Smith as above, firstly and empirically as such, is assumed to be an intentional activity that reflects the needs of humanity and, as a consequence, secures human progress. In order to achieve scientific progress, you should deploy your capacity for reason within the methodological rules of empirically based scientific method. Scientific statements are seen as pictures or snapshots of the things they refer to. Reality for the empiricist is made up of atomistic, discrete and observable experiences and events. Hence, one of the core "instruments" of the positivist is induction. Such a method refers to a logical process of constructing knowledge about observed relationships between variables in particular instances.

Such empirical method, as we saw in our own case (Anselm Adodo), was deployed to uncover "the facts on the ground", but those serving to expose the *reality* of "nature power", as embodied in the attitudes and experience of nature in and of itself, rather than those "business-like" views imposed on it. To that extent Adodo sought "the *real* truth" rather then the *western* inferred reality. This represented then, the pursuit of the truth in the best possible empirical light, documented as such in his subsequent book.

Table 14.5.1. *African Empiricism – Keynotes*

Search for Real Natural Truth.
Positivism to Naturalism: Seek after Home Grown "Positive Facts".
Collect Observational Data and Build Pragmatic Theories.
Control the Research through "Closed Place Based Systems".

14.5.2. Seek After Home Grown "Positive Facts": Positivism to Naturalism

The empiricist secondly seeks after the "positive" facts, rather than relying on pure faith or indeed dogma. Only that which can be observed, that is experienced by the senses, can be regarded as real. Knowledge is seen to be derived from sensory experience by means of experimental or comparative analysis.

The logical positivist uses induction to collect observational data and build theories to explain the observations. Thus the method of induction involves two movements simultaneously: from the particular to the general, and from observed events to theoretical constructions. For Houtondji then, as revealed in Chapter 12, what was critical was that such "positive facts" when then turned into theories, for example in the Pax Herbals case that of Communitalism as we shall see in the fourth, case story that follows, were home grown, in the *south-western* periphery as it were, rather than imposed by a *north-western* core.

14.5.3. Collect Observational Data and Build Pragmatic Theories

The logical positivist uses induction, analytically, to collect observational data, and then build theories, transformatively, to explain the observations. The method of induction refers to a logical process of constructing knowledge about observed relationships between variables in particular instances. This can be taken as a basis for making universal generalizations in as yet unobserved, particular instances. As a researcher you identify a limited number of variables and observe their behaviour and changes of one in relation with the other. Therefore, you identify factors, which are significant so their effect can be observed and you pinpoint, which factor actually causes the observed outcome to occur. As you evolve new theories, so you begin to transform the old into the new.

It is this process of transformation then, as again proposed by Houtondji and enacted by Chimakonam, as revealed our chapter on critical rationalism

(Chapter 11), that is crucial in our *south*-western context. All too often the data gathered in Africa, whether related to polity or economy, enterprise and community, are then moulded so that its fits into a prefabricated exogenous theory, be it related for example to entrepreneurship or to management accounting, at a micro level, or to GNP or parliamentary/electoral democracy – or otherwise – at a macro level. What remains key is that such data are transformed, inductively and deductively, if not also abductively and retroductively, altogether pragmatically, involving induction and deduction, abduction and retroduction, if you like an integral empiricism.

14.5.4. Control the Research Through Closed Placed Based Systems

Research, with a view to innovation, from an empirical perspective, happens within "closed systems", enabling you as a researcher-and-innovator, individually or institutionally, to isolate the objects you wish to investigate from all other objects, which would confuse the picture. Such a "closed system" research and innovation– means in addition to the identification of variables and the observation of their behaviour – that you avoid any interference from unexpected external forces. Exclusion clauses ensure that the mass of possible influences is screened out (ceteris paribus). It is you who controls the situation by manipulating variables.

Interestingly enough, and if you like the twist in our African tale, is that such a "closed" system should "close in" on a particular place, the local feel in which we are located, as one of us (Adodo) has intimated, before opening up to wider, exogenous horizons. This becomes increasingly difficult in our digitized, globalized, world. That said, and further to such a feeling local, needs to come an intuited local-global, and then newly globally more, leading onto the global-local, as revealed in these keynotes.

All too often then, in mimicking the "west", the "south", because of its own innate distance from such, takes the most limited form of western-ness rather than its more expansive and inclusive form, a system that opens after it is closed. We are now ready to conclude.

14.6. Conclusion

14.6.1. Empiricism Reviewed

The Empirical bereft of the Integral

We highlighted at this point the limitations of an empiricism, which acts in isolation and is bereft of an integral perspective. While the same applies to any one, single method or methodology, the fact that empiricism is the most commonplace, worldwide, makes these limitations more marked. Indeed, it was this isolated and unrelated (to context) perspective that gave rise, in the 19th century, to phenomenology, due to what Husserl perceived as "the crisis in European sciences".

That having been said, there are a number of strengths, that empiricism, well used, brings to the table. Specifically, it is overtly practical, seemingly evidence based, and coherently argued. It clearly presents a particular perspective, argues its case demonstrably, and incorporates many well-researched facts and figures to back up its overall argument. Indeed we have long lamented the fact that empirically based case studies are almost totally lacking in Africa.

However, its weakness often lies in its surface nature, unable to accommodate the depths of a particular nature and culture, as seen, as illustrated by one of us, Anselm Adodo, above, in place based reality, "through local eyes". Often, the actual faces or voices that (locally) belong to the researched context are not seen or heard. They remain silent. Moreover, and historically, there is no acknowledgment, or indeed reporting, on what has come before. Empiricism, in most cases, does not embed the research in its larger historical or societal context. Its mode of comprehension, while full of facts and figures, is bereft of a particular life world; history or philosophy are often left out of empirical account.

Reformative and Transformative Left Out of Account

In such a narrowly empirical form, there is little attempt to co-create a new world, simultaneous to investigating it, something that the more transformative minded pragmatists, like Pearce and Dewey, duly took into pragmatic account. As a result, a purely empirically based research project, based on induction to the exclusion of deduction, abduction and retroduction, thereby lacking integral credentials, is unable to pave the way for any form of social innovation, or indeed social and economic transformation. It is for that reason that we will now turn from empiricism to critical realism, from what is observable and measurable to, in addition, the underlying, generative forms and forces. It is therefore time, to enter the third emancipatory level of "critique", following case method and empirical methodology, to challenge the system as such. Here on our *south*-western path of African realisation, critical realism, intriguingly building, as we shall see now, on local aboriginal grounds, thereby *feeling local*, will probe beyond the empirical surface, and take us a step further to innovation.

Before entering our next chapter, however, we need to review our grounding, on the African path of realisation.

14.6.2. Original Grounding on the African Path of Realisation

For our original grounding we revisit Chapter 4, where we outlined not only survey and experimental method, as "western", our *south*-western grounds, but also case study method, or what we term in "southern" guise, a case *story*, such as the one illustrated by Cashbuild above, whereby, in devising such:

- You are able to ask good Questions – and to interpret the Answers.
- You are a good Listener – not trapped by your own Ideologies and Preconceptions.
- You are adaptable so that new Situations can be seen as Opportunities.
- You are unbiased by preconceived Notions, responsive to contradictory Evidence

14.6.3. Emergent Foundation on the African Path of Realisation

More specifically then, as far as the subsequent empirical foundation is concerned:
- You search for the real truth
- You see after natural positive facts
- You collect observational data and build pragamatically based theories
- You exercize control through place based closed systems

14.6.4. Pax Herbals Search for the *Real* Truth: *Natural* Realisation

As we have seen, there is a subtle difference between conventionally north-western empiricism, locally-globally and our south-western African equivalent, now newly globally, what we have termed *natural* realisation.

In fact, for Australian anthropologist Freya Mathews (2003), in her brilliant work on *The Love of Matter,* again for us, with her aboriginal affinities, coming form the *south*-west, she writes:

> What then is culture and why is it problematic in the present connection? It is problematic because the global ecosystem, or Nature, is physical and concrete, composed of particulars, while culture is abstract, a system of representations or symbols, composed for forms or universals .. It is no longer then controversial to state that a human individual is essentially a cultural being, and that culture is an emanation of Nature. However, and as such, it may be a metaphysical one way street, in the sense that it does not feed back into Nature, is not in itself part of an eco-matrix. In this case, the traditional Western view of the human condition, logically distinct even though causally dependent in nature, would be redeemed. Is culture an epiphenomenon, or is it in fact ecologically functional, ecologically connected with the rest of the Natural?

University to Communiversity/Capitalism and Socialism to Communitalism

Finally, and ultimately on the path of realisation, thereby engaging originally with case study method and foundationally with empirical methodology, albeit altogether in African guise, you seek to establish the basis for a socio-economic laboratory, by building up a case story of a Paxherbals (see case story 4 below), also doing the same for an adjacent learning community. All of such, moreover, establishes the both the original case for, and the empirical foundations for a communiversity, and communitalism, to follow.

Table 14.6.3. *Communiversity to Communitalism: W4fita Nhakanomics, Yurug-nomics, Economics of Love, Communitalism*

Feeling Local	Intuiting Local-Global	Thinking Newly Global	Acting Global-Local
Pax Natura	Pax Spiritus	Pax Scientia	Pax Economica

We now turn from empirical to critical realism, starting out in aboriginal guise.

14.7. References

Adodo A (2003) *Healing Radiance of the Soul: A Guide to Holistic Healing.* Edo State. Agelex Publications

Adodo A (2012) *Nature Power: A Christian Approach to Herbal Medicine. New Edition.* Edo State. Benedictine Publications

African Creation Energy (2014) *Heru-Copters: African Aeronautic Extension*

Blaikie N (2007) *Approaches to Social Inquiry.* Cambridge. Polity Press

Christie P, **Lessem** R and **Mbigi** L (1994) *African Management: Principles, Concepts and Applications.* Johannesburg. Knowledge Resources

Heron J (1994) *Feeling and Personhood.* Abingdon. Routledge

Hountondji P (2002) *The Struggle for Meaning.* Buckingham. Open University Press

James W (2000) *Pragmatism and Other Writings.* New York. Penguin Classics

Jung C (2022) *Psychological Types.* Abingdon. Routledge Classics

Lessem R and **Schieffer** A (2010) *Integral Research and Innovation: Transforming Enterprise and Society.* Abingdon. Routledge

Markie P (2004) *Rationalism versus Empiricism.* In Edward D. Zalta (ed) *Stanford Encyclopedia of Philosophy.* Palo Alto. Stanford University

Mathews F (2003) *For the Love of Matter: A Contemporary Panpsychism.* Albany. State University of New York

McDonald D (2017) *The Golden Passport: Harvard Business School, Limits of Capitalism and the Moral Failure of the MBA Elite.* Harper Business

Mill JS (1848) *Principles of Political Economy.* Oxford. Oxford University Press

Nonaka I and **Takeuchi** H (1995) *The Knowledge Creating Company.* Oxford. Oxford University Press

Peirce CS (1986) *Philosophical Writings.* Mineola. NY. Dover Publications

Smith A (2010) *The Theory of Moral Sentiments.* London. Penguin Classics

Smith A and **Sutherland** K (2008) *The Wealth of Nations: Selected Edition.* Oxford. Oxford World Classics

Smith M (2000) *Social Science in Question.* Buckingham. Open University Press

Chapter 15 From Empiricism to Critical African Realism. Discover Underlying African Reality

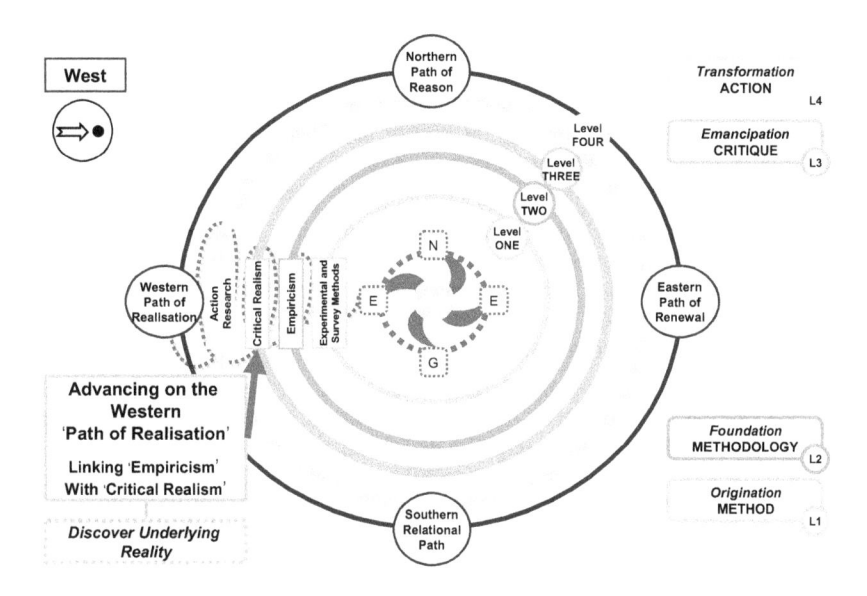

Figure 15.1: *Overview Chapter 15 – Level 3 / West*

So-called "bench laboratory science" – especially R and D – remains an elitist, university-centred practice. It does not come home to the villages and the streets. The dilemma of knowledge production in in Africa centres on how its structures, practices and concepts came to be informalised while inbound European ones were rendered formal. From the time that humans began making tools in stone, bone and wood, Africa hosted different forms of workshop.

Mavhunga C. (2017) What Do Science, Technology and Innovation Mean for Africa

Summary: African Critical Realism
• Following the path of realisation we now turn from empiricism, if not also naturalism, to critical realism (emancipation) as an evolution from experimental, survey and case study methods (origination) and conventional, albeit African home grown, empirical methodology (foundation).
• A local feel for such, in *south*-western terms, in this case in Yoruba-Nigerian, Ewo state territory, for one of us (Anselm Adodo) emerges as a form of communitalism for indigenous people, with their respective natural, communal, environmental and spiritual layered meanings
• The originator of critical realism is the Anglo-Indian social philosopher, Roy Bhaskar, who was influenced in turn by the New Zealander Rom Harre, and the Argentine Mario Bunge, setting the stage for a local-global approach, also reinforced by his Anglo-Indian dual identity, with altogether so called generative "real" mechanisms underlying surface events and behaviours
• In its newly global reach it is associated with an "eastern" turn, whereby its focus on "meta-reality" explicitly bringing in a spiritual dimension that was previously only implicit, and a dialectical orientation to supplement the pragmatic orientation. Such can altogether be aligned with our won approach to releasing African GENE-ius: Grounding, Emergence, Navigation, Effect.
• In the process, moreover, we reach back to traditional African "age sets", for African American historian, Chancellor Williams, and forward to Japanese organisational sociologists, Nonaka and Takeuchi, to their knowledge creating company
• The key global-local tenets of critical realism are its combined *objective and subjective* nature, its interpretive as well as explanatory orientation, its overall stratified, for us *African stratified reality*, nature, its *recognition of human fallibility*, as well as its *critical as well as emancipatory* orientation.

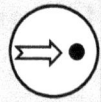

15.1. Orientation to Critical Realism

With critical realism we enter the third level of the *south*-western path of realisation. While we have positioned critical realism on the western path, it is a kind of a "mixed breed". Though it has global-local western (realistic) connotations, it also carries a local-global strong eastern flavour, adding to the visible surface of the research object its more invisible ground of local, for us *south*-western, origin. Herein, we give it a southern, indigenous and local feel, before we move into to its local-global *meta-real* eastern turn. In that sense it clearly transcends a purely positivist empiricism.

More specifically in fact, as can be seen in Table 15.1.1 below, on the overall path of south-western African realisation, by way of research and innovation, Paxherbals, as founded by one of us (Anselm Adodo), emerges empirically, and *meta-really*, as such, via nature power and healing radiance, towards communtalist navigation, culminating, through an Afrocentric south-west, in what is known as pan African – south (Shona), east (Swahili), north (ancient Egypt) and west (Yoruba) – toward a *Stratified African Reality*, as we shall explore in what follows.

Table 15.1.1. W*est African Social Research and Innovation: Path of Realisation: W3 Case Study to Action Research via CRITICAL REALISM*

Western Grounding Method and Origination	Western Emergent Methodology & Foundation	Western Navigational Critique and Emancipation	Western Effective Action and Transformation
Case Study (W1)	Empiricism (W2)	Critical Realism (W3)	Action Research (W4)
PaxHerbals (N1)	Nature Power/ Healing Radiance (W2)	Communitalism (W3)	Stratified African Reality (W4)

Adding thereby, critically, a deeper (subjective) experiential ground to the outer (objective) empirical surface, it enables you as a researcher, and our Centre for Integral Research and Societal Re-GENE-ration, as a research academy, to connect inner subject to outer reality, individually and communally, organisationally and societally. As such, it paves the way for ultimate societal re-GENE-ration contained within the *south*-western path, an integrated action research and innovation, which is finally embodied in Chapter 16, as our culminating case story, that of one of us, Anselm Adodo, and Paxherbals in Nigeria. We now turn to critical realism's origins.

15.1.1. The Origins of Critical Realism

Left Wing Intellectual, with an Interdisciplinary Approach and Political Credentials

Anglo-Indian research philosopher, the recently late Roy Bhaskar (1977) is unique in having given birth, almost single-handeldly, to a research philosophy, that is critical realism. He was also the catalyst for one of us (Ronnie Lessem) to break out of the conventional "western" empirical research mode, as a "southern" academic, early in the new millennium, thereby with a view to pursuing integral research and innovation. It also made Ronnie aware of the distinctively socio-political, if not altogether revolutionary, nature and scope of research methodologies, and especially such critiques as *Critical Realism*, thereby of especially import for a de-colonizing Africa.

Bhaskar was born in London, to an Indian father and English mother, both of whom were theosophists, heavily influenced by eastern philosophies, upon which, in his later years in particular, Roy Bhaskar would draw. As a young man in 1963 he went up to Baliol College, Oxford, on a scholarship to read Philsophy, Politics and Economics. Having graduated with first class honours in 1966, he began to work on a Ph.D thesis dealing with the relevance of economic theory for underdeveloped countries. This research led him to the philosophy of social science and then the philosophy of science. In the course of this the prolific social scientist and philosopher Rom Harre (1994) became his supervisor. Harre, of French Huguenot stock, but born and bred in New Zealand, is a philosopher, psychologist and anthropologist who spent much of his adult years teaching philosophy at the University of Punjab in India.

Bhaskar was also influenced in his early thinking by the Argentinian philosopher, Mario Bunge (1980). Bunge set out his thinking systematically in his "Treatise on Basic Philosophy", a monumental work in eight volumes, comprising semantics, ontology, epistemology, philosophy of science and ethics. In 40 books, and some 400 papers, Bunge developed a comprehensive scientific outlook, which he then applied to the various natural and social sciences. He was also *a left wing intellectual, and his interdisciplinary approach and political credentials appealed to the young Bhaskar.*

Emancipatory Body of Thought That Aspires to Move Beyond the Enlightenment

Bhaskar's own consideration of the philosophies of science and social science resulted in the development of *critical realism, an emancipatory body of thought that aspires to move beyond the Enlightenment, avoiding reductionist rationalism through enhanced historical self-awareness and use of dialectical thought*. To achieve this, it draws on pre-modern spiritual traditions as well as on positive aspects of the Enlightenment: its commitment is to scientific inquiry and to freedom.

Specifically then, what is required for Bhaskar (1993), as he states in *The Dialectic: The Pulse of Freedom*:

> What is required is a revolutionary transformation far more profound than any of us can imagine. Unless capitalism is overturned, by a revolution, which will be at once much more peaceful and deeper than the one that overthrew socialism, that will draw on resources and aspects of our being that are at once spiritual and cultural, set in the

context of a feasible transition, and done in a non-violent way – unless capitalism is overturned in that way, I can see very little prospect of humanity surviving much into the 21st century on this planet.

It is interesting to note that Bhaskar had no fixed academic abode. He remained a truly fee spirit, on the edges of academia, though he, with his close colleagues, developed an International Association for Critical Realism, established in 1997 which still flourishes today.

From East to West – The Odyssey of a Soul: The Philosophy of Meta-Reality

In the year 2000 in fact, Bhaskar (2000a) published his *From East to West: The Odyssey of a Soul*, from which we shall hear much more in our local-global considerations below, which significantly influenced – alongside John Heron's work – our GENE-tic approach to integral research and innovation. Therein Bhaskar first expressed his ideas related to spiritual values that came to be seen as the beginning of his so-called spiritual turn. This was initially very controversial, but has since won growing support after the publication in 2002 of his book on the radical development of critical realism which he called *The Philosophy of Meta-Reality*, here he made it clear that this latest phase of his thought applied to people of all faiths and no faith, i.e. was susceptible to a purely secular interpretation.

What he refers to as Meta-Reality, however, may be seen as a different philosophy altogether. In his (2002) *Reflections on Meta-Reality*, he states:

> This book articulates the difference between critical realism in its development and a new philosophical standpoint which I am in the process of developing, which I have called the philosophy of Meta-Reality.

The main departure, it seems, is a shift away from western dualism to a non-dual model in which emancipation entails "a breakdown, an overcoming, of the duality and separateness between things." In effect, in his midlife, Bhaskar turned very explicitly back to his "eastern" metaphysical roots, and combined such with his "western" realist approach, in a very distinctive way.

15.1.2. From Empiricism to Critical Realism

Ontology Is Stratified, with Underlying Reality Constituting the Generative Depths

Like in postmodernism, critical theory and feminism, so also in critical realism knowledge is socially constructed, but only in "transitive" part.

Table 15.1.2. *African Critical Realism – Core Assumptions*

A purely empirically based Truth is unattainable – all Knowledge is socially constructed, while at the same Time there is a naturally pre-ordered external Reality.
All Human Behaviour and Knowledge occurs within and simultaneously reconstructs culturally derived Meanings, in our case within an African context.
The Purpose of social scientific Inquiry is to produce causal Explanations, which can guide (and may be evaluated through) Human Interventions in our Social World.
Pragmatic-critical Realism demands a reflexive political Axis, focused on the Way in which Knowledge shapes Human Activities.

For, in critical realism unlike in postmodernism an objectively based reality does exist, "intransitively", and materially so to speak. So reality is partly naturally pre-existent and partly socially constructed. Insofar as reality is pre-existent, such a "realist" approach shares with empiricism its grounding in an objectively definable world. However, for such critical realists as Bhaskar (2002), that is not the end of the story. What is of profound importance for them is that *ontology is stratified, with underlying reality constituting the generative depths. Our emancipation, hence, is preconditioned by our coming to understand and work with such "real" depths.*

Free, Loving, Creative and Intelligent Energy Underlying Our "Real" Being

The philosophy of Critical Realism, and thereafter Meta-Reality, as we shall see, describes the way in which *this very world nevertheless depends on, is ultimately sustained by, and only exists in virtue of: the free, loving, creative and intelligent energy and activity of states of our "real" being.* In that guise critical realism is resonant with (see Sekem – case story 3) the *economics of love.* In becoming aware of this we begin the process of transforming and overthrowing the totality of structures of oppression, alienation and mystification and indeed misery, which we have produced. Such a vision opens up a balanced world, of a society in which the free development and flourishing of each unique human being is understood to be the condition, as it is also the consequence, of the free development and flourishing of all.

In that sense Bhaskar is taking psychologically and spiritually on, from where Marx and Engels as well as the Abouleishes left economically and socially off. In that context he rubs shoulders with his critical theory oriented counterparts. However, unlike them, there is a strong pragmatic and Anglo-Saxon edge to his argument. Alongside such, we can see the influence of his Indian heritage, where the notion of "levels of consciousness" (or indeed, for him and his Anglo-Saxon colleagues: the stratified nature of reality or ontology) predominates. We now proceed to ground such, uncharacteristically perhaps, in the aboriginal African *south*-west.

15.2. Feel Local: Grounded in Nature – Pax Africana: W3f

15.2.1. Capitalism, Communitalism, and Communiversity

For one of us (Anselm Adodo), rationally and empirically based Western theories such as Marxism, Capitalism, Socialism, and Communism, while focusing on economics, technology, and enterprise, fail to build their concepts on nature and culture, thereby making us *feel local*, thus leading to unsustainable and imbalanced development. An integral approach, such as *communitarianism*, which takes account of the totality of the above, set within a particular society, building up from nature and community, and embracing culture, politics, economics, spirituality and enterprise, is a surer path to sustainable and integral development in Africa. What then is *Communitalism?* According to Adodo (2017):

> Communitalism, as opposed to capitalism or communism, is an integral approach to knowledge creation and development that is grounded in a particular enterprise-in-community while ultimately effecting a whole society, emerging indigenously and exogenously as such. Such a communitalist perspective, built on the four Pax (4Ps), addresses the four key dimensions of development, which are identified as follows: Pax Communis (community), Pax Spiritus (sanctuary), Pax Scientia (university), and Pax Economia (laboratory).

15.2.2. Clinic-Oriented and Community-Oriented

In fact, for Adodo, there were two approaches to herbal medicine practice: the clinic-oriented approach and the community-oriented approach. In a clinic-oriented approach, emphasis is placed on the scientific identification, conservation, and use of medicinal plants. Laboratory research and screening are done to determine the chemical composition and biological activities of plants. Great interest is shown in quality control of raw materials and finished products and in the development of methods for large-scale production of labelled herbal drugs. The herbal drugs are labelled and packaged in the same way as modern drugs and distributed through similar channels, i.e. through recognised health officials in hospitals, health centres, or pharmaceutical supply chains. Huge sums of money are invested both by the government, private companies, and non-governmental organisations to promote further research in herbal medicine. Minimal interest is shown in the socio-cultural use of the plants.

In the community-oriented approach, the emphasis is on the crude and local production of herbs used for common illnesses. Knowledge of the medicinal uses of herbs is spread to promote self-reliance. Information is freely given on disease prevention and the origin of diseases. This approach aims at applying simple but effective herbal remedies to common illnesses. The target is the local community. No interest is shown in the mass production of drugs for transportation to other parts of the country or exportation to other countries. The cultural context of the plants used is taken into account, and local perceptions of health and healing often take precedence over modern diagnostic technology. Simple herbal recipes are used for the treatment of such illnesses as coughs, colds, malaria, and typhoid. The two approaches analysed above are two extremes. *There was a need to harmonise these two extremes to complement each other.* PAXHERBALS had then been established in 1996. It was registered as a private liability company in 2002 and described as *a Catholic research centre for the scientific identification, conservation, utilisation, and development of African medicinal plants.*

15.2.3. Pax Herbals to Pax Africana

Some 15 years later, inspired by his participation in Trans4m's PhD/PHD programme, Anselm took the next step, turning Pax Herbals towards Pax Afrikana:

- to serve as a centre for *genuine African holistic healing* that blends the physical and spiritual aspects of the human person.
- to become a *model comprehensive health care centre* where the western (North, West) and traditional (South, East) systems of healing are creatively blended.
- to be an example of how *proper utilisation of traditional medicine* can promote grassroots culturally acceptable, affordable, and relevant primary health care systems.
- to *disseminate knowledge* of the health benefits of African medicinal plants.
- to carry out research into ancient African healing systems with a view to modernising them and making them available to the wider world through education.
- to *demystify African traditional medicine,* purge it of elements of occultism, fetishism, and superstition, and promote its rational use to make it globally acceptable.
- to be a *truly indigenous/exogenous* herbal phytomedicine centre that combines respect for nature and community with wealth creation.

15.2.4. Pax Africana: A Multilayered Communiversity

Altogether, and integrally as such, Dr. Adodo has now thereby embraced worldviews, or realities, from all four corners of the globe. More specifically, then, in a specifically layered guise from Bhaskar's perspective, for us:

> Originally grounded in *Pax Natura;uth:* identified with AFRICA. Key features are: indigenous knowledge, agronomy, connection with the soil, respect and oneness with nature, and a community of life. The orientation is towards **communal learning.**
> Emergent Foundation in *Pax Spritus*: *South-East:* Identified with Africa and Asia. Key features are the emphasis on inner peace, wholeness, culture, inner security, spirituality, higher consciousness, intuition, feelings, and emotions as part of the human experience. The orientation is towards an individual **transformation journey.**

Emancipatory Navigation via *Pax Scientia*: *South-North*: Identified mainly with Africa and Europe. Fully in control of advances in scientific theories and social theories. Key features are: political systems; institutionalised research; economic, political, and social systems. Orientation to the Institutionalised **Research Academy**
Transformative Effect via *Pax Economia*: *South-West:* identified mainly with Africa and America. Known for business, enterprise, entrepreneurship, individual quest for profit, and competition. Key features are: practical application of technology for profit; business management; and dollarization of the world economy. The orientation is towards a **socio-technical laboratory**.

At *Paxherbals,* one of us (Anselm Adodo) and his 150 co-producers, supported by some 1000 distributors around Nigeria, cultivate their own herbs directly and also through accredited local out-growers. *Paxherbals* is the only herbal manufacturing company left in Nigeria that is locally producing its herbal medicines, despite the harsh economic climate, which makes it easier and more profitable to be an importer rather than a manufacturer. It is no wonder that the Nigerian market is flooded with herbal products imported from foreign countries. By so doing, Nigeria is creating wealth abroad and promoting poverty at home.

We now turn from *feeling local* in such a layered, aboriginal, *south*-western guise back to Bhaskar's local-global critical realism, drawing as we have seen from Harre in New Zealand, Bunge in Argentina, as well as his own Anglo-Indian heritage.

15.3. Intuit Local/Global – Realising Generative Mechanisms: W3i

15.3.1. From "West" to "East": Realism to Meta-Reality

Science and Philosophy Should Be Explicitly Concerned with Human Liberation

What then is this stratified, local-global critical-emancipatory perspective, in specific relation to critical realism, on our path of realisation research-wise, indeed following local Pax Africana suit, innovation-wise? For Roy Bhaskar it seemed in fact, in the late sixties when he was writing his doctoral thesis, that the most important problem facing mankind was that of overcoming world poverty. Times have hardly changed, though arguably the climate crisis, also today, looms equally large.

As such, and not unlike his kindred "critical theory" spirits, he was tapping into his humanistic roots. Human freedom, for Bhaskar, depended above all on understanding the truth about reality and acting toward it. The task of social innovation is thereby one, that his transformative approach to *Meta-Reality* (Bhaskar 2000b) would take on (see below). This indeed, as we shall see, is a route that we have also followed in turn, Pax Africana and Communiversity-wise, altogether also for us serving to recognize and release, herein, and in equally stratified guise, African GENE-ius. Interestingly enough, and as such, it was Bhaskar who served as the immediate catalyst (see below) for our initial journey into *integral research and innovation*.

So it is essential for the critical realists, that *science and philosophy should be explicitly concerned with human liberation*, or for us emancipation. The key to such liberation, though, was to uncover the generative forces, for us as arguably for Sekem (see Chapter 13) re-GENE-rative, that underlay our economic and social, as well as our physical reality. The further development of critical realism, what Bhaskar terms Meta-Reality, makes possible a re-evaluation of the old dispute between idealism and materialism. Capitalism at the moment is the dominant world order, as one of us above (Anselm Adodo) has pointed out, thereby *feeling local* in natural African guise. It is, however, faced with two pressing contradictions.

A New Synthesis Is Required Between "Leftist" Politics and "New Age" Psychology

A rising organic composition of nature, for Bhaskar, threatens to tear the world itself apart with ecological contradictions, something nature power, as above, seeks to redress, while, at the same time, a rising organic composition of ideas makes possible the notion of a new organization of the social world attuned to universal self realisation and harmony. *A new synthesis is what is required between "leftist" politics in the "west" and "new age" psychology* drawn from the "east", and we would add "nature power" and "healing radiance" form the "south".

Such a synthesis, for Bhaskar, will need to be set in a context of a local-global philosophy, which resonates with themes traceable back to the dawn of the great world civilisations – such as "global" Buddhism and Taoism, if not also for us *ubuntu* – rather than only drawing upon modern Euro-centric "local" times. What then, more specifically, is involved?

15.3.2. Reality is Ultimately Layered

Generative "Real" Mechanisms Force Us to Seek Knowledge

For Roy Bhaskar, the nature of reality, of "what exists" and the "essence of things", is intrinsically ontological (underlying the nature of reality) and must necessarily form the foundation for everything. This has been clearly spelt out by his fellow critical realists Berth Danemark et al (2002) and her Scandinavian colleagues in *Explaining Society*. A distinction can therefore be made, between ontological domains, in Bhaskar's case three such layers as opposed to four.

The observation of the "real" domain of stratified reality, the deep dimension of so-called generative mechanisms, is thus what distinguishes critical realism. *It is this deep dimension of reality, not immediately observable, the level of the real, that forces us to seek knowledge rather than just accumulate experiences and facts.* Since reality is differentiated, structures are stratified, and involve many different and sometimes conflicting practices and interests; there also exist several parallel conceptual frameworks and sometimes-competing interpretations. Indeed, for one of us, Anselm Adodo, the domain of the "real" is constituted of *Nature Power*.

Table 15.3.2. *Ontological Domains of Critical Realism*

① Empirical
② Actual
③ Real

Knowledge, independently of what it is about, is always a social product. Facts are relative to the conceptions we initially form of the phenomena. This issue, for us though, is that such a layered research ontology needs to be accompanied by innovative practice, not to mention, in our *south*-west, also "real" nature.

Real Powers and Mechanisms Operate Independently of Actions Here and Now

Natural and social science "facts" therefore are theoretically and/or ideologically determined. Critical realists argue however that *the fact that social phenomena are concept-dependent should under no circumstances be seen as if the social world only exists as a mental construction in people's minds*. For the social structures that are reproduced or transformed, when members of society act in accordance with their concepts of reality, are real. They contain *powers and mechanisms, for us naturally and culturally contextualised, operating independently of the actions here and now.*

Natural science, then, explores a basically value-neutral world, where the objects are neither good nor bad; they simply exist. *Social science, on the other hand, investigates an inherently value-charged world of social phenomena, positions, roles, identities and relations,* including for us such *natural* relations. When social science brings into question and analyses everyday knowledge, it therefore not only risks getting into conflict with alternative experiences and concepts, but also with deeply felt issues and ethical guidelines. Thereby it also challenges vital power and dominance relationships. These relationships are invariably hidden from immediate view. They therefore need to be conceptualised, from a perspective of hidden depth, as they cannot be directly perceived, experientially, from an empirical surface.

We now turn from local-global critical realism to newly global, for us, *Meta-Reality,*

which, as we shall see, had a major thinking on our own integral thinking generally,

and Pax Africana/Communiversity/Communitalism specifically.

15.4. Releasing GENE-ius: A Newly Global Meta-Reality
15.4.1. Adult Anglo to Midlife Indian

Critical Realism Underwent a "West-East" Metamorphosis

Interestingly enough, the birth and growth of critical realism took place during the 1970s and 1980s, when Roy Bhaskar was in his twenties and thirties – as indeed is the case for the young Karl Marx in his origination of communism. This took place during and after his doctoral studies at Oxford, in England, and following the student revolutions of the 1960s.

It was as he approached his midlife though, and was undergoing such a midlife crisis and resolution, in the 1990s and *into the new millennium, that his original philosophy, critical realism, underwent a "west-east" metamorphosis*. It newly evolved into his "Meta-Reality". In the same way as commentators refer to the early and late philosophical orientations of the great Austrian philosopher Ludwig Wittgenstein, the same can be said about the adulthood and midlife of Roy Bhaskar. The same ideed goes for Darwin in his *Origin of Species* (the young Darwin when competition rules his roost) and *The Descent of Man* (the nature Darwin when cooperation came to the fore). Interestingly enough, at the same time, one of us (Ronnie Lessem), now in his midlife, was first conceiving of his own integral approach to "four worlds" (see Chapter 13 above).

Dialectic – The Pulse of Freedom

In his early adult writings on critical realism, Bhaskar remained closely wedded to western pragmatism, though of course arguing against pure positivism and empiricism. While then, even at this initial stage of his philosophical analysis, he opposed a "naïve objectivity", preoccupied with surface analysis, he retained a practical and rational orientation, and one causally oriented towards "generative mechanisms" underlying events and experiences. In other words, while his underlying philosophy was critical of the purely empirically based "western" mainstream, the overall rational-pragmatic language remained true to his Anglo-Saxon and indeed European heritage. Moreover his doctoral supervisor at Oxford, Rom Harre, though New Zealand born and bred, was of "northern" French Huguenot origins.

Bhaskar's two seminal works in the 1970s, at this "adult" stage of his philosophical and psychological development, as already cited, were a *Realist Theory of Science* aimed at the natural sciences, and *The Possibility of Naturalism* focused on the social sciences. The break then came, explicitly and publically at least, in the early nineties, when he published his *Dialectic – The Pulse of Freedom*. At that point he turned from west to east (though still in a European context), in the same way as we here turn "south", serving to link in his case western European "realism" with central and eastern European "idealism". Here he was duly influenced by

Germany's Hegel, alongside of the Anglo-French Rom Harre. In the final analysis, though, Bhaskar retained his overwhelmingly realist orientation.

15.4.2. Dialectical Emergence

Mutual Exclusion of Opposites Passes over into Their Reciprocal Interdependence

The first explicitly eastern turn (albeit to begin with in European guise) was towards Hegel, and then Marx as well as Engels, for all of whom the dialectic came to the fore. The German 19th century philosopher saw splits, dichotomies, disharmonies and fragmentations as calling for restoration or unity in diversity, in his absolute idealism. *Negation, as such, always calls for a new and richer determination. The mutual exclusion of opposites passes over into their reciprocal interdependence.* For Hegel then the truth is a whole, and the whole is a process. Error lies in one-sidedness. Its symptom is the contradictions it generates and its remedy involves their incorporation into richer, more inclusive conceptual forms. Either the implicit is made explicit (telemony), or some want or inadequacy is repaired (teleology), both of which correspond with Bhaskar's notion of "negation".

Emergence: Dialectical Grasps Concepts/Forms in Their Systemic Interconnections

"Dialectical" then, in contrast with the analytical and reflective, grasps concepts and forms in their systemic interconnections, not just their determinate differences. It considers each development as a product of a previous less developed phase, whose necessary truth or fulfilment it is. So there is always a tension between a latent form and what it is becoming. For Bhaskar this is the power of *emergence*, upon which we have also "genEtically" drawn. In short, Hegelian dialectic is the actualised entelechy of the present, comprehended as everything that has led up to it. It involves a transformation of the consciousness of the dialectical observer as well as the expansion of the existing conceptual field. What it misses, for us, is "southern" natural and communal grounding, for his "west", "north" and now also "east".

15.4.3. Meta-Reality to Transformative Agency

Bhaskar's MELDA to Our GENE

The possibility of human emancipation, our emancipatory scientific and humanistic navigation, for the now "easterly" facing Bhaskar (Lessem and Schieffer 2015) depends not on "western" democratic freedoms and free markets, but on expanding the zone of "non-duality" within our lives. That is the level of what

Bhaskar calls a being's *"ground-state"*, albeit for us in "eastern" guise, which is its most essential level. It is the level upon which all other levels depend, which has much in common with a phenomenological "essence", and of course our grounding. It also serves to depend his prior notion of an underlying, generative reality. Altogether, in this newly "meta-real" case, every human situation, as such, must now be characterised by MELDA, which in fact has also had a profound influence on our own GENE-tic orientation:

M:an element of potential, which corresponds to the critical realist domain of stratified ontology, grounded in Meta-reality (M): our local original **G**rounding, which can be aligned, as above for us, with *Pax Natura*

E: creativity, that is the Emergence (E) of something new, even if this novelty is a repeat of the old, which would not otherwise have occurred: our local-global **E**mergent foundation, as also our *Pax Spiritus*

L: any human situation must be characterised by that form of bonding, solidarity, compassion, care and consideration that Bhaskar calls, altogether, Love (L), as indeed has been the case for Sekem's *Economics of Love* in thereby *north* Africa (see Chapter 13 above): newly global emancipatory **N**avigation, our *Pax Scientia*

D: each agent in the situation needs to be capable of Doing (D) something, spontaneously and correctly so that in each situation, creating an effect: our newly global-local transformative *Effect*, our *Pax Economica*.

Meta-Reality: Creativity, Love and Freedom

Bhaskar in his midlife then produced such books, as we have seen, as *Meta-Reality: Creativity, Love and Freedom, Reflections on Meta-Reality* (Bhaskar 2000) as well as *From East to West – Odyssey of a Soul*, taking forward this MELDA theme. In this last book, Bhaskar reviews several great world belief systems – including Ancient Greek, Judaic, Essene and Christian, Hindi (Vedic), Buddhist, Confucian, Taoist, Zen, Islam (Sufi) and modern materialist thought. We have then added in this chapter a Yoruba, African dimension. Bhaskar uses such a retrospective to cast light on the contemporary crises in western social and philosophical thought. These themselves reflect wider and deeper crises in society, which he relates to a dialectical chain of "avidya" (ignorance), "dualism" (split) and "maya" (illusion) itself grounded in ontological (existential) "insecurity".

While on the one hand, fellow critical realists (as Anglo-Saxon pragmatists) may consider that their founding father had become ever more "esoteric" of late, for us, overall, the reverse is the case. For, in turning "east", Bhaskar has become more practically transformative, and indeed newly globally integral, in his orientation. Indeed our own GENE effectively evolved out of Bhaskar's Meta-Reality, albeit that we add a "southern", integral African touch to now newly "eastern" orientation.

15.4.4. Releasing GENE-ius: Towards a Communiversity/Communitalism

Our (Lessem and Schieffer 2010b) approach to uncovering such an integral rhythm, or means of releasing GENE-ius, locally (Grounding), locally-globally (Emergence), newly globally (Navigation) and globally locally (Effect) both then in yourself and also, simultaneously and interactively, in your – in this case African – world, takes account of such (inevitably you will be a mix of worlds, but with one or other taking precedence). Thereby, for us, through:

- *Cycles of Life: "Southern" Humanistic (and more than Human) Reality:* you *experience* the world primarily through relationships: relationship to nature (including your inner nature) and to other human beings and to the community you belong to, and are enfolded within, as again in *Pax Natura*
- *Developmental Spiral: "Eastern" Holistic Reality:* you *imagine* the world primarily through an inner-directed cultural and spiritual perspective, seeking to understand the meaning of human existence, how life and the universe unfold, as in Pax *Spiritus*
- *Line of Argument: "Northern" Rational Reality:* you see the world primarily from a scientific, rational and systemic perspective, seeking to distinguish structures and processes within reality and to translate them into viable concepts and systems, as in Pax *Scientia*
- *The Point of It: "Western" Pragmatic Reality:* you act on the world primarily through experimentation and practical treatment of things, emphasising the application of ideas through action, pointing the way toward goal achievement, as in Pax *Economica*

The fourfold GENE rhythm, our (Lessem et al 2013) core integral "technology" as we shall see here, collectively also encompassing research-and-innovation (process and content) applying to both a PhD based research and innovation process, as well as to integral economic (Lessem and Schieffer 2010a) as well as integral enterprise (Lessem and Schieffer 2009) content, in similar guise, also incorporates, as you will see below, the elements of our Communiversity (Lessem et al 2019), ultimately leading, via Nhakanomics, Yurugu-nomics and the Economics of Love towards the Communitalism where we, South-West Africa wise, began:

- G = *Grounding and Origination: Cyclical – Experiential:* Communal Learning: You, individually and collectively, are *grounded* in a particular nature and community, which needs to be engaged with, if not also *activated*. For any living system, the "southern" grounds – herein *Southern* Africa as per our Integral *Kumusha* – represent its *local identity* and its *source of origin*. "Southern" grounding is about *being* in as well as feeling and *experiencing*, as well as *describing* a particular world, which thereafter continually cycles through, and indeed is recycled in *narrating* the stories we are. As such, and overall, you not only respond to a *call*, individually and collectively, but also begin to *activate* a community, altogether embodied, Communiversity-wise, in *Communal Learning*, in *Pax Natura* underpinned by *Nhakanomics*

- E = <u>E</u>mergent Foundation: Spiralling – Imaginative: <u>Transformation Journey</u>:
Moving to "eastern" emergence – herein *East* Africa as per our *Good African Story* – locates you and your community in a developing organisational and societal *context*, co-engaging with a *life world*, duly *interpreting* the imbalances therein, with a view to alleviating them. Here, we envisage dialectic interaction between "local and global", thereby coming to a newly imagined understanding, with a view to *catalysing development*. Such an emergent, spiralling process always includes a "stepping into the unknown" and "letting go" thereby becoming as it were a *local-global non-entity* – of some of the previous assumptions. New insights emerge, from out of the blue as it were, that provide clues for the transformative process. "Eastern" emergence is therefore essentially about *becoming*. It deals with *intuiting* and *imagining* the new *emergent* form, contained in spaces in between one existing form and another, altogether embodied in out *Transformation Journey*, via *Pax Spiritus* underpinned by *Yurugu-nomics*

- N = Emancipatory Navigation: Linear/Conceptual: <u>Research Academy</u>:
The move to "northern" navigation requires that the new insights gained are translated into new *concepts*, new knowledge, new technologies, new institutions, that now assume global, or universal, proportions. "Northern" navigation – as with *Sekem* in *North* Africa – is hence about *knowing* and about *making explicit* what hitherto had been rather implicit, through innovation driven *research* (method and substance). "Northern" *navigation* is about activating the *mind*-level, the conceptualising prowess of the human system, through *critical* emancipatory thinking, without losing touch with the emotional and spiritual levels that came before. At this point we conceive a newly *global* entity, as a new concept or even institution, forming the basis now for a universalizable line of argument, or activity, altogether embodied in our *Research Academy*, embodying *Pax Scientia* underpinned, following Bhaskar and Sekem, by the *Economics of Love*.

- E = Transformative <u>E</u>ffect: Point – Practical: <u>Socio-economic Laboratory</u>:
Moving to "western" effect – as embodied by our *PaxHerbals* in *West* Africa – finally now requires us to put all prior three levels into integrated, *practical* action. It is about pragmatically applying the new knowledge that has been developed, thereby actualising the research and innovation that it contains, thereby making a *contribution* to the *education* of you, your organisation and/or society. "Western" effect is hence about *doing* and about *making it happen*, thereby "to the point". This is the ultimate *transformative* level of the GENE-process, activating, metaphorically, the *body* or *hand*. This is the time where the newly global is actualised at a local level, through a *socio-economic laboratory*, *Pax Economica* ultimately underpinned by *Communitalism* as a whole.

Having completed the GENE-storyline, and Communiversity/Communitalism-line, so to speak, experientially-imaginatively-conceptually-practically, the process does not stop. Rather, it continuously moves on, in circular (iterative), spiralling (evolving) and linear (accumulative) as well as ultimately pointed (directive) form. Any transformative effect has to be continuously revisited, exploring whether it remains resonant with the "southern" grounds (e.g. the needs of nature and community) it seeks to serve. Any solution is considered a temporary one. Evolution is infinite. We now turn to Nonaka and Takauchi's analogous "knowledge spiral", while simultaneously revisiting our prior aboriginal grounds.

15.4.5. Transformative Agency to Knowledge Creating Company

Baa/Ba Means Space-and-Time in Layered Guise

In fact, via Bhaskar's Met-Reality and our GENE-ius, we can both reach back, newly globally in each case, to Ewo State in Nigeria (where one of us, Adodo, is based) in the *south*-west, and to Japan in the *east*. Ewo State, to which we referred in *feeling local* above, and other indigenous peoples conceive time not as a movement from past to future, but as a continuous channeling of consciousness from an intangible and tacit to a tangible and explicit expression.

The rock in the landscape was the ongoing tangible expression of the rock's consciousness, of nature power, as it had been since the time of creation. It was the same with people, animals and vegetation. They also did not make a distinction between time and space in their language. The suffix – *baa means both space of and time of. Today of course time is regarded by quantum physicists as part of a space-time continuum, as Einstein was to discover.*

Interestingly enough, moreover, the parallel notion of *ba*, in Japanese, had the same time-space connotations for the organisational sociologists Nonaka and Takeuchi (2008) that we cited in the last chapter, in the context of their *Knowledge Creating Company,* and also in Nonaka's (2008) *Management of Flow.* There are then, for him, in layered terms as for Bhaskar, evolving into MELDA (see above) four types of "ba", also analogous to our GENE.

These are (see Figure 15.4.4. below): originating Ba (southern), our original grounding via *Pax Natura;* dialoguing Ba (eastern), our emergent foundation Pax Spiritus; systemising Ba (northern), our emancipatory navigation via *Pax Scientia;* and exercising Ba (western), our transformative effect via *Pax Economica.* These, altogether, for Nonaka, are defined by two dimensions of interaction. One dimension is the "type" of interaction; whether the interaction takes place individually or collectively. The other dimension is the "media used" in such interactions; whether the interaction is through face-to-face contact or virtual media such as books, manuals, memos, e-mails or teleconferences:

- *Originating Ba is defined by individual and face-to-face interactions.* It is a place where individuals share experiences, feelings, emotions and mental models.

From such originating Ba emerges care, love, trust and commitment, for us, "southern", the ground for evolution within and among individuals and organizations, also in our case include (wo)man and nature (G).

- *Dialoguing Ba is defined by "eastern" collective and face-to-face interactions.* It is the place where individuals' mental models and skills are shared, converted into common terms, and articulated as concepts. Dialoguing Ba is more consciously constructed than originating Ba, involving the conscious use of metaphor and analogy, as well as negation and affirmation, to make the tacit explicit (E).
- *Systemising Ba is defined by "northern" style depersonalised and virtual interactions.* Information technology, through on-line networks, groupware, documentation and databanks, offers a virtual collaborative environment for the creation of systemising Ba (N).
- *Exercising Ba is defined by personalised, individual as well as virtual "western" style interactions.* Here, individuals embody explicit facts and concepts communicated through virtual media, such as written manuals or simulation programmes, making the explicit tacit (E).

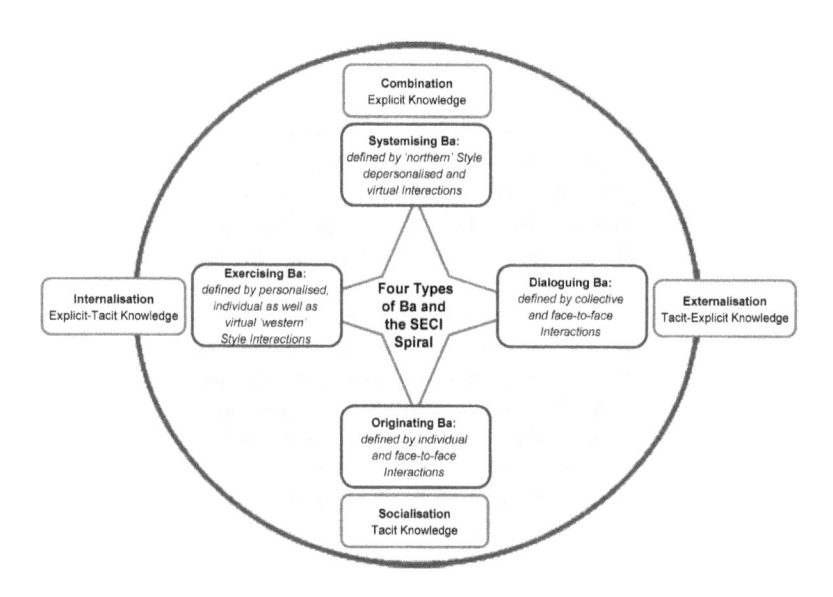

Figure 15.4.4: *Four Types of Ba and the SECI Spiral of Nonaka and Takeuchi*

The emergent, reformative world of Japanese style evolutionary spiral, arising out of an eastern, consciousness-based perspective – alongside the other worlds – is like a half-way house between "southern" community building and "northern" knowledge creation, in this case focused on the conscious evolution of organizations. The southern community building, in that layered guise, takes us back to the Dogon (see Chapter 10) with their *bummo/yala/tonu/toy* in turn.

15.4.6. Knowledge Creating Company to Traditional Age Sets

Age Sets, Communiversity, Pax Africana

Finally, in this newly global section, on the path of African realisation, we draw on African-American historian Chancellor Williams (1993) through his seminal work on *The Rebirth of African Civilization*. Written in the 1990s, his "age sets" anticipate the community (see items in CAP's below) of our integral day and age.

Childhood: Storytelling and Naming: 6–12: Being

LEARNING COMMUNITY/PAX NATURA

Each age set then had its own educational, social, economic, and political role. The children's set, to begin with, covers the years of game and play. *Primary education includes <u>storytelling, community songs and dances, as well as learning the natural names</u> of various birds and animals,* the identification of poisonous snakes, local plants and trees, and how to run and climb swiftly when pursued by dangerous animals.

Youth: Geography and History: 13–18: Becoming

TRANSFORMATION JOURNEY/PAX SPIRITUS

The next grade above childhood involved teenagehood (these periods varied, of course, amongst different societies). Now both education and responsibilities have stepped up, becoming more complex and extensive. The youth's entire future depended upon their performance at this level. *The boy was now required to learn his extended family history and the <u>trajectory of society</u>, including the geography and history of the region, the names of neighbouring states, and the nature of his relations with them. The girl's age group* differed from that of the boys. While they had the same intellectual education – history, geography, rapid calculation, poetry, music, and dance – education *in childcare, housekeeping, gardening, cooking, social relations, and marketing* was different.

Young Adulthood: Planting/Construction: 19–28: Knowing

Research Academy/Pax Science

At the next stage, the education of *male members involved hunting, community construction, preparing the fields for planting, and forming various industrial craft guilds,* including <u>engagement with secret societies</u>, each of which guarded the processes of the art. *The young women were generally responsible for planting and taking care of the farms, the operations of the markets, visiting and taking care of the sick and elderly, the formation of women's societies, and overall responsibility for the home.*

Midlife and Maturity: Elders' Council: 29–40: Doing

SOCIO-TECHNICAL LABORATORY/PAX ECONOMICA

There was not much difference thereafter between age groups C and D for both men and women, whose constitutional rights were inseparable. *At the age of 36, men and women were eligible for election to the most highly honoured body of society, the Council of Elders,* most especially reserved for age-set E, that is, from 40 years onwards, whose role was social, political, economic, and cultural altogether. By thereby combining "education" and "employment," as well as, if you like, "research" and "innovation," in contemporary guise, societies as a whole were integrated.

The Idea of a Community

As then set out more specifically in *The Idea of a Communiversity*, as per:

Learning Community

- a contextualised platform for learning and development, whereby human and more-than-human communities are enabled to reclaim or restore their potential
- communal stewards deeply immerse themselves in a particular natural and communal, local context, able to locally relate to other human beings and to nature.
- embodying the web of life, representing mother nature; the circle of physical and human nature, reflecting the original oneness of all creation in a particular context.

Transformation Journey

- individual and collective learning Consciousness-raising releases cultural and economic genius via a narrative of self, organisation, community, and society.
- A development catalyst is able to engage with the cultural and economic dynamics of a particular entity or place, co-evolving with individual, institutional, and societal factors.
- A spiral of conscious co-evolution represents the regeneration and renewal of the spirit, culture, and economy, locally and globally, of one place in relation to another.

Research Academy

Scholarship, research, and knowledge creation aim – internally and in an interdisciplinary guise – for social innovation, re-generating a society.

- promoting conceptual and analytical ability, individually and collectively, sharing knowledge in a group, and generating "newly global" models of transformation
- The resulting grid of knowledge represents a structure-seeking and organised process of transcultural knowledge creation across recognised disciplines.

Socio-technical Laboratory

a focal point for creative experimentation or a conducive space in which appropriate new practices can be conceived of, tested, and implemented.

- overarching facilitation of development, serving to translate knowledge into capacities globally and locally, thereby exercising overall governance.
- focused, goal-oriented, and co-creative, resulting in the active build-up of new infrastructure and institutions, now globally and locally.

As we can see from the above, the trans-modern community serves, transformatively, to re-generate the original pre-modern age-sets into an environmental, social, and governance, as well as economic, structure, and process, that draws upon and renews the gifts of a particular nature and community.

We now finally come onto the keynotes of Critical Realism and Meta-Reality, on the realisation path, in our case lodged in the south-*west*, *albeit* via Bhaskar, drawing also prolifically on the east, if not also the north.

15.5. Critical Realism – Keynotes: Toward a Layered African Reality

15.5.1. Critical Realism is Critical of the Status Quo

"Transcendental realism", so called for Bhaskar, signifies an ontology transcending the empirical level; in this sense relating to a critique of "flat" empiricism. In being critical of the merging of structure and agency. Bhaskar transcends such, as we do, through his transformational model of social action, embodied in his "meta-reality". Any universalist claims to truth need to be set, in addition to their objectively "intransitive" of natural, material reality, in the context of a subjectively cultural and social "transitive" character of science.

In our own African context such a transcendental orientation reaches back to our original Dogon cosmology, as well as to our own Pax African subsequently, altogether in the *south*-west, whereby we are equally critical of the academic as well as the economic status quo.

Table 15.5. *Critical Realism – Keynotes*

Critical Realism is critical of the westernised scientific status quo in Africa
You become involved with a stratified or layered African Reality.
You conceive Reality as both transitive (subjective) and intransitive (objective).
A hermeneutic cultural as well as an empirical material Side to Critical Realism.

15.5.2. Via Generative Mechanisms You Become Involved with Layered Reality

The most fundamental enterprise in science is to find the inherent mechanisms that generate events; it is these inherent properties the critical realists call "causal powers", for us thereby re-GENE-rative as such. Critical Realists distinguish three domains: the basic one is the domain of the "real" – here we find the generative mechanisms, existing irrespective of whether they produce an event or not. When mechanisms produce a factual event it comes under the domain of the actual, whether we observe it or not; when an event is experienced, it becomes an empirical fact. Insofar as reality is stratified, what is important is that new mechanisms are created in their respective strata, through emergent powers.

The generative mechanism, or "real" underlying domain, for us, in Africa, is our local natural and communal feeling, as such, with its duly generative powers, such as that of the proverbial "vital force", culminating in communitalism. Indeed it is such a *vital force*, drawn from a particular nature power, rather than westernised entrepreneurship, or indeed market forces, but on individual power which are generative in such a *south*-western guise.

15.5.3. Reality Is Both Transitive (subjective) and Intransitive (objective)

An external reality exists, for Bhaskar, independently of our conceptions of it. The purpose of science is to come as close to this reality as possible. It is such theories of reality (e.g. the laws of gravity) that constitute objective knowledge of it, that is its intransitive object – the transitive dimension is socially determined, subjective and changeable. What makes social science special, compared to natural science, is that social scientists seek knowledge about a socially produced reality, not just a socially defined one.

In our own context here, arguably, our African local is subjective, and the global is objective, albeit that the two are interwoven along the integral way.

15.5.4. There Is a Hermeneutic as Well as an Empirical Side to Critical Realism

For critical realism, society is made up of thinking and reflective, for us acculturated, human beings who are capable of continually changing their perception of social reality. Hence, you as a researcher are supposed to study other people's interpretations of the social world – the object of study is therefore socially defined. It is important to note, that social systems are rather open than closed: we cannot just isolate social events in order to manipulate a situation, with the purpose of studying what happens.

Moreover, such an interpretive if not also transformative perspective, via critical realism, applies not only to you as an individual researcher, but also to your society as a whole, thereby, for us, being a local, local-global-, newly global and ultimately global-local case in point. We are now ready to conclude.

15.6. Conclusion

15.6.1. Realization Through Stratification

Critical realism is the fourth one of our critical emancipatory orientations to research (level 3). While on the one hand, it follows in the pragmatic footsteps of experimental, survey and case study methods and empiricism, on the other hand, like the three other research paths, it is both critical and emancipatory.

Along the research path of realisation, critical realism has a pragmatic orientation, geared towards an ultimately transformative effect, as well as being located in globally objective, as well as locally subjective, in our case African, reality. However, it is more deeply imbued than experimental method and empirical methodology, in that it deals with an overtly stratified reality. Moreover, and like the other critical emancipatory approaches, it is more "worldly" than its predecessors. Moreover, as in each of the other cases, such a research path needs to be complemented by a path of innovation, for us here from nhakanomics (grounding) and yurugu-nomics (emergence) into the economics of love (navigation) and ultimately, now, communitalism (effect), with the south-west, as such, in Africa, building on the rest.

Secondly, in comparing and contrasting critical realism with the other three emancipatory orientations, we find that the realistic emphasis on *realization through stratification* compares and contrasts with that of postmodernism (*reason*), critical theory (*renewal*) and feminism (*relational*).

15.6.2. Original Grounding on the African Path of Realisation

Altogether then, for our original grounding we revisit Chapter 4, where we outlined not only survey and experimental method, as "western", our *south*-western grounds, but also case study method, or what we term in "southern" guise, a case *story*, such as the one illustrated by Cashbuild above, whereby, in devising such:

- You are able to ask good Questions – and to interpret the Answers.
- You are a good Listener – not trapped by your own Ideologies and Preconceptions.
- You are adaptable so that new Situations can be seen as Opportunities.
- You are unbiased by preconceived Notions, responsive to contradictory Evidence

15.6.3. Emergent Foundation on the African Path of Realisation

More specifically then, as far as the subsequent empirical foundation is concerned:

- You search for the African truth
- You see after positive facts
- You collect observational data and build African theories
- You exercise control through closed systems

15.6.4. Emancipatory Navigation on the African Path of Realisation

Herein then, and by way of emancipatory navigation:

- Critical Realism is critical of the westernised scientific status quo in Africa
- You become involved with a stratified or layered African Reality
- You conceive Reality as both transitive (subjective) and intransitive (objective)
- A hermeneutic cultural as well as an empirical material side to Critical Realism.

15.6.5. Communiversity to Communitalism

As we can see, ultimately, in Table 15.6.5, below, in the duly stratified terms set by Bhaskar's critical realism generally, and his Meta-Reality, specifically, our communiversity sets the stage for communitalism to follow.

Indeed one of us (Ronnie Lessem) can vividly remember asking Roy Bhaskar, at a seminar of his that Ronnie attended, whether critical realism invariably led to the kind of economic transformation Bhaskar was seeking. His response was non-committal. With hindsight we can now see that, for such to materialise the paths of, for us African, research and innovation, need to be mutually reinforcing. Lamentably, in Africa, if not worlds-wide, such mutual resonance between community (outreach), journey (education), academy (research) and laboratory (development) is seldom evident, in the social arena, which is why we engage with such here.

Table 15.6.5. *Pax Herbals' Search for the Real Truth: W2fita* **Via Nature Power, Healing Radiance and Communitalism**

Feeling Local	Intuiting Local-Global	Thinking Newly Global	Acting Global-Local
Pax Herbals	Nature Power/ Healing Radiance	Social Realisation	Search for the Real Truth

We now turn finally from critical realism to action research, starting out, as we shall see, with African American, Afrocentricity.

15.7. References

Adodo A (2017) *Integral Community Enterprise in Africa: Communitalism as an Alternative to Capitalism*. London. Routledge.

Bhaskar R (1977) *The Realist Theory of Science*. London. Verso Press.

Bhaskar R (1993) *The Dialectic: The Pulse of Freedom*. London. Verso Press.

Bhaskar R (2000a) *From East to West: The Odyssey of a Soul*. London. Sage.

Bhaskar R (2000b) *Meta-Reality: Creativity, Love and Freedom*. London. Sage.

Bhaskar R (2002) *Reflections on Meta-Reality*. London. Sage.

Bunge M (1980) *Causality and Modern Science*. New York. Dover Publications.

Danemark B et al (2002) *Explaining Reality*. Abingdon. Routledge.

Harre R (1994) *The Discursive Mind*. London. Sage.

Lessem R and Schieffer A (2009) *Transformation Management: Toward the Integral Enterprise*. Abingdon. Routledge.

Lessem R and Schieffer A (2010a) *Integral Economics: Releasing the Economic Genius of your Society*. Abingdon. Routledge.

Lessem R and Schieffer A (2010b) *Integral Research and Innovation: Transforming Enterprise and Society*. Abingdon. Routledge.

Lessem R and Schieffer A (2015) *Integral Renewal: A Relational and Renewal Perspective*. Abingdon. Routledge.

Lessem R et al (2013) *Integral Dynamics: Cultural Dynamics to Political Economy: The Future of the University*. Abingdon. Routledge.

Lessem R, Adodo A and Bradley T (2019) *The Idea of the Communiversity: Releasing the Natural, Cultural, Technological, and Economic Genus of Societies*. Manchester. Beacon Academic.

Mavhunga CT (2017) *What Do Science, Technology and Innovation Mean for Africa*. Massachusetts. MIT Press.

Nonaka I and Takeuchi H (2008) *The Knowledge Creating Company*. Cambridge: Harvard Business Review Press.

Nonaka I et al (2008) *Managing Flow: A Process Theory of the Knowledge Based Firm*. New York: Palgrave Macmillan.

Williams C (1993) *The Rebirth of African Civilization*. Chicago: Third World Press.

Chapter 16 From Critical Realism to Afrocentric Action Research. Become an African Scientist in Action

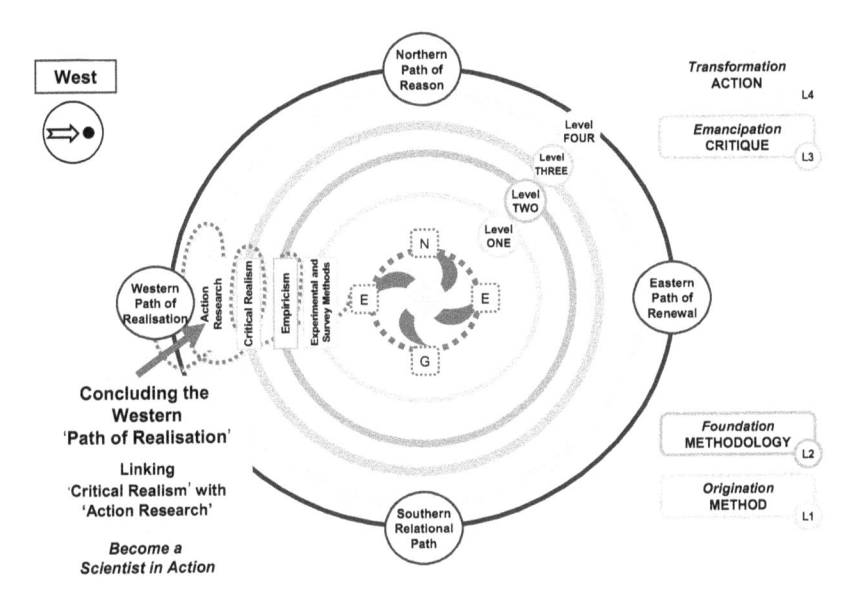

Figure 16.1: *Overview Chapter 16 – Level 4 / West*

Afro-centricity, , is a philosophical perspective associated with the discovery, location and actualizing of African agency within the context of history and culture. By agency is meant an attitude toward action originating in African experiences. Afro-centricity then is the belief in the centrality of Africans in post-modern history.

Molefi Asante (2003)   Afrocentricity – The Theory of Social Change

Summary: Afrocentric Action Research

- Finally we are concluding the western research path of realisation, by entering into its fourth "western integral" level: action research. In this particular case we speak of generic action research, as we also categorized PAR, Co-operative Inquiry and Socio-Technical Design as "southern", "eastern", "northern" expressions of such.

- Action research, in its generic form, was originally developed by Kurt Lewin, in the middle of the 20th century in the United States, and has been taken forward, in the 21st century, by Peter Reason in the UK. In America, late last century, Molefi Asante as head of Temple University's African Studies Department developed Afrocentricity as an approach to social change that had, for us, a local African feel

- Action research is a form of collective self-reflective enquiry undertaken by participants in social situations in order to improve the rationality and justice of their own social or educational practices, as well as their understanding of those practices and the situations in which the practices are carried out.

- Action research refers to the conjunction of three elements: action, research and participation. AR aims to increase the ability of the involved community or organization members to control their own destinies more effectively and to keep improving their capacity to do so within a more sustainable and just environment. Locally-globally it has been spread largely though PAR lodged in so called *Vivencia* drawn from "good life" in Latin America.

- Newly globally, again in African America, the principles of practices of Kwanzaa have been developed by Maulana Karenga in California, drawing on seven principles and practices of Form, Function, Force, Foundation, Field, Flow and Freedom each building on their African equivalents

- The keynotes of action research that underlie such, on the African path to realisation, are *appreciative inquiry*, of Kwanzaa in our case here; an Afrocentric approach to *social change*; soulful African *knowing how* more than that; and action learning *drawing on and from your own shores*.

16.1. Orientation to Generic Action Research

Table 16.1.1. *West African Social Research and Innovation: Path of Realisation: W3* Afrocentricity to Appreciative Inquiry

Western Grounding Method and Origination	Western Emergent Methodology & Foundation	Western Navigational Critique and Emancipation	Western Effective Action and Transformation
Case Study (W1)	Empiricism (N2)	Critical Realism (W3)	Action Research (N4)
Afrocentricity (W1)	Vivencia (W2)	Kwanzaa (W3)	Appreciative Inquiry (W4)

16.1.1. Action Research and Afrocentricity: Research to Innovation

We now come to the culmination of the path of realisation in Africa, as a re-GENErative process, focusing, in our GENEtic terms, ultimately, on its substantively transformative economic and enterprise effect, on the one hand, of *Communitalism*, in the form of a *Communiversity*, on the other, altogether, and contextually, centred in the healing wisdom of Africa. Such will be more fully illustrated, further to what we have already outlined on the path of realisation, with a view to innovation, in our next and culminating "south-western" chapter, on PaxHerbals in *West* Africa. PaxHerbals then, founded by one of us (Anselm Adodo) is also the Socio-Technical Laboratory that ultimately puts our *Communiversity* to work in West Africa, building on the learning communities, transformation journeys, and research academy – our Centre for Integral Research and Innovation in Africa and its Diaspora – that come before.

As such moreover, in this penultimate chapter, we focus, research-wise, on *action* research (transformative effect), that follows ultimately from research *method* (original grounding), *methodology* (emergent foundation) and *critique* (emancipatory navigation), in Africa. Furthermore, by way of innovation, thereby aligning such action research with social change, we pursue Afrocentricity, Vivencia, Kwanzaa and Appreciative Inquiry in turn.

We start as such, as has been our custom, with an orientation to generic action research. This follows, in turn, in "integral western" guise on the path now of realisation, action research wise, following prior PAR (relational path), Cooperative Inquiry (renewal path) and Socio-Technical Design (path of reason), albeit drawing especially, as we shall see in the *south*-west, on PAR/Vivencia.

Further to such an action research orientation, with a view to innovation, economically and enterprise-wise, we start by feeling local, originally naturally grounded in *Afrocentricity*; thereafter, intuiting local-global, our emergent cultural foundation is lodged in PAR laden Vivencia; the newly global form of scientific emancipatory navigation that follows is that of Kwanzaai and its seven principles: form, function, field, foundation, force, flow, freedom in duly African terms; finally, via our global-local keynotes, we serve to activate ultimately transformative economic effect is that of appreciative African inquiry.

16.1.2. Origins of Action Research

Kurt Lewin and the Origins of Action Research

The origins of action research, as we indicated in Chapters 7, 10, and 13, can be traced back to Kurt Lewin (2008) and John Dewey (2008). In a specifically "action research" context, Lewin's approach can be articulated in terms of a series of steps, each of which is composed of a circle of planning, action and fact-finding about the result of the action. Action research, in the United States at least, did suffer a decline in favour during the 1960s because of its association with radical political activism. However, it has subsequently gained a significant foothold both within the realm of community-based, and participatory action research; and as a form of practice oriented to the improvement of educative encounters. Herewith then, in aligning action research with Afrocentricity as we shall see, we reconnect with its hitherto radical orientation.

Action research as such is a form of collective self-reflective enquiry undertaken by participants in social situations in order to improve the rationality and justice of their own social or educational practices, as well as their understanding of those practices and the situations in which the practices are carried out. The approach is only action research when it is collaborative, though it is important to realise that action research of the group is achieved through the critically examined action of individual group members. Interestingly enough, and in that group oriented guise, all standard, individualised PhD work, for example, cuts dramatically across the action research vein. Finally, when set in historical context, while Lewin did talk about action research as a method, he stressed what was the contrast between this form of interpretative and ultimately action centred practice and more traditional empirical-analytic research that counted. We now turn to his leading compatriot, John Dewey.

John Dewey and the University Laboratory School

John Dewey, to whom we were first introduced in Chapter 7, moved to the University of Chicago at the turn of the 19th century to head the department of philosophy, psychology, and pedagogy. It was at this time that Dewey began to consider the philosophy of education in a serious and systematic way. In 1896, he founded the University Laboratory School, indeed anticipating our Communiversity Laboratory, now better known, for us in "watered down" university terms, as the "Dewey School".

The Laboratory School was not a model institution; rather, it truly lived up to its name. It was a place for educational experiments in the genuine etymological sense of experiment, that is, to make a trial of something, for us now, as we shall see, in prospectively "western" Afrocentric guise. Theories and practices were developed, tested, criticized, refined, and tried again. Experimentalism became increasingly important as Dewey's philosophy matured. For him, also influenced by Popper's critical rationalism (see Chapter 10) not only were these experiments falsifiable, but in a contingent evolving world, their generalizability was always subject to revision. There is no end of inquiry for Dewey; nonetheless, he believed it the best way to render human experience intelligent.

The Laboratory School was not the only site for educational research in Chicago at that time. Jane Addams and her work at Hull House, for which she eventually received the Nobel Prize, greatly influenced Dewey. Rosalind Rosenberg writes, that for Dewey, Hull House was a laboratory and an example of what he was trying to accomplish in education. Dewey visited Hull House even before moving to Chicago. Upon his arrival there, Dewey actively participated in the life of Hull House.

There he met some of the most influential early feminists whose involvement in the political issues of the day caused by massive immigration, the social and economic effects of urbanization, and rapid technological advance, exercised considerable influence. He also mixed with workers, trade unionists, and political radicals. Some of his most influential educational works emerged out of these laboratories. These works not only set out Dewey's practical pedagogy, but they also outlined the psychological and philosophical principles upon which it relied. These principles devolved from the trial and error experiments that occurred within and without the walls of the Laboratory School, anticipating the transformative effect of our communiversity today, as we shall see in the context of PaxHerbals in Nigeria in the final case story.

First though we turn Afrocentric to give action research a local African/American diasporic – thereby south/*western*, African American in this "west African – case, feel.

16.2. Feel Local – Path of African Realisation: Afrocentricity: W4f

16.2.1. Afrocentricity – The Theory of Social Change

The Essential Grounds of Afrocentricity in the West

Afrocentricity, for leading Afro-American authority on such, Molefi Asante (2003) Professor of African Studies at Temple University in Philadelphia, in his original book on *Afrocentricity – The Theory of Social Change*, embodies African history, mythology, Africa's creative motif, and its ethos exemplifying its collective will.

On the basis of Africa's story Asante builds upon the work of his ancestors who gave signs toward the continent's humanizing function.
For one of us (Anselm Adodo) then in that light, he claimed (Adodo 2012):

> In Ewo State, there were traditional healers everywhere, and traditional shrines could be sited in many corners of the village. There was a mission hospital and a government hospital in the village, but majority of the people also patronised traditional healers. At the time, herbal medicine was identified with witchcraft, sorcery, ritualism and all sorts of fetish practices. Because herbal medicine was associated with paganism, African-Christians patronized traditional healers, in secret, and the educated elite and religious figures did not want to be associated in any way with traditional African Medicine. Moreover for a religious figure, especially a catholic priest like myself, to be openly propagating traditional medicine was seen as a taboo of the highest order. In fact his goal was to change the face of African traditional medicine. In fact four years later in 2000, my book titled: "Nature Power. A Christian Approach to Herbal Medicine" was published. (Adodo 2012)

Economic freedom, for Asante then, and as has been clearly apparent in the Pax Herbals case, must always be connected to political and cultural freedom, of a particular society and its culture, or else freedom does not truly exist. As such (Adodo 2012)

> PaxHerbals then believes that the only way to sustainable development is for Africa to produce what it consumes and consume what it produces. But to produce, one must innovate. Paxherbals is determined to continue to champion the preservation of Africa indigenous knowledge, for the sake of posterity, of African medicine, and for the sake of Pax Africana.

The fragility of economic independence has been demonstrated throughout the U.S, Kenya, Soviet Union, Zimbabwe and South Africa. In addition, even the control of production and land can be tenuous if a people do not possess the political power to safeguard their economic freedom. In fact land on its own must never be equated with freedom; freedom, for Asante, is a mental state.

African nations, for Asante, which have gained political independence but have not secured their cultural and economic independence remain enslaved to alien forces. There is a Kiswahili saying (see Marimba Ami's *Yurugu*, Chapter 9): "muko vile mjiwakavyo wenyewe, si vile wengine wawawekavyo": "You are what you make of yourself, not what others make of you". Asante then turns to social science, and to levels of transformation in relation to such.

Levels of Transformation Towards Afrocentric Rhythm: The Beat of Your Life

Afro-centricity, for Asante, is a transforming power that helps Africans to capture the true sense of their souls. There are five levels of awareness leading to such transformation. The first level is called *skin recognition* when a person recognizes that his or her skin or heritage is black but cannot grasp any further reality. The second level is *environmental recognition,* whereby discrimination and abuse goes along with his or her blackness. The third level is *personality awareness,* when a person says "I like music or dance" that is African.

The fourth level is *interest concern,* with the problems of blacks but it does not yet represent a commitment to an African cultural based *Afro-centric awareness.*

The fifth level, is when the person becomes totally changed to a conscious level of involvement to his or her own mind liberation. Only when this happens can we say that the individual is aware of the collective conscious will. *Afro-centricity then becomes like a rhythm; it dictates the beat of your life.*

For one of us (Adodo) again (2012):

> .. we must reclaim our right to cognitive freedom, if we truly seek to be free. Africa must be aware of, and fight against the coloniality of knowledge and Epistemicide, which are modern forms of colonization, by evolving and e-ducing (origin of the word education) its own research methods and research methodologies suited to and geared towards African epistemological emancipation.

Afro-centric awareness is greater than the levels that have come before because each is a stage toward perfection, not perfection itself. Indeed culture, for Asante, is the most revolutionary level of awareness, in the sense that Cabral, Fanon, as we have seen (see Chapter 8) and Karenga as we shall see – the latter (Karenga) heralding our newly global Kwanzaa navigation on the path of African realization.

Such navigation, and then ultimate effect, includes dance, art, and music, science, and philosophy, engineering, architecture, and economics. It is difficult to create freely when you use someone else's motifs, styles, images and perspectives. Afro-centric awareness is a total commitment to African liberation by a determined effort to repair any psychic, economic or cultural damage done to Africans. It is further a pro-active statement of the faith we hold in the future of the African him or herself. What, for Asante constitutes the basis for action we seek?

The Bases of Action: Tradition and Innovation

The two fundamental aspects of the Afro-centric project are innovation – for us research and innovation – and tradition. Both are essential in the historical process of harmonizing the world. The generation of the new, the novel, is basic to the advancement of cultural ideas, but also so is the maintenance of the traditional. Innovation permits us, even requires of us, to promote new themes based on traditional motifs. For Adodo (2012):

> Through the utilization of common plants and weeds, PaxHerbal clinic and Research Laboratories has then been able to develop a natural science based approach to developing herbal recipes that has been of help to the local community and to millions of Nigerians. It also has a home-grown economic model that puts the interest of the local

community as its focal point. Rather than practice capitalist "free enterprise", which encourages the individual to acquire as much for himself as possible, we have developed an economic model based on what he has termed communitalism.

All real revolutions, for Asante, have taken place because of some appeal to the past for inspiration and direction. *Afro-centricity, moreover, is not Africanity. It is not the mere existence of the African person as such, but rather the active, self-conscious advancement of the humanizing motif in every sector of society.* It is an architect appealing to traditional motifs in the generation of the new and the modern. It is the economist examining and plying the relative and positive traditions of Africans in the economy. It is the political scientist and politician seeing in the traditional possibilities for dynamic change.

Holistic Plan to Reconstruct Every Dimension of the African World

Culture in relation to all of such then is not a narrow term. The Afro-centric

cultural project is *a holistic plan to reconstruct and develop every dimension of the African world from the standpoint of Africa as subject rather than object.* Culture then is the totalization of the historical, artistic, economic and spiritual aspects of people's lives. Afro-centricity assumes that African government officials will become conscious of the centrality of Africa in their deliberations, that a writer will seek to influence the African people, that we re-connect, in our minds, ancient Numibia and Kemet to the rest of Africa, that we speak on every subject affecting the world.

When Asante then calls for Afro-centricity, he is also calling for a new historiography founded on African aspirations, visions and concepts. The search is not for a naïve nationalism, nor for a superficial socialism, but for a deep, self-conscious, positive relationship with our own experiences. One day he says, on the continent of Africa we will see an Afro-centric university with its curriculum geared toward the Pan-African world as central, not peripheral to knowledge. As such we are following in his footsteps.

We can achieve the humanizing mission of the earth, for him, by remembering that the idea of culture and civilization first went down the Nile from the interior of Africa, where indeed, in Egypt, our associated enterprise Sekem is based. Our interiority is only significant because it reaffirms for us that if we once organized complex civilizations all over the continent of Africa, we can take these traditions and generate more advanced ideas. Let the artist imagine, let the scientist expand, let the priests see visions, let the writer be free to create, and let the Afro-centric revolution, for Asante, be born. As Reg Revans, as we shall see below, the founder of action learning, famously claimed, in seeking change and indeed transformation start by reaching within your own shores. We now turn to Asante's (Asante 2015) more recent work on Afrocentrcity, and now also Africology.

16.2.2. African Pyramids of Knowledge: Kemet, Afrocentricity, Africology

Afrocentricity to Africology

The shift then from Afrocentricity to *Africology* has gone almost unnoticed, not least because Asante himself has not clearly differentiated the two. In our (Adodo and Lessem 2021) own, recent work on *Africology: Deconstructing and Reconstructing Knowledge and Value in Africa*, we cited the work of Uganda's, recently late Dani Nabudere (2011), the originator of the term "Africology", from his *Afrikology: Philosophy and Wholeness: An Epistemology*:

> The word, "Afrikology" is not ethnic nor racial but a validation of a human knowledge of communal – including natural – living. It is "Afri-" because it is inspired by what I call "ideas originally produced from the cradle of human kind located in Africa", and so, it is not Afrikology because it is African (although to some extent it is). It is also "ko (logy)" because it is based on logos, the word from which the world was originated, but at the same time, an episteme, a worldly-wise eco-logical knowledge and consciousness Consequently, it does not strive for superiority but a reclamation and validation of its rightful position, as a whole. It seeks to avoid any claim to an overarching epistemic superiority, but stands for plurality of epistemic directions, for us "southern" and "eastern", "northern" and "western" communi-versity (harbouring di-versity). Knowledge therefore is an interpretation that is always situated within a living communal tradition and our inescapable historicity.

In other words, as we proceed from Afrocentricism to Africology, we turn from feeling local to intuiting local-global which will become more readily apparent in this next section as Africology and action research, so to speak, co-evolve.

Fields, Paradigms and Classifications of Afrocentricism/Africology

<u>Social, Historical, Cultural, Political, Economic, and Psychological Fields</u>

For Asante in fact there are seven general subject fields of so called Africology, altogether representing a groundedness of observation and behaviour in one's own historical experiences – without hierarchy and without seeking hegemony – sustained by a commitment to studying the life narratives, cultural values and possibilities of the African people trans-nationally and trans-continentally. In the West one would never assume to study literature without reference to the Greeks, so why should not the same apply to Africa with regard to its classical civilisations.

The Africological subject fields then, for him, are: *social, communication, historical, cultural, political, economic and psychological.*

<u>Paradigmatic Approaches to Research: Functional, Categorical, Ethological</u>

There are moreover for Asante, and at the same time, three *paradigmatic approaches to research in Africology: functional, categorical and ethological.* The functional paradigm represents needs, policy and action. In the categorical paradigm are schemes, gender, class, themes. The etymological paradigm deals with language, words and concept origin.

Classifying Cultural/Aesthetic, Social, Behavioural, and Policy Issues

Among Africologists, furthermore, the study of African phenomena is primarily an examination of *cultural/aesthetic, social, behavioural, and policy issues*. By cultural/aesthetic is meant the creative, artistic and inventive aspect of human phenomena that demonstrates the expression of values, arts and the good.

For Asante, his research methodology must be holistic and integrative; his epistemology participatory and committed. The Africologist is a working scholar committed to the advancement of knowledge about the African world. The task, for him, is *not like that of the Western social scientist who seeks to predict human behaviour in order to advance more direct control over nature but rather to explain nature as it is manifest in the African arena*. Africology does not deny rationalism its place but neither does it deny other forms of human inquiry their places in the acquisition of knowledge.

The African Pyramid Age Was the First Human University

In fact whole construction of pyramids, he goes on to say, throughout the African continent, and other large-scale projects were historically carried out with combinations of ideas, tasks and actions. That is why it is possible to claim that *the African pyramid age was the first human university where all the acquired knowledge of humanity was used in the grand constructions*. What happened later, much later, whereby European sciences must be criticized, therefore for Asante, for the exclusion of the "other", for their construction of the either-or paradigm, and for the anti-feminism posture. Furthermore, at least one African religion, Yoruba, indeed the heritage of one of us (Anselm Adodo) has grown to an international religion with some 100 million. adherents.

The Africologist, for Asante, then advances beyond the mechanistic moment and grasps the dynamic and rhythmic process, just like our transformational GENE, by which we live in the world. *The living in the world becomes the ground in which we find authentic empiricism*. In this respect Afrocentric inquiry is both particular and general. It is particular in the sense that it engages the scholar creatively as a person who lives in the world; it is general because it operates as social, action centred inquiry, encompassing psychological, cultural, and mythical dimensions of human life, thereby superseding the mechanistic model.

Turning the Table So That Africa Assumes Centrality

Moreover, South African born American historian Tsehloane Keto (Adodo 2012) wrote in his provocative historiography *The Africa Centred Perspective on History* that "different regions of the world that have evolved distinct cultures are entitled to develop paradigms based on the perspectives of the region's qualitatively significant human cultures, histories and experiences".

Thus for example for the Africanist who studies the economy of Kenya, the aim is to add to the economy and method a Western enterprise, more than to add the liberation of the African nation's economy from the grip of the West. *Only the Afrocentric scholar rises to a new level of consciousness which claims that it is the concrete act of turning the table so that Africa assumes centrality that grants African people a new economic, historical or linguistic vision.* Indeed, we make the future by virtue of realizing in our actions the predominant objective task for restructuring the present. The leap of the imagination one finds in the best Afrocentric scholarship gets its energy, for Asante, from the African aesthetic, rhythmic sensibility. What one seeks in a study are the mergers of facts with beauty; this becomes the creative quest for interpretation that "looks good".

The Soul of Method: Organic, Fluid Nature of Research Rhythm

Soul as such is what the researcher brings to the Afrocentric method, that is, the creative energy used to insure a successful project. In research, for Asante, the scholar must understand that everything is potentially active, powerful and possible and it is up to her or him to access the vitality of the project. One has soul or uses soul effectively when one is able to transform strong emotional attachments to ideas to something that is external to oneself so that it is recognized, seen and appreciated by others. *The concern is toward the direction of the truly organic, fluid, agreeable nature of rhythm, and the soul of method.* This is the Afrocentric version of generic action research. For one of us, Adodo (2012):

> What defines each person is not just one's tribe. The soil, the trees, the rivers, the mountains, the air and the animals who inhabit the environment define who we are. For me, an African community is not just a place where human beings live. A community comprises the plants, animals, the ancestors and the spirit. In times of crisis of identity, each society naturally goes back to its core values, images to rediscover its sense of identity. In other words, nature and community is the home of humankind and is the foundation of all science, innovation and development. Above all, humans find their identity by reconnecting with nature. At the very core of every society is a sense of the sacred.

Afrocentricity then, for Asante, as the intellectual movement that restored the place of Africans in world history remains fundamental to the Afrocentric revolution and place of Africa prior to Arab and European colonialism.

Economic Relations Become the Result of Cultural Relations

The acquisition of knowledge, as such moreover, occurs in a cultural context. What then is culture? For Asante it is *a world of voices, worldviews, cosmologies, institutions, ideas, myths, epics and symbols.* Since Eurocentric methods have been aggressive, it is necessary to demonstrate a humanistic method capable of allowing for the acquisition of data form all societies, African, American, European, Asian and Indigenous Peoples.

Asante's critique of polity and economy, as well as epistemology then, is not based, as such, on a fundamental rejection, for example, of Marx' analysis of capitalism but rather on *the inability of Marx to see the interrelationship of culture and economics*. Although social relations are central to Marx, by social relations he means essentially economic relations, not cultural relations. To be sure, in one sense all cultural relations are social relations but in the Afrocentric use of the term "culture" Asante means the generative expression of a people's myths, motifs and celebration of their history.

Economic relations become the result of cultural relations, the most elemental of human expressions. Afrocentricity totalizes culture, economic and social organization, demonstrating the essential character of human society from the centrality of Africa and the primacy of classical civilization. The second point is based on the dysfunctional Marxist hierarchy, for him, of social and economic organization: *communist, socialist, capitalist, mercantilist, feudal and communal. What this Darwinist concept of evolution does is to reserve for the "highest" form of economic and social organisation the white European nations. All of the African systems would be on the lowest step of the hierarchy.*

The African Must Find Centring in a Cultural and Psychological Sense

For Asante, moreover, European slave traders moved Africans off in physical terms; missionaries and settlers moved Africans off in religious terms; and capitalists moved Africans off in economic terms. This metaphorical conception of the human, African reality is clearly, for him, at the heart of the reclamation process. *To reclaim a centred place in economic, social and political contexts, the African must find centring in a cultural and psychological sense.* For Adodo (Tsehloane Keto 1995)

> Holiness, for me, is a state of union with God, with oneself and with others. Others include your fellow human beings as well as plants, animals, and indeed the whole of creation. When you discover that you are not just anybody or just a spirit, but a complete and whole person, then you will discover the meaning of holiness. The holy person is the one who has discovered the balance between the physical, the psychological and the spiritual.

In the final analysis, for Asante then as for us, we must propose a new ethic along the "newly global" lines articulated by his close associate Maulana Karanga, chair of African Studies at California State University, as we shall see below, one that brings restoration and reparation. How then, ultimately for Karanga, do we recover, repair restore, or indeed re-GENE-rate, the land, the people and the society: *serudj-ta?* First though, before proceeding from feeling local, in Afrocentric guise (Asante), to turning newly global as such (Karenga), we intuit locally-globally, now revisiting action research generally and participatory action research, specifically. We start, locally-globally then, with *vivencia*.

16.4. Intuiting Local-Global Vivencia on the Realisation Path: W4i

16.4.1. Destabilising Power Relations: Feminism to Cultural Studies

In turning from Afrocentricity/Afrologology specifically, to action research specifically, we (Lessem and Schieffer 2010) firstly, in our *Integral Research and Innovation*, revisited the "southern" grounds of "participatory action research", locally-globally, which are most closely aligned with "feeling Afrocentrically" locally. Though this does obviously overlap with our previous chapter (see Chapter 7) this is the nature and scope of action research, in that its different manifestations are strongly interwoven. In focusing on PAR then, as intimated earlier in Chapter 7, the local starting point was in Tanzania, via President Nyerere and his *ujamaa* before it spread locally-globally.

Feminist and participatory action research as such, particularly that in the "south", also aligned herein with Afrocentricism, both seek to unsettle and change the power relations, structures, and mechanisms of the social world. Unsettling such is multifaceted, ranging from redefining power to rethinking the very purposes of knowledge creation; turning the relationship inside out by promoting the approach of co-researchers in an effort to share or flatten power is at the heart of action research. Feminist scholars, at the same time, often disclose their biases, feelings, choices and multiple identities, clearly locating themselves within the research process. There we get glimpses of how we might each further transform ourselves as action researchers engaged in transforming the world, for example in the Afrocentric case:

- moving beyond traditional methods by
- creating knowledge for the sake of economic, political and social change in the Black community, and
- without forsaking rigorous social investigation.

PAR then, as we saw in Chapter 7, becomes a tool to dismantle the master's house, and to achieve social justice. It was also to be used as a building block to build "black" social institutions. Under these circumstances, the role of the "black" social scientist was to be both scholar and social activist. This stance of community members being responsible for building knowledge for the purposes of social equality and organizational change is one of the core values of action research. Co-inquiry emphasizes the research process as an elevating learning experience for all those involved in the research endeavor, stimulating dialogue between researcher and participant in the creation of new knowledge.

16.4.2. Promoting a Liberatory Transition: Towards Vivencia

The year 1970 was the first in a series of turning points for those (mostly in sociology, anthropology, education and theology) who were increasingly preoccupied with life conditions, which appeared unbearable in communities surrounding them. Fals Borda and Rahman (1991) then and their colleagues took for granted that these conditions were produced by the spread of capitalism and universalistic modernization. These were seen to be destroying the cultural and biophysical texture of rich and diverse social structures dear and well known to them.

They just could not be blind or silent when witnessing the collapse of positive values and attitudes towards humankind and nature. This seemed to require a radical critique and reorientation of social theory and practice. Conceptions of Cartesian rationality, dualism and "normal" science were challenged, as they could not find answers from the universities that had formed them professionally. Many therefore broke shackles and left the academies. During the course of 1970 some began to formalize *alternative institutions and processes for solving regional problems involving emancipatory educational, cultural and political processes.*

Soon after 1970 it became clear that the P(A)R crowd were looking for a new conceptual element to guide fieldwork. They wanted to go beyond social psychology (Lewin), Marxism (Lukacs), anarchism (Kropotkin), phenomenology (Husserl) and classical theories of participation (Owen, Rousseau, Mill). They also wanted to respect the critical methodology they had inherited from the hermeneutic philosopher Gadamer, and to remain disciplined researchers. At the same time they wanted to link such thoughts with their experiences in the field. Recognizing that knowledge was socially constructed, rather than objective truth, they postulated that the main criterion should be to obtain knowledge that would be useful for dealing with worthy causes. As such, the rebel, the heretic, the indigenous and common folk may prove to be more significant than themselves.

Discussing then the evasive problem of purpose in science and knowledge, they went back to Newton's operational rationality and Descartes' instrumental reason, oriented towards controlling nature, since labeled "scientism". On the other hand, Bacon and Galileo were more ready to acknowledge the role of practice and community to explain the functions of everyday life. Indeed popular knowledge has always been a source of formal learning. Overall though, *it was felt that science was in need of a moral conscience, and reason needed to be enriched with sentiment and feeling.*

Rejecting the academic tradition of doing research to promote academic advancement, they had to "de-colonise their minds". Their praxis-inspired commitment sought after role models such as Paulo Freire, Mahatma Ghandi and Julius Nyerere, seeking to theorize and obtain knowledge enriched through direct involvement and social action. Moreover, they followed Francis Bacon's original guidelines (1607): truth is revealed and established more through the testimony of actions than through logic or even observation'. They had to consider, then, researcher and researched both as real "thinking-feeling persons" whose diverse views on the shared life experience had to be taken into account. In fact, if applied in earnest, *such a participatory philosophy could produce social/collective transformations* between them. New "reference groups" were formed with grassroots leaders. Hard core data was combined with imaginative, literary and artistic interpretations.

In learning to develop an authentic attitude towards others, which was called *vivencia* (life wor)ld, now in Latin America rather then Husserl's Europe, meaning entering into the other's life experience (Husserl's life world), it became easy to listen to discourses coming from diverse origins. Participatory research, at an international conference in 1977, was defined as "vivencia" necessary for the achievement of progress and democracy, thereby becoming not only a research methodology but also a philosophy of life that would convert its practitioners into thinking-feeling-persons.

16.4.3. Liberationist Perspectives and the New Paradigm

The overall objective then was to use the knowledge gained to understand better, change and re-enchant our plural world. For Immanuel Wallerstein (1999) – founder of the World Systems group in America – the "two modernities" were those of technology and liberation, Fals Borda's orientation being towards the latter rather than the former. Thus to the Marxist orientation towards praxis is added the Aristotelean "phonesis", that is the pursuit of judgment and wisdom for the achievement of the good life. The two-pronged *commitment to liberation and service* then undergrids PAR lifestyle and practice. *It is not only a quest for knowledge, but also a transformation of individual and communal attitudes and values, personality and culture, an altruistic process:* the construction of a practical and morally satisfying paradigm for the social sciences to make them congruent with the ideal of service, especially in the south of the world, combining ethics and praxis, academic knowledge and popular wisdom, the rational and existential.

For Fals Borda this is the most overarching challenge we face. We have moved together from 18th to 19th century participatory and utopian theories to the threshold of another set of theories on chaos, complexity and postmodern liberation. This has been done with guidance from intellectual and political giants. Now alert philosophers of action, eloquent postmodernists and critical theorists have taken this story on, with a view to liberating peoples who are under the heel of oppressive power systems. *The need now is to construct an altruistic ethos for heterogeneous forms of cultures, times, spaces and peoples; that however implies a worldwide effort to combine political, economic and intellectual resources from north and south, east and west.* For a while, our concern for knowledge, power and justice and their relationships grew independently in our respective regions. In the final analysis, the effect of P(A)R work carries a liberating, political accent world-wide. The rising universal brotherhood of critical intellectuals tends to construct open pluralist societies in which oppressive central powers, the economy of exploitation, monopolies and the unjust distribution of wealth, the reign of terror, the dominance of militarism, and the abuse of the natural environment, as well as racism, is proscribed. As we arrive at a new millennium, it would be great to think, Fals Borda proclaims, that *P(A)R will be able to do its share to find better scientific, technical and social ways for improved living conditions, and for the enrichment of human cultures.* We now turn to power and knowledge.

16.4.4. Power as a Relation of Domination

The role of participatory action research is to empower people through the construction of their own knowledge, in a process of action and reflection, or "conscientization", to use Paulo Freire's (Freire 2017) terms from his *Pedagogy of the Oppressed*. Lack of empowerment occurs for several reasons. First there is the argument that the positivist methods distances those whose "stuffy reality" (expertise) *is* disconnected from those who experience knowledge through their own lived subjectivity. Second there is the argument that traditional methods of research – especially surveys and questionnaires – may reinforce the passivity of powerless groups, quantitative forms of knowing, moreover, reducing the complexity of human experience. Third, there is the critique that dominant knowledge marginalizes other forms of knowing. PAR on the other hand, recognizing that knowledge is socially constructed, allows for social, collective analysis of life experience. Participative research makes claims to challenge power relations in each of its dimensions through addressing the needs for knowledge, action and consciousness:

Table 16.4.4. *Participative Research: Challenging Power Relations in Three Dimensions*

Knowledge	⟹	as a Resource which affects Decisions
Action	⟹	which looks at who is involved in the Production of Knowledge
Consciousness	⟹	how the Production of Knowledge changes the Worldview of those involved

One of the most important contributions of PAR to empowerment and social change is in the knowledge dimension. Through a more open and democratic process, new categories of knowledge, based on local realities, are framed and given voice.

However, relatively powerless groups may merely speak in ways that echo the voices of the powerful. Treating situated representations as facts serves to characterize positivism. Actually, to fulfill its liberating potential, PAR must surface and reinforce alternative forms and categories of knowledge, which may not at first appear. Such knowledge must be embedded, moreover, in cycles of action and reflection. In other words, a process of critical consciousness needs to ensue. Ultimately, developing and using new forms of participatory knowledge on a large scale, as the World Bank has begun to do, thereby promoting and using new forms of participatory democracy, involves ordinary citizens in using their knowledge and experience to construct a more just and equitable society. At a time when inequality between rich and poor is greater then ever before, the challenges of going to broader scale with PAR are enormous, but so also are the risks of failing to do so.

16.4.5. Research of the People, by the People, for the People

PAR then is research of the people, by the people, for the people. The more obvious purpose of such is to bring about changes by improving the material circumstances of affected people. To this end, people engage in different kinds of activity: inquiring into the nature of a problem to solve it by understanding its causes and meanings; getting together by organizing themselves as community units; and mobilizing themselves for action by raising their awareness of what should be done on moral and political grounds. For the first of these objectives, the inquiry makes use of conventional methods, additionally facilitated by art and theatre, oral history, music and dance, to reveal the more submerged and difficult-to-articulate aspects of the issues involved. In all cases, however, group processes play an important role. Dialogue, in particular, looms large, whereby participants can share experiences and information, create common meanings, and forge concerted actions together.

Overall then, the kind of knowledge that the research generates needs to produce technically useful results while at the same time strengthening community ties and heightening transformational potential through critical consciousness. We now turn, thereby linking PAR in general, intuited locally-globally, and Afrocentricity felt locally, to Marunga Karenga's (1998) *Kwanzaa* and the practice of transformation, thought out newly globally, adding an explicitly cultural, *southwestern* overtone to our path of African realization. Indeed, such a philosophy and practice, for us at this duly culminating stage, draws on southern (Zulu), east (Swahili), north (ancient Egypt) and west (Yuruba) African traditions.

16.4. Newly Global Path of African Realization: Kwanzaa: W4t

16.4.1. Kwanzaa – Roots and Branches

For Maulana Karenga then, Chair of African Studies at the University of California, Long Beech, so called *Kawaida,* the philosophy out of which Kwanzaa is created, teaches that all we think and do should be based on tradition and reason which in turn are rooted in practice, or action. Tradition is our locally felt *grounding*, our cultural anchor and therefore our starting point. It is also the source of our cultural authenticity.

Reason is the critical, emancipatory thought about our tradition which enables us to select, preserve and build, newly globally, on the best of what we have achieved and produced, hence *navigating*, in the light of our knowledge and experience. Tradition, as such, is lived, living and constantly expanded and enriched, is or him thereby continually and locally-globally *emerging*. We now turn to Kwnazaa's Seven Principles.

16.4.2. Principles: Form, Force, Function, Foundation, Field, Flow, Freedom

First the Principle of Umoja – Unity: Form

Umoja – unity – is the first and foundational principle of the Nguzo Saba. In fact one of the ways to translate *Maat* is to define it as harmony – on the natural, cosmic and social levels. Likewise *Cieng* among the Dinka means both morality and harmonious living together. Relations, then, are the hinge on which morality turns, the ground on which it rises or falls. *In African complementarity, as such, three principles are key: equality, reciprocity and friendship.*

Unity begins in the family but extends to organizational affiliation, as we have seen in the PaxHerbals case, and then the unity of organizations. The ultimate level of unity for African people is that of the world African community.

Second the Principle of Kujichagulia – Self Determination: Force

The second principle is that of *Kujichagulia* or self determination. It is *a call to recover and speak our own special cultural truth to the world and make our own contribution to the flow of human history.* Kawaida then, building on the teachings of Franz Fanon (2021), states that each person must ask him or herself three basic questions: *who am I, am I really who I am, and am I all I ought to be?* In fact, for both of us this is what is driving us communiversity and communitalism-wise forward, the one (Adodo) inside out, the other (Lessem) outside in, altogether in relation to Africa.

The principle of self determination shelters the assumption that as fathers and mothers of humanity and human civilization in the Nile Valley, we have no business playing the cultural children of the world. Rather Africans seek freedom from want, toil and domination, and freedom to fully realize themselves in their human and African fullness. Afro-centricity, therefore, at its cultural best, is an ongoing quest for a cultural and spiritual anchor, a foundation on which we raise our cultural future, ground our cultural production and measure its authenticity and value. Moreover, it is and ongoing critical reconstruction directed toward restoring lost and missing parts of our historical self-formation as people.

Third the Principle of Ujima – Collective Work and Responsibility: Function

The third principle is that of "Ujima", that is collective work and responsibility. The principle supports the fundamental assumption that *African is not just an identity,* but also a destiny and a duty, that is a responsibility. It thus rejects the possibility or desirability of individual freedom in an unfree context. Instead it poses the need for struggle, in which all can be free. Indeed this resonated fully with out hitherto *Good African Coffee Story* (ICS2).

Moreover it rejects abstract humanism and favours that which starts with commitment to and concern for those humans amongst whom we live, and to whom we owe our existence, that is our own people. It also posits the liberation struggle to rescue and reconstruct African history and humanity, thereby contributing to the struggle for human liberation. Work, both personal and collective, is truly at the centre of history and culture. It is the fundamental activity by which we create ourselves, define and develop ourselves, and confirm ourselves as persons in the process.

Fourth The Principle of Ujaama – Cooperative Economics: Foundation

Ujaama stresses self reliance in the building, strengthening and controlling of the economics of our community, just as we have seen in the case of our Integral Kumusha in Zimbabwe. Closely related to the concept of self reliance is the respect for the dignity and obligation of work. *To respect work is to appreciate its value, and engage in its co-operatively for the good of the community.* This finds its modern philosophical expression in our social thought and struggles, as a people, around and for social justice, and ultimately to end poverty and vulnerability.

Fifth The Principle of Nia – Purpose: Field

The fifth principle is purpose (nia) which is a commitment to the collective vocation of *building and developing our community, its culture and history, in order to gain the historical initiative, and realize our legacy.* That legacy is one of having not only been the mothers and fathers of humanity, but also of human civilization. It is this identity which gives us an overriding cultural purpose and suggest a direction. This resonated clearly with Ibrahim Abouleish and the case of Sekem in Egypt, as an Egyptian, a Muslim, an anthroposophist, a world citizen.

Nia, moreover, suggests that personal and social purpose are not only nonantagonistic but complementary. In fact the highest form of individual purpose benefits the community. So our collective vocation of building and expanding our community honours the ancient teachings of our ancestors from the *Odu of Ifa* which says "surely humans were chosen to bring good to the world".

Sixth the Principle of Kumumba – Creativity: Flow

Creativity in the literature and culture of ancient Egypt involves an original act or imitation of the Creator, just as in the above Sekem case, as well as a restorative act, *constantly pushing back the currents of chaos and decay and revitalizing and restoring the natural, spiritual and cosmic energy of the world.* This concept of restoring *maat* includes the concept of *serudi ta* (restring the world) used in discussing the right relationships with the environment.

In fact the notions of *restoration* and *progressive perfection* are key concepts in the philosophy Kawaida. As reflected in "kumumba" is means "to do always as much as we can, in the way we can, in order to leave our community more beautiful and beneficial than we inherited it". Progressive perfection, specifically then, assumes an ability and obligation always to strive to leave what one inherits more beautiful and beneficial than it was before, thereby recovering and reconstructing "first fruits". In the Book of Kheti it is said "every day is a donation to eternity, and every hour a contribution to the future".

The Seventh Principle of Imami – Faith: Freedom

Faith is put forward as the last principle as unity is put forward as the first principle for a definite reason. It is to indicate that without unity we cannot begin our most important work, but without faith, as is the case for one of us (Adodo) as both an indigenous, nature empowered Yoruba and a Benedicitine monk, we cannot sustain it. Unity brings us together but faith in the Good, the Right and the Beautiful, sustains it, and commits is to working to the end.

In the context of African spirituality it begins with a faith in the Creator and in *the positiveness of the creation, leading to a belief in the essential goodness and possibility of the human personality, through self mastery and development* in the context of positive support. As a community-in-struggle there is no substitute for belief in our people, in their capacity to take control of their destiny and shape them in their own image and interests. Especially we must believe in the value and validity of our struggle for liberation and for a higher human life.

This must be tied to our belief in our capacity to assume and carry out with dignity and decisiveness the role of setting in motion a new history of humankind in alliance with other oppressed and progressive peoples to promote a new paradigm of human society and human relations. As Fanon says, *Africans should not try to imitate others but rather to invent, innovate, reach inside themselves and dare "set afoot a new man and woman"*, for us newly globally. We must dare to struggle, free ourselves culturally and politically and raise images above the earth that reflect our capacity for human progress and greatness. It is in that context that we can speak our own special cultural truth to the world and make our own contribution to the forward flow of history.

We now turn finally to the keynotes of such generic action research, albeit with an African orientation.

16.5. Action Research Keynotes: Appreciative Inquiry: W4a

16.5.1. You Start Out with appreciative Inquiry

The notable Peter Reason at the University of Bath in England and his colleague Hilary Bradbury have played a leading part in articulating (Cooperider 2004), as we saw in Chapters 7, 10, and 13, the wider reaches of action research. In so doing, they refer to David Cooperider's *Appreciative Inquiry* (Cooperider and Srivastva 1990), a noted communally based research method in its own right, as for them representative of a participative approach, for us firstly, to action research. For us then, the Kwanzaa approach to which we allude, newly globally on our African path of realisation, is a clearcut embodiment of such African "appreciative inquiry" into what is GENE-rically African, as illustrated here by our *Kumusha* in the south, *Good African Coffee Story* in the east, *Sekem* in the north, and *PaxHerbals* in the west of Africa.

In their original formulation of appreciative inquiry Cooperider and Srivastva (Greenwood and Morten 1998), twenty years ago, argued that action research had largely failed as instruments for advancing socio-organizational transformation, because of action research's preference for critique as opposed to appreciation. For if we devote our attention to what is wrong with organizations and communities, we lose the ability to sustain and enhance their life-giving potential. More than a method or technique, the appreciative mode of inquiry engenders a reverence for life that draws the researcher to inquire beyond superficial appearances to deeper levels of the life-generating essentials and potentials of social existence. That is, for Cooperider and Srivasta (Asante 2003):

> ... the action researcher is drawn to affirm, and thereby illuminate, the factors and forces that serve to illuminate the human spirit.

Table 16.5. *Afrocentric Action Research – Keynotes*

You start out with *appreciative Inquiry* as embodied Afrocentrically in Kwanzaa.
You undertake social Research for Afrocentric social Change.
Soulful knowing *how* is more important than mindful knowing *that*.
Action Research incorporates Action Learning from your own African shores.

16.5.2. You Undertake Social Research for Afrocentric Social Change

For Greenwood and Morten (Revans 2011), secondly for us, action research is *a set of self-consciously collaborative and democratic strategies for generating knowledge and designing action* in which trained experts – for us here Afrocentrically based – in social and other forms of research and local stakeholders work together.

Table 16.5.3. *Action, Research and Participation*

Action	⟹	AR is participatory because AR aims to alter the initial Situation of the Group, Organization or Community in the Direction of a more self-managing, liberated and sustainable State.
Research	⟹	They believe in Research, in the Power and Value of Knowledge, Theories, Models, Methods and Analysis.
Participation	⟹	AR involves trained social Researchers who serve as Facilitators and Teachers or Members of local Communities or Organizations. Because these People together establish the AR Agenda, generate the Knowledge necessary to transform the Situation, and put the Results to Work, AR is a participatory Process in which everyone involved takes some Responsibility.

The research focus is chosen collaboratively among the local stakeholders and the action researchers, and relationships amongst the participants are organized as joint learning processes. Action research centres on doing "with" rather than doing "for" stakeholders and credits these with the richness of experience and reflective possibilities that long experience living in complex situations brings with it.

Action research then is social research carried out by a team that encompasses a professional action researcher and the members of an organization, community or network, who are seeking to improve the participant's situation. AR promotes broad participation in the research process and supports action leading to a more just, sustainable, or satisfying situation for the stakeholders. The Table above shows how action, research and participation interconnect:

In fact, and as we have seen, in the Afrocentric version of such "social change", action reserch for Asante has much more overt cultural and political, it not also social and economic overtones, than in generic action research.

16.5.3. Soulful Knowing *How* Is More Important Than Mindful Knowing *That*

John Dewey, thirdly, believed that all humans are capable of scientific judgment and that society could be improved to the extent that these capacities are increased among all society's members. Consistent with this, he strongly opposed the division of public education into vocational and academic tracks, seeing this as the preservation of inequality and ultimately the weakening of democracy as a whole. Everyone could be a capable participant in experimental knowledge creation. He believed that limiting the learning of any individual ultimately limited society as a whole.

For Dewey, scientific research was not a process separate from democratic social action. Scientific knowing, like all other forms of knowledge, was a product of continuous cycles of action and reflection. The center of gravity was always the learner's active pursuit of understanding through puzzle-solving activity with the materials at hand. The solution achieved were only the best possible ones at that moment with the material at hand, hence the denomination of his philosophy as pragmatism.

For Asante (Lessem 1989) and Marenga, what ultimately counts, though, in an Afroecentric context, is a historical and cultural consciousness, of the African soul-force behind such action research, in fact for Karenga spread over seven-fold Form, Function, Force Field, Foundation, Flow and Freedom.

16.5.4. Action Research Incorporates Action Learning in Context

For Reg Revans, finally, one of Britain's most creative management thinkers, and originator of "action learning" (Revans, 2011) in the 1970s, with whom one of us (Ronnie Lessem) was closely associated, the salvation of individual countries and their enterprises is not to be found by observers scouring the world in the hope of turning up some miracle there. *Their salvation, their "Kingdom of God", is rather to be found within their own shores, their local source, and within the wills of their own people.* At the level of the individual enterprise, he further argues, it is not unreasonable to suggest that an essential part of any research and development policy is the study of the human effort, out of which the saleable products of the enterprise are largely created. Such a study involved "scientific method" (survey, hypothesis, test, audit and control = the core elements of the action learning cycle).

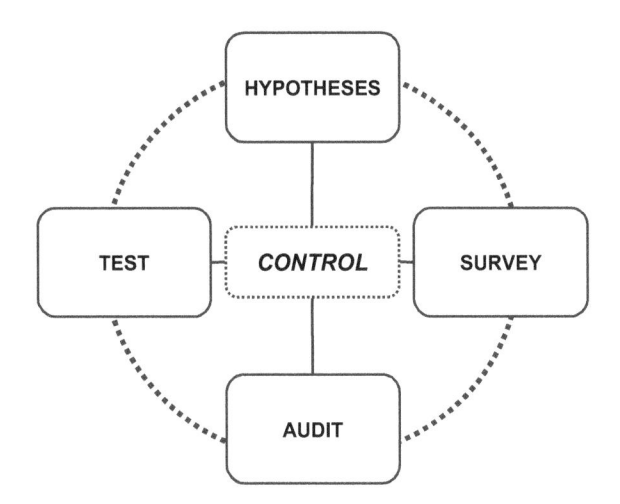

Figure 16.5.4: *Action Learning Cycle*

Learning moreover must demand not only research and analysis. It must demand power to get the knowledge needed to see one's part in what is going on. In particular, one needs to know the effect of one' behaviour upon those with whom one works. For Revans, this is best achieved within small "action learning" groups. In the Japanese context, he referred particularly to the establishment of small work groups, not only with a high degree of autonomy, but organized in a way that it gave people a continuing opportunity to develop. You learn with and from each other, in small groups or "learning sets", by supportive attacks upon real problems, through:

- an exchange of information – ideas, advice, contacts, hunches, concepts
- interaction between set members, offering each other support/challenge
- behavioural change resulting more often from the re-interpretation of past experience than the acquisition of fresh knowledge

In fact, for one of us (Ronnie Lessem) it was under Revans mentorship (Ronnie's PhD was on *Action Learning for Enterprise Development*), set in the context of community economic development in the the then impoverished East End of London, that he sought to uncover knowledge from his own inner city, English "shores" and facilitate its release through "intrapreneurship" (28), as a further evolution of his PhD studies.

16.6. Conclusion

16.6.1. Overlapping Approaches to Action Research

We find it remarkable that action research, as a whole, while a strong research movement in its own right, is so often cut off from the mainstream of research method and methodology. Its limiting factor, perhaps, is that this "western" approach to action research retains a somewhat analytic – albeit combined with action – orientation. In other words, it lacks some of the dynamic and transformative elements associated with social innovation, in our case here, for example, disconnected economy and enterprise wise from Nhakanomics, Yurugu-nomics, the Economics of Love and Communitalism. Actually, all too often, action research is considered in isolation of these. Moreover, notwithstanding what Revans maintained above, and as we have sought to remedy here, action research, overall, is devoid of any particular cultural and spiritual context, in our case Afrocentrically so. Finally, the conventional university setting – Revans himself was an academic renegade as such – is not conducive to suc communally based action research.

Table 16.6.1. *Action Research Social Innovation Laden Territory*

Forms of Action Research	Core Exponents	Dimension	Type of Transformation	Contribution to Integral Social Innovation	
Participatory Action Research / Appreciative Inquiry	Fals Borda (Columbia) / Cooperider (USA)	Communal	Social Transformation	Provides Underlying Grounds	SOUTH
Co-operative Inquiry / Participative Spirituality	Heron (UK)	Trans-personal	Spiritual Growth	Source of Emergence	EAST
Knowledge Creation / Socio-Technical Design	Morten Levin (Norway)	Organi-zational	Industrial Democracy	Provides Navigation	NORTH
Action Science	Revans / Schon (USA)	Individual	Action Learning	Ultimate Transformative Effect	WEST

Each of our four research paths, as distilled above, has ended with its own particular variation of action research, illustrating a particular southern (PAR), eastern (CI), northern (STD) or western (generic action research) flavour. Invariably though, the four approaches to action research overlap. In some respects, they are not easy to distinguish. Their closeness to each other underlines the integrated nature of generic action research. Not only then does it serve to integrate, transformatively, the three levels that came before (origination, foundation and emancipation), vertically as it were, it is also horizontally integrative. That is also the reason, why we re-introduced southern PAR as a global variation in this western chapter on action research. The above Table 16.6.1. gives a concluding overview on the action research territory.

As we have seen and in very simplistic terms, action research is a very "broad church". In fact, it may even be considered too broad, as it incorporates:

- Participative Action Research: our southern *grounding*
- Co-operative Inquiry: our eastern *emergence*
- Socio-Technical Design: our northern *navigation*
- Action Learning: our western *effect*

all under one "action research" roof. To the extent that it serves to integrate the research levels that come vertically before and is open to the full span of action research, horizontally, it serves to release the full GENE-ius of social innovation. Such is demonstrated by Figure 4.

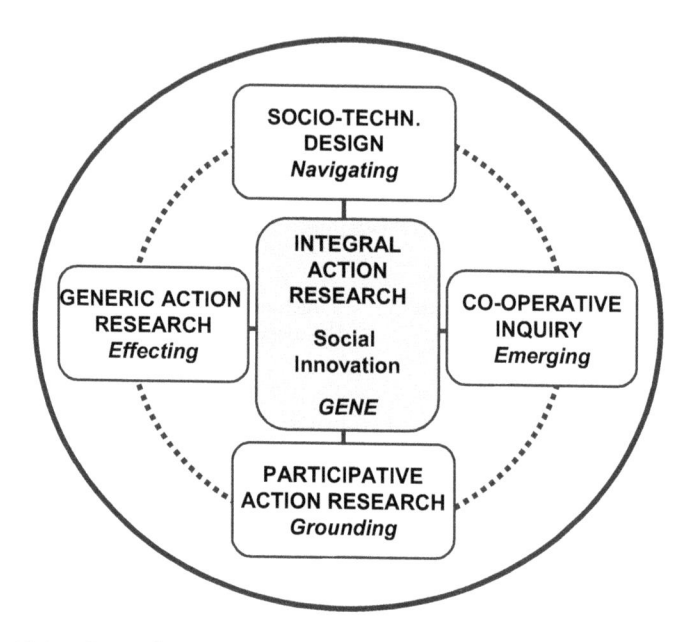

Figure 16.6.1: *Integral Action Research leading to Social Innovation*

However, as we have continually intimated, for social innovation, and ultimately societal re-GENE-ration, to acquire its full reach, the research process needs to be aligned with relevant substance and form, for us in African context.

16.6.2. Original Grounding on the African Path of Realisation

Altogether then, for our original grounding we revisit Chapter 4, where we outlined not only survey and experimental method, as "western", our *south*-western grounds, but also case study method, or what we term in "southern" guise, a case *story,* such as the one illustrated by Cashbuild above, whereby, in devising such:

- You are able to ask good Questions – and to interpret the Answers.
- You are a good Listener – not trapped by your own Ideologies and Preconceptions.
- You are adaptable so that new Situations can be seen as Opportunities.
- You are unbiased by preconceived Notions, responsive to contradictory Evidence

15.6.3. Emergent Foundation on the African Path of Realisation

More specifically then, as far as the subsequent empirical foundation is concerned:

- You search for the African truth
- You seek after *really* positive facts
- You collect observational data and build African theories
- You exercize control through place based closed systems

15.6.4. Emancipatory Navigation on the African Path of Realisation

Herein then, and by way of emancipatory navigation:

- Critical Realism is critical of the westernised scientific status quo in Africa
- You become involved with a stratified or layered African Reality
- You conceive Reality as both transitive (subjective) and intransitive (objective)
- A cultural hermeneutic as well as an material empirical side to Critical Realism.

15.6.5. Transformative Effect on the African Path of Realisation

Finally then, and now by way of ultimate transformative effect:

- You start out with appreciative Inquiry as embodied Afrocentrically in Kwanzaa.
- You undertake social Research for Afrocentric social Change.
- Soulful African knowing *how* is more important than mindful knowing *that*.
- Action Research incorporates Action Learning.

16.6.6. Pax Herbals Search for the Real Truth

In tracing a path finally from local Afrocentricity and local-global Vivencia onto newly global African Kanzaa, duly and ultimately supported by Appreciative Inquiry, we complete our path of African realisation, research and innovation-wise.

Table 16.6.6. *Pax Herbals' Search for the Real Truth: W2fita Via Nature Power, Healing Radiance and Communitalism*

Feeling Local	Intuiting Local-Global	Thinking Newly Global	Acting Global-Local
Afrocentricity	*Vivencia*	*Kwanzaa*	*Appreciative Inquiry*

*University to Communiversity/Capitalism
and Socialism to Communitalism*

All of such, moreover, establishes both the original case for, and the empirical foundations for a communiversity, and communitalism of one societal kind or another, to follow, ultimately centred, cosmologically, in the healing wisdom of Africa. In the process, we have not only encompassed all research paths and trajectories in Africa, alongside the social and economic innovation that each brings – when accompanied by Nhakanomics, Yurugu-nomics, Economics and Love or ultimately Communitalism, generically, but also established the Communiversity structure and process required to bring such about. In our final chapter we shall now reveal the Innovation Ecosystem required for such.

16.7. References

Adodo A (2012) *Nature Power: A Christian Approach to Herbal Medicine.* Ewu-Esan. Benedictine Publications.

Adodo A and **Lessem** R (2021) *Africology: Deconstructing and Reconstructing Knowledge and Value in Africa.* Manchester. Beacon Academic

Asante M (2003) *Afrocentricity: The Theory of Social Change.* New York. African Images

Asante M (2015) *African Pyramids of Knowledge: Kemet, Afrocentricity and Africology.* New York. Universal Write Publications

Cooperider D (2004) *Appreciative Inquiry Handbook.* New York. McGraw Hill

Cooperider D and **Srivastva** S (1990) *Appreciative Management and Leadership.* San Francisco. Jossey-Bass

Dewey J (2008) *Experience and Education.* New York. Free Press

Fals Borda O and **Rahman** MD (1991) *Action and Knowledge: Breaking the Monopoly with Participatory Action Research.* New York. Rowman and Littlefield

Fanon F (2021) *Black Skin White Masks.* London. Penguin Modern Classics

Freire P (2017) *Pedagogy of the Oppressed.* London. Penguin Modern Classics

Greenwood D and **Morten** M (1998) *Introduction to Action Research: Social Research for Social Change.* New York. Sage

Karenga M (1998) *Kwanzaa: A Celebration If Family, Community and Culture.* Timbuktoo, Mali. University of Sankore

Lessem R (1989) *Intrapreneurship.* Aldershot. Wildwood House

Lessem R and **Schieffer** A (2010) *Integral Research and Innovaiton: Transforming. Enterprise and Society.* Abingdon. Routledge

Lewin K (2008) *A Dynamic Theory of Personality.* Lewin Press

Nabudere D (2011) *Afrikology: Philosophy and Wholeness: An Epistemology.* Pretoria. Africa Institute

Reason P and **Bradbury** H (2005) *Handbook of Action Research.* New York. Sage. P 123

Revans R (2011) *The ABC of Action Learning.* Abingdon. Routledge

Tsehloane **Keto** C (1995) *Vision, Identity and Time: The Afrocentric Paradigm and the Study of the Past.* Dubuque, Iowa. Kendall Hunt Publishers

Wallerstein I (1999) *Social Science for the 21st Century: The End of the World as We Know It.* Minneapolis. University of Minneapolis Press

ICS4: Case Story 4: Africa South-West: Nigeria
Paxherbals to Pax Africana: Cultivating Health, Community and Identity in Nigeria
The Healing Wisdom of Africa: Natural Grounding to Economic Effect

C4.1 Introduction: A Natural Vision to Take Communal Root

C4.1.1. The Stories We Are Becoming

Anselm Adodo, at the outset of 2024, in association with the close-knit individual and institutional others, was about to enter the next, indeed fourth stage of his now explicitly societal, pan-African orientation, that of societal regeneration. Having pioneered the development of a community-based enterprise in Nigeria, now scientifically and technologically evolved as PaxHerbal over almost three decades, and furthered such of late through a communiversity, Pax Africana, he was now poised to develop a new association of individuals and communities, organisations and societies, through Re-GENE-Africa.

Indeed, he has developed Pax Africana as a communiversity during the course of his transformative PhD studies via Da Vinci Institute in South Africa and Trans4m worlds-wide; in the second decade of the new millennium, he was now poised, in the third decade, to co-evolve with such others a newly societal PhD, based on his own individual and organisational experience, oriented towards communitalism in Pan-African guise, now drawing explicitly on the healing wisdom of Africa on which PaxHerbal had centred itself. How, then, might he and his individual and institutional associates purposefully go about such? What communal, corporate, communiversity and communitalist heritage, in each associated case, would they be drawing upon? How then might they co-evolve?

C4.1.2. PaxHerbal: Setting the Nigerian Natural and Communal Context

Esanland's Rich Cultural Heritage: A Form of Education and Entertainment

The Esan people, a minority ethnic group among Nigeria's 200-plus ethnicities, encompass a populace of approximately half a million. Situated in the heart of Edo State within southern Nigeria, Esanland is marked by its rural and semi-urban character, comprised of small towns and villages encircling Benin City, the state capital, which lies about 200 kilometres away.

Comprising 35 clans, each headed by an Onojie, Esanland is divided into five Local Government Areas (L.G.A.): Esan West, Esan Central, Esan North East, Esan South East, and Igueben. The landscape of Esanland, with its flat terrain, is fertile ground for agriculture, boasting an array of fruit trees, cassava, yam, and diverse farm produce. Despite its agricultural potential, economic development in Esanland has been relatively limited compared to other regions of Nigeria.

Esanland's rich cultural heritage is deeply rooted in water rituals, farm festivals, and oral traditions, serving as a form of education and entertainment while preserving established customs. However, the advent of Christianity has significantly impacted traditional practices, leading to a decline in their prominence.

Ewu, a distinct village within Esanland, stands out for its unique religious diversity – comprising Christians, adherents of traditional beliefs, and Muslims in equal proportions, a rarity among Esan clans. Despite its agricultural potential, the village faces a significant challenge: a mass exodus of its youth seeking better prospects in urban areas. The allure of city life, with its modern amenities and opportunities, often draws the younger population away from their agrarian roots, leaving behind an ageing demographic.

Traditional Knowledge/Local Resources Underutilised; Young Generations Disconnected

The trend is reflective of a larger issue in rural Nigeria, where traditional knowledge and local resources remain underutilised while younger generations become disconnected from their land, culture, and environment. The education system's focus on imported knowledge neglects the wealth of local wisdom, hindering genuine and sustainable development.

The pervasive influence of religious fervour, particularly in the proliferation of churches, stands as a prominent symbol in Esanland. This rapid expansion of religious institutions contrasts sharply with the limited growth in education and industrial infrastructure.

C4.1.3. Moving Beyond Mono-Cultural Healing Traditions

Village of Ogwa Well-Known for Its Distinctive Healing Legacy

The village of Ogwa, located in the centre of Esanland, is well-known for its distinctive healing legacy, a history of bone setting handed down from generation to generation within a particular family. The ancestral gift of this family has become synonymous with the health and prosperity of the town. Its origins lie in the enthralling tale of Enahoro, a man who possessed a divine skill for bone healing.

According to Adodo, during his interaction with these traditional healers, it became abundantly clear that they did not waver in their commitment to preserving this precious knowledge. It is believed that the healing technique is an innate gift that is passed down from birth, a heritage that continues to be a family matter. This is why it is kept under strict confidentiality within the family.

The reason for this secrecy, in fact, is not just associated with protecting valued information; rather, it originates from a profound mistrust of external agencies, particularly the government. There is a reluctance, as such, to embrace change or modernise their therapeutic procedures without the consent of the elders, despite the fact that there are documented success stories that demonstrate the efficacy of their treatment.

Traditional Healers Consider Knowledge to Be the Basis of Their Livelihood and Status

The difficulty of combining indigenous and exogenous knowledge in local communities across Africa is brought into focus by this predicament. Government involvement becomes absolutely necessary in this situation; establishing rules that safeguard and compensate traditional healers for disseminating their knowledge could pave the way for a more open approach. In the same way that Coca-Cola or McDonald's protect their recipes, traditional healers consider their knowledge to be the basis of their livelihood and status.

That said, for Adodo (2017), and as an original backdrop to the formation of Paxherbals, he believes opportunities for education, creativity, and community development may be unlocked if traditional healers were encouraged to be more open with their patients. When cultures continue to be receptive to novel concepts, transformational knowledge, which is the core of the evolution of societies, flourishes. Having information is not enough; one must also be able to utilise that knowledge to advance economic and social conditions effectively. This is a lesson that is frequently overlooked in Africa. For him then:

> In order to move forward, it is necessary to have a dynamic combination of indigenous and external knowledge in a variety of fields, such as agriculture, medicine, and economics. To achieve sustainable development and reduce conflicts between cultures, it is essential to encourage a two-way flow of information rather than a one-way flow from the West to Africa. Regenerative education, which revolves around the development of theories and a passion for acquiring knowledge, has the potential to bridge this divide. The establishment of a research centre that is committed to the development of indigenous practices and the formulation of new theories of community-enterprise development that are anchored in local identity and culture has the potential to be immensely transformative.
>
> In addition, the acknowledgement and participation of the Nigerian government with institutes that conduct research on alternative medicine are essential components in the process of enhancing healthcare. Considering the nation's healthcare requirements comprehensively could be accomplished by incorporating traditional therapeutic traditions alongside the imported biomedical system. In the end, a harmonic combination of traditional knowledge and contemporary expertise offers a promising road towards holistic development. When it comes to developing a

convergence that holds the key to Africa's sustainable future, it is about cultivating an environment in which multiple knowledge systems coexist, supporting growth while preserving cultural variety.

C4.1.4. The Monastery as Healer

A Vision Took Root: The Earth, Our Primal Home, Held the Essence of Our Well-being

Almost three decades ago, amid seemingly inconspicuous weeds, a transformation brewed in the heart of the monastery garden. Life-giving herbs sprouted, weaving a narrative of hope and vitality. Here, in the African bush of Ewu village, a vision took root – a belief that the earth, our primal home, held the essence of our well-being. Paxherbal emerged from this sacred soil, a testament to the profound connection between humanity and nature.

Paxherbal's journey began with a mission to redefine health within the fabric of local communities. In a time when herbal medicine was unjustly linked to superstition and ritualism, Paxherbal stood as a lone beacon, dispelling the misconception that indigenous remedies equated to arcane practices. It reshaped perceptions, not merely about medicine but the essence of well-being – a harmony between mind, body, and soul.

Nurturing a Profound Understanding of the Language Spoken by the Earth

The Paxherbal tree, rooted in the Monastery of St. Benedict, has burgeoned into a towering presence in Ewu village. Its influence extends beyond Esanland, reaching across Nigeria. The concept transcends mere healing; it encompasses education, nurturing a profound understanding of the language spoken by the earth – its trees, soils, and streams.

Within the community today, an association of medicinal plant suppliers, our so-called EDEMCS, thrives. More than a hundred accredited cultivators partake in seminars, mastering the art of cultivation and harvesting. They've become catalysts for employment, cultivating not just medicinal plants but also economic growth in the local sphere. Under the watchful eye of the King of Ewu village, these suppliers adhere to ethical standards, ensuring sustainable practices that benefit both land and livelihood.

Union of Suppliers Becoming Pivotal Figures in Nigeria's Agricultural Landscape

This *union of suppliers* has evolved into more than cultivators; they've become enterprising, expanding their endeavours beyond medicinal plants and *becoming pivotal figures in Nigeria's agricultural landscape*. They have advanced their businesses through collaborations with local banks and micro-finance schemes, enriching their communities.

A Network of a Thousand Independent Distributors Spans the Nation

In parallel, a network of over a thousand independent distributors of Paxherbal products spans the nation. These individuals, equipped with a guidebook outlining the ethos of Paxherbal, embody the spirit of care and sincerity. They champion the cause, promoting health while respecting the boundaries of herbal medicine and knowing when to seek conventional medical aid in emergencies. Membership in this association demands dedication – rigorous training, attendance at conventions, adherence to fair pricing, and a commitment to uphold Paxherbal's values. The essence lies not just in distributing products but in fostering a culture of wellness and ethical practice.

Paxherbal's commitment to education extends further through involvement in a federal government student industrial training scheme. University students gain practical experience at the Paxherbal Clinic and Research Laboratories, forging a bridge between academia and real-world application.

A Testament to the Harmony Between Humanity and the Earth

Beyond the clinical and commercial facets lies a deeper ethos – a belief that society's roots intertwine with its natural surroundings. Paxherbal's approach transcends conventional research – it delves into the very essence of societal identity. It embraces indigenous and exogenous perspectives, weaving a narrative that amalgamates tradition and innovation, health and community.

In times of existential quandary, Paxherbal beckons societies to rediscover their identity, rooted in nature and community. The soil, trees, and rivers are not just elements but threads in the tapestry of human existence. In this holistic vision, Paxherbal redefines not just medicine but the very fabric of our being – a testament to the harmony between humanity and the earth. Amidst this contextual topography, Paxherbal's narrative extends beyond medicine; it is a narrative of unity, a reminder that the essence of a community isn't solely in its human inhabitants but also in the flora, fauna, ancestors, and spirits that coexist within it.

Southern Traditional Yoruba and Northern Christian Perspectives Converge

The Southern Traditional Yoruba and Northern Christian perspectives converge within Paxherbal, each contributing, altogether, to unique societal views. This convergence isn't just about healing but about communal enterprise, nurturing health within a community while fostering economic growth.

The association of suppliers has become a microcosm of this unity, where ancient healing practices blend seamlessly with modern enterprise. It is not merely about cultivating herbs but about sowing the seeds of progress within the fabric of tradition. Through meticulous training and ethical guidelines, these suppliers have revived ancient practices and woven them into the contemporary economic landscape.

Simultaneously, the network of distributors stands as a testament to the harmonious coexistence of divergent perspectives. Their commitment to the Paxherbal ethos is not just a business endeavour but a cultural synergy – an amalgamation of traditional healing practices and contemporary professionalism.

Seeds of Transformation: An Intricate Dance Between Humanity/ Environment

The commitment to education is not merely about training individuals; it is about fostering a deep-rooted understanding that health is not confined to hospitals and medications but is an intricate dance between humanity and its environment. The student industrial training scheme is not just an opportunity for practical experience; it is an invitation for young minds to immerse themselves in the symbiotic relationship between nature and health.

Paxherbal does not just provide solutions; it tells a story of a community reclaiming its identity, rooted in its environment, traditions, and holistic well-being. The herbs that sprouted in the monastery garden were not just plants; they were seeds of transformation, embodying the unity between humanity and the earth.

Community, Communiversity, Communiatlism: Communities, Nature, Well-Being

As Paxherbal continues to evolve, its narrative is not confined to the boundaries of Nigeria; it resonates globally – a testament to the enduring connection between communities, nature, and well-being. It stands not just as a clinic or a laboratory but as a beacon, illuminating the path towards a harmonious existence where health is not just the absence of disease but a symphony of mind, body, soul, and environment.

We now retrace steps, revisiting *Paxherbals*, historically, as firstly a technologically based and innovative operational **community;** before secondly moving onto its emerging role, as *Pax Africana*, as health beacon, a **communiversity** laden symphony of mind, body, soul and environment, which will take us onto *Re-GENE-Africa* as a focal point for societal regeneration, from capitalism and socialism to **communitalism**. We start then, historically, with the Paxherbals as an operational community, explicitly accompanied by technological innovation, beginning with its community interface.

C4.2. PaxHerbals: Clinical Operation/Technological Innovation

C4.2.1. Community Interface: Efficiency and Education

Community Interface to Governmental Relations

We start then with community interface. The operation of the PaxHerbal, as a clinic and laboratory as such, in Edo State Nigeria illustrates as we shall see, the principles of an integrated operation, inclusive of community interface, research and development, good manufacturing practices, quality control and governmental relations, altogether serving to fuse together communal (indigenous) and clinical (exogenous) medicine, ultimately centred in the overall healing wisdom of Africa, is not also the world at large. We start then with community and patient interface.

Optimized for Efficient Patient Flow Management and Time Efficiency

At the PaxHerbals clinic, to begin with, the waiting hall is meticulously designed to prioritise patient comfort and experience. Beyond its aesthetic appeal with soothing colours and comfortable seating, the space is optimized for efficient patient flow management and time efficiency. The Waiting Hall operates with a carefully structured scheduling system that minimises patient waiting times. This system ensures appointments run punctually, enhancing the overall patient experience.

Providing Patients with Opportunities to Engage with Educational Content

Moreover, patient education is an integral part of this area. The waiting hall features informative displays and materials related to various health topics, providing patients with opportunities to engage with educational content while they wait. The ambiance is carefully curated to create a tranquil environment, often incorporating soft music or calming visuals to promote relaxation and alleviate any potential anxiety or discomfort. Dedicated staff members are available in the waiting hall to assist patients, address queries, and guide them through their appointments. The staff's presence contributes significantly to patients' overall comfort and confidence in the clinic's services.

Seamless Communication Between Patients and Diagnostic Laboratory

Within PaxHerbal's diagnostic framework, the specimen room stands as a crucial link in the diagnostic chain. This specialized area is meticulously organized and adheres to strict protocols for the collection, handling, and preliminary processing of patient samples. Trained laboratory technicians in this area follow rigorous hygiene and safety standards to ensure the safe and sterile collection of various specimens, including blood, urine, and other bodily fluids. To maintain the integrity of these samples, meticulous procedures for collection, labelling, and preparation are followed.

The specimen room acts as the initial checkpoint for samples before they undergo diagnostic testing. Proper cataloguing and documentation ensure accurate tracking and prevent any compromise in sample quality during transfer to the diagnostic laboratory. Moreover, the specimen room facilitates seamless communication between patients and the diagnostic *laboratory*. Samples collected here are catalogued and swiftly sent to the laboratory for analysis, ensuring prompt delivery and accurate diagnostic testing.

Dispensing Medication and Providing Patient Education and Counselling

The dispensary at PaxHerbal serves as a pivotal point for the provision of prescribed medications to patients following their consultation. It operates as a meticulously organised space housing an extensive inventory of pharmaceuticals, both modern and traditional, catering to various health conditions. Highly trained pharmacists and staff manage the dispensing process with the utmost care and precision. They follow stringent protocols to ensure patient safety, meticulously verifying prescribed dosages and types of medications before dispensing them.

The dispensary is not merely a point for medication provision; it also serves as a crucial space for patient education and counselling. Patients receive guidance on medication usage, potential side effects, and general health advice within the dispensary. Pharmacists or qualified staff play a vital role in ensuring patient comprehension and adherence to prescribed regimens. Furthermore, the dispensary maintains comprehensive records of dispensed medications and patient details for both treatment and administrative purposes, contributing to PaxHerbal's comprehensive patient care approach.

C4.2.2. Technological Innovation at PaxHerbals

Diagnostic Laboratory: Routine Blood Chemistry Analysis to Sophisticated Screenings

We now turn to technological innovation at PaxHerbals in general, and, to begin with, to its diagnostic laboratory in particular. The Diagnostic Laboratory at PaxHerbal stands as the epicentre of comprehensive and precise medical testing and analysis. This specialized facility boasts cutting-edge technology and is staffed with highly skilled laboratory scientists dedicated to conducting an extensive array of diagnostic tests on patient samples. The laboratory is equipped to perform an extensive range of tests, spanning routine blood chemistry analysis to sophisticated screenings for infectious diseases, hormone levels, genetic markers, and more. It operates under stringent quality control measures to ensure the accuracy and reliability of test results.

Every step of the testing process, from sample processing to analysis and result interpretation, is meticulously carried out following established protocols. With its pivotal role in the diagnostic process, the laboratory handles the patient samples with the utmost precision. Upon receiving specimens from the specimen room, laboratory technicians conduct a variety of tests as specified by healthcare providers. These tests are executed with precision, and the results are meticulously documented. Once the analysis is completed, the results are relayed to consulting physicians for further clinical interpretation and decision-making.

Clinic Consultants' Offices as the Cornerstone of PaxHerbal's Patient-Centred Approach

The Clinic Consultants' Offices serve as the core space for direct patient-doctor interaction and assessment at PaxHerbal. These offices are meticulously designed to provide a comfortable and confidential environment where patients can discuss their health concerns and receive personalized medical attention from experienced consultants. Each office is equipped with essential medical tools and resources to support consultations and examinations. During patient visits, doctors or consultants conduct thorough examinations, attentively listen to patients' complaints, and discuss potential treatment options or further diagnostic steps based on the presented symptoms or medical history.

These offices go beyond being mere consultation spaces; they are designed to foster patient-doctor trust and collaboration. Patients can openly discuss their health conditions, receive guidance on lifestyle modifications, and discuss preventive measures to enhance their overall well-being. The Clinic Consultants' Offices represent the cornerstone of PaxHerbal's patient-centred approach, emphasising compassionate care and nurturing a strong doctor-patient relationship essential for comprehensive and effective healthcare delivery. We now turn to the herbarium, one of PaxHerbal's most unique features.

The Herbarium Dedicated to Harnessing African Ethnomedicinal Knowledge

The herbarium stands as *the nucleus* of PaxHerbals' plant science and biotechnology, dedicated to preserving and harnessing the wealth of African ethnomedicinal knowledge. This herbarium then is a repository of botanical specimens, serving as an invaluable resource for documenting, studying, and conserving medicinal plants integral to African traditional medicine. What is involved explicitly as such is:

- **Plant Collection and Documentation:**

    Each specimen is carefully identified, authenticated, and preserved using scientific methods. This systematic approach includes *recording plant* descriptions, geographic origins, traditional uses, and indigenous knowledge associated with each species. Detailed records are maintained, comprising botanical data, photographs, and information shared by local communities, ensuring the preservation of indigenous wisdom.

- **Botanical Research and Exploration:**
  This section serves as a hub for botanical research, enabling scientists to explore the vast diversity of African flora. Botanists and researchers delve into uncharted territories, discovering new plant species or identifying existing ones with potential medicinal properties. Advanced techniques like DNA barcoding and molecular studies aid in taxonomy, understanding plant relationships, and validating traditional uses.
- **Ethnobotanical Studies and Cultural Preservation:**
  PaxHerbal's herbarium contributes significantly to ethnobotanical studies. By collaborating with local communities, traditional healers, and indigenous knowledge custodians, it captures and documents the traditional uses of medicinal plants. This collaborative approach ensures the preservation of cultural heritage, fosters respect for indigenous practices, and facilitates knowledge transfer across generations.
- **Conservation and Sustainable Practices:**
  Recognising the importance of biodiversity conservation, PaxHerbal's Herbarium actively engages in conservation efforts. It advocates for sustainable harvesting practices, promotes the cultivation of endangered species, and safeguards rare medicinal plants. Additionally, it educates local communities on the significance of conservation, ensuring the sustainable utilisation of plant resources.
- **Contribution to Medicinal Discoveries:**
  The Herbarium's extensive collection serves as a goldmine for pharmacological and phytochemical research. Scientists leverage these documented specimens to isolate and study bioactive compounds with therapeutic potential. This invaluable resource accelerates the discovery and development of novel drugs or formulations based on traditional plant knowledge.
- **Education and Knowledge Sharing:**
  PaxHerbal's Herbarium acts as an educational platform, offering resources for botanical studies and ethnomedicinal research. It provides opportunities for students, researchers, and scientists to delve into the intricate world of African medicinal flora. Workshops, seminars, and publications foster knowledge dissemination, promoting a deeper understanding of indigenous healing practices.
- **Global Significance and Collaboration:**
  Beyond its local impact, PaxHerbal's herbium contributes to global botanical knowledge. It collaborates with international institutions, sharing data and participating in collaborative research projects. This collaboration ensures a broader understanding of medicinal plants, facilitates cross-cultural exchanges, and enriches global pharmacological knowledge.

In essence, the Herbarium Section at PaxHerbals stands as a cornerstone in preserving African ethnomedicinal knowledge. Its dedication to plant documentation, research, and conservation not only preserves cultural heritage but also fuels scientific discoveries.

Drug Formulation Serving to Combine Traditional and Modern Methods of Healing

PaxHerbal's Drug Formulation Laboratory operates at the intersection of traditional herbal medicine and cutting-edge scientific advancements. The laboratory follows a systematic and rigorous approach that integrates traditional knowledge with modern pharmaceutical techniques to develop effective herbal formulations. Here are the key technical aspects:

- **Pharmacognosy and Plant Identification:** Highly skilled botanists and pharmacognosists are engaged in the meticulous identification and authentication of medicinal plants. They employ various methods, including macroscopic and microscopic analysis, chromatographic fingerprinting, and DNA barcoding, to ensure the botanical integrity and quality of the raw materials.
- **Phytochemical Extraction Techniques:** Advanced extraction methodologies such as Soxhlet extraction, ultrasound-assisted extraction, and chromatographic separation are employed to isolate bioactive compounds from medicinal plants. These techniques ensure optimal extraction efficiency, maximising the yield of potent phytochemicals while maintaining their structural integrity and bioactivity.
- **Formulation Development:** Formulation scientists and pharmacists meticulously design herbal formulations using a range of excipients and delivery systems to optimise bioavailability, stability, and therapeutic efficacy. Techniques such as nanoparticle encapsulation or solid lipid nanoparticles might be employed to enhance the solubility and targeted delivery of active compounds.
- **Analytical Validation:** State-of-the-art analytical instrumentation, including nuclear magnetic resonance (NMR), mass spectrometry (MS), and liquid chromatography-tandem mass spectrometry (LC-MS/MS), is utilised for the in-depth characterization and quantification of bioactive compounds. This ensures consistency in product composition and potency across different batches.
- **Preclinical and Clinical Testing:** Before the formulations are released for production, extensive preclinical studies involving in vitro and in vivo experiments are conducted to assess their safety, efficacy, and mechanism of action. Clinical trials involving human subjects may follow, validating the therapeutic benefits and ensuring compliance with regulatory standards.
- **Standardization and Quality Assurance:** Strict adherence to standardized protocols and quality control measures is maintained throughout the formulation process. This includes establishing monographs for each product, setting

specifications for active ingredients, and implementing rigorous quality assurance practices to ensure the consistency and reproducibility of herbal formulations.

PaxHerbal's Drug Formulation Laboratory stands as a beacon of innovation, seamlessly blending traditional wisdom with scientific rigour to produce high-quality, evidence-based herbal formulations that meet global standards of safety, efficacy, and reliability.

Drug Innovation Research at PaxHerbal

PaxHerbal's commitment to innovation in herbal medicine involves a multifaceted approach encompassing rigorous research and development. The Drug Innovation Research Division employs a range of technical methodologies and scientific strategies to push the boundaries of herbal medicine. Here are the technical aspects:

- **Ethnobotanical Surveys and Traditional Knowledge:** PaxHerbal conducts comprehensive ethnobotanical surveys, collaborating with traditional healers and local communities to gather indigenous knowledge about medicinal plants. This ethnopharmacological approach helps identify potential candidate plants for further investigation.
- **Phytochemical Profiling and Bioactivity Screening:** Advanced analytical techniques like high-performance thin-layer chromatography (HPTLC), gas chromatography-mass spectrometry (GC-MS), and spectrophotometry are utilized for comprehensive phytochemical profiling. Concurrently, bioactivity screening using assays specific to various therapeutic targets is conducted to identify and validate the pharmacological properties of plant extracts and isolated compounds.
- **Extraction Optimisation and Process Development:** Research scientists optimise extraction techniques to enhance the yield and purity of bioactive compounds. They explore innovative extraction methodologies, including microwave-assisted extraction, subcritical water extraction, or enzyme-assisted extraction, to improve the efficiency of extracting therapeutic phytochemicals from medicinal plants.
- **Synergistic Formulation Development:** Through systematic experimentation and data-driven approaches, researchers investigate the synergistic effects of combining specific medicinal plants. They explore the principles of phytotherapy to determine the optimal combinations that exhibit enhanced therapeutic effects or reduced adverse reactions, thereby formulating potent herbal mixtures.
- **Dose Standardization and Pharmacokinetic Studies:** Rigorous dose-response studies and pharmacokinetic evaluations are conducted to ascertain the optimal dosage regimen for herbal formulations. This involves evaluating the absorption, distribution, metabolism, and excretion (ADME) profiles of active compounds to ensure therapeutic efficacy and safety.

- **Validation through Clinical Trials:** PaxHerbal conducts well-designed clinical trials involving human subjects to validate the safety and efficacy of herbal formulations. These trials adhere to internationally accepted guidelines and protocols, providing scientific evidence for the efficacy of the developed herbal products.

PaxHerbal's Drug Innovation Research Division stands as a pioneering force, employing cutting-edge scientific methodologies while respecting traditional knowledge systems. By leveraging innovative research strategies, they validate and elevate the status of herbal medicine, paving the way for evidence-based, globally accepted herbal therapies.

We now turn from the process of research and development, overall, at PaxHerbals, to its substance, agriculturally, plant taxonomy-wise, and ecologically in general.

Drawing Upon Agriculture, Plant Taxonomy and Ecology

PaxHerbals, known for their expertise in herbal medicine and sustainable practices, extends the principles of ecology, agriculture, permaculture, and taxonomy into a comprehensive and intricate framework within their laboratory:

Biomimicry and Symbiosis:

> *Ecological Modelling*: PaxHerbals integrates ecological models to mimic natural systems, fostering sustainable agricultural practices. Studying ecological patterns allows the emulation of natural processes like nutrient cycling, promoting self-regulating ecosystems.
>
> o *Symbiotic Relationships*: Understanding symbiotic interactions between plants, fungi, and microorganisms enables the development of companion planting strategies. This involves cultivating plants that mutually benefit each other by sharing resources or deterring pests.

Permaculture Integration:

> o *Agroecology Principles*: PaxHerbals emphasises agroecological approaches, blending traditional wisdom with modern agricultural techniques. This involves designing agricultural systems that mimic natural ecosystems to enhance biodiversity, soil fertility, and resilience to environmental stressors.
>
> o *Polyculture and Guilds*: Implementing diverse polyculture systems and guilds, where different plant species support and complement each other, maximises space utilisation and promotes ecological balance within cultivated areas.

Taxonomy and Plant Identification:

> o *Advanced Taxonomic Methods*: PaxHerbals employs advanced botanical taxonomy techniques, including molecular markers and morphological characterization, for accurate plant identification and classification.

- ***Ethnobotanical Surveys***: Integrating ethnobotanical surveys aids in identifying traditional medicinal plants used by local communities. This knowledge contributes to the preservation of indigenous plant species and their medicinal properties.

Sustainable Land Use Practices:

- ***Agroforestry Systems***: PaxHerbals implements agroforestry models, combining trees and crops in a symbiotic manner to optimise land use, improve soil fertility, and provide multiple benefits such as food, medicine, and timber.
- ***Soil Conservation Techniques***: Utilising erosion control methods, cover cropping, and organic soil amendments, PaxHerbals ensures sustainable soil management, mitigates soil degradation, and promotes long-term agricultural productivity.

Conservation and Cultivation:

- ***Biodiversity Conservation***: PaxHerbals emphasises the conservation of medicinal plant diversity by establishing botanical gardens, seed banks, and conservation programs. This ensures the preservation of rare and endangered medicinal plant species.
- ***Cultivation Protocols***: Developing cultivation protocols for medicinal plants involves optimising growing conditions, propagation methods, and harvesting techniques to ensure sustainable sourcing while preserving plant potency and quality.

PaxHerbals' integrated approach combines scientific research, traditional knowledge, and ecological principles to advance herbal medicine while promoting environmental sustainability and biodiversity conservation. Their comprehensive strategies encompass not only the scientific aspects but also ethical considerations for the preservation and responsible utilisation of medicinal plants.

Ethnobotanical Studies and Documentation: PaxHerbal's commitment to integrating traditional wisdom and scientific innovation extends into several pivotal practices and principles, underscoring the depth and significance of their approach. PaxHerbal invests in comprehensive ethnobotanical studies to systematically document indigenous knowledge related to medicinal plants. These studies involve meticulous documentation of plant species, their traditional uses, preparation methods, and cultural significance within local communities. By preserving this knowledge in a structured manner, PaxHerbal ensures its accessibility for future research and conservation efforts.

Collaborative Research and Knowledge Exchange

The company fosters collaborative research endeavours, inviting local healers, traditional practitioners, and academic scientists to exchange insights and co-create knowledge. This synergistic approach encourages a dynamic exchange of ideas, where traditional wisdom informs scientific investigations and vice versa. Through this collaborative platform, both parties contribute to a shared understanding that enriches healthcare practices.

- **Validation and Standardisation of Traditional Remedies**

PaxHerbal places great emphasis on validating traditional remedies through scientific validation and standardisation protocols. By employing modern analytical techniques, they identify and quantify active compounds present in traditional herbal formulations. This process ensures consistency, potency, and safety, aligning traditional remedies with contemporary quality standards without compromising their efficacy.

- **Cultivation, Conservation, and Sustainable Practices**

Recognising the importance of preserving biodiversity, PaxHerbal emphasises sustainable cultivation practices. They engage in cultivation programmes that promote the sustainable growth of medicinal plants, minimise environmental impact, and protect endangered species. Through educational outreach and support, local communities are encouraged to adopt sustainable harvesting practices, fostering a responsible approach to plant resource utilization.

- **Holistic Health Education and Awareness**

PaxHerbal prioritises community health education, empowering individuals with knowledge about traditional medicine, preventive healthcare, and lifestyle choices. Workshops, seminars, and outreach programmes disseminate information about the benefits of herbal medicine, encouraging individuals to embrace holistic wellness practices. This educational outreach aims to bridge the gap between traditional and modern healthcare systems, promoting informed decision-making for health management.

- **Advocacy for Integrative Healthcare Systems**

PaxHerbal advocates for the integration of traditional medicine into mainstream healthcare systems. Through advocacy efforts and collaborations with policymakers and healthcare institutions, they strive to create an inclusive healthcare environment that recognises the value of traditional practices alongside modern medicine. This advocacy aims to foster a healthcare system that offers diverse and personalised options for patient care.

In essence, PaxHerbal's holistic model for integrating traditional wisdom with scientific innovation goes beyond mere convergence – it represents a transformative synergy that honours cultural heritage, advances scientific knowledge, promotes sustainability, and strives for a more inclusive and effective healthcare landscape.

Research Collaboration with Government: Students Industrial Work Experience Scheme

Acting as a Bridge Between Academic Learning and Practical Application

The *Students Industrial Work Experience Scheme* (SIWES) was established by the Industrial Training Fund (ITF) in 1973 to address the challenge of inadequate skills among tertiary institution graduates for employment in Nigerian industries. It was designed as a skill training program to expose and prepare students from universities, polytechnics, and colleges of education for industrial work situations post-graduation. *Acting as a bridge between academic learning and practical application*, SIWES facilitated the acquisition of hands-on experience and exposure to equipment and machinery not typically available within educational institutions.

Before the inception of this scheme, a prevalent concern among industrialists was the lack of practical experience among graduates from higher institutions. Students in science and technology lacked hands-on training, leading to difficulties securing employment due to their limited working experience.

Recognising the disconnect between theoretical education and industry needs, the ITF initiated the SIWES programme in 1973/74. Initially solely funded by the ITF, the scheme's financial burden led to its withdrawal in 1978. Consequently, in 1979, the Federal Government entrusted the management of the scheme to both the National Universities Commission (NUC) and the National Board for Technical Education (NBTE).

In November 1984, the management and implementation of SIWES reverted to the ITF, while in July 1985, the Industrial Training Fund took over the scheme's management, with full funding responsibility shouldered by the federal government.

General Objectives of SIWES

SIWES primarily focuses on skill acquisition, preparing students for real-world work environments post-graduation. The scheme plays a pivotal role in fostering industrialization and economic development by imparting practical scientific and technological skills to students. The objectives include:

1. Providing avenues for Nigerian university students to acquire industrial skills relevant to their fields of study.
2. Exposing students to work methods and equipment not readily available in their educational institutions.
3. Bridging the gap between theoretical knowledge acquired in school and practical application in work settings.
4. Facilitating a smoother transition from academic learning to future employment opportunities.
5. Allowing students to apply theoretical knowledge in real-life scenarios, bridging the theory-practice gap.

Organizations Involved in SIWES Management and Their Roles

The Federal Government, the Industrial Training Fund (ITF), supervisory agencies (such as the National University Commission-NUC), employers of labour, and educational institutions all play distinct roles in managing SIWES.

Federal Government

- Provision of adequate funds for the scheme through the Federal Ministry of Industry.
- Mandating ministries, companies, and parastatals to provide attachment opportunities for students.
- Formulating national policies guiding the scheme's operations.

Industrial Training Fund (ITF)
- Formulating policies and guidelines for SIWES.
- Providing logistical support for the scheme.
- Organising orientation programmes for students before attachment.
- Assisting in industrial placement and supervising students during attachment.
- Processing students' documents and overseeing their progress.

Supervisory agencies (NUC, National Business, Technical Examinations Board-NABTEB)

- Ensuring the establishment and accreditation of SIWES units in institutions.
- Reviewing SIWES programmes regularly.
- Participating in SIWES conferences and seminars in collaboration with ITF.

Roles of the Supervisory Agencies

National Universities Commission (NUC)

- Ensures the establishment and accreditation of SIWES units in institutions under its jurisdiction.
- Approves and reviews the master and placement lists of students from participating institutions.
- Provides adequate funding to SIWES directorates in participating institutions.
- Directs the appointment of full-time SIWES coordinators or directors.
- Regularly reviews qualified programmes derived from SIWES.
- Participates actively in SIWES conferences and seminars in conjunction with the ITF.

We now turn from community interface, research and development onto good manufacturing processes and quality control at PaxHerbals.

C4.2.3. Good Manufacturing Processes and Quality Control

Good Manufacturing Processes

PaxHerbal's commitment to quality assurance and adherence to regulatory standards is upheld by its GMP supervisors. These individuals oversee and enforce stringent measures ensuring the hygienic, efficient, and compliant manufacturing of herbal products. Here are the technical aspects of their role:

- **Regulatory Compliance and Documentation:** GMP supervisors possess comprehensive knowledge of local and international regulatory requirements set by agencies like NAFDAC, WHO, and FDA. They ensure PaxHerbal's operations align with these standards, meticulously documenting processes, protocols, and procedures to maintain compliance.
- **Facility Design and Validation:** They are involved in the design and layout of manufacturing facilities, ensuring they meet GMP standards. This includes adherence to principles of cleanroom design, air filtration systems, and segregation of production areas to prevent cross-contamination. Additionally, they oversee the validation and qualification of equipment and utilities.
- **Process Validation and Control:** GMP supervisors are responsible for validating manufacturing processes, ensuring consistency, reproducibility, and reliability in the production of herbal products. They establish control measures to monitor critical parameters during manufacturing, guaranteeing product quality and safety.
- **Training and Quality Control:** They conduct regular training sessions for personnel involved in manufacturing to uphold GMP principles. This includes educating staff on proper hygiene practices, handling of raw materials, equipment maintenance, and adherence to standard operating procedures (SOPs). They also oversee quality control measures at every stage of production.
- **Audits and Inspections:** GMP supervisors perform regular internal audits to assess compliance with GMP guidelines. Additionally, they coordinate and facilitate external inspections conducted by regulatory agencies, ensuring PaxHerbal's readiness and adherence to standards during audits.
- **Continuous Improvement and Risk Management:** They spearhead initiatives for continuous improvement, implementing corrective and preventive actions based on risk assessment. They analyse processes, identify potential risks, and proactively address any deviations to maintain product quality and safety.
- **Documentation Review and Batch Release:** GMP supervisors meticulously review batch records and documentation before releasing products to the market. They ensure all manufacturing records are accurate, complete, and compliant with regulatory requirements prior to product release.

PaxHerbal's GMP supervisors play a pivotal role in upholding the highest standards of manufacturing practices, ensuring that herbal products meet stringent quality, safety, and efficacy criteria mandated by regulatory authorities. Their technical expertise and adherence to GMP principles guarantee the consistency and reliability of PaxHerbal's herbal formulations.

Quality Control

In the Quality Control Laboratory of PaxHerbals, a multi-faceted approach is employed to ensure the integrity and safety of herbal drugs. Here's a more detailed exploration of the technical aspects:

a. *Analytical Techniques:*
- **High-Performance Liquid Chromatography (HPLC):** HPLC plays a pivotal role in identifying and quantifying active compounds within herbal formulations. Using this technique, specific markers or active constituents are identified and quantified, ensuring batch-to-batch consistency and adherence to standardized profiles.
- **Gas Chromatography-Mass Spectrometry (GC-MS):** GC-MS is utilized for the analysis of volatile compounds present in herbal drugs. This technique aids in identifying a wide array of compounds, including essential oils, terpenes, and other volatile substances, contributing to the overall therapeutic profile of herbal products.
- **Microbiological Analysis:** Rigorous microbiological testing is conducted to verify the absence of pathogenic microorganisms. Culturing methods and advanced microbial identification systems, such as polymerase chain reaction (PCR) and next-generation sequencing, are employed to ensure compliance with safety standards and ascertain product sterility.

b. *Quality Assurance Protocols:*
- **Batch Sampling and Testing:** A meticulous sampling strategy is employed, where representative samples from each batch of herbal drugs are randomly selected. These samples undergo comprehensive testing and analysis to verify compliance with predetermined quality standards, ensuring uniformity and consistency across production.
- **Stability Studies:** Herbal formulations are subjected to extensive stability studies to evaluate their shelf-life, ensuring that potency, efficacy, and physical attributes remain unchanged over specified periods under various storage conditions. These studies involve accelerated stability testing, stress testing, and long-term stability assessments.

c. *Compliance with Regulatory Standards:*
- **Good Manufacturing Practices (GMP):** The Quality Control Laboratory operates in strict adherence to GMP guidelines established by regulatory bodies such as NAFDAC, WHO, and FDA. This ensures that every stage of the manufacturing process meets international standards for hygiene, documentation, equipment validation, and overall quality control.

d. *Instrumentation and Validation:*
- **Validation Protocols:** Validation of analytical methods and equipment calibration are paramount. The laboratory conducts rigorous validation protocols for analytical instruments to ensure accuracy, precision, and reliability of results.

e. **Documentation and Reporting:**
   o **Comprehensive Documentation:** Every stage of the quality control process is meticulously documented. This includes standard operating procedures (SOPs), batch records, and analytical reports, ensuring traceability and accountability throughout the production cycle.

PaxHerbals' Quality Control Laboratory integrates advanced analytical techniques, stringent quality assurance measures, and compliance with regulatory standards to guarantee their herbal formulations' safety, efficacy, and consistency. This commitment to quality control underpins the reliability and trustworthiness of their products within the herbal medicine industry.

Mycology at PaxHerbal: Unveiling Nature's Medicinal Treasures

The Mycology Section at PaxHerbal embodies a vital aspect of the company's research and production, centred on the cultivation and exploration of mushrooms. This specialised unit employs meticulous tissue culture techniques, maintaining stringent protocols within a controlled laboratory environment before transferring cultivated mushrooms to the fruiting site.

Cultivation via Tissue Culture

Precision Cultivation

Utilising tissue culture methodologies, the Mycology Section initiates and sustains mushroom growth through aseptic culture of mushroom cells or tissues. This controlled environment ensures optimal conditions for proliferation, emphasising high hygiene standards to guarantee the purity and quality of cultivated mushrooms.

Supervised Ramification

Under vigilant supervision, cultivated mushroom cultures are nurtured to ramify, encouraging mycelium development – the vegetative part of the fungus. This phase is pivotal for establishing a robust fungal network and laying the groundwork for subsequent fruiting and mushroom production.

Mycology's Role in Phytomedicine

Medicinal Mushroom Properties

Mycology research holds profound significance in phytomedicine due to the diverse medicinal properties exhibited by various mushroom species. Certain mushrooms contain bioactive compounds renowned for their therapeutic potential, encompassing antimicrobial, antioxidant, anti-inflammatory, and immunomodulatory traits.

Pharmaceutical Insights

Research in mycology aids in identifying, isolating, and characterising bioactive compounds from mushrooms. These compounds are valuable resources for developing pharmaceuticals, supplements, and herbal remedies, enriching the repertoire of natural therapeutic options in phytomedicine.

Health Benefits and Therapeutic Potential

Mushrooms cultivated through advanced mycology techniques offer an array of health benefits. Their potential to address immune-related disorders, cardiovascular diseases, cancer, and more expands the scope of natural remedies in healthcare.

The Mycology Section at PaxHerbal epitomises the intricate art and science of cultivating mushrooms through advanced tissue culture methods. Beyond cultivation, this research is pivotal in unveiling mushrooms' therapeutic potential, contributing to the development of natural remedies. PaxHerbal's commitment to exploring nature's pharmacopoeia underscores its dedication to harnessing natural healing for societal benefit.

Technical and Engineering Section at PaxHerbals: Towards Holistic Re-GENE-ration

The Engineering/Maintenance Section at PaxHerbal represents a dynamic fusion of innovation and resourcefulness, exemplified by the fabrication of specialised production equipment and the upkeep of company assets. This section not only ensures the seamless functioning of production units but also harnesses available resources to create custom machinery, such as automated conveyors, heaters, driers, ovens, and more.

Fabrication of Specialised Production Equipment

Automated Conveyors

The technical team at PaxHerbal exhibits an exceptional ability to design and fabricate automated conveyors tailored to precise specifications. These conveyors are vital in the production process, facilitating the efficient and systematic movement of finished products and goods between various production units. By customising these conveyors, the team optimises workflow, minimises manual handling, and enhances productivity within the manufacturing ecosystem.

Heaters, Dryers, and Ovens

Utilising available technological resources, the engineering experts at PaxHerbal engineer and assemble heaters, driers, ovens, and similar machinery essential for producing and processing herbal products. These specialised pieces of equipment are calibrated to meet stringent standards, ensuring precise temperature control and adherence to specific production requirements. By crafting these machines in-house, PaxHerbal minimises dependency on external sources and tailors the equipment to suit the unique needs of herbal product processing.

Tapping into Available Resources for Economic and Social Transformation

Resource Optimisation

The engineering prowess at PaxHerbal not only focuses on technical innovation but also emphasises resource optimization. By fabricating equipment in-house, the organisation reduces external procurement costs, maximises resource utilisation, and mitigates dependency on external suppliers. This approach aligns with PaxHerbal's commitment to sustainable practices and economic viability.

Empowering Local Expertise

The fabrication of specialised machinery within the company not only showcases technical proficiency but also empowers local expertise. The engineering team leverages local talent, knowledge, and available materials, thereby contributing to skill development and economic empowerment within the community.

Social and Economic Impact

The initiatives undertaken by the Engineering/Maintenance Section at PaxHerbal contribute significantly to both social and economic transformation. By reducing reliance on external equipment suppliers, the company enhances its self-sufficiency, fosters innovation, and positively impacts the local economy. Additionally, these efforts reinforce the organisation's commitment to technological advancement, driving progress within the herbal medicine industry while positively impacting societal development.

The Engineering/Maintenance Section at PaxHerbal stands as a testament to ingenuity and resourceful innovation. Through the fabrication of specialised production equipment and meticulous maintenance practices, the team not only ensures operational efficiency but also exemplifies the potential for utilising available resources towards economic and social transformation.

C 4.2.4 Collaborative Partnerships

PaxHerbal actively engages in collaborative partnerships with several esteemed institutions, fostering cooperative inquiry and advancing transformative initiatives in herbal medicine and healthcare. Some of its notable collaborations include the following:

- **Centre for Rural Development (CERUD), Lagos:** Advanced discussions on the establishment of a botanical park and rural health initiative in Lagos State.
- **Sickle Cell Centre, Ministry of Health, Edo State:** Partnership in the Treatment of Sickle Cell Anaemia.
- **Lagos State University of Traditional Medicine** is a long-term collaborator in the promotion, development, and modernization of African medicine.
- **National Institute for Pharmaceutical Research and Development (NIPRD), Abuja:** Collaboration in clinical trials and toxicological analysis of Pax products.
- **Irrua Specialist Teaching Hospital, Edo State:** Ongoing discussions in evidence-based treatment practices for diabetes, hypertension, malaria, HIV/AIDS, and other infectious diseases.
- **Nigeria Natural Medicine Development Agency (NNMDA), Lagos:** Collaborating in developing natural medicine.
- **Centre for Malaria Research and Phytomedicine, University of Port Harcourt:** Research partnership.
- **Ambrose Alli University, Ekpoma:** Student Industrial Training Programme, ongoing discussions on a certificate programme in herbal medicine.
- **Benson Idahosa University, Benin City, Edo State:** Advanced discussions on a certificate programme in herbal medicine.
- **Delta State University, Abraka, and Kogi State University, Ayingba:** student industrial training programmes.
- **University of Port Harcourt:** signed an MOU on a research partnership.

Partnership Goals/Aims

The collaborative efforts between PaxHerbal and its partners aim to achieve transformative goals in African medicine and healthcare. These include:

1. Pioneering the official integration of African herbal medicine into the national healthcare system.
2. Enhancing the capacity of communities and organisations in the scientific identification and conservation of African medicinal plants.
3. Institutionalising and improving holistic African healing and sustainable healthcare in Nigeria.
4. Demystifying the practice of traditional African medicine through research, documentation, and information technology.
5. Modernising, rationalising, and globalising the use of traditional African medicine.
6. Increasing the integrative network capacity of orthodox or traditional medical practitioners for better healthcare services.
7. Strengthening the capacity of Africans engaged in herbal medical practice.
8. Boosting the income-generating capacity of traditional African medicine practitioners.

9. Increasing linkage capacity among orthodox and traditional medical practitioners for legislative advocacy.
10. Exemplifying how proper utilisation of traditional medicine can promote a culturally acceptable, affordable, and relevant grassroots primary healthcare system.
11. Raising African awareness regarding the development and utilisation of African medicinal plants.
12. Cultivating and preserving common and rare species of medicinal plants in each state of Nigeria.
13. Enhancing the capacity of Africans on health-related environmental issues.

C4.3. PaxHerbals to Pax Africana: Community to Communiversity

C4.3.1. Taking CARE Underpinned by the Idea of the Holy

From Technological to Social Innovation

In the second decade of our new millennium, Father Anselm (Lessem et al 2019), having founded PaxHerbals some two decades hitherto, set out on a second major step on his journey, now from a community based enterprise to a communiversity, that is form PaxHerbals to what he termed Pax Africana (see Figure 4.3.2. below) Paxherbal's journey unfolds not just as a narrative of healthcare but as a transformational journey rooted in the intricate interplay between community, culture, and identity. Embracing the pillars of CARE – Catalysing Development, Communal Activation, Institutionalised Research, and Transformative Enterprise – as hitherto articulated by one of us, Ronnie Lessem (Lessem and Schieffer 2015), in his book on *Integral Renewal*, Pax Communis embodies this ethos.

The other functions of the emerging Communiversity were, in such terms, Pax Spiritus, Pax Scientia and Pax Economica. In that overall guise, Father Anselm specifically, and PaxHerbal generally, turns from technological to social innovation, now lodged in African cosmology, theology, and anthropology, as well as in economics and management, as well as in medical practice, botany and biology, agriculture and ecology. At the heart of every society, culturally and spiritually, resides a belief in the sacred, in this case Pax (Peace) an enigmatic force beyond human comprehension – an essence Rudolf Otto (1958), the German Philosophical Theologian, in his *Idea of the Holy*, termed the "numinous". This universal concept exists in various forms across cultures and religions, underpinning their approach to life. In Yoruba cosmology, this core image is embodied in the concept of Orisa, interwoven with the belief in Olodumare, the supreme God sustaining all existence. Olodumare, synonymous with reliability, omnipotence, and omniscience, represents the divine power that oversees the skies, known as Olorun – "owner of the sky."

C4.2.2. Olodumare Sent 401 Orisa to Earth, Each Assigned Specific Duties

The Orisa, including Ogun, Songo, Obatala, Orunmila, and Esu, play vital roles in Yoruba cosmology. According to Yoruba mythology, Olodumare sent 401 Orisa to Earth, each assigned specific duties. These Orisa personify different facets of life, offering the Yoruba a way to comprehend and navigate various phenomena, ensuring a sense of control and empowerment. Through rituals and sacrifices, the Yoruba harness nature's positive energies, directing them for their own benefit. The Orisa act as intermediaries, representing specific aspects of life – an appeal to them ultimately connects the devotee to Olodumare. However, an Orisa that fails to respond risks losing reverence and can be forsaken by the community.

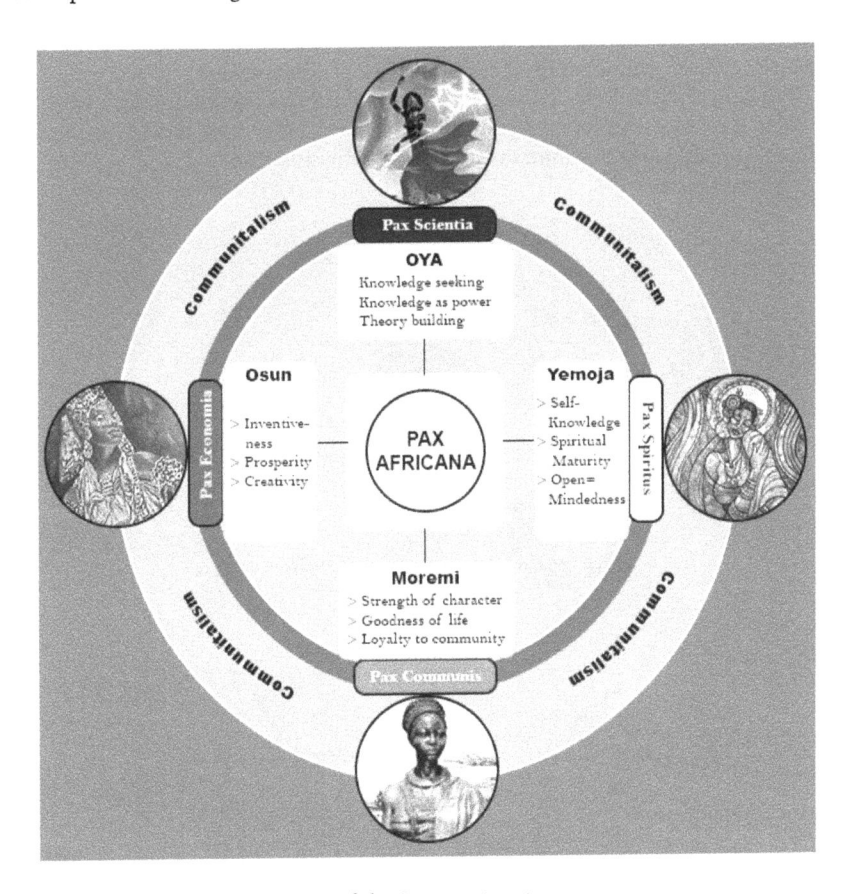

Figure 4.2.3: *Indigenous Origins of the Communiversity*

Linked intricately with creation, knowledge plays a vital role in Yoruba mythology. Moremi as such represents strength of character and loyalty to the community. Yemoja depicts self knowledge and spiritual maturity. Oya embodied knowledge as power, and theory building, Osun represents inventiveness, prosperity and creativity.

C4.2.3. Pax Communis, Pax Spiritus, Pax Scientia, Pax Economica

Pax Communis/Learning Community/Moremi Archetype

Within the realm of Pax Communis lies a redefinition of community, harkening back to its original essence – a fellowship held in common, bonded by intricate relationships and a moral core. It transcends the contemporary notion of individualistic societies, grounding itself in the essence of communality.

Drawing from indigenous roots, Pax Communis revives community spirit by tapping into ancestral connections, particularly with the Orisa, laying the foundation for a resurgence of community ethos – communitalism.

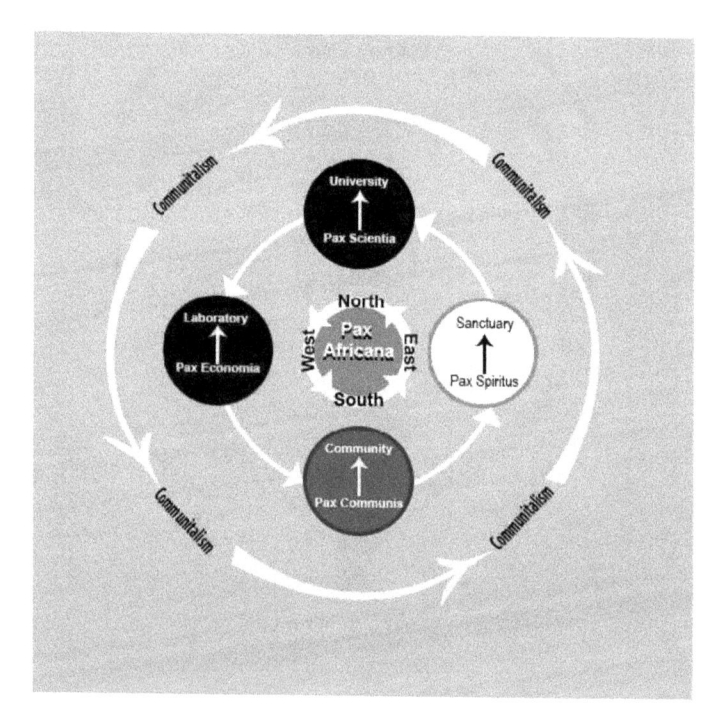

Figure 4.2.4: *Indigenous/Exogenous Pax Africana*

The archetype of Moremi stands tall as the embodiment of goodness within a community, intertwining goodness with beauty as inherent moral values. In Yoruba culture, goodness, encapsulated in "Iwa," intertwines with beauty, forming a holistic representation of character and virtue. A person of character embodies honesty, kindness, obedience, tolerance, and generosity – a tapestry of virtues that define a good existence. Here, the concept of "dara," combining creation and wellness, denotes the inherent beauty within goodness itself, while "buruku" signifies the absence of such virtues, leading to an unattractive, spiritually lacking existence.

The narrative of Moremi symbolises the embodiment of these virtues, echoing the values of Iwa and Dara in practical life. Pax Communis, thus, strives to resurrect the original meaning of community, infusing modernity with the timeless essence of goodness and beauty. The journey towards Pax Communis began with an inward and outward application of feminism's core principles. A journey towards integral societal transformation was initiated by activating the existing local community. Through dialogues and engagements with local farmers, an endeavour to give voice to the marginalised blossomed into the Ewu Development Educational Multipurpose Cooperative Society (EDEMCS). EDEMCS, primarily composed of passionate local farmers, embraced a bottom-up approach to development. They sought to leverage the potential inherent in their community, harnessing traditional systems and worldviews to carve a better future. This cooperative stands as a testament to the fundamental principles of sustainable development – self-reliance, community-driven initiatives, and preservation of indigenous knowledge.

Pax Communis delves into the symbiotic nature of communities, exploring the intricate relationships between humans, animals, plants, and the often-overlooked soil and oceans. It underscores the urgent need to expand our awareness of the rich diversity within our ecosystem, urging a deeper understanding and appreciation of the interconnectedness of all life forms. It serves as an invitation to immerse oneself in the immediate lifeworld, encouraging a rediscovery of community within the intricate web of life. This dimension fosters an appreciation for the interconnectedness among humans, animals, plants, and the unseen entities within our ecosystem, shifting the focus from nature and community to culture and spirituality.

As Pax Communis continues to evolve, it encapsulates not just the vision of community activation but the integration of traditional wisdom into contemporary societal frameworks. It stands as a beacon of communal resurgence, fusing the timeless essence of indigenous values with the dynamism of modernity – a narrative transcending healthcare, weaving a tapestry of societal transformation rooted in communal spirit and cultural integrity.

Pax Spiritus/Transformation Journey/Yemoja Archetype

Pax Spiritus, underlying an awakening consciousness, along a transformation journey, transcends the conventional dichotomy between the sacred and secular, integrating the spiritual dimension into communal perspectives. Rooted in indigenous wisdom and building upon exogenous foundations, it emerges as a bridge connecting ancient principles with modern ideologies. Yemoja, the revered Orisa of the sea and the moon, embodies the essence of Pax Spiritus. She transcends physical beauty, embodying wisdom derived from life's experiences – a mother figure revered for nurturing humanity and safeguarding the earth. Yemoja symbolises the power of resilience, patience, and wisdom, mirroring the dual nature of the sea – peaceful yet capable of immense destruction.

The Benedictine influence adds another layer to Pax Spiritus, illuminating a pathway to communal living grounded in humility, simplicity, and hospitality. The Rule of St. Benedict, initially intended as a guide for a peaceful Christian community, emerges as a testament to equality, respect, and solidarity among all individuals, irrespective of social standing.

Benedictine monasteries, often perceived as isolated entities, embody the essence of a caring community – a place of learning, beauty, and hospitality. They challenge the materialistic dogma of modernity, emphasising detachment from worldly possessions and embracing the true wealth found in solidarity and brotherliness. St. Benedict's emphasis on humility in daily tasks and the reverence for guests as embodiments of Christ reflect a profound understanding of human interconnectedness. The Rule underscores the significance of little things, echoing the sentiment that greatness lies in attention to detail and dedication in daily endeavours.

In the modern world, where material wealth often overshadows communal bonds, the Benedictine perspective offers an alternative – a reaffirmation that true wealth lies in human connections, respect for nature, and solidarity. It challenges the notion that capitalism is the only viable option (TINA), advocating instead that alternatives exist (TIAA). The Rule's call to welcome guests, especially the marginalised, echoes the essence of embracing diversity and offering hospitality without expecting reciprocation. It highlights the importance of humility in craftsmanship, advocating honesty and fair pricing – a reminder that ethical conduct matters in all endeavours. Pax Spiritus encapsulates a deeper understanding – the significance of finding meaning in daily struggles, embracing human diversity, and representing it inclusively. It seeks to rediscover the sanctuary – the monastery – as a symbol of identity and spirituality, transcending geographical boundaries and advocating for a rediscovery of moral cores worldwide.

This rediscovery, while taking different forms across cultures, is rooted in the quest to find meaning through spirituality. Pax Spiritus stands as a beacon, urging societies to delve into their moral cores, fostering a reconnection with their identity and purpose. The next dimension, Pax Scientia, delves into knowledge creation within the Nigerian context, furthering the journey of rediscovery and societal transformation.

Pax Scientia/Research Academy/Oya Archetype

The tale of Oya and Osun embodies a deeper symbiosis – a profound interplay between intellect and prosperity, a harmony of rationality and abundance that transcends the confines of mythology. Oya's portrayal as the archetype of intellect and research delves into the multifaceted nature of knowledge – a force capable of creation and transformation. As the representation of intellect (scientia), Oya exudes a unique balance of wisdom and calculated action. Her poised demeanour amidst emotional turbulence signifies her strength – an unwavering resilience derived from her deep-rooted expertise. Her skilful cooking, symbolic of her technical prowess, mirrors her ability to manipulate elements to create desired outcomes – a metaphorical reflection of the researcher's craft in manipulating information to derive insights.

The dichotomy between Oya and Osun reflects more than a mere narrative of personal relationships; it unveils a paradigm of intellectual pragmatism (Oya) juxtaposed with material prosperity (Osun). In this narrative, Oya stands as the epitome of calculated wisdom, a steady force capable of both shaping and adapting to change – a quality quintessential for transformative research.

Her leadership attributes, sought during the selection of leaders, highlight her discernment and analytical acumen – an embodiment of the guiding principles behind research-driven decision-making. As the archetype of the researcher, Oya symbolises the essence of our emergent Centre for Integral Research and Societal Re-GENE-ation (see below) – an institution poised at the intersection of intellectual inquiry and practical application, fostering a holistic approach to knowledge creation.

Pax Scientia, rooted in Oya's archetype, espouses a holistic understanding of research – a pursuit not limited to academic realms but entwined with societal implications. Our Integral Research Academy as an embodiment of this ethos, serves as a nexus where research transcends theoretical boundaries, converging with pragmatic solutions for societal development.

The union of Oya and Osun transcends the mythical realm, representing a harmony between intellect and prosperity, knowledge creation, and economic growth. Within this paradigm, Oya emerges as a beacon – a symbol of transformative knowledge, guiding the convergence of intellect and practical application towards collective societal advancement.The tale of Oya resonates beyond folklore – it reflects the intrinsic relationship between intellect and its practical manifestations, emphasising the need for research to transcend theoretical realms, impacting societal welfare. In this paradigm, Oya stands tall, not merely as a mythological figure but as an embodiment of the intellectual journey – a testament to the transformative power of knowledge harnessed for the greater good of society.

Pax Economia/Socio-economic Laboratory/Osun Archetype

Osun, portrayed as a significant Orisa embodying beauty, fertility, and prosperity, encapsulates the essence of transformative enterprise in Yoruba cosmology. Her depiction as an independent, ambitious, and skilful entrepreneur mirrors qualities intrinsic to successful business conduct. Osun's association with markets and trading places symbolises her pivotal role as the custodian of economic success. In the narrative, Osun's attributes echo an overlooked facet of feminism – a call for marginalised communities to cultivate consciousness, interpret their circumstances, and assert their rights. Her archetype emphasises the need for the oppressed to attain self-awareness, transforming them into advocates for their own justice rather than depending on the benevolence of the privileged.

Furthermore, Osun represents the nexus between good character and successful enterprise. Her negotiation skills and pursuit of her desires, while cautioning against selfish intentions, underline the significance of ethical conduct in business transactions. The market, often referred to as the "laboratory", becomes a realm where communal values, honesty, and good character must be nurtured – an intersection of Osun's influence with the ideals of Communis (community), Spiritus (sanctuary), and Scientia (university).

Paxherbal, as an exemplar of such a socio-economic enterprise, challenges the conventional dichotomy between health, spirituality, economics, and politics. It expands beyond the confines of mere biological health, embracing a holistic or integral healing approach. This holistic healing philosophy questions the conventional notion of profit, suggesting a shift from individual profit maximisation to a paradigm embracing caring and caregiving as fundamental economic activities. As a government-recognized institution, PaxHerbal stands at the forefront of imparting practical, hands-on experience to students. Here, they not only acquire theoretical knowledge but also gain invaluable insights into the practical application of scientific principles within a holistic framework.

PaxHerbal's emphasis on holistic approaches to research resonates deeply with students pursuing various scientific disciplines. It offers them a rare chance to explore the synergies between traditional wisdom and modern scientific methodologies. Through exposure to PaxHerbal's research methodologies and practices, students obtain a comprehensive understanding of how traditional medicinal knowledge can intersect and complement contemporary scientific advancements. Furthermore, PaxHerbal's integral role in academia extends beyond conventional learning. It provides students with an immersive environment that fosters critical thinking, interdisciplinary collaboration, and a deeper appreciation for the intricate connections between nature, health, and traditional healing practices, underscoring its pivotal role in shaping the future of scientific exploration and fostering a new generation of researchers adept at merging traditional wisdom with contemporary scientific methodologies for the betterment of society.

C4.2.4. From PaxHerbal to Pax Africana: Community Enterprise to Communiversity

Collaborative Learning to Promoting Societal Wellbeing

PaxHerbal embodies the essence of a Communiversity by encapsulating the principles of collaborative learning, research, and community engagement, ultimately geared toward societal betterment.

- **Collaborative Learning and Research:**
  At PaxHerbal, individuals from diverse backgrounds – students, educators, researchers, and community members – come together to collaborate on learning and research initiatives. Through hands-on experiences, practical training, and exposure to holistic healthcare practices, they collectively explore the intersection of traditional wisdom and modern scientific methodologies. This collaborative environment fosters a rich exchange of ideas and knowledge, promoting a deeper understanding of herbal medicine, natural sciences, and health approaches.

- **Stewards, Catalysts, and Educators:**
  PaxHerbal cultivates a community comprising stewards – individuals preserving traditional medicinal knowledge, catalysts – driving innovation in herbal medicine, and educators – mentors nurturing the next generation of holistic healthcare professionals. These roles intertwine, creating a dynamic network where expertise is shared, traditional wisdom is honoured, and innovative research methodologies are embraced.

- **Researchers and Learners:**
  The institution serves as a breeding ground for researchers and learners, where traditional healing practices intersect with rigorous scientific inquiry. Students, researchers, and practitioners engage in collaborative endeavours, conducting studies that explore the efficacy and safety of herbal remedies. This cooperative research atmosphere encourages continuous learning and innovation.

- **Community Engagement:**
  PaxHerbal extends beyond its academic boundaries to engage with the wider community.
  Local healers, community members, and indigenous knowledge custodians actively participate in knowledge-sharing sessions, workshops, and seminars. By involving the community, PaxHerbal bridges the gap between traditional healing practices and modern scientific approaches, ensuring societal well-being is at the forefront of their endeavours.

- **Promoting Societal Well-Being:**
  The core ethos of PaxHerbal revolves around contributing to societal well-being. By integrating traditional healing methods with scientific rigor, the institution seeks solutions that benefit society. Through education, research, and community outreach, PaxHerbal aims to improve healthcare practices, empower local communities, and preserve invaluable traditional knowledge for the betterment of society at large.

PaxHerbal epitomizes the concept of a Communiversity by fostering a collaborative ecosystem that unites diverse stakeholders in pursuit of knowledge, research, and societal advancement. Through its holistic approach to education, research, and community engagement, PaxHerbal stands as a model institution dedicated to the betterment of society through the convergence of traditional wisdom and modern scientific innovation.

Transition from University to Communiversity

Striking a Balance Between Scientific and Religious Endeavours

It is in Africa that the startling paradox of contemporary civilisation, which excels in the creation of wealth but is burdened by pollution, poverty, and inequality, finds a particular resonance. Africa is struggling with the issues of sluggish or no growth, which includes excessive poverty and a lack of important technological developments that are essential for the eradication of poverty. This is in contrast to the industrialised nations, which are struggling with the harmful ramifications of overdevelopment.

It is not the strong engineering, automation, or infrastructure development that characterises the landscape in Africa; rather, it is the spread of religious dogmas and churches that characterises the Africa landscape. Critical thinking and logic are frequently discouraged as a result of this rise in spirituality, which may potentially impede advancement. Finding a way to strike a balance between scientific and religious endeavours, that is for us between knowledge creation, scientifically and technologically, and conscious evolution, culturally and spiritually, centred in our healing wisdom, becomes crucial for the advancement of African nations, highlighting the necessity of having a mindset that is deeply rooted in both of these fields.

Preservation and Cultivation of Local Knowledge Rather Than Depending on Imported Ideas

The youth of Africa have a significant awareness of global events and trends, which overshadows their ignorance of the local environment, culture, and traditional knowledge. This is a manifestation of the knowledge deficit that exists in Africa. The actual development of the nation is contingent on the preservation and cultivation of local knowledge rather than depending simply on ideas that are imported from other countries.

With the death of each knowledge bearer, indigenous knowledge is disappearing at an alarming rate, which is comparable to the loss of a library. These efforts to preserve and disseminate this information through the educational system are of the utmost importance. The current educational paradigm in Africa, on the other hand, places a greater emphasis on exam-oriented learning rather than the preservation of indigenous knowledge. This paradigm places a higher priority on certifications than on holistic growth.

A flawed educational system that was passed down from colonial rulers is perpetuated to this day in Africa by the present educational framework, which does not accord with local knowledge. This inability to comprehend, reinterpret, and alter the system has the effect of impeding progress and preventing meaningful changes to the contexts of local environments.

When it was first coined, the term "universitas" referred to a group of academics who were discussing topics that were specific to their region. On the other hand, contemporary universities in Africa strive for international recognition without addressing the underlying difficulties that are faced locally. A disregard for the requirement of addressing local issues and cultivating talent that is tailored to African reality is a consequence of the pursuit of global benchmarks that are impossible to achieve.

The tendency of the educational system to adhere to globalised ideals and the absence of an emphasis on locally relevant information and problem-solving contribute to the perpetuation of the cycle of learning Western norms, which promote consumption and weaken indigenous traditions and culture.

Feel Local, Intuit Local-Global, Think Newly Global, Act Global-Local

The concept of communitalism is one that feels local, intuits local-global, and thereby and thereafter thinks "newly globally", that is in communitalist rather than in capitalist or socialist guise. Ultimately then Africa must develop its own global-local approach to knowledge generation, as PaxHerbal have done, in order to stimulate innovation, maintain cultural integrity, and handle local difficulties such as obsolete agricultural practices, political instability, and limited infrastructure. This must be done while maintaining an openness to global discoveries.

A shift in mentality is encouraged by the communiversity model, which promotes the investigation of indigenous knowledge and the concentration on finding solutions to local problems while simultaneously developing newly global knowledge for the purpose of holistic and sustainable development. Specifically, it represents a shift towards a more well-rounded educational paradigm that protects cultural identity while simultaneously embracing global learning for the sake of advancing Africa.

Given the essential role that science, technology, and innovation play in propelling economic progress, the emphasis that has been placed on higher technical education in Africa has become increasingly significant on the continent. Polytechnics in Nigeria were formed in order to meet the demand for technical education; yet, the exaltation of university degrees has frequently resulted in an attitude of inferiority among graduates of polytechnics. In order to close this gap and generate genuine societal transformation, educational institutions in Africa need to ensure that their students are encouraged to develop their innovative and enterprising talents.

Promoting Transformation Studies in Africa/TSA

Rather than producing people who create jobs, traditional university education in Nigeria and Africa tends to produce people who are looking for work. There is a need for this to change, with colleges placing a greater emphasis on the creation of graduates who are entrepring and capable of generating employment opportunities and contributing to the economic prosperity of their communities. It is the goal of this concept of a "communiversity" to go beyond the traditional dichotomies that exist in the process of knowledge creation and to generate graduates who are not only academically competent but also capable of making a real influence on society.

There has been a dramatic shift in the educational landscape as a result of the advent of Transformation Studies in Africa (TSA). An educational programme that focuses on transformation studies in Africa was approved by the University of Ibadan in 2017, marking a break from the conventional educational models that have been used in the past. This curriculum was designed by the Research Academy of Paxherbals with the intention of regaining cognitive freedom and confronting the coloniality of knowledge. Its goal is to build a new approach to research that speaks the language of Africa.

Towards a Centre for Integral Research and Societal Re-GENE-ration (Re-GENE-Afrika)

The objective of the *Centre for Integral Research and Societal Re-GENE-ration (Re-GENE-Afrika* we are developing together with our partners in Africa and worldswide is to bring about the development of separate Afrocentric research methods and methodologies that are independent of the prevalent Eurocentric systems. In addition to this, it places a focus on the growth of communitalism, which serves as a remedy for the economic imbalances caused by unrestrained capitalism and gives a voice to people that have been marginalised. The Educational Model of the Transportation Security Administration (TSA) running alongside such is constructed on an integrated research framework that focuses on four essential components: Communis, Spiritus, Scientia, and Economica. This concept encourages individuals to engage in interactive activities with various components in order to thoroughly solve transformational concerns.

We are now ready to take our next giant leap, building on PaxHerbal and Pax Africana that have come before to Re-GENE-Afrika in association with others, thereby, and self-consciously, building on *the healing wisdom of Africa,* now society-wide, also thereby promoting Nelson Mandela's envisaged long walk to African freedom, though now explicitly ecologically and culturally, as well as technologically and economically, as well as politically.

C4.5. Re-GENE: Community/Corporate/Communiversity/ Communitalism

C4.5.1. Towards Communitalism

Our Long Walk to Freedom: Regeneration Organisation and Society

Specifically as such Dr Father Anselm Adodo in Nigeria, together with fellow author Ronnie Lessem worlds-wide, and their partner in South Africa, Dr Sandile

Ndlungwane, who was closely associated with Nelson Mandela's (1994) *Long Walk to Freedom*, is now ready to take the next, societal step, from African community based enterprise, as opposed to "western" corporation; and then African communiversity as opposed to "north-western" university, to so called "communitalism" as opposed to capitalism and communism. In that respect they will be drawing on the seminal work of their late Dutch colleague Bernard Lievegoed (1991), in *The Developing Organisation*, who alluded to four phases of such development, or for us re-GENE-ration, that is pioneering, differentiation or scientific management, integration and ultimately association with others, our communitalism. for us ultimately pan-Africa wise.

PaxHerbal has, as we have seen, undergone its communally *pioneering* and corporately *scientific*/technological phases of development, proceeding onto further *integration*, through Pax Africana as a communiversity, and now seeks to pursue communitalism in regenerative *association* with others, both naturally-ecologically and also socio-economically. The ideology of communitalism, that is healing writ large, sheds light on the failure of Western ideologies such as Marxism and capitalism, which ignored nature and culture in their quest for development, if not regeneration, resulting in progress that is not sustainable.

As the basis for sustainable African development, we are co-evolving an associative, communitalist, overall healing-oriented model that takes into account issues pertaining to nature, community, culture, politics, economics, spirituality, and enterprise, building in macro guise, on such micro-enterprises as PaxHerbal. For Adodo (2012) as such, whereby communitalism is as much natural and cultural as it is social and economic in substance:

> Nature Power is inviting the world to come down to earth so as to regain our health. The earth is the primary source of our creativity, intelligence, and humanness. Before we set out to calculate, to create, to invent, to fabricate, the earth already was. Today, faced with globalization, high-technology and a fast-paced modern lifestyle, we are often tempted to forget our link with the earth and therefore become DIS-EASED. In the past we heard about physicians who provided health CARE to the sick. Our health, our life, our future in fact depends on the quality of the earth: soil, water, sunshine, forests and air.

Pax Africana and Re-GENE-Africa

Communitalism then is distinct from both communism and capitalism since it promotes the generation of knowledge that is inclusive and is based on communal enterprises. This perspective, which is shaped by the four Pax dimensions, proposes a comprehensive approach to re-GENE-ration (see above three case stories). Pax Communis (community/*community building/grounding*), aligned with Pax Spiritus (journey/ *conscious evolution/emergence*), Pax Scientia (academy/ *knowledge creation/navigation*), and Pax Economia (laboratory/*sustainable development/transformative effect*) are the four Pax dimensions.

The criticism of conventional educational institutions, which is founded on a so called Mode 1, as opposed to Mode 2 (Gibbons et al 1994) regenerative orientation, emphasises the universities' disconnection from the actual world and places an emphasis on the pursuit of knowledge without any linkages to the natural world or the community. This systemic detachment has been uniformly imposed, which has the effect of suppressing alternate means of knowledge formation and maintaining a rigid educational structure.

The idea that schools and universities should be rethought as simply vehicles for consumerist societies is strongly supported by Ivan Illich's (1995) call for deschooling, which has a great resonance with what we are seeking to achieve through Pax Africana, thereby de-colonising our society. With their reliance on Western educational paradigms, post-colonial African colleges are unable to successfully merge with indigenous institutions, which contributes to the perpetuation of a sense of detachment from the local identity.

The advent of a community movement, and communiversity, such as ours, poses a challenge to the conventional understanding of education, encouraging the development of an atmosphere in which individuals with varying intelligences can thrive. By integrating various forms of learning that are entrenched in community contexts, this movement goes beyond the confines of education that is centred on students attending universities.

In the university, knowledge is not confined to theoretical worlds but rather is actively applied and merged with reality. This is because the university acts as a laboratory of action and philosophy. In doing so, it promotes an understanding that education is inseparable from one's surrounding environment by highlighting the fact that education is not separate from communities but rather entrenched throughout them. Herein we highlight the significance of embracing one's local identity and acknowledging the origins of others, so highlighting the power that is associated with place.

Integral Research and Societal Regeneration

The move from Esanland, communally and enterprise-wise, and PaxHerbal corporately and management-wise, onto Pax African communiversity four world (Pax's) -wise, onto Societal Regeneration (Re-GENE-Afrika) represents an associative, societal and thereby communitalist move towards determining the future of Africa. REGENE AFRICA.

Not only does this communal-corporate-communiversity-comunitalist metamorphosis involve a change in name, but it also signifies a paradigm shift in the way that things are done. A diverse but associated community of enterprises centred in the healing wisdom of Africa is something that Re-GENE-Afrika is proud to embrace. It acknowledges, moreover, the importance of transcultural and transdisciplinary research and innovation, both technological and social, with a view to societal regeneration, recognising that the difficulties that Africa faces demand answers that are varied and holistic in nature. The goal is not simply to theorise; rather, it is to put into practice solutions that are both realistic and durable, and that are anchored in African nature, culture, and worldview, in its variegated guises.

As such, despite its lofty aspirations, Re-GENE-Afrika continues to maintain a firm footing in the actual world. The organization's vision is to steer Africa towards a future that is powered by the inherent resourcefulness and inventiveness of the continent. In order to accomplish this, it strives to build cutting-edge educational, technical, political, and economic models that are deeply founded in indigenous practices and beliefs. This goal is not merely about imitating foreign systems; rather, it is about building native solutions that resonate with the values and context of Africa.

The influence of Re-GENE-Afrika is not limited to the realm of academia. By doing so, the narrative of African development is being rewritten, and the very foundations of the continent's progress are being called into question. It seeks to construct a new trajectory for the continent by revamping not only the educational system but also the key pillars of Africa's development paradigm. This new trajectory will draw from Africa's rich cultural legacy while simultaneously embracing innovation and progress.

The transition from TSA to Re-GENE-Afrika is, in essence, a revolutionary step towards proactive problem-solving. It is a step towards a future in which Africa is able to realise its full potential by combining traditional African knowledge with modern technological advancements. The purpose of this new narrative is not only to make progress; rather, it is to redefine Africa's identity and to liberate the continent's genuine potential.

C4.6 Communiversity and Communitalism: from Nigeria to Zimbabwe with Love

In the ever-expanding tapestry of herbal knowledge and holistic healing, the story of Sister Yulita Chirawu stands as a testament to the transformative power of education and community-driven initiatives. Her journey, nurtured by Paxherbals, illuminates the profound impact of sharing wisdom and fostering local expertise.

Back in 2006, Sister Yulita embarked on a quest for traditional medicine wisdom, finding her way from Harare, Zimbabwe, to the nurturing grounds of Paxherbals in Nigeria. Introduced by a Catholic monk at the Benedictine Monastery near Harare, her path was set to embrace the essence of African traditional medicine. Paxherbals became her haven, her temple of learning, where she immersed herself for six months in a comprehensive training regimen. Here, she absorbed not just the principles of African traditional medicine but also imbibed the business models meticulously crafted by PaxHerbals.

Her purpose echoed a beautiful resonance: to transplant the PaxHerbal model, enriched by her learnings and tailored to the intricacies of Zimbabwe's local landscape. A vision was sown, nurtured by knowledge, and cultivated with a dedication that surpassed boundaries.

Fast forward to 2016, and Anselm Adodo, the visionary behind PaxHerbals, witnessed the blossoming fruition of Sister Yulita's efforts. The LCBL herbal centre in Harare stood as a thriving testament to her dedication and the fertile ground nurtured by Paxherbals. Its growth, its scale, and its impact left an indelible mark on Adodo, showcasing the profound success of Sister Yulita's work.

And now, in 2023, the blossoming dream has transcended into reality. The Zimbabwe Education Commission's approval for a school of herbal medicine at the LCBL centre stands as a beacon of hope, marking the birth of a community. This landmark achievement embodies the essence of communitalism principles, embracing education, healing, and community as interconnected facets.

Blessed Hands Herbals, nestled amidst Zimbabwe's verdant heart, has emerged as more than a herbal organisation; it's a catalyst for transformation. Rooted in faith and propelled by the LCBL Sisters' dedication, it seamlessly blends ancient wisdom with modern practices.

Their holistic approach, a synthesis of tradition and science, is the cornerstone of their success. Owning the entire supply chain, from garden to clinic, ensures unparalleled quality and a harmonious blend of traditional knowledge and contemporary methodologies.

The establishment of the first-ever herbal academy in Zimbabwe stands as a testament to their commitment to demystifying traditional medicine. Bridging the gap between ancestral wisdom and scientific validation, the academy fosters a new generation of herbalists and medical professionals, advocating for wider acceptance and integration of herbal remedies into mainstream healthcare.

At the core of Blessed Hands lies their herbal clinic, where trained herbalists, guided by Pax Herbal Clinic's teachings, offer personalised care for diverse ailments. This patient-centric approach empowers individuals to take control of their well-being, nurturing a sense of agency and hope.

Investing in the future remains their unwavering ethos. Their research endeavours explore Zimbabwe's rich flora for natural solutions to prevalent health challenges. Their dedication to diabetes, cancer, and blood pressure control reflects a commitment to integrate natural remedies seamlessly into conventional medical practices.

The Blessed Hands Herbal Clinic is not merely a treatment centre; it's a sanctuary where nature whispers remedies for ailments. From respiratory concerns to digestive harmony, their herbal arsenal offers solace and restoration. Their embrace extends to women's health and circulatory system support, offering hope in the face of health adversities.

Stepping into Blessed Hands transcends the clinical; it's an immersion into nature's healing embrace. Each patient's journey begins with a holistic diagnosis, delving into physical, emotional, and spiritual aspects for a complete understanding.

Nature's personalised remedies, drawn from Zimbabwe's rich flora and tailored to individual needs, stand as testaments to gentle healing. But healing at Blessed Hands extends beyond herbs; skilled therapists offer massages and reflexology, harmonising body and soul.

The vision for Blessed Hands extends far beyond their current horizons. Their aspiration to establish satellite clinics across Zimbabwe and neighbouring Southern African countries echoes their commitment to holistic healthcare accessibility.

The Herbal Academy, a pioneer in Zimbabwean herbal education, reflects the LCBL Sisters' dedication to preserving traditional medicine. From foundation courses to advanced studies, the academy prepares practitioners to champion natural remedies for the greater good.

Sister Yulita's journey, from PaxHerbals to leading the charge in Zimbabwe's herbal revolution, is a testament to the transformative potential of education and shared wisdom. Her story is woven into the expanding tapestry of the Communiversity, a legacy of empowerment, healing, and community thriving across Africa.

C4.7 Conclusion

C4.7.1. Re-GENE-Afrika's Aspiration for Re-GENE-ration

PaxHerbal's Transformation Journey: Integral Research to Societal Re-GENE-ration

A fundamental goal lies at the core of Re-Gene Afrika; this aspiration is for Africa to undergo a complete rejuvenation, rebirth, and revival within this time period. Initiating a comprehensive transition across every aspect of African society is not only about development; rather, it is about bringing about fundamental change. The goal that we have is a holistic tapestry that is weaved with the threads of societal advancement, cultural preservation, environmental sustainability, and educational empowerment. It also reflects, for one of us, Anselm Adodo via PaxHerbal in Africa, albeit in association with the others, Ronnie Lessem via Trans4m worlds-wide, in association with significant others, the transformation journey he, his community and organisation, if not yet African society re-GENE-ratively as a whole, has undergone (see Figure 4.6.1. below) over the past three decades.

Figure C4.7.1: *Transformation Journey in African Heartlands*

	PATH OF REASON	
	Pax Africana	
	Emancipatory **N***avigation*	
	COMMUNIVERSITY	
	Integration/Social Innovation	
	Yoruba/Benedictine/Integral	
REALISATION PATH	INTEGRAL RESEARCH	RENEWAL PATH
Re-GENE-Africa	Healing Wisdom of Africa	PaxHerbal
Transformative Effect	*Centreing*	*Emergent Foundation*
COMMUNITALISM	CO-CREATION	CORPORATION
Pan-African **Association**	**Quadruple Heritage**	Spirited Scientific **Management**
Integral/Benedictine/Yoruba Muslim/Secular	Indigenous/Christian/	Yoruba/Secular
	RELATIONAL PATH	
	Esanland	
	Original **Grounding**	
	COMMMUNAL	
	Pioneering Enterprise	
	Yoruba	

In pursuit then of ultimate societal regeneration, in retrospect, following Lievegoed's developing organisation, and thereafter society, Adodo started out, *pioneering* in and through Esanland, in his case though, unlike in Lievegoed's more individualistically pioneering, European one, individually *and* communally. Moreover, thereafter corporate-wise, as a now corporate PaxHerbal, such conventionally secular *scientific management* was also spiritually inspired, in his case, by the Benedictine mission of ora (prayer) and labora (work). The next phase of *integration*, as we have seen above, serve to combine indigenous Yoruba `(orisa), exogenous Benedictine (pax's) and our own integral worlds, in now communiversity guise. Penultimately then, and in *association* with individual and institutional others, pan-Africa if not also worlds-wise, we take an integral lead, combining southern, eastern, northern and west African forces, ultimately as such centred in the healing wisdom of Africa.

In such centring guise, moreover, we revisit the renowned work of the late Kenyan American philosopher Ali Mazrui (Mazrui 1986) on *The Africans* whereby he has drawn on Africa's "triple heritage" – indigenous, Muslim and Christian – where we have added *secular*. Moreover, while the Muslim heritage is missing, explicitly, from Pax Africana, it is certainly markedly present in our *Hausa* Nigeria, as well as in our third case story in Sekem in Egypt.

C4.7.2. Towards a Societal PhD: Integral Research/ Societal Re-GENE-ration

Our purpose is to ignite this vision via the empowering of communities, the nurturing of educational institutions, and the formation of collaborative partnerships that represent the essence of sustainable progress that is ingrained in the African mentality, most specifically the healing wisdom of Africa in its natural and cultural, technological and economic guises, integrally altogether. Moreover, as we have seen in the PaxHerbal case, this involves a transformation journey from community (pioneering) to corporation (scientific management) onto communiversity (integration) and communitalism (association).

Revisiting his own Paxherbal journey, through communally *pioneering* and scientifically *managing*, corporately hitherto, through a uniquely indigenous Yoruba and exogenous Benedictine-secular combination, the further move towards integration, via an emerging communiversity – Pax Africana – was promoted via a distinctive collaboration between community, spirituality industry and academe. This, in retrospect, he now viewed, in Africa, together with fellow author, Ronnie Lessem, as a *societal* PhD, as distinct form an academic or professional one. This will be elaborated upon in our final chapter.

Re-GENE-Afrika is not simply embarking on a mission; rather, it is a firm commitment – a commitment to a future in which Africa thrives in harmony with its environment, culture, and other forms of industry. All are welcome to accept this offer, which is a call to a future in which education does not only serve to amass information but rather serves as a driving force behind significant transformation.

C4.8. References

Adodo A (2012) *Nature Power: A Christian Approach to Herbal Medicine. New Edition.* Edo State. Benedictine Publication

Adodo A (2017) *Integral Community Enterprise in Africa: Communitalism as an Alternative to Capitalism.* Abingdon. Routledge

Gibbons M, **Limoges** C, **Nowotny** H, **Schwartzman** S, **Scott** P and **Trow** M (1994) *The New Production of Knowledge: The Dynamics of Science and Research in Contemporary Societies.* London. Sage

Illich I (1995) *De-Schooling Society.* London. Marion Boyars

Lessem R and **Schieffer** A (2015) *Integral Renewal.* Abingdon. Routledge

Lessem R, **Adodo** A and **Bradley** T (2019) *The Idea of the Communiversity.* Manchester, Beacon. Academic

Lievegoed B (1991) *The Developing Organisation.* Chichester. Wiley-Blackwell

Mandela N (1994) *The Long Walk to Freedom.* New York. Abacus

Mazrui A (1986) *The Africans.* New York. Praeger

Otto R (1958) *The Idea of the Holy.* Oxford. Oxford University Press

Part 6 University to Communiversity/ Capitalism/Socialism to Communitalism

Chapter 17 Cooperative Inquiry/Trans-Doctoral Program: Towards Societal Re-Gene-Ration in and Through Africa

At the opposite end from healing is the illness of not being able to accept or even tolerate those who are different from us. Worse, this inability encourages suspicion, fear, and resentment. Thus it is an illness of the collective psyche when different cultures don't understand one another. The history of humankind is plagued by this psychic disease that has caused much pain and disappointment in the world, as we still see today. Methods of healing, then, must take into account the energetic or spiritual condition that is in turmoil, thereby affecting the physical condition.

Malidoma Some (1987) The Healing Wisdom of Africa

We reject the power-based society of the Westerner that seems to be ever concerned with perfecting their technological know-how while losing out on their spiritual dimension. We believe that in the long-run the special contribution from Africa will be in the field of human relationships. The great powers of the world may have done wonders in giving the world an industrial and military look, but the great gift still has to come from Africa – giving the world a human face.

Steve Biko (1987)   I Write What I Like

Mode 2 knowledge production, is trans-disciplinary rather than mono or multi-disciplinary. It is carried out in non-hierarchical, heterogeneously organized forms which are essentially transient. It is not being institutionalised primarily within university structures. This means that knowledge production is becoming more socially accountable affecting the deepest levels what shall count as "good science".

Gibbons et al (1994)   The New Production of Knowledge

Peace comes when we transcend our fears by accepting our place in the universe, and accept others as they are. Fear is a source of violence and war. When we have peace, we stop harming others. We begin to relate to others and people with honour and dignity. We stop exploiting and cheating others. This is what Pax is all about: communitalism in action. How then does this work? Paxherbals believe that the only way to sustainable development is for Africa to produce what it consumes and consume what it produces. But to produce, one must innovate. Paxherbals is determined to continue to champion the preservation of Africa indigenous knowledge, for the sake of posterity, of African medicine, and for the sake of PAX AFRICANA, altogether, and integrally as such, thereby embracing worldviews, or realities, from all four corners of the globe, through Pax Natura (south), Pax Spiritus (east), Pax Scientia (north) and Pax Economics (west).

Anselm Adodo (2017)   Pax Africana

Given the condition of our times, a primary purpose of human inquiry is not so much to search for the truth but to heal, to make whole. The co-operative paradigm has two wings, that is political (value based) and epistemic (knowledge based). Co-operative inquiry, as such, does research with other people, as full co-inquirers, committed to both politically and epistemologically.

John Heron (Bhaskar 2002) Cooperative Inquiry

Summary : Trans-Doctoral Cooperative Inquiry into Societal Re-GENE-ration : *Trans-doctoral Program, Healing Context, Communiversity Form, Re-GENE-rative Process, Communitalist Sunbstance, Ecosystemic Polity, Integral Enterprise Product*

- The *trans-doctoral* PROGRAM proposed as a co-operative inquiry , is *trans-cultural*, in its pan-African CONTEXT; *trans-disciplinary* in its micro community building and macro communitalist SUBSTANCE; *trans-personal* in its individual, communal, organisational, societal, communiversity FORM; spearheaded by a *trans-formative* PROCESS, turning integral research into innovation, as social re-GENE-ration, experientially, imaginatively, conceptually, practically

- The *trans-cultural* CONTEXT of our *PAX AFRICANA* is embodied in the *HEALING WISDOM OF AFRICA*, constituted of healing the divides between ho   mestead and   workplace (Integral Kumusha), community and enterprise (Good African Story), (wo)man and nature healing the earth (Sekem), indigenous and exogenous knowledge (Pax Africana)

- Our *trans-discplinary* SUBSTANCE involves its southern   African nature and heritage (Nhakanomics) via Integral Kumusha in Zimbabwe, south-east African spirit and culture (Yurugu-nomics) via Good African Coffee Story, north-south African science (Regenerative Value Creation) via Sekem in Egypt, and western Africa enterprise (generic Communitalism) via Paxherbals in Nigeria, bringing peace/prosperity, cosmologically centred in the *HEALING WISDOM OF AFRICA*

- The FORM *of* delivery of such is an inter-institutional *COMMUNIVERSITY* serving to co-evolve nature and community (Learning Community), culture and spirituality (Pax Spiritus/Trans4mation Journey), social science and technology   (Pax Scientia /Research Academy) and economy and enterprise (Socio-technical Laboratory); transcends the conventional university

- Our individually and institutional PROCESS of integral research and societal re-GENE-ration that underlies such, begins with natural Grounding and origination (Pax Natura), Emerges through a cultural foundation (Pax Sp iritus); Navigates in emancipatory scientific guise (Pax Scientia); realizing its transformative   Effect economically (Pax   Economica), thereby transcending standardised approaches to individual education and research

- The people concerned with such,   our governing POLITY, are not conventional faculty and students, on one academic hand, nor is there the   conventional divide between industry, community and academe, on the other, but communal *stewardship*, academic *researchers and educators*, and industrial   *developers*, altogether aligned through *catalysation*, form now an *INNOVATION ECOSYSTEM*   spread across community,   enterprise and academe, duly and purposefully interconnected

- Ultimately the PRODUCT of our cooperative endeavours is the further development, within themselves ultimately prolifically w ithout, and on a pan -African basis, *to a quantitatively measurable as well as qualitatively measured effect*, of *INTEGRAL ENTERPRISES* like our affiliated *KUMUSHA and NATIONAL HEALTHCARE* (southern Africa), *COFFEE STORY* (east Africa), *SEKEM* (north Africa) , and *PAX HERBALS* (west Africa) , thereby turning marketing into *community building;* human resources into *conscious evolution ;* operations into *knowledge creation,* and finance exclusively, into the realization of sustainable development, goals, inclusively.

17.1. Introduction to Our Re-GENE-rative Constitution

17.1.1. Context, Process, Substance, Form, Program and Product

In this concluding chapter we turn to the prospective doctoral and trans-doctoral programs, and overall re-GENE-rative orientation, needed to take our story integrally on. Set in a trans-cultural ***African healing*** context, a trans-formative *process* of research and innovation, a trans-disciplinary communitalist *substance*, a transpersonal communiversity *form*, the integral *programmes* that follow, are altogether aligned with co-operative inquiry (see above), focused on societal re-GENE-ration.

What underpins such, moreover, is something very different from the conventional form of academic *polity*, that is rather our *innovation* ecosystem as we shall see, and a very different product from a mere business, economic, or other form of qualification, that is, rather, a community based *integral enterprise*. Such a *product* as such, ultimately both measurable and measured, in conventional terms, leads in micro-terms to sustainable development, and in macro terms towards societal re-GENE-ration.

17.1.2. Healing, Regeneration, Communitalism and Communiversity

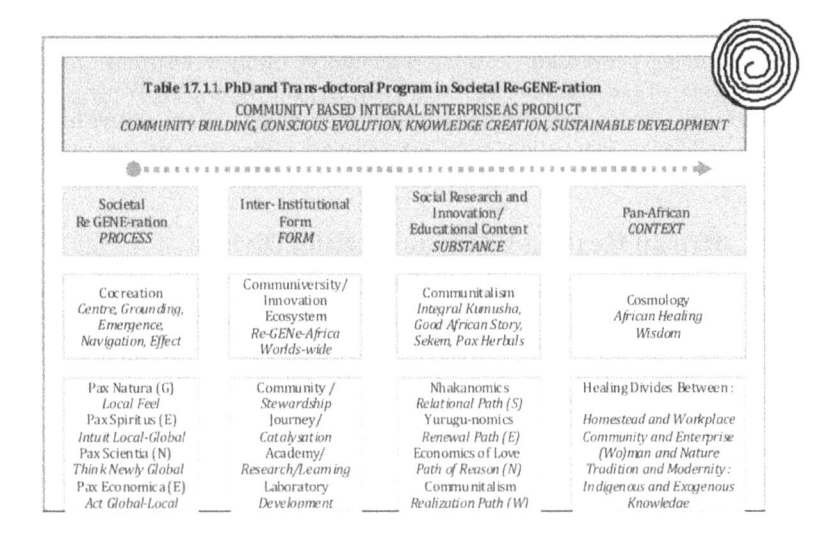

Table 17.1.1. PhD and Trans-doctoral Program in Societal Re-GENE-ration
COMMUNITY BASED INTEGRAL ENTERPRISE AS PRODUCT
COMMUNITY BUILDING, CONSCIOUS EVOLUTION, KNOWLEDGE CREATION, SUSTAINABLE DEVELOPMENT

Societal Re-GENE-ration PROCESS	Inter-Institutional Form FORM	Social Research and Innovation/ Educational Content SUBSTANCE	Pan-African CONTEXT
Cocreation Centre, Grounding, Emergence, Navigation, Effect	Communiversity/ Innovation Ecosystem Re-GENe-Africa Worlds-wide	Communitalism Integral Kumusha, Good African Story, Sekem, Pax Herbals	Cosmology African Healing Wisdom
Pax Natura (G) Local Feel Pax Spiritus (E) Intuit Local-Global Pax Scientia (N) Think Newly Global Pax Economica (E) Act Global-Local	Community / Stewardship Journey/ Catalysation Academy/ Research/Learning Laboratory Development	Nhakanomics Relational Path (S) Yurugu-nomics Renewal Path (E) Economics of Love Path of Reason (N) Communitalism Realization Path (W)	Healing Divides Between: Homestead and Workplace Community and Enterprise (Wo)man and Nature Tradition and Modernity: Indigenous and Exogenous Knowledge

Such ***regeneration*** (see Table 17.1.1.below) draws on our core, integral "social technology" underlying integral research and innovation in Africa, that is our GENE: Grounding locally, Emerging locally-globally, Navigating newly globally, with a view to Effecting globally-locally. This reverses the conventional logic of think global, act local.

Moreover and secondly, from the outset, *SUBSTANTIVE*ely, we seek to co-evolve, economically, one or other societal, **communitalist** alternatives to capitalism or socialism, starting out, enterprise wise, with community building rather than individual marketing. To that extent we invariably, and in *trans-disciplinary* guise, start out with the nature and culture of an enterprise and community, and build our approach to science and technology, polity and economy from there.

17.1.3. Communiversity Structure and Innovation Ecosystem Operation

Thirdly, the *FORM* of the conventional, stand alone university, especially in the social sciences and humanities with which we are primarily concerned, is unable to turn such integral research into societal re-GENE-ration, which is our intent. To realize such, in trans-personal guise, individually and collectively, we ground our so called **communiversity** in learning communities (further to community outreach), set alongside socio-economic laboratories (rather than individual secondments), further enhanced by transformation journeys (over and above education), altogether under the umbrella of a centre (integral research academy centred in an African society).

Indeed such a communiversity needs a different governance structure or polity, from conventional academe, where faculty and students are hierarchically arranged, involving *stewardship* (learning community); *catalysation* (transformation journey); *research and education* (research academy) and *development* (integral laboratory). Indeed, and in tune with the ethical underpinning of co-operative inquiry, research, and for us innovation, is undertaken *with* rather then *on* communities, ecologically and socio-economically, set within an **innovation ecosystem.**

17.1.4. African Healing Wisdom: Healing Divides

All of such takes place in a pan-African *CONTEXT* centred in the **Healing Wisdom of Africa** . Such prospective societal regeneration ranges from healing the divide between:

- **homestead and workplace** (*Nhakanomics* in Southern Africa);
- **enterprise and community** (*Yurugu-nomics* in East Africa)
- **(wo)man and nature** (*Economics of Love* in North Africa)
- **tradition and modernity** (generic *communitalism* in West Africa).

17.1.5. Community-Based Integral Enterprise as End Product

This brings us onto our end *PRODUCT,* that is a community based Integral Enterprise transforming marketing into **community building**; human resources into **conscious evolution;** operations into **knowledge creation**, finance into *sustainable development* as well as overall profitable into **healing strategies** Such community based integral enterprise, therefore, is altogether centred in the healing wisdom of Africa, serving to re-GENE-rate society, constituting a socio-economic laboratory within a communiversity, and substantively contributing, in micro guise, to the development of communitalism, in macro guise, and vice versa, in one societal context or another.

We now turn to each element of the above regenerative Constitution in turn, starting with our re-GENE-rative process which, as we saw in Chapter 15, took on from where Roy Bhaskar's critical realism and so called meta-reality left off, also aligned with John Heron's modes of Co-operative Inquiry, developed early in the new millennium (Bhaskar) in in the latter part of the old one (Heron). Moreover, one of us (Ronnie Lessem) had a strong personal connection. With each of these leading lights.

17.2. *Process* of Societal Re-GENE-ration

17.2.1. Meta-Reality to Transformative Agency

The possibility of human emancipation, for Bhaskar (2002) then, depended not on "western" democratic freedoms and free markets, but on expanding the zone of "non-duality" – our four worlds – within our lives, which can be aligned, in turn, with Heron's (1997) four modes of knowing: experiential, imaginal, conceptual and practical . Such also builds on what he termed a *"ground-state"*. It is the level upon which all other levels depend. It also serves to build on his prior notion of an underlying, generative reality. Altogether, in this newly "meta-real" case, every human situation, as such, must now be characterised by MELDA (see below), which had a profound influence on our own GENE-tic orientation. Indeed such MELDA can also be aligned with our *Pax Africana*, as below:

M: an element of potential, which corresponds to the critical realist domain of stratified ontology, grounded in Meta-reality (M): our local original <u>Grounding</u>, which can be aligned, as below for us, with *Pax Natura*, and with *unhu* laden <u>Nhakanomics,</u> and also with research philosopher John Heron's *experiential* mode of knowing (see Chapter 16)

E: creativity, that is the Emergence (E) of something new, even if this novelty is a repeat of the old, which would not otherwise have occurred: our local-global *Emergent* foundation, as also our *Pax Spiritus,* and with *asili* laden Yurugu-nomics, and *imaginal* knowing

L: any human situation must be characterised by that form of bonding, solidarity, compassion, care and consideration that Bhaskar calls, altogether, Love (L), as indeed has been the case for Sekem's <u>Economics of Love</u> in thereby *north* Africa aligned with *maat*: newly global emancipatory <u>Navigation</u>, our *Pax Scientia,* and *conceptual* knowing

D: each agent in the situation needs to be capable of Doing (D) something, spontaneously and correctly so that in each situation, creating an effect: our newly global-local transformative *Effect*, our *Pax Economica* giving rise to *orisa* laden Communitalism, as well as, for Heron, now *practical* knowing that needs to build on all that has come before.

We now turn to our re-GENE-rative process in more detail, standing on Bhaskar's and Heron's giant shoulders, also as prospectively aligned with the form of our communiversity (structural functions), and innovation ecosystem (operational roles).

17.2.2. Grounding to Effect

Our approach to the process of integral research and innovation, as a means of releasing GENE-ius, locally (Grounding), locally-globally (Emergence), newly globally (Navigation) and globally locally (Effect) both then in yourself and also, simultaneously and interactively, in your – in this case African – world, takes account of such (inevitably you will be a mix of worlds, but with one or other taking precedence). Our integral research and innovation trajectory, inclusive of *Pax Africana*, now also underlying societal re-GENE-ration involves:

- *Original Grounding*: Cycles of Life: "Southern" Humanistic (and more than Human) Reality: you experience the world primarily through relationships: relationship to nature (including your inner nature) and to other human beings and to the community you belong to, and are enfolded within, as again in *Pax Natura*
- *Emergent Foundation*: Developmental Spiral: "Eastern" Holistic Reality: you imagine the world primarily through an inner-directed cultural and spiritual perspective, seeking to understand the meaning of human existence, how life and the universe unfold, as in Pax *Spiritus* in the Pax Africana case
- *Emancipatory Navigation*: Line of Argument: "Northern" Rational Reality: you see the world primarily from a scientific, rational and systemic perspective, seeking to distinguish structures and processes within reality and to translate them into viable concepts and systems, as in Pax *Scientia*
- *Transformative Effect*: The Point of It: "Western" Pragmatic Reality: you act on the world primarily through experimentation and practical treatment of things, emphasising the application of ideas through action, pointing the way toward goal achievement, as in Pax *Economica*.

17.2.3. Generic Process Towards the Communiversity Form

The GENE rhythm then, our core integral "technology" encompasses research, on alternately relational, renewal, reasoned and realisation paths, and-innovation, via Nhakanomics, Yurugu-nomics and the Economics of Love towards Communitalism, towards societal re-GENE-ration, involving more specifically then, and building further on the above:

- G = *Grounding and Origination: Cyclical – Experiential:* Communal Learning*:*
You, individually and collectively, are *grounded* in a particular nature and community, which needs to be engaged with, if not also *activated*. For any living system, the "southern" grounds – herein *Southern* Africa as per our Integral *Kumusha* – represent its *local identity* and its *source of origin*. "Southern" grounding is about *being* in as well as feeling and *experiencing,* as well as *describing* a particular world, which thereafter continually cycles through, and indeed is recycled in *narrating* the stories we are. As such, and overall, you not only respond to a *call*, individually and collectively, but also begin to *activate* a community, altogether embodied, Communiversity-wise, in *Communal Learning*, in, for Pax Africana, *Pax Natura* underpinned by *Unhu* laden *Nhakanomics*

- E = *Emergent Foundation: Spiralling – Imaginative:* Transformation Journey*:*
Moving to "eastern" emergence – herein *East* Africa as per our *Good African Story* – locates you and your community in a developing organisational and societal *context*, co-engaging with a *life world*, duly *interpreting* the imbalances (incompleteness) therein, with a view to alleviating (completeness) them. Here, we envisage dialectic interaction between "local and global", thereby coming to a newly imagined understanding, individually and collectively, with a view to *catalysing development.*
Such an emergent, spiralling process always includes a "stepping into the unknown" and "letting go" thereby becoming as it were a *local-global nonentity* – of some of the previous assumptions. New insights emerge, from out of the blue as it were, that provide clues for the transformative process. "Eastern" emergence is therefore essentially about *becoming*. It deals with *intuiting* and *imagining* the new *emergent* form, contained in spaces in between one existing form and another, altogether embodied in out *Transformation Journey,* via *Pax Spiritus* underpinned by *Asili* laden *Yurugu-nomics*

- N = *Emancipatory Navigation: Linear/Conceptual:* Research Academy*:*
The move to "northern" navigation requires that the new insights gained are translated into new *concepts*, new knowledge, new technologies, new institutions, that now assume global, or universal, proportions. "Northern" navigation – as with *Sekem* in *North* Africa – is hence about *knowing* and about *making explicit* what hitherto had been rather implicit, through innovation driven *research* (method and substance).
"Northern" *navigation* is about activating the *mind*-level, exercising conceptual prowess, through *critical* emancipatory thinking, without losing touch with the emotional and spiritual levels that came before. At this point we conceive a newly *global* entity, as a new concept or even institution, forming the basis now for a universalizable line of argument, or activity, altogether embodied in our *Research Academy,* embodying *Pax Scientia* underpinned, following Bhaskar and Sekem, by *Maat* laden *Economics of Love.*

- E = *Transformative Effect: Point – Practical:* Socio-economic Laboratory*:*
Moving to "western" effect – as embodied by our *Paxherbals* in *West* Africa – finally now requires us to put all prior three levels into integrated, *practical*

action. It is about pragmatically applying the new knowledge that has been developed, thereby actualising the research and innovation that it contains, thereby making a *contribution* to the *education* of you, your organisation and/ or society. "Western" effect is hence about *doing* and about *making it happen,* thereby "to the point".

This is the penultimate *transformative* level of the GENE-process, activating, metaphorically, the *body* or *hand*. This is the time where the newly global is actualised at a local level, through a *socio-economic laboratory*, Pax Economica ultimately underpinned by *Orisa* laden *Communitalism* as a whole.

All of the above, ultimately, needs to be *centred* in the *healing wisdom of Africa*, cosmologically and strategically, thereby healing divides between: homestead and workplace; enterprise and community; (wo)man and nature; tradition and modernity.

Having completed the GENE-tic storyline, and Communiversity/Communitalism-orientation, experientially-imaginatively-conceptually-practically-integrally, the process does not stop. Rather, it continuously moves on, in circular (iterative), spiralling (evolving) and linear (accumulative) as well as ultimately pointed (directive) form. Any transformative effect has to be continuously revisited, exploring whether it remains resonant with the "southern" grounds (e.g. the needs of nature and community) it seeks to serve. We now turn fully from generic process to our trans-modern communiversity form, born out of pre-modern African tradition, constituted, as you will see, at the *birth of African civilisation.*

17.3. Communiversity *Form*: Epistemology and Polity Reconstituted

17.3.1. Functional Elements: Community, Journey, Academy, Laboratory

The Limits of Learning

We now proceed to reconstitute both Roy Bhaskar's Meta-reality, and John Heron's co-operative inquiry laden epistemology and polity in our so called communiversity guise. For whereas Bhaskar aligned research with societal regeneration, Heron considered the research process to be not only epistemological but also political, if not also, as for us, economic. Societal regeneration, for both then, as for us, needs to be co-evolved, inter/institutionally, trans-/personally and cross/sectorally via what we term a communiversity, aligning public, private, civic and environmental sectors.

What is important to recognize is that developing such a communiversity is easier said than done, because each of the communal, individual, institutional and enterprise constituents are inclined to paddle their own canoe, as it were. Learning is characteristically oriented to individuals rather than to whole communities,, and lacks the developmental thrust of a transformation journey. Academe in the social sciences and humanities tends to have its conventional "publish or perish" research agenda, rather than focusing on societal regeneration. Socio/economic laboratories – this is different in the natural sciences – are seldom to be found communiversity-wise as such.

Therefore, we have struggled for decades to establish an integral research academy within a conventional university, up to now to no ultimate avail, indeed in Africa, in MENA, in Europe and America. Having hitherto battled against standardised (northern), decontextualised (devoid of southern and eastern) and overly individualised (western) research activities, now the time has come to establish such an integral research academy, though now within a communiversity that takes distributed "mode 2" (see opening quote) knowledge creation seriously. In fact, for one of us, Anselm Adodo, three out of the four communiversity functions (community, journey and laboratory) are well established, in Nigeria, and it is only the research academy, set alongside, rather than within, a suitable, mode 2 oriented, university, that is still pending.

The Idea of a Communiversity

In fact, The Idea of a Communiversity (McNeely & Wolverton, 2008), firstly came to us via the seminal work of American historians McNeely and Wolverton (Lessem et al, 2019), *Reinventing Knowledge: Alexandria to the Internet,* in modern guise. Secondly it was regenerated, also duly informed by our overall GENE-ric approach, when, in traditional guise, we came across the pathbreaking work of African American historian Chancellor Williams (1993) on *The Birth of African Civilisation.* For therein he introduced the notion of *traditional age sets* in Africa, which immediately also rang a contemporary integral bell, illustrating why exogenous employment and indigenous livelihood have been torn asunder in the modern world.

Indeed we have now newly aligned such pre-modern age sets with our transmodern communiversity (in CAP's below), where community and laboratory meet, also duly aligned with the functionality of our *Pax Africana,* as our modal Communiversity in Nigeria. Each age-set, as such, had its an educational as well as a social, economic and political dimension to it, which, with a bit of the stretch of the imagination, as can be seen below, can be aligned with our communiversity (in CAP'S): learning community (childhood), transformation journey (youth), research academy (adulthood), socio-economic laboratory (maturity).

Grounding in Nature/Community: Childhood – Storytelling and Naming: 6–12

LEARNING COMMUNITY/*PAX NATURA*
The children's age set for Williams, to begin with, covers the years of game and play. *Primary education includes <u>storytelling, community songs and dances, as well as learning natural names</u> of various birds and animals,* and identification of poisonous

snakes, local plants and trees, and how to run and climb swiftly when pursued by dangerous animals.

Emergent Culture/Spirituality: Youth: Geography and History: 13–18
TRANSFORMATION JOURNEY/*PAX SPIRITUS*

The next grade above childhood involved teenage-hood (these periods varied of course amongst different societies). Now both education and responsibilities were stepped up, becoming more complex and extensive. The youth's entire future depended upon their performance at this level. *The boy was now required to learn his extended family history and <u>trajectory of the society</u>, including also the geography and history of the region, names of neighbouring states and the nature of the relations with them. The girl's age-group* differed from that of the boys. While they had the same intellectual education – history, geography, rapid calculation, poetry, music and dance – *education in childcare, housekeeping, gardening, cooking, social relations and marketing* was different.

Scientific/Technological Navigation: Young Adulthood: Planting/ Construction: 19–28
RESEARCH ACADEMY/*PAX SCIENTIA*

At the next stage education of *male members involved hunting, community construction, preparing the fields for planting, forming various industrial craft guilds,* including <u>engagement with secret societies</u>, *each of which guarded the processes of the art. The young women were generally responsible for planting and care of the farms, the operations of the markets, visiting and care of the sick and aged, the <u>formation of women's societies,</u> and overall responsibility for the home.*

Effective Political/Economic Midlife and Maturity: Elders' Council: 29–40
SOCIO-TECHNICAL LABORATORY/*PAX ECONOMICA*

There was not much difference, thereafter, between age groups C and D, for both men and women, whose constitutional rights were inseparable. At the age of 36, men and women were eligible for election to the most highly honoured body of society, the Council of Elders, most especially reserved for age-set E, that is <u>from 40 years onwards, whose role was social, political, economic and cultural altogether</u>.

By thereby combining "education" and "employment", as well as, if you like, "research" and "innovation", in contemporary guise, societies as a whole were integrated, albeit in pre-modern guise. As we can see the modern university has "skipped a beat", as it were, separating itself from prior community and subsequent enterprise, and we have sought to heal the pre/post modern divide, thereby centred in Africa's healing wisdom.

We now turn to the trans-modern communiversity, as we envisage it, taking on form where the pre-modern age sets leave off, though also drawing on modern pedagogical ideas, in more specific detail.

The Idea of a Communiversity: Functional Evolution

As then set out more specifically in *The Idea of a Communiversity*, we see:

<u>Locally Naturally and Communally Grounded in a Learning Community</u>

- A contextualised platform for *communal learning and development*, whereby human and more-than-human communities are enabled to reclaim/restore their potential
- *Communal/societal stewards* deeply immerse themselves in a particular natural and communal, local context, able to locally relate to other human beings and to nature
- Embodying the *web of life* representing mother nature; the circle of physical and human nature engaged respectively in human and more than human *community building*.

<u>Locally-Globally Trans-culturally Emerging through a Transformation Journey</u>

- Individual and collective *consciousness raising* releases cultural and economic genius, via a narrative, of self, organization, community, society, underlying a *transformation journey*
- A *development catalyst* is able to engage with cultural/economic dynamics of a particular entity/place, co-evolving with individual/institutional/societal others
- A spiral of *conscious co-evolution* represents the regeneration and renewal of the spirit, culture and economy, local-globally, of one place in relation to another

<u>Newly Global Emancipatory Scientific/Humanistic Navigation via Research Academy</u>

- Scholarship, research and knowledge creation – inter/institutionally and in inter-disciplinary guise – becomes a Centre for Integral Research and Societal Re-GENE-ration
- Promoting conceptual and analytical ability, through *research and education*, sharing knowledge in a group, generating "newly global" models of transformation
- the resulting grid of knowledge represents a structure-seeking and organised processes of transcultural *knowledge creation* across recognized disciplines.

Global-Local Transformative Political/Economic Effect via Socio-Economic Laboratory

- A focal point for *creative experimentation*/ a conducive space in which appropriate new practices can be conceived of, tested, implemented, in a *socio-economic laboratory*
- Overarching *facilitation of development*, serving to translate knowledge into capacities, globally-locally, thereby exercising overall governance
- focused, goal-oriented, co-creative, resulting in the active build-up of new infrastructure and institutions, now globally-locally, with a view to *sustainable development*.

We turn to the operationalisation our communiversity, via our so called innovation ecosystem, or transformative form of developmental polity.

17.3.2. Integral Polity – the Innovation Ecosystem: Stewardship to Development

Integral Governance/Innovation Ecosystem

For a conventional university geared towards *individual* education, if not also institutionalised research, its governing body, what we also term its "polity", is its academic hierarchy, with a council, senate, and departmental faculties to go with it. In our own comuniversity context, by way of such an alternative, integral governance, *communal* **stewardship;** *inter-institutional, cross-sectoral, transcultural* **catalysation**; *academic* **research and education**; and *laboratory* based **development** altogether ensue, with co-accreditation between all of the above necessarily following suit.

We now set out each of these ecosystemic roles in interdependent turn, located within what we (Lessem et al 2013) have termed an *innovation ecosystem*. Such an "ecosystem" then, is interdependent, and non-hierarchical in conventional terms, though it does contain and an integral trajectory, re-GENE-ratively so to speak, to replace such a power-laden hierarchy, typical of prevailing academe. This is more especially the case, ironically, in the global South with which we are primarily concerned.

Steward Forming Original Natural Grounding: Localised Learning Community

> **Steward : Local Grounding in Nature and Community**
> *e.g. Anselm Adodo, Ewo State Farming Community*
>
> - Actively engaged in thinking about the Future/rooted in a communal Past
> - Grounded in local learning community, as well as in Mother nature
> - An organic intellectual/grassroots thinker/practitioner in *Communitalism*
> - Supporting and promoting, individually/collectively from the communal ground up, the transformative platform/program and process of Journeying

Natural and communal grounding of our innovation ecosystem then, that is in our overall polity, is firstly promoted by "southern" stewardship, one of us (Anselm Adodo) being an example of such, in rural Nigeria, normally involving a senior community and/or religious leader such as he, leading business practitioner, public intellectual sometimes as government minister, together with communal others. How then is such local stewardship complemented by local-global catalysation?

Catalyst/Emerget Transcultural Foundation: Local/Global Trans4mation Journey

> **Catalyst : Local/Global Emergence via Culture/Spirituality**
> *e.g. Re-GENE Africa*
>
> - Promoting self, organizational and societal evolution, interconnecting indigenous and exogenous knowledge, underpinned by a shared moral narrative
> - Instead of well laid Course Curricula, the catalyst focuses on emerging, ever changing, intertwined Agendas in a Field of Possibilities.
> - Fostering inter-institutional Interaction with other Actors in the wider Environment, open to a Multiplicity of Worlds amongst Participants
> - Promoting interaction between learning communities, integral laboratories and a research academy, in an individual-societal transformation journey.

Local-global Emergence is secondly the realm of "south-eastern" catalysation, the role, for example, of a developmental group or entity, such as TCA whose task it is to promote the simultaneously co-evolution of community, laboratory and academy, alongside an individual's transformation journey. This is in fact the most crucial role in the establishment of an inter-institutional, indigenous-exogenous communiversity, and the one most often missing from conventional academe. However, that said, the role of the research academy, and transformative academics to spearhead such, is also key.

Research and Education via Research Academy/PhD; Trans-Doctoral Program

Navigating knowledge newly globally, and in now emancipatory, social scientific and technological guise, constitutes now "southern-northern" research and education, individually, and more especially institutionally. In our own Pax Africana case, this is where Nhakanomics, Yurugu-nomics, the Economics of Love and Communitalism comes into respective, African play, also building on prior, integral economic and enterprise foundations originally established by Trans4m.

Co-Researcher/Educator : Newly Global Navigation via Social Science/Technology
e.g. Centre for Integral Research and Societal Re-GENE-ration

- Researchers skilled at building from the ground up – from Mother nature and Moral narrative – towards developing social scientific Models
- Having experience of undertaking institutionalised Integral Research where they are required to turn social research into social innovation
- With conceptual Knowledge of, either, Community Building, Conscious Evolution, Knowledge Creation and Sustainable Development, and
- Nhakanomics, Yurgu-nomics, Economics of Love, Communitalism.

While such stewardship, catalysation and research as well as education is all important, for grounding, emergence and navigation, it still has to be out into transformative effect. In fact, the overall communiversity process is by no means a linear one, and each constituent of the innovation ecosystem could take the alternate lead.

Global-Local Political and Economic Development: Community-Laboratory

---

Developer : Promoting Global-Local Transformative Economic Effect
e.g. Pax Herbals Senior Practitioners

- Has an Economic /Engineering/Scientific or Ecological/Developmental Orientation
- Manages and develops Relationships within the Knowledge creating Community
- Builds in a measured way on Mother nature (community) via Moral narrative (journey), generating a scientific Model (academy, realising oikonomic Measures (laboratory)
- Draws on and from stewardship, catalysation and research to develop wellness associations communally and organisationally.

"South-western" development then enables the community and/or enterprise, in a particular context, aligned with our research academy to give such newly global reach, to realise a transformational global-local effect, as indeed we see in our

(Anselm Adodo) PaxHerbals case in Nigeria. So what prevents all of such arising in the first place?

People and Polity: Steward, Catalyst, Researcher/Educator, Developer

The Established Hierarchy Militates Against a Networked Communiversity

What militates against such a communiversity, and the process of integral research with a view to societal re-GENE-ration, innovation wise, to go with it, is the way conventional academe, on the one hand, and professional managers, community developers, or indeed government policy makers, on the other, conceive of themselves. In academe, firstly, the hierarchical structuring of institutionally empowered individual faculty and communally disempowered students militates again the kind of co-creation we seek. In the professions, managers and administrators all too often pursue a top-down as opposed to their starting, GENEtically, from the natural Ground up, albeit also building, middle-up down-across if you like, naturally-culturally-scientifically-economically.

Hence our focus, to begin with, is on communally empowered learning. However thereafter, so called community stewards, or senior, transformative figures in society tend to practically operate outside of the intellectual sphere promoted by academe, either seeing no need for the latter in their immediate activities, and/or being overawed by "the professors", especially those from the "global North". Thus our deliberate attempt to transcend that lofty academic-senior practitioner divide.

The Role of Catalysation as Vital: Linking together People, Institutions, Ideas

Moreover, developmentally minded practitioners in agriculture and industry have an altogether different temperament from the proverbial academic. Thereby, and most crucially, we see *the role of catalysation to be vital, linking together all the above people, institutions, and ideas,* indigenously and exogenously, across the public, private, civic and environmental sectors. Such, conventionally speaking, is, explicitly, rarely to be seen, individually and, especially, institutionally, left to uniquely "gifted" individuals .

The so called *innovation ecosystem* we then endeavour to put in place, as above – stewardship, catalysation, research and education, and development – becomes the essential operational, and altogether empowered, arm of the communiversity, replacing, at least centre stage, conventional academic faculty (empowered) and student (disempowered). Further to such, research or educational programs are accredited, so to speak, by steward, catalyst, researcher/educator and developer, individually and institutionally, alike, rather than exclusive by academic faculty.

The Natural Sciences Come Closer to the "Quadruple" Mark

This interactive and inclusive accreditation, in the social sciences and humanities, is virtually unprecedented. Conversely *the natural sciences come closer to this mark, through their science parks, and so called "quadruple helix" – government, industry, academy and community* – mutually and reciprocally accrediting advances in scientific research and technological innovation.

In our socio-economic guise, then, our innovation ecosystem overall then, through our constituent communities and enterprises, have a fundamental role to play in both operational and governance terms. We now turn from re-GENE-rative process and communiversity form, structurally and operationally, to economic, if not also political, substance, explicitly in Africa.

17.4. Communitalist *Substance* in Variegated African Guise

17.4.1. Nhakanomics, Yurugu-nomics, Economics of Love, and Communitalism

Herein, for example, we may seek to turn the substance of an African Studies program into one that facilitates the transformation of capitalism, socialism, and corporatism, centred in the healing wisdom of Africa, into, ultimately giving rise to communitalism, in one African guise or another. In other words, African Studies, as such, predominantly and conventionally lodged in the humanities, needs to be aligned with the social sciences and the professions, altogether integrally.

Taking on from where such illustrious predecessors of ours as Kwame Nkrumah (consciencism) and Julius Nyerere (ujamaa) individually, and politically-economically, left off, we may seek to turn ujamaa into south-eastern Yurugo-nomics and consciencism into south-western communitalism, amongst southern and southern-northern communitalist others. Community building at a micro level, we may be promoting nhakanomics, yurgu-nomics, the economics of love, and generic communitalism at a macro level. Such a substantive, integral orientation then spans enterprise (community building), economy (communitalism) and academe (communiversity) as well as African healing wisdom as a whole (cosmology).

Moreover, in Pan-African, or in what we rather term Pax Africana (see below) macro and micro guise, such <u>Nhakanomics</u> (Integral Kumusha), is a mere *southern relational* African stepping stone towards *east* African <u>Yurugu-nomics</u> (Good Africa Coffee Story) by way of *renewal*, the well *reasoned* <u>Economics of Love</u> (Sekem) in *north* Africa and ultimately working towards generic <u>Communitalism</u> (Pax Herbals) by way of *west* African *realisation*. It also altogether resonates with Bhaskar's MELDA:

- grounded in the *ivhu* (meaning soil in shona) aligned with *unhu* **M**eta-reality
- **E**merging from a seed – *asili* in Swahili – towards something more complete
- navigating via Egyptian *maat* toward the economics of **L**ove
- effectively and transformatively **D**oing good via the Yoruba *orisa* (energy forces)
- thereby **A**ctualising the healing wisdom of Africa.

17.4.2. From Individual Country in Pan Africa to Integral *Place* in Pax Africa

Ivhu, Asili, Maat, Orisa in South, East, North and West Africa

In the final Pax Africana analysis then, we take the ultimate, subtle step, of positioning each worldly part of an integral Pax Africana whole, in its own significant light as:

- Southern Africa building on Bantu *ivhu/unhu*: Nhakanomic regeneration
- East Africa building on Swahili *asil*: leads to Yurugu-nomic regeneration
- North Africa building on Egyptian *maat*: regeneration via Economics of Love
- West African on the Yoruba *orisa*: regeneration via generic Communitalism

one building integrally on the other. This involves both integral research (inner directed) in relational, renewal, reason and realisation guise, and innovation (outer directed wise): the latter from local origination (grounding) to local-global foundation (emergence), to newly global emancipation (navigation) onto global-local transformation (effect). We now elaborate on each.

Southern African Integral Kumusha: Ivhu, Community Building and Nhakanomics

For the Taranhike's then, in Zimbabwe in Southern Africa, in giving birth to their so called *Integral Kumusha* in rural Buhera, in the second decade of the new millennium, each of their three business enterprises, as we shall see, has had a critical role to play in transforming the rural homestead into also a workplace., that creates livelihoods. Therefore the Kumusha constitutes an indigenous Zimbabwean enterprise as opposed to the western exogenous form of corporation.

It is thereby built upon the four pillars of creating nhaka (a legacy) for future generations, adding up, at a macro level, to nhaka-nomics. The four pillars of *nhaka* are located within the integral approach together with the three business enterprises and the Buhera community as shown in the diagram below, constituting *Nhakanomics*.

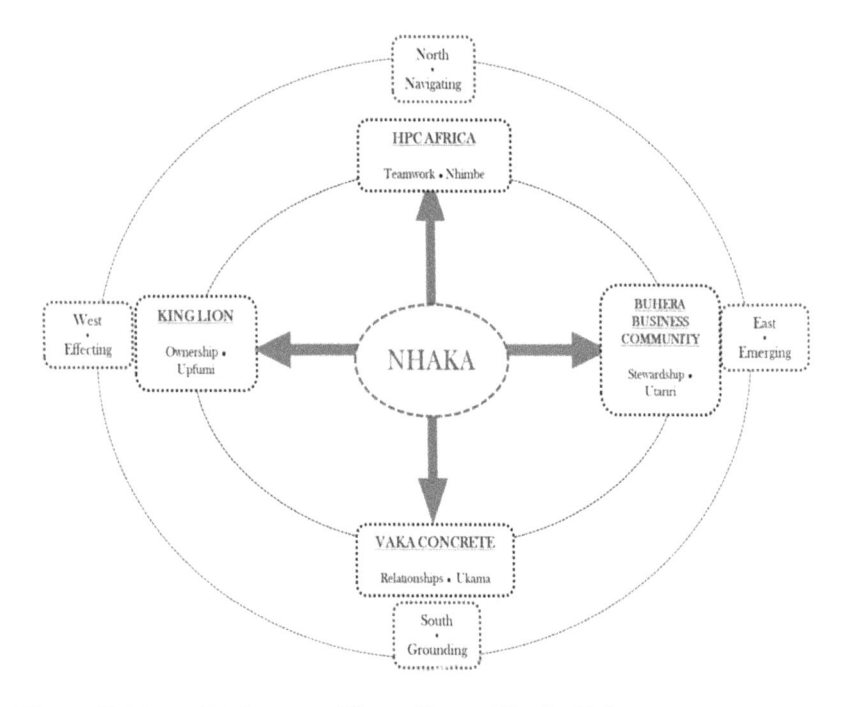

Figure 17.4.2a .1: Nhakanomics: Ukama, Utariri, Nhimbe, Upfumi

Integrally following the GENE, building on *Nhaka* through its integral *Kumusha concept*, Vaka Concrete with its building products is locally grounded (G) in building communities and building on nature via such relationships (ukama) within communities and the entire ecosystem; the Buhera Community as a whole exercises local-global emergent (E) stewardship (utariri), thereby renewing culture and spirituality; while HPC Africa's global north (N) has the newly global role of navigating technology and systems thereby creating knowledge and building teamwork (nhimbe); leading, hitherto, to King Lion's global-local effect (E) in its western role of promoting trade and enterprise leading to co-ownership (upfumi), albeit that more recently King Lion has been disbanded. We now turn from south to east Africa, from Nhakanomics to Yurugu-nomics.

East African Good African Story: Asili, Conscious Evolution, and Yurugu-nomics

As we now turn south-east, specifically to East Africa, we focus, generally thereby, on culture and spirituality based conscious evolution, enterprise-wise, and on developmental economics, economy-wise, while specifically now focused, locally-globally, on *Yurugu-nomics,* as an African-Arab fusion. Our *Good African Coffee Story,* originated by Andrew Rugisara, was the second case story on which we built, in our south-eastern Africa, Ugandan case.

For African American anthropologist and African Studies scholar, Marimba Ani (2000), in her book *Yurugu: An African Centred Critique of European Thought,* Yurugu, originally named Ogo, is described in Dogon (West African) mythology as acting with anxiety and impatience. In search of the secrets of Amma (the creative principle) of which he wants to "gain possession", Yurugu, in Kiswahili, is known for his arrogance and incompleteness. He is in a state of solitude, having been deprived of his female principle.

The universe loses its richness, in other words, as it is transformed into lifeless matter; the supernatural is reduced to the "natural", which means the merely physical and biological. Consequently time can only be lineal; space three dimensional; and material causality the ultimate reality. In European religious thought the human and the divine are hopelessly split. There is no sacred ground on which they meet. In such a setting the exaggerated material priorities of the culture are simply a result of the praxis of its participants, of the limited realities offered by the culture. The resultant materialism despiritualizes the culture.

Ani then introduces, more constructively in an East African, Swahili context, the concept of *asili,* a Kiswahli word that means "beginning", "origin", "source", "nature", "essence" or "fundamental principle". It can also be taken to mean "seed" and "germ", that is the source or initiating principle. It refers, as such, to the explanatory principle of a culture, the germinal principle or essence. The *asili* is like a template that carries within it the pattern or archetypal model for cultural development. We might say the DNA or "logic" of a culture, that forges a people into an ideological unit. It is not an idea, but a force, an energy. Ani has borrowed other Kiswahili terms to denote *utamaduni* or "civilisation", or indeed "culture"; *wazo* meaning "thought" and *roho* meaning "spirit-life". She then creates the concept of *utamawazo* to mean "thought" as determined by culture, and *utamaroho* as "the spirit-life of a culture", or the collective personality of its members. Whereas "utamawazo" is self conscious, *utamaroho* remains unconscious. Both originate from the meta-conscious *asili.* We speak of *utamaroho* as we might speak of temperament, character or emotional response. *Utamaroho* is not individual but collective.

Utamaroho does not categorize the ethoses of cultures into types, but as inseparable from *asili;* it focuses on the uniqueness of a particular culture with respect to its emotional rather than cognitive patterns. While the character of a culture's *utamawazoi* is expressed most obviously in literature, philosophy and academic discourse, and pedagogy, *utamaroho* becomes more evident in aesthetic expression whether visual, aural or kinaesthetic. At the same time *utamaroho* is the inspirational source from which *utamawazo* derives its form as "forms of thought". *Utamawazo* (thought), *utamaroho* (spirit life) and *asili* (seed) influence, reinforce and build on each other in a circular process. This circular process and synthesis is culture, and for us also in that context, economics, itself.

We now turn from East to North Africa, from Swahili to Kemet, that is to Egypt, and to Sekem therein.

North Africa's Sekem: Maat, Knowledge Creation, Economics of Love

In our (Lessem and Schieffer 2009) book on integral enterprise, in which Sekem was centrally featured,, we referred to knowledge creation specifically. Sekem (see Figure 17.4.2.2. below), literally meaning in the Coptic language the *Vitality of the Sun* was born, as a *social innovation* out of a fusion between ancient Egypt in Africa, the Islamic world in Asia, and Steiner's so called anthroposophy in central Europe, a latter day expression of balance, as per ancient Egyptian *maat*.

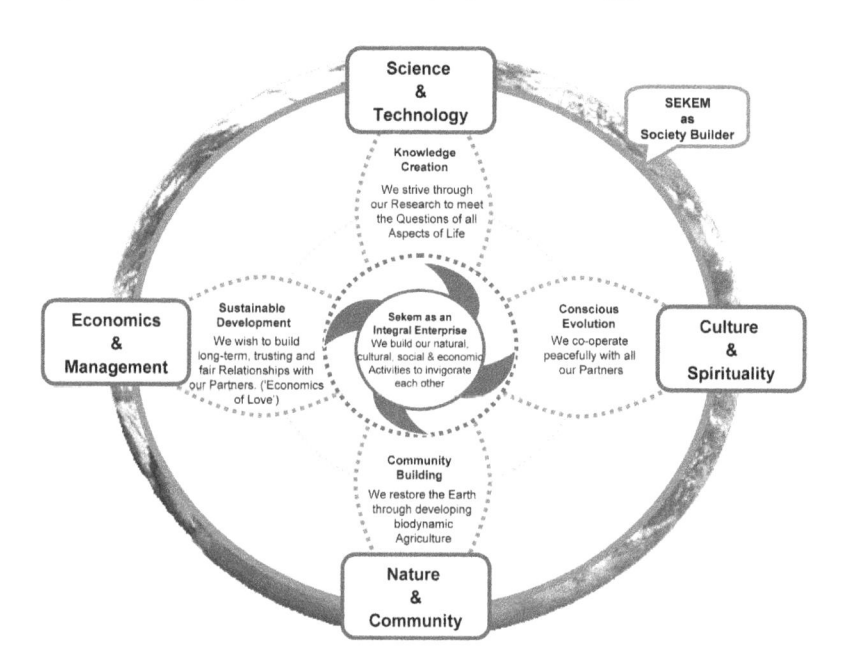

Figure 17.4.2b *.2: The Sekem Fourfold*

For Sekem's founder Ibrahim Abouleish (2005), already in his youth:

> I carry a vision deep within myself: in the midst of sand and desert I see myself standing as a well drawing water. Carefully I plant trees, herbs and flowers and wet their roots with the precious drops. The cool well water attracts human beings and animals to refresh and quicken themselves. Trees give shade, the land turns green, fragrant flowers bloom, insects, birds and butterflies show their devotion to God, the creator, as if they were citing the first Sura of the Koran. The human, perceiving the

hidden praise of God, care for and see all that is created as a reflection of paradise on earth. For me this idea of an oasis in the middle of a hostile environment is like an image of the resurrection at dawn, after a long journey through the nightly desert. I saw it in front of me like a model before the actual work in the desert started. And yet in reality I desired even more: I wanted the whole world to develop.

Set against the ancient backdrop, Sekem has further evolved the anthroposophically based threefold, associative economy, whereby economics is built upon fraternity (culture builds on freedom, and polity on equality), into a, for us, integral *fourfold* as above, adding nature as the fourth element. Indeed, in *knowledge creating* terms, being initially open to impulses from south, east, north and west, Abouleish evolved a knowledge network, locally and globally, second to none:

> SEKEM is starting to have a place in a worldwide association of people and initiatives who are concerned with a healthier more humane future on earth. The net of life created by us and our initiatives is becoming connected to a larger, worldwide net.

We now turn to West Africa and ultimately to Communitalism

West Africa: Orisa, Sustainable Development, Generic Communitalism

In our integral enterprise and economy, finally in African guise, we have referred to sustainable development, which further evolves community building, conscious evolution and knowledge creation that comes before, centred in the healing wisdom of Africa. The key philosophy of generic *communitalism* is "we are either happy together as a prosperous community or unhappy together" and thereby unprosperous. For *communitalism*, the health and prosperity of the individual cannot be separated from the health and prosperity of the local community. Global health must start from local health, not the other way round. In the process the link between individual, community and enterprise health and whole-making, integrally so to speak, will be made.

As a flourishing model of health and business enterprise, building on indigenous Yoruba energy forces, the *orisa*, then within a particular local community, in Edo State adjacent to Benin City in Nigeria, *Paxherbals* is actively activating the local community towards integral ecological and economic, scientific and cultural development. A flourishing agribusiness which allows all families in Ewu local community to engage in profitable cultivation of foodstuffs, medicinal plants and other cash crops will make the village into an economic hub. When there is an improvement in the material well-being of the community, the health of the members of the community will also improve. This is the essence of community medicine.

Unlike biohealth, which tends to focus on disease and neglect the root cause of diseases such as financial inequality, unjust wages, unfair working conditions, dysfunctional literacy etc., community medicine adopts an integral approach to health and well-being.

Diagram

NORTH — Science, System & Technology
- PAX SCIENTIA
- Conceptual Strength
- Institution Building

WEST — Enterprise & Economics
- PAX ECOMOMIA
- Practical Orientation
- Building Enterprises Polices

Center: PAX AFRICANA — Moral Core INTEGRITY

EAST — Culture & Spirituality
- PAX SPIRITUS
- Reflective and Intuitive
- Raising Consciousness, Holism

SOUTH — COMMUNITALISM
- PAX NATURA
- Closeness to nature
- Building healthy Communities
- Nature & Community

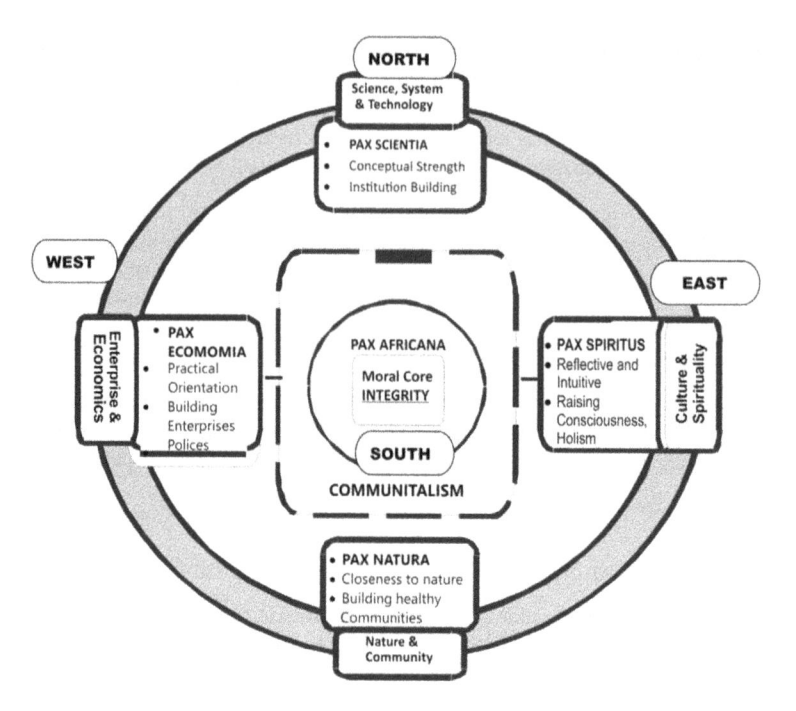

Specifically in West Africa then the term *communitalism*, for one of us – Anselm Adodo (2017) – is different from capitalism or indeed communism. *Communitalism* affirms that some aspects of capitalism, such is individual inventiveness, are worth pursuing and supporting, but such inventiveness must be put at the service of the community, so that both the individual and the community prosper, altogether, and integrally as such, for one of us (Anselm Adodo) thereby embracing worldviews, or realities, from all four corners of the globe. We now finally turn to the continent of Africa as a whole, cosmologically so to speak, to different expressions of *Africa's Healing Wisdom*. We now turn specifically to such.

17.6. Pan-African Cosmology: Healing Wisdom of Africa

17.6.1. Relational *Unhu*: Healing the Divide Between Homestead and Enterprise

SOUTHERN AFRICA: INHERENTLY AFRICAN

Unlike Pan-Africanism, whereby ostensibly every generically African nation was part of a pan-African whole, but without any explicit awareness of what part each would play, our four African worlds – south, east, north and west – each have a distinct role to fulfil in a Pax Africana whole, thereby prospectively – though currently far from such – bringing peace and harmony, in its broadest sense, to the continent.

As such southern Africa, more especially Zimbabwe, to begin with, embedded in *ivhu/unhu/ubuntu,* in altogether *Bantu* guise, brings its distinctive "southernness" to bear on Africa and the world. It was in that particular guise that South African freedom fighter Steve Biko (1987) claimed that Africa's role was *"to give the world a human face"*. The Taranhike's *Integral Kumusha* embodies such, *healing the divide between homestead and enterprise,* and thereby bringing both a natural and a human, homely quality to their rural enterprise and economy.

17.6.2. *Yurugu* Renewal: Healing the Divide Between Community and Enterprise

EAST AFRICA: FACING ASIA

As we may be aware, East Africa faces the Indian ocean, across to Asia and also the Kiswahili language therein, while essentially an African language, has strong Arab, middle eastern influence. While the Bantu as such are "southern" the Swahili speakers are "south-eastern". While unhu/ubuntu is innately southern African, as we have seen, from Marimba Ani above, *asili* is a typical Swahili term depicting a "seed force" within a culture, thereby a critical element of cultural, and for us also economic, renewal. Andrew Rugasira's *Good African Coffee Story* represents such here, in Uganda. Moreover, for Ani, as we have seen, *Yurugu* represents "incompleteness", in both Swahili and Dogon, whereby healing, whole-making and completeness align, ultimately with *healing the divide between community and enterprise.*

Reasoned Maat: Healing the Divide Between (Wo)man and Nature

NORTH AFRICA: FACING EUROPE

As we turn from Southern Africa, in itself, and then to East Africa, adjacent to the Indian ocean across to Asia, not to mention also the Arab region, so we come to the north of Africa, specifically to Egypt, where the blend of the African south (Kemet) and Arabia in the Middle East, also faces Europe. In fact historically Egypt and Southern Europe, especially ancient Egypt and ancient Greece, were closely intertwined. The symbolism of *maat,* representing harmony, moderation, balance and justice, alludes to the adoption of a well "reasoned" position.

The twin Egyptian/Greek god Thoth/Hermes also gave rise to Hermeticism, so called, and from there ultimately onto European anthroposophy, for its originator Rudolf Steiner (2011), the philosophy of freedom. The Abouleish's *Sekem* in Egypt is our constituent north African case, *healing the divide between (wo)man and nature.*

17.6.4. Orisa Realisation: Healing the Divide Between Tradition and Modernity

NORTH AFRICA: FACING AMERICA

Finally, in turning to *West* Africa, to Yoruba-land in Nigeria, of which one of us (Anselm Adodo) is part, we also connect with the American African diaspora, which has a strong Yoruba influence today. Herein the *ôrisa* have a pervasive influence as sources of energy, knowledge and power. Indeed the five major orisa, for Adodo, can be aligned with our four worlds and centre: Sango in our natural south, our *grounding*, was the orisa of thunder and rainstorms; Orunmila in the spiritual east as our *emergent* source of knowledge and wisdom; Esu responsible in our north for the general order of things, by way of *navigation*; Ogun in our enterprising *west* for transformative *effect,* related to iron and warfare; Obtala in our integral *centre* as the overall source of creation. One of us (Anselm Adodo), via *PaxHerbals* in Nigeria, duly embodies such, thereby *healing the divide between tradition and modernity.* We now turn to our end product as articulated in a previous book by Anselm Adodo (2017), *Integral Community Enterprise in Africa.*

17.6. End Product: Community Based Integral Enterprise

Extending Our Epistemological Reach

Substantively, to evolve in Africa form capitalism and socialism to communitalism, in one southern, eastern, northern or western guise or another, represents a giant leap.

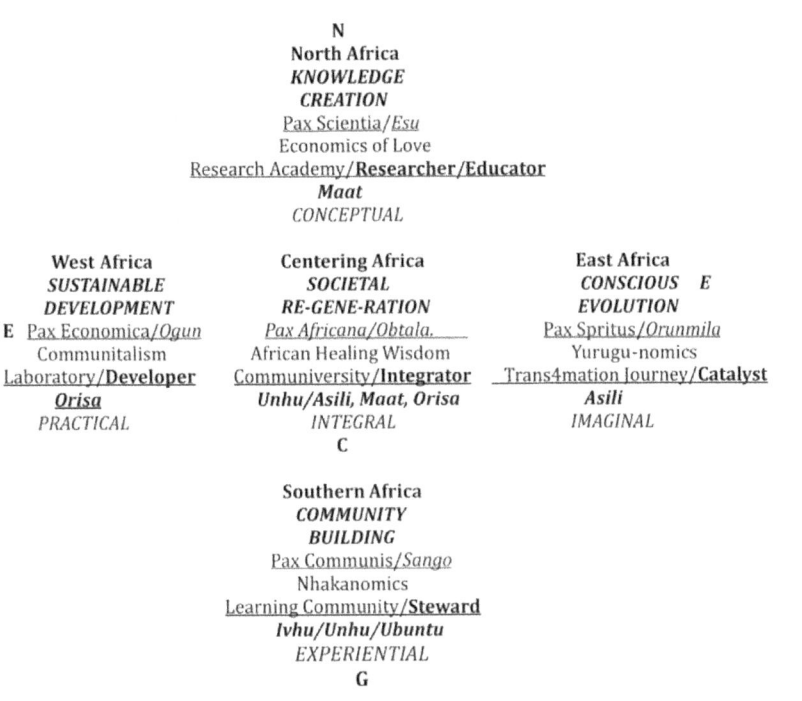

```
                              N
                         North Africa
                        KNOWLEDGE
                         CREATION
                       Pax Scientia/Esu
                      Economics of Love
             Research Academy/Researcher/Educator
                            Maat
                        CONCEPTUAL

   West Africa           Centering Africa          East Africa
   SUSTAINABLE              SOCIETAL              CONSCIOUS   E
   DEVELOPMENT           RE-GENE-RATION            EVOLUTION
E  Pax Economica/Ogun    Pax Africana/Obtala.    Pax Spritus/Orunmila
   Communitalism        African Healing Wisdom      Yurugu-nomics
   Laboratory/Developer  Communiversity/Integrator  Trans4mation Journey/Catalyst
      Orisa              Unhu/Asili, Maat, Orisa       Asili
   PRACTICAL                 INTEGRAL                IMAGINAL
                                C

                        Southern Africa
                         COMMUNITY
                         BUILDING
                      Pax Communis/Sango
                         Nhakanomics
                   Learning Community/Steward
                        Ivhu/Unhu/Ubuntu
                         EXPERIENTIAL
                              G
```

Figure 17.6.1: *Community Based Integral Enterprise/Societal Re-Gene-Ration*

It is therefore our view that such mesa (in between macro and micro) enterprises as our *Integral Kumusha* in southern Africa, the *Good Africa Coffee* company in east Africa, *Sekem* in north Africa and *Paxherbals* in west Africa, each now significant, practically, in their own societal context, can pave the way. However, as of yet, none of them have become a visible force, conceptually as well as practically, to the extent that they influence business academics and economic policy makers, locally and globally.

The key, in Heron's (1997) terms of Co-operative Inquiry (CI), epistemologically, is to comprehend such *practical* (socio-economic laboratories/managerially, politically and economically) in the light of what has come before *experientially* (learning community/ecologically and anthropologically), *imaginally* (transformation journey/philosophically, spiritually and psychologically), *conceptually* (research academy/scientifically and humanistically). This of course is easier said than done as each of the above represents different worlds, in our overall integral terms (see Figure 17.6.1. above).

Extending Our Political Reach

However, and again in CI terms, this is not adequate in itself. There is also a political, if not also economic dimension that needs to be taken into account. Whereas conventional university "politics" is noted for its departmental in-fighting, on the one hand, and renowned, in more societal contexts, for its student "revolts", as for example in the 1960s in Europe and America, people seldom look to such universities as catalysts for societal regeneration, as we do. The key to such, though, lies in a recasting of conventional academic roles, interactively and eco/systemically, as we have dome above in *innovation ecosystem* terms rather than hierarchically and bureaucratically.

Thereby teacher and student are replaced by researchers and educators, alongside stewards, developers and, most especially, catalysts. Indeed the catalytic role is to mediate between process, substance, form and context,

17.7. Conclusion

Such leads to the kind of end product to which we now finally turn.

17.7.1. Centred in African Healing Wisdom

Table 17.7.1. *Centred in Healing Wisdom*

CASE STORY RESEARCH PATH	SOURCE OF ORIGINATION	INTEGRAL ENTERPRISE	COMMUNI- TALISM	- HEALING DIVIDES
Paxherbals/ Realisation (E)	*Orisa/* Energy Source	Sustainable Development	Generic Communitalism	*Indigenous/ Exogenous*
Sekem/ Reason (N)	*Maat/* Balance,Harmony	Knowledge Creation	Economics of Love	*(Wo)man and Nature*
Good African Coffee Story/ Renewal (E)	*Asili* Seed/Nourish	Conscious Evolution	Yurugu-nomics	*Community and Enterprise*
Integral Kumusha/ Relational (G)	*Ivhu/Unhu* I am Because You Are	Community Building	Nhakanomics	*Homestead & Workplace*

The most radical step we have then taken in an overall, pan-African context (see Table 17.7.1. above), is to relocate economy and enterprise, communally away from capitalism (markets) and socialism (state planning), towards communitalism in one societal guise or another. In an African context, of healing wisdom moreover, we have sought to heal divides between *work and home, community and enterprise, (wo)man and nature*, as well as between *indigenous/tradition and exogenous/modernity*. Each of these forms of healing wisdom, moreover, is located in one or other of the four case stories we have presented, centred in the healing wisdom of Africa as a whole.

They serve to evolve integral research towards societal re-GENE-ration, via community based integral enterprise, such as our integral kumusha, southern Africa, Good African Coffee Story (east Africa), Sekem (north Africa) or Paxherbals (west Africa).

17.7.2. Whither Integral Research and Innovation?

Transforming Enterprise and Society: Towards the Integral Enterprise

In our original, 2010 version of *Integral Research and Innovation,* written almost a decade and a half ago, we subtitled our (Lessem and Schieffer 2010) work, with some wishful thinking, *Transforming Enterprise and Society.* Why might such have involved wishful thought?

A year before publishing this work, in 2009, our book on *Transformation Management* made the case of an emerging *Integral Enterprise,* Sekem (see Figure 17.4.2.2. above) in fact being a leading such example, we alluded to *community building, conscious evolution, knowledge creation and sustainable development* therein, replacing, in such an "integral" enterprise, marketing, human resources (HR), operations and finance in turn. Underlying such, specifically, was our belief that:

– Marketing, thereby *community building*, should be led by the communal "south"
– HR, thereby conscious evolution, should build on the spiritual "east"
– Operations, thereby *knowledge creation*, should be led by the scientific "north"
– Finance, thereby *sustainable development*, should build on the oikonomic "west".

Was this then pure wishful thinking by a group of "crazy" people who believed that the "west" should build on the "rest" rather than vice versa, and that the "south", "east" and "north" had something unique to offer the business world, in theory as well as practice, alongside the west. Indeed not. We reckon we were not crazy!

The Developmental Road Not Taken

The Developing Organisation: HRM to Conscious Evolution in the East

For in the latter part of last century, from the 1960s to the early 1990s, there was a genuine move, management-wise, towards worlds-wide integrality, in and around the business schools where one of us (Ronnie Lessem at Harvard) had been based. Most especially, already in the 1960s, the rise of organisation development, alongside the so called human potential movement, transcending human resource management, was strongly influenced by *eastern* philosophies. The book series we (Lessem 1991) launched with the U.K. publisher Blackwells, early in the 1990s, on *Developmental Management,* was then a celebration of that fact. The book by anthroposophically-spiritually inspired Dutch psychiatrist Bernard Lievegoed (1990) on *The Developing Organisation* epitomised such.

Value Sharing: Marketing to Community Building in the South

In that same series, moreover, we published the seminal work of Albert Koopman (1991), his so called *Transcultural Management,* based on the industrial democracy he had established in South Africa, based on *Value Sharing.* Such value sharing, moreover, was based on *profiting society* rather than merely "making profits", building thereby, as Koopman put it, on "the divine will of Africa". All of such served to evolve prior marketing, individually, into society building, communally. Sad to say both such a community building orientation, alongside organisation development above, has since significantly waned in their overall influence, for reasons to which we turn below.

The Knowledge Creating Company: Operations to Knowledge Creation in the North

At the same time, in the early 1990s, the soon to become renowned Ikijiro Nonaka (Nonaka and Takeuchi 2005) in Japan, which we identify as the "*north*-east", came out with his seminal work on the *Knowledge Creating Company,* together with his Japanese compatriot – both organisational sociologists – Hirotaka Takeuchi. For them, the company of the future was the one that conceived of knowledge as its primary resource. Ironically, for us though, while "knowledge management" has become all the rage, to this day, along with the "knowledge society", the subtle, for us integral approach that Nonaka and Takeuchi took, toward developing such a knowledge based, what they termed "hypertext" organisation, thereby purposefully building explicitly on such knowledge, mediated by a project layer as well as a bureaucratic system, got lost in translation!

Natural Capitalism: Finance to Sustainable Development in the Integral West

Finally in the American "west", again in the early 1990s, the most serious proponent of sustainable development, in the round, as opposed to the more narrowly based financial orientation, was economist and environmentalist Paul Hawken (1999), in his focus on *Natural Capitalism: The Next Industrial Revolution.* In fact he was the major intellectual influence on the late Ray Anderson (2008), who became a sustainability pioneer in the U.S, transforming his Interface Carpets into a model of sustainability worldwide. Hawken then alluded, in his seminal work, to *advancing productivity, pursuing biomimicry, enhancing flow, and promoting restorative economics*, altogether. This is indeed a far cry from the conventional wisdom, today, on sustainable development, especially that focused on the SDG's (Sustainable Development Goals), as currently advocated.

The Neoliberal Turn

So here is our concluding point. The Thatcher-Reagan neoliberal turn, from the 1970s onward, ultimately all around the world, giving rise to deregulation, privatisation, digitisation, financialization, consumerism and the like, stopped the integral evolution of management, worlds-wide – whereby southern, eastern and northern worldviews had come to influence the all pervasive managerial west – abruptly in its tracks.

In fact while business schools and schools of economics might be seen as ploughing their own separate furrows, for us, as for Harvard's renowned Rakesh Khurana, the two are intimately connected, in integral principle, though not in trans/disciplinary practice. For Harvard Business School (HBS) sociologist Khurana (2007) (he has since moved to Harvard College), in his *From Higher Aims to Hired Hands: The Social Transformation of American Business Schools and the Unfulfilled Promise of Management as a Profession*:

> Unforeseen by the intellectual architects of the revolution in economic sand finance was that by de-legitimating the old managerial order and turning executives into free agents, they had cut managers off from moorings not just to the organisations they led and the communities in which the organisations were embedded, but also in the end to the shareholders themselves. The resulting corporate oligarchy had no obligation other than to self-interest. The anomalies of executive pay and recurrent corporate scandals have been the recent result. What has been missing is any attempt to put the subject within a holistic, institutional context, thereby systematically challenging the dominant market logic with other models.

Developmental Management Set Against the Neoliberal Tide

Indeed our *Developmental Management* series, launched early in the 1990s, was then just such an attempt to counter the above neoliberal revolution, by putting the whole wide world – south and east, north and west – on the management and economic map. We were swimming against the heavy tide though, and that tide is yet to turn, notwithstanding ever advancing climate change, which is why, through our integral research and societal re-GENE-ration, we are seeking to renew fertile, developmental ground. As such we seek turn the tide, regeneratively, worlds-wide, through community building, communitalism, and our communiversity, and cooperative inquiry, ultimately centred in African healing wisdom.

Return to Co-operative Inquiry (CI)

So what does this mean in Co-operative Inquiry terms, for a doctoral or transdoctoral program? For John Heron (1997) as such, for us pursuing, interactively and developmentally their nhakanomic, yurugu-nomic, economics and love, and generically communitalist macro economic orientations, also in micro relation to community building, conscious evolution, knowledge creation and sustainable development in each micro/mesa enterprise case:

- *human flourishing is intrinsically worthwhile;* it is construed as a process of social participation in which there is a mutually enabling balance within and between people, of autonomy, hierarchy and co-operation, and is conceived as interdependent with the flourishing of the planetary system.
- *what is valuable as a means to this end is participative decision making*, through which people speak on behalf of the wider ecosystem of which they are a part, including the way that integral research is conducted within our research community.

17.6. References

Abouleish I (2005) *Sekem: A Sustainable Community in the Egyptian Desert.* Edinburgh. Floris Publications

Adodo A (2017) *Integral Community Enterprise in Africa: Communitalism as an Alternative to Capitalism.* Abingdon. Routledge

Anderson R (2008) *Confessions of a Radical Industrialist.* Toronto. Mclelland & Stewart

Ani M (2000) *Yurugu: An African Centred Critique of European Thought.* New Jersey. Africa World Press

Bhaskar R (2002) *Reflections on Meta-Reality.* London. Sage

Biko S (1987) *I Write What I Like.* London. Heineman African Classics

Gibbons M, **Limoges** C, **Nowotny** H, **Schwartzman** S, **Scott** P, **Trow** M (1994) *The New Production of Knowledge: The Dynamics of Science and Research in Contemporary Societies.* London. Sage

Hawken P (1999) *Natural Capitalism: The Next Industrial Revolution.* London. Earthscan

Heron JH (1997) *Cooperative Inquiry.* London. Sage

Khurana R (2007) *From Higher Aims to Hired Hands: The Social Transformation of American Business Schools and the Unfulfilled Promise of Management as a Profession.* New Jersey. Princeton University

Koopman A (1991) *Transcultural Management.* Chichester. Wiley-Blackwell

Lessem R (1991) *Developmental Management.* Chichester. Wiley-Blackwell

Lessem A and **Schieffer** A (2009) *Transformation Management: Toward the Integral Enterprise.* Abingdon. Routledge

Lessem R and **Schieffer** A (2010) *Integral Research and Innovation: Transforming Enterprise and Society.* Abingdon. Routledge

Lessem R et al (2013) *Integral Dynamics: Cultural Dynamics, Political Economy and the Future of the University*. Abingdon. Routledge

Lessem R, **Adodo** A and **Bradley** T (2019) *The Idea of a Communiversity*. Manchester. Beacon Academic

Lessem R, **Mawere** M and **Taranhike** D (2019) *Integral Kumusha*. Mazvingo. Africa Talent Publishers

Lievegoed B (1990) *The Developing Organisation*. Chichester. Wiley-Blackwell

McNeely I and **Wolverton** L (2008) *Reinventing Knowledge: Alexandria to the Internet*. New York. W.W. Norton

Nonaka I and **Takeuchi** H (2005) *The Knowledge Creating Company*. Oxford. Oxford University Press

Some M (1987) *The Healing Wisdom of Africa*. New York. Jeremy Tarcher

Some M (1997) *The Healing Wisdom of Africa*. New York. Jeremy Tarcher

Steiner R (2011) *The Philosophy of Freedom: The Basis for a Modern World Conception*. Forest Row. Rudolf Steiner Press

Williams C (1993) *Rebirth of African Civilization*. Chicago. Third World Press

Chapter 18 Towards a Societal PHD Community, Corporation, Communiversity, Communitalism

> *At the opposite end from healing is the illness of not being able to accept or even tolerate those who are different from us. Worse, this inability encourages suspicion, fear, and resentment. Thus it is an illness of the collective psyche when different cultures don't understand one another. The history of humankind is plagued by this psychic disease that has caused much pain and disappointment in the world, as we still see today. Methods of healing, then, must take into account the energetic or spiritual condition that is in turmoil, thereby affecting the physical condition.*
>
> Malidoma Some (1997)   *The Healing Wisdom of Africa*

18.1. Introduction

18.1.1. Towards a Societal PhD: A Communiversity Start-Up

Robbin Island University as Unfinished Business: Rhodes Must Fall

We finally turn to specific means of developing from healing cosmology and community based enterprise to spirited scientifically managed corporation onto integrated communiversity and ultimately communitalist association, (see Figure 18.1.1 below).

Communiiversity
Co-creation
Research and Innovation
<u>Knowledge Creation</u>
<u>Education</u>
CENTRE FOR AFRICAN RESEARCH & INNOVATION (CARI)
Emancipatory Navigation
RESEARCH ACADEMY
NORTH

Communitalism	**Healing Cosmology**	**Corporation**
Contribution	*Calling to Contribution*	*Societal Context*
Embody Development	Care-ing For Society	Awakening Consciousness
<u>Sustainable Development</u>	<u>Integral Enterprise</u>	<u>Conscious Evolution</u>
<u>Development</u>	<u>Innovation Ecosystem</u>	<u>Catalysation</u>
PAX AFRICANA, PHC, NHC	SOCIETAL PHD	REGENE-AFRICA/DA VINCI
Trans4mative Effect	**Re-Gene-ration**	**Emergent Foundation**
INTEGRAL LABORATORY	MEANS OF DEVELOPING INTEGRALITY (MDI)	TRANS4MATION JOURNEY
WEST	CENTRE	EAST

Community
Inner/Outer Calling
Community activation
<u>Community Building</u>
<u>Stewardship</u>
Original Grounding
LEARNING COMMUNITY
SOUTH

Figure 18.1.1: *Societal PHD and the Communiversity*

Building most specifically and in retrospect, on the case story of PaxHerbal, revisiting part of one of us – Dr Anselm Adodo's – PhD-laden transformation journey, we can conclude it was neither exclusively an academic nor a professional PhD, in the conventional sense. For the journey he undertook, not unlike that of Dr Daud Shumba Taranhike in Zimbabwe after him, was communal, individual, transformative, analytical, and specifically contextualised, naturally and culturally as well as technologically and economically, in Africa. Moreover, and in all those respects, it involved societal re-GENE-ration as well as individual, integral research.

West Africa to Southern Africa in Relation to Africa as a Whole

Such a thorough undertaking is much easier said than done; Pax Africana, for example, has been 25 years in the making. Such a societal PhD then needs to build on what has come before, adding communiversity and communitalist overtones, integrally and associatively, to what has come communally and corporately before. In fact, and by way of an originally well-known but by now probably long-forgotten example, the so-called Robbin Island University, as described in Nelson Mandela's (1994) Long Walk to Freedom, paved the way for a newly integral kind of university, if not also, emancipatory polity and economy.

Subsequently, of course, the socialist "political economy" toward which Mandela was aspiring never materialised in South Africa, arguably because the prior community-based enterprises and spirited, scientifically managed corporations – like a Cashbuild writ large, as we shall see below – were not in place, neither was a communiversity.

Rhodes Must Fall

In fact, the "Rhodes Must Fall" movement in the second decade of the new millennium, two decades after the birth of the new South Africa, represented a kind of implicit plea for university education to take on from where "Robbin Island University" had left off. Alas, give or take one or other course now being introduced in African philosophy or epistemology, the form and process of research and education in South Africa if not also in the continent at large, as well as the substance of economics and management, our primary field of substantive concern, has hardly changed at all. Moreover, as we indicated in Chapter 11, associated with Nyerere's *ujamaa* in Tanzania, in the 1960s, even the renowned development economist Walter Rodney (2018) *How Europe Underdeveloped Africa*, or the transformative sociologist Giovanni Arrighi (2009) – *The Long Twentieth Century: Money, Power and the Origins of Our Time*, based at the University of Tanzania's department of economics, could do nothing to "stop the rot" as it were.

Taking on from Where the Trans4m-Da Vinci PhD Left Off

Turning then from Africa at large to our own transformative activities, in Southern and West, if not also North, Africa, mainly through our PhD programs (case stories 1, 3 and 4), for all our achievements, these were invariably restricted, for three major reasons, in our view. First was the *focus on individual research and education*, necessitated by such degree programs, which largely precluded any explicitly communal, organisational or societal orientation. Secondly, such a form of education, *precludes any explicit orientation given toward catalysation if not also stewardship*, not to mention overall individual and collective integration. Thirdly our programs remained inhibited by the prevailing neoliberal, corporate *status quo*. In other words, our thereby "academic" PhD, for all its transformative overtones, was not enough.

18.1.2. A Communiversity as Inter-Institutional Agency for Societal Regeneration

Specifically then, as we have discovered over the past three decades during which our programs have been running, there is no institutional form, or, better, inter-institutional and inter-personal agency, serving to regenerate a particular society. Indeed, while the political, economic and civic powers that be focus on outer-directed development, and higher education, at its best, focus on inner development, seldom do the two meet. More specifically, and alongside such, sciences and humanities, natural and social sciences, and nature and culture go their separate ways. Moreover, even when one or other do meet, through "development" programs and processes, these are invariably dominated by theories, if not also practices, from the "north" and "west".

It is in that guise, building in the closest example we have to hand, that of our PaxHerbals in Nigeria, that we have proposed that a communiversity, as an inter-institutional agency, building *cosmology*-wise on the healing wisdom of Africa, specifically, as its centreing; is grounded naturally and originally in one or other learning *community*; emerging via a transformation journey thereby combining faith and reason via a spirited, scientifically managed *corporation*; navigating scientifically and humanistically in emancipatory guise, through a research academy as the capstone *communiveersity*; realizing a political and economic transformative effect through a form of *communitalism* transcending capitalism and communism, via a socio-economic laboratory.

How does this all practically work?

18.2.1. A Societal PhD

Our Common Future: Environment and Development

We centre ourselves, substantively to begin with, through what we term a "societal PhD", aimed at healing and regeneration, specifically in Africa, as generally intimated in the renowned report of the Brundtland (1987) Commission of 1987, named *Our Common Future – World Commission On Environment and Development*:

> Ecology and economy are becoming ever more interwoven – locally, regionally, nationally, globally – into a seamless net of causes and effects .. Those who are poor and hungry will often destroy their immediate environments in order to survive .. On the other hand, much of the economic improvement in the past has been based on the use of increasing amounts of raw materials, energy and pollution. Thus, today's environmental challenges arise both from the lack of development and from the unintended consequences of some forms of economic growth.

However, in our African case, as also highlighted in the PaxHerbal case story, if not also in that of the Taranhike's in their Integral Kumusha in Southern Africa, Rugisawa through his Good Africa Coffee Story in East Africa and the Abouleish's through Sekem in North Africa, such "healing" is ecological and cultural, as well as technological and economic, if not also political in its general nature and scope. In other words, healing and regeneration via communitalism in one form or another – *Nhakanomics* in Zimbabwe, *Yurugunomics* in Uganda, *Economics of Love* in Egypt, generic *Communitalism* in Nigeria, rather than free markets or state planning via capitalism or socialism, lead the way.

The Challenge for Africa: A New Vision

More specifically in Africa, the notable late Wangari Maathai (2009), the Kenyan environmentalist and Nobel Peace Prize winner, believed passionately in the need for African communities to discover the value of embracing their own destiny and determining their own futures rather than solely and passively relying on outside forces.

Centring Cosmology: On Nature Power and the Healing Wisdom of Africa

Turning from Bruntland and Maathai, environmentally, to one of us, Anselm Adodo (2012) cosmologically with his perspective on the healing wisdom of Africa via *Nature Power,* as again already intimated in the PaxHerbal case story:

> When there is an imbalance, there is disease. Society says: be rich, have pleasure, obtain power, and be famous, for these are the goals of life. This false conception of life, of all reality, is the root of all diseases. Having imbibed the mechanistic worldview, which sees natural things as mere objects to be exploited and the human body as a mere object of pleasure, we eat what we like, drink anything that comes our way and live as we want. The result of this is disease. We are no longer at ease. We have lost touch with our origins .. Nature Power then invites the world to come down to earth to regain our health. The earth is the primary source of our creativity, intelligence, and humanness. Before we set out to calculate, to create, to invent, to fabricate, the earth already was.

18.2.2. Focused on Re-Gene-ration

Underlying GENE

Our prospective Societal PhD program then, or better PHD – *Process of Holistic Development* – is specifically focused on *Re-GENE-ration* individually (integral research) and communally, organizationally and societally (societal regeneration), following the above cosmological centreing. This involves **G**rounding of communal enterprise locally and naturally; followed locally-globally by a spirited, scientifically managed **E**mergent corporate foundation; emancipatory **N**avigation ensues scientifically and humanistically, now newly globally via communiversity; finally leading to **E**ffecting transformation globally-locally, communitalism-wise, economically and educationally, if not also politically.

4 C's, CARE, Integral Enterprise, Integral Society

For the Individual, his or her Calling (iG), is set in a particular societal Context (iE), in which Co-creation (iN)then takes place, leading to an ultimate Contribution (iE), constituting our 4 C's. For the Community in which he or she is lodged, amongst fellow learners/ researchers and/or in the surrounding society, Community activation (cG) is followed by Awakening integral consciousness (cE), institutionalised Research and Innovation (cN), and Embodying development (cE), altogether, now individually and collectively, CARE-ing.

For the organisation, or thereby the integrative enterprise, this involves southern community building (oG) rather than individual marketing; eastern conscious evolution transcending human resources; northern knowledge creation overtaking operations; and western sustainable development superseding finance.

Societally, moreover, duly centred cosmologically in the healing wisdom of Africa, as indicated above, originally enterprising Grounding in nature and *Community*, is followed trans-culturally by a scientifically managed *Corporation*, as an Emergent foundation; thereafter, by way of scientific and humanistic Navigation, comes our *Communiversity* in and of itself; *Communitalism* of one kind or another (e.g. as an evolution of Consciencism, Ujaama, African Renaissance) transcending capitalism and communism comes effectively thereafter.

Innovation Ecosystem: Steward, Catalyst, Researcher/Educator/Developer

Inevitably, an individual researcher/ practitioner cannot actualise all of the above. This is where our so called *innovation ecosystem* comes in. Firstly then a senor *Steward* is required, be he or she an Adodo (Paxherbal) in Nigeria, or a Taranhike (Integral Kumusha) or a Ndudzo (PHC) in Zimbabwe, an Abouleish (Sekem) in Egypt, or a Rugisara (Good African Coffee Story) in Uganda, an Albert Koopman of late (Cashbuild) or a Dr Reinder Nauta (National Healthcare) in South Africa.

Role of the Enterprising Communal Steward
• Is actively engaged in co-creating the future, simultaneously rooted in his or her cultural past, with a view to transforming his or her enterprise-in-community • Paving the way for social Innovation • Normally has a strong Involvement with Community based or political Enterprises • Is a leading edge practitioner in his/her field, and will ideally have a track record in business, organizational and community development, as above.

Secondly comes the role of *Catalyst*, individually and more especially institutionally. This is indeed the most invisible, albeit crucial, role in an educational and developmental context, herein played by Regene-Africa.

Role of the Inter-Institutional Catalyst in Promoting Transformation
• Instead of well laid course curricula and ready-to-work action plans, s/he focuses on emerging, ever changing, intertwined agendas of individual and strategic Issues, located within a field of possibilities. • Uses instability and crisis to provoke continual individual and collective questioning and self, organizational and societal learning, knowledge creation and business development • Fosters creative Interaction with other actors in the wider environment, open to a multiplicity of worlds amongst participants, participating organizations and societies • Seizes on small differences in individual and cultural requirements and perceptions, and amplifies feedback, building these into significant differentiators.

As such, the individual researcher does not undertake what for us is now a *societal* PhD in individual isolation, nor does the educator function individually as such. Rather both form part of a research academy within the communiversity.

Role of the Educators, Researchers and Research Centre
• Academics, Researchers and Practitioners skilled at adapting Theory to Practice and particularly knowledgeable about the fundamentals of Integral Research • Rooted prospectively in the healing wisdom of Africa, also yearning for societal regeneration in a particular organisational and societal context • Open to collaboration with other researchers, and committed to building up a leading research institution in Africa, in the management and economic field • Participating in public-private-civic-environmental enterprise also with a view to seeking greater association and alignment between them

Rather such a PHD – Process of Holistic Development – involves the full cast of ecosystemic characters, as well as a research institute, our Centre for Integral Research and Societal Re-GENE-ration, as a whole. The university host for such, Da Vinci Institute in South Africa, moreover, builds on its "mode 2" knowledge creating foundations, originally laid in the 1990s by its co-founder, Nelson Mandela Himself. Finally, alongside such stewardship, catalysation and research as well as education, is the development activity undertaken by developers, individually, and by a socio-economic laboratory, organisationally,

Role of the Developer and the Laboratory
• Is in tune with the overall Purpose and Design of Societal Regeneration
• Manages and develops Relationships within the Knowledge creating Community, within the context of one or other form of Communitalism in Association
• Monitors and evaluates the Progress of Individuals and the Group
• Supports the transformational Process set in the Context of the Transformational Flow, promoting simultaneously self, organizational, communal Re-GENE-ration.

18.2.3. Cosmology, Communiversity, Innovation Ecosystem and MDI's

In the final analysis, with a view to institutionalizing healing and regeneration, inter-personally and inter-institutionally, as well as, overall, societally, by Means of Developing Integrality, this requires:

- A *Learning Community* – community activation to embodiment – replacing community outreach, requires *Stewardship* engaged with *Mother nature*
- A *Transformation Journey* – calling to contribution – transcending individual education, supported by *Catalysation* – serves to co-evolve a *Moral narrative*
- A *Research Academy* – origination to transformation – overriding individualised "research", supportive *Public Intellectuals* build together a social *scientific Model*
- A *Socio/Economic Laboratory* – community building to sustainable development – supported by *Facilitation and Development* – transcending individual secondments and placements – realizes *Measurable effects*.

A societal PhD, when looked at by itself, may seem like an individual achievement. However, when we view it as a standardized part of a bigger picture, it becomes like a vital, renewing "trojan horse" for us. It brings in a diverse group of people, communities, and businesses mentioned earlier. Let's now look at each of them one by one.

18.3. Learning Community: Stewardship: Pioneering Enterprise

Community
Inner/Outer Calling
Community activation
<u>Community Building</u>
Stewardship/Pioneering
Original Grounding
LEARNING COMMUNITY
SOUTH

18.3.1. Calling to Community Activation: Pioneering Community Based Enterprise

Pax Herbals to Pax Africana

<u>Inner Calling: I Was Born Into a Certain Place</u>

For one of us, Dr Anselm Adodo (2017):

> For the African, the community is a place of creativity, healing and relationship. Even though the community embraces both the visible and invisible, the natural and supernatural world, like the world of spirits, it should be noted that the point of interaction is always the visible community. The earth is where we live, relate, procreate and discover our creativity. As a person, I am born into a certain place, on a certain date, at a certain time, into a certain family. These facts play a key role in determining my destiny, my orientation and my sense of self. I am not just a vague entity. I belong to a place. No one becomes a global citizen at birth. Each person is a local entity, a local person.

<u>Community Activation and Pioneering Enterprise: For Whom the Bell Tolls</u>

For Adodo (Adodo and Lessem 2021) then, such an inner calling, as illustrated above, is aligned with, or co-evolved though, as revealed in his co-authored book: Afrikology: Reconstrucitng and Deconstructing Knowledge and value in Africa:

> Paxherbals is in St Benedict Monastery in Ewu, mid-western Nigeria. Life at the village of Ewu begins at 3.40 am daily, when the echoes of the huge metallic bell mounted on a wooden crossbar behind the Monastery church penetrates the morning mist to awaken the villages. All the young people in Ewu village born in the 1980s grew up accustomed to hearing this bell every morning, at precisely the same time. "O Lord open my lips, and my tongue shall declare your praise", so begins the Office of readings at Ewu Monastery. Meanwhile, Farmers are preparing to go to the farm, and market women are putting their wares together, also preparing their children for school. For them is an engagement with time, Chronos, in the here and now. For the monks of Ewu however, it is a time for spiritual engagement, with Kairos, sacred time.

We now turn from Nigeria to rural Zimbabwe.

The Chinyika Project

<u>Inner Calling: Moved by the Suffering of his People</u>

For Dr Chidara Muchineripi (Mamukwa et al 2014), in the first decade of the new millennium, according to his soul mate Dr Steve Kada, as participants on our masters and PhD programs from Zimbabwe:

.. out of his rural Chinyika community, a son was raised from the house of the Gutu chieftainship, and was moved by the suffering of his own people. He woke up to the call of his ancestors to save his people from the scourge of hunger and poverty. Chidara then, who had become a successful business person and management educator, had a wakeup call from his slumber of individual success, responding to his "fathers voice". Chidara then enrolled on the Trans4m masters (MSET), program unknowingly together with Steve, in 2005. That was the beginning of the establishment of the Chinyika Community Development Project. Chidara then reconnected with the voice that called his people to revisit the source of their food security in the past, the nutritious food and meals that came out of the sweat of their labour. A community that never starved.

Community Activation: Through a Democratic Process in the Traditional Manner

How then was such brought into the here and now, for Muchineripi (Lessem et al 2012):

> In order to coordinate these developments the leadership originally drew from the villages' horizontal structures. Through a democratic process in the traditional manner, the Chief, headman, counsellors, village development committees, extension services personnel were all involved, consulted and contributed to the selection of the project leadership. The leadership, headed by Mai Tembo (Mrs Tembo) clearly outlined its goals and strategy specifically to fight hunger through growing rapoko and in the long run eliminate poverty. They clearly distanced themselves from the very sensitive partisan politics, not aligning the project farming activities with any political groupings. The committees' main purpose has remained that of building a community consciousness that creates enlightened peoples actions to fight both mind and material poverty; to thereby decolonise the mind.

We now turn from rural to urban Zimbabwe, and from Chinyika to Providence Human Capital, like Paxherbals also drawing, in different guises, on the healing wisdom of Africa.

Providence Human Capital as a Pioneering Individual and Communal Enterprise

Inner Calling: The Corporate World Was Against My Ethics as a "Southerner"

For Dr Chipo Nduzo (Ndudzo 2021), in Zimbabwe in the second decade of the new millennium, immediately prior to her participation in our PhD program:

> The vision started with a dream. A dream to address the imbalances within me as an individual, cascading down to my organisation and then to my society as a whole. It was almost like a premonition, calling for change and I remember vividly just waking

up one day, packing up my small box and walking out of an organisation I had faithfully served for 10 years. I had resigned. I felt the corporate world was just filled with a lot of imbalances that I needed to address. The way business was being operated in the corporate world was against my ethics as a "Southerner", against my "Being", I needed to "Emerge/Become", to "Know" and eventually to "Act" so as to complete myself. That is how Providence Human Capital came into Being.

Community Activation: Toward PHC as a "Chitubu" Laden Integral Enterprise
For PHC (Lessem 2016), more specifically then, and in overall healing guise:

> Chitubu is a Shona word meaning Spring. A Spring is known to bring about medicinal, healing and rejuvenating powers, also an oasis in our Zimbabwean context in that it symbolises rest, being ever-green, though in the midst of a desert. Our "Health and Wellness" department became Chitubu Chehutano (an oasis of health and wellness) harnessed in nature and community. "Human Resources" transformed to Chitubu CheHungwaru (an oasis of Wisdom) harnessed in culture and conscious evolution. Payroll became Chitubu Cheruzivo (an oasis of science, systems and technology). "Finance" is now Chitubu Che Budiriro (an oasis of Sustainability).

18.3.2. Re-Gene-ration: Original Grounding in Nature and Community of a Society

Such a prospectively societal PhD, centred as in the above cases, in healing and regeneration, is infused with an inner, individual calling and galvanized through individually and collectively pioneering community activation, invariably grounded in a particular nature and community. This is most poignantly illustrated in the Chinyika case:

> The Karanga people who constitute the majority of the Chinyika people, in fact, are known as people of the soil. Their life depends on the soil, for they till it. They grow their crops on it and draw water from the ground. They bury their dead in the soil. Soil is their power. It gives them their identity. It is as if the rock came to life and talked through the people. The spirit engulfed everyone who sat or stood on the rock. One elder poetically asked:
>
> Why are the children, mothers and fathers starving?
> Why have the people forgotten what used to happen on this rock?
> Where your forefathers gathered rapoko and millet in abundance?
> Where children played around while fathers and mothers pounded rapoko ears with sticks and winnowed the grain from the chaff?
> Where granaries were filled with golden brown rapoko grains?
> Arise the children of Chinyika
> Arise and be who you should be!

18.2.3. Learning Community, Pioneering Stewardship, Rooted in Mother Earth

Such grounding then, supported by an individual, inner call and outer community activation, serves, communiversity wise, to build up a learning community, supported by engaged stewardship in such pioneering enterprise, altogether serving to enrich mother earth.

- *a contextualised platform for learning/development, and pioneering enterprise – human/more-than-human communities are enabled to reclaim/restore their potential*
- *communal stewards deeply immerse themselves in a particular natural and communal, local context, able to locally relate to other human beings and to nature*
- *embodying the web of life representing M̲other nature; the circle of physical and human nature reflecting the original oneness of all creation in a particular context.*

We then round out this section on Grounding in nature and community, generally, and building up a learning community – and community based enterprise – with Paxherbals (Ndudzo 2021), focusing thereby on the "community oriented approach" (the clinical comes later).

> In the community-oriented approach, the emphasis is on the crude and local production of herbs used for common illnesses. Knowledge of the medicinal uses of herbs is spread to promote self-reliance. Information is freely given on disease prevention and origin of diseases. This approach aims at applying simple but effective herbal remedies to common illnesses. The target is the local community. No interest is shown in mass production of drugs for transportation to other parts of the country or exportation to other countries. The cultural context of the plants used is taken into account, and local perception of health and healing often takes precedence over modern diagnostic technology.

We now turn from learning community to transformation journey, with a particular focus on turning such a community based enterprise into a corporation infused with *spirited* scientific management, to one degree or another, in. one guise or another.

18.3. Emerging Local-Global Transformation: Community/Corporation

Corporation
Societal Context
Awakening Integral Consciousness
Conscious Evolution
Catalysation/Spirited Scientific Management

REGENE-AFRICA/DA VINCI
Emergent Foundation
TRANS4MATION JOURNEY
EAST

18.3.1. Awakening Integral Consciousness in Societal Context

Shona Chitubu to Jacob's Well at PHC

Whereas a conventional PhD programme is focused on individual research and education, in our PHD (Process of Holistic Development), as we saw especially in the PaxHerbal case above, from the outset, there is an interaction not only between individual and community, but also between reason and faith, between science and spirituality, in a particular cultural context. In other words, awakening integral consciousness, as such, involves such an interaction between such indigenous nature and culture and exogenous science and technology. Such is a necessary step in the development from indigenous communal enterprise to exogenous scientific management, corporate wise, without losing overall authenticity. For Dr Chipo Ndudzo then, on the way to such:

> As Providence Human Capital we believe we need Daily Renewal, Daily Rejuvenation and Daily Healing. We chose the African indigenous shona name "Chitubu" because also of its exogenous, Christian significance, as Jacob's well. In the bible Jesus spoke to a Samaritan woman – breaking two "cultural" norms of His time because of both race and gender and we believe we can break all barriers, political, social and economic, in order to be a sustainable organisation. Jesus also promised Living Water, never drying and lives within Providence employees as they embody their own spiritual journeys.

What remains unfinished business, in the PHC case, is the link between such *chitubu* spiritually and indigenously, and the cultivation of wellbeing, scientifically and exogenously, thereby awakening an integral, scientific healing consciousness, and thereby a corporation evolved through such *spirited* scientific management.

Vaka (Ukama), Buhera (Utariri), HPC (Nhimbe) and King Lion (Upfumi) Enterprises

Turning, still in Zimbabwe, from urban PHC to Daud Shumba Taranhike's (Lessem et al 2019b) rural Integral Kumusha (shona for homestead), conceived of during his participation in. our PhD program and thereby PHD, it is built upon the four pillars of creating *nhaka* (legacy) for future generations. The four pillars of such an integral approach together with Daud's three business enterprises and his Buhera based rural community from where both he, and one of us, Ronnie Lessem, originate, are constituted of, <u>indigenous</u>ly and *exogenously*:

- Ukama/stewardship: enterprising *relationships*
- Utariri/catalysation: evolved through corporate *governance*
- Nhimbe/research and education: *teamwork* between business and academe
- Upfama/development: associative *co-ownership*

It is in fact the Taranhike's (Daud and his partner Christina) sincere belief that Zimbabwe's economic success cannot be achieved without addressing the socio-economic problems experienced in the rural areas.

There is a problem of rural-urban migration as the area is labelled as "a place for the poor". It is then the Taranhikes' burning desire to identify the imbalances that exist within this community and to work to correct these, and thereby facilitate real social transformation of the area in order to ensure that people become productive and contribute effectively to their own livelihoods and to the national economy. The Integral Kumusha concept, and practice, has been developed as an approach to cultural, socio-economic healing and regeneration, which will spur Zimbabwe and Africa at large, for the Taranhike's, onto prosperity, to manage its own affairs and ultimately stand proud among other nations and continents, serving to unlock and release the full potential of the individual, organisation, community and society. Through promoting a marriage between their natural, communal and cultural, enterprise in Buhera, and their businesses in Harare, the Taranhike's, also being devoted Christians, hope to build up a duly spirited approach to scientific management of their would-be corporation.

It is in that integral guise, moreover, that we have sought to forge an indigenous-exogenous link between *nhakanomics* and contemporary anthropology, via renowned British social scientist Timothy Ingold's (Ingold 2023) attempt to link faith and reason in his recent work on *The Rise and Fall of Generation Now*:

> Generation is a process – a bringing forth of life, not just at conception or birth but in every moment of existence. According to the book of Genesis it all began with Adam. "This is the book of the generation of Adam". The story of Adam and his descendants, while relentlessly patriarchal, is far from unique. Many peoples around the world take pride in reciting lengthy genealogies, extending from founding ancestors to generations alive today. Common to every list is that it is compounded of tales of begetting and being begotten. Anthropologists call this filiation. Such filiation is an entwining of threads; to recite a genealogy is to follow the twine.

The transformation journey, from communal to corporate with which the likes of one of us, Anselm Adodo, if not also the Taranhike's, have been engaged, is underpinned by what we have termed our (Lessem and Schieffer 2010a) socially scientifically based process of integral renewal, thereby from origination to transformation, from community to corporation, onto communversity and ultimately communitalism, in their *nhakanomic* guise. We now turn from Zimbabwe to South Africa.

18.3.2. Transformation Journey, Conscious Evolution and Moral Narrative

Community Based Enterprise in South Africa

As we have seen, albeit adjacent to our PhD, if you like aligned with our PHD (Process of Holistic Development) in South Africa, Albert Koopman (1991), in his own transformation journey prior to, and then during the regeneration of Cashbuild as an industrial democracy, as described in his *Transcultural Management:*

> .. was raised as a street fighter. My mother died when I was 13 and my father lived in Mozambique, 1240 miles from me. Set free at a very early age I had to learn to survive. That meant dealing with people, including people who had hang-ups, and people who wanted to do me in for what I believed. The one thing that I learnt as a result was that I was going to enter my life as a clean, moral fighter, someone who sterilised his bicycle chains before he entered the fight of interpersonal relationships.

Value Sharing at Cashbuild

He went on to say, having taken over the reigns at building supplies retail chain, Cashbuild, hitherto a conventional private company which he transformed, corporately, into an industrial democracy, as a would be "social scientist", infused with "the divine will of Africa":

> No stone was left unturned and over a period of one year we listened to why people worked, with whom they preferred to work, and what they saw would be the design of the perfect workplace. After spending extended periods of time living amongst our black employees, experiencing life within their communities, and consulting with them directly, I found I had to review my whole understanding of the people I employed, as well as how they saw their relationship with our business and with its philosophy. The degree to which aspects of indigenous "southern" culture were to become "spiritualised" in the workplace was to depend on the type of "northern" organisation imposed upon the individual, including the degree to which the organisation would allow expression of these elements.

As we shall see below, Albert Koopman at Cashbuild did come up with a newly global, Southern African scientific and humanistic model of enterprise, if not also economy, involving *Value Sharing,* but sad to say it has not endured, within business schools in South Africa at large, because of the lack of institutionalisation of such.

Communal Enterprise to Corporate Transformation

At the heart of our communiversity, its emergent foundation, lies not mere courses, or studies, but a transformation journey, from communal enterprise to corporate transformation, from pioneering to scientific management, in the Cashbuild case above underpinned by value sharing building in the divine will of Africa:

- *Individual and collective learning consciousness raising releases cultural and economic genius, via a Moral narrative, underlying the institution's vision and mission*
- *A development catalyst is able to engage with cultural/spiritual dynamics of a particular entity/place, duly evolved into "spirited" scientific management*
- *Promoting a marriage of faith – be it the "divine will of Africa" or Benedictine ora (prayer) and labora (work) – and reason as differentiated management functions.*

18.4. Newly Global African Emancipatory Navigation: CIRSRE

Communiversity
Co-creation
Research and Innovation
Knowledge Creation
Education/Integration
CENTRE FOR INTEGRAL RESEARCH & SOCIETAL RE-GENE-RATION
Emancipatory Navigation
RESEARCH ACADEMY
NORTH

18.4.1. Towards a Centre for Integral Research and Societal Re-GENE-ration

African Management: Principles, Concepts and Applications

In fact innovation driven institutionalised research, contextualised in Africa, individually and collectively applied to enterprise, economy and society, has been the Achilles heal of our PhD laden endeavours, thereby inhibiting our proposed *societal* PhD. For such needs to be furthered not only individually and communally, but also organisationally and ultimately societally, actively and reflectively.

Indeed prior to our PhD/PHD and programs, via our (Christie et al 1996) *African Management* project based in South Africa in the 1990s, we had developed some provisional principles, concepts and applications bearing upon such, but these were never tested out in practice. The outline contents of the African Management workshop, together wide the wide range of trans-cultural academic and business contributors, and text were:

Part 1: Philosophies

- Four Worlds: The *South African Businessphere* (Ronnie Lessem)
- *Transcultural Management* (Albert Koopman)
- The *Spirit of African Management* (Lovemore Mbigi)

- The *African Crucible*: Unity in Diversity (Beck and Linscott)

Part 2: Concepts

- The Need for an *Afrocentric Approach* (Reul Khoza)
- *Value Centred* Leadership (Christo Nel)
- Resolving *Structural Tension* (Loet Dekker)
- An Integrated *Organisation Perspective* (Peter Christie)
- A Population *Ecology Perspective* (Piet Human)
- A Learning *Community Perspective* (Louis van der Merwe)

Part 3: Applications

- *Worker Democracy*: Towards a New Union (Albert Koopman and Judy Maller)
- The *Organisation as Organism*: Case of the Valley Trust (Irwin Friedman)
- *Education for* Africa: *Robben Island to ITISA* (Aitken Ramadzuli)
- African Management: *Career in Community* (Mandla Adonisi)

The project was then disbanded at the end of the old millennium, and has never, to our knowledge, been resurrected by any university or research institute in Africa.

Integral Research and Development, Enterprise and Economy, and Communiversity

Thereafter, in the new millennium, Trans4m Centre for Integral Development, based in Geneva but operating worlds-wide, had developed its own, "newly global", *integral* – southern, eastern, northern and western as well as centred – approach to *research* (Lessem and Schieffer 2010a) and *development* (Schieffer and Lessem 2014), as well as to *enterprise* (Lessem and Schieffer 2010b) and *economy* (Lessem and Schieffer 2010c; Piciga et al 2016), and ultimately to our *communiversity* (Lessem et al 2019a). None of such, overall, was attuned, as a whole, specifically to Africa, as our orientation was invariably worlds-wide. Moreover, our communities, laboratories and transformation journeys were not altogether aligned.

Moreover, while Trans4m ran PhD and programs, together with Da Vinci Institute as we have seen, it failed to establish an enduring research academy. Neither did its partners in Zimbabwe, South Africa, Nigeria and Egypt, nor, outside of Africa, in Jordan in the Middle East, Pakistan in Asia, Germany and Slovenia in Europe, as well as in North America, succeed in such. To the extent, then, that the likes of a PaxHerbal, through one of us, Anselm Adodo, as we have seen above, was able to transform a community based enterprise into a spirited, scientifically managed corporation, there was no communiversity as such, that could serve to reflectively position such an active enterprise, if not also economy, duly centred in the healing wisdom of Africa.

Management programs there were aplenty, but would-be academies came and went, bereft of ongoing support from universities, or research institutes, in Africa or indeed worlds-wide, which either restricted themselves naturally or culturally to the humanities or, in the field of economics and management, were dominated by the "western" status quo.

18.4.2. Cocreation, Knowledge Creation, Societal Re-geNe-Ration

Drawing together the threads of hitherto thwarted attempts at African regeneration, adding also our own such failed African Management project, we now put them integrally together, now also centred in African healing wisdom, in a GENEtic whole (see Figure 14.4.2 below).

Centred then cosmologically in African healing wisdom, grounded in a learning community, and emerging corporately through a transformation journey together with others, you build up a research academy, against the odds, focused on the what has, and has not been, realised through consciencism, ujamaa, an African Renaissance and African Management. Integral research-wise a "southern" relational path of research and innovation, thereby employing descriptive method, phenomenological methodology, feminist critique and participation action research, providing the analytical individual underpinning for collectively transformative regeneration:

- *scholarship, research and knowledge creation aims – inter/institutionally and in inter-disciplinary guise– for social innovation, re-GENE-rating a society, newly globally*
- *promoting conceptual and analytical ability, individually and collectively, sharing knowledge in a group, generating "newly global" scientific Models of transformation*
- *the resulting grid of communal learning, individual transformation, institutionalised research, and laboratory based experimentation constitutes a communiversity.*

EMANCIPATORY NAVIGATION
NORTH
Science and Humanities
Consciencism
Philosophical Dialectics
Attunement of Forces Perpetually in Strife
Social Egalitarianism
Harmonious Growth & Development

TRANS4MATIVE EFFECT	CENTREING	EMERGENT FOUNDATION
WEST		*EAST*
Economics and Enterprise	Healing Wisdom of Africa	Culture and Spirituality
African Management	**Communiversity**	**African Renaissance**
African Businessphere	*Learn From Nature*	*I Am An African*
Transcultural Management	*Earth as Source of Creativity*	*Deep African Consciousness*
African Spirit Hierarchy	*Four Natural Forces*	*Black Renaissance*
The African Crucible	*As Vibrating Energy Fields*	*African Quest for Freedom*

ORIGINAL GROUNDING
SOUTH
Nature and Community
Ujaama
Family-hood
Sacredness of Life-Force
Mutual Respect, Common Property, Work Obligation
Everyone Participates in Government

Figure 18.4.2: *Consciencism, Ujaama, African Renaissance*

We finally now turn to transformative effect, to communitalism and our laboratory.

18.5. Global-Local Trans4mative Effect: Communitalism/Laboratory

Communitalism
Contribution
Embody Development
Sustainable Development
Development/Association
PAX AFRICANA, PHC, NHC
Trans4mative Effect
INTEGRAL LABORATORY
WEST

18.5.1. Pax Africana, Providence Human Capital and National Healthcare

Transformative Effect of the Integral Laboratory

The integral laboratory, then, lies at the cutting edge, as it were, that is serving to realise the transformative effect, of our societal PhD program and PHD process, in association with individual and institutional others, that is the realisation of communitalism, in one guise or another, in both micro and macro terms. As the institutionalized means of developing such integrality, oikonomic Measures, so to speak, arise out of it. In other words, while the program and process are centred in African healing wisdom, grounded in a learning community, emerge through a transformation journey and navigate through a research academy, it is via such a laboratory that the transformative effect is ultimately realised. This altogether requires a combination of pioneering stewardship, managerial catalysation, research and education by way of integration, development and association.

Pax Herbals as an Integral Laboratory: Communitalism in the Guise of Pax Economica

Starting here, by way of example, with "Pax Africana" our pilot communiversity in rural Nigeria, as a whole, and with "Pax Economica", by way of culmination, emerging out of Paxherbals, for one of us, its founder Anselm Adodo (2017), at the outset:

> PAX Herbals is not just a clinic. It is a centre of healing, of love, of service. Pax is not about mere eradication of suffering, or suppression of illnesses, or avoidance of pain. It is a fact of life that we all shall die one day, sooner or later. The mission of Paxherbals is to promote human health and human dignity, not just the eradication of pain, which in fact, is an essential aspect of being human. We the business of using our God-given natural resources to enrich ourselves. We want to re-write our history. We want to re-awaken the African Spirit. The African Spirit has been so suppressed and relegated that we are no longer even proud to call ourselves Africans. After all, Africa has been described as the "dark" continent. All that the world knows about Africa is civil war, poverty, famine, corruption. Nowadays, the Indian Spirit, The Chinese Spirit, Japanese Spirit have been revived. Pax is into the business of re-awakening the African Spirit by first affirming belief in African inner resources and genius.

We now turn from Nigeria to Zimbabwe, from Pax Herbals to PHC.

Providence Human Capital (PHC) as an Integral Laboratory

As stated then, by Chipo Nduzo (2021), in *The Providence Way*:

> Providence Human Capital (PHC) is a wholly owned Zimbabwean company which was founded in January 2016.

Its core business is to provide corporate services management focuses on people solutions. It provides Afrocentric flexible, innovative, customised, best practice solutions to its clientele. The services offered include outsourced Payroll Services, Human Resource Consulting, employee and Corporate Wellness, as well as Staffing Solutions. Though our services still take up a conventional guise, our delivery is heavily influenced by the philosophy of Unhu/Ubuntu and this is evident in the naming and norming of our departments that we have called the Chitubu Phenomenon.

Chitubu is a Shona word meaning an oasis which is known to bring about medicinal, healing and rejuvenating powers. It is also an oasis in. our Zimbabwean context in that it symbolized rest, being ever green and fertile despite being in the middle, metaphorically, of the desert. This was therefore the bedrock of our naming and norming of our departments, with Hunhu as our moral core.

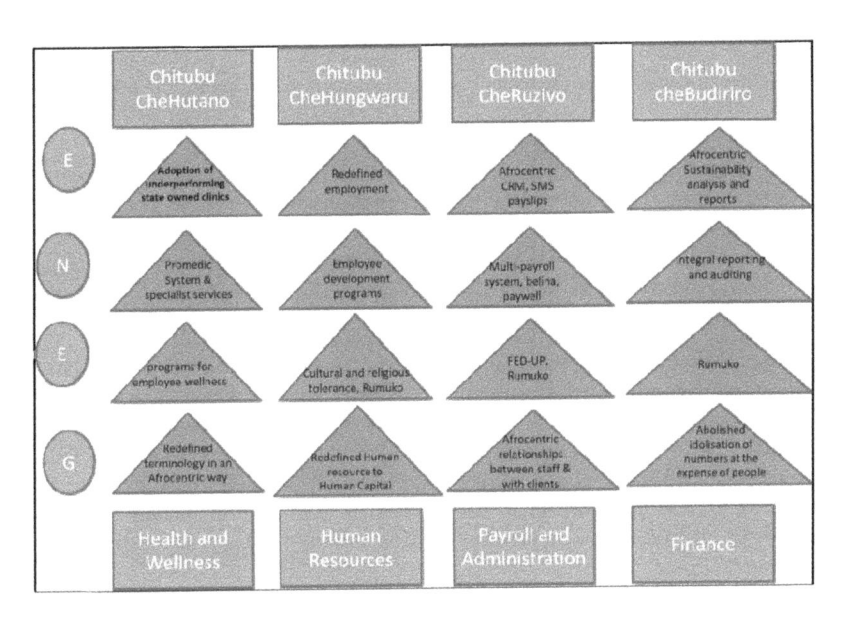

Figure 18.5.1: *The Communitalist Chitubu Phenomenon*

As such a Southern African oasis in the otherwise "corporate" African desert, PHC (Some 1999) could be seen as a genuine integral laboratory, centred in the healing wisdom of Africa, straddling nature and culture, the social and life sciences and enterprise, though it might not quite see itself in such purposefully experimental, scientific and humanistic guise. In other words, the step from enterprise to laboratory, from capitalism and socialism to commiunitalism, in socio-economic guise, may be seen in this case as a step too far. South Africa's National Healthcare is for us a third case in point.

National Healthcare: Strengthen the Bottom line, Builds Morale and Solidarity

In introducing the National Healthcare Group to South Africa, its founder, Dr Reinder Nauta (Ndudzo 2021), a longstanding friend and colleague of one of us, Ronnie Lessem, claims:

> Needed right now are consummate leaders who understand the importance of offering employees efficient health cover during these challenging times. Not only will it stand businesses in good stead by reducing absenteeism and strengthening the bottom line, but it also builds morale, solidarity, loyalty and ultimately good labour relations .. Our vision is to improve access to reliable and affordable healthcare cover for employees in the lower, and emerging income market, where many millions of South Africans have never yet in their lifetime enjoyed access to private healthcare services .. With technology, co-ordination of quality healthcare increasingly coming together to revolutionise the way people interact with healthcare for the better.

Nauta goes on to say:

> Now more than ever rapid transformation by the primary healthcare and corporate sectors is needed to ensure closer alignment to the healthcare policies and initiatives of Government. Given the pivotal role of corporate South Africa in the development and implementation of viable and sustainable solutions for employed, but currently uninsured individuals, we believe that businesses can assist in addressing many of the current healthcare challenges of our country.

The care delivery programme, for Nauta moreover, facilitated by the National HealthCare Group, is being implemented by a primary healthcare cooperative consisting of 3200 general practitioners, 2800 pharmacies, as well as all major pathology laboratories, radiology practices, dentists and optometrists. Interestingly enough, as such, and set somewhat nonchalantly alongside the otherwise fairly standard, for us "north-western" corporate speak, albeit of a socially responsible kind, is the mention of a *cooperative* of GP's and pharmacists, if you like in more "southerly" guise.

Altogether then, integral laboratory and facilitation wise, such could be seen as:

- *a focal point for creative experimentation/ a conducive space in which appropriate new practices can be conceived of, tested, implemented, and oikonomically Measured*
- *overarching facilitation of development, serving to translate knowledge into capacities, globally-locally, thereby exercising overall governance*
- *focused, goal-oriented, co-creative, resulting in the active build-up of new infrastructure and institutions, now globally-locally in the guise of communitalism.*

How then do the three cases in point, Pax Herbals, Providence Human Capital and National Healthcare, all concerned with healing and regeneration, compare?

18.5.2. Comparative Laboratory GENE-tics

As can then be seen from the above, each of our African laboratories, connect, in different guises (see Figure 18.5.2), with the healing wisdom of Africa. Paxherbals firstly, via its *nature power* and *healing radiance,* is closest to nature and community ("south"), as well as to Yoruba/Benedictine culture and sprituality ("east"). PHC secondly is closely aligned with African-shona culture, in *chitubu* guise ("east"), and with economy and enterprise, as Providence Human Capital ("west"). The National Healthcare Group, thirdly, is the most technology intensive, and also economically engaged.

All three, however, can be seen to draw, from their different angles, on the healing wisdom of Africa, for their centreing, Pax Herbals as PHC for local moral Inspiration, and National Healthcare more aligned with Universal truth (their Hippocratic Oath), while Pax Africana, combining clinical and community medicine, Synergises the two. We are now ready to conclude.

18.6. Conclusion: Individuality/Communiversity; Enterprise/Healing

18.6.1. Individual Research/Innovation Ecosystem; University/Communiversity

In conclusion, then, there are two major transformations with which we have been simultaneously engaged. The first has involved the evolution from an individual to a prospective *societal* PhD, thereby alternately viewed as a PHD (Process of Holistic Development). Such then becomes an alternative to the current academic, and professional PhD programs.

```
                            N
                       Science and
                       Technology

              National Health-         Pax
               Care Group.           Africana

              INTEGRATED        SPIRITED SCIENTIFICALLY
             COMMUNIVERSITY      MANAGED CORPORATION

    W    Economy and    The Healing       Culture and   E
         Enterprise    Wisdom of Africa   Spirituality
                            IUS

              COMMUNITALIST            PIONEERING
               ASSOCIATION      COMMUNITY BASED ENTERPRISE

                Providence          Pax
               Human Capital       Herbals

                       Nature and
                       Community
                            S
```

Figure 18.6.1: *Comparative Integral Laboratories*

As such, on the one hand, the conventional *PhD* relationship between individual researcher and supervisor is replaced by a more variegated exchange, interpersonally, through an *innovation ecosystem*, between *stewardship, catalysation, research and education, facilitation and development*. On the other hand, now institutionally, such an individual becomes part of a *learning community, while on a transformation journey together with that of his or her society, as a constituent part of a research academy, serving to co-evolve a socio-economic laboratory*, altogether as elements of a *communiversity*.

18.6.2. Healthy Society, Integral Enterprise and Individual Wellbeing

The second transformation is even more dramatic. For centred as such in *The Healing Wisdom of Africa*, cosmologically, in Malidoma Patrice Some's (Some 1999) sage-like terms, while thereafter grounded naturally in community, emerging trans-culturally as a corporation, towards scientifically and humanistically based communiversity of one African kind or another, the transformational communitalism in Africa, educationally, is not engaged with enterprise, or indeed economy, as we know it, but with overall healing.

As *such healing societally, integrality enterprise-wise, and wellbeing, individually, all come newly together, in African guise.* To that extent, we completely overturn the proverbial, geopolitical notion of the "global south", and the BRICS that go with it, subsumed by notions of economic growth, modernisation, neoliberal capitalism if not also "real" socialism, and the corporate enterprise, or indeed entrepreneurship and leadership, not to mention also the business schools and MBA programs that go with it. That said, it may appear unseemly to connect individual wellbeing, integral enterprise, or a healthy society with, for example, a mining corporation, with automobile manufacturing, or with financial and information services. However, for example in the former respect (mining and manufacturing), the *health of the planet* is not far removed from such. Moreover, in the latter respect (finance and information) *individual wellbeing* is a due consideration.

18.6.3. SDG's to MDI's

In the final analysis, we turn to the proverbial SDG's – Sustainable Development Goals – as *Measures* of overall effectiveness, in today's ever present "enlightened" terms, be it related to climate change or the alleviation of poverty, amongst altogether 17 such indicators, seemingly befitting the kind integral laboratory we have in mind. The problem though, for us, is that such quantitative indicators have nothing centrally to do with the healing wisdom of Africa, thereby grounded in Mother nature, emerging through a Moral narrative, navigating via scientific and humanistic Model, building up to such oikonomic Measures. This is what we term, alternately, our MDI's: **M**eans of **D**eveloping **I**ntegrality.

We conclude as such with the insights of renowned management thinker, Thomas Johnson, also co-author (Kaplan and Johnson 1987) of *Relevance Lost* in his (Johnson and Broms 2000) more recent book *Profit Beyond Measure:*

> Managing-by-means thinking then sets aside the assumption that quantitative growth is necessary for business success. The adoption of such means, or process-oriented thinking, will make it more likely, in fact, that today's environmental goals will be reached as a natural by-product of everyday management practice. Notably, a company that manages by means will profit only by nurturing fundamental human and natural relationships, thereby being aligned with our relational, if not also renewal, path.
>
> The "profit beyond measure" awaiting companies that manage by means encompasses, then, overall, the health and long-term survival of the ecosystem that supports all human life, including the human ecosystem. Management by means now proposes a way to organize work that is slower, quieter, and more likely to insure human survival in Earth's ecosystem, while being sufficiently profitable to ensure the long-term survival of companies. Instead of viewing business as an institution that commercializes human technology at any cost to human and natural relationships, management by means views business as a living system through which humans use and transform technology to achieve a fuller life in harmony with other forms of life and with the system that sustains life on earth.

In our proverbial African terms, we align such with its "healing wisdom". Whereas Steve Biko famously said the gift of Africa is to give the world a human face, for us, more specifically, it has gifted us, world-wide, healing wisdom, upon which we build pioneering community, spirited scientifically managed corporation, an integral communiversity and communitalist association.

18.6.4. Towards a Societal PhD

Finally, by way if conclusion, we compare and contrast the nature and scope the conventional versus our envisaged societal PhD, we can see the differences clearly outlined in the final Table 18.6.4. as set out below.

Table 18.6.4. *Conventional PhD Societal PhD*

University Faculty	Individual Researcher and Supervisor	Innovation Ecosystem: Steward, Catalyst, Research & Education, Development
Source of Accreditation	Academic Qualification	Societal Re-GENE-Ration
Overall Motivation	Professional Status	Contribution to Society
Research Orientation	Qualitative and quantitative research methods	Origination to transformation
Time Horizon	Three to six years	Several decades
Institutional Base	University Department	Communiversity
National Authority	Higher Education Authority	Centre for Social Innovation

18.7. References

Adodo A (2012) *Nature Power: A Christian Approach to Herbal Medicine.* New Edition. Edo State. Benedictine Publications.

Adodo A (2017) *Integral Community Enterprise in Africa. Communitalism as an Alternative to Capitalism.* London: Routledge.

Adodo A and **Lessem R** (2021) *Afrikology: Deconstructing and Reconstructing Knowledge and Value in Africa.* Manchester: Academic Beacon.

Arrighi G (2009) *The Long Twentieth Century: Money, Power and the Origins of Our Time.* London. Verso

Brundtland G (1987) *Our Common Future – World Commission on Environment and Development.* Oxford. Oxford University Press. p 43

Christie P, **Lessem** R and **Mbigi** L (1996) *African Management: Principles, Concepts and Applications.* Johannesburg. Knowledge Resources

Ingold T (2023) *The Rise and Fall of Generation Now.* Cambridge. Polity Press

Johnson HT and Broms A (2000) *Profit Beyond Measure. Extraordinary Results through Attention to Work and People.* New York. Free Press

Kaplan R and Johnson HT (1987) *Relevance Lost: The Rise and Fall of Management Accounting.* Cambridge. Harvard Business School Press

Koopman A (1991) *Transcultural Management.* Chichester. Wiley-Blackwell

Lessem R (2016) *Community Activation for Integral Development.* Abingdon. Routledge Focus

Lessem R and Schieffer A (2010a) *Integral Research and Innovation: Transforming Enterprise and Society.* Abingdon. Routledge

Lessem R and Schieffer A (2010b) *Transformation: Toward the Integral Enterprise.* Abingdon. Routledge

Lessem R and Schieffer A (2010c) *Integral Economics: Releasing the Economic Genius of Your Society.* Abingdon. Routledge

Lessem R, Adodo A and Bradley T (2019a) *The Idea of the Communiversity.* Manchester. Beacon Academic

Lessem R, Mawere M and Taranhike D (2019b) *Integral Kumusha.* Mazvingo. Africa Talent Publishers

Lessem R, Muchineripi P and Kada S (2012) *Integral Community: Political Economy to Social Commons.* Abingdon. Routledge

Maathai W (2009) *The Challenge for Africa – A New Vision.* London. Heinemann

Mamukwa E, Lessem R and Schieffer A (2014) *Integral Green Zimbabwe: An African Phoenix Rising.* Abingdon. Routledge

Mandela N (1994) *The Long Walk to Freedom.* New York. Abacus

National HealthCare. https://nationalhealthcare.co.za uncited

Ndudzo C (2021) *The Providence Way.* Harare. Self Published

Piciga D, Schieffer A and Lessem R (2016) *Integral Green Slovenia.* Abingdon. Routledge

Rodney W (2018) *How Europe Underdeveloped Africa.* London. Verso

Schieffer A and Lessem R (2014) *Integral Development: Transforming the Potential of Individuals, Organisations and Societies.* Abingdon. Routledge

Some M (1997) *The Healing Wisdom of Africa.* New York. Jeremy Tarcher

1. **Dr. Anselm Adodo** is a Benedictine priest who embodies diverse roles and expertise, spanning education, management, environmentalism, social work, health policy research, and naturopathic practice. His multidisciplinary approach to integrative medicine spans over two decades and is marked by prolific scholarly contributions across various fields. Dr. Adodo holds doctoral degrees in Management of Technology and Innovation from the DaVinci Institute, South Africa, and Medical Sociology from the University of Benin, Nigeria. His affiliations include roles as a Fellow of the Nigeria Society of Botanists, an Adjunct Research Fellow of the National Institute of Medical Research, Nigeria, and positions such as a Visiting Lecturer at the Institute of African Studies, University of Ibadan, Nigeria, and a Research Associate at the University of Johannesburg, South Africa. Authoring numerous books on ethnobotany, African studies, and integrative research, alongside research articles in esteemed peer-reviewed journals, Adodo stands as a pivotal figure bridging academia and practice. His expertise extends to curriculum review, mental health consulting, social innovation, and community development, making him a prominent figure in driving innovation and progress within integrative medicine and holistic healthcare. Anselm Adodo's commitment lies in inspiring individuals and fostering collaboration between academia and industry to pave the way for transformative advancements in healthcare paradigms.

2. **Professor Ronnie Lessem:**
Born in Zimbabwe and now based in the UK, was Co-Founder of TRANS4M (France), whereby he co-evolved, with Alexander Schieffer, *Integral Research* and *Development*, alongside *Integral Economics* and *Enterprise*, as their core products. At the same time they ran a PhD program with Da Vinci Institute in South Africa, in *Integral Development*, from which some three dozen candidates have graduated under the personal supervision, all drawing on *Integral Research* (Lessem and Schieffer, 2010). Such has since co-evolved, together with Drs Sandile Ndlungwane in Southy Africa and Anselm Adodo in Nigeria and, and subsequent to an earlier journal publication on *Linking College and* Community, into Re-GeNe-Africa in the South Africa, via *The Idea of the Communiversity* (Lessem et al 2019a), which focuses on the regeneration of particular societies, most especially in Africa, MENA and in Europe, and to a lesser extent in Asia and in America.

He studied economics at the University of Zimbabwe, the economics of industry at the London School of Economics, and Corporate Planning at Harvard Business School, gaining his Ph.D. in *Action Learning for Business* from City University in the UK. As now Professor of Management at Da Vinci Institute in South Africa, he has previously conducted research and taught for extensive periods at Bethel University in the United States, at City University as well as the University of Buckingham in the UK, at IMD in Switzerland in central Europe, at the University of Zimbabwe in Southern Africa, as well as at Yarmouk University in Jordan in the Middle East. He has also consulted with major multinationals on *Management Development through Cultural Diversity* and *Global Management*, and with companies in Africa and in MENA, to become *Integral Enterprises*, two of the 50 books he has written on such related subjects since the 1980s.

3. Professor Alexander Schieffer is an integral philosopher, academic activist, passionate educator, and mystic poet. He is Co-Founder of TRANS4M Academy for Integral Transformation (Geneva, Switzerland) and Co-Founder of Home for Humanity (France), a transformative community of "integral worldmakers", sharing the vision of "co-creating home on Earth". Having shaped Home for Humanity into a movement for planetary regeneration, he initiatied the One Home Journey – A collective future-building expedition to all countries on Earth to transform our divided world into a united home for humanity and the diversity of life on our Home Planet. A Professor of Integral Development at Da Vinci Institute, South Africa and St Gallen University, Switzerland, Alexander is also author and co-author of many books (including *Integral Development, Transformation Management, Integral Economics and Integral Research-and-Innovation*), as well as two poetry volumes and a novel. He is also Co-Editor of the Transformation and Innovation Series and the Integral Green Society and Economy Series, both with Routledge. In his early career, he was founder and CEO of First Asia Publishing in Singapore, prior to which he worked in international investment banking and management consulting across Europe. He has a Ph.D. from St. Gallen University, with a thesis on "The Development of Leadership Personality".

Index

A
Absorption, distribution, metabolism, and excretion (ADME) 544
Action learning 525–526
African critical realism
 – adult Anglo to midlife Indian 488
 – age sets, communiversity, Pax Africana 495–496
 – capitalism, communitalism and communiversity 483
 – clinic-oriented approach 483–484
 – community-oriented approach 483–484
 – communiversity to communitalism 491–493, 500–501
 – dialectical emergence 489
 – *Dialectic – The Pulse of Freedom* 488–489
 – emancipatory body of thought 480–481
 – emancipatory navigation 500
 – emergent foundation 500
 – free, loving, creative and intelligent energy 482
 – generative depths 481–482
 – generative mechanisms 498
 – generative "real" mechanisms force 486–487
 – *The Idea of a Community* 496–497
 – interdisciplinary approach 479–480
 – meta-reality to transformative agency 489–490
 – multilayered communiversity 484–485
 – original grounding 499
 – Pax Herbals to Pax Africana 484
 – *The Philosophy of Meta-Reality* 481
 – political credentials 479–480
 – powers and mechanisms 487
 – realism to meta-reality 485–486
 – realization through stratification 499
 – research and innovation 479
 – social reality 498–499
 – transcendental realism 497
 – transformative agency to knowledge creating company 493–495
 – transitive and intransitive 498
African Management project (AMP) 300
African postmodernism
 – Afro/modernity 385–386
 – autonomous person 388
 – civilizations 388
 – conventional rules and practices 378
 – discursive reality 383–384
 – economic deficit 389–390
 – epochal transition grounded theory 393–394
 net of life 394
 professional philosophy and reason 394
 radical integration and reconciliation 393
 transient workplaces 394
 university to communiversity/capitalism to communitalism 395
 – Foucault's new order of things 382–383
 – fruit of her womb 379
 – global south 386–388

- grounding of liberal society 388
- human beings 381
- integrativity and transience, Sekem 375
- life of the spirit 381–382
- meanings and workplaces 392
- modern core and traditional periphery 384–385
- multiple and shifting 392
- multiple discourses 376–375
- multiplicity of discourses 375
- number of pathways 378–379
- politics of life 390–391
- polity capable of great variation 378
- pre-modern 377–378
- pursue multiple discourses 391–392
- recognition of historic rights 390
- socially construct meaning 392–393
- social processes 388
- southern personhood, difference and ID-ology 388–389
- structured order of relations and fluid environment 379
- transformative 393
- work and social being 380–381
- worldview and ritual 381–382

African socio-technical design
- co-generative approach to organization development 417–419
- community and democracy 401–402
- east and west 405
- economics of love 399–400
  biodynamic agriculture 408–409
  healing wisdom 409
  Islamic stewardship of the earth 409–410
  nature, culture, society and economy 410–411
- *The Egypt Code* 405–406

- emancipatory navigation via transient workplaces 421
- emergent foundation 421
- friendly outsider 419–420
- gods, nature and psyche 404–405
- grounded in southern *Kemet* 404
- grounded theory 421
- group dynamics and action research 400–401
- industrial democracy 400
- integral design 399–400, 400
- integral enterprise 411
- ITISA 416–417
- Kolb's experiential learning 402–403
- learning community to socio-economic laboratory 420–421
- Lewin's experiential learning 400–401
- life-potential of Nun 404
- from maat to Islam 406
- managing in four worlds 412–413
- marriage 406–408
- miscontrued un-healing wisdom 422–423
- north and south 405
- participation and democracy, west 413–414
- participation and integrality, south/north 414–415
- polytheism 404
- reflection and experience 401–402
- re-GENE-ration and constituents, communiversity 403
- relationality and renewal 400
- research to innovation 421–422
- socialism to communitalism 422
- three-stage process 415–416
- transformative effect 421
- university to communiversity/capitalism 422

Index

- work organization 416
Afrocentric Action Research
- action learning 525–526
- Africa assumes centrality 512–513
- African pyramid age 512
- Africology 511
- appreciative inquiry 522–523
- communitalism 505
- communiversity 505
- cultural and psychological sense 514–515
- cultural and spiritual context 526
- cultural relations 513–514
- destabilising power relations 515
- division of public education 524
- dynamic and transformative elements 526
- economic relations 513–514
- emancipatory navigation 529
- empirical foundation 529
- fields, paradigms and classifications 511–512
- integral western 505
- Kwanzaa 519–520
- liberationist perspectives and new paradigm 517–518
- liberatory transition 516–517
- original grounding 528
- origins of 506
- path of realisation 505
- Pax Herbals search for the real truth 529–530
- people 519
- principles 520–522
- relation of domination 518–519
- scientific emancipatory navigation 506
- scientific knowing 524–525
- social change 523–524
- social innovation 527, 528
- soul of method 513
- transformative effect 529
- University Laboratory School 506–507
- way of innovation 505
America's Global Responsibility 69
Anthroposophy 141
Art of association 66–69

B
Bio-dynamic agriculture 409
British Holistic Medical Association 290
Building on societal legacy 180

C
Categorical imperatives 141
Centre for Integral Research and Societal Re-GENE-ration (CIRSRE)
- African management 624–625
- cocreation and knowledge creation 626–627
- communiversity 625–626
- enterprise and economy 625–626
- integral research and development 625–626
Centring cosmology
- Centre for Integral Research and Societal Re-GENE-ration 50–52
- circle/cycle 53
- cyclical process element 53–54
- developing capabilities 52
- East-India to China in Asia continual becoming 60
existence and non-existence 62
way of the east 61
Yin-Yang 62–63
- four worlds model 54–57
- *The Healing Wisdom of Africa* 49–50
- innovation paths creative synthesis 57–58
healing and regeneration 59–60
- integral cosmologies 73
- Integral Tree of Life 74–75
- integral west 66–69

- Islamic world 69–71
- modes 50
- north-Ancient Greek/ Judeo-Christian 63–66
- paths of integral research 47
- process 50
- region 72
- social design and social innovation 52
- transcultural research 52
- university and economy 49

Century of Awakening 192
Circular economy 375
Coding procedures 116
Communal and societal process 420
Communal learning 484, 583
Community and Individual Development Association (CIDA) 104, 300, 301
Community building 580
Community oriented approach 620
Communiversity 21
Conscious evolution 580
Context-dependence of value (CdV) 362–363
Cooperative inquiry 289
- Centred in Healing Wisdom 602–603
- communitalism 579–580, 592
- communiversity 579–580
- community-based integral enterprise 580–581, 600–602
- communiversity structure and innovation ecosystem operation 580
- context, process and substance 579
- developing organisation 603–604
- developmental management 605
- *East African Good African Story* 594–596
- economics of love 592
- form, program and product 579
- functional elements effective political/economic midlife and maturity 586–587
  emergent culture/spirituality 586
  grounding in nature/ community 585–586
  The Idea of a Communiversity 585, 587–588
  limits of learning 584–585
  scientific/technological navigation 586
- healing and regeneration 579–580
- *Healing Wisdom of Africa* 580
- integral polity
  global-local political and economic development 590–591
  integral governance/innovation ecosystem 588
  local/global trans4mation journey 589
  natural and communal grounding 589
  people 591–592
  research and education 590
- integral research 603
- *Knowledge Creating Company* 604
- macro economic orientations 605–606
- *Natural Capitalism* 604
- neoliberal turn 605
- Nhakanomics and Yurugu-nomics 592
- *North Africa's Sekem* 596–597
- Pan-African Cosmology community and enterprise 599
  homestead and enterprise 598–599
  tradition and modernity 600
- Pax Africana analysis 593
- societal Re-GENE-ration communiversity form 582–584

grounding to effect 582
meta-reality to transformative agency 581–582
- Southern African Integral Kumusha 593–594
- *Transforming Enterprise and Society* 603
- value sharing 604
- West Africa 597–598
Creative synthesis 55, 67, 68
Critical methodologies 90
Critical rationalism 29
Critical realism 29
Cultures of depth 175–176

D

Data processing 25
Deconstructionist 393
Democratic civilisation 166
Democratic modernity 164, 165–166

E

Economic growth 21
Egyptian Biodynamic Association (EBDA) 436, 438
Electromagnetic force 466
Emerging local-global transformation
- communal enterprise to corporate transformation 623–624
- community based enterprise 623
- societal context 621–622
- value sharing 623
Empiricism in South-West Africa
- action research 464
- African path of realisation 474
- animals 467
- approaches to social inquiry 465
- art of healing 468–470
- Austrians' logical positivist approach 460–461
- classical scientific method 460
- closed systems 461–462, 472
- collect observational data and build pragmatic theories 471–472
- creativity, intelligence and humanness 457
- defined 455–456
- experimental and survey methods 454
- feeling and personhood 455
- four natural forces 466
- healing potency of sound 459–460
- inductive, deductive and abductive 463–464
- influential force in modern science 453–454
- integral nature of social inquiry 466
- integral west builds 453, 472–473
- natural realisation 474–475
- natural road to wholeness 458–459
- *Nature Power* 457
- new species of plant 467–468
- open systems 461–462
- original grounding 473–474
- plants manufacture 467
- positive facts 471
- reformative and transformative 473
- rise of economics 456–457
- search for truth 470–471
- social innovation 454
- social sciences 463
- theory of plant signatures 468
- towards and integral Australia 466
- wisdom of the ancients 458
Environmental recognition 509
Experiential learning 292, 402
Extranet activities 104

F

Force of gravity 466

Formative research method 104
Free market approach 141

G
Gas chromatography-mass spectrometry (GC-MS) 544, 551
German ideology 269
Global integrity 55, 120
Global-local trans4mative effect
- Comparative Laboratory GENE-tics 631
- integral laboratory national healthcare 630
  Pax Economica 628
  Providence Human Capital (PHC) 628–629
  transformative effect 628
Global orientation to feminism
- aboriginal significance, relational 175
- act global-local 177–179
- in Africa
  The African Origin of Civilisation: Myth or Reality 159–160
  pre-colonial 160
- African sisterhood 163, 164
- common humanity 161
- compassion/love/peace 160–161
- critical emancipatory methodologies 156
- democratic confederalism 170–172
- democratic nation 170–172
- development of knowledge 174
- dual-sex character of political systems 161–162
- emancipatory movement and methodology 156–157
- environmental movement 159
- holistic knowledge framework 173–174
- indigenous academy 175–177
- indigenous knowledge 172–173
- integral research orientation 159
- Intuit local global (*see* Intuit local global)
- majority of African societies 162–163
- natural and social worlds, socially constructed 158
- science of women and life
  collective learning 170
  creation, liberation and life 168–169
  democratic civilisation 167
  divorce from a five thousand year patriarchal tradition 166
  freedom movement's educational endeavours 169–170
  ideological slavery 167
  moral and political society 167–168
  seizure of economy 167
  use of force 167
  vision of life and living 169
- self-organization and economy 163
- social to scientific and technological 157
- Southern Kumusha Guise 179–181
- southern relational path 155–156
- subsistence, communal and redistribution economies 162
- transformation of societies 174
- wrong with conventional science 158
Global School for African Leadership and Transformation (GSALT) 301
Global south
- adolescence 428–429
- adopting nature and religion 428
- Allah's ninety nine qualities 430
- Arab-Isreali Conflict 431
- concept of excellence and beauty 442–443
- concept of justice (*adl*) 443–444

- concept of knowledge
  (Ilm) 441–442
- concept of natural state
  (fitra) 441
- desert earth 427–428
- exogenous anthroposophy and
  Islam 445
- farming to phyto-
  pharmaceuticals 435–436
- global-local maturity 434–435
- indigenous healing wisdom 445
- inhibited recognition and release,
  GENEius 445–446
- integral enterprise
  Economy of Love 439
  fourfold structure of
    Sekem 436–437
  middle way of Islam 439–440
  strategy and structure 437–438
  sustainable development 438
- Integral Kumusha 425
- integral terms 447
- newly global midlife
  biodynamic agriculture 432
  cultural renewal 433
  destiny 432
- orient and occident
  meet 430–431
- Philosophy of Freedom 431–432
- re-GENE-rative value
  creation 446
- smallholder farmers 436
- social innovation 426
- social innovators 426–427
- societal challenges of Egypt 436
- socio-technical design 440–441
- souls of Egyptian people 433
- South X Alliance 425–426
- Stewardship *(Khalifa)* 444–445
- towards and integral worlds
  approach 446
- village of Mashtul 429
Good manufacturing processes
  (GMP) 549–550

Gross domestic product (GDP) 214
Grounded theory
- axial coding 117–118
- conceptual learning 115–116
- open coding 117
- path of reason 116
- research academy 115
- social innovation 118–119

H
Healing strategies 580–581
High Performance Capabilities Africa
  (HPCA) 217
High-performance liquid
  chromatography (HPLC) 551
High-performance thin-layer
  chromatography (HPTLC) 544
History of Systems of Thought 375

I
Industrial Training Fund (ITF) 548,
  549
Innovation ecosystem 39, 614–616
Integral Enterprise 603
Integral research and innovation
- academic research and social
  innovation 96
- analytical research/
  transformative innovation 79
- communal learning 79–80
- community 86
- communiversity 85
- developmental connection 87
- emergence 81
- four research moments 96–97
- fourth action centred or
  transformative level 98
- GENEtic process 84–85
- global-local economic action
  82
- grounding 80
- integral communitalism
  east African transformation
    journey 93–94

inner-directed research
trajectory 92
north African centre for social
innovation 94–95
outer-directed story 92
research-and-innovation
storyline 92
southern African learning
community 92–93
west African laboratory 95–96
– level of research method 98
– navigation 81–82
– origination to
transformation 88–91
– pragmatic-rational knowledge
generation 88
– process, form, context and
substance 84
– research academy 79–80
– socio-economic
laboratory 79–80
– traditional research
approach 97–98
– transformation 83–84
– transformational trajectory 88
– transformation journey 79–80
Integral research methodology 26
Interdependence and Transformation
in South Africa (ITISA) 416–417
International Participatory Research
Network 188
Interpretive phenomenological
analysis (IPA) 32
Intuit local global
– autonomous cantons 165
– critique/self critique 165–166
– democratic modernity 164
– Kurdish Liberation Struggle 164
– Rojava academies and learning
communities 165

K
Knowledge-creating company 28
Knowledge creation 580–581

Knowledge democracy 192
Knowledge-oriented process 93
Kyagalanyi Coffee Limited (KCL) 334

L
Lack of resources 33
Learning community 34, 41–42, 496
– The Chinyika Project 617–618
– culture and spirituality 222
– development plan 228
– economic development and
growth 208
– emancipation phase 213–215
– evolution of social
innovation 207
– foundation phase 212–213
– global local enterprise and
regenerative economy 222–223
– government and other
organisations 208
– integral approach 221
– Integral Kumusha 216–217,
223–226
– National Model Rural
Homestead 217
– Nature Power, Communitalism
and Nhakanomics 229–230
– navigating newly global science
and technology 222
– non-governmental organisations
(NGOs) 208
– opportunities 226–227
– origination phase 212
– Pax Herbals to Pax Africana 617
– pioneering individual and
communal
enterprise 618–619
– psychology 230–231
– research
approach 210–212
journey and transformation 209
method and methodology 207
process 212
questions 209–210

Index   647

- research to innovation
  journey 210–212
- rural to urban migration 208
- rural transformation 209
- security of the people and
  fields 219
- self-serving approach 207
- special garden of
  remembrance 218
- support from local
  leadership 220
- sustainable
  development 228–229
- traditional and conventional
  research 207
- transformation journey 231
- transformation phase 215–216
- Vakamusha 220–221
- water harvesting 218–219

Local global transformative
hermeneutics
- cabral's return to source 243–244
- critical edge of 240
- fractured split 241–242
- fusion of horizons 241–242
- reclaiming or discarding
  history 242–243
- turning over a new leaf and
  working out new concepts 241
- two-way dialectic 244
- urban-rural dynamic fusion 243

M
Macro-social transformation 194
Masters in Social and Economic
  Transformation (MSET) 300
Microbiological analysis 551
Middle East and North Africa
  (MENA) 139
Modernity 138
Moral and political society 170
Multi-National Finance
  Institutions 214

N
National Board for Technical
  Education (NBTE) 548
National Universities Commission
  (NUC) 548, 549
Newly global navigation
- choosing an appropriate
  communalist ideology 246–247
- emancipatory
  navigation 251–253
- evolving viable and appropriate
  democratic political
  institutions 246
- indigenous culture
  adaptive capacity 248–249
  cultural borrowing 251
  growth of human culture 249
  imposition deprives 249
  individualism and
    communitarianism 250–251
  modernity 250
- revitalise tradition 247–248

O
Orientation to co-operative inquiry
- academic analysis to
  transformation journey 313
- authenticity criteria 300
- changing east-west
  paradigm 289–290
- collaborative
  participation 292–293
- contemporary action
  research 290–291
- cooperative inquiry 291
- cosmology and economy 289
- deconstructing
  and reconstructing
  knowledge 293–294
- Dogon as a cosmological
  cycle 294–296
- eastern transformative effect 289
- four inquiry outcomes 298

- grounding and
  consummation 299
- healing and whole
  making 291–292
- inquiry outcomes 298–299
- integral "green" society and
  economy 303–305
- Integral Green
  Zimbabwe 300–303
- integral path 313–315
- political and epistemic 297
- political perspective 311–313
- self-generating culture 292
- transformative African effect
  informative inquiry 307
  knowledge-oriented
    process 306–307
  participative reality 308–309
  reasons for political
    participation 305–306
  transformative inquiry 307
  truth and reality 309–310
  validation of practice 310
  validity 308
Orientation to critical rationalism
- African philosophy 352–353
- construction of the future 369
- deprived of theory building/
  deprived of African economic
  theory 357–358
- effect of integrative African
  society
  deductive strategy 366
  derive theories 365–366
  empirical science 365
  social engineering 366
- extraordinary science 369
- Ezumezu
  integrality 363–364
  methodology 361–363
  philosophical reason 359
  philosophy of logic 360–361
- hierarchy of cultural
  practices 356

- higher learning from the
  village 348
- impoverished science and
  detached philosophy 356–
  357, 367
- inner changes and outer
  learning 348–349
- integral research and
  innovation 369–370
- intellectual independence 351
- liberation of the future 358–359
- net of life 349
- peripheral perspective 368
- pervasive influence of Greek
  European logos 351–352
- *Popper's Logic of Scientific
  Discovery* 349–350
- *Popper's Philosophy of
  Science* 350
- professional philosophy
  ethno, sage, statesman and
    professional African
    philosophers 353–354
  Europe and Africa 354
  successive revolutions 355–356
- public intellectual, ultimately on
  a worldwide stage 348
- question of method 352–353
- south-north African social
  research and innovation 347
- towards African
  reappropriation 368
- unbranded index for thought 352
- villagisation of knowledge 353
Orientation to critical theory
- Africa and twentieth
  century 267–268
- African renaissance 269
- African renewal
  problems of everyday life 281
  suffering of people 282–283
  uncovers power relations 282
  Yurugu-nomic
    Orientation 281–282

- black consciousness 269
- cultural alternatives to
  Yurugu 279–281
- cultural dimension 283
- East Africa E2fita 284–285
- epistemic freedom in Africa
  African Academy 270
  circulation of
    knowledge 271–272
  epistemological
    decolonisation 271–272
  five decolonial
    imperatives 270–271
- European *versus*
  African 278–279
- global south 272
- grounding in Asili 275–276
- interpretive methodology/
  trans4mation 284
- liberal constitution 274
- making of self and
  others 273–274
- metaphysical orientation 283
- narrative method/trans4mation
  journey 283–284
- negritude 268–269
- origins and meaning of
  European
  critical thinkers 266
  critique 266
  East African social research and
    innovation 265
  interpretation of religious
    texts 265
  political activism 267
- planting European memory 268
- reflections on the
  post-colony 274–275
- regenerative *versus*
  modernization 273
- rivers 268
- unique civilization 272–273
Orientation to hermeneutics

- African heritage and effective
  history 244–245
- Cooperative/Good African
  Story 235–236, 257–258
- global local renewal
  constructed 253–254
  European interpretive to African
    transformative 255–256
  individual and collective Asili
    Source 256–257
  multi-culturalism 254–255
- global origins 236–238
- interpretive methodology/
  trans4mation 257
- local tradition and
  destiny 239–240
- narrative method/trans4mation
  journey 257
- newly global navigation (*see*
  Newly global navigation)
- Nzonzi 239
- universe or multiverse 245–246
Orientation to phenomenology
- African Life World 149
- Black Consciousness 136–137
- centred Islamic
  reconstruction 142–144
- *The Crisis of the European
  Sciences* 132–133
- developmental biology 145
- ecological adaptations 144
- ethnic politics 144
- feel local and intuit
  local-global 134
- humanity and nature 145
- Humanity's Search for
  Home 137–139
- Integral Kumusha in
  Zimbabwe 134–135, 150–151
- land, soil and
  connectivity 135–136
- linking ecological
  psychology 145

- newly global southern phenomenology
  building and dwelling perspective 147
  house as organism 148
  Ingold's dwelling perspective 147
  philosophy of freedom 147–148
  radical empiricism 148–149
  westernised neo-liberal economics and enterprise 146
- organism 144–145
- phenomenology operates 133–134
- radical detachment from the east 140
- radical doubt in the north 140–141
- radical empiricism 142
- reductive positivism and naive empiricism 150
- research to innovation 131–132
- social organization 144
- southern African research to innovation 132
- southern relational foundation 149
- think newly global and act global-local 134
- unique cultural history 150

Originating integral research and innovation
- analytical method 105–106
- building blocks of research matter 103–105
- case study method 121–123
- communiversity/communitalism 123–124
- empirical phenomenology 109–110
- experiential learning 109
- grounded theory (*see* Grounded theory)
- human integrity 107–108
- imagination 112
- Integral Kumusha 110–111
- integral method 106–108
- learning community 108–109
- narrative research method 112–114
- origination and culture 106–107
- partnership with some authoritative agent 113
- practical learning 120–121
- self realisation 119–120
- social research/innovation paths 113–114, 124
- sustainable development 125
- transformation journey 111–112
- transformative origination 105–106
- vital force, GENE 105

Origin of Species 488

P

Participatory action research (PAR)
- awareness, people's own resources 200
- community 186, 200–201
- critical awareness 199
- feel local
  adult educators and community developers 189–190
  beginning of this story 188
  transformative learning 188–189
- Integral Kumusha to Nhakanomics 204–205
- integrating education with life processes 187
- knowledge creation 190–193
- knowledge in action 183
- people's liberation 186–187
- radical transformation of social reality 201–202
- Rahman's people's self development 193–195
- relational path 203–204
- retrospect 202–203

- social existence 197–199
- social innovation
  development expertise 195
  flexible funding 195
  local knowledge 195
  Naam structures 195–196
  reasons for their success 196
- transformative effect 185

Pax Herbals to Pax Africana
- collaborative learning 562–564
- collaborative
  partnerships 554–555
- communitalism 533, 538
- community and
  communiversity 538
- community-based enterprise 533
- communiversity 533
- economic and social
  transformation 554
- efficiency and education 539–540
- fabrication of specialised
  production equipment 553–554
- form of education and
  entertainment 533–534
- GMP 549–550
- humanity and earth 537
- indigenous origins,
  communiversity 557
- language spoken by the
  earth 536
- mycology's role in
  phytomedicine 552–553
- Nigeria's agricultural
  landscape 536–537
- partnership goals/aims 555–556
- patient education and
  counselling 540
- Pax communis/learning
  community/Moremi
  archetype 558–559
- Pax Economia/socio-
  economic laboratory/Osun
  archetype 561–562

- Pax Scientia/research academy/
  Oya archetype 560–561
- Pax Spiritus 559–560
- quality control 551–552
- Re-GENE
  communitalism 566–569
  from Nigeria to
  Zimbabwe 569–571
- seeds of transformation 538
- societal PhD 573
- societal regeneration 533
- Southern Traditional Yoruba
  and Northern Christian
  perspectives 537–538
- technological innovation
  African ethnomedicinal
  knowledge 541–543
  agriculture, plant taxonomy and
  ecology 545–546
  Clinic Consultants' Offices 541
  collaborative research and
  knowledge exchange 546–547
  diagnostic laboratory 540–541
  drug formulation 543–544
  drug innovation
  research 544–545
  *Students Industrial Work
  Experience Scheme*
  (SIWES) 548–549
- technological to social
  innovation 556
- thousand independent
  distributors 537
- tissue culture 552
- traditional healers 535–536
- traditional knowledge/local
  resources 534
- transformation journey/Yemoja
  archetype 559–560, 571–573
- transition from university to
  communiversity 564–566
- village of Ogwa 534–535
- vision took root 536

People's Organizations (PO's) 201

Personality awareness 509
Phenomenology 29
Political economy 611
Political kingdom 271
Positivism 460
Postmodernism 29
Primitive mentality 354
Providence Human Capital (PHC) 628–629
Psychoanalysis 267

R
Relational thinking 145–146
Research Academy 485, 496–497, 583
Robbin Island University 611

S
Savings and Credit Cooperatives (SACCO's) 329
Sekem – A Sustainable Community in the Egyptian Desert 427
Sekem Development Foundation (SDF) 436, 437
Skin recognition 508–509
Social and contextualised innovation 35
Social design processes 52
Social enterprise 319–320
Social innovation 596
 – analytical trajectory 38
 – commercial activities 23
 – communitalism 20–21
 – communiversity 20–21
 – dysfunctional research 24, 25
 – emancipation succeeds foundation 30
 – form and context 21–22
 – integral research and innovation 20–21
 – inter-institution building capitalism-communitalism 34
 composite research-and-innovation team 33–34
 individual research predominates 31–32
 integral research and societal regeneration 32–33
 research-innovation 34
 university-communiversity 34
 – lacking in integrity 27–28
 – learning community 41–42
 – method and methodology 25–27
 – new research-and-innovation paradigm 18
 – organisation and society 43
 – origination precedes foundation 29–30
 – process and substance 21–22
 – public and civic sectors 24
 – reason and realisation 40–41
 – relational and renewal 40–41
 – research academy 42–43
 – self and community 43
 – social and economic arena 24
 – Social Science for the 21st Century 44–45
 – social sciences and humanities integral research trajectory 36–37
 integral trajectory and technological innovation 34–35
 societal re-GENE-ration 36–37
 societal re-GENE-ration 37–38
 – technology 22–23
 – transformation journey 41
 – transformative action 31
 – transformative trajectory 38–39
 – tree 43–44
Social research methodology 84
Societal PHD community
 – *The Challenge for Africa* 613
 – communiversity 609–610, 612, 616
 – Conventional PhD 634
 – cosmology 616

- emerging local-global transformation (see Emerging local-global transformation)
- environment and development 612–613
- healthy society 632–633
- individual research/innovation ecosystem 631–632
- individual wellbeing 632–633
- innovation ecosystem 616
- integral enterprise 632–633
- inter-institutional and inter-personal agency 611–612
- learning community (see Learning community)
- Means of Developing Integrality 616
- mother earth 620
- *Nature Power and the Healing* 613
- original grounding 619
- Re-Gene-ration 613–616
- Rhodes Must Fall 611
- SDG's to MDI's 633–634
- university/communiversity 631–632
- West Africa to Southern Africa 610–611

Socio-economic enterprise 20
Socio-economic laboratories 34, 583–584
Socio-technical laboratory 485, 497
Spectrophotometry 544
Spiritual Science 408
Spiritual science of anthroposophy 440
Standard operating procedures (SOPs) 552
Statistical research methods 26
Students Industrial Work Experience Scheme (SIWES) 548–549
Sustainable development 580–581

T

Technical and technological innovation 21–23
The Crisis of the European Sciences 132–133
The Descent of Man 488
The Future of Muslim Civilisation 406
The Good African Coffee Story
- African farmers 336–337
- African Renaissance 332–335
- analysis and transformation 339–340
- burden of history 325
- commitment to community 336
- *Common Man's Charter* 326
- community 328–329
- creative origination 329–332
- critical theory 319–320
- cultures and communities 337
- current economic situation 327
- Developmental Path of Western States 323–324
- external orientation of colony 323
- first community liaison officer 328
- goodness, trustworthiness and authenticity 338–339
- incomplete transformation 340–341
- institutional capacity 322–323
- integral African communitalism 341
- integral research and innovation 317–318
- interpretive to transformative 335–336
- knowledge oriented process 320–321
- local, local-global and global-local 318
- logistical difficulties and poor infrastructure 329

- neocolonialism 322
- newly global emancipatory navigation falls 340
- plantation economics 325–326
- potentials and possibilities 327–328
- power relations 321
- private sector 321–322
- *Savings and Credit Cooperatives* (SACCO's) 329
- socio-economic cleavage 324–325
- South *versus* North and West 341–342
- vision, mission and values 318–319

The Logic of Scientific Discovery 350

Theories of the South 272

Theosophy 408

The Philosophy of Meta-Reality 481

The Real Wealth of Nations 178

The Regeneration of Africa 272, 386

The Theory of Social Change
- essential grounds of afrocentricity 507–508
- every dimension of the African world 510
- levels of transformation 508–509
- tradition and innovation 509–510

Tradition-informed understanding 254

Transcultural Management 604

Transformation journey 484, 496, 583

Transformation Studies in Africa (TSA) 566

Trans-sectoral research orientations 34–35

Tribal Trust Lands (TTLs) 208

Truth and Reconciliation Commission (TRC) 112

U
Unity in diversity 54

V
Vivencia 186

Z
Zimbabwe National Statistics Agency 207–208